EPIPHANY

A Theological Introduction to Catholicism

Aidan Nichols, O.P.

A Michael Glazier Book
THE LITURGICAL PRESS
Collegeville, Minnesota

A Michael Glazier Book published by The Liturgical Press

Cover design by Ann Blattner.
Cover image: "The Adoration of the Magi." Whalebone, English, early twelfth century. Reproduced by the permission of the Curators of the Victoria and Albert Museum, London.

1   2   3   4   5   6   7   8

Library of Congress Cataloging-in-Publication Data

Nicols, Aidan.
    Epiphany : a theological introduction to Catholicism / Aidan Nicols.
      p. cm.
    "A Michael Glazier book."
    Includes bibliographical references and indexes.
    ISBN 0-8146-5504-1
    1. Catholic Church—Apologetic works. 2. Catholic Church—Doctrines.
    3. Catholic Church—Liturgy. I. Title.
BX1752.N53 1996
282—dc20   96-35209
                                               CIP

Contents

Preface   5

1   A Christian Philosophy   7

2   Revelation and Its Sources   30

3   The Historian's Jesus   65

4   The Church's Jesus   106

5   The Trinity   151

6   The Nature of Salvation   169

7   The Church   206

8   The Religious Life   238

9   The Rites of the Church   272

10   Mary and the Saints   337

11   The Cosmic Setting of Salvation   368

12   The Good Life   391

13   Ways to Holiness   433

14   Catholicism and Other Religions   456

15   Coda   470

Suggestions for Further Reading   471

Index of Names   481

Index of Main Subjects Treated   488

Preface

This book has been written in the conviction that the Catholic faith constitutes a unique source of illumination for the good, the true, and the beautiful—the three interconnected transcendentals of medieval Christian philosophy. That faith is destined to be, and humbly offered as, light for all peoples. The language of light is perhaps the most symbolically dense, the most metaphysically pregnant we possess for our account of reality. From the thirteenth-century bishop Robert Grosseteste of Lincoln with his ontology of light to the hero of Ruskin's *Modern Painters*, J. M. W. Turner, with his evocations of light as the very expression of Being, no more persuasive symbol has come down to us. Fittingly, it was by this metaphor that Jesus Christ, the Origin of Catholic Christendom, was hailed by an elderly Jew when as a tiny babe his parents presented him in the Jerusalem Temple—for Jews the center of the world. Suitably also the Church has applied this symbol of "epiphany"—shining forth—to his first, pre-verbal contact with the Gentiles, as his mother held him out to the representatives of the non-Jewish nations.

I have subtitled this book "*A* Theological Introduction to Catholicism," for it would of course be unforgivable hubris to claim that one work could encapsulate all the illuminating richness Catholic Christianity can offer. I am, however, confident enough of its *catholic* quality in both senses of that word, since I have brought together here much that clearer thinkers, and better scholars, have thought and written.

This is a traditional theology, though not, I believe, an altogether unattractive one. It is also a consciously non-liberal theology, but not, I think, an illiberal one, for its subject is the generosity of God in his revealing Word and sanctifying Spirit. I offer it to my fellow clergy in the hope that they may find it of use in the enriching of their ecclesial culture, and to all interested readers, but most especially to the laity. It is not a neutral work, since it aims to arouse a "Christian maximalism" and the boldness to seek in Catholicism's theological tradition inspiration for present and future. *Si quid male dixi, totum relinquo correctioni Ecclesiae.*

Blackfriars,
Cambridge,
Easter 1996

1
A Christian Philosophy

The Catholic Church understands her faith as the answer to all human aspiration (that is one fundamental meaning of the word *catholic*) and so as the true philosophy—echoing, and fulfilling, the philosophers' articulation of the true, the good, and the beautiful in all metaphysical generations. Catholicism's own use of philosophy has been marked by a recognition of its many abidingly valuable elements ever since antiquity. If the Presocratic philosophers sought to fathom the coming-to-be and fundamental order of the cosmos, then the Church's doctrine of divine creation, through the Word and by the Spirit of God, could help. While for Thales the world was "full of gods," the Church proclaimed the presence by causality of the one God throughout the material universe. The pre-existent divine Son, disclosed through Jesus Christ, was the true "beginning," *archē*, sought by Anaximander of Miletus; the all-encompassing "world-air" of Anaximenes was God's Holy Spirit; the divine transcendence affirmed on the basis of the Jewish-Christian Scriptures was the truth glimpsed by Xenophanes whose god "without toil" shook all things. Heraclitus actually divined that the underlying coherence of things is to be found in the Logos, the Word or Reason which gives measure, proportion, and unity to things, and reveals itself in language, the embodiment of the common wisdom that is in all human beings, however much the false opinions of private individuals may obscure it. Pythagoras's rules of abstinence—contemplation, orderedness, purification—foreshadowed the Church's own ascetic teaching. Her theological masters agreed with Parmenides that the most important word in all discourse is *being*—though being's fullness abides in the uncreated Source of everything that is, and so reality is not indivisible, as Parmenides had supposed. Melissus at least saw that reality was infinite, and the One incorporeal. Empedocles foreshadowed

Catholicism's incarnational realism and confidence in the senses: "Think on each thing in the way by which it is manifest"; like Pindar in the Orphic odes, he was concerned with the Church's basic salvational problematic: the fall and restoration of humankind. Anaxagoras, by distinguishing mind so sharply from the rest of finite being—it alone is self-ruled and mixed with nothing—prepared the way for her doctrine of the soul and its immortality. Hesiod found *erōs*, love, to be the first of gods, and friendship, *philia*, the efficient cause of every union of cosmic forces: looking ahead to the last line of the greatest Christian poem, Dante's *Commedia*, with its naming of God as "the Love, *amor*, that moves the sun and the other stars." For Homer, the proper excellence, *aretē*, of things (including human beings) uncovers a world where purposes are inbuilt and humans must develop the virtues necessary to realize them. Whereas the Sophists argued that moral standards, *nomos*, have no basis in nature, *phusis*, Plato, alerted by Socrates, contends that *phusis* is not over against *nomos*: all human laws are nourished by the one divine law.

The ethical, indeed sacred, character ascribed to the world-order in ancient Greek thought as it moved from religion to philosophy is paralleled in the ancient Confucian concept of *tao* and the Buddhist notion of *dharma*. Both are at once the moral order and the order of the world. Ancient thought was at one and the same time cosmological and mystical: understandably, for all human beings are concerned with the world they inhabit and with what their own destiny will be. Antiquity's cosmological speculations on the periodic growth, culmination, and destruction of the world find a healing resolution in Catholicism's doctrine of the "last things." Similarly, the Church's understanding of how fallen humanity appropriates salvation through the liturgy of the sacraments fulfills the dream of the ancient mystics of the Orpheus cult that our souls, fallen from the stars after a primal sin, are saved by sympathetic, ritual contemplation of a suffering god who dies and is reborn.

Historically, Plato—duly corrected by Aristotle—has been the philosopher who best supplied the Catholic faith with its rational preamble. Plato took from Socrates a concern with definitions—not just to secure a preliminary agreement about the use of words, but to work out formulae that reveal by clarifying the essential natures of things. Plato grasped in advance the later theological idea of *transcendentals* (features of divine being mirrored in various ways in created being) by arguing that there are super-properties which never actually characterize physical things but bear some relation to properties that do. For Plato the very word *being* connotes not only existence but also genuineness, stability, ultimacy. The real, *to on*, is at once cognitively dependable and valuable, though it transcends our usual specifications of value as moral, aesthetic, and even religious. The drawback in Platonism, for the Church, is its downplaying of the sensuous world: Plato would surely have upgraded his estimate of its significance had he realized that, while it is unpromising material for logical analysis, it is the best possible material for empirical knowledge.

The great contribution of Aristotle to a *preparatio evangelica* in the ancient world lay in his much clearer awareness that, in the words of a Christian successor, the philosopher-theologian Thomas Aquinas, "Nothing is in the intellect that is not first in the senses." Awareness of the unity of matter and form, and thus of how the world of matter is a revelation of an intelligible world, was a precondition for any philosophical articulation of a religion of incarnation. All that remained was for the doctrine of creation to transform Aristotle's God from a mere contemplator into a true maker: One whose thoughts are not recognitions of intelligible necessities independent of itself but are truly creative of things, events, and even logic. Moreover, Aristotle's closeness to reality in its pith gave him profound insight into the structure not only of biological nature but also of the human city. His account of the virtues that belong to human coexistence would be not annulled but enhanced and completed by the gospel, on the principle that "grace builds on nature."

With the later Platonists ancient wisdom reached the notion that forms, *eidoi*, are ultimately thoughts in the divine Mind. Teetering on the brink of the idea of creation, the Neoplatonists in particular saw the One as a ceaseless fount of emanation of all reality lower than itself. God alone lacks the complexity which is the presupposition of disintegration; he possesses the perfection that renders change or development otiose, the unlimitedness that excludes lack and want. In Neoplatonism, such goodness, unity, truth, and beauty as we encounter in this world signify the presence in and beyond phenomena of the indescribable Origin of them all.

Into this Greco-Roman world, the world of late antiquity, a paradigm of created nature, its triumphs and its falls, Christ brought the light of the Wisdom of God. For this reason, the Catholic Church has taken it as a priority to strive with all her power to advance knowledge truly so called—while at the same time taking great care that all human learning be imparted according to the rule of her faith. This is especially true of philosophy, on which, in great measure, the right treatment of the other arts and sciences depends. If the human mind is solidly grounded in true principles, it can be the source of great blessings, both for individuals and for the community. A right use of philosophy is regarded by the Church as among the greatest of those natural helps given humanity by God's kindness and wisdom as he sweetly orders all things. The light of faith does not quench, or lessen, the strength of the understanding, but perfects it, giving it new vigor and fitting it for greater works. The Church demands the formal study of philosophy from her future ordained ministers. She reveres the great pagan philosophers whom her own masters have used in articulating her vision. And she encourages the baptism of a "perennial" tradition: the making of a Christian philosophy where natural wisdom is fructified by those revealed truths which are capable of taking on philosophic form. "Absolute reason" refuses all revelation, as of set purpose; "pure reason," beloved of rationalism, belongs only with a state of pure nature which has never, in the concrete, existed; "natural reason," on the other hand, remains open and *disponible* where revelation is concerned: it is able to enter into a relation with some historically realized situation of humankind, whether fallen or renewed. Revelation completes philosophy, proposing to the philosophical search other truths—deriving from faith—that can coordinate with the truths of reason to form a unity in the mind of the believing person.

How to understand the nexus of complementarity (subordination?) involved, however, is a matter of dispute among Catholic scholars. Whereas the idea of a "Christian philosophy" usefully calls into question the supposed sufficiency of philosophic thought, showing up its intrinsic indigence and consequent need for an openness to revelation, going too far down this road would wholly destroy the autonomous content of philosophical tradition.

Scholastics with historical inclinations, like Etienne Gilson, stress the contribution that some of the central dogmas of Christian faith made to Greek thought in its centuries-long travail of giving birth to European philosophy, whereas those Thomists who above all stress the distinction between nature and grace are skeptical of the very idea of Christian philosophy, which they see as impugning both the autonomy of the natural order and the gratuity of its supernatural counterpart. For those closer to the Augustinian tradition, like Maurice Blondel, the solution lies in recognizing the vital compenetration of the supernatural with the natural, and so affirming the essential openness of philosophy which can invite faith to bring to it a fuller resolution of the human problem.

We shall look at how a Christian philosophy is structured under the principal headings of "God" and "humankind"—admitting that reflection on neither can profitably be advanced without due attention to that key term of all metaphysics, "being."

God

For Catholicism, certain salient features of the concept of God can be put in place already by rational reflection, especially on what is implied in the notion of a ground-for-the-world that is in itself infinitely distinct from anything within the world. For the philosophers, God is essentially the principle of all present being. For the Church's Scriptures, God's essence is far from exhausted by this function. He is, after all, essentially free with respect to the world, as is definitively revealed in Christ's resurrection. Yet the philosophers' exploration of divine causality lent itself in various ways to the proclamation of the Christian God—notably in matters of God's unity and otherness, his spiritual nature and his incomprehensibility. Philosophy helped Augustine to write in his *Confessions:*

> What is this God? I asked the earth and it answered: "I am not he"; and all the things that are in the earth made the same confession. I asked the sea and the deeps and the creeping things, and they answered, "We are not your God: seek higher." I asked the winds that blow, and the whole air with all that is in it answered, "Anaximenes was wrong; I am not God." I asked the heavens, the sun, the moon, the stars, and they answered, "Neither are we God whom you seek." And I said to all the things that throng about the gateways of my flesh, "You have told me of my God, that you are not he; so tell me something of him." And they cried out in a great voice: "He made us."[1]

The very immanence of the divine ground within the world implied in the fact that Augustine could "interrogate" the creation about God, demands, in other words, its transcendence of the world. No part of the whole can be present to the whole as such. Only what transcends the whole can be present to it. Hence there is no true divine immanence in the universe unless God transcends the world.

---

1. Augustine, *Confessions* 10.6.

The notion—crucial as it is to the Church's doctrine of God—that this ground is an uncreated ground, standing over against all that proceeds from it by way of creation, is open in principle to reason, though, de facto, it was only by means of the scriptural revelation that it entered the philosophical tradition. The doctrine of creation states that God is the ground of the existence of everything there is, the universal ground of all possibility and necessity, so that all being exists by virtue of the creativity of God.

To grasp the divine omnipresence it is vital to see that between God and the existents he causes there is no intermediary. There is no action or energy passing out of God. The divine causality is one with the divine being. Thus there are simply two realities: God himself, in himself—and all other beings. The divine immanence (the "innerness" of God to the world) is the being of the creature as dependent on God's causality, which is God himself. Such an understanding is at once an affirmation of God's transcendence (nothing "goes out" of God to become mingled with the creature) and of his immanence (the being that is of and in all beings is the presence of God to them). Thus the medieval Italian mystic Angela of Foligno was able to write: "I saw that every creature was filled with him,"[2] for he is the being of all creatures. The sixteenth-century Spanish spiritual theologian John of the Cross echoes this vision when he calls God the "center of the soul," the center proper to each rational creature, while the twentieth-century French Jesuit poet-scientist Pierre Teilhard de Chardin went further in naming him the "Center of centers," *Centrum super centra*. God's immanence—even the most insignificant movement in the evolutionary process of the world's becoming is impregnated with his presence— derives from his transcendence. The Catholic doctrine of God is thus the exact contrary of immanentism, of pantheism.

God's creative action is not simply, however, the ground of all being. It is also the principle of the rational order of creation, and the bestower of its developing life. God is, therefore, not just the source of creation but the origin of creation's capacity to give a response to its Creator.

For Catholicism, the world contributes nothing to God, but God gives everything positive to the world. To be the creative and sustaining cause of all being—including rational structure, evolutionary novelty, and responsive relationship to himself—adds no new quality to

2. *Il libro della beata Angela da Foligno* (Rome, 1950) 36.

God. God is not related to creatures by anything added when they come into being. It is in his own being and acting (which are one with himself) that he is freely yet totally related to his world. God's involvement is the very being and working out of creation. The existence and activity of creatures are real and actual divine effects; they are the reality of God's being immanent.

Yet the concept of God, however much it may delight natural reason, does not itself arise from reasoning. It is, merely, purified by reason, and then, in the (Old and) New Testament revelation, disclosed in its true and highest character. In the first place, the idea of God arises from the religious imagination of humankind. This is entirely predictable if in fact we were brought into existence by an almighty creativity who has left us a trace of himself in the power we call "imagination." It is imagination's peculiar property that it can range from fairly humdrum processes of ordinary perception to the highest activities of mind in knowing as well as in creating literary and artistic forms.

In the first place, we can think of imagination as the "odd-jobber" of our mental life. Just as we need an odd-jobber for prosaic bits and pieces of household management, so in intellectual management we find we need such functions as imagining-how, imagining-that, and imagining-as. The common factor here is interpretation: we are faced with something given in our ordinary situation which is for some reason problematic, and we need to interpret it, to see it anew. Thus for the eighteenth-century Scottish philosopher David Hume imaginative interpretation enables us to live in the (as he would say) distinctively human world where persons remain identical over time, and events have causes. For his German contemporary Immanuel Kant, imagination enables the mind to order the perceptual field of sense experience into distinctive unities. For the early twentieth-century English thinker R. G. Collingwood, it makes possible the writing of history by allowing us to reenact the thoughts of people in the past. In such ways, the image-making faculty allows us to move more easily in the empirical realm, interpreting the problematic data of experience in more coherent and intelligible ways.

But Kant in particular drew attention to a kind of imaginative encounter which at once is rooted in the world of sense and opens a door to a religious or spiritual dimension. There are certain images heard or seen by us that we might agree to describe as beautiful: these are, for Kant, images that present us with some kind of satisfying form or inner order in which the mind takes pleasure. But there are also (again, following Kant) aspects of the world that trigger a sense of the sublime, a sense that the real transcends our capacity to image it. We express this in certain highly charged representations: in cult and drama, painting and sculpture, narrative, symbol, and metaphor—representations that strain after something beyond the confines of experience. After Kant, F. W. J. Schelling will take this one step further by saying that the artistic or religious innovator of genius brings forth symbols that are able to manifest the infinite in the finite, the universally significant in the particular. Here imagination takes on a religious inflection. Its images enable us to grasp nature and consciousness as pointing towards infinite being, infinite spirit. By attending to epiphanies in finite beings we come to apprehend the infinite: the God of imagination.

Not all such religious symbols operate, of course, in a theistic way. Buddhism, for instance, is fairly clearly not a religion of the one God, although the "plenary Void" of Nirvana might be compared with the preference of much Greek Christian theology for negative descriptions of God ("he is not this, not that"). Extreme respect for the mystery of the divine Being is not agnosticism. However, it seems altogether too easy to restate all talk of transcendence—a depth to, source of, meaning beyond the empirical order—as talk of the one God of the theistic tradition. There is a conflict between religions, and we must choose. It is the theist's conviction that the religious imagery of this tradition, where the divine is evoked on a personal model as Creator, Lord, Redeemer, commends itself better than all other imageries to the rational intelligence. It has the greatest power to make sense of finite experience, to connect the various epiphanies of religious experience, and to express in coherent fashion the relation between the world and that other world which is God.

The history of the sense of God, then, is a history of images—images generated by the urge of mind and heart to uncover the infinite in the finite, whether in nature, history, or moral or mystical experience. The history of the concept of God, by contrast, is a history of the purification of all images of God by thought, by reason. Both moments are necessary, yet the God of imagination always retains a certain priority. Without images of God there is nothing to criticize. No concept of God can emerge until these images have been provisionally accepted, and then tried and tested in the crucible of philosophy.

Catholic Christians believe that one particular succession of theistic images is uniquely important, because it prepared the sense of God entertained and communicated by Jesus Christ. This gallery of images is what we know as the Old Testament. Beginning from the pagan, or generally Semitic, image of a divine realm behind, yet involved in, all natural activity (fertility, sun, storm) the people of the Old Testament started off their collection of images with a perception of Elohim, or El—the primordial Hebrew words for God. In the patriarchal period they added the image of the divine as friend and protector, active in succoring the lives of the clans and their chiefs: the God of the Fathers, the shield of Abraham, bull of Isaac, rock or mighty One of Israel. Millennia later, Aquinas, as a "master of the sacred page" will say that in calling God "rock," "fire," "husband," and so forth, the ancient writers posited a likeness of relation, an analogy of metaphorical proportionality. Two terms, differing completely with respect to their nature, may have between them a certain dynamic or functional equivalence. The mysterious reality at the root of divine action acts as if it were these things. At the Exodus, Moses received the divine name as YHWH—notoriously hard to translate but conveying the idea of One who is supereminently real and who commits himself to moving forward in history with the people he has called to be his own. Prophets, wisdom writers, priests, lawyers, theologians of the Davidic city of Zion, apocalyptists, novelists like the author of the Book of Tobit: all of these made their own contributions to what we can think of as the picture gallery of the Old Testament. These pictures were not identical. But they were bound into a unitary complex by the common life and worship of a people. Through them, that people apprehended their God imaginatively, in liturgy, prayer, and story. Jesus will decisively transform these images when he reconstellates them around the image of the Abba, the "dear Father." To say that the God disclosed in this gallery is the true God is to say that the providence behind the world has—in this specific tradition—used in a unique way the image-making faculty of humankind, disclosing the Creator in a gradual way suited to human capacities, building up to the climax attained through the consciousness and work of Jesus Christ.

To pass from the God of imagination to the God of reason is simply to consider the reasons for thinking that this imaginative sense of God truly attaches us to reality. For the most part, such reasons are explications of the experiential epiphanies grasped by the imagination, though some derive from pondering the conditions of possibility for the existence of a world—and thus such experiencing subjects as ourselves—at all.

The First Vatican Council (1869–70), framed its declaration on this topic in these words: "The one and true God, our Creator and Lord, can be known through the creation by the natural light of human reason."[3] In other words, the images of God in the Judaeo-Christian tradition decant into a concept of the Creator Lord, the sovereign, transcendent source of nature and history. And this concept can be shown actually to be exemplified in reality "by the natural light of human reason." It has sometimes been supposed that the council committed Catholics to seek a proof of God's existence in strict logical form, a demonstration in a quasi-mathematical sense. Yet the key words of the text are ample, broad, capable of multiple interpretation: a knowledge "through the creation" (through some, or perhaps each and every, aspect of finite being), "by the natural light of human reason" (human reason *tout court*, with no attempt to lay down in advance what mode or style of human rationality that might be). This open invitation turns into more general form Paul's rebuke of unbelievers in the Letter to the Romans: "God's everlasting power and deity, however invisible, are there for the mind to see in the things he has made" (Rom 1:20), a rebuke which itself draws on the fuller remarks of the author of Wisdom (13:1, 3): "What folly it argues in man's nature, this ignorance of God! So much good seen, and he, who is existent Good, not known! . . . Such great beauty even creatures have, reason is well able to contemplate the Source from which these perfections came."

In the context of the astral and nature cults of Mediterranean religion, this is at once an attack on idolatry and a plea for the recognition of an underived Source disclosing itself in the world of finite forms. But we should not be too hasty in taking this affirmation of fontal being to mean that only some form of the cosmological argument or the argument from design will serve our turn. In Catholicism, many kinds of argument for the existence of God can find house and home.

An account of the God of reason involves, in fact, sifting numerous suggestive experiences to see whether, taken cumulatively, they do not make God's existence so overwhelmingly probable as to justify our giving it unconditional assent. John Henry Newman, in proposing this as the proper form for the rational justification of Christian theism, spoke of "a cable, which is made up of a number of separate threads, each feeble, yet together as sufficient as an iron rod. An iron rod rep-

---

3. DH 3004. The letters stand for the most commonly used collection of doctrinal authorities, H. Denzinger, *Kompendium der Glaubensbekenntnisse und kirchlichen Lehrentscheidungen*, 37th ed., ed. P. Hünermann (Freiburg, 1991). Cited below as "DH."

resents mathematical or strict demonstration; a cable represents moral demonstration, which is an assemblage of probabilities, separately insufficient for certainty, but when put together irrefragable."[4]

What kinds of experience may be regarded as raw materials in the argument for the existence of God? They would include (1) the "erotic" (desiring) nature of human existence, combined with the realization that nothing finite will ever satisfy the human animal; (2) the discovery that truth is an absolute standard for a conditioned mind; (3) awareness of the finitude of beings—their transience and contingency—bringing with it the insight that the entire universe of being exists by grace and favor; (4) the apparent authenticity of much mystical experience; (5) our sense of the irremediable ambiguity of humankind, "glory and refuse of the universe" as Pascal judged, a walking tragedy which only the healing goodness of an infinite God can resolve; (6) moral obligation as an implicit awareness of the presence of the all-holy foundation of morals; (7) the need of human society (and individuals) for a hope that refuses to be bound by the limits set by calculation, and so implies some transcendent ground of hoping; (8) in G. K. Chesterton's words, "joy without a cause," a reaction of joy to the fact that there should be such a thing as life at all, for "existence . . . has the wild beauty of a woman, and those love her with most intensity who love her with least cause."[5] In this romantic epiphany, religion finds its justification by being the vindication of joy, play, thanksgiving, our sense of basic security in the world, and of all that embodies these things in human living.

If these areas of experience were to be assessed singly, we could not be sure that a reductionist account of them would not suffice to meet the demands of reason. For each of them a naturalistic explanation might serve, though some would mount a stronger resistance thereto than others. But the mind, engaging with the materials of life, does not assess areas of experience singly. It has a marked tendency to integrate them and let them fall, if they will, into a pattern. And the pattern formed by the kinds of materials considered here is manifestly theistic: their uncreated pole is a reality supremely desirable, all-knowing, the fount of existence, offering itself in communion to humankind, the resolution of our restlessness, ethically all-holy, provident in giving us grounds for hope, the secret joy at the heart of being. And this (to echo

4. Cited in W. Ward, *The Life of John Henry Cardinal Newman, Based on His Private Journals and Correspondence* (London, 1912) 2.243.

5. G. K. Chesterton, *Charles Dickens* (London, 1966) 41–42.

Aquinas) all human beings call God. The simplicity or elegance of the God of reason lies in the way this God is simultaneously the key to so many arresting features of self and world.[6]

Reason has less to say on the question, if God be the patterner of our existence, then what is the divine pattern like? It is harder to grasp the inner shape of the divine life. This is as it should be, for, on the analogy of the person, we should have to say that a reality of this kind must be supremely a subject: an initiator of relationships. And the whole point about subjects is that they cannot simultaneously be affirmed as both subject and object in the same way. I cannot enjoy a deeply personal relationship with someone and put the same quantity of mental energy into considering them as an interesting specimen of human zoology. It is because God is so totally a subject that the great Protestant opponent of Catholic natural theology, Karl Barth, was so unwilling to permit the obtrusive interference of rational theology in revelation. If the God of reason encroaches on the terrain of the God of love, he does indeed become an abstraction, a mental idol, just as the God of imagination uncriticized by the God of reason can be "away with the fairies." Nevertheless, just as the God of reason cannot be thought of without the help of the God of imagination—for in the beginning was the image, the symbol, the story—so the God of love cannot disclose himself as truly the God of love without the God of reason. We need to know that the Old Testament Lord of covenant love and faithfulness, the New Testament Father of Jesus, really is the God disclosed to all human beings in the structures of the cosmos and the human spirit.

In speaking of the infinite, we must be prepared for concepts made to measure for the finite to be a poor fit. Aquinas, building on both the Platonist tradition and its Christianization in the patristic age, speaks of language applying to God through a dialectic of affirmation and negation. We know that God exceeds all that we understand of him; and to this extent, we know him. There are, nonetheless, concepts available to us that are distinguished by their ability to capture aspects of the life of finite spirits—knowledge, for instance, or love—in a manner sufficiently supple for us to use them in speaking of infinite Spirit, so long as we do not claim to know their mode of application to the infinite. The same may be said of the "pure perfections," concepts drawn from our grasp of being as such—unity, goodness, beauty—which can

6. For a fuller account, see A. Nichols, *A Grammar of Consent. The Existence of God in Christian Tradition* (Notre Dame, Ind., and Edinburgh, 1991).

be made to speak of eternal and self-existent Being. We see the direction in which these concepts can be true of God, though we cannot see its term. This is already a dark knowledge of God which allows us to speak of God as he is in himself, yet discipline such talk by a sense of his mystery. By denying *(via negationis)* the usual sense of language in our assertions about God *(via affirmationis)* we learn how the unlikeness between the Creator and the creature is always greater than the likeness *(via eminentiae)*.

Such perfections of the maker are co-implicative. Here oneness, goodness, and beauty cannot be set over against each other. As the absolute plenitude of being, God is able to draw to himself all desires, to satisfy all needs, to resolve all thought; his pure being is necessarily transparent to itself, totally lucid in its self-possession.

> By the very fact that they acquaint us with the divine essence, our concepts, while remaining themselves, are absorbed in its abyss. In God what they signify escapes—without our being able to know how—our mode of conceiving. The divine essence is thus really reached by our metaphysical knowledge—but without handing itself over to us. It is known, but its mystery remains intact. . . . In the very fact of our knowing it, it escapes our grasp, and infinitely surpasses our knowledge.[7]

The First Vatican Council summed up the rational knowability and the simultaneous unfathomable mystery of God when it summarized the preceding tradition by confessing

> One living and true God, Creator and Lord of heaven and earth, almighty, eternal, immense, incomprehensible, infinite in intellect and will and every perfection: who, since he is one unique and altogether spiritual substance, must be proclaimed to be really and essentially distinct from the world, in and of himself most blessed and unspeakably exalted above all things which exist and can be conceived outside him.[8]

The same council also emphasized the freedom and graciousness of God in creation: he created, in his goodness and almighty power, "not to acquire but to manifest his perfection," through the good things he granted to creatures. "All things are from him, and through him, and to him" (Rom 11:35), wrote Paul. As powerful, God calls the world into being, sustains it, and moves it toward the fulfillment of his purpose. As wise, he fully comprehends its reality, and the ways whereby it can

---

7. J. Maritain, *Distinguer pour unir, ou, Les degrés du Savoir* (Paris, 1932) 453.
8. DH 3001.

reach the goal he sets for it. As loving, he intends the communication of his life and goodness to created things.

We have seen that, as the sole fount of being, God is the source of the most intimate reality of each thing. The divine activity undergirds the entire network of created causes, forming them into the unity of a single universe, and drawing them to the goal he proposes. God makes creatures not only to exist but also to act: they share with one another the goodness or reality they receive from him. Acting according to its own nature and capacities, the creature is already an instrument of the power of God. In the case of creatures endowed with freedom, however, all activity contains at least an implicit response to God. This is eminently true of the human being.

Humankind

Human beings are for Catholicism proper objects of metaphysics. They are also metaphysical subjects: their bodily being is the expression of a spiritual being that can be exercised independently of the body (though more frequently is not). The giveaway sign of humankind's special status is its capacity for history. The human being does not only, like the other animals, inhabit nature. He or she can also advance creatively into the novelty of events. The human creature has a capacity for history—not merely for reading and writing books about past events, but for enacting the events whose significance it is the historian's business to exhibit.

The fully human act is the emergence of radical novelty, distinct from the cyclic repetition of the organic world. Such an act can already be called, at the level of human affairs, a "revelation." This is not only because it is the conclusion of a deliberative process conducted in the mind and heart of free agents, illuminating their own being to themselves and showing up the requirements of some situation in a new light. Human action is also "revelation" because normally, though not necessarily, it finds translation into bodily visibility. Every person is an artist, revealingly translating interior novelty into manifest exteriority. The human gesture, made in the public world, is the medium in which our inner life is realized in the world around us. Human language makes explicit the content of such gestures, giving them intelligible sense. This is how mutual self-disclosure, and thus creative communion with others, is achieved.

God, the source and ground of the world, since he is the fount of all being, its order, development, and responsiveness, could make use of this crucial aspect of the human condition. He could insert into the historical process not only awareness of a plan for uniting human beings to each other in himself but also the actuality of that plan. A series of (divinely) efficacious gestures could furnish a share in the divine life in a new community for all peoples, the Church.

> And this is the drawing-up of our faith, the foundation of the building, and the consolidation of a way of life. God the Father, uncreated, beyond grasp, invisible, one God the maker of all: this is the first and foremost article of our faith. But the second article is the Word of God, the Son of God, Christ Jesus our Lord, who was shown forth by the prophets according to the design of their prophecy and according to the manner in which the Father disposed, and through him were made all things whatsoever. He also, at the end of times, for the recapitulation of all things, is become a man among men, visible and tangible, in order to abolish death and bring to light life, and bring about the communion of God and man. And the third article is the Holy Spirit, through whom the prophets prophesied and the patriarchs were taught about God and the just were led in the path of justice, and who at the end of times has been poured forth in a new manner upon humanity over all the earth renewing man to God.[9]

A view of human nature as open to God will not simply, then, leave space for the operation of a general providence that takes foresight for human destiny as for the rest of created being. Rather will it concern the direct interaction of God with humankind, as the origin affects the process at certain definite points in time and space, centrally in the incarnation of the Word and the manifestation of the Spirit.

The incarnation of the Word is not simply a theophany, a revelation of God to humankind. As the manifestation of the divine interiority—the mystery of the divine essence—in the gestures of the Word in public space, and the words of the Word in human discourse, it must also be a new creation, the introduction of a new spiritual principle that gradually leavens and transforms human nature.

Such supernatural gradualism is opposed to revolutionary utopianism in all its forms. Karl Marx and G. W. F. Hegel both played at being the Redeemer God, since neither of them was prepared to tolerate the imperfection of the world. Unaware that the best we can achieve in civil society is a fragile equilibrium of freedom and restraint, Hegel sought the perfect identity of reason, necessity, and freedom in

---

9. Irenaeus, *Demonstration of the Apostolic Preaching* 6.

the rational state, Marx in the communist society. For both, the world must be humanly transformed into a perfect condition. With Hegel, this takes place, after a certain point in historical evolution, through speculation; for Marx, via revolutionary praxis. Both exemplify the Promethean temptation of Western thought since the Renaissance. Neither can be fully refuted or replaced except by restoration of the concept of the human being as "pontifical": as a bridge *(pons)* between the divine and the world of matter, and thus at once a channel and a recipient of grace. For only God can so work on the disorder of things that—without interference, much less conflict, with the created pattern—he can by his creative and redeeming purpose restore the world to a goodness beyond its own devising. Our freedom is not independence from God, but his giving us a genuine role in what happens. By contrast, the self-divinization of the human being, which arose from certain currents in the thought of the Renaissance, led to a practical idolatry of the human: "man is God to man," *homo homini Deus*. With such presuppositions as these, the achievements of humankind in ethical heroism, artistic creativity, or scientific genius are no longer seen as touches of the Absolute, visitations of a *daimōn*, a rumor of angels, but, rather, as just what one should expect of human powers. By the nineteenth century, the idea that what is given to God is *ipso facto* taken away from human beings had become imaginatively pervasive. It was taken for granted that the dignity of human beings lies in their autonomy, their being dependent on, responsive to, and indebted to none but themselves for good or ill. Such a Promethean picture of humankind is close to Lucifer's *Non serviam*, "I will not serve." It is at once a cause and a symptom of the collapse of any imagery of God as truly the Creator of the human race, the primal Freedom which grounds and sustains our derived freedom. There can be no move from the life of humanity to theistic images of the divine, seriously entertained, till this Promethean picture is replaced by a pontifical alternative. In this latter world-view, the human being would be the pontifex, the bridge-builder between the visible and invisible worlds, between created and uncreated, the goal knowledge and love, whose service is perfect freedom. Human persons are not absolutes. They are called beyond themselves, and their receptivity to this call constitutes their glory.

The final authority governing the human mind is thus not the flux of phenomena (as in positivism), nor the historical process (as in Marxism), nor the mind itself (as in existentialism), nor the principles of reason (as in idealism), but God. The predicate *true* finds its full meaning only in relation to the all-encompassing truth, which is equivalent to an absolute mind. The same goes for the final good that governs the human will.

> When ethics and living are in question, I do not think it is necessary to look any further for what is the sovereign good of man to which everything must be related. For it has been shown by reason—insofar as we are capable of it—and by that divine authority which exceeds our reason, that it is nothing else than God himself. What indeed could be the highest good of man if not that whose possession makes him perfectly happy? This good is God himself, to whom it is certain that we can only be attached by direction, love, charity.[10]

The human being relates to this divine truth and divine goodness in a way that accords with human nature: that is, through history. The history concerned is of two kinds: the general history of human culture in which the person's relation with God is possible only in a diffuse and indirect way, and the special history of revelation, with its salvific goal— sacred history, where this relation exists in a focused and direct form.

In the sacred history that Christianity at once assumes from Judaism and proclaims through its own gospel, the human person both passes through historical time so as to enter, at death, an eternity which already, in life, surrounds him or her, and also, *qua* individual member of the human race as a whole, waits for the future parousia of the Lord, when all God's ways with the world will reach their goal. "Time ends in eternity even before the end of time."[11] The principal events of this episodically unfolding sacred history are found in the divine economy which the Christian faith reflects in and the sacraments of that faith, which are the continuing extension of the special divine action in later time. By contrast, the religious significance of the history of human culture at large is not so unambiguous. That history does not follow a single thread of progress, as simple evolutionary theories suppose. Just as cultures, like individuals, may die and pass away for ever, or die and be reborn, so the civilizations through which the sacred history passes know what the Judaeo-Christian Scriptures call their "times," crises of internal disruption caused by hubris of one sort or another, to which they may react by either dissolution or purification. Such "times," or crucial moments, not only subsume and perpetuate

---

10. Augustine, *On the Customs of the Catholic Church* 14.24.
11. T. Dilworth, *The Shape of Meaning in the Poetry of David Jones* (Toronto, Buffalo, London, 1988) 200.

that crisis par excellence which was the death and resurrection of the Word made flesh, but also anticipate the final verdict of God in history. For the individual person, immersed in history, judgment is an ever-present reality, while the world of creatures as a whole has still to learn that judgment hangs over it. In both senses, the history of the world is the story of a perpetual judgment, of which the parousia will form the consummation.

But what are the elements of human nature to be thus purified and transformed in what Dante calls *la vita nuova,* the "new life"? According to Catholic anthropology, the human being was created as a duality-in-unity: soul and body, at once animated body and embodied soul. While it is the essential task of soul, as the spiritual principle in humanity, to give life to the body which shares after its own fashion in our being "in God's image, to his likeness" (Gen 1:27), nonetheless it is the soul's special originating mark that, in its utter simplicity (so unlike the complexities of biochemistry) it is created immediately by God, and in that simplicity will escape the decay to which organisms are subject; it will not perish, then, at its separation from the body in death. This in turn, however, should not be taken to mean that the Creator ever envisaged the soul without reference to the body which it is to animate. Rather must we think of God as creating precisely that soul and no other which, in union with the body that human procreation and heredity have provided, can enter into the unique and unrepeatable unity of a particular human being.

We have not yet fathomed, however, the deepest basis of the unity of soul and body, in a principle which also serves as the highest index of their purposeful engagement. Human beings share the dignity of being persons: able to enter into communion with other persons and to be called by grace to covenant relations—a union of knowledge and love—with their Creator. The Church's anthropology is not exclusively or even primarily speculative, but has in view a practical aim, namely, the moral, ascetic, and mystical life whereby human persons are united with God and so with all their fellow creatures. To be a spiritual being—even an embodied one—is to be able to penetrate other beings to their ontological interior, to make them part of one's own life without violation of their integrity.

The twelfth-century monastic theologian William of St. Thierry, who explored, in the steps of Augustine and Bernard, the essential mystery of our nature, set forth in his *On the Nature and Dignity of Love* the two very different directions in which the human being can travel.

The heart should "govern body and soul like a king in his realm," yet under the influence of distorted desire it can "flow down into the belly and even lower." Alternatively, the heart can take an upward direction, allowing love to be purified until it is fit to be united to God. Then "holiness of life and the transfiguration of the inner man become visible." The flesh can become, in the faces of the saints, transparent to the future glory.[12]

Through the five senses the soul feels, knows, and understands, coordinating their deliverances as a unity. The wonderful conjunction of body and soul has its closest bond in the imagination (the image-forming faculty, which is not more of soul than it is of body and vice versa). For William, five loves correspond to the five senses. First, diffused through humanity as is the sense of touch throughout the body, comes the love of our near relatives. Normal and unremarkable, it may be taken for granted, needing more curbing than development. Next, comparable to the sense of taste, comes social love, based on common interests, for taste, like the imagination, is bodily yet quasi-spiritual. The altruistic love of our fellows for their own sake, *amor naturalis*, William compares to smell, for this is more spiritual still: scent, though it enters the soul through the body, leaves soul not body affected. Spiritual love he likens to hearing, and defines by it the love of our enemies. Hearing signifies obedience, and the love of those we dislike is something we can only achieve by obeying the commands of the gospel. Needing constant practice, it brings about in us in time the likeness of the Son of God. The love of God, finally, resembles sight, the highest of the senses, a fitting analogue for the highest of loves, that of God for his own sake. On this scheme, no one is complete who has not developed the entire fivefold hierarchy of love, in which even the most elementary and self-interested love is drawn through an ascending scale to love what is Godlike in human beings, to love in a Godlike way, and eventually to love God himself as perfectly as he may be loved.[13]

As later Catholic anthropology will insist, all the functions that make up properly human behavior are unified by the person who thus appropriates soul and body with all their powers and commits them to action. By reflecting on consciousness, on what it is to be a subject in action, we are led to explore the experience of being an agent, what the

12. William of St. Thierry, *On the Nature and Dignity of Love* 3–13.
13. Ibid., 19–24.

philosopher-pope Karol Wojtyla has called the "experience of effi-cacy." To a degree the person transcends nature, for, as the image of God, humanity enjoys free determination, and the power to initiate ac-tion; as Aquinas pointed out, echoing the seventh-century Church Father John of Damascus, the human person is *autoexousion, causa sui*. At the same time, the free act must also have a cognitive dimension, for freedom does not dispense persons from maintaining their place within the order of truth. Indeed, moral agents cannot possess them-selves via an act of really responsible self-determination unless that act respects the essential structure—the ontological truth—of their own personhood, including, via the soul, the natural finality of the human body and its characteristic rhythms. Moral action, when it is in corre-spondence with the true, serves to establish the unity of body and soul in the personhood of each human being.

This should not be understood, however, in some hermetically in-dividualist sense. As etymology indicates, a *person* is a communicator, an individual subject in dialogue, and so from the start of existence a member of a community. A person is a respondent. Concern with com-munion (as distinct from mere social coexistence) distinguishes Catholic anthropology from its competitors, whether in European totali-tarianism or in Anglo-Saxon individualism. The ultimate relationship—and the reason why ecclesial society, the Church, is of greater moment, for human nature, than civil society in all its forms—will be, then, with the Creator, who calls me into existence by name, and continues to call me into association with himself in his divine community.[14]

Yet in social communion too (namely, by reflecting on their experi-ence of responsible action), human beings can become aware of that unique, inalienable dignity which is theirs as personal subjects, whose very self-fulfillment demands self-giving—a self-giving through which they are able, wondrously, to share in the life of other centers of freedom. Such self-donation forms a bond of true communion between human beings. Here is the deepest ground of the "third way" in the so-cial doctrine of the Church, which we shall consider later in this study. It was owing to a failure to recognize the dignity of human beings as personal agents that the materialisms of classical liberal capitalism and Marxian socialism dehumanized their objects, making people the ser-vants or the products, respectively, of impersonal forces.

---

14. K. Wojtyla, *The Acting Person* (Boston, 1979); "The Person: Subject and Community," *Review of Metaphysics* 33 (1979) 273–308.

Such an account of human identity highlights what in the human sciences today goes for the most part by default—the result, we may well think, of too exclusively empirical a view of definition and method. Yet such sciences can never prove the absence of Godward relationship, but only fail to demonstrate this relatedness, which is quite another matter. Since every material sign of the human being's Godly dimension is, for empiricism, equivocal, such empirical methods cannot constitute the final court of appeal in discussion of the human mystery.

A Catholic anthropology, furthermore, holds out hope for the practical, and not just theoretical, resolution of the human "affair." Pierre Teilhard de Chardin, for instance, holds that while compulsions, at once geographical and psychological, oblige human beings to live and think in ever-closer proximity, they do not necessarily love each other the more on that account: far from it. In *L'Avenir de l'homme* he insists that only the appearance, at the summit and heart of the world, of an "autonomous center of congregation" can inspire, release, and preserve, within a spiritually dispersed humanity, the power of true unity. Only a "veritable super-love" can, of psychological necessity, control and synthesize the host of other earthly loves. Without such a center of universal convergence, there can be no real coherence among humankind. A world that culminates in the impersonal can bring us neither the warmth of attraction nor the hope of "irreversibility" (immortality). And without these, individual egoism will always have the last word—echoing Albert Camus's statement that if humans found that the universe could love they would be reconciled.[15] This is where the incarnation belongs. Here one can find God in humanity and humanity in God, as the Cistercian doctors pointed out long ago. For Bernard, the charity-love that flows from the incarnate Lord enables us to show effective compassion to fallen human nature, both in ourselves and in others. For his English contemporary Aelred, that same charity creates the concord of brethren living in unity, enjoying their collateralness and companionship. For William of St. Thierry, the love of Christ in other human beings verges on an act of adoration for him present there, since through the incarnation everything human has become a vehicle for the divine.

The catalyst in such transformation of human powers can only be the Holy Spirit joining human wills to himself—he who is in his own

15. P. Teilhard de Chardin, *L'Avenir de l'homme* (Paris, 1959).

substance the will of Father and Son. The Trinitarian understanding of God presents us with the Holy Spirit as both Giver and Gift, Giver in the changelessness of eternity, Gift in the changeableness of time. The presence of the Holy Spirit in God's own being flows over, through grace, as a presence in our souls where he causes in us that literally "ecstatic" (outgoing) co-presence of Father and Son which is the archetype of all relationship whatsoever. The centrality of the soul in its origin, between God and the body, gives way to a centrality in the Holy Spirit, between Father and Son, in the midst of the divine Trinity. This is the final transformation which, being eternal, has no end.

The anthropology of Scripture read in Tradition is therefore a theomorphic anthropology: the human person is called to bear the form, *morphē*, of God himself, to be a living image of the unseen *Elohim*, the God of Israel who is also the God of all the world. Though this carries the danger of encouraging idolatry of the human, the New Testament successfully scotches that threat. As the Letter to the Colossians says, Jesus Christ, the Word who, becoming flesh, became the self-emptying poor man of Nazareth, is the "image of the invisible God" (1:15). Christ is not only the definitive revelation of God in the finite, providing a key to God's purposes in his creation, he is also the perfect fulfillment of the humanity spoiled in Adam, and thus the measure and goal for human beings. And so the anthropology of the Church is necessarily a Christological anthropology.[16]

If reflection on the problem of humanity leads the Catholic mind to Christ, so also does thinking of the mystery of God. As we have seen already, rational reflection on the divine produces a *docta ignorantia*, an "enlightened ignorance" wherein we know principally of God what he is not. The modest understanding that the search for the God of reason achieves must give way to some other mode of knowledge if the promise of divine presence held out by the images of the God of imagination is not to be judged empty. In the history of revelation propitious conditions are created for the embodiment of the transcendent Creator within his own world. As the fifteenth-century metaphysical theologian Nicholas of Cusa has it, the *maximum absolutum* of God, the totality of underived being, becomes—at a midpoint of history, in the incarnation, which is comparable only with the original creation of the world—conjoined with the *maximum contractum* of the world, the to-

---

16. For this theme, see A. Nichols, *The Art of God Incarnate: Theology and Image in Christian Tradition* (London, 1980).

tality of derived being: "The maximal and minimal coincide: maximal humiliation with exaltation."[17]

Christ is at once *viator* and *comprehensor:* himself a traveler, and yet the One who comes to meet all human beings at some point on life's way. He is "the man who loves and the God who is beloved."[18] The person who receives this as the truth, says Nicholas, is converted in spirit, and finds himself journeying towards the God who is not only lovable but love itself.[19] It is "the most sweet Jesus," he remarks in the epilogue addressed to his patron, Cardinal Cesarini, who opens to us "the goal of the mind's desire." In sympathetic identification with the human consciousness of Jesus Christ and in receipt of all that flowed from his mission, we come to share that inner exchange which is the life of God itself. We discover the commerce of Jesus and his Abba ("dear Father") in the Holy Spirit: an everlasting interpersonal communion of self-giving goodness, offered to us also, insofar as we can bear it, in grace and glory. Here the God of reason gives way at last to the God of love. But our exploration of that must await the chapter of this book on the revealed, Churchly doctrine of God—the Holy Trinity.

17. Nicholas of Cusa, *On Learned Ignorance* 1.4.
18. Ibid. 3.12.
19. Ibid. 3.9.

2
Revelation and Its Sources

Revelation

Monotheism proposes a world distinct from God but not separate from him. Creation carries within it an iconic power—a capacity to image, or echo, its Creator. This in turn means that the world has a fundamental (and therefore God-given) possibility of being an epiphany of the divine presence, and that presence's transforming power. Unbelieving humankind misses its opportunity, failing to recognize and praise the Creator, which is why Paul says that our moral sense becomes a wayward guide (Rom 1:18-23). But suppose God were himself to liberate this iconic, epiphanic power vested in beings in their substance and process and, with special intensity, in human beings in their identity and story? This, for the Church, is what the almighty maker of the world has done through the prophets and other inspired persons of the old covenant, and finally, at the heart of the new, in his Son Jesus Christ whom the apostolic witness proclaims the Word par excellence—the very self-expression of God and so the key that unlocks the significance of God's many "words," the center of revelation history.

The idea that in Jesus and as Jesus what appears is the Source of being itself cannot indeed be grasped without revelation. Nor is this surprising. Owing to the negative phenomena of evil and finiteness—which are no mere epiphenomena, though the one entails defect and the other is sheer deficiency of being, but true *phenomena* in the root meaning of that word: striking realities—history is incapable of fulfilling itself by its own resources. There may be signs and pointers to meaning *in* the world but there are no signs of a meaning *of* the world, of the world as a whole. Of course when the concept of history is too narrowly defined to permit a disclosure by way of revelation, then criticism must necessarily oppose the gospel's revelatory claim. But when historical critics take a view of reality (and so of history) that is open to transcendence, they need not oppose the idea of revelation.

Humankind is situated in history, and yet is not totally subject to history's conditions. Like other living things, human beings are endowed with a nature, yet not in such a way that they can dispense with the free, creative, spiritual self-constitution of their existence on that nature's basis. The revelation the Church claims to transmit corresponds well to the condition of so spirited an animal. She regards this revelation as located in history but unconfined by history's limits, for through humankind the world is open to the transcendent, the absolute. It likewise fits humanity's "dialectical" relation to history that, on the one hand, the truth of revelation either expands until the close of the climactic revelatory epoch of the incarnation or, in the time of the subsequent Church, is further refined, while, on the other hand, the revealed truth is, thanks to the gift of the Spirit, truly "in" Christians, really interior to them, as their own persons here and now. For the human species occupies in developmental mode the span between the beginning, the origins of the race, and the end, the final truth of the kingdom, and yet does so without prejudice to the ability of each of its members to apprehend (over against the rest if need be) what is true, beautiful, and good.

Catholic Christianity understands itself, then, as a revealed religion. It is a way of life, worship, and prayer created by divine initiative, and entered upon out of obedience to a more than human demand. This unveiling of initiative and demand is what constitutes revelation from the side of its divine subject. Such disclosure necessarily involves, moreover—and indeed this is its highest office—the disclosure of the Subject himself, for, as the Scholastics rightly insisted, *agere sequitur esse*, "action manifests being." Although an historical revelation that was not the disclosure of the Source of all being could hardly be called a manifestation of God, this particular disclosure—or, rather, this Christologically unified set of disclosures—was made through the medium of historical events. Nor should this perplex us, incorrigible searchers after timeless truths of reason though we are. After all, if temporality is the mode of being of the cosmos, the Lord of the cosmos is necessarily the Lord of history also.

Such revelation in history implies some consciousness, on the part of revelation's recipients, that the human situation has been changed from beyond. And this in turn implies a transformed awareness which may come about through reworked concepts, or refashioned images, or, most probably, through both of these together, for at its highest, human penetration of the real is at once conceptual and perceptive, thought that makes images its vehicles, imagining empowered by thought.

If revelation is a disclosure of initiative and demand then the relation between human recipient and divine Subject is best understood on the analogy of our experience of persons, who are also acting subjects, after their own fashion. Granting privilege to this analogy enables us to call the revelatory transformation, in its unlooked-for quality, the "gift" of God, or, in the Latinate English which sometimes produces so lovely a word, his "grace." Since the demand that issues from the initiative tells us what we ought to do, and, as the philosophers remind us, "ought" implies "can," we rightly describe such grace as the communication of new life, of fresh resources for our nature's being. And so revelation has at one and the same time existential, cognitive, and ontological dimensions. In other words, it changes the human situation, our awareness of it, and our very being itself.

That the divine initiative, demand, and grace, are found in history implies their "economic" or step-by-step manifestation, and this in turn suggests the structure of the overall process, which is one of promise and fulfillment. At one point in this sequence, a moment of initiative, demand, and grace—a revelatory moment—was experienced as plenary. In that moment, the known resistances to the communion of God with humankind—sin and death—were absolutely negated, and human nature in one case, that of Jesus Christ, became fully conformed to the divine will in its final and architectonically conceived aim, and therefore identical with the terminus of the divine promise. That human nature not only altogether received but also in receiving wholly expressed the Father's very life, his self-communicating Word, and thus embodied a unity of the world with and in God only prospective at the moment of creation and unachieved—indeed traduced and parodied—ever since. At that point, the ascension of the risen Lord, revelation was complete. As John of the Cross remarked, God has no further word to say to us than this Word thus spoken in his Son.[1]

Nor is this wholly unexpected: here we need not say, *Credo quia absurdum*, "I can only believe because it is unthinkable." Goodness is self-diffusive, and the higher its order the more abundant and intimate its self-communication, as heroic love can testify. It is not unfitting, then, to think of the Creator of the world as communicating himself in

---

1. John of the Cross, *Ascent of Mount Carmel* 2.22.3–5.

the eternal generation of his Word, nor to conceive that the Word so be-gotten should enter into the created order for our salvation and, be-coming incarnate, exist for us in a "sacrament" (a humanly visible form where the outer gives expression to the inner and leads into its mystery), living and teaching, acting and suffering, embracing our self-inflicted distance from God and triumphantly overcoming that es-trangement in the events of the first Easter.

At that first Easter, though, the plenary revelation embodied in the glorified humanity of Jesus was not yet adequately registered by other people. That happened only with the communication at Pentecost of a share in the new communion of God and humanity as divinely en-compassed in Jesus Christ. This communication came about in and through the creation of a community, the Church, equipped by the Spirit to "remember" (to ponder in her corporate memory and on that basis to articulate) the fullness of divine truth brought by the Revealer. In this perspective, it is only with the dying of the last constitutive member of the apostolic generation—the last apostle—that the revela-tion comes to its term.

In still another sense, however, revelation has still not reached its goal: namely, in as much as the plenary moment of Christ, in his dis-closure of the true finality of history and cosmos, is not yet extended in all its implications to each and every one of the living, the departed, and those yet to be born, nor to the material continuum (the special case of Mary of Nazareth apart) of which his transfigured body is the renewed foundation.

Apologetics

But why do we thus "believe in" Jesus Christ? As with belief in the ex-istence of God himself, we are dealing here with the convergence of a number of factors, all of which point to the conclusion that Jesus of Nazareth was a unique divine "legate" (spokesman for the mystery of the divine) in the course of world history's development. In the first place, his figure sums up in an integrative fashion the pre-history of Israel's religion and the characteristic emphases of the other great world religions. His is a revelation than which no greater can be thought. The faith of Israel that God has entered into a voluntary covenant with this people (Moses), dealing righteously with its moral transgressions (Amos) yet always faithful and merciful (Hosea), high uplifted in his being (the apocalyptic literature) yet giving life and energy to his creatures by his word, wisdom, and spirit (the sapiential literature) and comprehending all the nations and all time in his plan (the later prophets), found its completion in one who himself performed "all righteousness" (Matt 3:15) on behalf of and in human flesh, teaching an exigent moral code yet providing the motive force to meet its demands, separated from sinners yet compassionate to their weaknesses, looking to the salvation of the nations and to a rebirth of all things.[2] At the same time, while ancient polytheism in the Gentile world never recovered from the criticisms of philosophers, the ethical systems that replaced it lacked the power to move multitudes effectively to seek the Good. Jesus taught of a God who had all the dramatic interplay with creation of the ancient myths, yet, so far from being dethronable by the critiques of the philosophers, crowned their insights. More widely, if Judaism and later Islam emphasize the transcendence of God, Hinduism stresses his immanence; they meet in the religion that describes the Word of God as becoming incarnate in this same Jesus Christ. And while Buddhism offers suffering as the key to life, only Christianity can dare to speak of the divine One who suffered under Pontius Pilate.[3]

The second reason for accepting the claims of Jesus as a revealer is that he shows to human beings the true purpose of their nature, illuminating the meaning of the human condition as a whole as well as such concrete, particular problems as labor and solitude, otherness and communion, freedom and duty, suffering and death, sin and salvation, so that all falls into a pattern, whose basic form is that of vocation to be children of God, called by grace to share his life and glory. In the image of the Father who "is working always" (John 5:17), disciples order their work to the glory of God, notably by making this world a place of greater fellowship, thus preparing it to enter the kingdom. Jesus also shows what solitude can be, lovingly if painfully accepted in union with God's overflowing presence. Since, moreover, in Jesus the Father has adopted human beings as his children, "others" are not "Hell," as Jean-Paul Sartre maintained, but Christ. Our difference from others is overcome in a communion that gives access to our own deepest identity. Again, Jesus' gospel is full of practical directives, for so long as we are still on the way to goodness, our freedom is vulnerable and can fail; yet he invites us to enter a realm where that freedom can unfold to the point of becoming deiform, and law give way altogether

2. H. E. W. Turner, *Why We Believe in Jesus Christ* (London, 1952) 4–6.
3. Ibid., 10.

to love. On the other hand, it is clear that the power of evil, shown forth nowhere more fully than in the cross, is not to be appeased or harmonized with the rest of life, but neither is it to become the occasion for a rebellion that would condemn God in the name of justice. The disfigured but all-merciful face of Christ shows that victory over evil is won by a love that rises above hate. This is, however, a true victory in a genuine spiritual warfare: the New Testament speaks with deliberate paradox of the "wrath of the Lamb" who never minced words in his evocation of human malice and its predestined outcome.[4]

Third, Jesus was experienced as altogether authoritative in both word and deed. "He taught them as having authority and not as the scribes" (Matt 7:29); "never did man so speak" (John 7:46). Though the language of authority discomforts a libertarian society like that of North Atlantic civilization at the end of the second millennium, the fact is that human beings (when not misled by ideologues) seek submission to true authority, for it is human nature to want it, and real frustration not to find it. The idea of authority is part and parcel of the meaning of transcendence. The words of Jesus, though he stood in the line of the Old Testament prophets, went beyond theirs since he called men and women to find rest in discipleship (Matt 11:28-30), representing himself as the agent of the divine judgment (Matt 25:31-46), among whose criteria are attitudes to his own mission and message (Mark 8:38). To be his disciple is already to share the coming kingdom. He is something greater than Jonah and Solomon (Matt 12:41-42; Luke 11:30-32); many prophets and kings have desired to see what his disciples see and have not seen it (Matt 13:16-17; Luke 10:23-24). He treated his miracles as signs of God's own order breaking through into the world order as we know it. Though not to be overvalued for themselves they constitute fresh evidence of his authority. He himself avoids calling attention to them as signs of his power, for the emphasis within the miracles themselves lies on their content of love. They are responses to human need.

Fourth, there is the aesthetic dimension of Jesus' career: the attractive radiance of the form of life that was his. That form of life can be summed up as "love suffering and transfigured," a phrase that refers to his life, death, and resurrection all in one. The apologist will ask the unbeliever: is not this form of life an incomparable "translucence" (shining through) of the eternal in the temporal, and so of all epiphanies

4. R. Latourelle, *Man and His Problems in the Light of Christ* (New York, 1983).

in our experience the most powerful and authoritative? We are justified in answering this question affirmatively in as much as many cultures have shared the intuition that the divinity is essentially self-giving goodness; that this notion is, to say the least, compatible with the rational idea of God in theism; and that, in the majestic humility of Jesus, the hypothesis it contains is uniquely exemplified. The public "profile" of the life of Jesus encourages us, therefore, to see him as a man specially authorized by the divine Subject, inspired, engraced by him. For this reason, his inner mystery, his inner selfhood which was the locus of his communion with God, must be of compelling interest for us.

Fifth, the Church claims that communion like his with the Father is still possible for us. The resurrection means that he is living now. Those resurrection appearances that took place in Jerusalem were evidential, proving that Jesus was really alive. Those in Galilee were more vocational, telling the disciples what they were expected to do as a result of their encounters with the living Jesus. More broadly, we can describe the evidence for the resurrection as falling into three categories, two of which are objective (the empty tomb, the appearances), and the third subjective (the extraordinary change in the disciples which resulted from both of the former). The resurrection showed not only that Jesus was still overflowingly alive but also (and even more) that he was available for continuing discipleship, as Friend and Master, to human beings everywhere. It vindicated humankind's hope for a life everlasting (for what can a Creator mean by bringing into existence a creature capable of immortal hope and a voluntary attachment to God?). It initiated a victory over the destructive powers of sin as well as death, acting as the charter of a new society, the Church, which is the fellowship of the resurrection with a gospel that proclaims the annulling of the separation between humankind and God, and between one human being (or constellation of human beings) and another.

Finally, the Church herself is the sign of salvation. Exhibited in the whole being of Jesus—his teaching, wisdom, holiness, miracles, passion, death, and resurrection—this salvation still makes itself known, albeit fitfully, through the Church. In this sense, she is part of the evidence for the truth-value of Christian believing. The First Vatican Council speaks of her as a sign lifted up before the nations: a motive of credibility, and a witness to the divine message, thanks to five qualities which make her, of all the institutions in human history, something unusual, exceptional, and even astonishing. The quintet is: marvelous expansion, eminent holiness, inexhaustible fruitfulness (in good works), catholic or universal unity, and invincible stability. These qualities, taken cumulatively, convergently, are an argument for accepting Christian truth; they make the Church, in her own lesser order, an analogue of the sign of Christ. Although the Church is *semper reformanda*, always to be reformed (which means in the first place that the life of each and every member of the Church needs such reform), she is not only the Church of sinners (to think so would be to render the tabloid press the criterion of all relevant data). She is also the Church of saints, a body manifesting extraordinary positive qualities. She shows herself as a community that has, historically, defeated normal human prediction. Despite her diversity and the complexity of her message, she has triumphed over internal division and the negative effects of human particularity (catholic unity, that is, faithfulness to the same gospel and communion in a single corporate life). Despite her immersion in the historical process, she has triumphed over the limits of time and history (invincible stability and marvelous expansion: an institution so thoroughly inserted in history and its tensions has preserved not only identity and consistency but also dynamism). Despite the ravages of human sinfulness, she has triumphed over the processes of attrition and mediocritization that afflict even the most highly motivated groups and individuals over time (holiness, and fruitfulness "in all good").[5]

Moreover, her teaching speaks authoritatively to all the questions that life suggests, refining answers over centuries of discussion and addressing them in a language that strikes home to the human heart. She rehearses sublimely the mystery of the human condition and the universality of the promised redemption. That in all of this the Church remains fully conscious of her human wounds does not obliterate, but rather confirms, her force. She has won the minds of great thinkers, the loyalty of great servants from missionaries to philanthropists, the love of great saints. The community founded by Jesus Christ has been the greatest civilizing agent of all the institutions of human history, even though her gospel is not simply a humanism and cannot adequately be evaluated in these terms alone.

The Act of Faith

Since Catholic Christianity is founded on revelation, its *sacra doctrina*, "holy teaching," can only be grasped by the reception of revelation:

5. R. Latourelle, *Signs of Christ and His Church* (New York, 1975).

faith. The classic account of what faith is for Catholic theology comes in the *Summa theologiae* of Thomas Aquinas.[6] There faith is said to be a theological virtue—a habit or disposition by which God attaches us to himself. Directly, though mysteriously, it places us in contact with him. Indeed, it is itself such a contact. In this contact, the human mind is satisfied through the gift of access to what Thomas calls *prima veritas*, the "first truth"—the mind of God which is both perfect intelligence and complete intelligibility, the source and criterion of all the truth of the created world. At the same time, the human will is satisfied through being put in touch with the supreme good—God's own beatitude, or happiness, which cannot fail to make happy those who receive it. So faith is a beginning of the life of glory. It is a rudimentary start to that wholly fulfilled existence which will be ours when we enjoy the vision of God. (The distinction between mind and will here is a relative distinction within the unity of a person. Both aspects of ourselves, intellectual and affective, knowing and loving, are engaged simultaneously in the act of faith.) And when that act becomes a habit—a set of the whole personality—then mind and will are developed in this gracious relation to God. Faith is itself "gracious," a divine gift, a share at our level of reality in God's own knowledge of and delight in himself.

The object of faith, then, is not ultimately a series of propositions (what the Bible says, what the Creed teaches, etc.), but the reality of God himself communicated in Christ who is the providential way to God witnessed to in the Scriptures, which in turn are summed up, on the Church's authority, in the articles of the Creed and commentary on them in other doctrinal determinations. Strictly speaking, then, we do not believe in the Bible or the Creed or the Church's authority, but through all these things (and, when we consider them as media of the historic revelation, in no other conceivable way) we are attached to God himself, in whom is our faith, in whose reality the act of faith terminates.

In other words: faith is a certain kind (the most central kind!) of mystical experience. It is a mysterious, not fully expressible yet real, contact with God in Christ. It is a touch of God in his self-manifestation and, in that way, a participation in the inner love-life of Father, Son and Holy Spirit: not, however, as an inarticulate feeling but through, with and in a real conformation of our minds to divine truth.

---

6. Thomas Aquinas, *Summa theologiae* 2–2.1–7.

If this is what faith is, how do we come to get it? Two things must coincide. First, we must hear the preaching of the Church, which is the communication of the gospel here and now. Second, we must allow scope for the inner action, the interior drawing or attraction, of the Holy Spirit. No one who has not heard the Church speaking of God in Christ can be said to have faith in the full sense of that word; the same must be said of anyone who resists the pull of God's *beata veritas*, the beatifying truth of his own being, expressing itself on the occasion of this preaching.

In more recent times, and chiefly in the nineteenth century, the Catholic Church set out to clarify the relation of faith, so understood, to human rationality, that is, to what we are doing when we are engaged in knowing in a secular way. Faith is said to transcend reason, but not to go against it. On the contrary, in the typical instance of the alert and informed pagan in the process of conversion to the gospel, faith has a rational preamble, a series of arguments and evidences that demonstrate faith's coherence with the deliverances of reason. As we have seen, Catholic theology regards the existence of God, the world's source, as philosophically demonstrable, and likewise our possibility of "hearing" this God should it please him to communicate with us. Historical evidence, so Catholicism maintains, is at least compatible with, and even points to, the actual speaking of God in Israel, his self-identification in Jesus Christ as a divine legate, and the energizing, from beyond normal human resources, of the apostles at the first Pentecost. Consideration of these things clears away the undergrowth of error from ignorance, and makes faith rationally feasible. Yet faith itself remains a supernatural gift, a direct intervention of God illuminating our minds and quickening our wills, so that through the language of Scripture, the Creed, and the liturgy (the three principal forms of discourse in Tradition), we can gain a hold on God himself.

Faith transforms the affirmations of natural theology made possible by reason alone. Believing that God exists, persons of faith will already, by anticipation, believe implicitly all that the subsequent revelation of the mystery of the Holy Spirit will some day disclose to them. Similarly, believing that God is the rewarder of those who seek him—and these two propositions, for the Letter to the Hebrews, sum up the minimum *credo* of the good pagan (Heb 11:6)—they will already believe, by anticipation, and darkly, all that the mystery of the redemptive incarnation will later make manifest to them.

The God of the imagination is too close to poetry, the God of reason too close to philosophy, to meet the demands of the concept of faith. And what are those demands? First, through the media of the divinely instituted religion (through Jesus' mission and its mediations in the Scriptures, the sacraments, and the preaching of the Church) there is direct encounter between the Lord of Israel—the Father—and myself. Second, this encounter is to be understood on the model of personal relationship. Third, the meeting concerned is transformative: it actually brings about changes in me, in my habitual way of seeing things (my conceptual understanding) as in my behavior (my life).

Through faith, I enter more and more into the sphere of activity of the Father, I am drawn into his life, a life which is already relationship, and to this process no end may be preset. The imagination produces my images of God, reason purifies them, but then, within the mental space carved out by these purified images, I become aware that I am not so much an "I" looking for a divine "Thou" as a "thou" engaged by the divine "I." In the case of the imagination, what I am aware of reflexively through the images is my own capacity to symbolize the infinite God in finite terms. In the case of reason, what I am aware of is that God exists—a conclusion inferred through a variety of premises. But in the case of faith, what I became aware of, through the economy of Word and sacrament, is the self-offering of the true God himself in fellowship and communion as the God of love.

What kind of awareness is the awareness we call faith? Although Protestantism is frequently chary of the word *mystical*, faith-encounter with the God of love can only be described with the help of the vocabulary of mysticism, that is, the language of direct (though not unmediated) meeting with divinity. Anyone who possesses Christian faith must be the subject of a mystical experience at once intellectual and affective in kind.

To say that the absolute, the unconditioned, has a relation to a conditioned, finite being such as myself would normally be simply to say that God, whoever he may be, is my Creator. This is a reasonable claim, since as we have seen it is reasonable to hold that the world and the self are patterned in the way they are by a fontal being on which they depend. But to say that the absolute has desired to enter into a relation of communion with me, that I am conscious of the absolute God as it were before me, facing me, rather than as the ultimate condition of my being, behind my back: this claim can only be paraphrased with the aid of mystical terms.

The content of this continuous state of mystical awareness which we call Christian faith is the loving possession of the gospel truths proposed for our assent by the Church. But this Godward expansion of mind and heart has an indispensable center in sympathetic identification with the consciousness of Jesus Christ, the Word made man. For this reason, faith involves at the same time the awareness of God as Father and Spirit as well as Son, and of the intimate co-presence of Father, Son, and Spirit: the Holy Trinity.

But why should we be interested in the consciousness of Jesus Christ in the first place? It is because in him there lie hid all the treasures of wisdom and knowledge (Col 2:3) that faith is justified: its deliverances derive from One who did not himself believe but knew. Yet faith does not merely know about Jesus Christ, through his verbal self-testimony. It knows Christ Jesus, the public agent of revelation at its climax, in his inward uniqueness.

There are, however, those who would want to dismiss all such references to "inner selving," or interior awareness, and even to consciousness itself, as a matter of philosophical muddle-headedness. Reports of these things, they would object, are but garbled versions of the propensities of particular organisms to behave in certain ways, and should be rewritten in this form as soon as possible. But while people certainly vary in their capacity to describe their own inner world, and some have a richer, and more interesting, inner life than others, anyone who has ever experienced a profound relationship with another person knows full well that to write off this whole area of life is perverse. Fortunately what poets, lovers, and spiritual directors have always known, many philosophers can still admit. Consciousness is the answer to the question, What is it like, being he, she, or it? It is that reality whose being is one with its own (non-discursive) knowing of itself.

> I find myself both as man and as myself something more determined and distinctive, at pitch, more distinctive and higher pitched than anything else I see. . . . And when I ask where does all this throng and stack of being, so rich, so distinctive, so important, come from, nothing I see can answer me. And this whether I speak of human nature or of my individuality, my selfbeing. . . . And this is much more true when we consider the mind; when I consider my selfbeing; my consciousness and feeling of myself, that taste of myself, of I and me above and in all things, which is more distinctive than the taste of ale or alum, more distinctive than the smell of walnutleaf or camphor, and is incommunicable by any

means to another man. . . . Nothing else in nature comes near this un-speakable stress of pitch, distinctiveness, and selving, this self being of my own.[7]

Ontologically incommunicable, it can yet be known, thanks to the empathy triggered by observation. Such empathetic imagining of the consciousness of others is not infallible. It can make mistakes. Nonetheless, imagining a thing as it really is must count as a peculiarly basic way of knowing a fact, while the singular importance of consciousness, subjectivity, lies in its being the necessary medium for the apprehension of value, the worth of facts. Apprehended value can attach only to what occurs within a stream of consciousness—with the exception of the divine consciousness, for that, as the consciousness of an infinite subjectivity, is not a stream but a simultaneous possession.

Though the light of faith whereby our intellectual powers are rendered proportionate to their revealed Object and the gracious quickening of the will which draws us to it are themselves unique, and our grasp of Jesus' identity controlled and steadied by our participation in that corporate subject which is the apostolic community, in other respects our faith knowledge of him is comparable with our knowledge of any other human consciousness: namely, by empathetic identification working on sensuous epiphanies in deed and word. There can be no imaginative access to the subjectivity of another without a free, self-restraining, humble, other-oriented establishment of concern. Such an attentive and concerned disciplining of self is necessary for imaginative entry into the existence of another person, whether this person be part of the past or of the present.

It is the peculiar nature of our access to the subjectivity of Jesus that it partakes of both these latter categories. The empirical cues that enable empathetic identification to go forward are a matter of both ancient texts (the Gospels, especially) and current experience (for instance, the seven sacraments, which the Church holds to be extensions of the historical action of Jesus, since, in the words of Pope Leo the Great, "all that was visible in the life of the Redeemer has passed over into his sacraments"). The case of Jesus Christ is unique in that he is both an historical figure, epistemologically laid to rest with the last contemporary account that speaks of him, and a person living in a metahistorical dimension that yet impinges through his Church-body on our world.

7. Cited from Hopkins's notes on the *Spiritual Exercises* of Ignatius in G. Storey, *A Preface to Hopkins*, 2d ed. (London and New York, 1992) 33–34.

For this reason, the specifically Christian material to be used in setting out to describe the God disclosed in faith is Scripture read in Tradition. Texts and other monuments witness to Jesus Christ as, in the Spirit, the revealer of the Father, within the worshipping community of the Catholic Church, defining herself as she does by continuing relation with his living person. These cues, when read aright, bring us to the inward self: the outer reveals the inner, the public realm the intimate foyer of the heart—that heart which, as the privileged locus of the human sense of God, is rightly called the sacred heart par excellence.

Scripture

For Catholicism, exegetical method cannot be equated with the historical method *tout court*. The exegesis of the Bible, the Word of God, is or should be theology (believing interpretation) from the beginning. In studying Scripture we seek what in their faith the biblical authors wished to express in their texts—something that always goes beyond the historical events concerned when the latter are taken in their sheer historicity. So true exegesis has to include two essential dimensions: the horizontal one of historical research and philological analysis, and the vertical one of the ontological depth, or opening onto mystery, of the sacred texts. By identifying fact with truth (rejecting or neglecting the metahistorical aspect of Scripture), modern historicism closes itself off from the self-revelation of the Word. Through representation, which moves on the level of phenomena (things thought, said, formulated), interpretation has to go beyond things and words to attain to ontological truth, to place in the light what is not immediately visible, to bring out the root experience behind what is spoken. Just as in metaphysics one cannot speak truly of beings without referring at the same time to being, in which they share, so also interpretative language even as it speaks of something determinate always says in addition something more. As the recent (1993) guidelines of the Roman pontiff's biblical commission, "The Interpretation of the Bible," have it: over and above the deliverances of the historical-critical method, valuable though this is, there stands the special "pre-understanding" of the Catholic exegete, in continuity with the selfsame religious tradition coming down from Israel and the primitive Christian community. "Their [exegetes'] interpretation stands thereby in continuity with a dynamic pattern of interpretation that is found within the Bible itself and continues in the life of the Church. This dynamic pattern corresponds to the requirement that there be a lived affinity between the interpreter and the object, an affinity which constitutes in fact one of the conditions that makes the entire exegetical enterprise possible."[8]

Furthermore, authentic interpretation always carries some reference not only to the source of its texts, what lies within and behind them, but also to their goal, to the final term of what they describe. For this reason too, biblical interpretation, as understood by Catholicism, cannot but be ecclesial. Only the Church understands the goal of God's revealing (and therefore Scripture-inspiring) activity, so only she can interpret the Spirit by the Spirit. Ecclesial exegesis takes place at the highest level: on the presupposition of God's design for this literature.

Moreover, we should not abstract the question of inspiration from the multiform action of the Spirit in the economy of salvation. The production of Sacred Scripture is conditioned by three wider factors: the existence of a community (Israel, the Church) called to salvation, the historic experience of this community, and the particular vocation of some individuals to occupy key positions within it and fulfill crucial roles in divine salvation's coming in history. The theology of inspiration considers both authors and texts within the historical and cultural milieu in which they were placed, but also within the tradition unfolded throughout the economy of salvation. Hence, ultimately, its Christological reference, since Christ is the center of tradition's history. Had Jesus himself written, the religion which came from him would have been "koranic" in kind. The sacred text, recognized as "come from heaven," the product of unmediated transcendence, could only have been conserved in fundamentalist fashion, imposing itself in a wooden way as the straightforwardly applicable norm of faith and practice during all subsequent generations. But the definitive revelation came in Jesus, and by his mediation, under quite another form: a living person who spoke and acted, leading a human existence of a type that can be called at once prophetic, didactic, sapiential, apocalyptic, and messianic (the latter in a sense at variance from that which his contemporaries imagined), right up to the final drama and its *dénouement* in the death on the cross. So as to found on his faithfully obedient person a new world where salvation might be extended, at least as offer, to all human beings, the Father raised Jesus up as Lord and Christ, giving him the name which is above every other name (Phil 2:9). There is the global event within whose spaciousness the texts of the two interrelated Testaments must be evaluated. Through all of that, God spoke his definitive word.

8. *The Interpretation of the Bible*, preface to part 3.

The ancient Scriptures have thus been "fulfilled" by way of what the contemporary French exegete Pierre Grelot has called a "surplus of meaning" which is from now on the key to their interpretation "in the Spirit."[9] This surplus does not obliterate all trace of their original bearings, but draws out from the letter of the text a dynamic quality which the Holy Spirit placed there with a view to the realization of salvation in the Christ who was to come. In taking up the Old Testament in a way that transcended its imaginable limits, Jesus (in Origen's words) turned the Scriptures into the gospel. At the same time, by fulfilling the divine *mystērion* (the age-long unfolding of God's liberty), of which his resurrection was the climax, he became the object of the good news, having first been its proclaimer.

The earliest disciples had no different canon of Scripture from Jews. What they possessed was, rather, a distinctive manner of reading the shared sacred texts. They approached the Bible in the light of the accounts of the crucified and risen Messiah passed down in the Church, the new Israel, for it was in the name of this Messiah that they prayed, and into his reality that they were introduced by baptism and the holy Eucharist. His words, the memory of his actions, the vehicles of his atoning sacrifice: all these were entrusted to his witnesses so that they might carry out the two tasks he had laid upon them—the foundation of the Church as the community of salvation, and the transmission of the gospel which the Church is called to proclaim in missionary fashion to the world.

The ministry of the direct witnesses, the apostles, had its prolongation in the diverse forms of service of the Word carried out under their presidency; and this labor produced new texts—our "New" Testament—inseparable from the communitarian life of the gospel churches. The production of these texts was not a systematic affair, but depended rather on the concrete circumstances that led the apostles and other depositories of the apostolic tradition to respond in this way to the practical needs of local communities for the sake of their instruction and perseverance in faith and evangelical practice. Here too, if revelation was to receive authoritative witness in written form, inspiration had to serve as a "charism" (a divine gift of both stimulus and guidance, to mind and to heart), encompassing the entire prehistory, whether oral or written, of the texts the New Testament preserves.

9. P. Grelot, "Dix propositions sur l'inspiration scripturaire," *Esprit et Vie* 96, no. 8 (1986) 97–105.

The only finally decisive criterion for discerning inspiration is the use of certain books as authority-bearing vis-à-vis the Word of God in the community which guards the true faith, hinged as that community is on the ministries—episcopacy and papacy—that animate and watch over it. It is in the name of the apostolic tradition that ecclesiastical tradition recognizes the authority of these books, thus integrating them into the Church's fundamental structure as a heritage handed down by her own first leaders.

Catholicism, then, reads the Bible in the Spirit as a canonically and narrationally unified whole centered on Jesus Christ and telling the story of the dealings of the Father with his people and his world in ways (and here we come to a new point) that are typologically applicable to the present. This is indeed how Scripture came into existence, at any rate as the Church's canon. To constitute the New Testament, writings were selected on the basis of a *sensus fidelium* formed by the liturgically embedded Christological and Trinitarian reading of the sacred books of Israel. To read the Bible otherwise is not to read it as Scripture at all.

This principle governs the Catholic understanding of the Old Testament. Though Christ and his teaching cannot be explained exhaustively on the basis of preexisting factors in Judaism, nonetheless we must be prepared for the possibility that the "elder dispensation" was providentially commissioned to assemble much conceptual material with a view to its incorporation into the fabric of the Christian Creed—much as King David is said to have collected great stones and timber for the building of the temple he was destined never to see.

"A rose is a rose is a rose," wrote the poet Gertrude Stein, but the Christian Doctors would not have agreed. In terms of God's providence (literally, his foresight in planning the course of his self-communication to the world) the ultimate significance of a thing, what it points to, may not be located within itself at all. It may be something that will happen centuries later, when the original rose has withered and returned to the earth. Thomas Aquinas says of the biblical history: "God has the power, not only of adapting words to convey meanings (which men also can do), but also of adapting things themselves [*etiam res ipsas*, the 'very realities of history'*]. In every branch of knowledge, words have meaning, but what is special here is that the things meant by the words mean something [*etiam significant aliquid*, 'point to something other than themselves'].*"[10]

---

10. Thomas Aquinas, *Summa theologiae* 1.1.10.

Thus many events, recorded in the historical books of the Old Testament, as well as in its explicitly prophetic writings, were significant not primarily for themselves but for what they foreshadowed. They were important not so much for their value as literal history (though this is never, in the nature of the case, insignificant) but as types and images, in and through which the Holy Spirit indicated what was to come, when God would bring in the new covenant to fulfill the old. They denoted what was to be enacted in the gospel events, and Christian believers, looking back on the events recorded in the Old Testament in the light of their fulfillment, found themselves in the position of the spectator of a drama who already knows how the play will end. Grasping the plot, they could recognize and appreciate the subtlety of the dramatic irony by which the divine dramatist had made the very stage of the action prefigure the final *dénouement* described in the New Testament books, even though this would not be understood by the characters themselves in their historical setting.

In terms of salvation, the God-given destiny of humanity, the people who composed the types and shadows have only limited significance: Melchizedek, a pagan Canaanite prince entering into some sort of friendship-treaty with Abraham, the wandering sheikh in whom Israel came to see her founding patriarch; the Hebrew slaves, slaughtering and eating the paschal lamb, taking a spring festivity where the firstborn of the flock was offered to the gods and making of it an act of thanksgiving for their escape from Egypt across the Sea of Reeds; and the survivors of those slaves, close to starvation in the semi-desert of the Sinai peninsula, coming suddenly on a food sufficiently similar, at least, to a secretion of the tarfa tree *(tammarix mannifera)* to share its name ("manna")—all of these people have their experiences not, ultimately, for their own good, but that they may be pointers to a wider future they could never have imagined: the incarnation, and the Church which flows from it. Adapting the language of the Creed, they lived not so much for themselves but "for us . . . and for our salvation." As the fourth-century Latin Father Hilary puts it: "Christ originates, and purifies and hallows, and calls and chooses, and redeems the Church, by valid, authoritative prefigurations through the whole course of the world's history . . . in the sleep of Adam, in the Flood of Noah, in the blessing of Melchizedek, and the justification of Abraham. Everything which Christ would fulfill had been prefigured since the beginning of the world."[11]

11. Hilary, *Treatise on the Mysteries* 1.1; cf. A. Nichols, "Imagination and Revelation: The Face of Christ in the Old Testament," *The Way* 21 (1981) 270–77.

The Gospels use the same approach. When, in Matthew's Gospel, we see Christ presented as a second Moses, announcing the new law of the kingdom from a hilltop in the Sermon on the Mount; when, in Luke's Gospel, we are invited to respond to him as to a second Elijah, raising a widow's son at Nain as Elijah had at Zarephath, we get a glimpse of what the catechesis of the earliest Church was like: typological through and through. And if we look forward to the Fathers and the medievals, we find that liturgy, visual art, music, and the common piety of the people of God are all soaked in typology. Even in a milieu distanced from Catholic Christendom, such as that of the post-Reformation Anglo-Saxons, there are witnesses. Handel's *Messiah*, with its ransacking of Scripture for texts to speak about Christ, is unintelligible without typology. Simple folk in the England of George Eliot and Thomas Hardy were brought up on it, in florid type in the page headings of the Authorized Version of the Bible, which told them plainly that, in the Song of Songs for instance, Christ was addressing the Church "black" with sin "but beautiful" as justified by God's grace. The Catholic liturgy, old style or new, quite simply depends upon typology for its own imaginative structure.

> The principal purpose toward which the plan of the Old Covenant was directed was to prepare for the coming both of Christ, the universal Redeemer, and of the messianic kingdom, to announce this coming by prophecy, and to indicate its meaning through various types. The books of the Old Testament, though they also contain some things that are incomplete and temporary, nevertheless show us true divine pedagogy. . . . In them the mystery of our salvation is present in a hidden way.[12]

Though this approach may be unpopular in modern departments of biblical studies, largely nonecclesial as these are, it has much to commend it from the viewpoint of theological doctrine. First, while the Bible has no theology of itself, the Church can and should have a theology of the Bible. Such a theology, drawing on subsequent Christian experience and wisdom, will state the unity of God's plan in Scripture, and suggest how all its parts relate to the single center, Jesus Christ. Second, we must resist the false choice between the original meaning of an event or text, present in the minds of its contemporaries, and a purely artificial, external, imposed meaning. It is a matter of common experience that the full scope and bearing of an event can only be assessed retrospectively. Third, the prophets themselves recognized that

12. *Dei Verbum*, 15.

their words were to some degree open: only God, expressing his will through events, would determine their final meaning and truth. Fourth, the single most pervasive theology of the Hebrew Bible, that of the Deuteronomic school, insists that the God of Israel is constant, steadfast, reliable, having a single style in all his wonderful works. If this is true, then we can expect one event, one work of God in history, to throw light on another. And the sense of a common style is aesthetic: neither pure reason nor historical scholarship can establish (or demolish) it.

This is not to say that rational evaluation of the affirmations of the biblical writers, or an historical testing of their reports, is always out of place. While holding to the inerrancy of the saving truth which God inspired the sacred writers to express in the biblical books, the Church does not treat such inerrancy as covering necessarily every element of description or reportage their message contains. Pope Leo XIII, in his encyclical on biblical inspiration, *Providentissimus Deus*, conceded that in scientific matters the sacred writer "speaks according to the appearance, in such a way that his statements must not be taken as formal affirmations," while in the succeeding pontificate of Pius X the Pontifical Biblical Commission admitted that "in certain cases narratives thought to be properly historical had only the appearances of history."

This is a topic on which at times Church authority has been more sensitive (and defensive) than was needful, yet it was (and is) correct in principle to scrutinize scholarly initiatives not only closely but slowly, when so much is at stake. In 1884 Cardinal Newman had already written: "It seems unworthy of divine greatness that the Almighty should in his revelation of himself to us undertake mere secular duties, and assume the office of a narrator, as such, or an historian, or geographer, except so far as the secular matters bear directly upon the revealed truth." That last clause introduces an important qualification: a revelation given in history, and bearing on the destiny of both history and cosmos, will necessarily entail some factual assertions about both. Newman went on, accordingly, to speak of the need for an authoritative interpreter to act as a complement to the inspiration of the text: "satisfactorily to distinguish what is didactic and what is historical, what is fact and what is vision, what is allegorical and what is literal, what is idiomatic and what is grammatical, what is enunciated formally and what is only of temporary and what is of lasting obligation."[13]

13. J. H. Newman, "Inspiration in Relation to Revelation," 11, 15; reprinted in J. D. Holmes and R. Murray, S.J., eds., *John Henry Newman on the Inspiration of Scripture* (London, 1967) 108, 111.

This brings us to the subject of Tradition, and its organ of self-interpretation, the Church's teaching office or "magisterium."

Tradition

Tradition, in the Catholic doctrinal sense, is not simply whatever has been, *de facto*, received from the past. Holy Tradition is, rather, the treasure-house of the revelation of Christ entrusted to the Church. For this reason, the Church has to guard the integrity of Tradition, to keep it unimpaired by false accretions or wrongful mutilations, and to approach it, always, with humility and reverence, and the confidence of faith. For the revelation of God in Christ found in Tradition is a perfect work, though the mortal eyes of the faithful have yet to see that perfection. In the age to come, we shall recognize with full vision the reality we were told to remember on earth.

Unde et memores . . . "Wherefore, remembering": these words of the Latin Rite introduce the section of the Eucharistic Prayer known as the *anamnēsis*, the "remembering." In her central act of worship, the Church both remembers her Lord and, by the power of his Spirit, actualizes anew the mystery of human salvation in her own depths. Thus her memorial of the Lord corresponds to her own deepest awareness of herself. The Church remembers that God was faithful to his promises: he willed that the reality of his eternal love, prefigured by the ancient covenants, awaited by patriarchs, felt by prophets, should be attested in the reality of history in the fullness of time in the person of his Son, so that his eternal love should become the hope of all future generations.

The primary content of Tradition is the apostles' witness to Christ's sufferings, death, and resurrection, considered—against their background in the Jewish doctrine of God and in their outflow through the Holy Spirit's work in the Church—as the crowning events of humankind's salvation. Tradition reproduces what happened then not chiefly in its historiographical detail but rather in the form of its presence now in the life of the Church, that is in its abiding significance. Likewise, the perpetual making present of the words of Jesus in the Church's Tradition requires an intelligent reception and transmission of what the apostles left behind. It presupposes the action of the Holy Spirit who makes Tradition a living doctrinal substance which is to be preserved from falsification and disintegration, and assists in the process of producing an ever-deeper understanding in the Church. The *evangelium a Jesu Christo promulgatum* (in the words of the Council of Trent) is the true object of Tradition. Tradition is the form in which the gospel is proclaimed in the sphere of the Church.

Catholic theologians frequently distinguish between Tradition, which denotes the meaning of what is written in Scripture (and so Scripture's plenary content), and certain unwritten traditions, especially in matters of worship and discipline, that are considered to have originated from the apostles themselves as the heads of the first community and, as such, endowed with an irreplaceable, unrepeatable authority to determine its basic structure as a believing, worshipping, acting, and praying people. "You will sit on twelve thrones, judging the twelve tribes of Israel" (Matt 19:28)—the new Israel, the universal Church. The whole body of the Church, then as now, is engaged in preserving and transmitting the tradition; but it is apostolic authority alone that gives to the material, as transmitted, a normative value. The later Church with her papally centered episcopate constitutes nothing of the apostolic tradition. Instead, she guards it, passes it on, judges the adequacy of locally or temporally limited expressions of it, and where need arises (in the case of doctrinal "development") warrants the adoption of new insights into the original deposit as integral features of the doctrine of faith. For the Church, authentic Tradition is always a summons to rediscover the religious experience of the apostles in its vernal spontaneity and freshness.

Of course the Scriptures themselves are transmitted, and can therefore be called an aspect of Tradition. Scripture is one of the two forms of the Tradition, given so that the Church might preserve the purity of the gospel, and be confirmed in her proclamation. As the Council of Trent puts it, Scripture is "subsequent to the forming of the foundation of the confession of faith," being given as "a most powerful testimony and safeguard in the confirming of [faith's] teachings."[14] But the fact that Scripture as testimony to the Word of God in revelation is itself ordered to the transmitting of the gospel (Catholic Christianity can never be a "religion of the Book"), does not mean that Catholics lack reverence for Scripture. They are not bibliolaters, but they can call Scripture (with the nineteenth-century South German divine Johann Adam Möhler) the Church's "heart-blood, her very breath, her soul, her all,"[15] or say (with his twentieth-century successor Joseph Geiselmann): "Holy Scripture as the guardian of the Gospel is the doorway of the Holy Spirit to the Bride of Christ. It is the most precious jewel the Creator Spirit bestowed, along with the Word of Christ, on all her life

14. DH 1505.
15. J. A. Möhler, *Symbolik, oder Darstellung der dogmatischen Gegensätze zwischen den Katholiken und Protestanten,* ed. J. R. Geiselmann (Cologne, 1958–61) 438.

to come."[16] Nor is this irrelevant to the individual, for each member of the Church must become a bearer of tradition in his or her own way. As Cardinal Newman, writing while still an Anglican, put it, the "heart of every Christian ought to represent in miniature the Catholic Church."[17] That they can only do when the faith given in tradition is realized seriously in the heart. The Christian becomes a witness of tradition only when faith has become devotion. Realizing the truth of the gospel leads inevitably to personal holiness, which is the integral form of all the qualities required in the witness. Tradition is (to cite Newman again) always "the tradition of the saints."[18] The charity whereby the heart is dedicated to God's truth simultaneously forms the believer into the image of Christ.

But if the deep sense of the normative text of Scripture, found in the last analysis by what the French philosopher-theologian Maurice Blondel called "the spiritual labor of Catholic consciousness,"[19] enables the Church to furnish from out of her "total experience" an "autonomous principle of discernment," a special place is given in this task to the *consensus patrum*, the accord of the Church Fathers. How may we understand this?

The texts of the New Testament do not so much describe a religion as show a religion in the process of being born. The whole complex of events that made up the life, teaching, death, and resurrection of Jesus Christ and the coming of his Spirit at Pentecost amounted to an explosion of spiritual energy of which our New Testament is, so to speak, the precious debris. Some of the texts, perhaps, are emotion recollected in tranquillity: for example, John's Gospel in its present form; others, like the Book of Revelation, are anything but recollected; some, like the Letter of Paul to Philemon, are more or less postcards tossed off in a tornado.

The New Testament testifies to the extraordinary impact its central events made on some contemporary Jews and Gentiles, but it does not constitute a religion. Some modern theologians, captivated by the notion that the secular world is already, in its own right, full of goodness and beauty and hence revelatory potential, have been unhappy with the idea that Christianity is a religion. But it is surely clear that if the way of life taught by Jesus and gifted by him once risen from the dead

---

16. J. R. Geiselmann, *The Meaning of Tradition* (London and New York, 1966) 37.

17. J. H. Newman, *Sermons Bearing on Subjects of the Day* (London, 1918) 132.

18. John Henry Newman, *Parochial and Plain Sermons* 3 (London, 1880) 257.

19. M. Blondel, *The Letter on Apologetics and History and Dogma* (London, 1964) 264–82.

in power and the Holy Spirit was to be continued in a community, it could only be as a structure of belief, worship, and discipline (and if this is not a religion it is hard to imagine what could be). The patristic period, in brief, was the age in which the religion of the gospel became articulate as a way of belief, worship, and discipline—"traditional Christianity" as lived in the mainstream of historic Christendom and showing, under a variety of cultural carapaces, a remarkable unity and continuity across space and time.

The age of the Fathers, then, was the moment when the apostolic teaching was given an exact form, partly with a view to excluding interpretations of it felt to be at variance with the basic thrust of Jesus' teaching and significance. The Fathers determined the fundamentals of Christian faith, the basic dogmas about God, Christ, and salvation. They forged for the future the elements of a whole Christian language. To think of a Church without Athanasius's work in establishing the divinity of Christ, Basil's activity in affirming the Godhead of the Holy Spirit, or Augustine's achievements in determining the independent and sovereign activity of God's grace, is to imagine a Church quite different in credal structure from the Church to which Catholic Christians in fact belong. The same is true of the liturgical life of the Church. In the East, the classical pattern of the liturgy was fixed by the fourth century, at least in what touches the central act of the Eucharist, the Great Prayer of consecration; and the same held for the West by the mid-seventh century at the latest. Again, the fixing of the canon of Scripture is an achievement of the patristic Church. We take it for granted that the Old and New Testaments contain certain books and not others, although if we look at a standard Protestant Bible—one lacking the Deuterocanonicals—we can see at a glance that something curious has happened to their Old Testament. We could perhaps imagine a Bible minus two lengthy narratives on the Maccabean wars, and even that delightful Hellenistic novel the Book of Tobit (though these have their importance for our understanding of, respectively, the intermediate state and angelology), but what of a New Testament shorn of the Fourth Gospel or consisting solely, as the heresiarch Marcion wished, of the Pauline Letters plus an abbreviated version of the Gospel according to Luke? What of a New Testament including that somewhat bizarre Jewish-Christian production *The Shepherd of Hermas*, in which Christ is held to be no more than an angel? Determining the canon of Scripture is not the least contribution of the Fathers to the determining of the shape of Christianity as a whole.

Indeed, in the patristic reception of the scriptural revelation all sub-sequent tradition finds its marching orders. The various media whereby a revelation thus crystallized transmits itself in tradition—not only Creeds, the liturgy, and the canon of Scripture but also iconography and hagiology, those beautiful expressions of the sense of the faithful, as well as the institutional forms of councils and the pri-matial ministry of the Roman bishop in his teaching office—all emerged in this decisive moment.[19a]

Finally, the teaching of the Fathers provides a model for the sort of theological reflection this book exemplifies. First, patristic thought is theocentric: God is the primary reality, and in a sense the one reality; all else is only real by virtue of relationship to him. It is the Spirit of God who brings the creature to its freedom, its fullness. Second, pa-tristic thought is Christocentric, for the Spirit is given by Christ. Third, patristic thought is ecclesiocentric: Christ acts as head of the Church, through which salvation comes to human beings. Fourth, patristic thought is mysteriocentric: the Church's life is accomplished through the celebration of the mysteries, the sacraments. Patristic theology, in other words, concentrates on essentials, as does the best scholastic the-ology after it, and notably that of Thomas. We can contrast this with much modern theology where a journalistic element, concerned with those things that are actually felt to be currently important as distinct from those things that ought to be felt to be eternally important, has crept in and to some extent distorted the whole. When that happens, the pattern of the divine epiphany is obscured.

Tradition and the Magisterium

While the Church continues to live from the Fathers and their achievement, she also, and decidedly, lives after them and therefore needs some organ of internal guidance in her reading of her own deep mind.

Nothing shows up more clearly the metahistorical character of the help given the Church by the Holy Spirit than the charism of infalli-bility. Owing to this resource from beyond history the faith of the

19a. On all these "monuments" of Tradition, and aids to discernment of their reve-latory significance, as indeed on the sources of revelation at large, see A. Nichols, *The Shape of Catholic Theology. An Introduction to Its Sources, Principles and History* (Collegeville: The Liturgical Press, and Edinburgh: T&T Clark, 1991). That study pro-vides the formal understanding of what Catholic theology is which underlies (and jus-tifies) the content of the present work.

Church today can be identical with that of the apostles, and the privilege of normative truth and certainty enjoyed by them can also, in differing historical modalities, be shared by the Church now. The Holy Spirit's assistance is not just a guarantee against all infidelity vis-à-vis the memory of the Lord. It is the interior light of the very fidelity concerned. Though it can be translated into negative terms of resistance to exterior menaces and perils, in itself it is the very principle, living truth, and highest consciousness of the Church's faith existence.

In their different ways, all the main lines of historic Christianity expect to be able to identify the content of the gospel; indeed, if it is only as available now as water running through sand it is hard to see why one postulates a divine intervention to bring its presence into history! The Orthodox speak of abiding truth, Protestants of an enduring message. Catholics too, and par excellence, believe that it is possible to trace with certainty what the gospel teaches (faith) and commends (morals). In a fast-changing world, the self-identification of Christians can only be achieved through identifying the elements that endure through all changes. Otherwise, the very term *Christian* becomes riddled with ambiguity.

Such identification is made, according to Catholics, by the teaching office of pope and bishops in virtue of their apostolic and, ultimately, dominical mandate. This is true above all of those cases where their authority is most fully engaged, in the exercise of ecclesial infallibility—that freedom from error in what is taught and believed that Christ willed his Church to possess. The gift of infallibility is a liberating one: not only because the truth always "sets you free" (John 8:32), but also because through establishing the limits of the abiding elements in Tradition, it also indicates those numerous things that are legitimately subject to a variety of understandings. In this way, the infallibility of the Church fosters a positive pluralism, rather than a destructive wrangling over truth.

Dogma is the fruit of that process whereby, within the communion of the Church, the thinking mind adores the self-revealing God and thinks within the mystery of grace in a renewed way. Paul told his hearers that their minds were to be renewed by the grace of Jesus Christ. This was not just a moral exhortation, encouraging people to be good, though it has moral implications and conditions. More than that: the Fathers, at any rate, understood Paul to be speaking about the difference made to the very way the human mind operates by the redemption and transfiguration of the world through Jesus Christ and his Spirit. Outside the sphere of salvation, reason is adapted to the fallen state of humankind. It is, often, happily and successfully so adapted, but adapted nonetheless it is. Fallen reason can generate truth—speculative truth in pure reason, truth about conduct through practical reason, and that other truth for which we have no name in productive reason (i.e., in making things, from pots and pans to states and governments). Yet it remains fallen reason, and the telltale signs are scattered throughout the history of thinking. Our apparently inextinguishable urge to locate ourselves in relation to reality as a whole, to go beyond what experience alone can tell us, ends up frequently enough either in hubris or in impotence. Thought either leaps into speculative delusions about how much it can know or else falls back into a state of supine resignation to not knowing. And so the history of philosophy is a history of reaction against metaphysics, and of reactions against the denial of metaphysics.

The Christian message insists that thought cannot go beyond the limits of fallen humanity, of a fallen world, unless it undergoes a death and a resurrection. The "death" in question is a discipline, an asceticism, provided for the human mind by ecclesial experience (worship, meditation on the Scriptures, prayer, religious love) all of which purify little by little the eye of the human intellect. The "resurrection" involves the transformation of fallen reason into that understanding which mirrors the Word of God, in whose image and to whose likeness we were originally made. In this resurrection of the mind we rise into the life of the Holy Spirit. The mind becomes spiritual, penetrating into the ultimate significance or bearing of things, as it becomes attuned to the Spirit of God.

Doctrine, then, together with dogma, its most hard-won form, and the theological thinking these stimulate, is the vision of the world that results from this Easter "passover" of the mind from death to life. It is the festival of the mind celebrating the mystery of existence in God. It is a wondrous medium that permits us to see in Christ, by the Holy Spirit, the final truth of the world beyond the illusions (be they hypermetaphysical or antimetaphysical) of what the Bible calls this *aiôn*, this age of the world.

The idea of the development of doctrine (and so ultimately of dogma) is invariably associated with the name of Newman. For Newman, the entire process of dogmatic development begins with a comprehensive intuition which is in many respects covert or tacit, and which continues, by way of thought both implicit and explicit, to the point where the dogma is formulated in all the sharpness of a propositional truth.

According to Newman, the appearance of the divine Messiah aroused in the apostles' faith-consciousness a comprehensive intuition of the essence—the "idea"—of Christianity. Within this initial impression lay dormant certain implicit orientations and unexpressed elements, typical of a knowledge that is experienced rather than consciously thought out. What the Church handed on was primarily this comprehensive apostolic intuition, whose living presence in the collectivity created an atmosphere in which the Christian idea could be transferred to, and impressed upon, new members. That idea or impression forms the link between the unsystematised revelation and the definitions of dogma, and eventually, then, in dependence on articulated doctrine, systematic theology itself. Newman's presentation suggests that there are two sorts of "reasoning" involved here: first, implicit reasoning, subject to multitudinous influences, slow in maturing, personal, incommunicable; second, explicit reasoning, which is purposeful and reflective, technical and logical in character, less rich in content, yet an authentic extension of the original idea (as formed by what, in the context of his argument for the existence of God, he had called the "illative sense"). Through intimate contact with, and affective experience of, the reality of faith, we can make judgments that contain right conclusions even though the formal reasoning adduced in their service may be non-demonstrative.[20] Though Catholic divinity insists on the coherence and consistency of the end result of this process (its "homogeneity"), it need not maintain that all was plain sailing at the time.

> Newman was much struck by the sureness and definiteness with which doctrine develops and matures, along with every variety of hesitation and interruption. Truth finds its own equilibrium, through ways that are often unforeseen. The risks and changes of the most unfavourable situations, the conjunction of efforts apparently entirely independent one of another, even mutually opposed—through the ebb and flow of all this, even through outright forgetting, or neglect at least, harmony is established.[21]

20. A. Nichols, *From Newman to Congar: The Idea of Doctrinal Development from the Victorians to the Second Vatican Council* (Edinburgh, 1990) 17–70.

21. H. de Lubac, *The Splendour of the Church* (London and New York, 1956) 8–9.

However, in a world that always threatens to level dogma down, revealed truth would hardly be perspicuous without some accredited organ for the articulation of these advances and recuperations. Hence the need for a visible Church with a divinely shielded (and hence infallible) teaching authority, the final principle of dogmatic development. The content of the tradition of the gospel has its form in the apostolic succession.

> It is only a dead religion to which written records are sufficient; a living religion must be able to adapt itself to changing environment without losing its own identity. One thing, therefore, is absolutely certain—that if Christianity is a real Revelation, the Teaching Church must at any rate know her own mind with regard to the treasure committed to her care, and supremely on those points on which the salvation of her children depends. She may be undecided and permit divergent views on purely speculative points; she may allow her theologians, for instance, to argue, unchecked, for centuries as to the modes by which God acts, or as to the best philosophical terms for the elucidation of mysteries, or as to the precise limits of certain of her own powers and the manners of their exercise. But in things that directly and practically affect souls—with regard to the fact of grace, its channels, the things necessary for salvation, and the rest—she must not only know her mind, but must be constantly declaring it, and no less constantly silencing those who would obscure or misinterpret it.[22]

The object of the Church's teaching authority is the content of Christian revelation and all that is necessary and useful for the preaching and defense of this revelation. In determining the content of revelation, and demarcating it from other matters on which the teaching office is not competent, the magisterium is judge of its own authority: else it would be subject to the judgment of individuals, and defeat its own, Christ-given, purpose. May it not then exceed its own powers, requiring the assent of faith to alleged truths that may in fact be false or, if true, beyond the scope of revelation? Catholic faith holds that the bearers of the teaching office cannot err in this way, thanks to the assistance given the Church by the Holy Spirit. The magisterium does not, however, "make it up as it goes along": those who exercise it must refer to the Scriptures and the monuments of Tradition (the Fathers, the liturgies, the witness of sacred art, the lives of the saints, the sense of the faithful) in order to ascertain whether a proposed truth does or

---

22. R. H. Benson, *Confessions of a Convert* (London, 1920) 91–92.

does not belong to the divine revelation given in Christ and "closed" (thanks to its eschatological fullness) with the deaths of the apostles. The congruence of a proposed dogma with the earlier state of the Church's tradition is discerned primarily by the magisterium itself, only in a secondary way by individual believers and theologians. There is room for nuance here, for the teaching office can propound its own doctrine as obligatory in various degrees: the so-called theological notes of a teaching.

The Magisterium and Theologians

If the primary concern of the individual theologian is propositional coherence, as defined by the context of one's approach to revelation, the magisterium by contrast possesses no system of theology as such. Instead, it—or rather *those* who by episcopal consecration in the ministerial order have received what Irenaeus calls the *charisma veritatis*—enjoy a kind of habitual knowledge of the overall proportions of revealed truth. When the magisterium makes a pronouncement, sufficient to the day will be some especially apt form of words which, in the particular historical situation, expresses the abiding mystery. The Church's magisterium does not identify itself with the limits of some individual theological system on which it may draw. It does not underwrite such a particular theology's own perspective and cast of mind. Rather, it discerns how a form of words created, it may be, within such a theology can serve the magisterium's own purpose: providing a window that opens onto the complete vista of revelation in some crucial—and usually disputed—respect.

The functions of the magisterium and of Catholic theology are, evidently, complementary rather than competitive. Theologians attempt to cast the revealed truth into a satisfying pattern, from one vantagepoint, with some unifying concentration of interest. They do so by becoming learned in the Scriptures and the monuments of Tradition, and utilizing the resources of philosophy and the arts and sciences to throw light on that primary datum. Bishops, by contrast, are responsible for the global transmission of the faith; they are its adjudicators, its promoters and its guardians.[23]

Unfortunately, in recent years, the self-denying ordinance of Church authority, which now intervenes relatively rarely in such matters, has not been matched by a similar sense of responsibility in

23. *Christus Dominus*, 15.

numerous theological writers. Cardinal Cahal Daly of Armagh has written:

> The freedom which the Council sought to restore to all the members of the Church, and in particular to theologians, is a freedom in faith, a freedom to serve the believing community in the unity of charity which marks the body of Christ. This freedom calls for a greater sense of responsibility than ever on the part of all members of the Church. As freedom increased, the sense of personal responsibility was required to grow in keeping with it. As control by Church authority over the thinking and practice of Catholics diminished, the taking over by members of the Church, each in their own place and sphere, of personal responsibility for the purity of Catholic teaching and the fidelity of religious observance ought to have increased. When, for example, Church authority ceased to enforce the old regulations about prior theological control of religious writing, concern for the Catholic orthodoxy of the writing should have been taken over by writers themselves and by their theological colleagues, by editors, publishers, competent book critics, et cetera. This sense of shared responsibility has not always been evident.

The same philosopher-bishop went on, adverting to the attempts of some today to justify their departures from tradition because of the abuses of Church authority in the past: "The actual sufferers of twenty-five years ago [Daly is writing in 1976] were enhanced in their persons and strengthened in their faith and their love of the Church—the correct word is sanctified—by their nobility in suffering. The men who today presume vicariously to avenge them are diminished in their persons and damaged in their thinking by their very bitterness."[24]

This is a tragic waste of effort and emotion, for the hierarchy and the theologians are called together to serve the people of God in its grasp of the common truth of the Church. The first has a priority over the second: it is the apostolic ministry that is called to "proclaim the message, and, welcome or unwelcome, insist on it . . . with patience and with the intention of teaching" (2 Tim 4:2). This burden they cannot surrender to theologians, or anyone else, for they received it from God and not from human beings. But, as Pope Paul VI remarked in an address to theologians in the year after the council's close:

> Without theology, the magisterium would lack the instruments which are essential for the conducting of the great symphony in which the en-

---

24. C. B. Daly, "Theologians and the Magisterium," *Irish Theological Quarterly* 43, no. 4 (1976) 225, 226, 228.

tire Church community express their thinking and their living in Jesus Christ. . . . Without the help of theology, the magisterium could undoubtedly preserve and proclaim the faith; but it would have great difficulty in acquiring that full and deep knowledge which it needs in order fully to accomplish its task.

The pope ended by summarizing the *desiderata* for theology today:

The Council exhorts theologians to develop a theology which will be at once pastoral and scientific: a theology which will be closely in contact with the sources, both patristic, liturgical, and, particularly, biblical: a theology which will always have profound respect for the magisterium of the Church and in particular the magisterium of the Vicar of Christ; a theology which will be relevant to human existence as historically lived and as actually experienced; a theology which will be openly ecumenical, but at the same time openly and sincerely Catholic.[25]

Experience

A high doctrine of Scripture, Tradition, and the magisterium, adopted at revelation's behest and in revelation's service, does not mean that experience is sheerly nullified in favor of these authorities. Experience has its assured place in the Catholic Christian's grasp of the truth of creation and redemption.

A sound philosophical grasp of the idea of experience is, however, vital, as the French priest-theologian Jean Mouroux showed in his study *L'Expérience chrétienne*.[26] Mouroux draws his readers' attention to two principal and widespread errors. The first sees experience in terms taken from such empiricist philosophers as John Locke and David Hume. Empiricism regards the human mind or spirit as a kind of blank sheet or empty blackboard: a *tabula rasa*. Objects impinge on the mind as do ink marks on the first or chalk marks on the second. While the mind registers certain impressions (and the feelings associated with them in our passions), it makes no more contribution to what is "written" on it than does any such surface. Here the mind is reduced to the level of a thing—in reality, however, it has its own drive toward intelligibility and understanding. The human intellect is constantly scanning the horizon for elements of meaning, going forth to meet its objects, to penetrate them and squeeze out what it can, as a bee draws

25. Paul VI, Message to the International Congress on the Theology of the Second Vatican Council, in *Documentation catholique*, 16 October 1966, cols. 1738–39, 1732.

26. J. Mouroux, *L'Expérience chrétienne: Introduction à une théologie* (Paris, 1952).

nectar from a flower. But at the other extreme, in idealism, the mind may be seen as so totally active that it becomes the sole source of all experience. According to this contrary misconception it resembles a kind of skin inside which everything we experience is contained. If we are hot, we can get out of our clothes and go for a swim, or take a shower; but we cannot get out of our mind. So in idealism, for all intents and purposes, reality is what the mind takes it to be—what is posited by a mind itself conceived as virtually God-like. As God the Creator puts forth the world from within the divine mind and in contemplating his creation in a sense contemplates himself, so the mind puts forth its own mental creations and endows them with the status of reality. Were individuals to do this, they would soon be judged mad, but idealists are speaking of the transcendental "I," the structure of human consciousness as such. Yet surely finding ourselves surprised by the way other beings disappoint (or exceed) our expectation is so pervasive a feature of mental awareness that it could itself be called a structuring dimension of human consciousness. The idealist account of experience may not, like its empiricist rival, reduce the mind to a thing. But it treats it nonetheless as a closed system of acting.

We are looking, then, for a fuller statement of what experience is, avoiding the errors of empiricism and idealism alike. The process of assimilating perceptions must be, over against empiricism, a personal activity, not just a thing-like passivity; and it must also be, over against idealism, an encounter with agencies beyond us.

Revelation, in presuming its own intelligibility, presupposes a certain degree of spiritual experience on the part of the race. From the very fact that it has recourse to human language, it appeals to a certain spiritual experience among human beings, for concepts, as the crystallization of habits of thinking, are the echo of multiple experiences. Some experience, then, is a condition of possibility for the intelligibility of revelation.

But does the knowledge of faith itself include some further experience of its own? At least at the level of the Church as a whole there must be contemplation of the realities proclaimed in the gospel if there is also to be both correctness and plenitude of understanding. It is sometimes said that dogma is itself the fruit of Christian experience. The doctrine of the Holy Trinity, for example, may be called the product of the Church's experience of issuing from the Christ who revealed himself as the Father's Son in sending upon her the Holy Spirit. In the Gospel of John, faith itself is said to be a kind of seeing, and those who see Jesus see the Father also. Some aspects of this disclosure of God's saving plan in Christ belong exclusively with the beginnings of the Church, with the apostolic experience. But others endure throughout the whole time of the Church, as the reactualizing in her of God's self-gift. So, for example, Paul speaks of the Christian life as an existence "with Christ" and "in Christ," and this is surely meant to appeal to the experience of the believer. Again, there is Paul's teaching in the Letter to the Romans on the indwelling of the Holy Spirit (the Spirit of Christ) who unites himself intimately with our spirit. The notion of the mystical and moral senses of the Bible in the Fathers and the medievals derives from a sense that the main historical events of God's saving intervention in the world are unlimited in their efficacy and so can form the basic pattern for the personal life of each Christian. They are reproduced over and over again, refracted in a myriad of souls. Angelus Silesius, a German mystical writer of the Counter-Reformation, wrote, "Were Christ to be born a thousand times in Bethlehem, but not in you, you would be lost forever."[27]

The very sacramental foundations of the Christian life are built on this basis. In baptism we die and rise again with Christ, and this act must be lived out in many small dyings and risings in a progressive "imitation of Christ." In these ways, we can and must vindicate the Church's dogma in our own experience.

On the other hand, there are also senses in which the appropriate metaphor for faith is not seeing but hearing: receiving a word on trust as the authentic report of a reality not open to our inspection. The Church's dogmatic word is grounded on the word of the apostles, itself founded on Christ as substantial Word, Logos, of the Father. "God is very Truth, who can neither deceive nor be deceived" (as the English Victorian *Catechism* puts it). However much we assert, in a Johannine perspective, that faith naturally becomes knowledge because, through charity, it achieves communion (and so the union of God and the human person), we can never entirely rule out this other aspect of faith: simply accepting on the word of one who is faithful and true. That must remain the support of all faith experience. From one angle, it follows from the disparity between God and humanity in terms of understanding, the reception of reality into the mind. From another, it expresses the fact that we are not yet at the end, the eschaton, when, as Paul puts it, "eye has not seen, nor ear heard, neither has it entered the

27. Angelus Silesius, *Cherubinischer Wandersmann* 1.61.

heart of man, what things God has prepared for those who love him" (1 Cor 2:9). Dogma, then, may not be cast without remainder in terms of experience. Experience needs to be supplemented by such things as the prior tradition, the Scriptures themselves as a relatively independent norm, and the deliverances of those commissioned to teach authoritatively in the Christian community.

In any case, the role of tradition, text, and community in the construction of experience is properly human. As a linguistic animal, the human being exists but rarely in the world of immediacy. Rather, we inhabit worlds mediated by meaning and value. Our world is always foregrounded for us through interpretation: a world come close in words. To be human is to share a conversation that constitutes the human race as a whole. To be a Christian is to be constituted by an analogous conversation, the holy discourse of the Church's tradition.

3
The Historian's Jesus

Some prolegomena

So far as non-Christian sources for the life of Jesus are concerned, there is little to be said. The rabbinic materials—texts that have come down to us from the Judaism of the period after Jesus' lifetime—contain no clear reference to him. Within the first hundred years after his death only three secular authors mention him. The Roman historian Tacitus remarks that Christians were named after a certain Christus, condemned to death by Pontius Pilate. A senior administrative official, Pliny the younger, in a letter to the emperor Trajan, describes Christians as singing hymns to someone named Christus, as to a god (which is therefore not, strictly speaking, a reference to the earthly Jesus of history). The third such reference is more informative. The Jewish historian Flavius Josephus, writing, it would appear, independently of the four Gospels but confirming their basic presentation, tells us that during the procuratorial rule of Pontius Pilate there appeared on the religious scene in Palestine a certain Jesus. He enjoyed a reputation for wisdom as expressed in teaching and wonder-working, and acquired a large following which led the Jewish leaders to bring criminal charges against him. Pilate had him crucified but his followers continued in their devotion to him till Josephus's day. For any further first-century information about Jesus one must turn to the New Testament itself.

The New Testament consists of four Gospels or presentations of the essential features of the life, work, and message of Jesus, followed by an account of the beginning of his Church (the Acts of the Apostles). Then comes a set of letters from various individual apostles, and the whole is brought to a close by a vision of the end of time, the Revelation of John. Of these books by far the most important for any reconstruction of the life of Jesus are the Gospels. We are enormously fortunate to have them, for they constitute one of the richest biographical sets of sources there are for any historical figure from the world of antiquity. Though it has been fashionable until recently to deny this, the four Gospels would have been understood by their authors' contemporaries as biographies. The fact that they have a message to present about Jesus does not rob them of their status as biography, in the sense in which that literary genre was appreciated in the ancient world.[1]

We are, however, told by many scholars and popularizers of scholarship that using the Gospels to write a life of Jesus is problematic. Two objections are commonly raised. (1) The evangelists, like the other New Testament authors, were not interested in simply recording bare occurrences for their own sake. On the contrary, those who formulated and preserved the tradition about Jesus did so because they believed his religious claims and considered that they had later seen for themselves the reality that justifies those claims: the risen Lord of the first Easter. In early Christian tradition, therefore, the facts of the historical events were coupled with a new interpretation of those events, stemming from resurrection faith; the history of the pre-Easter Jesus was swallowed up by faith in the post-Easter Christ. (2) The gospel writers did not in any case share the high regard of the modern historian for knowing precisely when and where this or that event took place. Each evangelist goes his own way, except for a broad four-point outline consisting of the witness to Jesus of John the Baptist, a public ministry in Galilee, one or more journeys to Jerusalem, and the death and resurrection there. This is, fortunately, something, but in terms of an overall explanation of how Jesus' life and preaching led to his death (and its amazing sequel), it is not very much.

These are indeed difficulties, but not insuperable ones. First, the objection that the Gospels were from the outset an interpretation by faith for faith (intended, that is, to awaken or encourage faith in others), does not render them valueless as history. An interpretation, after all, is always an interpretation of something: it presupposes some kind of datum. The New Testament authors, responsible as they were both for preserving the traditions about Jesus and for applying them to the practical needs of the Church, were necessarily conscious that their work would be in vain if there was no historical basis for their teaching.

---

1. R. A. Burridge, *What Are the Gospels? A Comparison with Graeco-Roman Biography* (Cambridge, 1992).

Second, although the evangelists clearly did not regard exact chronology as paramount (literary and theological considerations, as well as, no doubt, confusions or failures of memory, led to much discrepancy in this regard), it is possible to recognize in the Gospels a great deal of authentic historical detail (not simply a grand sweep; though here each section of a Gospel must be judged on its merits). Moreover, the events recorded in the Gospels both in themselves and in certain of their interrelations often reveal a close acquaintance with Palestinian geography as well as with the complex religious and political situation of the time. Furthermore, they frequently appear to form sequences that reflect an unfolding development in the attitudes of Jesus himself, attitudes towards the various social groups—whether family and kin, the twelve disciples, Jewish sects and movements, or pagans—that constituted his immediate world.

Too often it is forgotten that behind all exegetical assessment of the gospel texts there stands a living person affected by and responding to the events of the time and the society in which he lived. It is the primary task of the historian to recover the features of Jesus in his public life and teaching, and not to become diverted by an obsession with the analytical dissection of the texts, the delineation of what may have been various stages in their transmission, or the search for the Christological emphases that may have characterized the local communities in the Church where those texts were stabilized in their present form. Fascinating though these adjunct activities are, the historian's chief task is to arrange the relevant data in a narrative form, explaining that data by fashioning a connected story which seems coherent and plausible to the ears of enlightened (which does not by any means signify atheistic) common sense. The making of such coherent, explanatory stories about the human past is the discipline of history. Thus, for instance, no narrative reconstruction of the life of Jesus is plausible that so reduces the amount of what we know historically about him as to leave no clue as to how he aroused the reactions he did.

In these matters of history and exegetical method there is a guideline for Catholic students in the "Instruction on the Historical Truth of the Gospels" written during the Second Vatican Council by a team of scholars under the aegis of the Pontifical Biblical Commission. Its framers open by noting that "Today the labors of exegetes are all the more called for by reason of the fact that in many publications, circulated far and wide, the truth of the events and sayings recorded in the Gospels is being challenged."[2] How, then, should these "labors" proceed?

In the first place, the "Instruction" says, the Catholic exegete will wish to draw on the resources furnished by the inherited patrimony of gospel interpretation, especially as that is found in the Fathers of the Church and her Doctors (the latter being theologians distinguished by three marks: learning, orthodoxy of doctrine, and holiness of life). We can take it for granted that such patristic and classical interpretation of the Gospels assumes their substantial historicity. Second, the Catholic scholar will also be happy to use the new aids provided by the historical method, though with a pinch of caution added. Because, as the "Instruction" points out, with particular reference to form criticism (on which more anon):

> Certain exponents of this method, led astray by rationalistic prejudices, refuse to admit that there exists a supernatural order, or that a personal God intervenes in the world by revelation properly so called, or that miracles and prophecies are possible and have actually occurred. There are others who have as their starting-point a wrong notion of faith, taking it that faith is indifferent to historical truth, and is indeed incompatible with it. Others practically deny a priori the historical value and character of the documents of revelation. Others finally there are who on the one hand underestimate the authority which the apostles had as witnesses of Christ, and the office and influence which they wielded in the primitive community, whilst on the other hand they overestimate the creative capacity of the community itself. All these aberrations are not only opposed to Catholic doctrine, but are also devoid of any scientific foundation, and are foreign to the genuine principles of the historical method.[3]

What then are the main elements of the historical method, so far as the Gospels are concerned? There are usually held to be four "tools," known (in order of their emergence in the last two hundred years) as source criticism, form criticism, tradition-historical criticism, and redaction criticism. In describing them I will keep in mind our particular interest: the historicity of the Gospels as a necessary condition for answering the question, How do we know about Jesus Christ?

Critical Tools

Source criticism deals with the literary relation between the Gospels and their written sources, if any are detected. Comparing the four

2. *Instruction on the Historical Truth of the Gospels*, 1.
3. Ibid.

Gospels leads to the conclusion that the first three share much common material (they are *synoptic*, a term first used when the practice arose of arranging their contents in parallel columns), while John is something of a sport. Comparing the Synoptics leads to one of four conclusions. The first, adopted by perhaps a majority of modern scholars but under increasing attack, is that Mark's Gospel is primary, along with an anonymous source for the sayings of Jesus shared by Matthew and Luke—though this source, known as *Q* from the German word for "source," *Quelle*, could be either a written document, now lost, or just a pool of remembered sayings, an oral tradition. In itself, there is nothing wrong with taking a special interest in Mark. Augustine wrote, *Credimus in quem credidit Petrus,* "We believe on him whom Peter believed,"[4] and early tradition regarded Mark's Gospel as the direct echo of Peter's catechesis in Rome. Q, however, is much more problematic, since, as a sayings source, it has nothing about Jesus' death and resurrection (the narratives of which figure so prominently in the canonical Gospels). Books can now be written, accordingly, that claim that for the "Q community"—a (hypothetical) Church with as much right to be regarded as authoritative as any other in the New Testament world—Jesus was a wisdom teacher pure and simple; his death and resurrection were not regarded there as normative for faith. Some source critics would go further and claim that the only reliable Synoptic historical material we have about Jesus is Mark and Q—and this would reduce our knowledge of him considerably. There is however no logical force behind this extension of the first solution to the Synoptic problem. Even if Mark and Q were the earliest sources to be crystallized out of the apostolic tradition, that does not mean they must necessarily be our only historical evidence. What about the material that is distinctive of Matthew and Luke? It cannot just be assumed that those evangelists spun it out of Mark and Q by creative imagination.

A second major possibility alongside the two document hypothesis is now steadily regaining ground, and this is the so-called two Gospel hypothesis, according to which the order of the Synoptics is Matthew, Luke, Mark, with Mark writing on the basis of Peter's preaching in order to unify the presentation of the gospel made in the very Jewish Matthew and the very Gentile Luke. Apart from the greater consonance of this theory with what the early ecclesiastical writers say about the order in which the Gospels were composed, it also solves many

4. Augustine, *City of God* 18.54.

puzzles that arise if one adopts the two document hypothesis, notably the fact that there are many "minor agreements" between Matthew and Luke over against Mark. This is the Achilles' heel of a theory according to which Matthew and Luke did not know each other, but are only connected through Mark.

A third main possibility, associated with the name of Anglican exegete Austin Farrer, is to retain the priority of Mark but dispense with Q, holding instead that Luke used Matthew as a primary source alongside Matthew's predecessor, Mark.

A fourth and final view is that the Synoptics, despite their large volume of shared material, are in some way independent of each other. For those who take this line, the sharing of formulae in the Synoptic Gospels is to be explained in the first instance by the fact that Jesus formed the disciples into a group whose task it was to spread memorized versions of his teaching and summaries of his actions. After all, this is what appears to be happening in the Synoptic evangelists' own accounts of the relation of Jesus to the Twelve, and it fits extremely well with the known practices of the Pharisees, and later on the rabbis, in a Jewish world where written and oral culture, learning from texts and learning by word of mouth, existed side by side. On such presuppositions there could be many different earlier versions of the canonical Gospels, and our best bet will be, then, a multiple source theory. The Swedish Lutheran convert to Catholicism Harald Riesenfeld and the French Dominican Père Marie-Emile Boismard represent, respectively, the first and second parts of this composite proposal. In the absence of any clear consensus about the direction of literary influence among the Synoptics, this may be the most prudent course to follow.

In any case, in discussing the Gospels we cannot be content with the Synoptics alone. There is such a thing as the "tyranny of the Synoptic Jesus," an undesirably exclusive recourse to Matthew, Mark, and Luke over against John in composing a narrative outline of Jesus' life or an overview of his teaching. In the nineteenth and early twentieth centuries, when not so much was known about the archeology and cultural history of the Israel of Jesus' time, it was not recognized that John's exact knowledge of customs and places in Palestine makes him a promising source for the historian's Jesus. The different tones in which the Johannine Jesus speaks may be explained in part by a difference of audience—one notes particularly the engagement of the Jesus of John's Gospel with the learned theologians of the Jewish parties of the day, and the fact that the lion's share of his private or "esoteric" teaching to the Twelve in that Gospel is given on the occasion of his final meeting with them, the Last Supper.

Once source criticism—on the basis of a majority vote of Protestant scholars for the two document hypothesis—had put forward the claim that we can infer the editorial techniques of Matthew and Luke by seeing what they did to Mark, it was fairly inevitable that people should ask whether there might perhaps be signs of similar editorial work within Mark himself. An editorial framework was duly discovered, and, when removed, left behind a series of disconnected units of various kinds. Mark, it was now said, is a snapshot album—unconnected snaps of Jesus at various points in various postures, the interrelation (and, therefore, significance) of which we can no longer discern. And just as source criticism had been in fact the application to the New Testament of the methods of historians of texts from the Greco-Roman and medieval European worlds, so now a new method arose which applied to these disconnected units the methods of historians of folklore. The tale, the saying, the miracle story, and so forth, were already well known as typical forms of popular folk-culture from Norway in the north to the Australian aboriginals in the south. Focusing on such formal aspects enabled the scholars to identify (to their own satisfaction at least) the original function the units possessed at the oral stage before the author of Mark or the compiler of Q got hold of them. The overall conclusion of *form criticism* has been summed up as: "In the beginning was the sermon." The units tell us next to nothing about the life of Jesus; rather, they tell us about the life of the community that believed in him. Such radical form criticism, undermining as it does any pretension to know anything much historically about Jesus Christ soon aroused attack, and deservedly so.

In the first place, we can say that the application of the form criticism of folklore specialists whose material has developed over hundreds of years to texts which have a prehistory of only a few decades is distinctly dubious. Secondly, form criticism cannot show, in point of fact, that units were not transmitted for their own sake. Were early Christians really so uninterested in what the Jesus of history had actually said and done? Was the principal effect of Pentecost to turn the apostles' memories into blanks? Thirdly, it is a non sequitur to say that because the form of a unit shows how it was used in the earliest Church (before Mark, say) therefore it originated in the post-Easter period as the "theology of the community." At the most, form criticism has shown how "Jesus material" in the Gospels was affected by the use made of it in the early Church's preaching, liturgy, and apologetics. It has not shown that the early Church had no interest in passing on authentic historical matter about Jesus Christ. The great Catholic historian of ancient education Henri-Irénée Marrou pointed out that the idea and techniques of form criticism are suspiciously indebted to the German romantics, notably J. G. Herder, in ascribing popular literature to the collective, spontaneous creation of communities—an almost unconscious expression of the soul or genius of a social group. This romantic theory is today largely abandoned as illusory by other literary historians, not excluding specialists in folklore.

Assuming that form criticism has at any rate some value, we are faced with the question, How can we distinguish words and ideas that the Church has introduced into the forms from the original oral record? Form critics had their own suggestions here. At their most rigorous they put forward two main criteria: a saying of Jesus may well be authentic if (a) it is something a first-century Palestinian Jew could plausibly have said and (b) it is not the kind of thing the early Church set out to say about Jesus but rather something which left that Church slightly embarrassed. The conclusion is that a typical authentic saying of Jesus might be Mark 13:32, where Jesus admits that he does not know the time of his parousia! These criteria are far too restrictive. They state in effect that no saying of Jesus is authentic if in first-century Palestinian-Jewish terms it is original (in other words, Jesus was utterly conventionally minded!), or if the early Church agreed with it (in other words, the apostles got absolutely everything wrong!).

The *tradition-historical critics,* however, accepted from the form critics that something like these criteria were the right ones and then tried to answer the question, If the language and ideas of the units identified by form criticism did not come from Jesus and the apostles, then where did they come from? Their answer was that the language and ideas at issue came from the surrounding culture within which the early Christian communities lived and prayed.

We can indeed accept that the historical tradition about Jesus was affected by picking up things from the environment, just as it was modified by such internal demands of the life of the Church as preaching. But since we have rejected radical form criticism, we necessarily also reject radical tradition-historical criticism. The problem the latter was devised to answer largely disappears anyway with the rejection of the former.

If form criticism is even partly right about how Mark and Q originally found their materials, it will be possible to ask, Why did Mark (since no one possesses a copy of Q) organize his materials the way he did? That is, we can ask not only about the prehistory of the Marcan units, as in tradition-historical criticism, but also about their subsequent history—and this is *redaction criticism* (named after the German loan-word from the French for "editor," *Redakteur*). Redaction critics are interested in the author of Mark considered as an original theologian, and likewise with the authors of Matthew and Luke in their editing of Mark and Q. Here we may throw in John for good measure, insofar as it is possible to conjecture what his materials might have been.

Once again, the acceptability of redaction criticism turns on just how radical is its use of form criticism. Once radical form criticism is accepted, redaction criticism makes the Gospels tell us more about the evangelists than about Jesus, just as tradition-historical criticism makes the Gospels tell us more about the contemporary culture than about Jesus, and form criticism makes the Gospels tell us more about the Church than about Jesus. But can we really suppose that the evangelists felt this sovereign freedom to make things up as they went along? As one critic has recently remarked: "For all his claims to apostolic authority, Paul does not feel free to create teachings and put them in the mouth of Jesus. We might ask, Who in the first generation did?"[5]

In its effort to keep the ship of gospel study on an even keel, the Pontifical Biblical Commission proposed a three-stage scheme as corresponding better both to Catholic teaching and to historical probability. At stage one, it suggested, Jesus deliberately created a group of disciples, a kind of rabbinate, so as to pass on the tradition about him in a culture where oral transmission was still vital in the communication of knowledge. Stage two involves the apostles themselves as they recounted Jesus' life and words but did so in the light of what they knew to have been their final outcome.

> It need not be denied that the apostles when handing on to their hearers the things which in actual fact the Lord had said and done, did so in the light of that fuller understanding which they enjoyed as a result of being schooled by the glorious things accomplished in Christ, and of being illuminated by the Spirit of Truth. Thus it came about that, just as Jesus himself after his Resurrection had "interpreted to them" (Luke 24:27) both the words of the Old Testament and the words which he himself

5. J. P. Meier, *Jesus: A Marginal Jew* (New York, 1991) 46.

had spoken, so now they in their turn interpreted his words and deeds according to the needs of their hearers. "Devoting [themselves] . . . to the ministry of the word" (Acts 6:4), they made use, as they preached, of such various forms of speech as were adapted to their own purposes and to the mentality of their hearers; for it was "to Greek and barbarian, to learned and simple" (Rom 1:14) that they had a duty to discharge.[6]

Here then the oral forms were enclosed within the actual word-of-mouth preaching of the apostles. Finally, stage three was reached when those whom the commission calls "the sacred authors" began to operate and to compose the Gospels out of the material coming to them from the apostolic tradition. The commission speaks of these evangelists as setting down the gospel message in written form in response to the needs of their respective Churches.

Here the "Instruction" seems pointedly to refrain from identifying the apostles (and their co-workers) with the "sacred authors" or evangelists, and in this it appears to have had an influence on *Dei Verbum*, the Dogmatic Constitution on Divine Revelation from the Second Vatican Council. After declaring that the four Gospels are our principal sources for the life and teaching of the incarnate Word, our Savior, *Dei Verbum* continues:

> The Church has always and everywhere maintained, and continues to maintain, the apostolic origin of the four Gospels. The apostles preached, as Christ had charged them to do, and then, under the inspiration of the Holy Spirit, they and others of the apostolic age *[ipsi et apostolici viri]* handed on to us in writing the same message they had preached, the foundations of our faith: the fourfold Gospel, according to Matthew, Mark, Luke and John. . . . Holy Mother Church has firmly and with absolute constancy maintained and continues to maintain, that the four Gospels just named, whose historicity she unhesitatingly affirms, faithfully hand on what Jesus, the Son of God, while he lived among men, really did and taught for their eternal salvation, until the day when he was taken up (cf. Acts 1:1-2). For, after the Ascension of the Lord, the apostles handed on to their hearers what he had said and done, but with the fuller understanding which they, instructed by the glorious events of Christ and enlightened by the Spirit of truth, now enjoyed.

But in the following section, where it would be natural to find a confident assertion of apostolic authorship for Matthew and John, and that of "apostolic men" for Mark and Luke, the language is rather subdued.

6. *Instruction on the Historical Truth of the Gospels*, 8, 2.

The sacred authors, in writing the four Gospels, selected certain of the many elements which had been handed on, either orally or already in written form, others they synthesized or explained with an eye to the situation of the churches, while keeping the form of proclamation, but always in such a fashion that they have told us the honest truth about Jesus. . . . Whether they relied on their own memory and recollections or on the testimony of those who "from the beginning were eyewitnesses and minister of the Word," their purpose in writing was that we might know the "truth" concerning the things of which we have been informed (cf. Luke 1:2-4).[7]

By borrowing the phrase "the sacred authors" from the biblical commission's text, *Dei Verbum* leaves open (probably deliberately) the possibility that the authors of the Gospels were in fact second-generation Christian writers and scribes. At any rate, by prescinding from the question of how, when, and where the apostles committed their preaching to writing, *Dei Verbum* made it officially possible for Catholic scholarship to adopt a broadened notion of apostolic authorship—though we should note that the historical authority of the Gospels will suffer if that notion is expanded too far: if, for instance, an "apostolic writing" comes to mean merely a writing in which the Church recognizes the apostolic faith. For that may be said of, for example, the autobiography of Thérèse of Lisieux, or the Code of Canon Law of the Oriental Churches! The most recent Roman pronouncement to take a position on the point, the 1994 document of the biblical commission on "The Interpretation of the Bible," steers a *via media* in calling the New Testament writings a "genuine reflection of the apostolic preaching" while insisting that this does not necessarily mean all were composed by the apostles themselves.

How then, can we know about Jesus Christ? We can obtain an historical knowledge of him by looking at the Gospels, but we must be canny about how we approach them. Though we can admit that they are deeply affected by the faith of those who wrote them, this does not mean that, as believers, the evangelists or those on whom they relied were uninterested in what actually happened. We can also admit that the evangelists were not historians in the modern sense, and even that, in quite a short time, the tradition about Jesus had been directed to the practical needs of the Church. But this does not mean that the evangelists or those on whom they drew were wholesale inventors of facts,

7. *Dei Verbum,* 18–19.

continually put words on Jesus' lips, and retained no sense of the location or order of events and sayings. We can accept that chronological order was not a paramount consideration for them or their sources. Otherwise they would no doubt have taken steps to ensure the transmission and writing down of a more consistent scheme. Arrangement of material by topic was sometimes more important, and this led inevitably to a certain displacement of episodes. But enough of what the contemporary non-Catholic exegete E. P. Sanders has termed "chronological clues" are left to reconstruct an outline chronology using the imaginative hypothesizing essential to all historical explanation.[8]

In sum, the idea that the evangelists, or the early Christian community, were the inventors of much or even most of the story of Jesus is historically implausible. To explain the rise of the Church, a figure of enormous originality and power must be postulated by the most religiously skeptical of historians—and it is paradoxical that Christian scholars can sometimes appear less ready to accept this than some of their secular colleagues. Some would call what follows "novelistic," but I prefer to make my own some words of a distinguished Protestant biblical scholar of a new generation:

> This approach may rightly be regarded as conservative if by that is meant that it places a premium on considerations of historical plausibility, continuity, and common sense, at the expense of readings which tend to atomize texts into a profusion of sources in mutual social and religious contradiction. We must indeed affirm the multiformity of our evidence, and refuse to rule out the possibility of finding such contradictions. Nevertheless, my inclination here will be to look in the first instance not for clinical detail in source criticism but for a *whole picture* of both the teaching and the actions of Jesus which makes plausible sense in a first century Palestinian narrative framework.[9]

The Life

Jesus was born in Mediterranean Asia, in a territory known anciently as Canaan, and in his own lifetime as Palestine. It consisted of three regions: Galilee in the north, Samaria in the center, Judaea in the south. Jesus lived there during a period of Roman rule, though this rule was

8. In what follows I shall be indebted to the work, along these lines, of the German archaeologist-exegete Bargil Pixner, monk of the Dormition Abbey, Jerusalem. See: B. Pixner, *With Jesus through Galilee according to the Fifth Gospel* (Rosh Pina, 1992).

9. M. Bockmuehl, *This Jesus: Martyr, Lord, Messiah* (Edinburgh, 1994) 21.

directly exercised, in the period of his public ministry, only in Judaea. Otherwise it functioned indirectly through petty subkings or tetrarchs (rulers of a quarter of a kingdom, whether literally or metaphorically). The Jewish community, though humiliated by this foreign presence, was still permeated by the religious ideas of the Hebrew Bible, which provided the foundation for its culture. These ideas were, however, differently expressed in the various movements characteristic of the rather pluralistic and fluid Judaism of the day. Of these three were notable: (1) the Sadducees, the priestly aristocracy and their followers: conservative and minimalizing in their attitude to the Old Testament but culturally innovative and pro-Greek, and on good terms with the Romans who left certain powers of governance with their council, the Sanhedrin; (2) the Essenes, who were deeply opposed to the acceptance of pagan elements by the Sadducees and withdrew, exteriorly or interiorly, from official society, seeing themselves as the only true Israel who had renewed their Sinai covenant with God and now were awaiting the Day of the Lord, a definitive separation of the righteous from the unrighteous; (3) the Pharisees, an enthusiastic reform party, which maximized the divine revelation by treating the oral law as equally authoritative with the written Bible. They had a revolutionary nationalist wing, the Zealots, which boasted a sufficient following among have-nots to precipitate open warfare with the Romans after Jesus' death.

The father of Jesus' own family was a craftsman, and his circle of relations appears to have lived in the style of the *sortis media*, neither rich nor poor. More significant is the fact that they knew themselves to be descended from the ancient kings of Judah, the Davidides, to whose line the messianic hope of Israel was intimately linked. The name of the town where the family lived, Nazareth, and the word for an inhabitant thereof, Nazarene, come from the Hebrew root *netzer*, which refers to the springing of the Messiah as a fruitful "shoot" from the stump of Jesse, David's father (Isa 11:1). Nazareth had been founded in the period just before the Roman occupation; its first inhabitants would have been Jewish exiles intent on resettling the largely paganized Galilee on their return to the Land. Near the end of the second century of the Christian era, the Palestinian writer Julius Africanus records that the blood relations of Jesus in two villages had preserved the Davidide family trees: Kochba, the village of the star, and Nazara, village of the shoot—both names deriving from terms closely associated with the dynasty of David. This explains an incident in the

Gospels of Luke and Mark: in Jericho, when the blind beggar Bartimaeus is told that "Jesus the man from Nazara" is passing by, his spontaneous reaction is to call out, "Jesus, Son of David, have mercy on me" (Luke 19:37; Mark 10:47).

The circumstances of Jesus' birth and certain episodes in his childhood were remembered as extraordinary. The narratives of his conception, birth, and infancy have been, alongside those of the resurrection, the main target of skeptical critics in their approach to the Gospels. Not only does the supernatural play a major role in these stories (in the form of angels, visions, dreams, and strange astronomical phenomena), but even the realistic elements in the narratives make, in context, a palpably theological demand upon their readers. Thus some would maintain that the matrix of the infancy narratives (the term normally used to cover all the stories from the annunciation up to, but excluding, the baptism) lies in popular legends which the evangelists found already in circulation. Without necessarily claiming that these stories were historically well founded, the gospel writers saw that they could serve as vehicles for their own theological message.

Alternatively, it may be held that the infancy narratives are a form of the imaginative interpretation of the Old Testament known to Jewish tradition as *midrash*. This is a recognized genre of book or text in the Palestinian Judaism of the period: examples lie to hand in the Dead Sea Scrolls. But while practitioners of midrash certainly tried to apply Old Testament prophecy to events or developments of their day, there is no reason to think that they considered themselves justified in creating events *ex nihilo*.

In point of fact, when we listen to Luke's account of his own historical method in the prologue to his Gospel as a whole, he makes it clear that his approach consisted in the provision of an orderly framework for materials derived from what today would be called oral history.

> Inasmuch as many have undertaken to compile a narrative of the things which have been accomplished among us, just as they were delivered to us by those who from the beginning were eyewitnesses and ministers of the word, it seemed good to me also, having followed all things closely for some time past, to write an orderly account for you, most excellent Theophilus, that you may know the truth concerning the things of which you have been informed (Luke 1:1-4).

Again, though Matthew makes no comparable statement, the body of his Gospel, while taking perhaps certain liberties with the chronology of events in Jesus' lifetime, is generally regarded as giving access nonetheless to authentic Jesus material—thus raising the question whether someone would knowingly synthesize in the same work historically valueless with historically invaluable information.

In any case, what is more probable than that, as writers who believed Jesus to be the Jewish Messiah and the Savior of all peoples, Luke and Matthew would have been curious about his origins, ancestors, birthplace, family circle, and any memories that pointed to his later fate? (It is the absence of such material in Mark and John that requires an explanation.)

However, none of this is meant to deny that the infancy Gospels were also meant to convey a theological message about Jesus' identity and future mission. Scenes have been presented as carefully constructed tableaux, often using props drawn from the Old Testament, so as to convey to reasonably well-informed Jews, or Gentile converts to Judaism, the significance of the child who would be the Messiah of Israel and the answer to the hopes of the nations. It is admittedly difficult for scholars to establish what should count here as historical reportage and what as deliberate dramatization by the evangelist (or his source). Only some wider epistemological framework, skeptical or not, can provide an orientation. The Catholic historian will find this in the mind of the Church which has determined, in her use of the Bible in the liturgy and the construction of doctrine, that the events described in the infancy Gospels are historically based, even though literary techniques may also have been used to draw attention to certain key aspects of their theological meaning.

> If the Church is to limit her decisions to what pleases critics she must surrender all claim to divinity. And if she did so she would only please the critics of today. What about those of tomorrow? No one who watches the ebb-and-flow of Biblical criticism can fail to see how the "accepted" positions of a few years ago, the rejection of which stamped a man as a hopeless obscurantist, are now being called in question. How long before "Q" will hear his Requiem sung?[10]

With these preliminary points made, what may the historian assert about the man Jesus before his public ministry began? First, that there was some mystery about his conception and birth: Mark refers to Jesus as "son of Mary" (6:3)—a strange designation in so patrilinear a cul-

---

10. H. Pope, "Assent to the Decrees of the Biblical Commission," *Blackfriars* 6, no. 61 (1925) 225.

ture. John calls Jesus "son of Joseph" (1:45; 6:42), but he also records a dialogue which seems to imply, in an ironic play on the concepts of earthly and heavenly fatherhood (8:19-41), that he is not. Matthew and Luke, for whom Jesus' Davidic descent through Joseph is crucial, have to settle, by implication, for a purely legal sonship by adoption in putting forward the notion of parthenogenesis from Mary.

Second, he was born in the Judaean town of Bethlehem, once celebrated as David's birthplace, where in all probability Joseph's extended family maintained some form of property. (The "inn" where no room was to be had is more correctly a "house," presumably that of the Bethlehemite members of the clan.) The birth took place during a census. Luke's Greek may plausibly be construed as identifying this bureaucratic intervention of Roman authority as the last before Quirinius became governor of Syria (in A.D. 6). There may well have been a census in 7 B.C., connected with the requirement of an oath of allegiance to the emperor and his procurator: Augustus not only wanted a general stock-taking in the empire, but saw a particular need to tighten control over Palestine and Rome's Eastern frontier. As to the manger-cave, many Palestinian houses had feeding troughs for animals in the vicinity of their main entrance: doubtless this was where Mary laid her new-born child amid the confused as well as straitened circumstances of a clan-gathering in the ancient Near East.

On Matthew's account, Joseph and Mary remained in Bethlehem for up to two years: their stay included an astronomically inspired encounter with wandering astrologers from the pagan cultures to Palestine's east. Though reconstruction is more than usually hypothetical, reference may be made here to the conjunction of Saturn and Jupiter in the constellation Pisces in 7 B.C., and the conjunction of both those planets with Mars early in the following year. There is evidence that Pisces was associated with both the Hebrews and the end of the world, Jupiter with global rulers, and Saturn with the Amorites, the earliest inhabitants of Syro-Palestine; the combination could well have suggested the emergence of an eschatological ruler in that part of the world. A conjunction of planets would of course resemble "stars," rather than "a star": and the Protogospel of James, a noncanonical text that may include some material from early Jewish-Christian tradition, has exactly that.

The negative reaction of the Judaean king Herod the Great to such inquiries is in keeping with attitudes of the period. Where affairs of state were concerned, an astrology still undifferentiated from astronomy was taken very seriously in the ancient world. Astrologers could be forbidden from making predictions about the emperor's health; Domitian executed men born with imperial horoscopes. The massacre of the innocents (the destruction, on Herod's orders, of Bethlehemite children of approximately Jesus' age), was the typical reaction of a cruel and insecure ruler faced with a potentially subversive astrological prediction in a village whose name was charged with symbolism and situated on the doorstep of his key fortress of Herodion.

The "flight into Egypt" of Jesus' nuclear family may have been no more than a short journey across a frontier. Alternatively, it might have entailed a stay in some major center of Egyptian Jewry, accessible, numerous, vibrant, and in frequent contact with Jerusalem as this was.

Visits to Jerusalem by Palestinian Jews were not in the nature of the later pilgrimage by Muslims from the Maghreb to Mecca, a once-in-a-lifetime occurrence. Rather were they frequent features of a well-regulated liturgical life for the devout. Jesus' presentation in the Temple, and his conversation with its resident clergy on the eve of his Jewish coming-of-age, as recorded by Luke, are out of the ordinary only inasmuch as the convictions of the evangelists about the ultimate identity of this child (or youth), based on the events of his adult life, give them a significance they could not otherwise possess. It is to that adult life we must now turn, leaving till the next chapter an account of the inner meaning of these and others of the chief episodes of Jesus' life, a commentary on the fuller, indeed divine, meaning invested in them, as the Church sees them.

The youth grew up to inherit his foster-father's profession (Mark 6:3), but he was soon caught up in the mission of the first postbiblical Jewish prophet, Johanan ben Zechariah. In the context of this attempted religious renewal of the Jewish nation, he began to express in a "public ministry" his identity and role.

At a certain point in early manhood, then, Jesus left his native place so as to associate himself with the spiritual revival initiated by his cousin John the Baptist. John saw his work as a call to repentance in the spirit of the prophet Elijah, and chose to concentrate his activity in places hallowed by Elijah's memory. He preached by the river Jordan near Jericho where Elijah had ascended to heaven in a whirlwind of fire (2 Kgs 2:11-12), and baptized at Aenon near Salim where Elijah had thrown his cloak around Elisha, his successor, as a sign of his transmitting to him the prophetic spirit (1 Kgs 19:19). John first spoke of Jesus to representatives of the Pharisee party at Batanea, "Bethany beyond the Jordan," near the ravine where Elijah had hid from King

Ahab in preparation for his great campaign to purify Israel from its sins and errors. Just as in Jewish tradition Elijah was linked to the fulfillment of God's promises for Israel at the end of time (when, it was thought, he would reappear), so John's preaching and the baptism of repentance he offered had as their theme the imminence of an all-encompassing divine judgment. In permitting himself to be baptized by John, Jesus identified himself with these expectations.

To begin with, then, Jesus shared the Baptist's aim which was the reconstitution of God's sacred people, Israel, in view of the coming consummation of world history known in Greek shorthand as the *eschaton*—the last age, the final epoch, the ultimate moment in historical time as hitherto known. Jesus met some of his first disciples—Andrew, Peter, Philip, John—in the context of the Baptist's activities, as the latter tells us in his gospel (1:38b-39), and the Baptist singled Jesus out as having a special role to play in the great events that were coming (John 1:30). The background lay in the biblical conviction that history, understood as including all our individual life-stories as well as great public events, is the unfolding of a divine purpose for the world. As such it must be construed as a plan, with a beginning, middle sections, and an end. The Baptist taught that the end was close at hand, and would take the form of a painful judgment and thus purgation and remaking of Israel. Therefore he preached repentance—the renouncing of any and every claim on God's justice based on one's own righteousness. When the end came, only such repentance would make it (for the individual Israelite) a positive experience rather than a negative one, what the prophets had called "weal" rather than "woe." Jesus, in seconding this affirmation, also approved the method John used to communicate it: a call to repentance which, if answered, led to a symbolic purification in the Jordan. When the Baptist was arrested by the civil authorities, however, Jesus evidently took this as a signal that one significant stage in the events of the endtime had finished. He ceased baptizing and withdrew further north to his native region of Galilee. There he embarked on a new proclamation and ministry of his own.

The Gospels differ as to where to place the public beginning of Jesus' ministry. Luke takes it to be Jesus' preaching in the synagogue at Nazareth, his home town, where he aroused the scornful opposition that befalls prophets in their own country; John locates it at Cana some few miles to the south, the first miracle of Jesus rather than the first sermon. John also reports that Jesus' Nazarene origin did not commend itself to all Jews outside of Nazareth (John 1:46—no doubt

Davidides were as slightly ridiculous then as, say, members of the house of Habsburg fallen on hard times would be today). However, Nathanael of Cana, when he actually met Jesus and witnessed this first miracle at a wedding feast in his native town, rapidly changed his mind. Luke and John agree in saying that after the initiation of his ministry, wherever we place it, Jesus transferred his base to Capharnaum, a town on the Sea of Galilee, the native country of his future apostles.

Although the three Synoptic Gospels speak explicitly about only one visit of Jesus to Jerusalem, they hint at others, and John is quite definite that Jesus did go up to Jerusalem for the feast of Passover during the first and last springtimes of the two to three years of his public ministry, and that he attended the Temple for the feasts of Tabernacles and Dedication in the intervening year when Passover found him still in Galilee. Such relatively frequent pilgrimages to Jerusalem are only what one would expect of a devout Jew of this period. After, then, some initial activity in Galilee which need not demand more than few weeks for its performance, Jesus journeyed to the Jewish capital and immediately confronted the guardians of its holiest shrine in the episode of the cleansing of the Temple. John records that the spiritual vigor of this act brought many Jews to his side; perhaps prominent among them were Essenes, who had theological difficulties with the Temple cultus as practiced by the dominant, Sadducee party. Jerusalem would remain of the highest importance to Jesus, not only for the obvious reason that it was the holy city of Judaism, but also because one of his major rivals for the definitive interpretation of the Hebrew Bible—the priestly party of the Sadducees—were there in strength.

On the other hand, Galilee was the great stronghold of the other principal contender for the right to interpret the divine revelation to Israel. There the Pharisees, both moderates and rigorists, had a devout following as had their revolutionary wing, the Zealots. In Galilee too Jesus would touch the fringes of the pagan world, the Gentiles, whom his proclamation of imminent salvation also concerned. Hearing, then, of the many converts being made by those of his disciples who were continuing to practice John's baptism of repentance, Jesus left Judaea for Galilee by way of Samaria where his conversation with a Samaritan woman reinforced the point that the messianic kingdom would not be restricted to the Jewish people (John 4:42). At the fishing ground of Capharnaum, Jesus relocated certain disciples he had already met in the Baptist's company. The news that John the Baptist had been imprisoned by the Roman satrap Herod Antipas—in the Machaerus fortress, far away by the Dead Sea—was the cue for his urgent message to these men: "The Kingdom of God is near" (Mark 1:5). Calling two sets of brothers (Andrew and Peter, James and John), Jesus walked the two miles to Capharnaum, his adopted home. There he began to build up a spiritual family in the form of a circle of friends in which he was the rabbi surrounded by his special disciples. Jesus borrowed this concept from the Pharisees, but the closed number of twelve disciples of predilection was his own contribution. It harked back symbolically to the twelve tribes of Israel, a new version of which was in the making. Jesus had no home of his own (Matt 8:20), but seems to have lived in the house of Peter. Recently excavated, it was venerated by Jewish Christians who scribbled the names of both Jesus and Peter on its walls.

Jesus now began to develop a highly personal style of teaching through parables and pithy sayings, and such was his originality that he made an immediate impact. The main motifs of his preaching were: the reign or kingly rule of God; his own role in bringing in that reign; the unique importance of the epoch on which humanity had just entered, thanks to his presence and words; and the task consequently entrusted to his followers. He also taught ethics, reworking in the light of these themes a number of the moral dictates come down from Jewish tradition. Though many of his ideas and values were taken over from the Hebrew Bible, he tended to express them in an absolutely new way. As a result, his teachings caused ill-feeling between himself and the various religious leaders of the Jewish people.

Jesus was first registered as something quite exceptional when he illustrated his message with actions that exceeded normal human capability: notably, exorcisms, healings, and intensifications of the bounty of nature. Contrary to Jesus' intentions, these miracles were popularly interpreted as feats of power indicative of a political renaissance for Israel, and so by implication divine vengeance on the Romans for their rule. It was fortunate, then, that he had gathered around him the group of pupils called the "disciples" for whom he could correct such misconceptions. From their number he chose twelve apostles (the word can be paraphrased as "mandated representatives") to whom he gave a more intimate teaching. This centered on his relation with God, whom he characteristically called "Abba" ("dear Father") and the Spirit of God, whom he referred to as the Paraclete, or Counsellor, and so dealt more fully with his own identity, his special role in the mission of the Spirit from the Father. This more intimate or esoteric teaching also concerned the founding of a new Israel: a new community termed in Greek (a language Jesus probably knew) *ekklēsia,* "the Church." Several remarkable women lent this apostolic group their support.

The novelty of Jesus' approach and the impact he made naturally gave rise to questions about his identity and intentions. The narratives of his baptism and its sequel, the temptations, were partly autobiographical answers to these questions which (we may suppose) the inner core of the disciples were invited to memorize, as they (evidently enough) were trained to commit to memory his formal teaching. Jesus' immersion in the waters had been accompanied by a profound experience of the Spirit of God, and of his own unique sonship of the Father (two vital themes of the esoteric teaching). His free act of solidarity with sinners, as he went down under the waters, may have given him the notion of redemptive solidarity in a suffering and death freely offered for them. Certainly, the gospel tradition knows nothing of the view that only late in his ministry was Jesus aware that he must suffer and die. These experiences led him to forsake his former trade and way of life and go out into the desert. There he felt Satan—the angelic figure appointed in the Hebrew Bible to test God's righteousness—entice him to try out the various possibilities implicit in the power of the divine sonship he now experienced. Seeking the Father's will through prayer and fasting, he dismissed these promptings as presumptuous and evil. But this did not mean that Jesus had thereby rejected the idea that he himself was central to the working out of the phase of salvation history inaugurated by the Baptist. He referred to John as his Elijah, the "greatest among those born of women," that is, the announcer of the start of the final fulfillment of history (Matt 11:11). Yet the least person in the kingdom of heaven (i.e., the period of God's actual reign as now ushered in by Jesus) must be greater than John. Whereas John had only announced that beginning of the new age, Jesus was actually realizing it by his teaching and activity.

That activity would be concentrated in the area sometimes called the "evangelical triangle," the piece of land between the three towns of Capharnaum, Korazin, and Bethsaida, on the northwestern shore of the Sea of Galilee. Here, as Matthew records (11:20), most of his miracles were to be performed. Of special importance was the local mountain of Capharnaum, a ridge of hills called by the Gospels "the lonely place" or "the mount." With its superb view over the lake and the surrounding villages, this craggy hill with its own cave, well suited to contemplative withdrawal, enabled Jesus to gather large crowds without inconvenience to local farmers. Its spring covering of anemones and iris led him to reflect on the lilies of the field (Matt 6:28), whose beauty surpasses Solomon's in all his splendor. Matthew prefaces his account of Jesus' sermon on this mount by detailing the regions from which people were streaming to hear him: from Galilee, the Decapolis (ten nearby towns with Greek-speaking settlers), Jerusalem, Judaea, and the region across the Jordan (4:25), while news of him had reached even Syria, far to the north (4:24). Jesus also delivered his new interpretation of the Torah, the divine revelation to Israel, from a boat— almost certainly in the inlet now called the "bay of the Parables," halfway between Capharnaum and its fishing ground, where the land slopes down like a Roman theater to the water's edge. Using the extraordinary natural acoustic, his voice could reach thousands in, for instance, the parable of the seed falling on different kinds of earth (a scenario easily imagined by the hearers, for the countryside around them illustrated it). Here we can see the Land as, in Bargil Pixner's words, a "fifth Gospel"—something recognized since at least the fourth century when the historian Eusebius produced his *Onomastikon*, an explanation of biblical place-names in their scriptural contexts, using records of roads, distances, and so forth available in the provincial headquarters at Caesarea. The *Onomastikon* extends Eusebius's other treatise, the *Demonstration of the Gospel:* the testimony of the holy places tends both to substantiate and supplement the testimony of the Bible. As another Greek Christian of the early centuries, Cyril of Jerusalem, would write: "Reverence the place, and learn from what you see."

Already in the early part of the ministry sources of tension can be detected, despite the popular acclaim Jesus undoubtedly received. Clashes with pagans and with his own kinsfolk occur in what is probably the first year of Jesus' public life. Mark describes his crossing over to the pagan, eastern shore of the Sea of Galilee as a challenge to a world under the control of the Evil One. Jesus' quieting of the threatening wind with, it is insinuated, the evil spirit of chaos behind it is followed by his encounter with a possessed man, who embodies both the depravity and the strength of paganism. Challenged by Jesus, the demons maintain their right to remain if not in a human being then at least in the swine, animals associated with paganism because the early Canaanites had sacrificed them to their gods. The confrontation ends with an act of self-destruction at the rock precipice which falls away suddenly into the lake. But the local inhabitants, discovering that the exorcist was an intruder from Israel, implore him to leave the area. Jesus' first attempt to bring the message of salvation into heathen territory had failed, though the exorcised man was commissioned to spread the good news of his visitation among his compatriots. A less conflictive encounter with an individual pagan, back on Jewish soil, is the healing of the woman with a hemorrhage. Almost certainly a pagan—a statue of her meeting with Jesus was erected some while after at Caesarea Philippi, an action only conceivable then in a Gentile context—she knew herself doubly unclean in the ritual outlook of Jews: she was both a hemorrhaging woman and a Gentile. This explains her secret stealing up to Jesus to touch his garment, though he at once makes personal contact with her lest she should feel she had somehow stolen her cure. More encouraging relations with pagans would be established in the middle period of the ministry, but these rather tense and uncomprehending moments point ahead to the final rejection of the earthly Jesus by the pagan world in the shape of the Roman governor of Judaea two years later.

The other early source of conflict was Jesus' relation with his kinsfolk. Though his spiritual family, the disciples, sometimes coexisted harmoniously with his natural family (e.g., at Cana, and again before Pentecost in the upper room), there was also tension between them. To the relatives in Nazareth it seemed that they had lost their son and cousin to the new family of the Twelve. The Nazarenes would have regarded Jesus' kinship with their clan as giving them legitimate demands on his person. If, as seems natural to think, the account in Luke of Jesus' initial preaching at Nazareth implies a space of time between a first enthusiastic welcome ("all spoke well of him," 4:22) and a subsequent rejection, the reason may be that the son of Joseph preferred now to work down at Capharnaum with the fishermen, whereas for centuries it was they, the clan of the Nazarenes, the Davidides, who had been divinely elected. The result was an open breach with his kinsfolk, and even an attempt at assassination (Luke 4:24). However, as we can see when his brethren tried to persuade him to go to Jerusalem for the feast of Tabernacles on the ground that he had disciples there also (John 7:3), some links were still maintained. John reports, though, that these brethren did not really believe in Jesus: they offered him their admiration and counsel but not their discipleship. Looking ahead, we can say that not till Calvary was the tension between the two groups—the spiritual family and the natural family—fully overcome. That was when Jesus gave his mother into the keeping of the "beloved disciple." By Pentecost, the families were united, Peter heading the Twelve and James, "the brother of the Lord," heading the clan. Paul records in 1 Corinthians 15:1-7 that the risen Jesus appeared precisely to these two leaders, one of whom became head of the universal Church, the other that of the Church of the Jewish Christians in Israel itself.

By the end of the first year of the ministry it was clear that Jesus' message differed from that of the Baptist in two respects. First, he placed less emphasis on the negative moment of God's judgment of Israel and more on the positive moment, soon to be realized, of her restoration. Second, he stressed the concomitant salvation of all the other nations for whom Israel was meant to be a light. In his public preaching, Jesus proclaimed God as not only judge but Savior. He spoke of salvation as not simply the result of human decision and effort but also as the gift of God. Indeed, he spoke of the human decision for salvation and the effort to gain it as part and parcel of that very gift. The only thing he asked was that this gift of salvation be accepted as a total gift—in other words, in the most radical poverty of spirit, something which went against the grain of the Jewish religious parties in his day, who preferred to rely on their own works, and notably the observance of the Old Testament Law. This aspect of his teaching, exemplified in the parable of the two men who went up to the Temple to pray, would be especially well understood by Paul.

But what was this "salvation" that Jesus held out to his hearers, and saw his own preaching as inaugurating? He saw it as the coming of a new paradise, as is made clear by his sayings on marriage. Divorce is now prohibited, for the norm of paradise is restored, and this is possible because a cure for human hardness of heart (the problem that had led the Old Testament to allow divorce) is now to hand. Thanks to Jesus' presence and influence, the disciples are becoming changed people. The rigor of Jesus' ethical demands upon them (no hatred, no lustful thoughts) only makes sense on the understanding that human nature is being transformed, thanks to communion with Jesus.

That this was not self-delusion was shown in the miraculous signs of salvation Jesus worked. The exorcisms he carried out were meant to point to God's imminent triumph over evil, the dawning of his reign. The miracles of healing and such nature miracles as the calming of the storm and the multiplication of the loaves and fishes point to the restoration of physical nature, its harmonization with what is good for human beings, and a superabundant fulfillment for the life of the old creation.

The coming about of the reign of God, at which Jesus aimed in his public teaching and action, had, then, its cosmic aspect, but its center lay in the relations of persons to God. In his table fellowship with sinners, regarded by the Jews of the day as ritually unclean, Jesus reversed the hitherto normal biblical order by putting communion before conversion. Without acquiescing in the sins of these reprobate characters, Jesus first of all extended fellowship to them in the Father's name, and that turned out to trigger repentance and so conversion. His extraordinary freedom displayed itself not in an abstract criticism of accepted standards but in making himself accessible to those who needed him, regardless of conventional limitations. The meals he took with the disreputable he regarded as anticipations of the banquet between God and humanity at the end of time. That Jesus understood this offer of communion with God through him as including (eventually) the Gentiles is shown by the parable of the mustard seed which grows into a great shrub in which birds can rest. "Birds" was, at the time, a common metaphor for the Gentiles; "nesting" was a technical term for their eschatological assimilation to Israel. What can we conclude then on the basis of the public or exoteric teaching and actions of Jesus? That his proclamation of the reign of God was aimed at bringing about the actual communication of that reign as a new paradise in which, most importantly, human nature, thanks to his presence and influence, is transformed. Miraculous signs attest that this is actually happening as evil is depotentiated, human bodies and psyches healed, the maladjustment of natural forces to human happiness rectified, and the created order itself transcended in enacted symbols of ultrafruitfulness. The transformation of the human being by the grace of God is also symbolized by the offer of table fellowship, and Jesus predicts that his preaching, even though it sparked few conversions, will be the means for the entry of the Gentiles into the salvation promised in the first instance to Israel. We can add that, because this program necessarily involved the restoration and integration of the depressed elements in society—the poor, the sick, the simple—a later age whose own outlook was sociological and humanistic rather than metaphysical and religious could misconstrue Jesus as a social reformer.

It was probably at Passover of the second year of the public ministry that news reached Capharnaum of the execution of John the

Baptist, and Herod Antipas's fear that Jesus might be another John. The antagonism of the Herodians, the supporters of the puppet king, grew apace. Henceforth Jesus would avoid crowds and never remain too long in any one place. When the disciples, sent out in pairs by Jesus in the missionary extension of his preaching of the imminence of the kingdom, returned to base at Capharnaum, flocks of people wanted to see the Master with their own eyes, thus bringing new danger. Jesus accordingly took the disciples away in search of solitude, but when the boat turned in toward the fishing ground and the crowd caught up with them Jesus had compassion on them as "sheep without a shepherd" and began to teach them (Mark 6:34). It was here, in the lakeside spot now called Tabhga, that the first feeding of the multitude took place; it is recalled by a venerable Jewish-Christian inscription on a large slab of rock, visible today beneath the altar of the Benedictine chapel of the multiplication. The twelve baskets of bread and fish mentioned by the evangelists, and the way the people are made to sit in groups of hundreds and fifties, as their ancestors had been accustomed to do in the Sinai desert according to the Book of Exodus, point to this as a feeding of Jews rather than local pagans. This renewal of the miraculous feeding of the Exodus generated a religious and nationalist enthusiasm which found expression in an attempt to have Jesus proclaimed Messiah. He bundled off the disciples to safety in the less paranoid atmosphere of the lands of Herod's brother Philip, at Bethsaida, while he himself retired to the cave below the cliff where he was accustomed to pray in solitude to the Father. But that night one of the sudden fierce winds characteristic of the Sea of Galilee arose, blowing from the direction of Bethsaida, and Jesus, concerned for the Twelve, hurried down to the lake. This is the *mise en scène* for the walking on the water. Taking the shortest course to the land, the disciples and their Master made for Gennesaret, where, however, he was once again the target of the crowds, this time carrying their sick with them (Mark 6:54-55). So the group set off for the borders of a largely pagan country, Phoenicia, which lay outside the lands of the petty Jewish subkings altogether.

Here at the midpoint of his ministry, Jesus made a new opening to the Gentiles while at the same time becoming more distanced from the Pharisees. It was probably at the only city on his route, Gischala in northern Galilee, though the name is absent from the Gospels, that Jesus had a serious set-to with the stricter Pharisees. The topic was food laws; Jesus opposed a rigorist interpretation, for only what comes from within can make a person unclean (Mark 7:15). Mark interpreted this exchange to mean that Jesus declared all foods clean—an unheard-of challenge to the authority of the Law.

This was the point at which Jesus would come to spend a lengthy period among Gentiles. Phoenicia represented an opening to the pagans. The meeting with the Syro-Phoenician woman, who besought him to cure her sick daughter, though he had been "sent only to the lost sheep of the house of Israel" (Matt 15:24), appears to have greatly affected him. Did he think of the words spoken about the Suffering Servant of the Lord in the Book of Isaiah? "It is too small a thing for you to be my servant to restore the tribes of Jacob and bring back the preserved of Israel. I will also make you a light for the Gentiles, that you may bring my salvation to the ends of the earth" (Isa 49:6).

For Paul, as the "apostle of the Gentiles," such passages of Isaiah—notably chapter 53, with its teaching that universal salvation would come through the redemptive death of the Servant of the Lord—would be all-important (see 1 Cor 15:1-3; 2 Cor 5:14-21). It seems no accident that Mark describes Jesus as returning at this juncture to the Gentile Decapolis (7:31). The news of the cured demoniac had spread widely and an enthusiastic crowd of pagans awaited him on a hillside by the lake's eastern shore. In a second feeding of the multitude, this sign of the dawning of the messianic era, already worked for Jews, is now renewed for Gentiles who "praised the God of Israel" (Matt 15:29-31). The baskets were seven in number—perhaps for the seven heathen peoples mentioned in the Book of Deuteronomy as having once inhabited the Land. The message is that the gates are now thrown open for all nations to enter God's presence.

The increasingly innovative nature of Jesus' behavior was a growing worry to other Jewish parties, and when he arrived back on the western shore of the lake, he was met by Pharisee and Sadducee representatives who asked him for a "sign," a legitimizing confirmation of his mission. He replied that none would be given except the sign of Jonah. In Church tradition this is taken to refer to the resurrection, for just as Jonah was three days in the living tomb of the whale so was Jesus three days in the living tomb of the earth. Originally, however, the "sign of Jonah" may have referred to the conversion, on the occasion of Jonah's preaching, of the pagan city of Nineveh. Jesus is saying that the conversion of the Gentiles will be the sign that the messianic kingdom has come.

In the latter part of the second year of his ministry Jesus visited Jerusalem for the feast of Tabernacles. In the courtyard of the Temple, stimulated by the stirring symbolism of the feast—the water carried from the Pool of Siloam for ceremonial lustration of the altar of burnt offerings—Jesus spoke of himself, of his own heart, to bystanders in exalted terms as a source of water for all who believe in him (John 7). Naturally, such statements only increased the anxiety of the Sadducee and Pharisee leaders.

Back in Galilee, amid encouraging reactions from pagans, but deepening suspicion from the Jewish movements, Jesus took the disciples on a tour intended for their reeducation. It led them into the subalpine north of Galilee, where the mount of the transfiguration would be the climax of the program. The expedition, which began with a sea-crossing from Capharnaum to Bethsaida, seems to have originated in Jesus' awareness both of a mounting confusion among his disciples and of a resultant thinning out of their ranks. In the discourse on the bread of life, which following the miraculous feeding in John 6, many of the disciples sorrowfully go away. Mark may be alluding to this when he remarks of the beginning of the expedition north that the disciples had forgotten to bring bread save for the one loaf in the boat—namely, Jesus himself. At the heart of the reeducation lay concepts of messiahship. The route took them past both Tiberias, a city founded by the Herodians in the honor of the Roman emperor, and, at the opposite pole of the political spectrum, Gamla, seat of the Zealot movement, itself founded by the extreme Pharisee Jehuda of Gamla in A.D. 6. The idea of the Messiah in this northern section of the lake was indeed colored by revolutionary militancy, which explains Jesus' extreme reluctance to allow the disciples to acclaim him as Messiah. He now proposed to enlighten them in a suitably gradual fashion—as made clear by the symbolic action of healing a blind man, at Bethsaida, in stages (Mark 8:22-25).

For alongside his public, exoteric teaching lay a private, esoteric message delivered to the disciples alone. The turning-point, beyond which Jesus begins a deeper and more mysterious-sounding instruction of the disciples, is Peter's confession of Jesus' messiahship at Caesarea Philippi. In his response to Peter, Jesus defines his aim as the messianic task of building a living "temple," as on rock, secure against decay, the temple of the last days. He was referring here to the eschatological temple which, in the Hebrew Bible, symbolized the final meeting-place of God and humankind, the site of their definitive communion. In the symbolic thinking of the period, this temple was conceived as miraculous, everlasting, the center of a new heaven and a new earth, the goal of pilgrimage for all nations. How did Jesus understand his role in creating this permanent divine-human communication? As the final revealer of God's will and the agent through whom that will was to be realized, the construction of this temple fell to him personally, but he could not achieve it until first he had become victorious over the anti-God powers at work in the world—sin and death—and thus been enthroned at God's right hand. At his trial, Jesus was accused of having said, "Destroy this temple and I will rebuild it in three days" (Matt 26:61). Why should that particular statement have been taken as blasphemy? In an oracle from the Second Book of Samuel, God is made to say of the future messianic king: "He shall build a house for my Name, and I will establish the throne of his reign forever. I will be his father, and he shall be my son" (2 Sam 7:13-14a). "Forever": originally this was deliberate hyperbole, court rhetoric, but Jesus treated it literally. Unless he had referred to himself as an ever-living or eschatological Messiah, we cannot understand why his disciples, after the first Easter, took the resurrection appearances as proof that their crucified teacher had turned out to be the Christ of Israel, the "once and future king." At his trial before the Sanhedrin, we shall see Jesus refusing to conceal his messianic character for fear of implicitly abandoning this eschatological claim. In any case, now helpless in his enemies' hands, the title "Messiah," "Christ," had lost its liability to political misinterpretation: Jesus would become a suffering Messiah, a Messiah of the Cross. Yet to claim to be Messiah, albeit forever, would not itself be regarded by other Jews as blasphemous. Something more was involved. The last line of the oracle suggests what it was: "I will be his father, and he shall be my son."

Jesus understood his eschatological messianic sonship in a sense entirely his own. He spoke of himself as "the Son," absolutely or unconditionally, and so uniquely. When speaking with the disciples he was always careful to say "my Father and your Father." "Our Father" was what he told the disciples to say, not what he said with them. Part of his unique sonship, as Jesus understood it, was a sharing in the divine prerogatives vis-à-vis creation. From the moment of Peter's confession onwards, we find the two themes of Jesus' messiahship and his cosmic enthronement joined together. In these contexts he often spoke of himself in terms of the figure called the "Son of Man," that angelic representative of suffering Israel, described in the Book of Daniel as receiving glory and power from God to triumph over the forces hostile to his people. This constellation of ideas re-occurs at the climactic moment of Jesus' trial: "Again the high priest asked him, 'Are you the

Christ, the Son of the Blessed?' And Jesus said, 'I am; and you will see the Son of man sitting at the right hand of Power, and coming with the clouds of heaven.' And the high priest tore his mantle and said, 'Why do we still need witnesses? You have heard his blasphemy'" (Mark 14:61-62). It was as a messianic pretender who also claimed to share in the divine attributes that Jesus was condemned for blasphemy.

After Peter's confession, Jesus' esoteric teaching became an initiation of the disciples into the meaning of his suffering and death. As the Messiah, whose enthronement, itself stunningly supernatural, transcendent, would not come about without his own violent death, he had the power to (as he put it) "ransom" the mortal and the dead. The Son of Man had come "to give his life as a ransom for many" (Mark 10:45), which is a Semitic way of saying for all—not just for a remnant of Israel, but for all Israel; and not just for all Israel, but for all the world. His death and subsequent enthronement would purify the world from sin, and by thus overcoming its alienation from God the Creator give it entry into a new life.

It was under the lee of Mount Hermon, the northernmost point of their journey, that Jesus had thus begun to teach the disciples his understanding of messiahship, entailing as this did identification with a Son of Man who could only be glorious if he was first humiliated and killed (Mark 8:31-32a). Their amazed and negative reaction, vocalized by Peter, was followed by the experience of Christ's transfiguration on the mountain's summit. The disciples were able not only to see their master as belonging to the company of the greatest figures of Israel's history, Moses and Elijah, but also to glimpse something of his deeper mystery. But even after further discussion of his coming passion (Mark 9:31), the whole trip ended up with a debate among the Twelve as to which of them was the greatest, a depressing upshot which prompted Jesus' saying on the necessity of service and of spiritual childhood (Mark 9:35-36). Only serving their fellow human beings and particularly those disregarded by others, the "little ones," would give the Twelve a share in his work and lead to their being honored by the Father who had sent him.

In the discouraging aftermath of the transfiguration, Jesus soon decided to abandon Galilee. He was deeply disappointed with reactions in Korazin, Bethsaida, and Capharnaum, in which he had invested so much hope and energy (Matt 11:20-24); despite admiration, there was little true obedience. His efforts at dialogue with the moderate Pharisees (his friends Simon and Nicodemus were doubtless in this camp) had come to little: these pious men with their insistence on the traditions of the fathers could not accept his interpretation of the Torah. Gradually, the Pharisees at large began to see his popularity as a danger. Likewise those in the northern townships under Zealot influence soon realized that he was no candidate for the kind of messiahship in which they believed. It was easy for them, therefore, to form an unholy alliance with the Herodians to move him on (Mark 3:6). Jesus did move on—to Batanea, Bethany-beyond-the-Jordan (cf. John 10:40-42), from where he paid one more visit to Jerusalem, for the feast of the Dedication of the Temple, the last visit before his death. We are now in the last winter of Jesus' life. As during the autumn trip for the feast of Tabernacles, Jesus was moved by the exploitation of the great symbols of the Scriptures in the Temple liturgy; notably, at Hanukkah, the symbolic lights with which the Temple and its precincts were set ablaze led him to declare himself personally identical with the light of the divine glory to which they referred (John 12:1). Once again, the consequences (namely, mounting hostility from the Jewish leaders and their theologians) were entirely predictable. There was a threat of stoning for blasphemy; however, Jesus extricated himself and returned to Bethany beyond the Jordan which was to be his last home.

The Gospels locate three events in the life of Jesus at this Bethany: a controversy, an urgent personal summons of what proved to be a lethal kind, and what we may call a lyrical intermezzo. In this politically peaceful region, ruled by the unambitious tetrarch Philip, Pharisees and Essenes differed on a major socio-religious theme: marriage (the former permitted divorce, the latter did not). Mark, who records Jesus' adjudication in favor of the Essene position, also speaks of the "house" where the disciples pursued this topic further (10:10). We know from the tenth chapter of Luke's Gospel that Jesus had earlier visited the sisters of Lazarus not at the Bethany in the Jerusalem district, where we otherwise find them, but at Bethany-beyond-the-Jordan. It is conjectured that this house, then, was the summer residence of Jesus' friends. This would explain how, from their city home near Jerusalem, they knew of Jesus' hiding place and so could send him the message, "Lord, the one whom you love is sick" (John 11:35). Here we come to an event—the raising of Lazarus—which, more than any other, set into motion the wheels of enmity against Jesus, bringing him to his death. The hostility of the supreme spiritual authority of Judaism, the high priesthood, which Jesus was soon to incur stands out all the more sharply by contrast with the idyllic scene at Bethany-beyond-the-Jordan word-painted by Matthew and Mark: Jesus blessing children.

The raising of Lazarus—this spectacular and well-attended miracle—focused the antagonism of the Sanhedrin who resolved to be rid of Jesus. He returned with the disciples to a village, Ephrem, in the desert area some twelve miles north of Jerusalem. From there, according to John, he would make his final entry into Jerusalem. The Synoptic Gospels have Jesus set out from Jericho, further down the valley, as he begins this final journey. The fourth evangelist's account converges with the Synoptics only when they come to describe Jesus' entry into the city, thus leaving those of his readers who knew one or more of the Synoptics to conclude that Jesus and his disciples went down from Ephrem to Jericho. There was indeed a Roman road between the two, making possible a relatively easy ascent from the Jordan valley into the hills where Jerusalem stands. As Jesus passed through Jericho he healed the blind beggar Bartimaeus (and one other, unnamed): beggars would have lined up at this point where the pilgrim routes from north and east converged. Luke tells us how crowds of pilgrims and curious citizens thronged around Jesus so that a chief tax collector, Zacchaeus, had to climb a "sycamore" (actually a mulberry-fig) to get a glimpse of him, its dense foliage (the species still flourishes there) concealing him from those beneath. Jesus called him down and invited him to his dwelling with the gripping words, "Salvation has come today to this house" (Luke 19:9a).

Why did Jesus make this detour via Jericho? It may have been to end where he had begun. There at the Jordan his ministry had started. Where the Baptist had been his forerunner, coming to an untimely death as a witness to God's commandments, Jesus would imitate him in his own violent death. In the desolate solitude of the mountain wilderness he had renounced Satan who had offered him "all the kingdoms of the world and the glory of them" (Matt 4:8). He could look to the right and left of that road and again see the mountain where he had chosen the way now leading to his death, a death that would also inaugurate God's kingdom, whose glory would outshine those worldly realms. The pilgrims who joined him would be his witnesses as to how he had entered Jerusalem poor and with his majesty unrecognized yet implicitly declaring himself the Messiah of the coming divine reign. Following the Roman road, Jesus climbed over the crest of the Mount of Olives and down into Bethany. We must suppose that the pilgrim crowds learned he would be following their number the next day:

many would come out to meet him waving their palm branches in acclamation. Mounting an ass at Bethany, when the worst of the ascent (from a mounted animal's viewpoint!) was over, Jesus descended into the awaiting city. Somewhere on the route, with its wonderful vista, Jesus, "seeing the city, wept over it" (Luke 19:41). The anointing by an unnamed sinner (later identified with Mary Magdalene) is placed by Mark and Matthew after the entry into Jerusalem.

As the Passover approached, Jesus made arrangements for celebrating it with the disciples; it was the last such celebration of his life.

The Death—and beyond

Jesus must have had many friends and admirers in the city, so the choice of venue was an *embarras de richesse*. His instructions to the disciples on how to find the house he selected were cryptic: he sent two disciples ahead with the words, "Go into the city, and a man carrying a jar of water will meet you: follow him, and wherever he enters, say to the householder, 'The teacher says, "Where is my guest room [refectory, *katalyma*] where I am to eat the passover with my disciples?"'" And he will show you a large upper room furnished and ready" (Mark 14:13-15). Probably Jesus did not wish Judas to know the site till the last moment, so as to avoid any early warning to the Sanhedrin, whereupon he might be arrested. The water-carrier was in all likelihood a servant sent to fetch fresh water from the Pool of Siloam, by way of substitute for the cistern water in normal domestic use. Eventually, the upper room of Zion, where the disciples gathered on returning from the Mount of Olives after the ascension, came to be regarded as the scene of this Last Supper.

Then, on the last evening of his life, Jesus announced the solemn beginning of a new covenant between God and the world, a covenant made in his death, with his life offered up as a sacrifice of expiation— along the lines of the Suffering Servant in Isaiah 53:12, his soul "poured out unto death" for "the sins of many." A crisis stage was coming: an ordeal that would mean Jesus' own death but also the persecution of his followers; intensified suffering for Israel which had, in the main, rejected the public offer of salvation; and the destruction of Jerusalem and the Temple. The crisis was to be resolved, however, in the triumph of the Son—referred to by Jesus as "the day of the Son of Man," a phrase that is probably the counterpart in the private teaching of the term "the reign of God" in the public proclamation. To anticipate such an exaltation, Jesus must have supposed for himself, after his ordeal, a stupendously transcendent condition, which would be constituted by, on the one hand, his resurrection and ascension, and on the other, his final parousia, the second coming. The two were evidently telescoped in his awareness. The moment of the parousia was, to his consciousness, extraordinarily close. By his work, he was the bearer of God's lordship over time. The whole time of the redemption was as it were concentrated in his person, since where he acts the terms on which the salvational future will proceed are already laid down. During his disciples' missionary journeys, he had seen "Satan fall like lightning from heaven" (Luke 10:18), even though that final victory remained to be accomplished. The disciples shared something of Jesus' consciousness in this regard. Their confidence in the imminence of his return coexisted perfectly happily with their knowledge that Jesus had established an "apostolic succession" for his Church, and had promised to intercede with the Father, so that the Spirit, in whose power he had worked and taught, might come to counsel the apostolic fellowship, both defending them against the last, peculiarly vicious death-throes of the evil powers in their antagonism towards the Church, and leading them into all truth, bringing to mind all he had said to them (what we now call the "development of doctrine"). To ordinary consciousness it would be contradictory both to expect the final outcome of history and to provide for an indefinite future—but the disciples did not by now have an ordinary consciousness. They had, instead, begun to share in Jesus' consciousness.

At the Last Supper, Jesus ordered his disciples to celebrate the new covenant, to be made between God and humankind in his blood, by a sacramental re-presentation of his sacrificial death. Equipped with this rite, for as long as the ordeal lasted they would themselves be the eschatological temple in its earthly aspect, the house built on rock, which the power of Hades would try in vain to overcome. The Church, which the disciples constituted in relation to Jesus, would be the mystery of the kingdom, the reign of God, the day of the Son of Man, insofar as that kingdom, reign, day, are already manifested in time. Until the definitive ingathering of the saved at the end of time (the plenary coming of the new heaven and the new earth) the redemptive purposes of Jesus would be incorporated and continued in this community.

Having instituted the sacrificial meal of his own memorial, and sung a hymn, the Messiah went out with his friends onto the Mount of Olives (more precisely, into a garden just across the Cedron, on its lower slopes, an olive orchard where the Gethsemani church stands today). After his agony, endured while the disciples largely slept, noises and lights announced the arrival of the betrayer. Tradition locates the betrayal in the grotto on the edge of the garden, possibly where the eight waited, and the three together with Jesus returned when Judas and the guards approached. Whereas Mark and Matthew give the impression that the high priest and the elders had merely collected a motley crew with "swords and staves" to apprehend him, Luke and John make it more official: they were Jewish temple police, though John uses a Roman military term. Jesus was taken for a preliminary private hearing of the case against him before the high priest Annas, father-in-law of the reigning high priest of the year, Caiaphas. Only in the morning could a proper judicial sentence be passed by the Sanhedrin, and that in the Temple precincts. In the courtyard of the high priest's house, however, there took place an event recorded by all the evangelists: Peter's denial that he knew Jesus, and his subsequent tears of repentance.

The Sanhedrin condemned Jesus for blasphemy, but in order to win over Pilate stressed the political menace implicit in a Jewish Messiah. As the superscription on the cross—"The King of the Jews"—shows, Jesus was condemned as a rebel against Roman rule. The hearing took place, and judgment was given in the praetorium—either the procurator's palace (originally built by Herod the Great) or the Antonia fortress (also Herodian) where the Via Dolorosa begins today, close by the Franciscan monastery of the scourging of the Lord. According to one tradition at least, it was on the forecourt of the Antonia that Jesus was shown to the people: "Behold the Man!" There he was judged, mocked, crowned with thorns, and scourged while Pilate ceremoniously washed his hands. Though Pilate was seemingly far from convinced that Jesus deserved the death penalty, he swallowed his scruples under the combined pressure of the religious authorities, the ever-hostile tetrarch, Herod, whom he consulted, and the Jerusalem crowd, anxious, in all probability, for their economic position (largely dependent as that was on the employment and prosperity generated by the Temple, whose supersession Jesus had predicted). In the account given by John, the timing of Pilate's judgment is significant. "In condemning Jesus at noon, the very hour when the Passover lambs began to be killed in the Temple precincts, Pilate fulfills at the end of the Gospel the word spoken about Jesus at the beginning by John the Baptist, identifying him as the lamb of God who would take away the world's sin."[11]

11. R. Brown, *The Death of the Messiah* (London, 1994) 1.34.

He was led out to Golgotha, the "place of the skull." During the time of the two Jewish wars, the memory of this place—essentially an abandoned quarry—would be preserved. The emperor Constantine cleared away the pagan temple erected over this "cave of the Redeemer" and built there the Church of the Holy Sepulchre, which later excavation shows to have been surrounded by rock tombs. Today within the walls of the Old City, in its own time Golgotha was outside the city wall—but close enough for people to see, and reflect upon, the crucifixion victims. The date was, in all probability, Friday, 7 April (14 Nisan) of the year 30 of what would eventually be called the Christian era.

Crucifixion was a widespread penalty in antiquity; among the Romans it was used chiefly on slaves, violent criminals, and the unruly elements in rebellious provinces. Valued for its deterrent effect, it was also an expression of sadism and the lust for revenge. The public display of a naked victim in a prominent place was linked in the Jewish mind with human sacrifice; hence the horror expressed in Deuteronomy 21:23 at the very thought of such a victim. In this context, the crucified Messiah was a lived demonstration of the solidarity of the love of God with those tortured and put to death by human cruelty.

As we have seen, the significance of that death in Jesus' own mind was strictly salvational. It had absolutely nothing of the character of political adventure. Jesus uses the political significance of his situation, and the possible political consequences of his actions (e.g., the entry into Jerusalem on Palm Sunday, mounted on an ass), so as to secure his rejection on his own terms. Only such rejection could set him free to be the Messiah according to the very truth of God's self-revelation. He had foreseen this outcome, and, though dreading it in itself, also welcomed it as the crucial turning-point in the ushering in of the reign of God.

Jesus' body was laid in a "new tomb" by Joseph of Arimathea, a figure otherwise unmentioned in the Gospels. Though privately buried, the corpse of Jesus, which, according to Israel's sacred law was accursed, could not be allowed to contaminate other corpses in a family grave. Given the need for speedy burial before the Sabbath, the choice of a hitherto unused tomb, close to the site of the execution, was understandable. It appears to have been a shaft tomb of a distinctive first-century type. The body was laid in an antechamber, wrapped in linen sweetened with spices. Jesus' corpse was anointed royally, according to John, for he has Joseph and Nicodemus use a simply enormous quantity of myrrh and aloes. Apparently, though, Joseph ran out of time for the full process of embalming; this was noted by various women disciples who looked on, the Twelve having scattered. The tomb was sealed by a circular stone. The spot would eventually be cleared, and the rock cut away to allow access and, not least, scope for building; by the late third century the actual tomb would be wholly encased in a round church of its own. But this would dignify no sacred remains. For, in all the Synoptic accounts, on the first day of the week Mary Magdalene and some other women went with fresh embalming materials to the tomb of Jesus and found the stone rolled away. A young man (or two, sometimes presented "angelologically" as a divine messenger or messengers) explained, "He is raised; he is not here."

The resultant resurrection faith is linked to the events of the ministry for two reasons. First, it confirms the claim of authority made by the pre-Easter Jesus, and second, it reveals the latter's unity with God, and so God's unique presence in him. After his death, and counter to all natural possibility, Jesus' disciples experienced him as returning to them. At the first Easter they encountered him with all the characteristics of a real human being, only now he was beyond the common frontiers of human experience as though in a new life. They felt obliged to regard his personality as somehow continuous with that of God himself, and, though strict monotheists (believers in one God alone), worshipped him with the titles "Lord" and "God." For his part, he finalized their instruction on continuing his mission until the Easter encounters ceased with the overwhelming spiritual experience of Pentecost: the pouring out of the Spirit of God, now experienced as the Spirit of both Father and Son.

The Christian religion thus began when, all human hopes, enthusiasm, and comradeship annihilated, the disciples of Jesus were involved in certain events on the morning after the Sabbath of his entombment in a garden outside Jerusalem, and either concurrently or at some subsequent point by the Sea of Galilee, in an upper room in Jerusalem, and on the road to an unimportant Judaean village called Emmaus. The Catholic Church, as a reality that may be studied by the historian, began with an empty tomb. Whatever construction the historian may put on the fact, it started with an extraordinary transformation of the broken and distraught friends and disciples of the crucified. They were changed into men and women blazing with confidence that God, in a manner beyond the gropings and imaginings of the human spirit, had "visited" (i.e., acted upon) history. It began with some such words, reported by the eyewitnesses, as "I know that you seek Jesus who was crucified. He is not here, for he has risen as he said" (Matt 28:5-6); "Why do you seek the living among the dead? He is not here but has risen" (Luke 24:5). The truth-claims of Catholic Christianity are those of an interpretation of history. We are invited to say of this history—which the Church lives by repeating it in preaching, in the sacraments, and in the prayer whereby she communes with her risen master—whether it is based on a mistake or is just an insoluble enigma, or whether the career of Jesus was in fact extended, by the grace of a power thus disclosed as the Spirit of his Father, into a new and limitless future with God, a future in which our human nature has at last found its hidden meaning, thus making superfluous all humankind's other faiths and ideologies.

To the critical reader the discrepancies in the scriptural accounts of the appearances of the risen Jesus have sometimes seemed as notable as their points of contact. Yet without straining the evidence, some kinds of order may be introduced into the apparent chaos. For instance, all the gospel accounts narrate the same basic sequence of events, though they differ on their location. The same elements are always there: a situation where Jesus' followers are bereft, an appearance of Jesus, his greeting, their recognition, his word of command or mission. Moreover, the geographical complexity of the appearances—Galilee or Jerusalem—is not so off-putting as it might seem. The Jerusalem appearances, so Père M. J. Lagrange suggested, were chiefly intended to convince and reassure the disciples. The Galilee appearances were principally meant to link their minds to memories of the past. For the risen Christ is the glorified earthly Jesus, just as the earthly Jesus was the one destined to be the glorified risen Christ. There is no contradiction between the historian's Jesus and the Church's Jesus (whom we shall be contemplating in a moment).

If the majority of the resurrection appearances took place in Galilee, why then did the apostles return to Jerusalem? Because as observant Jews, they would naturally have gone up to the holy city for the next pilgrimage feast, "Weeks" or Pentecost. It was in Jerusalem, on that feast, that there took place an overwhelming manifestation of the Spirit they had received from the risen Christ. Now the Twelve through Peter began to proclaim the good news they perceived in faith. God had fulfilled his promises to Israel in Jesus whose crucifixion was not a defeat, for God had raised him and thus stamped his message and life with the seal of divine approval.

An ultimate agnosticism about the resurrection requires one to consign to the realm of the inexplicable the origins of the major transformation of the Greco-Roman world whose heirs we are. If we are not prepared to countenance the Church's own account of her beginning, with the reversal that turned Jesus' disciples, that smashed and headless group, into missionary apostles, we shall be hard pressed to make sense of the new Christian element running like quicksilver through the Mediterranean basin and beyond. Some would have it, with Goethe, that "They are celebrating the resurrection of the Lord for they themselves are resurrected." But what "they" (the disciples) in fact experienced was fear and doubt, and what awakened joy and jubilation was something other than themselves. They were the ones marked out by death, but the crucified and buried one was alive. We can put it like this: Those who survived him were the dead; the dead one was the Living.

The triumphant return to life of the Lord Jesus has been deemed "not proven" by many who have approached it with an historian's eye. Yet the faith-account handed down in the living witness of the Church of all generations remains a plausible construction of the evidence. Moreover, the kind of event that faith-witness depicts is, importantly, one open to public scrutiny, one that would submit to falsification. The discovery of the skeletal remains of Jesus—along the lines of a celebrated novel by Piers Paul Read—would surely falsify (i.e., disprove) the Christian faith. It is, on an orthodox view of that faith, an intrinsic feature of the divine sacrifice by which the Father sent his Son on his mission of liberation that God freely made himself vulnerable to human beings, even in the very truth-claims of his own self-revelation.

Conclusion

> There was once a man, within historical times, who, as a child of the Jewish people, knew only of one God of heaven and earth, of a unique Father in heaven, and stood in reverential awe before this heavenly Father; a man whose meat was to do the will of this Father, who from his earliest youth in good and bad had sought and loved this will alone, whose whole life was one prayer; a man, further, whose whole being was so firmly united with this Divine will, that by its omnipotence he healed the sick and restored the dead to life; a man, finally, who was so intimately and exclusively dedicated to this will, that he never swerved from it, so that not even the slightest consciousness of sin ever oppressed him, so that never a cry for penance and forgiveness passed his lips, so

that even in dying he begged pardon not for himself but for others. And this man from the intimacy of his union with God could say to afflicted mortals, "Thy sins are forgiven thee." And it was this holy man, utterly subject as he was to God throughout his whole life, absorbed as he was in God, awestruck as he stood before him, who asserted, as if it were the most natural and obvious thing in the world, that he was to be the judge of the world at the last day, that he was the suffering servant of God, nay more, that he was the only-begotten Son of God and consubstantial with him, and could say of himself, "I and the Father are one."[12]

The mystery of Jesus is so deep that it has taken a number of New Testament interpretations of it to constitute the New Testament canon, to satisfy the Church that she has in the Scriptures an adequate written basis for her future. Theologians, mystics, poets, and artists down the ages have all made their attempts to plumb Jesus' mystery. Of course, part of Jesus' elusiveness comes from the fact that we today do not share the dominant ideas and symbols of the particular culture in which he was born. But if a redemptive incarnation were to take place at all, it had to happen in some particular culture, and so there had to be a risk—and more than a risk, a moral certainty—that with distance in space and time the form of the redemptive incarnation would become harder to identify with and so to understand. The role of the Paraclete or Counsellor, promised by Jesus, is to overcome this problem by leading the disciples into all truth, which means first and foremost all the essential truth about Jesus Christ.

To the Catholic Christian, the Jesus Christ of the Church's dogma is this infallible portrait of the incarnate Redeemer, an interpretation of the New Testament materials made under the leading of the Holy Spirit, so that the community of the kingdom, constructed on the basis of the Holy Eucharist, will appreciate the essentials of that person who is the kingdom's center and really present in its Eucharistic feast. The Christ of dogma, the Christ of the Church, is an unerring interpretation of what was given in and with the Jesus of history. We seek the history, therefore (using the tools of scholarship), in the context of the Church's tradition, just as we also seek the personal origin of the Church's tradition within scholarly history. If we differentiate the two it is only for the purpose of revealing more clearly their interconnection.

Once . . . we accept the faith perspective of the authors of the New Testament and the judgement of the Church which has canonized this

12. K. Adam, *The Son of God* (New York, 1934) 203.

apostolic faith response as a witness guaranteed by God, a new avenue of knowing the reality of Jesus is opened up for us. This faith is then pursued not merely as a safeguard against reducing the figure of Jesus to pre-fabricated clichés, but as a positive hermeneutical tool which can answer the question raised by the quest for the historical Jesus: who is this man? We also begin to understand that it is not a great tragedy for us—in fact it might be providential—that we do not have personal writings by Jesus himself (or transcripts of his discourses for that matter). God's intention was to bring a community of faith around Jesus so that the understanding of Jesus would become inseparable from accepting the witness of this archetypal community. In fact, the reality of Jesus, "who he was and what he intended," or more precisely, who he was in God's plan of salvation and what God revealed to us through his person, deeds, and words, becomes accessible to us only through the divinely guaranteed documents of the apostolic Church, that is, the New Testament. If Jesus wanted to reach all humankind through a community whose faith, life, and ritual are to continue the faith, life, and ritual of this archetypal apostolic community, then the fact that Jesus himself authored no book or letter makes complete sense. If Jesus' reality could be reached without the faith response embodied in the documents of the apostolic Church, an individualistic relationship between isolated individual believers and Jesus would become a distinct possibility. Then our faith would not necessarily be an ecclesial faith.[13]

13. R. Kereszty, "Historical Research, Theological Inquiry, and the Reality of Jesus: Reflections on the Method of J. P. Meier," *Communio* 19 (1992) 595.

4
The Church's Jesus

Investigating the figure of Jesus as he appears via the materials of the historian is vital. How can we be expected to commend our faith to informed unbelievers if we cannot show that the historian's Jesus is at any rate something like what the Church believes? Yet the historian's Jesus is incomplete: the full picture of who Jesus was is inseparable from the special experience of the Church, the continuation in space and time of the apostolic fellowship with its sharing in Jesus' unique consciousness of himself.

As we have seen, the historian can argue that Jesus thought of himself as the ever-living messianic Son of the Father sharing in the latter's prerogatives vis-à-vis the world. The historian may go so far as to say that Jesus understood the God of Israel to be living in him and even as him. Through the work of the Paraclete, in the development of doctrine, the Church can see the picture more fully. The man Jesus is the taking-on of humanity by the eternal Word who, in obedience to the Father, entered our sinful flesh for our salvation. His entire life-story is, therefore, a revelatory sign of salvation, a disclosure of the mystery of God in his plan to bring true welfare—healing and wholeness—to humankind. While his life has its high points and decisive moments, each of these shares in the mystery of that life as an entirety, and so, in the last resort, can be validly understood only from out of that fullness.

Just as the God of Jesus Christ is only accessible via the man Jesus, so the humanity of Jesus is only seen aright from the perspective of the God of Jesus Christ. Without the eyes of faith (that is, without the empowerment of our intellectual gaze by the Holy Spirit who is the communion between the Father and the Son), there can be no sufficient understanding either of the God of Jesus Christ or of Jesus Christ himself. And the faith of the Church, as expressed in Scripture and Tradition, is the Spirit's means of drawing our minds and hearts into their communion.

The overall impression made by the life, personality, death, and subsequent transfigured appearances of Jesus turned erstwhile supporters of a strictly monotheistic religion, Judaism—which holds to a rigorous separation between Creator and creature—into apostles of a Trinitarian religion, Christianity—in which the one God is adored not only as the unique source of all other being (the Father), but also as the subject of a human life (Jesus, the Son) and as their mutual love (the Holy Spirit). Such was the transforming power of this revolution in religious understanding that it turned upside down the cultural world of its day, and has not ceased since to affect a variety of cultures (massively or peripherally, directly or indirectly), to the point that its influence (at any rate, in the form of its ethos) extends throughout practically the whole world. The members of the Church of Christ testify to the continuing presence of Jesus as the Son of God in worship, in mystical prayer, and in daily life. Catholic theology, as the exercise of reason on the resources of faith, has elucidated the coherence of this fundamental proposition that God was, and remains, incarnate in a human being. It finds no contradiction in the affirmation that the personal existence of God the Son, who, as God, is our Creator, can be realized as both the subject of the divine nature and the subject of a human nature, solidary with our own. The *who* of my personal existence is not, after all, exhausted by the *what* of my human nature, whether we are thinking of the nature I share with all my fellow-humans, or the particular way in which I receive that nature, in the culture, place, and time where I was born. I am more than my nature; the question, What am I? no matter how fully answered, still does not satisfy the further query, Who am I? the question of personal identity.

It is the faith of the Church that the two natures were indeed held together in Christ's own person.

The Incarnation of the Word

During the public ministry, awareness that Jesus is the divine Son in the full sense is always an exceptional act of divine revelation. Jesus tells Peter it is not flesh and blood but the Father who has revealed to him that he is the Son of the living God (Matt 16:17), and Paul echoes this when he tells the Galatians (1:15-16) that it was God who, by grace, was pleased to reveal his Son to him. At the baptism of Christ, as also during his transfiguration, it is the voice of the Father that marks out Jesus as the "beloved Son." Only after the resurrection does Christ's divine sonship appear more manifestly in the power of his exalted humanity (cf. Rom 1:4; Act 13:33), enabling the apostolic community as a whole to confess how they saw the glory that is his as the only Son of the Father, full of grace and truth (John 1:14).

The first seven ecumenical councils of the Church (and the lesser synods that prepared and complemented them) unfolded little by little this basic datum of the apostolic faith, that Jesus, while true man, is also one with the Father as his Word. If the Council of Antioch (284) defined against the heresiarch Paul of Samosata that Jesus is Son of God by nature, not adoption, the first ecumenical council, Nicaea I (325) anathematized the teaching of Arius that he came out of nothing (as creatures do) and thus was of another substance than the Father. The relevant clauses of the Nicene faith were solemnly reiterated and embodied in the final version of the ecumenical Creed, at the second ecumenical council, Constantinople I (381). Not all, however, was pellucid yet. While Nestorius saw in Christ a human person conjoined with the divine person of the Son of God, Cyril of Alexandria persuaded the third ecumenical council, Ephesus (431), that there is no other subject of Christ's humanity than the person of the divine Son who assumed it in making it his own. The fourth ecumenical council, Chalcedon (451), taught that in the single hypostasis (underlying subject, and so, for beings endowed with spiritual activity, person) of our Lord Jesus Christ the two natures are united inseparably but without confusion, while the fifth ecumenical council, Constantinople II (553), cleared up a possible ambiguity in the text of Chalcedon by insisting that this single hypostasis was indeed that of one of the Holy Trinity— who was, therefore, the subject of (even) Christ's sufferings and death. With this "neo-Chalcedonian" conviction thus integrated into the public doctrine of the Church, it was safe enough at the sixth of the councils, Constantinople III (691), to speak freely of a duality of wills in the Redeemer, such that he chose in a properly human fashion to do, in his living service of the Father as man, all that, as the divine Word, coresponsive with the Spirit to the Father, he had willed as God from all eternity. Finally, at the seventh ecumenical council, Nicaea II (787), the union of divinity and humanity in Christ was pronounced so close that veneration of the painted image of the body of Jesus could count as homage to the uncreated person of the Son.

The faithfulness of this doctrinal development to what was given in the ministry of Jesus appears when we consider the way Jesus claimed the title *Kyrios*, "Lord"—the typical name of God in the Greek translations of the Hebrew Bible—during his discussions with the Pharisees about the meaning of Psalm 110 (cf. Matt 21:41-46: David calls the Messiah his "Lord"; how can he be merely his son?), and made gestures expressive of dominion over creation—both the physical world, in mastering nature, sickness, death itself, and the spiritual world, in dealing with human and angelic sin. And if, during his ministry, some people use the title "Lord" simply through respect and trust, others, moved by the Holy Spirit, may use it in recognition of his divine mystery (Luke 1:43; 2:11), while, in encounter with the risen Christ, it becomes outright adoration ("My Lord and my God!": John 20:28). Since, as the New Testament affirms, everything found a fulfillment in him, this can only be because, from the beginning, everything was likewise made dependent on him (Col 1:15-21). He is the everlasting Word through whom all things were made.

The basic proclamation of belief in the incarnation was well stated by the twelfth-century Cistercian theologian and homilist Guerric of Igny: "The Most High himself . . . came down to his mother's womb, he who always abides in the bosom of the Father, with whom he lives and reigns through every age."[1] Guerric accepted Bernard of Clairvaux's proposal that the Son's union with our flesh is the true meaning of the kiss offered by the divine bridegroom to Israel in the Song of Songs; the incarnation fulfills the articulate hope of Jewry and of the dumber longings of humanity at large. In his sermons Guerric celebrated that union in a series of contrasts. The Ancient of Days becomes a child; the God of majesty empties himself. Here we see a speechless infant; yet he gives all eloquence to human tongues. He comes before us as one who knows nothing; but he is God's Wisdom and Word, teaching knowledge to human beings and angels. The child wrapped in swaddling clothes is he who is robed in light boundless and unapproachable.

This is what Paul in the Letter to the Philippians calls the *kenōsis* or self-emptying of the Word (2:7). It entails no discarding of the divine nature or attributes, for with God, as James remarks, there is neither change nor shadow of alteration (1:17). In its wondrous simplicity God's nature has everything that God is, and what God does alters his

---

1. Guerric of Igny, *Sermons on the Annunciation* 1.6.

world, not him. So the *kenōsis* is a change in creation. It is the assumption by the divine Son of our human nature, our sinful flesh. As Bernard says, he took not Adam's nature before the Fall but my nature, in its slave-like condition of susceptibility to the fallen passions and to death. This verifies the words of Paul on the *kenōsis:* "Though he was in the form of God, he did not count equality with God a thing to be grasped, but emptied himself, taking the form of a servant, being born in the likeness of men. And being found in human form, he humbled himself, and became obedient unto death, even death on a cross" (Phil 2:6-8). Christ's human nature could have been pervaded from the first moment of its existence by his divine glory and happiness, as it was at the transfiguration and would become with his resurrection. But instead he chose to live out his earthly life under the conditions of the Fall. As the writer of the Letter to the Hebrews puts it: "We have not a high priest . . . unable to sympathize with our weaknesses, but one who in every respect has been tempted as we are, yet without sin" (Heb 4:15).

Yet Guerric (to return to our Cistercian guide) realizes that the incarnate Word is not set before us simply to be the object of faith and wonder. Rather he will act so as to solve our basic problems, redeeming us from the power of evil and winning for us eternal happiness. "The Son, doing the work of God, suffering the lot of man, is a sign to us that he will bring over to God the man for whose sake he is conceived and brought forth, indeed for whom he suffers."[2] What Guerric calls "the craft of mercy" blends divine bliss and human misery in a "sacrament of union." Through the mediator, by the power of his resurrection, bliss is to absorb misery, life swallow up death, and the whole person pass glorified to a sharing of the divine nature.

The sophisticated metaphysics invoked by Catholic theology to express the reality of this union have been worked out in the service of this salvational plan of God for (at least in hope) all our futures. It was to this redemptive end that the person of the eternal Word so activated the human nature of Jesus as to make it one being with himself, with the result that what stands before us in the gospel narratives is a person at once divine and human. For Thomas Aquinas, the unity of Christ flows from the fact that there is in him only one *esse*, "act of being," the eternal act of existence of the Word. Identical with the divine nature itself, this everlasting energy of existence becomes in the

2. Ibid. 3.4.

incarnation the *esse* that sustains and, even more, *is* the unique act of existence underlying Christ's human nature also. There is no human nature in Christ apart from that nature's existence in the *esse* of the Son; there is no man Jesus apart from his existence in the *esse* of the uncreated Word. Here we begin perhaps to understand the conundrum bequeathed us by the historian's Jesus, the conclusion of the investigator of Jesus' self-understanding: namely, Jesus knew that the God of Israel existed not only in him but also as him.

On the basis of this union, we can say that what Jesus does and suffers is, simply and directly, what God does and suffers—no symbol but brute fact. The Council of Ephesus, in defending devotion to the mother of Jesus as *Theotokos*, the "God-bearer," vindicated the "communication of idioms" whereby we can say, "The Eternal One was born in time" and "God hung for us on a tree." It remained for the Council of Chalcedon to provide a theological account of this in its doctrine that the attributes of the two natures may be "exchanged." We may speak, for instance, of a crucified divinity and an omnipotent humanity, so long as these adjectives are being applied to the single hypostasis or person who is in both these natures.

Moreover, all this concerns not only Christ but us as well, we who are the Word incarnate's fellow human beings. Hilary of Poitiers, that great defender of Christ's divinity in the fourth-century Latin Church, the Athanasius of the West, wrote, "He became our flesh universally." Christ is the universal man, the new Adam in whom our humanity is remade. Yet for the Word's relation to the humanity of Jesus to become a relation with all human beings individually it has to be reproduced, so to say, in another mode. From the moment of the hypostatic union, when our Redeemer began to exist in the womb of Mary, such was the mighty effect of his solidarity with us that humankind was recreated in him as in a new principle of being. But this did not happen in such a way as to be automatically effective for all. We benefited personally only when, with the resurrection, his eternal sonship became fully effective in and through his history and the accomplishing of his destiny on the cross, and that efficacious power began to be received by us in the free response we call "faith."

Just as the mysterious constitution of the God-man, as one person in two natures, was not brought about by God simply for our contemplation (and therefore his own glory), but in order that Christ might act, energetically, to save us from evil and raise us up into the blessedness of God's life, so the identity of the new Adam is inseparable from his mission. That is already clear at the annunciation when the angel communicates to Mary the name she must give her child: Jeshua, that is, "God saves," for, in Paul's words (2 Cor 5:19), God was in Christ reconciling the world to himself.

But why did God send his only Son into the world? The Word was made flesh so as, in the first place, to manifest the Father's infinite love (1 John 4:9), but also in order to make us sharers in the divine nature (2 Pet 1:4), free from sin and raised up to gracious union with our maker. Both creation and incarnation reveal a primordial freedom whose action consists supremely in giving—though the grace of the incarnation, as the communication of the Godhead itself, altogether exceeds the gift of our created being. Christology, by conceiving the unity of divinity and humanity in Jesus as an act of divine liberty in its self-insertion into the history of salvation to be that history's center, changes both theology (our understanding of God) and anthropology (our understanding of the human being).

First, the incarnation reveals God as sovereignly free even vis-à-vis his own nature. It is not in the nature of the aweful and infinite divinity to be united with its frail and fallible creature. But God now shows himself not to be the prisoner of his nature (if we may dare express it so), but to transcend that nature in the freedom of his triune love. The world has, as the philosophers surmised, an infinite principle, but that principle is the Trinitarian love and so is radically free in the world's regard. In the Creed we say of the Word that "he came down from heaven," and this poetic language discloses the deepest metaphysical truth of things: the divine movement of love towards the world, and above all towards humankind.

Second, the incarnation discloses to us what, by divine grace, we are capable of: union with God.

> Nothing could so provoke us to love God than that his very Word, through whom all things were made, should assume our nature, for its healing, and be himself both God and man. We have, in this fact, the greatest sign of his love for us, and to know oneself to be loved strongly urges to love in return. Moreover, man's mind and affections are tied to material things; he does not easily rise above them. Yet anyone can know and love another man. To meditate upon the sublimity of God and be borne to him by worthy love is for those only who by divine help and long and laborious effort are lifted from the corporeal to the things of the spirit. But, that he might provide a way to himself for all, God wished to become man, so that even the lowly could know and love him as one like

themselves. Thus, through that which they could grasp, they might eventually advance towards perfection. Again, because God has become man we have the hope of obtaining a share in that perfect happiness which belongs by right to him alone. Man knows his limitations. If someone had promised the happiness of knowing and joyfully experiencing God for which the angels even are scarcely fitted, he would hardly have dared hope for it, unless he had been shown the worth of human nature, which God so highly prized that he became man to redeem it. So it is through his taking flesh, that God has given us the hope that even we may reach union with him in blessed happiness.[3]

So the incarnation presents a double aspect to us. It is God who reveals himself, but in this very act of self-disclosure, it is also revealed what we ought to be, what we are called to be and indeed what in our deepest essence, which the wounds of the Fall leave intact, we actually are. So the Fathers will say that the incarnate Son is at one and the same time the manifestation of God and a re-presentation of the original humanity, created in God's image, which Adam was meant but failed to be.

The first Adam was taken from the dust of the earth (the Bible's version of the truth of the evolution of the body discovered by Wallace and Darwin); the incarnation of the Word, the second Adam, is also the crowning of matter, and its evolution. The earth has provided the flesh of the "humanity assumed," as the point of insertion into the natural world of God's own eternal life. As Ephrem the Syrian, the early Church's greatest poet, sang:

From the thirsty earth
a Fountainhead sprung forth
capable of sustaining
the thirst of all peoples.
From the virgin womb,
as though from the rock,
a seedling has sprouted
to provide a great harvest.[4]

The French priest-paleontologist Pierre Teilhard de Chardin stressed this in his account of the incarnation as a new epoch in evolution, which now begins to take the form of "Christification." There will be

3. Thomas Aquinas, *On the Reasons for the Faith* 5.
4. Ephrem, *Hymns on the Nativity* 4.84–85.

no more true progress for humanity, in its place in nature, without assimilation of the grace Christ brought by his life, death, and resurrection.

Reminding ourselves that the Lord of all, He Who Is, became human brings us up with a shock against the question of the mind of Christ. What could be the understanding of the world on the part of one who was fully human and yet entirely divine? Unless we are to think of the divine mind and the human mind of the Word incarnate as hermetically sealed from each other, we must postulate not only the integrity of each but also their intercommunication. The content of Christ's human mind will therefore include not only that experiential knowledge acquired by him in the course of his development from infancy to adulthood in a way substantially the same as our own (though more consistent and unimpeded)—that is, through the senses. It will extend also to an infused knowledge directly communicated to his human nature from the divine person who is its subject. As the divine person of the Son, he was in continuous possession of the divine knowledge which is an inherent attribute of the Godhead (and distinct from the divine nature itself only to our apprehension, not in reality). As completely man, he had a human mind subject to all the limitations that belong to human nature. The conditions under which his human mind could apprehend what was in his divine mind may be thought of as analogous to those that regulate the process of translation from one language to another. Without "translation," divine knowledge could have no more meaning in a human mind than the words of a language would to one for whom it was totally unfamiliar.

We should expect that, as Jesus grew in wisdom, his human mind would grow in its capacity to draw on the divine mind so intimately united with it. Thus Jesus' human intellect would go from strength to strength in power of understanding *pari passu* with the development of his human holiness in moral force, as the latter passed from one immaculate state and stage of life to another—until finally, in the resurrection, his human mind and will reached total transparency to the divine mind and will possessed everlastingly by the Son as the gift of the Father in the Holy Spirit. We can think, then, of the human intelligence of the Lord as receiving from his unimpaired divine knowledge as the Word whatever at each fresh juncture it was capable of receiving. In dependence on the Father's economy, his wise plan, Jesus' human mind would thus transmute into human knowledge, and so make available for the Lord's use in his incarnate mortal life, whatever it was thus able to receive.

The exegetical and doctrinal tradition of the Catholic Church ascribes to Jesus not only an awareness of the saving plan of the Father for the world (without which he could not have carried out his mission at all), nor simply an understanding of the foundation of his role in his procession from the Father, his unique Sonship (without which he would have been bizarrely unaware of his own deepest identity), but also an immediate vision of the Godhead: the Beatific Vision. Even here, however, we must think in terms of a real development in Christ; that vision will not be enjoyed in the same manner by the soul of a baby as by that of a mature man.

The upshot is that while in some ways Jesus was in continuity with his culture—resembling to some degree, for instance, the Jewish teachers of his time—in other respects he towers above them by discontinuity. He "speaks of what he knows" (John 3:11), appropriately for one who is the truth of God incarnate. The freshness and intrinsic authoritativeness of his teaching astonished his hearers (Mark 1:22, 27), and this will not surprise us for it manifested the creativity of one who is no less than the Creator, come into his own world. Hence Jesus' extraordinary, effortless confidence, and a behavior that is as bewildering, often, as much to friends as to enemies.

Jesus, as the humanity assumed by the Logos, was not, however, a superman or Titan. His sinlessness meant that he did not *achieve* ethical perfection. He came into this world already full of grace, bringing to our sinful flesh, as he assumed it, that gift of wholeness which as man he received in his conception by the Holy Spirit. Since, consequently, he was without moral limitation, his sympathies could be universal, and lead him to relate to sinners in unexpected ways. The greatest miracle of the public ministry is the moral miracle of his own personality.

> He realized in the entire sphere of human relations that imaginative sympathy which in the sphere of art is the sole secret of creation. He understood that leprosy of the leper, the darkness of the blind, the fierce misery of those who live for pleasure, the strange poverty of the rich. . . . His entire life also is the most wonderful of poems. For "pity and terror" there is nothing in the entire cycle of Greek tragedy to touch it.[5]

His human personality was the visible sacrament—at once ethical and aesthetic—of the invisible mystery of the incarnation.

5. O. Wilde, *De profundis*, 2d ed. (London, 1969) 86, 87, 89.

We could call the life of Jesus preeminently a charitable life except that the word *charitable* is now, in English, offputting. One says "as cold as charity," whereas originally *caritas* came from *carus*, meaning "held warmly in affection." Perhaps we should use the Greek, and call his human personality "agapeistic." For Jesus' summary of the Torah as love of God with one's entire being and of one's neighbor as oneself accurately expressed the law of his own life. Only perfect love achieved complete solidarity. This is what his baptism signified: association with his fellows in their direst need. But Jesus did not love people ineffectually, leaving them as they were. Rather, he established himself as the nucleus through which the demands of God's righteousness and the grace of God's forgiveness are alike disseminated through the body of humankind. This task he took to its consummation when, on the tree of Calvary, he gave himself for us with the words, "It is finished" (John 20:30).

In Jesus we see humanity raised to its highest capacities, so that it becomes the instrument and organ of God's great act of love for our salvation. Because the human perfection of Jesus upon earth is relative to the accomplishment of God's work through his humanity and that work is unique, Jesus' life cannot present in all respects a comprehensive example for the imitation of other human beings. That is why the Church has the saints: to spell out what the work of Christ means for every human condition and walk of life. Our judgment of Jesus' ethical perfection is based, then, less on minute examination of his particular deeds and words in relation to some generally accepted rule of human conduct, and more on recognition of the fitness of his whole existence to be the human instrument of the divine love for that saving purpose which his life revealed.

The "high" Christology to which the Catholic Church is committed by the seven ecumenical councils of the patristic era does not, therefore, prevent a full exploration of Jesus' humanity. In the Church's history, devotion has focused ever more sharply on the Lord's human figure, from the cradle to the cross. Notable already in the twelfth century with Bernard of Clairvaux, spreading in the thirteenth thanks to Franciscanism, the stress on Jesus' "kindness"—his kinship with human beings—reached an early climax on the eve of the Reformation. From that age modern piety has inherited many of its forms: meditation on the life of Christ, the Way of the Cross, the Seven Words from the Cross, and so forth.

Thus on the one hand the Church confesses the authenticity of the human experience of the Lord—his temptations, prayer, weariness, tears, fear, suffering, dereliction, death, as well as his religious exultation, feasting and fellowship, friendship with both men and women, compassion, welcome for children, tender and inquisitive attitude towards nature—yet, on the other hand, she also proclaims his everlasting Godhead, for in him the two natures are united without confusion, but without division.

The Mysteries of Christ's Life

To the eyes of faith, conscious of who Jesus is, his two natures are fused. The life of Christ, portrayed dramatically by the evangelists in the main episodes of their narrative, becomes the "sacrament" of his divinity. What was visible in his earthly life leads into the invisible mystery of his divine Sonship and mission. As the seventeenth-century French spiritual writer John Eudes put it:

> We must continue and accomplish in ourselves the states and mysteries of Jesus, and pray him often to complete and accomplish them in us and in all his Church. . . . For the Son of God has it in mind, by making us share in his mysteries, to extend and continue them in us and in all his Church, by the graces that he wills to communicate to us, and by the effects that he chooses to produce in us through these mysteries. And by this means he wishes to fulfill them in us.[6]

Those mysteries—what the twelfth-century theologian Arnold of Bouneval called "the cardinal works of Christ"—are laid out in the course of the Church's liturgical year: to present Catholic Christology by way of these mysteries, as celebrated liturgically, is the main approach adopted by the contemporary *Catechism of the Catholic Church* and will be echoed here.

The Mysteries of the Birth and Infancy

The unique manner of Jesus' virginal conception does not make him what he is: true God and true man. Jesus is the God-man only because of God's free decision from all eternity that the eternal Son should be identified with the man from Nazareth. However, the virginal conception of Jesus is essential to the gospel as a sign that God gives in history of his new creative art. Whereas in human generation the partners

6. *Oeuvres complètes du vénérable Jean Eudes* (Paris, 1905) 1:310–12.

are highly active, achieving something themselves in procreation, in the work of salvation only God takes the initiative; only he achieves. In the case of Jesus, the male is removed entirely, while the virginal woman is present simply as the one upon whom—though also with whom—God acts.

At the annunciation, Mary gives the consent long prepared, and wholeheartedly embraces the saving will of the Father, dedicating herself as the *ancilla Domini*, the "Lord's handmaid," in the service of the person and work of Christ. "By her obedience she became for herself and for all the human race the cause of salvation."[7] In this moment, the most stupendous metaphysics and the earthiest biology combine. The eternal God, by his Spirit, fertilizes an ovum in the womb of the Virgin Mary, uniting that embryonic human being to the person of his uncreated Word. The divine Son entered the human environment as a fetus—and the feast of the Annunciation (25 March) is not the least reason for Catholicism's reverencing unborn human life.

Since the Son's taking flesh from the Virgin is the outcome of God's great love for humankind it was fitting, so Aquinas points out, that the active principle in his conception should be the Holy Spirit, who is personally the love of the Father and the Son. Aquinas describes Mary's cooperation as having from the first a bridal quality: "In order to show that there is a certain spiritual wedlock between the Son of God and human nature, in the Annunciation the Virgin's consent was besought in lieu of that of human nature as a whole."[8] For Bernard, when the angel speaks, all Israel, all humankind, indeed all creation wait breathlessly for a reply:

> In his sorrow, Adam is asking this of you, O loving virgin. . . . Abraham and David too implore. The holy men of old, your ancestors, those who dwell in the valley of the shadow of death, earnestly beseech this of you. . . . The whole world, on bended knee before you, is waiting for it . . . for on your word depend consolation for the afflicted, redemption for captives, liberation for the condemned, in short, salvation for all the sons of Adam. . . . O Virgin, give your answer quickly![9]

At this moment something happened so different from all other events since time began that it resembles a new beginning for the world. The Creator assumed the life of a creature so as to bring his creation back

7. Irenaeus, *Against the Heresies* 3.22.4.
8. Thomas Aquinas, *Summa theologiae* 3.70.3.
9. Bernard, *Homilies in Praise of the Virgin Mother* 4.8–9.

to himself from within, by providing us with a new model for our activity, Jesus Christ his Son, and a new set of resources for our acting, his Holy Spirit.

In Christmastide, the Church celebrates Jesus' birth and the mysteries of his infancy. Jesus is born in lowliness, in the marginalized condition of a family without a roof, but in this poverty the glory of heaven is revealed, as the bells rung at the Gloria of Christmas night proclaim.

> The Lord of all comes in the form of a servant. He comes as a poor man, so that he will not frighten away those people he is trying to capture like a huntsman. He is born in an obscure town, deliberately choosing a humble dwelling place. His mother is an ordinary girl, not some great lady. And the reason for all this lowly state is so that he may gently ensnare mankind and bring us to salvation. If he had been born amid the splendour of a rich family, unbelievers would surely have said that the face of the world had been changed by the power of wealth. If he had chosen to be born in Rome, the greatest of cities, they would have ascribed the change to the power of her citizens. . . . [But] he chose nothing but poverty and mean surroundings, everything that was plain and ordinary and (in the eyes of most people) obscure. And this was so that it could be clearly seen that it was the Godhead alone that was to transform the world.[10]

When we humble ourselves and can be born again "from above" (John 3:7), Christ is formed in us (Gal 4:19), and the "wonderful exchange" between God and humanity, transacted at the birth of the Son as a human being, is continued in the world. John Henry Newman wrote in a Christmas sermon:

> The Word was from the beginning, the only-begotten Son of God. Before all worlds were created, while as yet time was not, he was in existence, in the bosom of the Eternal Father, God from God, and Light from Light, supremely blessed in knowing and being known of him, and receiving all divine perfections from him, yet ever one with him who begat him. As it is said in the opening of the Gospel: "In the beginning was the Word, and the Word was with God, and the Word was God" (John 1:1). If we may dare conjecture, he is called the Word of God as mediating between the Father and all creatures; bringing them into being, fashioning them, giving the world its laws, imparting reason and conscience to

---

10. Theodotus of Ancyra, *On the Day of the Lord's Nativity.* This homily was preached at the Council of Ephesus (431).

creatures of a higher order, and revealing to them in due season the knowledge of God's will. . . . He indeed, when man fell, might have remained in the glory which he had with the Father before the world was. But that unsearchable Love, which showed itself in our original creation, rested not content with a frustrated work, but brought him down again from his Father's bosom to do his will, and repair the evil which sin had caused. . . . Thus he came, selecting and setting apart for himself the elements of body and soul; then, uniting them to himself from their first origin of existence, pervading them, hallowing them by his own divinity, spiritualizing them, and filling them with light and purity, the while they continued to be human, and for a time mortal and exposed to infirmity. And, as they grew from day to day in their holy union, his eternal Essence still was one with them, exalting them, acting in them, manifesting itself through them, so that he was truly God and Man, one Person—as we are soul and body, yet one man, so truly God and man are not two, but one Christ.[11]

This means, from God's side, his unconditional self-committal to humanity. Contrasting the old and new covenants in this regard, Basil wrote in a sermon for Christmas night: "To the prophets he came; and he went from them. But this night he is coming as the One who has assumed our human nature in its entirety, and for ever, for by making our flesh his, he has raised up to himself all of humanity." So the effect is, from our side, the union of fallen humanity in a transformative fashion with its own all-holy maker. "Tonight Adam's condemnation is over. People can no longer say to one another, Dust you are and unto dust you will return. Now they must say, You are united to him who is in heaven, and unto heaven will you be lifted up."[12] The implications are at once ontological (a matter of being ethical, of acting) and sacramental (a matter of worshipping). Basil's own emphasis in this address is concerned with a metaphysical transformation: though heaven does not lose the One who contains the heavens, earth welcomes into its bosom the One who is in heaven. For Ephrem, the entry of the Word, unchanged, into our nature ethically reorders the existence and action that flow from that nature.

> On this day that claims all things, let no one threaten or disturb. This day belongs to the Gentle One; let none be bitter, none be harsh in it. This day belongs to the Meek One; let none be high nor haughty in it. This is the day of pardoning; let us not be unforgiving. This is the day of gladness;

11. J. H. Newman, *Parochial and Plain Sermons* (London, 1880) 2:29–30, 32.
12. Basil, *Homily on the Sacred Generation of Christ* 6.

let us not spread sadness. This day is too mild for us to be harsh in it. This is the day for peaceful rest; let us not be wrathful in it. This is the day when God came to sinners; let no-one think himself and despise the sinful. This is the day when the Lord of all came to his servants; let all men who are masters love their servants with a love like his. This is the day when he who once was rich for our sakes became poor; so let the rich man amongst us bring the poor man to share his table. Today for us came forth the Gift for which we had not asked; let us therefore give alms to those who cry and beg of us. Today was the day that opened for us a gate on high to our prayers, let us also open the gates of forgiveness to those who have offended us and ask to be our friends.[13]

For Aelred, the sign of the swaddling clothes, the lowly integument of the Word incarnate, points us ahead to where, in the Church, he will remain accessible: in the sacraments, and above all, the holy Eucharist. Recalling that, in Hebrew, "Bethlehem" means "house of bread," he identifies the city of the incarnation symbolically with

Holy Church, in which is administered the body of Christ, the true bread. The manger at Bethlehem is the altar of the Church; it is there that Christ's creatures are fed. This is the table of which it is written, "You have prepared a table for me." In this manger is Jesus, wrapped in the swaddling bands which are the outward forms of the sacraments. Here in this manger, under the species of bread and wine, is the true body and blood of Christ. We believe that Christ himself is here, but he is wrapped in swaddling bands; in other words he is invisibly contained in these sacraments.[14]

And to sum up, the Pseudo-Chrysostom in his homily for Christmas night finds the whole redemptive outreach of God in his Word, and its response in the multifarious sorts of human being, precontained in the divine condescension of Bethlehem:

See how kings are coming to adore the king of heavenly glory. Soldiers come, to serve him who leads all the warriors of heaven's army. Women come, to worship him who was born of a woman to change the pains of childbirth into joy. Virgins are coming, too, to the virgin's son, and with joy they see that he who is the giver of milk himself sucks from a virgin mother the food of infancy. Infants are coming, to worship him who became an infant to perfect praise from the mouth of infants and of babes. Children come, to the child who through the rage of Herod raised up

13. Ephrem, *Hymns on the Nativity* 1.88–96.
14. Aelred, *Sermon 2, on the Birthday of the Lord,* with an internal citation of Psalm 23, 5.

martyr children. Men come to him who became a man to heal the miseries of his servants. Shepherds come to the good shepherd who had laid down his life for his sheep. Priests come to him who has been made a high priest according to the order of Melchizedek. Slaves come to him who took upon himself the form of a slave that he might bless our slavery with freedom. Fishermen come to him who chose fishermen to be made fishers of men. And tax-collectors come to him who from amongst them named a gospel-writer. And sinful women, to him who exposed his feet to the tears of the penitent. In short all sinners have come to Bethlehem, here to look upon the Lamb of God who takes away the sin of the world.[15]

The event of the *circumcision* on the eighth day after Jesus' birth must be interpreted in terms of the principle that the Son of God has taken nothing into his human existence that lacked some special meaning for salvation, in its own fashion. This has to be especially true of what concerns his relation to the divinely willed rites and uses of the old covenant. The circumcision, though now incorporated in the Church of the Latin Rite into a "Solemnity of Mary, the Mother of God" is, evidently, a Christological occurrence. Today Jesus took his place within the people of the covenant, entering on a life of obedience to the Torah, and of participation in the cultus of Israel, both of which issued from his Father. The Son of the promise made to the patriarchs is subjected to the Law that accompanies the promise, so that by fulfilling all that the Law required he might bring the promise to pass in its fullness. Just as the ordinary Israelite became a bearer of the promise through circumcision and so (appropriately enough) was required to become spiritually "circumcised" in his manner of living, so the Son must suffer in all the dimensions of his being in order to enact our redemption. For the rabbis, the blood of circumcision carried the same religious value as the blood of the paschal lamb: it was worth the blessing of the covenant between the Lord and Israel. Jesus' circumcision looks ahead, to the bloody sacrifice of Calvary where he will fulfill all the "types and shadows" of Israel's history.

The *Epiphany*, the feast of the manifestation of the Word made flesh to the Gentiles in the persons of the wise men come from the East, anticipates the universality of God's salvation as offered by Jesus to all the nations. Today (6 January) the hidden God is seen on the wintry earth. And the Magi bring before the face of the invisible God now

---

15. Pseudo-Chrysostom, *Homily on the Birthday of Christ* 1.

made visible the questions their gifts signify. Gold as the metal from which royal insignia were wrought and by which the trade of antiquity was conducted stands for questions about the nature of power, and its use for the human good. Frankincense as the material of worship, burnt aromatically in divine worship, represents the theological questions that probe the being of the gods. Myrrh, as the stuff used for mummifying the dead, raises that great question mark of mortality which, set against human activity as a whole, is the philosophical question above all others. The Church then sees in the Magi types of the whole *humanum* in its search for final truth. On Epiphany humanity finds that God really can be found by humankind. In his kindness God even allowed astrology, foolish as it may be, to succeed (this once) for those who, in purity of heart, knew no better, and set out on this strange journey equipped with only some fragmentary knowledge of the Jewish expectation of salvation, and a prescientific astronomy. That does not prevent today's feast from celebrating the epiphany, or shining forth, of the Wisdom of God in Jesus Christ as something that can draw to itself the doubting intelligentsia of the pagan world of all times and places—so beautifully portrayed in the Anglo-Saxon ivory which forms the frontispiece of this book.

In the West, by the third century the Magi were held to be kings, thus fulfilling Old Testament prophecies of how the rulers of lands afar would hail the divine Lordship in the last age. Bede would suggest that they represented the continents of Europe, Africa, and Asia (the only ones known to him) and Christian art would take this cue in its depiction of their varied ethnicity. Their gifts were now reinterpreted Christologically as gold for Christ's kingship, frankincense for his divinity, and myrrh for the bitterness (the root meaning of the word) of his suffering and death. In the East, by contrast, up to a dozen wise men are reckoned, and their retinue lavishly described. But on any arithmetic, this is a feast of fullness.

> Let the whole pagan world enter into the family of the patriarchs, yes, let it enter, and let the children of the promise receive in Abraham's seed the blessing which his children according to the flesh rejected. In the three Magi let all the nations worship the Author of the universe; and let God be known, not in Judaea alone but throughout the whole world, so that everywhere his name may "be great in Israel."[16]

16. Leo the Great, *Sermons on the Epiphany* 3.2.

The Jewish Law required a mother to present herself for purification after childbirth at Nicanor's gate of the Jerusalem temple. It also commanded the biological father to redeem his firstborn son, since the firstborn of human or beast was holy to (the property of) Israel's Lord. On the feast of the *Presentation* (2 February), called in the Eastern Churches the "Meeting of the Lord with Symeon," the old man Symeon and the elderly prophetess Anna greet the infant Jesus as the Christ long awaited: he is acclaimed as a light for the nations and the glory of his people Israel. This he can be in the last analysis only because, in the words of the Creed, the Son (now made human as this infant) is "Light from Light." That affirmation of the Fathers of Nicaea had, in part, the aim of preventing any projection into God of the creaturely, or corporeal, ingredient in our words *father, son, offspring, generation*. But it also had the effect of making clear that, as light is never without its radiance, so the Father is never without the Son, the Word. As the eternal radiance of God, the divine Son is himself eternally light, without beginning or end. Today the Church's faithful carry lighted candles in liturgical procession, witnessing to the entry of the Light into the world.

> The Mother of God, the pure Virgin, carried the true Light in her arms and offered him to those who were lying in darkness; so let us hasten to meet him, enlightened within by his brightness and carrying in our hands a light that all can see. . . . This is our mystery, so it is right for us to come together with lights in our hands to signify the light which has shone on us and to point to the brightness he has brought with him for us men.[17]

More somberly, however, the Child, being incapable of "redemption" by an adoptive father, must, under the Law, later redeem himself. Thus the presentation has its dark hues to set beside the bright. Jesus' life commission will be the surrender of his life in a death which makes him the firstborn par excellence. To be the "firstborn from the dead," and to be recognized thereby as the "firstborn of all creation," he must first make the offering of the Cross. So his mission will constitute a "sign of contradiction," and a sword will pass through his mother's soul at the costly redemption made on Calvary's tree. The flight into Egypt, and the massacre of the innocents, caused by the opposition of the Herodian monarchy to messianic rumors, continue this theme, pre-

---

17. Sophronios of Jerusalem, *Orations* 3.6–7.

figuring the full realization of John's judgment on the Messiah's fate: "He came to his own, but his own did not receive him" (John 1:11).

Still in Christmastide, the Church also celebrates Jesus' years of uneventful daily living—of labor, and of life in the family and in the social community. The obedience of the divine Son-made-man to his mother and adoptive father, and to the ordinary familial and communitarian norms they represented, constitutes both a beginning of his work of reestablishing what the disobedience of Adam had destroyed (cf. Rom 5:19), and the gospel foundation of the Church's own concern for the structures of the family and of society, seen as pregiven in the natural law. The only event that interrupts the silence of those years is the episode of the finding in the Temple, where Jesus gives his parents a glimpse of his divine sonship, subsequently stored up by his mother in her heart—a source of her standing as the Church's model contemplative. The feast of the *Holy Family* (the Sunday after Christmas) celebrates these themes. Instituted in the late nineteenth century, it nevertheless gathers up the Church's long-established beliefs in Mary of Nazareth as the all-pure Mother of God and in Joseph as holy Joseph, participating in the divine calling and blessing that distinguished his predecessors, the patriarchs. The feast considers these convictions in relation to Jesus himself, so as to explore and celebrate the relations that bind these three individuals together. Nothing can make the family of Nazareth into a typical human family—which is why it is an archetype of the Catholic home, not an instance or example of it. Yet as numerous remarks in the gospel tradition show (most notably the episode of the losing and finding of the child in the Temple), the holy family was not sacred because it knew no troubles, difficulties, even crises. It was sacred because of the resources of grace it brought to these negative moments, and because of the way in which human freedom struggled with and triumphed over those negativities by continuing conversion, self-denial, sacrifice, until it became, in Mary, the nucleus of the Church of the resurrection.

The hidden life of Jesus at Nazareth is also a life of labor, a working life, and Catholicism has seen in this fact a consecration of work, a divine declaration that toil is more than its penal aspects. Labor also has dignity, a dignity that derives from the creativity of the human agent who is its subject. At the same time, the Church marvels at the contrast between the infinite work of the God-man in his divine nature, and the finite work in which he consented, in his humanity, to find meaning and fulfillment. The priest-poet John Gray's *Ad matrem* is to the point:

> Mary is busy sewing. Jesus stands
> Beside St. Joseph, working through the day.
> He did not come into the world to play
> At being man, but worked with both his hands. . . .
> Thus He who built the world now condescends
> To learn the joiner's trade, and handled saws
> And chisels for His bread, who made the laws
> Which guide a million points to their ends.

The Lucan episode of Jesus' loss and re-finding in the precincts of the Jerusalem Temple anticipates the moment of his coming of age, when in the following year, thirteen years old, he would be bound by all the commandments of the Law. He marks this crisis of growth by asserting the rights of his heavenly Father. During the Week of Unleavened Bread, which followed the Passover celebration, some of the Jewish doctors would give lectures of a more popular nature than was customary on the Temple terrace, as a way of honoring the festal season. It would have been normal for the family to have begun its return to Galilee two or three days after Passover. Doubtless because Jesus was almost of age, his parents would not have been surprised had he not been with them from the start. Probably they missed him at the first night's halt and spent most of the next day making sure of his absence. On the third day they found him. . . .

The Mysteries of the Public Life

The New Testament itself alludes to the growth of the Child not only in stature but also in wisdom. The incarnation, we can say, is augmentative: the Word seizes and appropriates those new sides of the human being which are generated in authentic human development. But the moment of breakthrough par excellence in Jesus' developing awareness of his mission is surely his baptism: in both East and West a major "Christophany" or disclosure of who Jesus is.

The public ministry of Jesus began with his *baptism* at the hands of John, when he both received and inaugurated his mission as the Suffering Servant. John spoke in the "person" of "all the voices" of the Old Testament hope,[18] and Jesus as the God-man replied "in the person of the Word." To "fulfill all righteousness" (Matt 3:15)—to submit

18. Augustine, *Sermon 288*.

himself to the will of the Father—he undergoes this anticipation of the "baptism" of his sacrificial death. His self-identification with sinners is accepted by the Father whose voice expresses delight in the Son's action. At this point the Spirit, which Jesus possessed from the moment of his conception, begins to "rest" on him—to constitute him as the source of the Spirit's presence and activity for all humanity whose mediator with the Father he is. The waters of the Jordan are sanctified by the descent into them of the Son and the Spirit, the beginning of the new creation. In their own baptism of water and the Spirit individual Christians become identified sacramentally with Jesus who in his archetypal baptism anticipates his death and resurrection. This is a mystery of humility and repentance where the Christian is reborn to become a "son in the Son." "If the sun with stars and moon is bathed in the Ocean, why should not Christ be bathed in the Jordan? He is the king of heaven and the ruler of creation, the rising sun, who shone upon the dead in Hades and upon mortals on earth. He alone is the sun who rose in heaven."[19] As the sun descends daily into the bath of the ocean, so the true Son descended into the waters of Jordan, prefiguring his going down into Sheol, the waters of death. But though the waters seem to snuff out the sun's radiance, as the grave swallowed Christ, the sun's light is not lost in itself. So Jesus' light is not lost in itself, but shines out for the saints, to the old covenant, and, ultimately, for all the redeemed.

After the baptism, Jesus lives for a period in the wilderness, reliving the temptations of Adam in paradise and Israel in the desert. The abyss of the physical water, as the Swiss theologian Hans Urs von Balthasar remarks, changes into the spiritual abyss that interprets it. The Gospels present him as the new Adam who, unlike the first, stayed faithful: the perfect Israel of God fully obedient to the divine will. Christ's work of "recapitulating"—summing up, and thus fulfilling—all human existence in God involves a negative recapitulation of the Fall of Adam, and hence a super-positive action. As Irenaeus presents Christ's work of deliverance, a movement backwards, taking over again what man has done awry, is also a movement forwards: the bringing into existence of something new, a man of earthly flesh and blood who is simultaneously the image of God and recipient of his unending life. In the *temptations,* Christ takes his stand against the devil, forcing his way back, as it were, through the Fall and emerging on its

19. Melito, *On Baptism.*

far side, in God's sinless creation. But the place of his final emerging will be the resurrection on the third day.

In the case of Jesus, the temptation could only be from without, not from within, and the result was never uncertain. That did not make his struggle any less intense, nor did the suffering of temptation without the possibility of sinning mean that the internal tearing was less. On the contrary: since the incarnate Word had the most perfect and delicate spiritual fiber of any human being, his mental anguish was more exquisite than that of sinners.

From this point on—as our exploration of "the historian's Jesus" in the last chapter has indicated—his ministry of preaching and acting unfolds: his message is of the unconditional nearness of the Father's love and mercy, which will become the sovereign norm of the world (the kingdom) for those who accept it by faith and repentance. That message is embodied in his own practice: his warmth towards those who, though morally guilty, accept the grace of forgiveness and begin to live out the feast of the kingdom, his judgment of those who are hardened in self-righteousness.

The message is sealed by acts of power in which the Son reverses the disintegrating effects of the activity of the evil angels, in his exorcisms restoring men and women to the sanity which is their birthright since they were created in the Logos, the archetype of rationality; sealed too by miracles of healing and recreation in which power goes out from the Son to make good the deficiencies of the nature made through him and also to provide signs of the yet more wonderful remaking of human nature, his raising of it to share in grace and glory.

The *transfiguration* signifies precisely this. On a high mountain, the glory of God which is Jesus' everlasting possession as the Father's only Son breaks through briefly in his human features and appearance. It discloses to the disciples the transparency of Jesus, in his humanity, to the Godhead—something to be further manifested in the resurrection when, through the cross, the kingdom of God is at last inaugurated on earth. Jesus is flanked by the figures of Moses and Elijah, who, according to Jewish tradition, were taken forward at their deaths into the coming glory of the divine reign. Their appearance at this juncture is highly significant. In the Hebrew Bible, they embody the holy war against evil (personified in Pharaoh in the one case, Jezebel and the gods of Canaan in the other). They are, then, suitable presences for the "last days"— Jesus' final confrontation with Satan, with sin and with death.

Acclaimed by the Father as his "Beloved," to whom the disciples must pay heed, Jesus uses the opportunity of this visionary disclosure to point his followers to the sacrifice of his dying. That sacrifice is necessary if his humanity is to become (at the end of time) the perfect organ of God's self-expression to the world.

The feast of Christ's transfiguration, as kept liturgically by the Church, may be described as the foundation of all Christian theology. For theology begins with the flooding of the mind by the uncreated light, and the concentration of the heart on the person of the Savior. We cannot create this foundation: rather, we live within it, resting upon it. So this feast (6 August) is one to exult in, filled as it is with that beauty, love, and joy of God now within our reach in Christ, our friend and brother. The transfiguration is the sign of humanity on the way to final redemption in God, the dawn of a history of joy in the midst of the unanswered suffering of the world.

> When we are one with the Son, and lovingly return toward our Beginning, then we hear the voice of the Father, touching us and drawing us inwards; for he says to all his chosen in his eternal Word: "This is my beloved Son, in whom I am well pleased." For you should know that the Father with the Son, and the Son with the Father, have conceived an eternal satisfaction in regard to this—that the Son should take upon himself our manhood, and die, and bring back all the Chosen to their Beginning.[20]

And so we come to the passion, death, and resurrection of Christ, the true center of the Catholic faith.

The Mysteries of the Lord's Passover

Considered simply from the viewpoint of the nature assumed, the re-creation of humanity is complete from the moment when the hypostatic union was first established, at the annunciation. But in terms of its applicability to ourselves, the re-creation of humanity is initiated only at the moment when, in his death upon the cross, Christ overcame the powers that enthrall us, though they never enthralled him. By his incarnation he took a perfect human nature to himself. By his passion, however, he actively identified his nature with ours, not by a metaphysical union alone but by the personal sacrificial offering thereof in obedience and love.

---

20. Jan van Ruysbroeck, *The Sparkling Stone* 12 ("Of the Transfiguration of Christ on Mount Thabor").

Owing to this union of life and being, in Jesus Christ God himself took on the existence of a slave and, appropriately, died as man the slaves' death on the tree of martyrdom (Phil 2:8), given up to public shame (Heb 12:2) and the "curse of the law" (Gal 3:13), so that, in the death of One who was personally God, life might win victory over death. Jesus "was given up for us all" on the cross, in a death which can only, therefore, be termed "sacrificial."

Here the Church gives priority not to analysis but to praise.

> The prophets announced many wonderful things about the Passover mystery which is Christ. To him be glory forever, Amen!
>
> He descended from heaven to earth for the sake of suffering mankind, clothed himself with a human nature through the Virgin Mary, and appearing in our midst as man with a body capable of suffering, took upon himself the suffering of those who suffered. By his Spirit which could not die, he slew death, the slayer of men. Led forth like a lamb, slain like a sheep, he ransomed us from the servitude of the world, just as he ransomed Israel from the land of Egypt. He freed us from the slavery of the devil, just as he had freed Israel from the hand of Pharaoh, and he has marked our souls with the signs of his own blood. He has clothed death with dishonor and he has grieved the devil, just as Moses dishonored and grieved Pharaoh. He has punished wickedness and taken away the children of injustice, just as Moses punished Egypt and unchilded it. He has brought us from slavery to freedom, from darkness to light, from death to life, from tyranny to an eternal kingdom.
>
> He is the Passover of our salvation. He was present in many so as to endure many things. In Abel he was slain; in Isaac bound; in Jacob a stranger; in Joseph sold; in Moses exposed; in David persecuted; in the prophets dishonored. He became incarnate of the Virgin. Not a bone of his was broken on the tree. He was buried in the earth, but he rose from the dead, and was lifted up to the heights of heaven. He is the silent lamb, the slain lamb, who was born of Mary the fair ewe. He was seized from the flock and dragged away to slaughter. Toward evening he was sacrificed, and at night he was buried. But he who had no bone broken upon the Cross, was not corrupted in the earth, for he rose from the dead and raised up man from the depths of the grave.[21]

Here we reach the theme of the atoning efficacy of Christ's death, a theme explored in liturgy, preaching, and devotion down the Christian centuries, and expressed in art, music, and literature, both high and low.

---

21. Melito, *On the Pasch* 65–71.

If Christ's death was a universal sacrifice, it must somehow have atoned for the sins of the human race at large: humankind and God, estranged from each other as they were through sin, were restored by Christ's dying to a condition of "at-one-ment." The early Christians illuminated the meaning of Christ's sacrifice not so much through rational investigation as by relating it to the ritual sacrificial practice of the Jewish people, as set forth in the Old Testament. The New Testament, and notably the author of the Letter to the Hebrews, sees Christ's sacrifice as fulfilling and superseding these sacrifices. Hebrews, while having principally in mind the expiation sacrifice of Yom Kippur, seems to refer to others as well. Its message is that the functions served by these rituals have now been taken over by the sacrifice of Christ, a sacrifice which took place "once for all"; its effects continue even now, since the sacrificed Christ still stands before the Father, pleading efficaciously for the sins of the world. The blood of Christ has thus achieved what the blood of the myriad animal sacrifices could not. Christ has "washed away our sins with his blood" (Rev 1:5).

In his sacrifice, Christ acts as our head or representative. In his cry of dereliction on the cross he voiced the pain of every desolate and lost human being. But since he is a divine person, this action has infinite saving power. By it he brings light to the blackest vault of human misery.

> One can say that these words of abandonment are born at the level of that inseparable union of the Son with the Father, and are born because the Father "laid on him the iniquity of us all" (Isa 53:6). They also foreshadow the words of St. Paul, "For our sake he made him to be sin who knew no sin" (2 Cor 5:21). Together with this horrible weight, encompassing the "entire" weight of the turning away from God which is contained in sin, Christ, through the divine depth of his filial union with the Father, perceives in a humanly inexpressible way this suffering which is the separation, the rejection by the Father, the estrangement from God. But precisely through this suffering, he accomplishes the Redemption, and can say as he breathes his last, "It is accomplished" (John 19:30).[22]

In his "Why?" there is no protest, rebellion, or despair. Christ accepts his sacrificial death willingly, and so places the final conclusion of humanity's rebellion within his freely given loving obedience to the Father's will—thus locating it within the existence of the uncreated. Hereafter, everyone can transform the necessity of death into a free-

---

22. John Paul II, *Mystici doloris* 18.

dom of self-renunciation, can repeat the "moment" of Christ which is the very inversion of Adam's rebellion. Everyone can rest the possibility of existence no longer in mortal nature but in personal relationship with the Father.

> The Cross is indeed a feast and a spiritual celebration. Once the Cross meant punishment, now it is an object of honour. It used to be a symbol of condemnation. Now it is the source of healing and salvation. For the Cross is the cause of countless good things; it has delivered us from error, enlightened our darkness, reconciled us with God. We had become his enemies, strangers afar off; the Cross has made us his friends, close at hand to him. The Cross for us is the destruction of enmity, the pledge of peace, the treasure-house of thousands of good things. Thanks to the Cross we no longer wander in desert places, for we know the true Way. We no longer have to stay outside the king's palace for we have found the Door. We are not afraid of the fiery attacks of the devil, for we have discovered the fountain of water. Thanks to the Cross we are no longer widowed but have found the Bridegroom. We are not afraid of the wolf, for we have a Good Shepherd. Thanks to the Cross we are not troubled at the prospect of the usurper, for we are seated by the King himself. And so we are keeping holiday, celebrating the memory of the Cross. St. Paul himself invites us to the feast which honours the Cross. "Let us keep the feast," he says, "not with the old leaven of malice and wickedness but with the unleavened bread of sincerity and truth." He says why: "Christ our passover has been sacrificed for us." He orders a feast in honour of the Cross, because on the Cross Christ was slain. There the Sacrifice was offered; and so there we find the abolition of sin, reconciliation with the Lord, festivity and joy. Christ our Sacrifice has been slain, slain on a gallows high and lifted up, a new altar for a new and altogether extraordinary Sacrifice. He is at once victim and priest, victim according to the flesh, priest according to the spirit.[23]

But the use of the language of sacrifice to speak of the atonement need in no way exclude what has long been called the "judicial" or "satisfaction" theory of what was done on the cross of Christ. The truth that the cross shows the willingness of divine love to suffer the consequences of sin on our behalf, need not exclude the further truth that, on the cross, the sinless manhood was offered so that, having passed into the heavenly world, its sanctifying and life-giving power might be available (by humble and thankful receptivity) to sinful humankind.

23. John Chrysostom, *Homily 2 on the Cross and the Thief* 1, with an internal citation of 1 Cor 5:7.

The main concept the symbolism of Christ's sacrifice offers to rational theology is, in fact, that of an all-inclusive, substitutionary satisfaction for the sin of the world.

As analyzed by the classic divines of the Latin Church, sin consists of two elements. There is a *conversio*, a turning towards something, but equally, by a kind of negative complement that transforms the moral charge of the action, there is also an *aversio*, a turning away from something. In every sin, no matter how aberrant, the *conversio* is always to something good. Though people can be mistaken in placing their good, their flourishing, in objects that actually are not their good, the error this involves cannot be total. Absolute or unconditional evil does not exist, and so the object of sinful choice always includes an element that in some way befits the human good. This is why novelists, playwrights and filmmakers, can render sin intelligible. The element of malice in sin is the *aversio*, whereby in making a particular choice I orient myself morally in a different direction from that which God has imposed upon me—not arbitrarily but by the creative act which brought me into existence, and which is found in concrete form in my nature (apart from original sin), as well as by the supernatural vocation which takes its own, more intimate, concrete form in my personal election to grace. In the *aversio* I refuse to recognize God as my last end, as the absolute good to which all other goods must be referred. I negate God practically even though theoretically I continue to profess his existence. This is why sin contains an infinite malice. "As for the evil which is sin, the good to which it is opened is the Uncreated Good itself. Sin is the contrary of the accomplishing of the divine will and love by which the divine Good is loved in itself and not simply as participated in by creatures."[24] Just as the freely willed openness of the person to God through desire and love has an infinite positive dimension which will ultimately be realized in the Beatific Vision and the beatifying love of God, so (precisely because the free creature is thus ordered to a communion of life with Father, Son, and Spirit) there is in the closure on self which is sin an infinite negative aspect. The enclosure of sin involves a refusal of the infinite Object to which the person is open by nature and grace. Sin, then, is an infinite offense and it attacks the very order of the universe, because humanity—and this must mean individual human beings—is responsible for the ordination of the world to God.

24. Thomas Aquinas, *Summa theologiae* 1.46.6.

As Anselm pointed out, it is unthinkable that God should accept the disorder sin brings with it (though this does not mean, as Anselm also thought, that God must obtain a sufficient reparation for sin: since God is transcendent, he cannot be confined by any created state of affairs, even that of sin and its possible reparation). How then did God will to overcome the rupture in our relations with him which sin involved? He who at the dawn of history created human freedom by creating our first parents free, proved able to redress the sinful human will from within by grace, and thus to reestablish the order disturbed by sinning. As the disorder was in the free will, it was at the level of the free will that the redressal had to take place. The Son of God achieved this in his coming among us. As one of our race, he was capable of making the human gesture of reparation. As the divine Word, the initiative he thus took had an infinite value. Moreover, he could make an (infinitely valuable) act of reparation or satisfaction on behalf of all human beings, since the Father had made him the new head of all humanity—the second or last Adam—by making the destiny of all human beings turn on the work of the incarnate One. Thus Paulinus of Nola's poem *Verbum Crucis*, "The Word of the Cross":

> Look on my God, Christ hidden in our flesh.
> A bitter word, the cross, and bitter sight:
> Hard rind without, to hold the heart of heaven.
> Yet sweet it is; for God upon that tree
> Did offer up his life: upon that rood
> My life hung, that my life might stand in God.
> Christ, what am I to give Thee for my life?
> Unless take from Thy hands the cup they hold,
> To cleanse me with the precious draught of death.
> What shall I do? My body to be burned?
> Make myself vile? The debt's not paid out yet.
> Whate'er I do, it is but I and Thou,
> And still do I come short, still must Thou pay
> My debtors, O Christ; for debts Thyself hadst none.
> What love may balance Thine? My Lord was found
> In fashion like a slave, that so His slave
> Might find himself in fashion like his Lord.
> Think you the bargain's hard, to have exchanged
> The transient for the eternal, to have sold
> Earth to buy Heaven? More dearly God bought me.

"For our sake," writes Paul, "God made him to be sin who knew no sin" (2 Cor 5:21). The sin-bearing of the sinless Son manifests therefore the gratuitous superabundance of the divine justice. But it also reveals the breathtaking proportions of the divine mercy. Within the moral order as it stands, it would be irresponsible—immoral—for one person to take the place of another. No one can take on another's moral responsibility. No one, therefore, can be a responsible substitute for another's guilt. That God in Christ has actually taken our place, substituted himself for us, tells us that the whole moral order as we know it in this world needed to be redeemed, and set on a new basis. This is what the justifying act of God in the sacrifice of Christ was about. The atoning mediation perfected in Christ is to be grasped not in the light of abstract moral principle but only in the light of what God in Christ has actually done in descending into the dark depths of our twisted human existence and restoring us to union with himself. In this interlocking of incarnation and atonement, of creation and redemption, there took place a soteriological suspension of ethics, in order that the entire moral order might be regrounded in God himself.[25]

It is easy for us to suppose that the sinner can return to God in virtue of the same freedom by which he has turned from him. But Scripture sets its face against any such supposition, as does the whole dogmatic tradition of the Church. Reconversion to God can only be an act of charity, an act which alone can overcome the refusal of loving communion with God which we made in sinning. But just because by sin we have become deprived persons—deprived of the grace which alone can transcend our natural limitations—an act of true charity is the one thing that, without divine reconciliation, we cannot bring off.

The satisfactory value of the passion and death of Christ comes from his charity, the defining characteristic of his agapeistic life. More precisely, it derives from his penitent charity, for all humankind was included in him, not with its sins but in its character of having sinned. Christ's charity, therefore, was permeated by penitence because of the sins of the men and women he freely bore in his own person. This charity pressed him on to a work of satisfaction that would be really proportionate to it. And he found this "external work" in the gift of his own life. "I have a baptism to be baptized with, and how I am straitened until it is accomplished" (Luke 12:50). Or again: "How I have

25. See T. F. Torrance, *The Trinitarian Faith: The Evangelical Theology of the Ancient Catholic Church* (Edinburgh, 1988) 146–90.

longed to eat this Passover with you before I suffer" (Luke 22:15). He must suffer, for, as the Johannine Christ explains, the cross on which he will be lifted up is his "hour." It is for this that he came. In his Good Friday sacrifice, Christ offered his life to the Father by immolating it in obedient penitent love, as the all-inclusive, substitutionary satisfaction for the sins of the whole world.

The dialogue between Anselm of Canterbury and the monk Boso in Anselm's treatise *Cur Deus homo* brings out perfectly the gratuitous, *gracious* quality of the divine action.

> Anselm: To whom will it be more appropriate for him to transfer the fruit and recompense of his death than to those for whose salvation, as we have learned from reliable arguments, he made himself man and to whom, as we said, he gave by his death an example of dying for the sake of justice. It is useless, surely, for them to imitate him if they will not share in his merit. Or whom will he more justly make heirs of what is due him, and which he does not need, and of the super-abundance of his own fullness, than his kinsmen and brethren, whom he sees bound by so many and such great debts, perishing in penury, in an abyss of miseries, so that what they owe for their sins may be pardoned, and what they have need of because of their sins, may be granted them?
>
> Boso: Nothing more reasonable, nothing more agreeable, nothing more desirable can be proclaimed to the world. In fact, I derive such great confidence from this that even now I cannot describe the tremendous joy with which my heart exults. For it seems to me that surely God rejects no person who draws near to him under this name.[26]

And indeed at Easter the Father manifests his acceptance of the Son's sacrifice in the twofold but intimately related events of the resurrection and the outpouring of the Holy Spirit on forgiven humankind. The disciples rightly interpreted the resurrection of their master as signifying forgiveness and reconciliation, and they tasted its power in the gift of the Spirit, whereby charity was set abroad in their hearts. In principle for all human beings—in practice for all those who turn to Christ in order to appropriate the fruits of the redemptive sacrifice—God is reconciled with them. Sin, to return to our departure point, is washed away in the blood of the Lamb.

Taken in conjunction, then, the sacrificial and judicial theories simply give greater precision to the truth of Melito's classic statement

---

26. Anselm, *Cur Deus homo* 2.19.

from which we started: namely, that by the cross God-made-man has won the victory that redeems humanity from the powers of evil—the fundamental affirmation of the Gospels and the liturgies of the Church. And thus, finally, the fullest truth is found in the great principle vindicated by Peter Abelard that the cross is the supreme demonstration of the love of God.

There is yet more to be said, for in manifesting the triune love, the atonement founded a new worship, and brought the Church to birth. In electing to substitute himself for the ritual victims by which human beings have expressed their desire for forgiveness and renewed relationship with God, the Son manifested his self-giving love, and thereby revealed what is most divine in him. He showed forth, first, the divine nature as generous, fruit-bearing goodness. Second, he revealed that life of communion between the divine persons in which the divine nature has its concrete form, where selfhood is defined by self-giving. The diffusive, self-surrendering goodness had already manifested itself in creation: God makes room for the world, graciously enabling his own act of existence (albeit at an infinite remove) to terminate in creatures which have their own limited yet real autonomy vis-à-vis himself. At the same time, the manifestation of the divine self-giving on the cross goes far beyond this, since here the Son enters into the abandonment of death and hell. Though God is not changed by the crucifixion we are brought to see that in God there is sacrifice: the eternal event whereby the Father becomes the Father of the Son, the Son consents to be as sheer relation of obedience to the Father, and in this moment, the Spirit to be the mutual love of them both. The suffering of the cross is thus, in the words of Balthasar, "the manifestation of the Trinitarian Eucharist of the Son." Thus Calvary shows us what the eternal God is like.

Christ's death was not a piece of ritual yet it *was* a cultic act (i.e., a deliberate act of adoration of the Father), albeit carried out for a unique end: the forgiveness of the infinite malice contained in the *aversio* of sin, a forgiveness that restored human beings to participation in the divine life, since at no time has God not willed for them grace and glory. Thus the circumstances in which the death was embraced—the betrayal by friends, the rejection by the religious leaders, the hostility, or cynical indifference, of the men of power—all of these purely secular conditions were taken up into an act of cult, a supreme act of worship, whose hidden fruitfulness made it the central event in the history of the world. Because Christ's sacrifice was a supreme act of worship, it was capable of becoming the foundation of the Christian liturgy. Aquinas remarks that by his sacrifice on the cross, Christ inaugurated the cultus of the Christian religion. His sacrifice is the objective basis of our worship.

Furthermore, if the sacrifice of Christ is thus the goal of the incarnation (i.e., governing the whole life of Christ who "must" suffer and is constrained until this "baptism" is accomplished) then the whole of the subsequent history of grace in the Church, and notably the sacraments, flows through that sacrifice, taking no other course. The saving power of the cross extends via the resurrection through all subsequent time. The Church is born from the cross: so the Fathers loved to interpret the lance-thrust of John 20. From the riven side of Christ flow water and blood, the life-giving stream of baptism, the nourishment of the Eucharist. And so in her deepest reality, the Church is nothing but humankind's taking hold of the fruits of Christ's sacrifice.

This is how Augustine saw things in his comments on Psalm 21:

> This psalm that we have been singing puts the picture before us. "Eli, Eli, lama sabachthani?"—the very words the Lord cried out on the cross. "My God, my God, why have you forsaken me?" What can he possibly have meant by that? How could God have forsaken him? He himself is God, God the Son of God, God the Word of God. In the beginning was the Word, and the Word was with God. And the Word was made flesh. And the Word made flesh hung on the Cross and cried out, "My God, my God, why have you forsaken me?" It would only make sense if he were including us in himself. The body of Christ is the Church, and we, the body of Christ, were being crucified there. Similarly the psalm goes on to say, "Far from my salvation are the words of my crimes." His crimes? He did no sin, neither was any guile found in his mouth. How can he talk about his crimes, except by way of praying for our crimes and treating our sins as though they were his sins, and so making his righteousness our righteousness. Then he says, "I am a worm and no man, the reproach of men and the outcast of the people." We are coming to the story of his sufferings. First of all we shall see what he suffered and then why. What was the use of it all? Our fathers hoped, and they were delivered from Egypt. Thousands have called upon God and been delivered. But not so our Lord. He was scourged and there was none to help. He was spat on and there was none to help. He was knocked about and crowned with thorns and there was none to help. He was nailed to the cross and no one came to rescue him. Why, brethren? What was to be gained by suffering such as these the psalm describes to us? Listen as the psalm goes on and answers my question. You must be ready to ask your-

selves if a man has any right to call himself a Christian unless he has some part in the stake for which Christ suffered. What was his stake, for which all his bones were counted and his garments divided and his coat made the stake in a dice game? Tell us, Son of God, what was the use of your passion? Certainly you endured it because you yourself were prepared to do so. But what was it all about? I will tell you, he answers, and tell you plainly. It is no secret, even if men are too deaf to hear it. It is all there in this psalm. "I will tell your name to my brethren; in the midst of the Church I will sing to you; and all the ends of the earth shall turn to the Lord." The Church is the reason for his suffering: that is what he bought. The Church was the stake in his game. The Church is what he shed his blood for, the great Church in the whole wide world from the rising of the sun to its setting.[27]

Such a rich and many-faceted doctrine of the atoning significance of the passion and death of Christ has given rise, naturally enough, to a devotional cultus to the "Man of Sorrows." The Sacred Heart, the wounded heart of the Savior, is, in the words of Pope Pius XII, the "lawful symbol of that boundless charity which moved our Savior to shed his blood and so to enter into mystical marriage with the Church."[28] Karl Rahner wrote in his meditation for what Germanophone Catholicism delights to call the *Herz-Jesu-Fest* (feast of the Sacred Heart, kept on the Friday following the second Sunday after Pentecost):

Only in this heart do we know who God wills to be for us. Only by it, the heart of Christ, is the riddle, into which all the wisdom of the world leads us, changed into the mystery of love that gladdens and blesses. In the heart of Christ our heart is all-knowing because it knows the one fact without which all knowledge is vanity and spiritual nuisance and without which all the practical experience of our heart causes only despair: in the heart of Christ our heart knows that it is one with the heart of God. It knows that it is one with the heart of God in which even the thief and the murderer find pardon, one with the heart in which our deepest, darkest nights are transformed into days, because he has endured the nights with us. It knows that it is one with the heart in which everything is transformed into the one love. If he is our heart, our diversity can enter into the apartness of God without being burned to nothing in it. In him our dispersion can be collected without being confined and constricted, our heart can gush forth into the expanse of the world without being lost. The heart of Jesus is God's heart in the world, in which alone

---

27. Augustine, *Enarration on Psalm 21*, with additional internal citation of Matt 27:46.
28. Pius XII, *Haurietis aquas*, 39.

the world finds its God as its blessed mystery, in which alone God becomes the heart of our hearts, in which our being finds its centre: at one and the same time unified and all-embracing.[29]

If devotion to the Sacred Heart is especially connected with the present experience of grace (which enabled it to play an indispensable, positive role in the struggle against Jansenism, with its soteriological minimalism), the cultus of the Sacred Wounds relates the passion to the final consummation of human history: when Christ comes as judge he will display his wounds, to the elect as pledges of love, to sinners as bitter reproach. In preparation for that end, acts of penitent charity form an inseparable part of the practice of this devotion, that wounds of judgment may become wounds of mercy for humankind.

If, finally, the Lord's wounds and his pierced heart have spurred the creativity of Christian piety, and, in its train—for as the philosopher Paul Ricoeur noted, the symbol gives rise to thought—sacred theology, it is the *crucifix*, the figure of the Lord's body, that must count as the supreme icon of Christ's abiding solidarity with suffering humankind. This can range from the Christ robed in the royal and priestly tunic of the (Syrian) Rabula Gospels, or crowned in the Catalan "majesties" to the "Lily" crucifixes of the English Middle Ages where the figure of Christ hangs on the lily plant, symbolizing the fulfillment of the Annunciation in the Passion, and, finally to the anguished realism of their German counterparts in the sixteenth century.

The *burial* of Christ is not a common topic for theological reflection. Yet both the Apostles (or Old Roman) Creed and the Creed of Nicaea-Constantinople take the trouble to note it distinctly from the death. As I have written elsewhere, regarding the treatment of this subject in *The Catechism of the Catholic Church*:

> The mystery of the Burial belongs with the mystery of the Descent into Hell: the Father willed that the Son should experience death in its fullness, for our sake, and that means in the first instance the natural yet unnatural separation of soul from body of which the body's laying in the sepulchre is the potent sign. But, as the procession of the faithful accompanying the flower-covered bier of Christ on the evening of Good Friday in the Byzantine rite attests, the Burial of Christ, insofar as it forms an integral part of our happy salvation, is by no means a matter of unrelieved gloom. Beautifully, the *Catechism* describes it as manifest-

29. K. Rahner, *The Eternal Year* (London, 1964) 127–28.

ing the Sabbath rest of God—this time not after his work of creation is completed, but on finishing his work of redemption with its power to "bring repose to the whole world."[30]

Having been separated from his body, the soul of Christ "descended" into what the Hebrew Bible calls *sheol*, the abode of the dead. Here is at once the lowest pitch of the suffering of the passion and the beginning of the resurrection. For, on the one hand, death is the absolute opposite of the God who is "the God not of the dead but of the living," and yet, on the other, for Tradition, Christ's soul was immediately in glory following its separation from the body and actively communicated its state of beatitude to the waiting souls of the just (as in the great Byzantine Easter icons where Christ takes Adam and the patriarchs by the hand). An ancient homily, now used in the Office of Readings of the Roman Rite for Holy Saturday, puts into words the silent message of such icons.

> Today a deep silence covers the face of this earth. A deep silence and a profound stillness. The king is asleep. Earth shook and trembled because the King, God, fell asleep in the flesh. Hell trembled. For a moment God slept, and he woke up those who were in hell. He came to seek man, the beautiful Shepherd seeking the lost sheep. He came to visit to the uttermost those who were seated in darkness and in the shadow of death. He came to deliver Adam and Eve from their prison and their suffering, he who is at once both God and son of Eve. He took man by the hand and said to him: "Awake O sleeper, and rise from the dead, and Christ shall give you light." I am your God. For your sake I am become your son. And to you and your descendants in chains I say: "Come forth." To those who find themselves in darkness I can say: "Be enlightened": to those who are sleeping: "Rise." To you I say "Awake, O sleeper," for I have not made you to stay chained up. To you I say, "Rise from the dead," for I am the life of the dead. Get up, my image, created to my likeness. Get up, let us go away from here, for you are in me and I in you: together we are one and indivisible.
>
> I am God; for you I have become your son. I am the Master; for you I have taken the form of a slave. I am above the heavens; for you I have come down to earth, and even down under the earth. For you, man, I have become like a helpless man, free among the dead. You came out of the garden; for you I have been delivered up to the Jews in a garden, and

30. A. Nichols, *The Splendour of Doctrine: The 'Catechism of the Catholic Church' on Christian Believing* (Edinburgh, 1995) 90–91.

crucified in a garden. See on my face the spit I received to give you back your first breath. See on my cheeks the marks of the blows I received to re-create your face in my likeness. See on my back the cuts made by the whip, the lashes I received to remove from your back the heavy weight of your sins. See my hands fastened to the cross by nails, fastened there for you who stretched out your hand to the tree in the garden.

Rise, let us go from here. The enemy tricked you out from the earthly paradise. I want to take you, not back there, but to heaven. I forbade access to the tree of life, but I myself am the Life, and now I am united to you.[31]

The descent into hell redeems the past. The redemptively causal power of Christ's humanity works not only forward in time, but backward also.

Yet, because the liberation of the dead is also prospective, and touches our own future, the commemoration of the Lord's burial is also a personally liberating matter. Indeed, the celebration of the death and burial of the Jesus who is soon to be hailed as the ever-living One gives us a final theme in the theology of the atonement before we pass on to consideration of the resurrection itself.

Today, brethren, we are commemorating the burial of our Savior. He has gone down to hell, and he has burst it open. He has fired the world below with his splendor; he has roused from sleep those who were lying there. We who have not yet gone down to the dust, we who still remain on earth, we too rejoice and exult; we need fear death no longer, for it will not prevail against immortality. "You will not leave your holy one to see incorruption," the Bible says. It may well be that Jews and Greeks will laugh at our wisdom—that the Jews will go on looking for the Christ, that the Greeks will bring their hopes to an end in the grave. But though we weep now, soon our sorrow will be turned into joy.

Death has seized our Lord Jesus Christ, but it is not going to be able to keep its hold on life. Death has swallowed him up, not knowing who he was. Death binds him fast today, but it is because he himself wills it that the Lord is bound. Tomorrow death must release him, and many more besides. Tomorrow he will rise again, and hell will be emptied. Yesterday on the Cross the splendor of his passion darkened the sight of the sun, and at noonday it was as midnight. Today death is losing its dominion, suffering itself a kind of death. Yesterday the earth mourned as it looked on the hate of those who put Christ to death. Today "the people

31. "From an Ancient Homily on the Holy and Great Saturday," in *Liturgia horarum iuxta Ritum Romanum* (Vatican City, 1977) 2:383–89.

who walked in darkness have seen a great light." Yesterday the earth quaked as though it were collapsing, threatening to open and engulf those who dwelt on it. The mountains were cleft asunder. The rocks were split. The temple, like a living thing, threw off its veil. The elements wept for him, as though chaos were about to dissolve the world again.

This was altogether quite new, and quite unheard of: By his word the Lord stretched out the heavens; by soldiers he is stretched out on the cross. He placed the sands as the bounds for the sea; now bonds hold him fast. He has given us wells of honey, but we give him gall to drink. We crown him with thorns, though he crowns the earth with flowers. He is struck on the head with a reed, though of old he struck Pharaoh with ten plagues and submerged his head in the waves of the Red Sea. The cherubim do not dare to gaze on his face, but his guards spit on it. Yet while he suffered all this, he was praying for those who tormented him, and saying, "Father forgive them, for they know not what they do." . . .

Let us leave them in their unbelief for now. Let us watch not with them but with faithful Mary Magdalene. With her we stand weeping by the tomb. "Weeping may last for a night but joy comes with the morning." So with her we prepare to say, "I have seen the Lord."[32]

The mystery of the Lord's resurrection gives Catholicism its radiance and joy. Resurrection must not be reduced to resuscitation. The resurrection does not simply signify that Jesus was restored to physical life in the world and to the society of his friends, living on for some further weeks until a final withdrawal expressed by Luke as Christ's ascension. The resurrection includes that, but also goes far beyond it. The resurrection—as the Church, rather than the historian, comprehends it—tells us that something has happened so world-shaking that from now on everything else we know about reality must be related to this, not the other way round. The universal significance of the resurrection is brought out in symbolic language in Chromatius of Aquileia's homily for the "Lord's Vigil," Easter Eve.

So angels in heaven and men on earth and the souls of the faithful departed in the world below, all celebrate the Lord's vigil. In heaven the angels are getting ready to celebrate it, since Christ by his death has destroyed death and trodden hell underfoot and saved the world and delivered man. There is joy in heaven over one sinner who repents. But the whole world is redeemed. The angels must really be going to rejoice tonight. Men on earth are getting ready to celebrate the vigil, for it was

32. Amphilochius of Iconium, *Oratio 5 on Holy Saturday*, with internal citations of Ps 15:10, Isa 9:2, Lk 22:34, Ps 30:5, and Jn 20:18.

for them, for the salvation of the whole human race, that Christ suffered death and by his death killed death. The souls of the faithful departed in the world below are getting ready to celebrate the Vigil, for Christ went down into the world below just so that death and hell would no longer have any dominion over them. Christ who dies is the Creator of heaven and earth and hell—surely all should celebrate the Vigil tonight.

But there is still more to say. It is the Lord's Vigil. The Father himself is getting ready to celebrate it with the Son and with the Holy Spirit, for it was according to his will that the Son underwent death to bring us life. So tonight is not going to be a feast just for angels and men, but also for Father, Son, and Holy Spirit—the salvation of the world is the joy of the Trinity itself. So tonight we must celebrate the Vigil with all possible devotion, the Vigil in which death is destroyed, the world redeemed, and we and all mankind set free.[33]

The Son made man is brought from under the control of human destructiveness, as of death, into a new order of existence: a re-creation in which the Father at last fulfills the promise inscribed in our being at the original creation, but constantly spoiled by us. Humanity is now open to the intimate and irreversible redemptive and transfiguring action of God. But unless there were some element of physical continuity between Jesus and the risen Lord of Christian faith, if it were not the earthly—and hence the bodily—life of the rabbi from Nazareth that was this transformation's immediate and foundational subject, the proclamation of a new creation would have no purchase on the cosmos. The Lord Christ is raised up in all the dimensions of his human being to share the glory of the Father. Thus the resurrection confirms the claim to authority made by Jesus and reveals his unity with the Father, just as he had said. Fittingly, then, the Church celebrates on Easter night the vindication of her Lord, and the confirmation of the truth of his message and saving work, the seal on the good news of the mercy and love of God.

> Tonight the great marriage-hall will be full of guests,
>   all dressed for the wedding of the Lamb,
>   no guest rejected for want of a wedding garment.
> Tonight the bright new lamp-light will be shining,
>   the light in the lamp of the wise virgin Church,
>   the light of Christ that will never again be extinguished.
> Tonight the fire of grace will burn in us all,

---

33. Chromatius of Aquileia, *Sermon 17 on the Great Night*.

spiritual,
divine,
  in our bodies and in our souls,
fed with the oil of Christ.
Therefore we pray you,
    God, our Sovereign, Christ, King for ever in the world of spirits,
   to stretch out your mighty hands over your holy Church
   and over the people that will be forever yours.
Defend them.
Protect them.
Fight and battle for them against the rulers of the darkness of this world.
Raise now the sign of your victory over us,
  that tonight with Moses we may sing the triumph-song.
For yours are victory and power for ever and ever.[34]

Christ is the first fruits of a wider harvest. He is the Head who draws his body with him to where he is. So the resurrection is a mystery of hope for the Church. As the Fathers say, when a baby is born it is usually born head first, but when the head is born the whole body follows naturally, for it is the birth of the head which is the hardest part. As the glorification not only of the human soul but of matter also, the resurrection promises the transfiguration both of humanity and of the cosmos in which our life is set.

Last night did Christ the Sun rise from the dark.
  The mystic harvest of the fields of God,
And now the little wandering tribes of bees
  Are brawling in the scarlet flowers abroad.
The winds are soft with birdsong; all night long
  Darkling the nightingale her descant told,
And now inside church doors the happy folk
  The Alleluia chant a hundredfold.
O Father of thy folk, be thine by right
The Easter joy, the threshold of the light.[35]

The risen Lord possesses a universal dominion (Phil 2:7-11), which all creatures must acknowledge. In him, God reestablishes the harmony of the world, making all things converge on himself. Though its effects have not yet spread through the world, nothing less than a cosmic revolution has taken place in the risen Christ. Moreover, not only nature but history too is now placed in the hands of the exalted One. The

34. Hippolytus, *Homily on the Holy Pasch* 62–63.
35. Sedulius Scottus, *Carmen paschale.*

glorifying of the Lamb brings about a continual crisis ("judgment") in the world process whose development forms the innermost history of humankind. Moreover, in Christ humankind is lifted above the realms of the angels, whose entire host is now drawn into the Savior's exaltation, and, in Paul's metaphor, fastened to his triumphal chariot (Col 2:15). As the Father's heir the glorified Christ inherits the whole life of God insofar as bodily humanity can live it. Redeemed humanity enters into this patrimony through him, the Church moving toward the fullness that she will attain when she has come to the stature of Christ in glory. Since now the Spirit plays unchecked in the Lord's humanity, in him the divine spontaneity and liberty breaks into the world. Through that uniquely efficacious sign of the new and everlasting covenant, the "circumcision" of his death and resurrection, Christ now ceases to be confined to the Jewish nation and can become the foundation of the Catholic Church. The resurrection is the Father's acceptance of the sacrifice of Christ: with his glorification his priestly activity is inserted into the eternal now of God (this is why Scripture compares him to the "timeless" Melchisedech, without father or mother). The offering of Calvary, as it exists transfigured in the Father's welcoming embrace, is prolonged in eternity: one who wishes to penetrate the sanctuary of God can join oneself to Christ, who enters in his condition as victim.

To understand what the *ascension* entailed we must briefly consider the relation between God and space and time. The universe's creation out of nothing implies the absolute priority of God over all space and time. God does not enjoy a spatial or temporal relation to the cosmos, but a transcendent and creative one. Even the relation between the actuality of the incarnate Son within this world of space and time, and the Father from whom he came, cannot be made spatial or temporal. But space and time as a continuum of relations given with created existence are order-bearing, and indispensably so, for without them nature would be indeterminable and unintelligible. So they are the medium in which God makes himself present and known to us. We must bear in mind, however, how God's nature and acts and those of humans differ in the way they relate to these orderly functions of contingent events. In the incarnation, Jesus Christ does not just fit into patterns of space and time as formed by other agencies, but rather organizes them around himself, giving them transcendent reference to God in and through him. As Aquinas remarked, Christ is, as man, the way for us to tend to God; in more modern terminology, he provides in the movement between annunciation and exaltation his own distinctive and continuous "space-time track," travelling through the cosmos, fulfilling the divine purpose within it and pressing on to the consummation of God's plan in the new creation.[36] Just as the bodily resurrection is a stumbling-block, or may be, if we look at it merely as one phenomenon to be correlated with others according to the laws of physics and chemistry, removing it from the "field of force" set up by God in the incarnation, whereas it appears quite differently if considered in terms of the incarnate Son's whole "space-time track," so we should think of the ascension as a movement from humanity's place to God's "place"—the former being bounded at one end by the nature of humankind and of its space, the latter being limited only by the boundless nature of God and the limitless "space" which he makes for himself in his eternal life and activity. Christ ascends in order to fill all things with himself, so that what follows on the ascension is not absence but a new mode of presence. He left us in the mode of our presence to each other so as to return to us in the mode of God's presence to humankind.

The Letter to the Ephesians says that Christ ascended in order "that he might fill all things" (4:10). To fill heaven and earth was, for the Old Testament, one of the marks of deity (Jer 23:24). The ascension of Christ is the assertion of God's control over the created order, the endless repercussiveness of the resurrection triumph over sin and death. At the same time, it is the affirmation of all humanity's reflected glory, the second Adam's being taken into God: "It was not merely one man, but the whole world that entered" (Ambrose). In this unique bursting forth of the power of the resurrection, the world of our space and time, wounded by sin and death but now healed and redeemed in the humanity of the crucified and glorified Lord, enters the very radiance of the Father, to the wonderment of the angels. Christ ascends so as to be unspeakably closer to us, to fill the universe with his intimate and transforming presence. The priestly activity of his Church in submediating his glory should not therefore be seen either in purely thisworldly terms or simply in those of preparation for a consummation still far off. Rather do we stand within the movement of ascension, the lifting up of human life to God, and it is only within this movement that the Spirit will come upon us.

---

36. I gladly acknowledge here the help of T. F. Torrance, *Space, Time, and Resurrection* (Edinburgh, 1976).

The *descent of the Holy Spirit at Pentecost* is also a Christological mystery in that the Spirit is not the Spirit of the Father only but of the Father and the Son. The visible mission of the Holy Spirit in history also enters into the cycle of the mysteries of Jesus, and, with the exception of the final parousia, gives them their crown.

Jesus told his disciples, "It is to your advantage that I go away, for if I do not go away, the Counsellor will not come to you" (John 16:7). With the outpouring of the Holy Spirit through the exalted Lord the kingdom begins. The First Letter of Peter has as its theme the spiritual house being built on the foundation of Christ as cornerstone. He is the new temple, the dwelling place of the glory. When everything is placed under his feet, he is given to the Church as her head. The Church is Christ's mystical body because she is united in all her members to the Savior's risen body.

The Holy Eucharist is the rite that expresses and effects this unity. In his death and resurrection Jesus becomes able to impart his life unconditionally. Whereas the old covenant is composed of people related to Christ according to the flesh, the new covenant, now inaugurated, consists of those related in the Holy Spirit to his glorified body. Ancient Israel passes theologically into the new Church of Christ.

The members of the Church from now on will live "in" the risen Christ: in a sphere of existence where a person's whole being is energized by a new principle. As a result Christ becomes a co-subject of our actions: "the love of Christ presses us" (2 Cor 5:14). In the Christocentric coinherence of Pauline theology, the personal sufferings of our Lord are undergone by the believer, and the apostolic sufferings of Paul are those of the Lord. Human beings become open to the person of Christ as the Spirit raises them to the divine mode of living. This new life can also be spoken of as life "with" Christ: the believer, by uniting himself or herself to the glorified Christ of the present, communicates in the saving acts he did in the past. Our identification with Christ (supremely in baptism, the sacrament of faith, and the Eucharist) involves a communion with those acts that form the permanent basis of the Savior's new existence. The believer ascends into the heavenly places, and as a result acquires a new knowledge and a new ethos: the eyes of the heart behold the Lord in the glory of the resurrection whose riches are destined for the saints (Eph 1:18-20), while the whole of the Christian life becomes obedience to God's righteousness, to the law of the Spirit, who brings forth virtues as a plant its fruits (Gal 5:22). The Church's very being "demands charity even before her teaching does,"

for that being lies in the Christ of Easter who is "eternally a renunciation and a giving."[37]

The Parousia of the Incarnate One

The Creed affirms that the Son once made human will come again in
glory, to judge the living and the dead, in such a way that "his kingdom will have no end." The eschatological good of salvation which
Christ has won by his saving incarnation, life, death, and resurrection
is possessed by the Church—but only in faith and hope, as she looks
forward to the end of all things, when her Lord will return, to be a
source of everlasting joy for the redeemed, for those who have corresponded with God's grace in seeking the true, the good, and the beautiful in this life, and to be a sign of judgment for the unredeemed.

It is part and parcel of Jesus' own teaching that we do not know
when the end will be—even though the Church is its anticipated realization. Nor do we know what the world's transformation will involve, which is why Scripture presents it under a plethora of images.
Yet the sacraments, the signs of the Word made flesh, tell us all that is
essential, as do the New Testament images, the signs of the divine
Flesh-taking made word. The Second Vatican Council in its decrees on,
respectively, the mystery of the Church and that Church as set "in the
modern world," sums it up:

> When the Lord comes in his majesty, and all the angels with him, death
> will be destroyed and all things will be subject to him. Meanwhile some
> of his disciples are exiles on earth, some have finished with this life and
> are being purified. Others are in glory, beholding clearly God Himself,
> triune and one, as he is. . . . When Christ shall appear and the glorious
> resurrection of the dead takes place, the splendor of God will brighten
> the heavenly city and the Lamb will be the lamp thereof. Then in the
> supreme happiness of charity the whole Church of the saints will adore
> God and the Lamb who was slain.[38]

> We do not know the time for the consummation of the earth and of hu-
> manity. Nor do we know how all things will be transformed. As de-
> formed by sin, the shape of this world will pass away. But we are taught
> that God is preparing a new dwelling place and a new earth where jus-
> tice will abide, and whose blessedness will answer and surpass all the

37. F. X. Durrwell, *In the Redeeming Christ* (London and New York, 1963) esp. 3–19,
144–61.
38. *Lumen gentium*, 49, 51.

longings for peace which spring up in the human heart. Then, with death overcome, the children of God will be raised up in Christ.[39]

We shall return to the subject of this definitive epiphany of Emmanuel, God-with-us, in the soteriological perspective opened by these quotations, when in chapter six we investigate "The Nature of Salvation."

---

39. *Gaudium et spes,* 39.

5
The Trinity

This chapter, though it has for its subject the deepest and most glorious mystery of the Christian religion, will be, paradoxically, nearly the briefest in the book. This is because this whole study is meant to be permeated by Trinitarian thinking and its source, the Trinitarian reality.

In the Old Testament

The experience of Israel contains some adumbrations, or foreshadowings, of the later Trinitarian faith of the Church. For the Hebrew Bible had spoken of the Spirit of the Lord, as also of God's Wisdom and Word. The Spirit shows the selective initiative that characterizes personal, as distinct from impersonal, acting. Less clear is whether he relates to the Lord himself as a person, but there are some indications that he was so hypostatized for a short period in late Judaism. To the Wisdom of God the biblical writers ascribed both prophetic inspiration and the achievements of reason. Sent from the divine throne, this Wisdom interpenetrates, while not superseding, the human spirit. Both the Old Testament and its Aramaic paraphrases, the Targums, speak of the Word of God as participating in the creation of the world and the guidance of God's people—hypostatizing, in both, God's power of fulfilling his commands. For the Jewish philosopher Philo, Wisdom and Word are identified, and seen as the mediator between God and the human world. "Read dogmatically rather than exegetically, that is to say in light of both the New Testament and later doctrinal development, the Jewish Scriptures betray a revelatory climate that lends itself to what is to come."[1] But it is from the teaching and impact of Jesus that the doctrine of the Trinity takes its true rise.

In the Life of Jesus

If Jesus is the founder of Christianity, the center of his own relationship with God lies nonetheless in his sense of his source: the One he called on as *Abba*, "dear Father" (Mark 14:36). Those around him realized that this relation was unique. Not only did they offer Jesus a kind of discipleship granted to no other Jewish prophet or holy man. They also realized that, though themselves devout Jews, they could not, in comparison with the prayer of Jesus, be said to pray at all. That is implied by the request, "Master, teach us to pray," (Lk 11:1) which prompts the giving of the Lord's Prayer. Jesus' chosen address for God was novel in Jewish devotion, and its Aramaic keyword was left by Christian reverence as the exclusive preserve of Jesus himself. Listening in to the prayer of Jesus, we find an extraordinary sense of intimacy with God, combined with an awareness that he stood in a unique relation of sonship to God as Father. The disciples' appeal to the Father was only possible because of their relation to Jesus.

God was to Jesus what he was not to anyone else. This is the origin of Jesus' grasp of his mission, as most certainly it is the heart of his message. The preaching of Jesus has its principal content in the kingdom of his Father, and his divine love and mercy. The mode in which the kingdom is proclaimed consists in its being made accessible by the parables of the Son—parables both spoken and enacted, both words of Jesus and his deeds. Only the unique Son has the right of access to this kingdom, but he mediates such access as sheer gift to the disciples. "No one knows the Father but the Son and those to whom the Son chooses to reveal him" (Matt 11:27; Luke 10:22). In this striking saying from the Synoptic tradition, Jesus expresses his awareness of being, in a singular way, the recipient and mediator of the knowledge of God. The saying points us on, therefore, to the Gospel of John, and the faith of the Church as expressed in the early councils. From this consciousness of being the only Son of the God he alone knew as Father, the specifically Christian doctrine of God—faith in the Holy Trinity—takes its rise.

---

1. W. J. Hill, *The Three-Personed God: The Trinity As a Mystery of Salvation* (Washington, D.C., 1982) 5.

For, in dependence on this sense of God as Father, Jesus was also aware of a unique endowment of the Spirit of God. The Spirit, whose outpouring Jewish tradition considered a mark of the "fullness of time," the imminent consummation of history, was conceived as the agent of union between God and the world. This Spirit Jesus knew as a power working in him, and coursing through him to others. In his ministry of healing, his preaching, and, in and through these, his capacity to draw others into his own relation with the Father, he could see the singular way he possessed the Spirit of God, and the Spirit possessed him. The Spirit was the power of the *Abba* prayer, uniting him to the Father in a union of love. The Spirit was also the power that enabled him to draw within the ambit of that prayer the disciples, whom he taught to say, "Our Father."

In the Paschal Mystery

What was thus implicit in the public ministry of Jesus became explicit at the first Easter, with its host of attendant visionary and charismatic experiences. In the resurrection appearances of Jesus, and the Pentecost experiences of the Spirit, the absence from the empty tomb in the Easter garden is grasped as a Trinitarian presence. The resurrection is the manifestation of Jesus' renewed presence and activity as truly the Son of the Father in the power of the Spirit. It also entails the full breaking through of the power of that Spirit (now named indifferently the Spirit of God and the Spirit of Christ) into this world, so as to draw others into a share in the Son's relation to the Father. As Paul writes, at that moment Christ was "manifested as Son of God in power with the Spirit of holiness" (Rom 1:4). In the light of this supreme event of human history, the first disciples saw more clearly how the mutual implication of the Father and the Spirit in the person of Jesus had been a reality of his earlier life. The incidents of the baptism and the transfiguration were recollected as Trinitarian "epiphanies"—events that imaged the unique relation of the Son to the Father and the Spirit. In the Gospels of Luke and Matthew, such recuperative memory extends to the birth of Jesus. Finally, in the Gospel of John, the evangelist affirms this divine dimension of Jesus' life as being present from the beginning. The Son was always in relation to the Father and the Spirit, even in that eternity to which nothing can be prior. The Son and the Spirit, these irreplaceable bearers of the disclosure of the Father, themselves belong from before all worlds to the realm of the uncreated, where God is all in all.

The dialogue between Father and Son is, in the Holy Spirit, a dialogue of *agapē*, of love. The intimate trust in the Father which Jesus expresses in sayings recorded in the Synoptic tradition is translated by John, very reasonably, into the language of shared knowledge and love; this may even reflect an esoteric teaching given discreetly by Jesus to the inner circle of his disciples. Jesus' tender, yet unbreakable, confidence in the Father—found most poignantly in Luke's record of his dying prayer on the cross, "Father into your hands I commend my spirit" (24:46: the Jewish child's night prayer)—has as its necessary precondition the loving knowledge of the Father claimed by the Christ of John. Similarly, the self-giving obedience to the Father's will shown by the Jesus of the Synoptics, that sense of "Thy will be done" contained in the little Greek word *dei* (it must be so), John renders in an idiom of total surrender and receptivity by Son to Father.

Should these words not be the very words of Jesus, they are not for all that a theological imposition. Rather are they an elucidation, a drawing out of what was tacit in what was said: the *ipsissima vox* within the *ipsissima verba* of the Lord. Only a really ripe reflection could enable the immediate disciples to grasp the mystery of Jesus' identity (which they sensed from the first in his presence) in its full implications. As the English Benedictine theologian B. C. Butler wrote, the actual Jesus of history may well have been more Johannine than appears in the Synoptic tradition.[2] We understand, often, only in retrospect.

Verba or *vox*, the Son enjoys his unique relation of knowledge and love with the Father because he is the perfect recipient of the Father's own self-giving goodness. He is the one mirror in which this goodness is not distorted.

The *Homoousion* of the Son

These reflections on New Testament Christology bring us within reach of the epoch-making teaching of the Council of Nicaea (325) that the Father and the Son are *homoousion*, "of the same being." The Creed produced by that council, which eventually commanded and unified the mind of the Church, secured the gospel against distortions, grounding the Church unambiguously in the self-revelation of the Father through Jesus Christ his Son and in one Spirit (whose own divinity would not, however, be effectively confessed until the Council

2. B. C. Butler, *An Approach to Christianity* (London, 1981) 180–213.

of Constantinople, in 381). All were agreed that the Father is the source, *archē, fons et origo,* of the divinity: it is to the Father that the Son is turned, in the most complete obedience and receptivity. But—and here was the clarified perception of Nicene orthodoxy, owing so much, as it did, to Athanasius—so total is this receptivity on the Son's part that he must be the fullness of the Father's life, as received and exercised. For many, it took a long time to grasp the difference between, on the one hand, subordination, inferiority, or even, as in the Alexandrian heresiarch Arius, the merely creaturely mediation of further creation— views of the Son that the Church finally rejected—and on the other hand, sheerest receptivity. Jesus can be the bearer in history of the good news of the Father and his kingdom because in eternity the Son is the recipient of the Father's total self-gift. Were this not so, the Son could not divinize us; he could not bring us salvation. This concern for the reality of salvation prompted Athanasius's defense of the Son's divinity in his treatise *On the Synods:*

> Since he is the deifying and enlightening power of the Father, in whom all things are deified and quickened, he is not alien in essence from the Father, but coessential. For by partaking of him we partake of the Father; and that because the Word is the Father's own. Whereas if he were himself also divine by participation, rather than receiving from the Father his essential Godhead and imagehood, then he would not deify—for he would be one of those things that are deified. It is impossible that he who merely possesses by participation should impart of that partaking to others, since what he has is not his own but the Giver's.[3]

Father and Son define each other in coeternal deity. As Son, Jesus exists solely from the Godness of the Father. He is, as the Nicene-Constantinopolitan Creed puts it, "God from God, Light from Light." The intrinsic generosity of the divine nature comes to fruition in and as Father and Son, differentiating itself in a movement whereby each possesses in fullness the being, *ousia,* of God. "As soon as one understands the divine *ousia* as self-giving love, one perceives something of the Father and the Son. Total love giving itself, yearning for an object to be given to, for a subject in which to inhere: this is the Father. Total love received, given, expressed and therefore expressive: this is the Son."[4]

---

3. Athanasius, *On the Synods* 51.
4. G. H. Tavard, *The Vision of the Trinity* (Washington, D.C., 1981) 69.

In the light of the *homoousion* it is possible to see what is truly distinctive in the New Testament knowledge of God. By contrast with Judaism and its stress on the unnameability of God, the Christian faith is concerned with God as he has named himself in Jesus Christ, incarnating in him his own Word, so that in Christ we know God as he is in his own inner being. The incarnate Word is the principle of all revealed knowledge of God, of what he has done and continues to do in the universe, as understood by faith.

The effect of this is to redraw, in the first place, the outlines of a doctrine of God, "Creator of all things, visible and invisible." The Fatherhood of God, revealed in the Son, determines how we are to understand God as the almighty Creator (not the other way round). It is because God is inherently productive in his own being that he is also the Creator. God is the ultimate fountain of being only as he is, from all eternity, the Father of the Son.

In the second place, the Nicene doctrine also speaks of Christ himself. Athanasius brought this teaching to its sharpest focus in his account of Christ as the incarnate correlate of that ultimate origin that God is in his triune being as Creator. The Lord's humanity taken from the Virgin Mary is the "economic" or salvation-historical form which the divine Origin has assumed in the personal stooping down of the eternal Son, as he enters creation, to actualize within it the providential activity of the almighty Father. While the Arians appealed to Proverbs 8:22 in its Greek translation, "the Lord created me a beginning of his ways for his works," in order to justify their view of the Son as the creaturely instrument of the rest of creation, Athanasius used the same text to serve his teaching that, in his human nature, Jesus was created as the new foundation for God's providential and redemptive operations toward us. The Son, through whom all creatures are made, deliberately became man "in the form of a servant" (Phil 2:7) so as to carry out God's saving and renewing work in our regard. Christ is thus the basis of a new beginning in the creation and the archetypal pattern of God's gracious provision for it. If the Arians searched the Scriptures for any and every passage indicating the creatureliness, human weakness, mortality and subordinate, indeed, servile, condition of Jesus, all in complete contrast to the transcendent Godhead of the Father, Athanasius took the same texts in order to show that it was precisely in this condition of a servant that the everlasting Son came among us, becoming one of us, and one with us, so as to be our Savior. Thus Athanasius was able to articulate simultaneously two truths about the

Son. First, in his humanity he is the creaturely form that the divine saving economy has taken among us: the way that leads human beings to the Father. Second, in his divinity, as the divine principle in this creaturely economic form, he is the Head of all creation, the principle in whose terms we are to understand all the works of God.

Homoousion is then, rightly, one of the key terms and crucial proclamations of Catholicism, vital to the Creed which, Sunday by Sunday at the Eucharistic assembly, all Catholic Christians profess. In its insistence that, though eternally distinct, the Father and the Son are the same being, it rules out at once unitarianism and polytheism (and their moderated patristic versions, Sabellianism and Arianism). Furthermore, since what God is in himself, and what he is in the incarnate Son are one and the same, God is identical with the content of his own revelation, and so we have access to the Father through the Son (and, as the Council of Constantinople will add, in its tacit affirmation of a second, pneumatological *homoousion*, "in the Spirit"). The *homoousion* guards the great truth that, in the incarnation, the everlasting, transcendent God has revealed his own self to us, and is, indeed, fully identical with that self-revelation in Christ. The gospel could not be the gospel without this affirmation. There is no unknown God behind Jesus Christ, but only he who has made himself known in the Son's incarnate person as he who is. Nor is this simply a matter of the revelation of the being of God. The actions of Jesus Christ are thus recognized as really and truly divine activity. Only if the actions of Jesus Christ are God's own acts "for us men and for our salvation," do they possess absolute finality and ultimate validity for all human beings. For such attributes belong necessarily to actions which only the Creator of the world can perform.

The *Homoousion* of the Spirit

What place in this dialogue of love should be given to the Spirit? In the Hebrew Bible, and in the later Wisdom literature, there is already talk of the Spirit of the Lord, the Creator Spirit who gives life and breath to all that lives, yet remains gloriously above the whole development of nature and guides it. The same Spirit is said to animate every human being—both in his or her ensouledness, as a living being, in this created order, and in the future life, that of the glorified soul, the risen body—and also to empower particular individuals in more spectacular ways, as with the judges, or the prophets, called as they were to fulfill high-profile roles among the Israelite people of God. The specifically Christian doctrine of the Holy Spirit, however, as with the entire doctrine of God, must await the era of the New Testament. If it was the Son of God who became incarnate (not the Father, not the Spirit), it is only through the Son that we have knowledge of the Spirit, as of the Father. Our understanding in faith of the Holy Spirit must be controlled, therefore, by our knowledge of the Son.

During Jesus' ministry, the Spirit is the power of the Father's presence overflowing from Jesus to others. The largest number of New Testament references to the Holy Spirit fall, however, in the period of the resurrection and ascension, the immediate prelude to the time of the Church, when the dialogue of love between visible Son and invisible Father will no longer be conducted on the earth's surface, in our space and time. For both Paul and John it is the Holy Spirit who carries forward the dialogue of Father and Son so as to incorporate within it the disciples of Jesus, the Father's adopted sons and daughters. In the Fourth Gospel, Jesus speaks of the Holy Spirit, the Paraclete, as the Creator of communion between the Son and his disciples, and between the Son and the Father. In the Pauline letters, the Spirit gives the Church all those gifts that Christ willed for his community—not only charismatic and hierarchical gifts, impulses to prophesy and preach, but also the more fundamental realities of the new covenant: wisdom and holiness, charity, new life, and new freedom both here and hereafter. Above all (and here Paul shares the Johannine understanding), the Spirit makes us children of God (Rom 8:12-17; Gal 4:6), enabling us to stand in the Son's own relation to the Father.

> Those who are bearers of the Spirit of God are led to the Word (that is, to the Son) but the Son takes them and presents them to the Father, and the Father confers incorruptibility. So without the Spirit there is no seeing the Word of God, and without the Son there is no approaching the Father. For the Son is knowledge of the Father, and knowledge of the Son is through the Holy Spirit. But the Son, according to the Father's good pleasure, administers the Spirit charismatically, as the Father wills, to those whom he wills.[5]

The last five clauses of the Nicene-Constantinopolitan Creed depended originally on the affirmation of belief in the Holy Spirit. They describe the Holy Spirit in action. First he fills the Church which be-

---

5. Irenaeus, *Demonstration of the Apostolic Preaching* 7.

comes therefore one, holy, and Catholic, and is preserved in the apostolic preaching. Second, he gives efficacy and power to the sacraments which, accordingly, become ways in which we commune with "holy realities," the *communio sanctorum*. Third, he bestows justifying grace: entry into God's covenant in Christ with humanity, thanks to baptism (what the Creed calls the "forgiveness of sins"). Fourth, he guarantees full personal immortality ("the resurrection of the body"). Fifth, he also gives his warrant to eternal life, an abiding share in the divine life itself ("life everlasting"). Thus the sanctification lost in Adam and regained in Christ consists in recovering our conformity with the Son and Father through the Holy Spirit.

> [The Son] truly bestows the Holy Spirit on the souls of believers, sending him to dwell there, and, through him and in him reforms them to their pristine condition—namely, into himself, into his likeness through sanctification. And so in this way he calls us back to the archetype of the image, namely the "character" of the Father. For that character, expressive of a true and perfect likeness, is the Son. But the pure and natural likeness of the Son is the Spirit to whom we also being configured by sanctification are refigured into the very form of God.[6]

Owing to the unity of action of Word and Spirit in the work of redemption, it is not surprising that in the earliest centuries the doctrine of the Spirit remained comparatively undeveloped. But this situation could not last. Once again, as the First Council of Constantinople made clear in its confession of the divinity of the Spirit, the extender of the love-relation of Father and Son to others must himself belong to the realm of the uncreated. In any case, even for the Old Testament, God's Word and Spirit are presented as not less than God, though, admittedly, they are not yet seen as in relation to God, while in the New Testament, just as God's Word is related to God as Son to Father, so the Holy Spirit is presented as being from the Father, and from the Son. We can say that, as Jesus' sending by the Father and his prayer to the Father disclose economically his eternal relation to the Father, so the Spirit's sending by Father and Son and the prayer he prays in us (Rom 8:26ff.) reveal his eternal relationship to Father and Son. Though the New Testament speaks of the Holy Spirit in personal terms—he is the "other Paraclete" of John 14–16—and his divinity seems taken for granted (1 Cor 2:10-11; 3:16), it took the Pneumatomachian (Spirit-

---

6. Cyril of Alexandria, *Dialogues on the Trinity* 7.

slaying) heresy of the patristic period to irritate the Church into producing the pearl of this doctrine.

Athanasius, having already appealed in the course of his defense of the Son's divinity to what an agent of divine salvation must be, made the same move, in relation to both salvation and creation, on behalf of the Holy Spirit.

> Since all has come to be through the Word, you rightly think that the Son is no creature. Now is it not a blasphemy, then, that you describe as a creature the Spirit in whom the Father, by the Word, consummates and renews all things? . . . He who unites the creature to the Word cannot himself be numbered among creatures; he who confers filiation by adoption cannot be a stranger to the Son. . . . Just as the grace accorded [us] comes from the Father by the Son, so there can be no communion in that gift on our part except in the Holy Spirit: it is through participation in him that we have the charity of the Father, the grace of the Son and the communion of the Spirit himself.[7]

So the Holy Spirit, like the Son, must be from the being of God—a being now enriched by its passage (as it were; no time is involved) to self-affirmation as Father and Son, and so self-enabled to express itself indefinitely further, in creation and redemption. For the divine works of creation and redemption, though deriving from the being and will of the whole Trinity, do so by originating from the Father, being mediated through the Son, and fully achieved only in the Holy Spirit.

As the One who completes the work of salvation, the Holy Spirit is the vital principle of the people of God, the soul of the Church. He is the eschatological power which impels the Church, and through her all history, towards the fulfillment of the creation.

This does not mean, however, that the Spirit is a corporatist power, indifferent to individual persons. Augustine, who most stressed that the Holy Spirit is appropriately given as God's most intimate self-communication to his redeemed people (since it is his role in the Holy Trinity to be the gift of Father and Son to each other), also found in the constitution of each individual human person an analogy for the triune God. There are, Augustine thought, only two fundamental acts of spiritual existence: knowledge and love; it is the latter that we must associate with the Spirit if he truly is in his hypostatic being the mutual love of Father and Son. Just as the Creator Spirit crowns the divine act of our creation by bringing us into existence as possible centers of lov-

---

7. Athanasius, *Letters to Serapion* 1.23, 25, 28.

ing responsiveness to the Father, so our redemption is the actualization of this possibility, thanks to the "second gift" of that Spirit, his filling us with grace as the Spirit of the Son.

In the theology of the Western Church, reflection on the person of the Spirit has carried down the ages the insight that the primary model for our understanding of the Holy Trinity and its action must be caritative, a sustained reference to the pattern of love. The Spirit is God's "bond of love," *vinculum amoris*, the love of the Father resting on the Son, and at once returned by him to the Father and turned outwards, for the sake of those who will be sons and daughters in the Son, *filii in Filio*. Father, Son, and Holy Spirit are love originated, love received, and love in action, the everlasting self-differentiation of the God of love. Wherever the writings of Augustine were treasured, this was not forgotten—as for instance in the twelfth-century Scottish theologian and mystic Richard of St. Victor.

For Richard, the Trinitarian persons are *amans, dilectus,* and *co-dilectus,* the lover, the beloved, and the co-beloved. Richard sees the *dilectio,* love, which the Father is, as given to a *dilectus,* or well-beloved, the Son. Since it cannot rest on him without ceasing to give itself, it also flows into a *co-dilectus,* who is loved in common by Father and Son, and constitutes love's channel to the human beings who receive the God of revelation by faith. The relation between love given (the Father) and love received (the Son) is eternally fruitful, its fruitfulness consisting in a new personal life, the Spirit, bearing the same fruitfulness forward into the world.

The Holy Spirit, then, has his being from the Father. But the form of that being is shaped by the relation of the Father and the Son. The self-giving of the Father and the receptivity of the Son condition the existence of the Spirit, and stamp his activity towards ourselves with its characteristic hallmarks, namely, the power to recreate love where it has died or become sterile (charity) and the ability to respond to this recreative power set liberatingly within our minds and hearts (faith) and to persevere in so doing (hope). The Spirit of the Father rests on the Son, as the Greek Fathers insist; but the Father is who he is only as Father-of-the-Son, and so the Spirit is who he is through the Son, or even, as the Latin Fathers affirm, from the Son. Theologians and philosophers, mystics and poets may, from time to time, try out other vocabularies for the being of the triune God, but the language of love, based on the New Testament, sums up their deepest common conviction. The vocabulary of theological ontology, found in the dogmatic definition of Trinitarian belief, is there to guard this more "familiar" (indeed nuptial) language of the Church's inner life as bride of Christ.

One Being in Three Persons

The vocabulary of *ousia* (being) and *hypostasis* (person) in which the dogma of the triune God is couched sometimes arouses objections on account of its Hellenic, philosophical origin. But these terms underwent a semantic shift as the Church turned them to her use. They must be understood in the light of the gospel to whose service they were pressed. They now express the truth that God is, in the internal relations of his transcendent being, the very same Father, Son, and Holy Spirit which he shows himself to be in his revealing and saving activity in space and time. *Ousia* (what the triune persons share) now refers to being not simply as that which is, but to what it is in respect of its internal reality, while *hypostasis* (that reality, three of which possess the divine *ousia*) refers to being not just in its independent subsistence but in its objective distinctiveness too. In the Church's teaching, moreover, these terms have an essentially personal meaning: the "of the same being" of Father, Son, and Spirit, refers to personal relations within the one being of God. The three are consubstantial, yet distinct from one another—indeed, hypostatically so. The great Doctors of the Cappadocian Church of the fourth century—Basil, Gregory Nazianzen, and Gregory of Nyssa—stressed the irreducibility of the hypostatic order to that of essence. God as personal being may exceed his own nature. The hypostatic existence of Father, Son, and Holy Spirit admits the possibility of divine actions in which God might freely assume (for instance) a fully human existence while remaining God (i.e., One whose nature remains completely transcendent). At the same time the essential eloquence and dynamism of the divine being, as revealed in the processions from the Father of Son and Spirit, made it possible for Athanasius to speak of the totally interpenetrating or co-indwelling character of the persons' relations, later called the doctrine of the divine circumincession or coinherence.

The application of the term *person* here deserves special mention. *What* are the three who are involved in the circumincession of mutual love and knowledge in the divine Trinity? We know *who* they are: Father, Son, and Spirit, but what is the genre of being to whom these three possessors of the single divine reality belong? The classic answer of the Fathers, East and West, *persons*, and if we ask what a *person* might be in this unique context, we shall find no better answer than that of Thomas Aquinas: subsistent relationship. The term is coined for its transcendent object, but it remains rooted in the finite realm, in our own experience.

For ourselves too our relationships are, to a degree, constitutive of who we are. There can of course be no functioning human mind in this world without a biological substrate of body, especially of brain. And bodies are individual. Nor could I speak of "my own relationships" unless the mind is individual also. Nevertheless, the laws of subjectivity are neither material nor simply mental, and, by their *Diktat*, I can only become more myself by allowing myself to be constituted by another. This is the seeming paradox of all human love. In Shakespeare's words:

> So they lov'd, as love in twain
> Had the essence but in one;
> Two distincts, division none;
> Number there in love was slain.[8]

We can distinguish, then, between individuality and personhood. In us, personhood requires individual existence as its base. However, to be a person is not to be an isolated monad but, on the contrary, to find oneself increasingly defined by others. Augustine had already seen this. Persons are *ad invicem*, "turned towards one another," not *ad semetipsum*, "turned toward self." When Aquinas refers to the Trinity as subsistent relationship, he means that in Father, Son, and Spirit this process of becoming constituted in what one is by the relationships one has reaches its full term; or, rather, this process in human beings has its source and archetype in God. What in us is a process or series of intermittent events, is in them an archetypal and eternal event.

In their case there is no individuality, no way of specifying the persons which does not consist in pointing to a relationship. The Son points with all he is to the Father. He exists within this pointing, itself eternally expressed by the Spirit, the bond of the love of Father and Son and the channel of its outflow.

Augustine's ruminations on the divine image in the human being are intended to throw light on this uncreated mystery by drawing our attention to a created case where a triad of vital processes are mutually self-implicating. When the human mind activates the self-presence of

8. W. Shakespeare, *The Phoenix and the Turtle.*

the person and, in Augustine's term, "remembers" itself, this act of self-minding (to use a Scottish speech-form) generates a mental word of self-understanding whereby I say explicitly "me"—from which intimately conjoined acts there issues a third that unites both in a novel fashion as the person affirms or wills the "self" he or she remembers and understands.

Yet no monadic individual can represent the fruitfulness of the divine One, and in book 14 of *De Trinitate* Augustine accordingly allows his own analogy to crumble. The truth of self-memory, self-understanding, and self-love cannot be had till all these acts are referred to God, for the self is grounded in God who is "interior intimo meo." In the template of Augustine's teaching, the schema of Bible and Fathers, the only proper way for an image to find its exemplar is to realize its likeness. By letting these acts be self-directed, indeed, every person falls, defacing the Godly image. The true self is ever open to God. By closing itself to God, the "I" centered on its own ego loses its real self-possession, all its coherence, and tumbles downwards and outwards, scattering itself in fragments. The one-in-three of human personality cannot be redeemed without the saving, historical intervention of the divine one-in-three of whose mystery its own constitution is a faint echo.

> The remedy for this state of affairs is the divine missions, and particularly the sending of the Son in the flesh. For as man fell and the image was fragmented by downward and outward movement from the inner and upper citadel of the mind to the outer and lower reaches of the senses and their appetites, so he can only be raised up, and the image restored, by a reverse movement inward and upward; the restoration must start with the flesh. It must start with the humiliation, to the spiritual mind (the Platonist in Augustine felt this far more keenly than we may do), of having to believe in the flesh of Christ, in the incarnation of the eternal Word, and his death on the Cross.[9]

The Eternal Trinity in Time

The nexus of the Trinitarian relationships is known to us because, in history, it was projected in and through the concrete circumstances of the life of Jesus of Nazareth, the Spirit-anointed humanity assumed by the Son. More especially, it is the crucifixion, as the sign par excellence of these relations, that we hail as the supreme icon of the Holy Trinity.

9. E. Hill, "Introduction," in *The Works of St. Augustine*, vol. 1.5, *The Trinity* (Brooklyn, N.Y., 1990) 55.

The suffering love of the Son on Calvary expresses in time the eternal self-giving which is God. Though the cross is the distinctive love-act of the Son, the whole Trinity was there engaged. The Calvary drama's protagonist was the God who, one in essence, is the Father who sends the Son to experience the passion and the Spirit to inspire and sustain that onerous offering. The cross is God's tree. The poet G. M. Hopkins wrote in a notebook: "This sacrifice . . . is a consequence and shadow of the procession of the Trinity, from which mystery sacrifice takes its rise."[10] On the cross, the Son makes the Father present as love and mercy. The Father is seen in him, as he manifests himself as Son. But Christ offered himself to the Father, remarks the author of the Letter to the Hebrews, "through the eternal Spirit" (9:13). Proceeding from the Father, the Spirit directs towards the Father the sacrifice of the Son. He consumes the sacrifice with the fire of the love that unites Father and Son in the communion of the Trinity. It was, surely, by contemplation of the cross as for this reason glorious that John could sum up the Christian faith in the simplest of all creeds, "God is love" (1 John 4:8b).

By taking us through flesh-and-blood history into the mystery of God, and then back out again into time, the story of Jesus gives us not only our key to the deity, but also our project for living, our social program. The Trinitarian God disclosed in that story is the archetype of that charity, or self-giving love, which, in classical Christian ethics, must in some way inform all virtues. Even in such matters as politics, therefore, contemplation of the God of love always precedes action, if action is to be Christian and gracious, and not exhaust itself in a vain attempt to wrest transfiguration from a barren earth. The triune God of love is not only our goal in eternity. He is also our banner in time. He is both the mystical heart of Christian experience and faith's agendum for the transformation of this world.

This brings us to the deepest aspect of our relationship to the Trinity: its "inhabitation" in us. "The complete Trinity dwells in us, the whole of that mystery which will be our vision in heaven. Let that be our cloister. . . . Throughout the whole day, let us deliver ourselves to Love: by doing the will of God, in his regard, with him, in him, for him alone."[11] To the question, What is being lived out in me? the Catholic Christian replies by, first, acknowledging the Father as the source of

---

10. C. Devlin, ed., *The Sermons and Devotional Writings of Gerard Manley Hopkins* (London, 1959) 197.

11. *Ecrits spirituels d'Elisabeth de la Trinité, présentés par le R. P. Philippon, O.P.* (Paris, 1949) 41.

one's Christian life; second, recognizing in hope that the pattern of one's life is the life and death of the Son incarnate, who attained his victorious resurrection through the Father's good pleasure; and third, affirming—and here lies the final wisdom—that, thanks to the gift of the Spirit, the origin and destiny of one's life is the God who is love.

> For the souls delivered to his action in their very depths, the mystical death of which St. Paul speaks . . . becomes so simple, so sweet. They think much less of the work of destruction still left to them as of plunging into the *foyer* of the love which burns in them and is none other than the Holy Spirit—that same love which, in the Trinity, is the bond between the Father and his Word. . . . They live, in St. John's words, "in society" with the three adorable persons. Their life is common, and that is what the contemplative life is.[12]

If such words of Elizabeth of the Trinity flow from a life of Christian discipleship at its most mystically intense, what they express is shared in lowlier ways by all the redeemed. The Trinitarian economy means that, thanks to the advent of the divine persons, we are being radically changed. Their presence to us (through baptism) is prior to any conscious psychological act we may perform, yet that presence is for the sake of our psychological transformation (for our consciousness is our existence at a higher pitch of the perfection of being). To say we are sharing in the life of the Trinity must mean that we begin to transcend the limitations endemic to our human way of knowing and loving, and it is through this transforming effect of the divine indwelling that we have access to the Trinitarian persons themselves. The Holy Trinity is the inversion, and the cure, of our corrupted consciousness, for it is at once both perfect self-knowledge and self-affection, and perfect mutual knowledge and mutual affection. All creatures are known and loved by the triune God; it is the special privilege of Christians that such love-knowledge is reciprocated by a conscious share in the life of the Trinity and the hope for a consummation of that sharing in the age to come.

The associative thinking called "appropriation" helps us to reflect about what those persons are, and what they have done for us. Most importantly, it has been the common teaching of the Church's theologians since the eighteenth century that each of the divine persons takes possession of the justified according to their personal properties. Thus,

---

12. Ibid., 192.

for instance, the Holy Spirit enters the lives of human beings, in the post-Pentecost economy, only *for* the Son and the Father: therein lies the deepest reason why his grace-union with humankind, unlike that of the Son, is not hypostatic.

A Trinitarian Monotheism

Yet for all the richness of the Church's doctrinal vision of the divine threefoldness, the faith of the Catholic Church remains a monotheism in the line of Judaism and even Islam. All in God is one save that which is indicated by the relations of opposition which define the persons. As the *Quicunque vult*, a Western patristic creed later ascribed to Athanasius, has it:

> Thus the Father is God, the Son is God, the Holy Spirit is God; and yet there are not three Gods, but there is one God. Thus the Father is Lord, the Son is Lord, the Holy Spirit is Lord; and yet there are not three Lords, but there is one Lord. Because just as we are obliged by Christian truth to acknowledge each person separately both God and Lord, so we are forbidden by the Catholic religion to speak of three Gods or Lords.[13]

Whether we are thinking of the divine nature (or essence), or of the unbreakable communion of the persons in their reciprocal relations which mirrors the unicity of the nature on the hypostatic level, or finally of the role of the Holy Spirit as bond of unity between the Father and the Son (which reflects, in terms of the origins of the persons, both the nature the persons embody and the communion of life they share), oneness is as typical of the Godhead as is triadicity. The *Quicunque vult* concludes resoundingly, therefore: "In all things . . . both Trinity in Unity and Unity in Trinity must be worshipped. So the one who desires to be saved should think thus of the Trinity,"[14] for salvation would be incomplete without the immersion of human thought in saving truth. In this "most simple and sublime . . . most devotional formulary to which Christianity has given birth," so Newman thought, "we warn first ourselves, then each other, and then all those who are within its hearing, and the hearing of the Truth, who our God is, and how we must worship him, and how vast our responsibility will be, if we know what to believe, and yet believe not."[15] And the unity toward

---

13. DH 75.
14. Ibid.
15. J. H. Newman, *Essay in Aid of a Grammar of Assent* (Westminster, Md., 1973) 133.

which concern for the divine oneness presses us is not only, as the Augustinian theologoumenon of the triune image might have it, the unity of the individual human person. It is also as the entire Catholic tradition testifies, that of the human continuum at large. The Catholic sense of the urgency of the task of uniting all human beings, all the world, is bound up with the unity of God. "Do we not have one God and one Christ and one Spirit of grace poured out upon us, one calling in Christ?"[16]

Such considerations bring us by a natural progression to the topics of the next chapters: salvation and the Church. For these can hardly be described without allusion to that divine hallmark which is unity—a point urged persuasively yet in vain by Cardinal du Perron on that sovereign representative of early Stuart Anglicanism, the wise and foolish James VI and I:

> God of his inestimable bounty and incomprehensible wisdom has vouchsafed to watch over us and to prepare and direct us even in this life towards that eternal happiness that it has pleased him to promise us and reserve for us in the other; and to this end he has chosen the method which best corresponds with the excellency and dignity of his nature. And since he is one, the principal of all unity, and even unity itself, instead of saving us by so many distinct and separate ways, he has obliged us to embrace the means of our salvation and its conditions in unity. "He is one," said St. Augustine *(In Psalmos 101),* "the Church is unity, nothing corresponds to the one save unity." That is, he was not content to win us and possess us separately as so many scattered and dispersed individuals, but willed that by the terms of that same covenant between him and ourselves we should be bound up together in a common society, to constitute, under the authority of his name, a sort of spiritual body, and a form of Estate and Republic. Jesus died, said St. John, "not only for the nation, but to gather together in one the children of God, that were dispersed" (John 11:52).[17]

---

16. *1 Clement* 46.6.

17. J.-D. Duperron, *Réplique à la Response du Sérenissime Roy de la Grande Bretagne* (1620) preface, cited in H. de Lubac, S.J., *Catholicism: Christ and the Common Destiny of Man* (London, 1952) 235–36.

6

The Nature of Salvation

The context of the salvific process is the outreach of the triune God in creation and providence—God's original making of the world, and his continued sustaining and guiding of it.

Creation and Providence

In creating, God constitutes what is on the basis of what is not, thus establishing the reality of the world *ex nihilo,* "from nothing." This doctrine, given earliest expression in the Second Book of Maccabees (7:28), was taken as foundational by Christians. Their conversion to an understanding of creation as "out of nothing" was not unconnected with their proclamation of Christ's resurrection. In that stupendous event, God's unconditional power over life and death, being and non-being, had been exhibited in a way no one could overlook. But as we saw in the opening chapter of this book, the all-creative Word of God does not merely distinguish and separate the created from the uncreated. He also produces community and continuity between them. Since creation comes into being through God's word it never withdraws beyond the range of that Word; indeed, it remains ever open to him.

An abyss of difference separates creatures from the Creator, and yet creature and Creator are intimately co-present. This is the mystery of the contingency of all created being. The universe is not self-supporting, but neither is it mere appearance. The ontological grounding of the world takes place beyond the world, in God, and yet the world's reality, order and measure is truly its own, received from the Source of all, and sustained by that Source's Word and Spirit. Just as the single divine nature belongs to the Trinitarian persons according to a certain *taxis, ordo,* "order," so likewise the creative power of the one God is exercised in a fashion appropriate to each of the divine three.

Ultimately, the meaning and truth of the world lie in the Father, Son, and Spirit who originate, undergird, and nurture it by their divine activity. To do justice to this doctrine, we must move beyond both a deistic theism, which would see the world as separated from God, and a panentheism, which would see it straightforwardly as "in" him, to an understanding of the world as, in its very difference from God, embraced within the powerful presence of that creative Word and Spirit. Our createdness is as it were the 'place' which related us to him, because it is the place where he, differing from his creatures in his power as Lord and Creator, loves his creatures and enfolds them in his grace.[1] The createdness of beings, considered as their gift of sharing in the limitless being of the Creator, conjoins eternity and time. Eternity gives rise to time; from it time ceaselessly flows; eternity bestows on time its meaning. The whole order of time—creation as temporal—receives being through the eternal act which is God.

Providence is creation continued. The Old Testament people who founded the biblical doctrine of creation saw the world as a thing in jeopardy, and so in constant need of deliverance by the Creator's power. Through his efficacious will, the personal Lord was close to creation. So his conserving causality could not be sundered from his personal purpose.

The doctrine of providence does not for all that deny some role to chance and necessity in the story of the cosmos. Providence, we can say, incorporates and masters both. When things occur "by chance," owing to the failure of some cause or its prevention by another, such irregular chains of causal agency depend quite as much on the first cause for their existence as do any other. On the other hand, what is fate save the operation of some predetermining *intermediary* cause? Fate is not so primordial a factor as to fall outside the scheme of providence.

Whatever words the text of the world may contain, providence encompasses them all. Yet this is not to say that providence can be "read off" from the way the world goes. Far from it: nature and history show ugly faces which the great theodicists, from the Attic tragedians to Dostoevsky, have contemplated in fear and pity. Supernatural revelation, a word in history from the God of all things, must address at least this, if not only this.

Scripture regards creation as the beginning of God's history with humankind, as the understanding heart of the sentient creation.

1. R. Guardini, *Freedom, Grace, and Destiny: Three Chapters in the Interpretation of Existence* (London, 1961) 119–43.

Congruently, it treats historically God's solicitude for the world he has made. The purpose of God's dispositions is his kingdom, that sweet rule over creatures which manifests his own divine triunity. The careful action whereby the primal liberty of God causally directs the historical process is signalled in the miracles that attend Israel throughout history (Job 10:14; 1 Sam 3:11; 2 Kgs 21:12; Jer 19:3). Old Testament writers deal with evil as divine punishment for sin, and an instrument for instructing and purifying humankind, yet they also look forward to an apocalyptic annihilation of evil at the world's consummation (Amos 2:16; Isa 2:20; Mic 2:4)—increasingly so as the Jewish canon approaches its closure in *Sturm und Drang*.

The protology of the New Testament (its account of the foundational beginnings of cosmos and so of history) in no way overthrows the wisdom of Israel. For the Gospels, too, God's dominion over creation is, first and foremost, his fatherly care (Matt 5:45). The "primordial"—the original order of creation—retains its archetypal authority for the present, as the evangelical prohibition on divorce makes clear. And yet with Jesus Christ a supreme novelty enters the Judaic picture. What comes first can no longer be depicted without painting in the revealer of the Father's purpose from the beginning. The risen Lord exhibits the goal to which the world was always ordered, embodying time's end before time's termination. And if, to change the metaphor, the finale has thus identified the overture's true leitmotif, we also have the key to the score's intervening pages. In the cool, clear idiom of Christian Scholasticism, Jesus Christ is creation's exemplar, its final purpose, and its moving cause. Nor is this mediaeval eisegesis but rather a restatement, descriptively, of the truth once given by the New Testament authors doxologically (as prayer and praise).

> He is the image of the invisible God, the first-born of all creatures; for in him all things were created in heaven and on earth, visible and invisible, whether thrones or dominions or principalities or authorities—all things were created through him and for him. He is before all things, and in him all things hold together. He is the head of the body, the Church; he is the beginning, the first-born from the dead, that in everything he might be pre-eminent. For in him all the fullness of God was pleased to dwell, and through him to reconcile to himself all things, whether on earth or in heaven, making peace by the blood of his Cross (Col 1:15-20).

The One who is the revelation, from the beginning, of creation's goal in God is also its consummation, in the anticipated ending of the first

Easter, and therefore the instrument, in the in-between time of human history, of all the purposive coherence it possesses.

We shall return to this topic when we consider the setting of redemption in the cosmos—both material and spiritual—in chapter 11.

The Need for Redemption

So much for creation, as reconceived through revelation in Christ. The substance of our topic—the nature of salvation—concerns, rather, that revelation's departure point, God's redeeming act whereby through Jesus Christ he delivered humankind from the evil of sin, reuniting it graciously with himself. Here once again the Old Testament prepared the way. God aroused in his people the hope for a Messiah, thus disposing them to expect a future, definitive saving intervention, changing the terms on which the historical process unfolds, and intersects with eternity. Types and foreshadowings accumulated as he freed them from Egyptian slavery (Exod 19:5-6), established the Davidide monarchy (2 Sam 7:8-16), sent them prophets (2 Kgs 17:13), and brought them back from captivity in Babylon (Isa 40:1-11). This hope became more focused as the divine promise took on clearer outline, first in the covenant with Abraham (Gen 12:1-3), then in its successor, the covenant with David (2 Sam 7:6-17), and the announcement of a new covenant to exceed them both (Jer 31:31-34), and finally in prediction about a mysterious Servant of YHWH, whose sufferings would remove sin (Isa 52:13–53:12), and the vision of a "Son of Man" who would inaugurate in history the universal kingdom of God (Dan 7:14). At the same time awareness grew of the transcendence of God who can act at all times and everywhere since he is not confined by time and space. In his eternity he is beyond the perishable world of time (Lam 5:17-20; Ps 90:1-3); in his immensity he transcends all limitations of place (1 Kgs 8:27; Ps 139:8-10). And since his Spirit contains all things (Wis 1:7) and his Wisdom orders all things (Wis 9:1), he can be our Savior no matter how radical our need.

The doctrine of the incarnation discloses that the world was indeed so precariously situated that God the Son had to unite it to himself in order to save it. Human beings, brought from non-existence to existence by the gift of God, naturally waste away when they turn from God. By destroying the relationship of creature with the Creator sin destroys the creature itself. Through sin we are wounded, psychically, bodily, and spiritually, and the world is in our persons (but not only there) despoiled. The incarnation reveals that human creatures had become infected by a deep corruption exceeding the corruptibility of natural existence, a corruption that worked for their utter ruin. Not only were they perishable, they were also affected by the evil that divine judgment must inevitably oppose, and that only God's own atoning and redeeming activity can overcome. The novelist George Bernanos wrote in his *Le crépuscule des vieux:*

> Here you have this child in its cradle, all grace and innocence, fresh and clear as a running brook, new like the spring, and sincere as the light of morning. Its little life leaps on its way, with such purity and candor. Who is it then—who, I ask you—that works away inside it with so sinister a care and clairvoyance, with the precision of a surgeon who knows where to put his scissors and forceps in order to reach the most delicate nerves, day by day, and hour by hour, until twenty or thirty years later you find this radical little creature transformed into an anxious and solitary animal—envious, jealous, avaricious—eaten up alive by the absurd hatred of itself, and choosing the terrible and sterile pleasure that destroys it in preference to joy and freedom and all the good things of the earth?[2]

The metaphysical implications of this condition, centering on the radical need for the restorative grace of God, are brought out by Thomas Aquinas in his treatise on sin and grace in the *Summa theologiae.*

> For someone to rise up from sin is to be restored to those things that were lost by sinning. Now we incur a threefold harm by sinning: a stain, the corruption of natural goodness, and the debt of punishment. We incur a stain in that the disorder of sin drives out the beauty of grace. The good of nature is corrupted, because our nature becomes disordered when our will is not subject to God; when this order is destroyed, it follows that the whole human nature of the sinner remains disordered. By the debt of punishment the one who sins mortally deserves eternal damnation.

Aquinas goes on, by way of indicating the divine agenda in the work of our redemption:

> It is clear that only by God can each of these be repaired. Since the beauty of grace comes from being lit up by God's light, this beauty cannot be restored in the soul unless God shine on it again. Hence the habitual gift,

---

2. G. Bernanos, "Une vision catholique du réel," in *Le Crépuscule des vieux* (Paris, 1956) 43–44.

the light of grace, is required. Likewise, the natural order cannot be restored by the human will becoming subject to God, unless God should draw the human will towards himself. Again, the debt of eternal punishment can only be remitted by God, against whom the offence was committed, and who is the judge of men.[3]

God could not truly love the good unless he hated and shunned evil. A mere declaration of amnesty would hardly be more than an ignoring of evil. In the forgiveness of sins there must be *fitting* forgiveness. So the scope of human evil and the dimensions of redemption must be duly pondered in any account of the nature of salvation.

Humankind as issuing from the creative hand of God at the moment when our rational species appeared on earth was, by definition, in a condition of integrity of being. But Church tradition sees more, still, in the affirmation of Genesis that the human being, so created, was "very good." For the Council of Trent, God made the first human beings in holiness and justice—sharing supernaturally, that is, in his own qualities. The world they experienced would have been aglow with the presence of God, in a paradisal way that now only poets can imagine: the grass orient and immortal wheat; man and woman strange, seraphic pieces of life and beauty, moving jewels; horses whinnying as they walked out onto the fields of praise. At the beginning of human experience was a moment of glory haunting all subsequent culture in myths of a golden age. Original sin chiefly consists in the loss of the share in the divine life enjoyed by Adam, and hence of the harmony and wholeness that stemmed from such grace. With the Fall the powers of human nature cease to be harmoniously united; its structure disintegrates, for our humanity was never intended to be a purely natural reality. From the origin it was disposed toward the vision of God by the supernatural gift of charity. The eating of the fruit of the tree of the knowledge of good and evil represents the possibility that we will take our nourishment—realize our life—not in communion with God but unrelated to and independent of God, feeding ourselves only for our own preservation, for the survival of our physical individuality.

It is when we think through the implications of the Church's ascribing sin to the newly born that we realize how the loss of divine friendship can be said to wound our nature. No infant has a will freely set against God, for there can be no salvifically relevant use of the will unless and until we start to decide rationally, committing ourselves not

3. Thomas Aquinas, *Summa theologiae* 2–2.109.8.

in impulse but decision. Yet the state of children is still sin: the lack of God's life and, therefore, of the wholeness of our nature is a lack of what ought to have been present but is not present, for all whom Adam "represented."

Owing to human solidarity, one person can represent many. This is true in social settings at all levels, from the family, through those associations we call precisely not only clubs but "societies," to the great society of a country, the civil society of a state. There seems no reason why the same principle cannot be extended into macrosociety, even to the level of the race as a whole. From the "leader principle" both benefits and disasters have flowed. But with Adam, as with Christ, we are dealing with a mystery of supernatural vocation for which all other forms of representation are at best analogies. Grace was given Adam—"our Sire," as Milton calls him—as the source of grace for others. His refusal to undertake the mediation of grace as humanity's representative means that human beings are born gracelessly, with their spiritual wills indisposed to communion with the holy God.

This Catholic teaching on original sin is sometimes treated as a purely Western, and indeed Augustinian, doctrine, unechoed in the rest of traditional Christendom. For the latter, we hear, it was only as the de facto result of Adam's transgression that the human world became infected by bad example and bad influences. On the *occasion*, merely, of this episode did human beings begin to decline. Adam's sin, it is alleged, was not as such the foundation of our sinfulness; he did not carry us all in him, so that we come into the world bound for a tragic experience. But the Greek Fathers too can be quite clear that human solidarity with Adam is more than just that of the first link in a chain. We read in them that in Adam *we* were disloyal, *we* were banished from paradise, just as in Christ these corporate conditions were reversed.

To a secular mind, the difficulty with this doctrine will be not only the concept of vicariousness but also the question of historicity. The story of the Fall could be read as a symbolic account of human rebelliousness against God, of how all our cultural developments (as for the Genesis writer, clothing, metal-working, city-building) are spoilt by an element of vengefulness and pride. Yet sin must have entered human life at some historical moment, whether identifiable or not. For unless evil marred the creation of humanity contingently (i.e., historically), it could only have done so essentially (i.e., by God's own creative act), which is unthinkable. In claiming Adam (with Eve) as historical figures, the Church is confirmed by the New Testament, especially by Paul's appeal to Adam's fall as the act which Christ's redemptive act inverted. Revelation presents both as historical events with metahistorical meaning.

Naturally, if the human race emerged in the form of a single couple, that couple could scarcely have been culturally advanced. No archaeologist will find evidence of a lost Eden. That would not prevent such a human pair existing in the greatest charity when "it was all/ Shining, it was Adam and maiden."[4] Nor need their sin have been some carefully calculated rebellion. A false step might seem small yet be crucial. Pascal, in his *Pensées*, proved adept at describing the result, as when he wrote, "What sort of freak then is man! How novel, how monstrous, how chaotic, how paradoxical, how prodigious! Judge of all things, feeble earthworm, repository of truth, sink of doubt and error, glory and refuse of the universe."[5] This unresolvable duality of human beings as they are can only be explained by a duality in origin: the original fallenness of an originally good nature. From now on, as in A. H. Clough's poetic fragment *The Mystery of the Fall*, human beings are as Cain: marvelling at the facility with which crime can be committed even as they live in chafing awareness of unreasonable limitations to their freedom.

Redemption in Christ

Humanity, then, grew old in wickedness, but God did not leave it to itself. It was renewed in the "child," Jesus, who grew up aright, and became, in a garden, the first-born from the dead, so that we might have a new birth, and the new man, dwelling in us, might redeem the old humanity. At this the *Exsultet,* sung on Easter night, proclaims: "O happy fault, O necessary sin of Adam,/ which gained for us so great a Redeemer!" Adam's sin was a "happy fault," providentially allowed so as to provide the context into which Christ might come as our Redeemer, to show us God's love and power in an unsurpassable way. By a wild excess of love, in his generous goodness, God willed to give himself to us not simply in the vision of himself in heaven, but also in that union between him and our nature which is the incarnation—to the extent of dying for us on the cross and sharing his divine life with us in the resurrection. In order that our race might be given such

4. Dylan Thomas, "Fern Hill," in *Collected Poems,* 1934–1952 (London, 1952) 150–51.
5. Blaise Pascal, *Pensées* (Harmondsworth, 1966) 64.

bounty, it was allowed to be in desperate need of such bounty. It was permitted to fall in Adam, so that it might be restored in the new Adam, and, in Paul's words, "grace abound all the more" (Rom 5:20).

The restoring of God's creation, and notably of ruined humanity, was the reason for the incarnation of his eternal Son and Word in Jesus Christ. By taking our frail, contingent nature upon himself—he who is the one source and origin of all creaturely being—he transferred to himself our origin, so as to secure our being from final dissolution. At the same time, he took upon himself our alienated and corrupt nature, so as to redeem us and renew our being. By transferring our contingent existence into himself, in whom divine and human, uncreated and created, realities are indissolubly united (as Chalcedon declared), Christ secured our nature's origin and end in his own eternal being. In this sense, the incarnation saves us by completing the work of creation and consummating the world's contingent relation to God.

> He made his appearance as God, with the assumption of human nature, a unity composed of two opposites, flesh and Spirit. The former he deified, the latter was already deified. . . . He who is comes to be; the Uncreated is created, the Unconfinable is confined, he who enriches becomes poor. He takes upon himself the poverty of my flesh so that I may receive the riches of his divinity. He who is full is emptied: he is emptied of his glory for a little while, so that I may share in his fullness. What a wealth of goodness! What a mystery is this. . . . I had my share in the divine image, and I did not preserve it. He shares in my flesh in order that he may rescue the image and confer immortality on the flesh. He enters upon a second fellowship with us much more wonderful than the first. Then he imparted an honor; now he shares a humiliation. The latter is a more godlike act, and thoughtful men will find it more sublime.[6]

The Flesh-taking is indeed the foundation of all the other mediations whereby the Word incarnate brought God's redemption to humankind.

In the last chapter we explored the divine presuppositions of that mediating work, and before that we scanned its historical outworking in the mysteries of Christ's life. For as that life unfolded the Word-made-human constructed on the basis of his incarnation his own reality as Savior—in the public ministry as Messiah, prophet, high priest; in his death as sacrifice, Redeemer, victor, exemplar; in his resurrection

---

6. Gregory Nazianzen, *Oration 38, On the Theophany* 13.

as intercessor, judge, and consummator of all God's redemptive ways. It is not only on the cross that the incarnate One saves, but through his resurrection, ascension, and outpouring of the Spirit.

> His ascent bodily is his descent spiritually; his taking our nature up to God, is the descent of God into us; he has truly, though in an unknown sense, taken us to God, or brought down God to us, as we view it. Thus when St. Paul says that our life is hid with him in God, we may suppose him to intimate, that our principle of existence is no longer a mortal, earthly principle, such as Adam's after his fall, but that we are baptized and hidden anew in God's glory, in that Shekinah of light and purity which we lost when Adam fell—that we are new-created, transformed, spiritualized, glorified in the Divine nature—that through the participation of Christ, we receive, as through a channel, the true presence of God within and without us, imbuing us with sanctity and immortality. . . . This is the one great gift of God purchased by the Atonement, which is light instead of darkness and the shadow of death, power instead of weakness, bondage and suffering, spirit instead of the flesh, which is the token of our acceptance with God, the propitiation of our sins in his sight, and the seed and element of renovation.[7]

The new covenant, thus enacted, brings into being a worldwide divine family, in which Christ Jesus shares with us his own divine sonship, thus making us the children of God. By making disciples and giving them the new Law, Christ established the lines of that community in which deliverance from the evil of sin and reunion with the Father might take place, and when realized in the members be lived in freedom. Likewise he established the new cult with its priesthood, so that by means of the Church's liturgy humankind might be enabled and inspired to hate the malice of sin and love God's goodness.

Of course, even when by our new birth of baptism we appropriate this rich redemption through the Church, the temptation to sin—called by theological tradition *concupiscence*—remains. But from now on, concupiscence is simply the provider of occasions, and materials, for our transfiguration into Christ, as each person retraces the history of the Savior from his baptism in the Jordan, through the temptations in the wilderness, his public life, to his passion, death, and resurrection. The postbaptismal disorder in the psyche is left to us as something to fight against through Christ's grace, so that we may share for ourselves in his paschal triumph.

7. J. H. Newman, *Lectures on Justification* (London, 1900) 218–19.

The Father by his Spirit enabled Christ as man to undertake and accomplish the work of deliverance from sin and reunion with himself by inspiring him with the loving obedience whereby the Word incarnate freely performed in his human existence that work of liberation and atonement. God raised the same Christ from the dead so that the crucified and risen Lord might be able to communicate to all humankind his gifts of salvation, unity and peace. It is in terms of the overall, Christ-centered, divine "plot" of history that we can make sense of the gift, loss, and reacquisition of original righteousness.

> How are we to understand the prohibition of the tree? It teaches us that man can only enjoy the garden, and life, if, in the submission of faith and obedience, he respects the wisdom which unites—from above—the moral order with the order of the Promise. Since knowledge has a "nomic" or ethical aspect, the prohibition means that it is forbidden to evade those obligations the Word of God defines, namely, the commandments. But because of its prophetic meaning, the prohibition also proclaims that it is forbidden to anticipate God's gracious designs. . . . Man must accept, then, two limitations before God—a humility of obedience, and a humility of faith vis-à-vis a future whose secret God reserves to himself, a faith open to God's supernatural initiative, a forward-moving faith that accepts time's dispensation.[8]

In our own lives personal sin—our very own ratification of the Fall in the myriad ways that novelists (as well as the Scriptures!) describe—looms larger than sin's archaeology. But the genesis of sin is vital to its understanding, and to the understanding of redemption.

> The deepest longing of man is to ascend to God, to become like God, indeed to become equal to God. Whereas daily life chains and constricts him in the narrow confines of everyday life on this earth, a pressure ignites within man to tear away the chains of this slavery and to break through to the mysterious depths that lurk behind this world, to a world in which he can be free, whole, wise and immortal—free of the limitations of his narrow ego and holding dominion over the total context of events, superior to fate and death. In all peoples an estate, a class, a caste, has formed that was meant to give visible, representative and, as it were, sacramental expression to this general longing. But we know that the snake got a hold of this very innermost drive of man to press on to God, and poisoned it. Original sin does not sit somewhere on the periphery of human nature. Rather, the very promise *"eritis sicut dii"* [you

8. L. Ligier, *Péché d'Adam et péché du monde* (Paris, 1960) 1:192.

shall be like gods] is the perversion of the original core of this nature it-self.[9]

Self-apotheosis will always be criminal lunacy. It remains the case, however, that "the [true] life of man is the vision of God" (Irenaeus). Beyond God's positing of creation is his reordering of creation to himself, called by Catholicism the *supernatural*. The life graciously bestowed on human creatures is more than natural existence.

The vocabulary of the *supernatural* was coined by the Greek and Latin Fathers for a good enough reason. The message of revelation is that the incomprehensible God, who lies infinitely beyond his creatures (though he is also intimately present to them, to preserve and guide them), has chosen to share his own life and happiness with us, by lifting us up so that we can come to know him as he is. In this life we are made nothing less than children of the Father by faith (a sharing in the Father's Word or self-expression) and charity (a sharing in their Holy Spirit), so that, led by the Spirit, we may grow in the Son until, in the next life, faith gives way to sight. Then, in and through the Word, we shall truly know the Father and live by sharing that divine self-knowledge. We shall delight in that vision, which means that we shall share more fully in the divine joy which the Holy Spirit is. This lifting up of the creature to share the life of the Creator is the greatest of all God's works; the rationale of the term *supernatural* should surely be self-evident.

The supernatural is the main category that, beginning modestly enough in the age of the Fathers, Catholic theologians have used to express how grace is the "second gift" of God. This second gift does not simply make us better endowed human beings, even human beings with better endowments given in a supernatural way. It makes us more than human, indeed more than creaturely. We become "sharers in the divine nature" (2 Pet 1:4). If by the first gift we are brought from nothingness into being, as creatures with (in our case) human capabilities, then by the second gift God makes us adopted sons and daughters, giving us his Spirit so that we may share in the life of his Son. Nature (i.e., what we are capable of by virtue of our own resources, not without God, but apart from his self-communication) is not grace (i.e., what we have become capable of through that very

9. H. U. von Balthasar, "Patristik, Scholastik, und wir," *Theologie der Zeit* 3 (1939) 69, cited in E. T. Oakes, *Pattern of Redemption: The Theology of Hans Urs von Balthasar* (New York, 1994) 110.

self-communication). The gifts of nature are given us as our own; the gifts of grace are bestowed as a sharing in what remains proper to God, and so reach us only through salvation history, with its power to change the form and goal of our natural existence. Here begins a familial, nay, a nuptial, intimacy. In the words of the English Jesuit theologian Edward Yarnold, "Our Creator becomes our bridegroom."

The more faithful exponents of the mind of Aquinas have argued that humanity has a natural desire for this supernatural life. As Henri de Lubac, one of Aquinas's most penetrating twentieth-century disciples, saw clearly, the life of glory is not a banquet set before a person who feels no hunger. In other words, heaven is not some arbitrary reward, conditional on our progress in this life, but otherwise unrelated to it. Nonetheless, there remains as an abiding source of Christian admiration the complementary truth which the baroque Scholastics and Neoscholastics so firmly held: though by the first gift, creation, God equips us to receive the second, he could, without a shadow of contradiction, have left us with nature alone. Yarnold draws on G. B. Shaw's *Pygmalion* for dramatic illustration:

> Professor Higgins did more than train Eliza Doolittle to take a place in high society; he transformed her so that it was possible for her to fall in love with him, and him with her. Let us suppose that he behaved honourably, and did nothing to encourage hopes that he had no intention of fulfilling; he could have trained her and then turned her out. That he should wish to give himself to her in marriage . . . would be a further gift totally distinct from his education of her, though impossible without it. The first gift prepares for the second, though the second remains a *second* gift.[10]

Where nature and grace are at issue, traditional divinity distinguishes (1) the state of "pure nature," which we know by faith has never been realized in human history, for the latter was a history of salvation from the very start; (2) the state of integral nature, in which a series of gifts—exemption from concupiscence, suffering, and death—bore fruit in a perfect equilibrium for human living; (3) the state of original justice, surpassing even integral nature, in which the original humans were created, blessed not only with quasi-angelic gifts of limpid self-possession but also sanctifying grace (viz., a lifting up to the strictly supernatural level where alone the vision of God can be bestowed; (4)

10. E. Yarnold, *The Second Gift: A Study of Grace* (Slough, 1974) 39.

the state of fallen nature, that of Adamic humanity after the loss of these gratuitous gifts—a sinful state where nature stands opposed to the gracious will of God, his plan for humankind; (5) the state of redeemed nature, which is our own. We possess sanctifying grace but not the quasi-angelic gifts of Adamic humanity; these latter are, for us, replaced by the economy of the sacraments under the sign of the cross. This is to our advantage from the viewpoint of our growth in charity. The materiality of the sacraments keeps us rooted in the good humus of earth even as our faces (not a mixed metaphor: *flowers* are plants' faces) are turned towards heaven. "Though all this is marked by the tragedy of sin, which weighs down matter and obscures its clarity, [materiality] is redeemed in the Incarnation and becomes fully 'theophoric,' that is, capable of putting us in touch with the Father. This property is most apparent in the holy mysteries, the sacraments of the Church."[11] Thus the Roman liturgy can say of our nature that it was wondrously created by God yet in Christ was even more marvelously restored.

Aspects of Grace

God does not merely provide our salvation through his grace. He is so generous that he enables us to deserve that salvation; he enables our merit. This he does by the way that, in the concrete, he predestines us—namely, through our justification, which is his gratuitous sharing with us of his own righteousness. "He works out his justification toward us, in us, with us, through us, and for us, till he receives back in produce what he gave in seed."[12] And again, "He makes us gradually and eventually to be in our own persons what he has been from eternity in himself, what he is from our baptism toward us, righteous."[13] Newman's words point to the distinct, though internally connected, concept of *sanctification*, but it is nevertheless true that for Catholicism (as for Protestantism) justification is the work of grace alone, although (in opposition to classical Protestantism) it does not come by faith alone. Justification happens in us through faith operant in charity. This must be so if Christ and his Spirit (the Word and the Love of the Father) are the agents of our justification. Over against the view that would make faith itself, or "spiritual-mindedness, into the end of religion," Newman insisted that "Christ is our renovation by dwelling in

11. John Paul II, *Orientale lumen*, 11.
12. Newman, *Lectures on Justification*, 93–94.
13. Ibid., 104.

us by the Spirit; he justifies us by entering into us. He continues to justify us by remaining in us. This is really and truly our justification, not faith, not holiness, not (much less) a mere imputation; but through God's mercy, the very Presence of Christ."[14]

Our justification means first of all our forgiveness and consequently (so radical is sin) our regeneration, a new birth into a life of friendship with the blessed Trinity. Romano Guardini wrote that this mystery is as marvellous as the mystery that the world arose from nothing: A new creation takes place. God draws man to himself with all that he has done, he draws him into his ineffable power and man comes forth again renewed and guiltless.[15] Repentance is therefore an appeal to the deepest mystery of the creative power of God.

For repentance there must be. *Metanoia*—"conversion," a "turning again"—though itself the gift of grace is the necessary condition of our sharing in the righteousness of God. There can be no personal appropriation of salvation without repentance. He who worked our salvation in the cosmic acts of the assumption of our nature by the Logos also struggled and suffered for us in his (now humanly realized) person. My salvation cannot simply rest, then, on the objective metaphysic of the new life of grace communicated to me by the Church in her sacraments; I am called on to make a demanding and heartfelt, and ever-repeated, act of repentance. The Byzantine Church expresses this in Lent in the profound poetry of Andrew of Crete's *Great Canon:*

> Give heed, O heaven, and I will speak, and will lift up in song
> Christ, who of a Virgin, in flesh is come among us.
>> Have mercy upon me, O God, have mercy upon me.
> Give heed, O Heaven, and I will speak: Earth, give ear to a voice
> Repenting unto God, and singing his praises.
>> Have mercy upon me, O God, have mercy upon me.
> Give heed, O God, to me in pity, with merciful eye,
> And accept now my fervent confession.
>> Have mercy upon me, O God, have mercy upon me.
> I have sinned alone, above all men, I have sinned against thee:
> But, as God and Saviour, pity thy creation.
>> Have mercy upon me, O God, have mercy upon me.
> A storm of ills hems me in: but let mercy weigh the scales,
> And stretch out thy hand to me as unto Peter.
>> Have mercy upon me, O God, have mercy upon me.

14. Ibid., 150.
15. Guardini, *Freedom, Grace, and Destiny*, 124–31.

The Harlot's tears, O Merciful Christ, I pour out unto Thee:
Be gracious, O Saviour, to me in thy compassion.
    Have mercy upon me, O God, have mercy upon me.
My soul's beauty I have dimmed with pleasures of the passions,
And all my mind to mud wholly is changed.
    Have mercy upon me, O God, have mercy upon me.
I have torn my robe, that first robe which my Fashioner for me
Wove at the beginning, and now I lie naked.
    Have mercy upon me, O God, have mercy upon me.
I have put on a torn coat, which the serpent wove for me
By his evil counsel, and I am confounded.
    Have mercy upon me, O God, have mercy upon me.
I looked upon the beauty of the tree, and my mind was deceived.
Now I lie naked, and I am confounded.
    Have mercy upon me, O God, have mercy upon me.
Upon my back all the leaders of the passions have ploughed,
Lengthening against me the furrows of their lawlessness.
    Have mercy upon me, O God, have mercy upon me.
I have lost the first-created beauty, and all my comeliness.
Now I lie naked, and I am confounded.
    Have mercy upon me, O God, have mercy upon me.
Only for the outward adorning I took thoughtful care,
Neglecting the inward God-patterned Tabernacle.
    Have mercy upon me, O God, have mercy upon me.
I have crusted over with passions the beauty of the Image:
But seek me like the piece of silver, Saviour, and find me.
    Have mercy upon me, O God, have mercy upon me.
I cry like the Harlot, I only have sinned, I have sinned against thee.
Saviour, accept now my tears like hers as ointment.
    Have mercy upon me, O God, have mercy upon me.
I have sinned like David and waxed wanton, and am deep in the mire.
But wash me also, Saviour, clean with my tears.
    Have mercy upon me, O God, have mercy upon me.
I cry like the Publican, "Be merciful": Saviour, be merciful to me.
For none of Adam's offspring has sinned as I against thee.
    Have mercy upon me, O God, have mercy upon me.
No tears have I, no repentance, Saviour, nor any compunction.
Do though in thy Godhead bestow these gifts upon me.
    Have mercy upon me, O God, have mercy upon me.
Shut not, I pray, thy door against me, Lord, Lord, in that day,
But open it to me, when I come to thee repentant.
    Have mercy upon me, O God, have mercy upon me.
Lover of man, who willest that all should be saved, bring me back,

And in thy goodness accept me repentant.
Have mercy upon me, O God, have mercy upon me.

Grace is operative in our lives, but it is also co-operative with us. This is the basis of the distinction between justifying grace and merit. God doing what we cannot do—make evil will become righteous will—is the work of operative grace. In his justifying activity, operative grace works on our very being. But as Augustine says, grace is needed not only for the beginning of *bonum velle* but also for its continuance. Co-operative grace enables us to do the good with love (without love it would be an intolerable burden). Such grace makes it possible for us to act rightly, moving towards our end. In other words, co-operative grace works not on our being but on our doing. Though we cannot claim salvation for what we have done, our acts must have a significant connection with our salvation. In the New Testament there is, in this sense, a concept of reward. Our deeds "earn" a place in the kingdom, making us into the kind of person who is able to live under the rule of God. Such continuance in grace can be merited, for, thanks to his covenant, God can be relied on to fulfill his promises. Though we cannot merit the grace that moves us, once moved we can merit the end. It is only fitting (congruent) that a man or woman who has done good should not be abandoned by God.[16]

The distinction between operative and co-operative grace (like that between justification and sanctification, justifying grace and merit) can also be expressed in terms of a distinction between healing and elevating grace. On the one hand, grace is God's restoration of us from a state of sin to a condition of righteousness, delivering us from the dominion of darkness, transferring us to the kingdom of his beloved Son (Col 1:13). Grace, in affecting us inasmuch as we are sinners, is *gratia sanans*, "healing grace." In addition, and without direct reference to sin, grace can be thought of as the work of the Holy Spirit making us adopted children of God, raising us up to share the divine life: *gratia elevans*, "elevating grace." The grace that "makes us gracious" (*gratia gratum faciens*) for Aquinas includes both a habitual gift, orienting us to the Father by the love we have received freely in Christ, as poured out by the Spirit, and also what he terms the "gratuitous moving of God" (*gratuita Dei motio*), what later generations would call "actual grace," grace to help with particular acts that the ethical and spiritual

16. B. Lonergan, *Grace and Freedom. Operative Grace in the Thought of St Thomas Aquinas* (London, 1971).

life calls for at different times, impulses that enable us to express our new nature by living as befits the children of God. Habitual grace has the lion's share of sanctifying grace, however, for by the latter the descendants of Adam recover habitual friendship with God, finding themselves once more habitually attuned to their supernatural end.

Actual and habitual grace are both aspects of "created grace," the transforming effect on us of the presence of God himself. God not only comes personally to human beings, to be present to them, but also raises their personality and capacities above those of a creature. His presence is a transforming presence, such that we become a "new creation" (Paul) undergoing a second birth (John). God's presence (uncreated grace) supports us from within our personalities, and this explains how gracious actions can be both our's and God's: they flow from a grace-filled personhood.

Created grace must never be conceived apart from the divine indwelling. It is not something between God and ourselves, a ladder or path into his presence. Created grace's very being is union. Created grace is at once the fruit and the bond of the indwelling, originating in the indwelling and sustained by the indwelling; it raises us into an ever-deepening actualisation of the indwelling on earth and in heaven.[17] Grace's two poles, uncreated and created, mirror the apparent paradox that the divine essence is incommunicable, for God "alone has immortality and dwells in unapproachable light, whom no man has ever seen or can see" (1 Tim 6:16) yet there is from that essence a true communication of life, which is sharing, not manipulation: "God's love has been poured into our hearts through the Holy Spirit who has been given to us" (Rom 5:5).

Even in the heart of the free spiritual person, the turning to God which enables our reception of salvation is prepared at all points by divine grace. For Catholicism, justification (the individual person's incorporation within the justice, righteousness or right order, of God) happens on the basis of Christ's atoning sacrifice in baptism, by which we are included in that saving reality. This concerns the admission of Christians into the favor and covenant of God, not their final forgiveness and title to everlasting happiness, which turns on a lifetime of continuing responsiveness to grace, or at any rate in limit cases on "death-bed conversion." Those whom God in his foreknowledge knew would remain true to membership in Christ's mystical body, the

17. E. Mersch, *The Theology of the Mystical Body* (St. Louis, Mo., and London, 1952) 600–633.

Church—those who would remain faithful to the privilege of professing the gospel—are described as "elected." But the number and identity of the elect is known only to God, and Catholicism hopes (though cannot, on the basis of Scripture and Tradition, confess or teach) that it may include all human beings. The spiritual grace (regeneration) given in holy baptism suffices, when renewed by the collaboration of our freedom, to institute a holy life, and there may be gracious surrogates for baptismal regeneration in the case of non-Christians, as we shall see in Chapter 7, where I speak about the mystery of the Church.

The Fathers and medievals centered their doctrine of predestination on Christ and the Church. It is Christ, the man assumed by the Logos, who was eternally intended by God for the salvation of the human species. It is the Church, symbolized in the immaculately conceived Mary, that was predestined in dependence on Christ as his preordained instrument. But this is not to say that Catholic theology is wholly silent about any extension of predestining grace to individual persons other than Jesus and Mary.

Although the issue had already been raised by Augustine, and caveats against a deterministic form of the doctrine were promulgated by various local councils of the Church in opposition to extreme Augustinian theologians of the Carolingian period, it was the sixteenth-century Reformation that put the issue at the head of the doctrinal agenda. The Reformers tended to a voluntarist understanding of the "decree" of predestination: the divine will is righteous merely by positing itself, proposing itself as determining such and such. (An alternative theology of God holds that it is the divine essence as subsistent goodness that is the measure of God's willing.) They also accepted the conviction of Augustine in his more pessimistic moments that human nature is thoroughly depraved, drawing from this the conclusion that human beings cannot deserve salvation—nor damnation, for deserving eternal punishment implies the possibility of choosing against evil, which a totally depraved creature cannot do. So the only possible explanation of damnation is that this too is God's eternal decree.

The Catholic response to this position, at the Council of Trent and during the struggle with Jansenism (a Catholicized version of Calvinistic predestinarianism), insisted that God predisposes no one to evil, but wills the salvation of all human beings. Christ did not die solely for the elect, or the faithful. Moreover, God offers to all sinners a grace that really suffices for their salvation, withholding the grace of conversion from no one even at the point of death. Only those people are deprived of this grace who refuse to accept it; God permits this but he is not the cause of it.

Nevertheless, God *has* decreed eternal punishment for the sin of final impenitence, and reflection on that caused much theological heartache in Catholicism in the early post-Tridentine era. If the grace of God is sufficient for salvation, should it not also be efficacious in causing the impenitent to become penitent, even, if need be, in the moment of death? How is it that God mercifully grants efficacious grace to some and yet justly refuses it to others?

Here three schools of thought divide up Catholic divinity between them: Molinism (named after the Spanish Jesuit Luis de Molina) is closest to Pelagianism, Bañezianism (named for another Spaniard, the Dominican Domingo Bañez) to Calvinism, with the Congruists (of whom the best-known representative was the Italian Doctor of the Church Robert Bellarmine) attempting a *via media*. For Molina, God knows all possible beings and all possible world orders in which those beings might find themselves. Willing one such world order, he chooses those human beings to be saved whom he foresees (by his "middle knowledge," *scientia media*, of future free acts) would make good use of the graces he would grant them in these particular circumstances, persevering and ultimately meriting eternal happiness. Since God's choice of the world order in which they would thus merit salvation is itself entirely gratuitous, Molina believed he had done justice to the orthodox doctrine of predestination, Pelagian or semi-Pelagian overtones notwithstanding. God shows to these human beings, so placed, a special predilection he does not show to others.

Molina's belief that for God causally to determine human freedom (even to the good) destroys that freedom, since every person must determine on his or her own power not only to withhold co-operation from God but also to furnish it, necessarily brought him into conflict with Thomists—and indeed with all those who accepted the normal interpretation of the conciliar tradition of the West whereby the will to respond to grace is itself graced. Bañez took up the cudgels. For him predestination to glory is decreed *ante praevisa merita*, "before the prevision of any merits" whatever. By his absolute dominion over creatures and his inscrutable counsel (note the voluntarist-sounding language), God elects some to glory and gives them in their lifetime graces that are intrinsically efficacious, that infallibly predetermine their wills to salutary actions, actions that appropriate his salvation. Though God does not reprobate others to damnation he nonetheless does exclude them from such efficacious election, granting them merely "sufficient grace," and so permitting them freely to sin and to perish unrepentant.

The Congruists, fearing that this was but Calvinism by the back door, argued that, by *scientia media*, God could foresee how souls would react to particular graces, and on this basis conferred on the elect those graces he saw would be efficacious ("congruent" with salvation), while on others he simply bestowed sufficient grace—thereby excluding them from an efficacious election to glory. The Jansenist crisis, which this kind of debate prepared in its own fashion, led to a deep revulsion in many parts of the Catholic Church from any attempt to provide a theological explanation for reprobation (i.e., the divine role in permitting final impenitence). What is known with certainty, from the work of Christ, is that only the divine Goodness moves the Father's will.

Predestination is for all Catholics subjectively uncertain—short of some private revelation. There are nonetheless held to be probable signs of predestination which exclude all excessive anxiety: purity of heart, delight in prayer, patience in suffering, the frequent reception of the sacraments, love of Christ and the Church, devotion to the Mother of God who is the epitome of human responsiveness to the Word. Yet none of this guarantees us against a failure finally to persevere—hence our need to work out our salvation continually in fear and trembling. The question Are you saved? can only be answered by asking in turn, Do you mean past perfect, present, or future conditional? I *have been* saved by Christ's life, death, and resurrection into which I am plunged in baptism. I *am being* saved by daily sharing in the life of Christ. I *will be* saved if I endure to the end (Matt 10:22).

How are we to reconcile the universal salvific will of God with a possibly restricted predestining grace? Reconciliation can only be sought in the incomprehensible union of infinite mercy and infinite justice with the sovereign divine freedom. If God grants final perseverance to one, this is by his mercy; if he does not accord it to another it is by a just punishment of previous faults and final resistance to his last call. This is an immense mystery, in which these three attributes (mercy, justice, freedom) are only united in the unsearchable Godhead itself. J. B. Bossuet wrote:

> From all eternity God has foreseen and predestined all the particular means by which he was to inspire in his faithful their fidelity, their obedience, their perseverance. That is what predestination is. The fruit of this doctrine is to put our will and our liberty in the hand of God, to pray him to direct them in such a way that they do not go astray, to thank him

for all the good that they do and to believe that God works this good in them without either enfeebling them or destroying them, but, on the contrary raising them, strengthening them and giving them their own good self-use, which is of all goods the most desirable. . . . We must believe that no one perishes, no one is reprobated, no one is left aside by God or by his aid, except through his own fault. If human reasoning finds a difficulty here and cannot conciliate all the parts of this holy and inviolable doctrine, faith must not abandon the effort to conciliate them wholly, expecting that God will make us see everything in the Source.[18]

Here if anywhere *apophasis*—the simultaneous recognition of the limits of our knowledge and the unlimitedness of God's essential mystery—must prevail.

But what of the public, historical dimension of this personal salvation? A philosophy of history becomes a theology of history if it accepts that the source of history is the Father, that the norm of history is his Son, Jesus Christ, and that the fulfillment of history is the work of the Spirit, whom the Father and Son send forth. Balthasar wrote of the Spirit's work in world history:

The work which he undertakes, the shaping and fashioning of what the Son bequeathed to him, is a work of supreme divine freedom. He is presented with two data: the life of Christ, and "world history"; and it rests with him so to dispose of the infinite wealth in the life of Christ that it can blossom out in the variousness of history, and that at the same time, history, thus made subject to this norm, shall be able to discover the fullness within itself.[19]

As this account suggests, Balthasar stresses in the first place the transcendence of the Son and Spirit vis-à-vis history. They do not simply uphold the structure of history as it develops, via nature, from the Creator's hand. As divine persons, they are capable of relating history in a new manner to the God who is not only its source but its goal. As Balthasar puts it: "The Spirit . . . makes history into the history of salvation . . . prophetically oriented towards the Son," while the latter's "action is what history is for; his uniqueness sets it free to attain its proper character." Yet at the same time, Balthasar is careful to underline that the redemptive action of the Holy Trinity does not just disre-

18. From a letter of J. B. Bossuet cited in R. Garrigou-Lagrange, "Prédestination," *Dictionnaire de théologie catholique* 12/2 (Paris, 1953) 3020–21.
19. H. U. von Balthasar, *A Theology of History* (London and New York, 1964) 98.

gard, much less ride roughshod over, the natural pattern of history. The Spirit "leaves history its own immanent laws and structure, but orders it and all its laws in subjection to the laws of Christ."[20] The relation of history's natural structure to its supernatural pattern as disclosed by Christian faith is like the broader relation of nature to grace. Grace builds on the historical expression of nature, elevating it in the process. It does not overthrow it. The Spirit operates in the order of created spirit not, Balthasar insists, as "another," but rather, echoing Nicholas of Cusa, "as One exalted above all otherness." The Spirit is so transcendent that he can be wholly immanent, his divine creativity so utterly indifferent to maintaining its difference from our human creativity that his sovereign work can go undetected by the secular historian. Yet what he achieves is a real transformation, for he uses the natural structure of history as a means by which to attain his goal. The key to an appreciation of that goal is, for the Christian, the life of Jesus, since the Son made man is history's "norm." If the distinctive form of Christ's temporality, his participation in history, lay in his unique receptivity to the will of the Father for the world, which enabled history to reach its anticipated fulfillment in him as its personal norm, then the proper content of that norm lies in those exemplary responses to the human challenges of Christ's environment in which the divine will was concretely expressed. Seasons of grace in the public life of society are always for Catholicism breaths of air from the springtime of the gospel: moments of repentance, reconciliation, feast-making.

The salvific lesson of the mysteries of Christ's life for the public history of the world is not only, however, a matter of the qualitative transformation of time. As his resurrection and ascension, the climactic events of the Christological cycle of the liturgy, show, the ultimate issue of Christ's life is the throwing open of humanity's time, now and in the future, to God's eternity.

De novissimis: The Last Things

The scope of grace includes this world, but reaches more fundamentally beyond it.

> This is the sacrament, the hidden meaning, of the Old Testament, where the New Testament lay concealed. In the Old Testament the promises and gifts are of earthly things; but even then men of spiritual perception realized, although they did not yet proclaim the fact for all to hear, that

---

20. Ibid., 59, 99.

by those temporal goods eternity was signified; they understood also what were the gifts of God which constituted true felicity.[21]

The blessings of the new covenant are above all eternal blessings even though there be one single gracious purpose which disposes in order both earthly and eternal felicity.

In treating of life after death, the Catholic Christian will tread warily. For on the one hand, overemphasis on the unity of the human being as a body and soul composite (the Council of Vienne taught that the human soul is itself the vivifying principle of the human organism) may make the meaningful assertion of the person's eternal destiny very difficult. On the other hand, upholding a destiny beyond death by endowing the soul with the prerogative of immortality may seem to impair the original dogmatic affirmation of the unity of the human person. The Fifth Lateran Council, presided over by Pope Leo X (once a pupil of the philosopher Marsilio Ficino) went further: Though the soul is the form of the body it is still naturally immortal. Philosophical reasons may be found for crediting such immortality; at any rate, according to the disciplinary measures attached to the decree, Catholic lecturers in philosophy must show the non-groundedness of any arguments to the effect that the soul is naturally mortal. This is an example of theological doctrine serving as a "negative norm"—a determination of what at least can *not* be true—for the secular sciences. The strongly Christian-Platonist Pico della Mirandola, layman and Dominican tertiary, who was present at the council, may have assisted it to drink from those ancient springs.

The resurrection of the human being under his or her bodily aspect would not be a supernatural fulfillment of the *humanum* were there not something in humanity, by virtue of creation, that made us apt for everlasting life. The positive possibility of human immortality is a metaphysical implication of the soul's non-material nature. If the soul is spiritual, then nothing would seem to induce its corruption. Everything we know of human spirituality—the way our intelligence, in its activity, transcends the material conditions of our senses—signals a continuing existence for the soul beyond biological death. In Thomas More's *Utopia*, the sovereign decrees that none should conceive so poor and base an opinion of human dignity as to think that souls perish with the body.

---

21. Augustine, *City of God* 4.33.

From one aspect the soul can be seen to be our formal principle *(forma substantialis)*, but from another it forms the ground of what is eternal in us *(forma subsistens).* As a spiritual being, the human person lives by way of an immortal soul; and yet this same immortal soul can simultaneously vivify a material body. For Aquinas, the separated soul lives and acts eternally on that acquired material of knowledge and habits which it possessed in its union with the body. Aquinas's notion is prolonged in modern Catholic thanatology (the theology of dying) which treats death, over and above its classical description in terms of the separation of body and soul, as an existential act of the human person. And so the human spirit's post-mortem being would be what it has made of itself, not least in its final self-determination, "at the hour of our death."

The doctrine of the indestructibility of the soul must be completed by the doctrine of the resurrection. Because ultimate bliss also means the perfection of the blessed, and because the soul does not possess the perfection of its nature—not even the Godlikeness it is capable of achieving—except in conjunction with the body, the indestructibility of the soul seems actually to require the coming resurrection. But since, conversely, what exists by nature (i.e., owing to creation) is always primary, and is the basis for every divine gift that may be accorded to creatures, if the soul were not by nature indestructible there would simply be nothing and no one able to receive the immortality that truly conquers death. Hopkins's sonnet "That Nature is a Heraclitean Fire and of the Comfort of the Resurrection" acknowledges the unique place of mind in nature yet finds in the resurrection of the body the only warranty for the transfiguration of the whole human being:

> Million-fuelèd, nature's bonfire burns on.
> But quench her bonniest, dearest to her, her clearest-selvèd spark
> Man, how fast his firedint, his mark on mind, is gone!
> Both are in an unfathomable, all is in an enormous dark
> Drowned. O pity and indignation! Manshape, that shone
> Sheer off, disseveral, a star, death blots black out; nor mark
>   Is any of him at all so stark
> But vastness blurs and time beats level. Enough! the Resurrection,
> A heart's-clarion! Away grief's gasping, joyless days, dejection.
>   Across my foundering deck shone
> A beacon, an eternal beam. Flesh fade, and mortal trash
> Fall to the residuary work; world's wildfire, leave but ash:
>   In a flash, at a trumpet crash,

> I am all at once what Christ is, since he is what I am, and
> This Jack, joke, poor potsherd, patch, matchwood, immortal diamond,
>   Is immortal diamond.[22]

The awareness of the prospect of dying is, for Christian spirituality, something to be cultivated by preparation for a "good death," and the frequent prayer that we will be delivered from death sudden and un-provided. The behavior of some saints appears neurotic, because they have not put up the "normal" defenses against awareness of human finitude, the dread of death, the ravages of sin and time. Not surely-seated in the body, such saints appear to humanist sensibilities to have failed in their humanization; in more candid terms, however, they have failed confidently to deny our real situation on this planet. In con-fronting death, we confront not only the biological fact of mortality but also our failure to develop our potentialities in lost opportunities, our incompleteness, and the unfinished nature of things. We either die too soon or too late, while we are still asking questions or when we are too tired to ask any more. We never realize our full capacities to be alone and to be together.

For many people it is death that establishes the serious quality of life, that forces them to explore the deeper, darker depths of human experience, the wider dimensions of sorrow, sadness, pathos, and poignancy. There most of all we meet the depths of the God who en-tered Gethsemane in his incarnate presence amongst us. Death is a merciful provision by God to prevent aimless or Godless existence per-petuating itself indefinitely without ever coming face to face with the realization that all is not well. The tradition of the desert saints knows this:

> Abba Pachomius thought always on the fear of God, the judgement to come and the tortures of the fires of hell so that his heart became like a solid copper door made to resist all thieves. He told the brothers: "When it is time for you to go to bed, turn and address yourself to each part of your body. O feet, before you can no longer walk, stand and work dili-gently in the presence of your Lord. O hands, there will come a day when you will be joined together unable to make the slightest move-ment, so now before that hour comes work for your Lord. O body, be-fore we leave one another, I to remain for ever in the shades of hell and you to return once more to dust, stand and then prostrate yourself be-

---

22. W. H. Gardner and N. H. Mackenzie, eds., *The Poems of Gerard Manley Hopkins,* 4th ed. (Oxford, 1970) 105–6.

fore your Lord . . . begin to feel as I feel in the midst of my tears . . . be submissive to your master, be alert, seeking neither rest nor health. If you obey me not, what a misfortune that you were ever linked with me; because of you I too will be condemned. Penetrated by this spirit you will become a true temple of the living God."[23]

John Climacus remarks that, as bread is of all foods the most indispensable, so death is of all considerations the most important. "The remembrance of death is painful to the undisciplined, or rather to the unscrupulous and pleasure-loving, but to the disciplined it brings freedom from anxiety, prayer unceasing and vigilance of spirit."[24]

Catholics "practice" dying by acts (great or small) of mortification, willingly sacrificing good and legitimate things so as to learn the art of giving oneself away. Every Christian death must be a self-surrender to the love of God. Death as we know it is always painful, a fragmentation of our being, which God wished to spare us. But Christ, in going before, has made this way redemptive. If we follow him in trust, our death, while remaining painful, also becomes beautiful: *un mort chrétien*, a "good death." "Death, as the offspring of sin, is evil, but by the grace of Christ, who deigned to undergo death for us, it has been rendered to us in many ways useful and salutary, lovable and desirable."[25]

The greatest Catholic poem of death is Newman's *Dream of Gerontius* (especially in its oratorio form, composed by Edward Elgar). Just as in the *Apologia pro vita sua* Newman records his belief that God had "called" him to his youthful conversion, to the reform of the Church of England, and, finally, to the Roman communion, so in the *Dream* God "calls" the old man (the *gerōn*) to death and judgment: "Jesu, Maria: I am near to death, / And thou are calling me; I know it now."[26] Whereas in his youth, as a Calvinistic Evangelical, Newman had believed himself sure of salvation, in 1865 as a Catholic he could only trust that, since he had followed the light given him, God would save him. But the first step of that salvation would be one of purification— through the fire of God's love. While in the *Apologia* Newman had appointed the English reading public to be judges of his honesty, and his Catholic views were sometimes judged unfavorably by fellow members of the Catholic community, now in the *Dream* only God's

23. *The Asketikon of Pachomius* 10.
24. John Climacus, *The Ladder of Paradise* 6.
25. Robert Bellarmine, *The Art of Dying Well* (1620).
26. J. H. Newman, *The Dream of Gerontius* (London, 1905) 7.

judgment matters. The *Apologia* recounts how Newman left home—his position in Oxford, the Anglican Church, and English society—for Catholicism; but even that Church could not be a final home. The human being's home is heaven, with purgatory its antechamber. This is the burden of the first words of the angel to the separated soul in the *Dream*, and of the last words of the angel of the agony. The guardian angel is a motherly figure, despite its masculine pronoun (Elgar rightly gave its part to a mezzo-soprano).

The doctrine of purgatory is at the heart of the *Dream*. In Naples, Newman had been disturbed by seeing images of souls in flames, and wanted to eliminate what he regarded as popular misunderstandings of the doctrine. In the *Dream* he focuses on the soul's spontaneous re-alization of its unworthiness in the presence of God, and on pain with hope. The "fire" of purgatory is the burning presence of the love of God which an unpurified soul cannot yet endure. The *Dream* makes use of the Roman liturgy for the last rites, and notably of the great prayer of commendation for the departing. Indeed, even Gerontius's friends take on a liturgical significance at his bedside, becoming "as-sistants," ministers at a rite. For while in one sense death is the mo-ment when I am most utterly alone, in another I am then least alone, most suffused by the presence of the Church which lives from the Passover (through death to life) of Christ.

The doctrine of purgatory stems from the Church's practice of prayer for the departed. "Remember, Lord, those who have died and have gone before us marked with the sign of faith, especially those for whom we now pray. . . . May these and all who sleep in Christ find in your presence light, happiness, and peace" (Roman Canon). Among the Eastern liturgies, the Coptic Rite may stand for all: "Remember all those who have fallen asleep, of the priesthood and of the order of laity, and grant them rest in the bosom of Abraham, of Isaac and of Jacob, in a green place beside the waters of repose, from whence pain, sadness, and groaning have fled." Again, in a Mass of Requiem, "In the first place, remember your servant N., for who today we offer these gifts. Let him be well remembered at your holy altar and pardon him his sins and transgressions." United to the sacrifice of Christ and to his intercession, then, the Church offers prayers for the dead. She does this during the Mass, but also at funeral services and other liturgical com-memorations of the dead. While the fundamental personal situation of the departed, vis-à-vis God's judgment, cannot change, since their earthly existence has ended, the Church expects the "holy souls" to pass from a condition of nonenjoyment of the blessed life (resulting from the effects of sin) to one of joy and peace in Christ. Such prayer bases its efficacy on Christ's victory over the death-dealing powers, and his gift of life to the world, but also, thanks to the work of Christ, on faith in the Spirit's activity in the communion of saints—the intimate union of all the baptized in the body whose head is Christ. Though such prayer does not alter the eternal destiny of the dead, by the intercession of the Church as united to the Lord's sacrifice it causes them to benefit more fully from that sacrifice's fruits.

In her dogmatic teaching, the Catholic Church speaks with discretion of this intermediate state. In 1979 the Congregation for the Doctrine of the Faith in its *Letter on Certain Questions concerning Eschatology* declared: "The Church believes there may be purification of the elect previous to the vision of God, which is nevertheless totally different from the pains of the damned." About the "place" of this purification, its duration, and its manner the teaching office of the Church falls silent, leaving the question to spiritual tradition. In that tradition we find a number of images: in the Alexandrian Fathers, Athanasius and the Cappadocians, purification by fire (where "fire" may represent the intensity of desire for God); in the Cappadocians and Ambrose of Milan, an opening of the paradise gates guarded as these are by the cherubim and the flaming sword; in Athanasius and the Desert Fathers, stages along the roads leading to heaven.

The crucial thing to note is that, in the Church's vision, the "holy souls" deserve our prayer because of their goodness. Their presence in purgatory is a proof of their faith, hope, and charity. The alms Christians bestow in the cultus of the dead is par excellence charity to the poor: the holy dead are the most deserving poor of all. The souls in Thomas More's *Supplycacyon* put it simply: "Remember, friends, how nature and Christendom [= baptism] bindeth you to remember us."[27] The Gaelic tradition of the western isles of Scotland calls purgatory the "Hell of the Holy Fathers," and sees Christ's people purified there

> Till they are whiter than the swan of the songs,
> Till they are whiter than the seagull of the waves,
> Till they are whiter than the snow of the peaks,
> And whiter than the white love of the heroes.[28]

27. Thomas More, *The Supplycacyon of Soulys against the Supplycacyon of Beggars* (London, 1529).

28. A. Carmichael, ed., *Carmina Gadelica: Hymns and Incantations* 3 (Edinburgh, 1940) 371.

The Protestant rejection of purgatory (and prayer for the dead) is seen by Catholicism as based on a mistaken interpretation of the mediation of Christ. Christ's mediation of human salvation is indeed unique and all-sufficient, but it is not separated from the prayer of his Church. The head and the body are one, and the head's glory as Savior is the greater in that he encourages the body to share in the communication to the whole human mass of the effects of his redeeming work. What the Lord has done for us in his mighty salvation he grants to us to do ourselves. The continuum of life in Christ is more primary than the biological continuum. As sharers, *in via*, of the life of Christ who called himself "the way," we (super)naturally wish both to pray for the holy souls and to seek their prayers.

The eternity of *hell* is for the Church a consequence of human inward obduracy. It springs from one aspect of the essence of freedom, which is the possibility, while we are yet wayfarers, of a constant revision of our decisions. Eternity is in this perspective the definitive achievement of history. "The just God is 'active' in the punishment of Hell only insofar as he does not release man from the reality of the definitive state which man himself has achieved on his own behalf, contradictory though this state be to the world of God's creation."[29] In Matthew 25:31-46, the parable of the last judgment, whereas at their encounter with the Son of Man, the good go to a place intended for them, thus fulfilling their destiny, the bad go to a place never intended for human beings at all. This parable reflects other parables of Jesus, of which Mark 9:43-45 may stand as representative. Here, just as the refusal to amputate a diseased limb may result in the corruption of the whole body, so the refusal of self-denial may result in the total corruption and dissolution of the personality. Jesus evidently believed final impenitence to be a possibility: it is possible to lose the capacity for seeking truth, for recognizing justice and mercy. But equally clearly, Jesus believed that all were capable of salvation: the "many" of Mark 10:45 does not mean "not all" (cf. 1 Tim 3:5-6).

The Catholic Church does not in fact pronounce either on who may be damned or even on whether the category "the damned" contains any human individuals at all. Neither, however—as the affirmation of the real possibility of hell demonstrates—does she teach universalism. In this ambivalence (not contradiction) her teaching reflects the witness of the New Testament itself. Thus Paul, for example, sometimes

---

29. K. Rahner, "Hell," *Sacramentum Mundi* 3 (New York and London, 1969) 8–9.

speaks of all creation as coming to a glad acknowledgment of God, and at other times doubts his own salvation (as in Rom 9:27). Yet some would hold that it is precisely because God will not torture us or violate our personalities that he is bound in the end to break down our resistance. Over against the more usual interpretation of Christ's descent into Sheol in 1 Peter 3, namely that he made his proclamation to those who long ago had refused obedience, giving them a second chance of salvation, Balthasar revived Nicholas of Cusa's notion, sharpened by Luther, that Christ endured the torments of the lost, thus, in principle —or so one might argue—annihilating hell by redeeming it via his own atoning work—a speculation hard to reconcile with the doctrinal tradition's firm stand against any *presumption* of exceptionless salvation.

The lesson of hell is not the cruelty of God, but, rather, the awful responsibility of human freedom, and the darkness and agony into which our daily acts may be insensibly leading us. The doctrine of hell warns us of the horror of life without God and the torture a daily turning from light to darkness will bring. Hell is the self-made judgment whereby we confirm the inherent outcome of a refusal to remain and grow in divine friendship.

The goal of God's salvific self-involvement in his creation— *heaven*—is that we should know him as he is and enjoy him for ever. "We shall see him as he is" (1 John 3:2). "Now we see in a mirror dimly, but then face to face. Now I know in part; then I shall understand fully" (1 Cor 13:12). In enabling us to know him as he is, God invites us to share his own happiness. "This is eternal life, that they know you, the only true God" (John 17:3). Our filiation as "sons in the Son" will at last be manifest for what it is: an adopted share in the mutual love of the Father and his Son, Jesus Christ. "See what love the Father has given us, that we should be called children of God. Beloved, it does not yet appear that we shall be, but we know that when he appears we shall be like him, for we shall see him as he is" (1 John 3:1-2). Appropriately, then, the vision of God will be mediated to us (as is the whole of our salvation story) by the humanity of the Savior, the Lord of the thorn-crowned head and the five wounds. In the Revelation of John, the last book of the Bible, the central figure of the heavenly tableau is "the Lamb that was slain": a crucified man bearing the marks of wounds that have not healed, yet in no way diminish his radiance. No book of Scripture, unless it be the Psalter, has been illustrated more often, and none has inspired so many works of art (sculpture, painting, etching, not to speak of tapestry and stained glass). The Christian imagination seized on the notion that the picture-space of heaven is organized by a figure where God is seen in the human, and the human in God, for the sevenfold Spirit of the Lord has anointed Jesus as the Savior, and flows from the victorious sacrifice of the crucified Christ. The "sharing in the divine nature" which the Second Letter of Peter holds out as the foremost of God's "precious and very great promises" (2 Pet 1:3-4) has of necessity a Trinitarian dimension. Furthermore, it involves a loving understanding of the will and plan of the only God: a perfect gaze on the Christological and pneumatological structure of redemption history.

> After this I looked and behold a great multitude which no man could number, from every nation, from all tribes and peoples and tongues, standing before the throne and before the Lamb, clothed in white robes, with palm branches in their hands, and crying out with a loud voice, "Salvation belongs to our God who sits upon the throne and to the Lamb." And all the angels stood round the throne and round the elders and the four living creatures, and they fell on their faces before the throne and worshipped God, saying, "Amen! Blessing and glory and wisdom and thanksgiving and power and might be to our God for ever and ever! Amen" (Rev 7:8-12).

In God, as the origin and goal of all reality that is not God, all other reality will be known and loved by the saints, in the manner and measure in which it concerns them. In knowing the holy mystery which grounds the world and the world's incorporation into the divine life of Father, Son, and Spirit, knowledge itself will be raised into the bliss of love. With Aquinas, we may speak of the very essence of God providing the form in which our minds may know his mystery (which otherwise infinitely exceeds them). By way of the sacrament of Jesus' humanity, we come, in the Word, to share God's self-knowledge, being related to him as the Son is to the Father. With his intellectualist emphasis Aquinas considers this as a transformation of our minds: as in everyday understanding concepts through which we know the world give the mind shape and structure, conforming it to the realities of things, so here at the climax of our journey of understanding we receive God himself as the structuring form of our intelligence. Of course at the same time (and here the Franciscan school's characteristic emphasis usefully supplements that of the Dominican) our wills need divine strengthening, if they are ever to be attuned to their almighty object. Not the light of the glory only but the fire of the kingdom must set human powers ablaze. We are like packets of seeds, or boxes of fire-works, as Chesterton said of the Thomist doctrine of beatitude. In the fruition, the trees burst into flower, the rockets into flame.

But just as the personal, interior history of God's predestining grace is not without its correlate in the public, exterior narrative of world history, so here too: the fulfillment of the gift of grace lies not only in the personal, interior eschatology of the beatific vision, but also in the public, exterior transformation of the world which is the Parousia, the "end of history." With the Lord's parousia this world will come to its end in the universal judgment. If we ask what "the world" is, the answer must be that it is the total set of relations of which we form part. The Church, making her own the voice of Scripture, proph-esies that this total set of relations will come to an end, and a new set take its place. What this new set will be like is foreshadowed in the sacraments of the Church, where the onset of the kingdom is antici-pated.

The world inaugurated by the general judgment will be a world of wholeness and holiness, a world healed and restored; it will also be a world with bitter knowledge of the judgment on sin, of excommuni-cation, and gifts that were fruitless because the human person was not open to profit by them. It will be, then, at once a more wonderful world, and a more terrible one: heaven and hell. Scripture speaks of it both as a banquet where all the nations will feast together in the pres-ence of the Most High, and a day of lamentation when the tribes of the earth will wail for him whom they have pierced. Its common factor, therefore, is that it will be a world of the most lucid moral and spirit-ual clarity where the mercy and the justice of God are freely revealed and the thoughts of all hearts laid bare. As the final revelation of the victories of Christ's grace, it will be the disclosure of the personal econ-omy of the Spirit who enabled these victories, of his unique hyposta-sis in the multiform faces of the saints.

And yet even here there is still a deficiency: we have hardly touched on the *resurrection of the body*.

The life everlasting experienced as the resurrection of the body (not simply for the individual but for the entire communion of the re-deemed) is the ultimate Christian hope. Bodily death in its hideous-ness is not only punishment for sin; it is also the dreadful symbol of sin's essential deformity. It is not just the repulsiveness of decompos-ing flesh that makes death ugly. The separation of soul from body mars the beauty of human nature which God made as a matter-spirit unity.

The divine bridegroom's aim in assuming human nature, and in dying and rising again in it, is to draw the Church, his bride, into his own beauty—first in soul by grace, then in body in glory. The Word, "the Beauty that beautifies the universe" (Bonaventure) in creating the world, is now the world's "Re-beautifier" in redeeming it. Christ rises from the dead as "the first fruits of them that sleep" (1 Cor 15:20). What Christ as God can originate (the raising up of the dead to everlasting life), he wills as man to mediate (for it is through his human voice that the dead will rise [John 5:28]). And since what he as head exemplifies his members are to become, when he returns in the glorious parousia he will shape our lowly bodies, as our crown of beauty, into the likeness of his lovely one. In Christ rose the whole reality of human nature, all that goes to make up its comeliness. "This corruptible and mortal must put on incorruption and immortality through configuration to the glory of the body of Christ, who is our head. It would be unbecoming for the head to be beautiful and immortal while the members were corruptible and ugly."[30] The final and complete redemption of the human being is the resurrection from the dead. Even in heaven, the faithful departed long for this consummation.

> And I heard in the divinest light
> Of the smaller circle a simple voice
> Perhaps like that of the angel who spoke to Mary,
>
> Answer: "As long as this festivity
> Of paradise shall last, so long our love
> Will shed around us such rays as clothe us.
>
> When our flesh, then glorified and holy,
> Is put on us once more, our persons will be
> In greater perfection as being complete at last:
>
> Because there will be an accession of that light
> Which is freely given us by the highest good,
> Light which enables us to see Him;
>
> In this way the vision must grow clearer,
> And the warmth produced by it must grow too,
> As well as the rays which shine out of it.
>
> But, like charcoal which gives out a flame
> And yet glows more brightly than the flame itself

---

30. Bonaventure, *Sermons for Passion Sunday* 1; see J. Saward, "'The Flesh Flowers Again'": St. Bonaventure and the Aesthetics of the Resurrection," *Downside Review* 110 (1992) 1–29.

So that it keeps its outline and appearance,

So the radiance which surrounds us now
Will be outshone by the brilliance of the flesh
Which now lies buried in the earth;

Nor will so much light weary us at all;
For the organs of the body will be strong
To everything able to give us pleasure."

One and another chorus seemed to me
So quick and eager to say "Amen!"
That it was clear they wanted their dead bodies;

Perhaps not just for themselves, but for their mothers,
For their fathers and others who were dear to them
Before they turned into eternal flames.[31]

The resurrection of the human body of God's Son is in principle the glorification of the entire visible universe, the regeneration of the cosmos. The sacramental economy of the Church depends on this truth. Matter can be sanctified and sanctifying not only because, through creation, it is good and beautiful and integral to human nature, but also because, through the incarnation and bodily resurrection of the Word, God has raised it to an incomparable grandeur and promised it an indestructible glory. This is how Augustine described the "eternal felicity" of the city of God in its "perpetual Sabbath":

How great will be that felicity, where there will be no evil, where no good will be withheld, where there will be leisure for the praises of God, who will be all in all. What other occupation could there be, in a state where there will be no inactivity of idleness, and yet no toil constrained by want? I can think of none. And this is the picture suggested to my mind by the sacred canticle, when I read or hear the words, "Blessed are those who dwell in your house; they will praise you for ever and ever!"

All the limbs and organs of the body, no longer subject to decay, the parts which we now see assigned to various essential functions, will then be freed from all such constraint, since full, secure, certain and eternal felicity will have displaced necessity; and all those parts will contribute to the praise of God. For even those elements in the bodily harmony of which I have already spoken, the harmonies which, in our present state, are hidden, will then be hidden no longer. Dispersed internally and externally throughout the whole body, and combined with other great and marvellous things that will then be revealed, they will

31. Dante, *Paradiso* canto 14, lines 34–66.

kindle our rational minds to the praise of the great Artist by the delight afforded by a beauty that satisfies the reason.

I am not rash enough to attempt to describe what the movements of such bodies will be in that life, for it is quite beyond my power of imagination. However, everything there will be lovely in its form, and lovely in motion and in rest, for anything that is not lovely will be excluded. And we may be sure that where the spirit wills there the body will straightway be; and the spirit will never will anything but what is to bring new beauty to the spirit and the body.

There will be true glory, where no one will be praised in error or in flattery; there will be true honor, where it is denied to none who is worthy, and bestowed on none who is unworthy. And honor will not be courted by any unworthy claimant, for none but the worthy can gain admission there. There will be true peace, where none will suffer attack from within himself nor from any foe outside.

The reward of virtue will be God himself, who gave the virtue, together with the promise of himself, the best and greatest of all possible promises. For what did he mean when he said, in the words of the prophet, "I shall be their God, and they will be my people"? Did he not mean, "I shall be the source of their satisfaction; I shall be everything that men can honorably desire: life, health, food, wealth, glory, honor, peace and every blessing"? For that is also the correct interpretation of the Apostle's words, "so that God may be all in all." He will be the goal of all our longings; and we shall see him for ever; we shall love him without satiety; we shall praise him without wearying. This will be the duty, the delight, the activity of all, shared by all who share the life of eternity.[32]

In their "clothing" in the garments of incorruption after the resurrection, bodies are protected from natural corruption. To express this in a language less distant from that of natural science (for it is a transfigured biology with which we have to do), their matter would suffer no degenerative change, but since in all material organisms entropic change there must be, the human body would need some fresh source of energy: this could be created by God *ex nihilo* (the simplest account) or (as some have suggested) there could be a God-given version of an energizing device—beyond the capacities of contemporary engineering techniques but theoretically discussed in modern physics—that would provide for nutritional needs and the disposal of metabolic by-products. An implanted device with a tiny black hole or naked singu-

32. Augustine, City of God 22.30.

larity at its center might be able to exploit the properties of matter or singularity to achieve this. Such a physics of "superradiant scattering" has already been worked out on earth; how much more readily may the divine ingenuity envisage it in the kingdom!

The nature of Catholic eschatology soars up to leave behind the question of optimism or pessimism in regard to the world and its history. Orthodox Christians are more aware than others that human nature has need of purification, to be brought to perfection through Christ's cross and resurrection. They can accept neither a philosophy that would canonize and eternalize a world ruined by sin and condemned to death, nor one that would, in its pessimism, contradict the meaning of the incarnation of the Son of God who came into the world to bring joy, in a life triumphant over death.

7
The Church

The topic of "the Church" naturally follows that of "salvation." Our Christological enquiry has prepared us for the discovery that there can be no salvation without the mediation of the Church's head, the incarnate Word. Against some modern theologians—notably those concerned to find parallel ways of salvation in the great religions of the East—we have to say that never can the saving work of the Logos be found in splendid isolation from that of Jesus Christ. Some would speak of unevangelized people as "anonymous Christians," a phrase acceptable enough if it be taken to mean that the graces human beings receive are always the grace of Christ, even though this goes unrecognized by them. But the term is sometimes taken to imply that the real substance of Christianity is available without any explicit knowledge of or belief in the gospel, and that only the name of Christian is lacking to the unevangelized who follow the dictates of personal conscience. How could such a position ever be reconciled with the salvific importance which Bible and Tradition attach to the proclamation of the gospel and to explicit faith in Christ?

Now we must take a further step and say that, in the salvation of non-Christians, the Church is always involved, since saving grace is itself always ecclesial. The mediation of Christ, though it excludes other agents' parallel efforts, includes participated forms of mediation, which draw their efficacy from his unique work. Under Christ (in "submediation"), the Church is the divinely appointed way of salvation. Though the gifts of grace and salvation may be given to people who are not, and do not consciously wish to be, her members, without her neither grace nor salvation is possible.

The Church exists to perpetuate Christ's redemptive work, equipped for this task as she is by her apostolic heritage of faith, sacraments, and ministry, together with the promised assistance of the risen Christ, who acts through the gift of the Holy Spirit. Not only is she, in the words of Pope John Paul II's encyclical *Redemptoris mater,* the "first beneficiary" of salvation, since Christ won his bride at the price of his own blood. She is also, as the Second Vatican Council loved to say, the "universal sacrament of salvation." Ever since the moment of Pentecost, believing the gospel and entering the ecclesial ark of the gospel community is the way of salvation desired by God for all members of the human race.

Catholic discourse about the Church is lyrical. But to avoid misunderstanding we must begin by setting out what it is we are speaking of in cooler, even canonical (and hence legal), language. To be fully incorporated in the Church it is a necessary (though not, as the philosophers say, a sufficient) condition to be a baptized Christian in union with bishops themselves in communion with the Roman pope—in a word, a Catholic. "Those baptised are in full communion with the Catholic Church here on earth who are joined with Christ in his visible body through the bonds of profession of faith, the sacraments and ecclesiastical governance,"[1] and even then we must add the negative rider "and who are not legitimately excommunicated" for some grave offense against the Christian life. These are necessary conditions for adherence to the Church's saving fellowship. They remain insufficient, however, for unity with her at the deepest level, which requires the gift of the indwelling Spirit and perseverance in charity. Henri de Lubac was not speaking of some purely ideal Church when he chiselled this mosaic of texts from Scripture, the Fathers, and the medievals:

> She is the dwelling-place prepared on the mountain-tops and foretold by the prophets, to which, one day, all nations are to come to live in unity under the law of the one God. She is the treasure-chamber in which the apostles have laid up the truth, which is Christ; the one and only hall in which the Father celebrates the wedding of his Son; and since it is in her that we receive our forgiveness, it is through her that we have access to life and the gifts of the Holy Spirit. We cannot believe in her as we believe in the Author of our salvation, but we do believe that she is the Mother who brings us our regeneration.[2]

---

1. *Codex Iuris Canonici* (1983), canon 205; *Codex Canonum Ecclesiarum Orientalium* (1990), canon 8.

2. H. de Lubac, *The Splendour of the Church* (London and New York, 1956) 20.

Two most important nuances must now be added. First, other Christian Churches and ecclesial communities have, happily, some at least of the divinely instituted means of grace—most notably, the Scriptures, certain sacraments, and spiritual traditions. Considered as means of salvation these derive their efficacy from that "fullness of grace and truth which has been entrusted to the Catholic Church."[3] "On her own recognisances," then, the Catholic Church herself in this sense lives and acts by way of these schismatic (or partially schismatic) communities.

Second, and more widely, non-Catholics, and non-Christians, have the possibility of being "ordered"—oriented—to the true Church by what Pope Pius XII called an "unconscious will and desire." As the Second Vatican Council put it: "Since Christ died for everyone, and since the ultimate calling of all human beings is one and divine, we are obliged to hold that the Holy Spirit offers everyone the possibility of sharing in this Paschal mystery in a manner known to God."[4] Perhaps this happens by way of a divine illumination in the moment of "passover" at the hour of every person's death—a view that has the merit of reconciling the modern teaching that God's salvific will extends to every individual with the thesis (supported by many Fathers and medieval divines) that no one can be saved in the Christian era without explicit belief in the Trinity and the incarnation.

In the language of Scholasticism: within the mystery of the Church's outreach to all human beings both "final" and "efficient" causality are at work. Those ignorant of the Church are nonetheless, when they respond to grace, moved toward her (final causality), while she for her part, as an "instrument for the redemption of all,"[5] acts as a moving agent (efficient causality) in their salvation. For those whom she cannot reach with her proclamation she offers prayer, the holy sacrifice of the altar, and the spiritual sacrifices of her children, and in all these ways sets up hidden filaments of connection with those beyond her bounds. The body is always involved in the dispensing of grace, for the head has joined it indissolubly to himself.

In the Catholic understanding of the Church, the vertical is the primary dimension of her consciousness. That dimension makes her aware that she has come from God—sent by the Father, through the incarnate Word and the Holy Spirit, on her own "horizontal" mission to

3. *Unitatis redintegratio*, 3.
4. *Gaudium et spes*, 22.
5. *Lumen gentium*, 9.

the world God created and redeemed. When we look at the Church with that illumination of the mind which revelation and dogmatic thought make possible, we see that her structure is that of a communion, and a communion that makes manifest the yet more fundamental structure of the Christian mystery as a whole: namely, the way Christ shares with us the life of the triune God himself. The dogmas that enable us to grasp what the Church is are twofold: they are Christological and Trinitarian.

In Jesus Christ, divinity and humanity were not only perfectly united: they also actively penetrated each other. God made his own life shareable, so that it made its way into the humanity of Christ: "in him . . . all the fullness of the Godhead dwells bodily" (Col 1:19). The Church, though prepared in Israel, and indeed from the beginning of the human race, nay, the foundation of the world, truly came forth only at the moment when the energies of that divine humanity began to pass into other men and women—when, with the resurrection and ascension, the Crucified entered completely into the glory for which his perfect love equipped him, and, with Pentecost, the power of his Holy Spirit sent that glory into the history of the world.

The Church of the Father, through Christ, in the Spirit

Energy and *power* are impersonal terms, but the divine form of them which the Spirit communicates to us is nothing other than the life of the Trinity itself, the original mystery which throws light on everything else, all that is originated from it. Perhaps the most important reality on which the mystery of the Trinity throws light is the human individual. In its light we see that individual as a person—a point where absolute unity and absolute diversity coincide. A person is neither an isolated individual nor the source of those conflictual oppositions and damaging multiplicities that isolated individuals generate. Rather is the person diversity in unity. Persons are infinitely different yet endlessly united, whereas individuals tend either to become like each other or to become enemies. We know from the Trinity, however, that the full realization of personal existence consists in unique selves united in one Being. Father, Son, and Holy Spirit are defined by their differences, yet the Father is never alone, never without his Son, and the duality of Father and Son is itself transcended by the Holy Spirit. Each exists by giving to the others what it is, and the extension of that kind of personhood to the world is the sign of the work of the Holy

Spirit on earth. Human beings become different from each other without being opposed to each other, since they "propose" (put forward) others in the same moment that they propose themselves. Christian existence is, therefore, a spirituality of the self-in-communion. It stands equally over against Western individualism and over against the Oriental exaltation of a self lost in beatific solitude.

The Church, accordingly, is the sphere where such communion is created. It is the extension of the unity in diversity of the Holy Trinity to the world. Its center can only be, then, the Eucharist, which we call precisely "holy communion," and of which Paul wrote to the Corinthians that by participating in it those who are many become one body, since they all share in the one bread. Because such communion in the holy gifts brings about in us the presence of the Spirit of Christ, it is also the foundation for a communion of holy people. The *communio sanctorum*, which we affirm in the Creed, means in the first place a sharing in the *sancta*, "holy things," but for that very reason it also means a sharing in the life of *sancti*, "holy people," the "communion of saints." Christian consciousness is not individual but personal, and therefore ecclesial. It does not belong to the individual who has separated himself or herself from the rest of humanity, and in that way darkened the revelation of Trinitarian love, but to the person who realizes in the Holy Spirit his or her Eucharistic co-being with all the rest. That is why thinking with the Church is the proper form of Christian theology, and attentiveness to the consensus of the Church the distinctive virtue of Christian teachers.

It is as the nexus of the work of Son and Spirit that the mystery of the Church is best understood. If the Son is the authoritative teacher of truth in the world, the Spirit is the living freedom of God. When freedom defines itself over against authority, regarding the latter as something external and to that degree alienating, a pseudo-freedom arises, made up of protest and revolt. Christ's obedience to death was not a surrender of his freedom to such an outside force, but the expression of his total unity in the Spirit with the Father. The life of the Church, as a life by the Word in the Spirit, lies beyond the dichotomy of freedom and authority. That prophet of the mid-twentieth-century ecclesiological renaissance, Romano Guardini, wrote:

> Individual personality starves in a frigid isolation if it is cut off from the living community, and the Church must necessarily be intolerable to those who fail to see in her the pre-condition of their most individual

and personal life; who view her only as a power which confronts them and which, far from having any share in their most intimate vital purpose, actually threatens or represses it. Man's living will cannot accept a Church so conceived. He must either rise in revolt against her, or else submit to her as the costly price of salvation. But the man whose eyes have been opened to the meaning of the Church experiences a great and liberating joy. For he sees that she is the living presupposition of his own personal existence, the essential path to his own perfection. And he is aware of profound solidarity between his personal being and the Church; how the one lives by the other, and how the life of the one is the strength of the other.[6]

The Church is "full of the Trinity."[7] The Church cannot be thought without thinking at the same time of those mysteries that form the heart of Christian revelation. This Trinitarian life in Christ is, however, given to the Church not so that she can enclose it within herself, but, on the contrary, so that she may communicate it to all humanity. For the problem of unity-in-difference to which by grace she holds the key is the fundamental problem of human living at every level—from the individual psyche, through marriage and the family, to civil society and the international order. The world, it is true, could not become such a communion without becoming the Church, just as the Church could not fully become that communion she is called to be without becoming the kingdom. But this is precisely what we pray for each day in the Our Father. We pray for a total integration of the human creation, not obliterating the precious distinctiveness of its selved parts, but rather enhancing them. "Thy kingdom come, on earth as it is in heaven" is a prayer which was answered, for in the exaltation of the Crucified, earth and heaven were joined.

Not surprisingly, then, Catholicism favours speaking of the mystery of the Church as the "sacrament of Christ." At Pentecost, the Spirit of Christ is sent upon the apostles so as to form the social body of the Church as the continuing instrument of God's saving work. In Israel, God's Word, his self-communication, was already ordered to the creation of a unique community, a transformed people, in and through which God's plan for history would be realized. But if Jesus is in a total and absolute way God's communication of his Word, his own inner life, and is this in an embodied human existence, then he could not but

---

6. R. Guardini, *The Church and the Catholic* (London, 1935) 46.
7. Origen, *Excerpts on the Psalms* 23.1.

transform the community of the promise. On the biblical view of how God's self-disclosure and humanity's salvation come about, he could not but found a community. If he really is God's self-communication, then he must necessarily be, in his own person, the foundation of the Church. For that communication is always "community-shaped," taking the form of a divinized community in whom God is then known. Augustine, in his homilies on the Psalms, declares that the Word was made flesh in order to become the head of the Church. And the Letter to the Ephesians speaks of the passion as Christ giving himself up for the Church that he might "present her to himself in splendor" (5:27), holy and immaculate. The Church is the visible sign and mediation of the embodied grace (the "sacrament") which is Christ.

The sacramental idea enables us to articulate a grasp of the Church as signifying, in historically tangible form, the redeeming grace of the Savior. The symbolic structures that constitute the Church as a sign of Christ's redeeming work are, on the one hand, the seven sacraments and, on the other, the concrete expressions of faith, hope, and charity found among those attached to Christ through the sacramental pattern. Because the Church is the milieu where the redemptive work of Christ becomes efficacious in the Holy Spirit, she is the primordial sacrament of the grace of God for all human beings. Such ecclesial sacramentalism carries a necessary load of paschal realism: if the Church is really endowed with so high a calling, she can expect to tread no other road than that of the Easter Savior whom, in the divine drama of continuing time, she represents. In history she both suffers and is (for a time) glorified, in likeness of her Lord, until that final trial and triumph which Christ promised for the end of time.

> She, too, was betrayed and crucified; "dying daily," like her great Lord; denied, mocked, and despised; a child of sorrows and acquainted with grief; misrepresented, misconstrued, agonizing; stripped of her garments, yet, like the King's daughter that she is, "all glorious within"; dead even, it seemed at times, yet, like her natural prototype, still united to the Godhead; laid in the sepulchre, fenced in by secular powers, yet ever rising again on Easter Days, spiritual and transcendent; passing through doors that men thought closed for ever, spreading her mystical banquets in upper rooms and by sea shores; and, above all, ascending for ever beyond the skies and dwelling in heavenly places with Him who is her Bridegroom and her God.[8]

---

8. Benson, *Confessions of a Convert*, 109.

Theologically, for Catholics, the Church cannot be understood save in relation to the mystery of the Son; but the same is true with respect to that other expression of the Father's resourcefulness, his fontal being: the mystery of the Spirit. The Church was born at Pentecost, when she was generated by the Holy Spirit who is himself the living bond of love between the Father and the Son; and the Holy Spirit, as *anima Ecclesiae,* the Church's native spirit, remains the divine principle of her own fecundity. It is the Spirit who endows the Church with memory and consciousness, those essential features of personality which allow (and require) us to speak of Church as "she." The graces that God gives through the Church, the virtues he nurtures in her, are all made possible by the life-giving Spirit, sent thanks to the reconciling work of the Son. Alessandro Manzoni's poem *Pentecost* brings out this pneumatic basis of the Church:

> Mother of the Saints; image of the heavenly city; perpetual guardian of the ever-living Blood; you that for so many centuries have suffered, fought and prayed; that set up your tents from sea to sea;
>
> realm of those who hope; Church of the living God; where were you? what dark corner received you at your birth, when your King, drawn by villains up the hill to die, encrimsoned the clods of his sublime altar?
>
> And then, the sacred body now issued from the dark, when he breathed in the power of the new life; and when, the price of our pardon in his hands, he rose from this dust to the Father's throne;
>
> you, who suffering had watched him suffer, aware of the mysteries of his being, you, deathless daughter of his victory, where were you? Awake to nothing but your fears, safe alone in being forgotten, you stayed in seclusion and secrecy until that sacred day,
>
> when upon you the renewing Spirit descended, and kindled in your right hand the ever-burning torch; when as a beacon for the nations he placed you on the mountain, and on your lips set flowing the fountain of speech.
>
> As swift light pours down from one thing to another, bringing our diverse colours wherever it rests, such was the multiple echo of the Spirit's voice: Arabians, Parthians, Syrians heard it, each in his own tongue.
>
> O worshippers of idols, scattered on every shore, turn your eyes to Jerusalem, hear that holy cry: weary of its vile abasement, let the earth return to HIM: and you who are starting the course of happier times,
>
> wives whom the sudden throb of a hidden burden rouses; you now nearing the release from childbirth's pains; to the lying goddess of maternity raise no song: sacred to the Holy One is that which grows within you.

Why does the slave still sigh as she kisses her little ones? and look with envy at the breast that suckles the freeborn? Does she not know that to his kingdom the Lord raises the wretched whose lot he shared? that in his agony he had all Eve's children in mind?

A new freedom the heavens announce, and new peoples; new conquests and a glory won through nobler trials; a new peace, firm against terrors, firm against sly flattery; a peace the world scoffs at, but cannot take away.

O Spirit! We—whether suppliants at your high altars, or lonely travellers through wild forests, or roaming the open seas; from the freezing Andes to Lebanon, from Ireland to rocky Haiti, scattered on every shore, in heart at one in You—

we implore You! Come down again, gentle Spirit; gracious to your worshippers, gracious to him who knows you not; come down and remake us; revive the hearts grown faint with doubt; and may the victor be a divine recompense to the vanquished.

Come down, Love; calm in our souls all anger born of pride; inspire thoughts which the hour of our death will leave unchanged, when the past comes back in memory; and may your gifts be nourished by your kindly strength; as the sun draws out from the torpid seed the flower,

that will droop and die on the common grass, nor rise with the coloured splendour of its unfolded petals, unless, poured down through the air, that soft light return to it, giver of life, untiring nourisher.[9]

And if the Church is all of this, the special creation of the Father in the image of the communion of the triune life, the sacrament of Christ, born of the Holy Spirit, then she must have the most intimate relation to the reign of God—God's kingdom, the center of Jesus' preaching. The Church is the bearer and present form of that kingdom. She is the point at which the powers and blessings of the age to come (God's effective rule over his creation, and thus its fulfillment in him) break through into present time, and from her pass into the world. As Pope Paul VI wrote in the *Credo of the People of God,* "We profess that the Kingdom of God begins here on earth in the Church of Christ," echoing the words of the Swiss theologian Charles Journet: "The kingdom is already on earth, and the Church already in heaven."[10]

---

9. From the translation by Kenelm Foster in "'Pentecost' and Other Poems," *Comparative Criticism: A Year Book* 3 (1981) 203–4.

10. C. Journet, *L'Eglise du Verbe incarné* (Bruges, 1951) 2:57.

Aspects of the Church

In the Creed, we confess the Holy Spirit as unifying, sanctifying and preserving in the wholeness (catholicity) of the apostolic faith the Church to which we belong: "we believe in one, holy, catholic, and apostolic Church." Since the Church is, then, a new creation by the Holy Spirit, analogous to the first creation when he moved over the chaos waters, and to the moment of the annunciation, when he brought about the incarnation in Mary's womb, there is, naturally enough, a spirituality of the Church. A text for the consecration of a church building says:

> You hallow the Church you have founded by unceasing activity. This is the true house of prayer, the temple of the dwelling-place of your glory, the seat of incommutable truth, the sanctuary of everlasting love. This is the ark which has brought us into the harbour of salvation, hauled up from the flood of this world. This is the beloved and only bride, which Christ acquired with his blood. In her womb we are reborn by your grace; we are nourished with the milk of your Word; we are strengthened by the Bread of Life, and cherished by your manifold mercy.[11]

By contrast, there is in Protestantism, to the Catholic eye, an inadequate sense of the continuing reality of the incarnate One in his body. In Protestant thought the Church is seen as the gathering *(congregatio)* of men and women who have already come to faith, through learning to know God in Christ. In Catholicism, the Church herself is the gatherer *(convocatio)*, calling people to the kingdom, her life the very form in which we come to faith, and learn, in Christ, the knowledge of God.

The chief symbol in which Catholics express their instinct for the Church as (under God) their life-giver is *Ecclesia mater*: "Mother Church." In this figure, the Church stands forth as mediatrix of salvation in continuity with the divine action. God's vivifying, environing, and securing maternity comes to expression in her activity. Just as the old Israel was portrayed as bride and mother by Hosea, and Jerusalem as future mother of many nations in Second Isaiah, so in the Letter to the Galatians, the Church is the fecund mother of all who are born in the Spirit by virtue of union with Christ. In his treatise on the Church's unity the North African Doctor Cyprian defines the aim of his pastorate as ensuring that "our Mother should have the happiness of clasping to her bosom all our people in one like-minded body . . . [for]

---

11. Consecration rites are a neglected source of Latin ecclesiology: see R. W. Muncey, *History of the Consecration of Churches* (London, 1930).

nothing that is separated from the parent stock can ever live or breathe apart."[12] If then she alone communicates divine sonship, "One cannot have God for Father if he has not the Church for Mother."[13]

The Church as communion is thought of by Catholic theologians on two levels. Externally, the ecclesial communion is constituted by the totality of the means of grace—the Word preached and taught, the Word celebrated in sacramental form, the Word present in the pastoral office of the apostolic succession of her bishops and priests (and deacons)—as that is exercised within, not over against, the holy people formed by the Word preached and taught, by the sacraments celebrated. Internally, that communion is the life of grace of which these visible realities are the sign. Together they constitute the Church. So far we have been speaking by and large of the internal communion but the bond of union is more than sharing some identical attitude or enjoying mutual friendly affection: it is also the public peace and unity, papally guarded, of bishops and faithful. We must now turn to a fuller account of the visible face of the Church.

If the Church is a mystery, from the Father, through Christ, in the Spirit, her mystery is embodied in a social form. She is, ineluctably, an institution. Jesus, in commissioning the Twelve as leaders of a company of disciples, founded a visible community endowed with a common mission and the means whereby to realize it. At the very beginnings of the formal discipline of ecclesiology (the study of the Church) in the early fourteenth-century Latin West, the Church is spoken of, accordingly, as a "kingdom," differing from other kingdoms only in the supernatural character of its foundation and its end. In the context of the Reformation, Catholics would stress ever more emphatically the visible character of the Church (over against Luther's dichotomy of the invisible-spiritual and visible-natural orders, with the latter consigned to the reign of sin). In the writings of Robert Bellarmine, for instance (a good example of a "doctor raised up by God to defend the walls of Jerusalem"),[14] the Church is defined as all those professing the right faith, communicating in valid sacraments, and obeying legitimate pastors. And since relation to lawful pastors is needful in order to find out what should count as "right" faith and "valid" sacraments, there is a natural highlighting of the element of government in this ecclesial kingdom which prepares the kingdom of

12. Cyprian, *On the Unity of the Church* 23.
13. Cyprian, *Letter* 74.
14. A. Gréa, *L'eglise et sa divine constitution,* 2d ed. (Paris, 1965) preface.

God. Thus the eighteenth-century English bishop Richard Challoner, commenting on the *types* or foreshadowings of the Church in ancient Israel, remarks that:

> All these glorious characters set down in the Scriptures, relating to the Church of Christ, or the people of God of the New Testament, evidently point out to us a society, founded by Christ himself, with all power and authority from him; and by his commission, propagated far and near throughout the world; a society which from this beginning should ever flourish till time itself should end; ever one, ever holy, ever orthodox; founded upon a rock, proof against all the powers of hell; secured against error by the perpetual presence and assistance of Christ, her King, her Shepherd and her Spouse; who is the Way, the Truth and the Life; ever taught and directed by his Spirit, the Holy Ghost, the Spirit of Truth; furnished by him with a perpetual succession of church guides, pastors and teachers, divinely appointed, and divinely assisted; favoured by a solemn oath of God himself, promising his peace and loving kindness for ever; and assured by him, that his Spirit, the pure profession of his words, his light, and his sanctuary, should be with her for ever more.[15]

It is a basic task of ecclesiology today so to revalue the institution as to let it appear as the plausible organ of the Church as mystery. For, as Pope Leo XIII pointed out in his letter *Satis cognitum:*

> Christ is one by the union of the two natures, the visible and the invisible, and he is one in them both; in the same way, the mystical body is only truly Church on condition that the visible aspects draw their strength and vitality from the supernatural gifts, and other invisible elements, and it is from this union that the proper nature of the external aspects themselves results.

Not the least significant aspect of this enterprise is a more truly ecclesial reading of the phenomenon of canon law, now seen as a real raid on revealed truth, captured by a distinctive means and logic, as the Church-mystery enters the social nexus with binding force. If the Church is a society she must have a law. So much is obvious, but the unique qualities of this society must also be brought out if canon law is not to be simply the engrafting of secular law-forms, naturalistically, onto the Church's stem. The philosophical notions that underlie much modern

---

15. R. Challoner, *A Caveat against the Methodists* (London, 1760) 4, cited in *Challoner and His Church: A Catholic Bishop in Georgian England*, ed. E. Duffy (London, 1981) 111.

law-making are not applicable to canon law, whose self-understanding can never prescind from a strictly theological dimension. The society canon law directs is a sacramental mystery; an Enlightenment concept of the autonomy of natural reason cannot do it justice. This difference must be borne in mind in interpreting the canons as an aspect of the Christian reality.

Canon law is intended to be a schooling in ecclesial life together, contributing to the visibility of the people of God.

> Being, as she is, a body which is at one and the same time mystical and visible, she frees us, by the very fact of her existence, from the illusions of a spiritual vocation conceived as solitary and disembodied. . . . And she reminds us ceaselessly of our social vocation and the reality of our earthly condition. In so doing she recalls us to worship of the true God; the man who separates himself from the community of brotherhood turns imperceptibly from God to worship himself.[16]

The early Church had soon felt the need for a discipline in such areas as the admission of catechumens, reconciliation of the lapsed and the treatment of heretics, marriage, baptism, Eucharist, sacred space and time, the relief of the poor and the sick. The bonds of faith were complemented by the bonds of a common life. After Constantine the Church found it convenient to model some aspects of her law on civil law (for now Roman law was the law of Christians), but with an admixture of the ecclesial inventiveness of popes or bishops meeting in conclave. Gradually the idea of the "reception" of laws took hold as the canons of one council were tacked onto those of another. Canon collections were increasingly regarded as tools for the reform of the Church in godly order. In the West the composite *Corpus Iuris Canonici,* as unsystematic as Eastern canon law, and requiring a special class of interpreters (so difficult was it to consult), was replaced at the end of World War I by a codex where old laws became merely instruments of interpretation, their quality as law depending on their newly allotted place in the codex as a whole. Despite the opposition of some of the cardinalate, the new idea of the codex was born in part from admiration for the nineteenth-century civil codes. Still more recently, by shifting emphases in Catholic ecclesiology the Second Vatican Council, though it created no canons, made a revision of canon law inevitable.

---

16. Lubac, *The Splendour of the Church,* 131.

The two great codices which are its fruit (that of the Latin Church, and that of the Eastern Churches in communion with Rome) translate the council's ecclesiological vision of a Church both one and many in different respects into a program of practice.

So far as the single Catholic Church throughout the world and the many local Catholic Churches are concerned, the history of ecclesiology shows two ways of thinking through this crucial relation of the one and the many. One can have either a universalist or a particularist ecclesiology. That is: one can give a formal priority to the concept of the Church universal, or to the Church in particular. The first of these two perspectives has its full justification in the account of Pentecost in the Acts of the Apostles, where a single faith and life, born of the Spirit, are evidently meant to encompass all languages and cultures and so all particular Churches. This approach will lay its main stress on those elements in the Church's tradition that guard the principle of universality: letters of communion, the collegial symbolism at the ordination of a bishop, conciliarity, the unity of the episcopal college safeguarded by its communion with the bishop of Rome. Various particularities are seen as the explication, unfolded over time and across space, of the richness of a primordial unity. The second perspective, giving priority to the concept of the Church-in-particular, is also justified on grounds of Tradition.

> The Church of Christ is really present in all legitimately organised local groups of the faithful which, in so far as they are united to their pastors, are also quite appropriately called churches in the New Testament. For these are in fact, in their own localities, the new people called by God, in the power of the Holy Spirit and as the result of full conviction. In them the faithful are gathered together through the preaching of the Gospel of Christ, and the mystery of the Lord's Supper is celebrated "so that, by means of the flesh and blood of the Lord the whole brotherhood of the Body may be welded together." In each altar community, under the sacred ministry of the bishop, a manifest symbol is to be seen of that charity and "unity of the mystical body, without which there can be no salvation." In these communities, though they may often be small and poor, or existing in the diaspora, Christ is present through whose power and influence the one, holy, Catholic and apostolic Church is constituted. For "the sharing in the body and blood of Christ has no other effect than to accomplish our transformation into that which we receive."[17]

17. *Lumen gentium*, 26, with internal citations of a prayer from the Mozarabic liturgy; Thomas's *Summa theologiae* 3.73.3; and Leo the Great, *Sermons* 63.7.

In this perspective, it is the bishop's responsibility to ensure that, in the celebration of the Eucharist, his Church acts in such a way that the other Churches are able to recognize therein their own fullness of identity. At the same time, his Church must be able to recognize its own essential features in the others, as well as its true identity with them. Thus, since each bishop must ensure that the local communion is distinctively Christian, he has to make it aware of the universal communion of which it is part. And so the two perspectives meet, and are complementary.

In particularist ecclesiology, the whole Church is present in a particular Church; in universalist ecclesiology, by contrast, the whole Church is present only in the integration of all the particular Churches. If one thinks the universal Church from a particularist ecclesiology, one has the idea of the communion of Churches; through participation in this communion, the particular Churches express or "focus" the being of the entire Church. If, however, one thinks the particular Churches from a universalist ecclesiology, one understands the local Church as a portion of the people of God, existing through incorporation into the Church universal.

It would be quite wrong to attempt to suppress either perspective, since both are well based in the sources of revelation. Yet in a given period there may well be a need to express one more firmly than another in order to restore a balance between them. This should not be done in such a way as to create fresh imbalance! Some statements may fit only awkwardly into one or another perspective, and yet be required by Christian faith in the mystery of the Church. If in recent memory the particular Church has been unjustly neglected in Catholic practice, today it is likely to be distortingly exalted, as local culture and the values of pluralism and differentiation are, in the contemporary context, prized above unity of religious believing. In 1992, therefore, the Roman Congregation of the Doctrine of the Faith, in promulgating a letter on the Church as communion, thought fit to insist that

> the particular churches, insofar as they are part of the one Church of Christ, have a special relationship of mutual interiority with the whole, that is, with the universal Church, because in every particular church, the one, holy, catholic and apostolic Church of Christ is truly present and active. For this reason, the universal Church cannot be conceived as the sum of the particular churches, or as a federation of particular churches. That Church is not the result of the communion of the churches, but is,

in its essential mystery, a reality ontologically and temporally prior to every individual particular church.[18]

In aphoristic mood, the "Letter" proposes that the formula *Ecclesia in et ex ecclesiis*, "the Church is formed in and from the churches," is inseparable from its sister axiom, *Ecclesiae in et ex Ecclesia*, "the churches are formed in and from the Church." If all this sounds highly abstract, the text ends by making clear that it is dealing with something highly concrete: how Catholics should think of themselves.

> Every member of the faithful, through faith and Baptism, is inserted into the one, holy, catholic and apostolic Church. He does not belong to the universal Church in a mediate way, through belonging to a particular church, but in an immediate way, even though entry into and life within the universal Church are necessarily brought about in a particular church. From the point of view of the Church understood as communion, the universal communion of the faithful and the communion of the churches are not consequences of one another but constitute the same reality seen from different viewpoints. Moreover, one's belonging to a particular church never conflicts with the reality that in the Church no one is a stranger. Each member of the faithful, especially in the celebration of the Eucharist, is in his Church, in the Church of Christ, regardless of whether or not he belongs, according to canon law, to the diocese, parish or other particular community where the celebration takes place. In this sense, without impinging on the necessary regulations regarding juridical dependence, whoever belongs to one particular church belongs to all the churches, since belonging to the communion, like belonging to the Church, is never simply particular, but by its very nature is always universal.[19]

Laity, Hierarchy, Primacy

The Church's Scriptures present the Christian people as a prophetic and royal priesthood. Peter hails the recipients of his first letter as "a royal priesthood . . . that you may declare the wonderful deeds of him who called you out of darkness into his wonderful light" (2:9). This priesthood of all the faithful is established by the Son for the Father; as John remarks in Revelation: "[He] has made us a kingdom, priests to his God and Father" (Rev 1:6). The royal priesthood which the laity are is for the Father's glory: that is, for the realization of his purpose.

18. *Letter on Certain Aspects of the Church Understood As Communion*, 9.
19. Ibid., 10.

The Fathers of the Church are unanimous in taking the origin of this priesthood to be Christ. The Christian, after all, is a sharer in the Christ (Heb 3:14). The human being assumed by the Son of God to be his very own human expression is the "Anointed One" *(ho christos)*. He or she is divinely commissioned for a threefold office, at once prophetic, royal, and priestly. By incorporating all three functions in his own person, the incarnate Son reveals that he is the long-expected Messiah of Israel. He embraces and fulfills the three different kinds of messianic figure—the prophet, the king, the priest—found amongst the Old Testament people of God. Clearly, if Christians are sharers in Christ, they too must be in some way prophets, kings, priests.

The Lord does not only have a name, "Christ," that describes his messianic functions. He also has a proper name, "Jesus," which means "Savior"—a name that points to the goal which the messianic functions serve. We are incorporated into Christ Jesus, our salvation, through baptism, which brings us forgiveness of sins and newness of life. Augustine reports how "throughout the world, every day, you can see mothers hastening with their infants not toward the Christ simply speaking, the Anointed One, but toward Christ Jesus—the one who is also the Savior."[20] The body whose members we become in this way belongs to that head who is prophet, priest, and king. So it is through his mystical body, through the Church, that Christians enjoy their prophetic and royal priesthood.

So far we have not mentioned the Holy Spirit. Yet Irenaeus tells us that, if it is the Father who anoints and the Son who is anointed, then it is the Holy Spirit who is personally the anointing itself.[21] Preaching at Caesarea on the coast of Palestine, Peter had told his hearers how God "anointed Jesus of Nazareth with the Holy Spirit" (Acts 10:38), while in Luke's Gospel Jesus' own sermon at the Nazareth synagogue began from the text, "The Spirit of the Lord is upon me, because he has sent me to preach good news to the poor" (Luke 4:16ff.). So too, the Christian's sharing in the Christ comes about through the work of the Spirit. John writes that "You have been anointed by the Holy One, and you all know" (1 John 2:20): the faithful are "theo-didacts," taught by God, and their "sense" for the Christian realities is recognized by Catholic theologians as an important clue to the contents of Tradition.

The prophetic and royal priesthood is acquired sacramentally, in Christian initiation by baptism and confirmation. Baptism, the gate-

20. Augustine, *Against Julian* 1.7.31.
21. Irenaeus, *Against the Heretics* 3.18.

way to sacramental life, invests us with our priesthood. Confirmation "seals" our baptismal rebirth, strengthening and perfecting the life of grace we have received. It also makes us public representatives of the people of God, visible representatives of its prophetic, royal, and priestly offices. Catholics can never be private Christians, though our life is rooted in the interior mystery of baptismal rebirth. By baptism we die to this world order, and our life henceforth is "hidden with Christ in God." Yet, though the deepest roots of our new being lie far from view in the soil of the divine life, we must manifest a healthy Christian growth in the eyes of all the world. By confirmation we are mandated by the Church to teach, to "rule," and to sanctify for the salvation of the human race. By these sacraments of initiation, we become related to Jesus Christ, the mediator between God and humanity. Our very being is affected in such a way that all our future action is to be touched by this new relationship. Catholic theology calls this the "character" (mark) we acquire in baptism and confirmation. By this character, we are equipped for communion with God by (prophetic) understanding, (royal) ruling-in-serving, and (priestly) sanctification of the world. This character is, then, nothing other than our prophetic and royal priesthood itself.

The universal priesthood comes to its climax and fulfillment in the Eucharist. In the Eucharist, the faithful make a spiritual sacrifice of their own persons: when the ministerial priest, at the consecration, has brought about, through God's power, the real presence of the victim of Calvary, they co-offer Jesus Christ to the Father in the Holy Spirit. Then, in holy communion, they enter into union with him, now no longer humiliated, but, since his Good Friday sacrifice was accepted by the Father at the first Easter, in a condition of power, radiance, and glory. From that communion they draw the resources to exercise their priesthood in the workaday world.

By the baptismal character, all the good works of the laity are ordered in some way to worship, to the Eucharistic action which is the climax of the Christian life. For the act par excellence of Christian worship is the renewal of the sacrifice of the cross. The personal oblation of their bodies, to which Paul exhorts the faithful in Romans 12:1, is related by the Fathers to the obligations (for the laity in the world) or the counsels (for the lay religious) which follow from the royal priesthood. That priesthood, like that of Jesus Christ its source, is a "victim" priesthood, offering itself in worship of the Father for the salvation of the world, in a fashion which makes the Eucharist its most appropriate expression.

The first task of the laity we must mention is that of the *prophetic* office. In confirmation, the faithful accept the duty to defend the faith they professed by baptism. They must be concerned to know, proclaim, live, and defend the Christian message, the word of God. Our witness does not spring from our lips alone. When we imitate Christ, those about us see it, and they cannot fail to be impressed by the beauty of the faith. All lay persons are bound to present this spontaneous radiance to those around them. "You are the light of the world. . . . Neither do men light a lamp and put it under a measure. . . . Let your light shine before men, in order that they may see your good works and give glory to your Father in heaven" (Matt 5:14, 16). Christians should desire that their very presence become a blessing for their family, neighborhood, workplace, and place of recreation.

In addition to such indirect proclaiming and persuading to the gospel, the royal priesthood is committed to its direct communication. We neglect the commission given us at our confirmation if we let slip, perhaps by silence, opportunities to make known even the least portion of God's revelation that he is love, that he has sent his Son, who has risen from the dead, and that his Spirit dwells among us. For this purpose, we must be as well-instructed as our possibilities allow. We must strive to grasp our faith as completely as possible, precisely so that we can hand it on to others.

Reading a book like this is one way! Another is thinking through the application of Catholic principles to the issues of our day, where, in a post-Renaissance, post-Reformation, post-Enlightenment society, truth and error are strangely commingled. The laity, after all, are educators, parents, and catechists and they should be (like, say, G. K. Chesterton) apologists. They can also outdo this author, and be better theologians!

By the *royal* office, we carry out various, analogically related, kinds of "ruling." We master the disorder of sin in our own persons, and exercise our spiritual kingship for the good of others. We do this by using whatever influence we may have in our spheres of life and work so as to unite human beings in free obedience to their head, Jesus Christ. The royal mission mandates us to spread the spirit of the gospel, expressed in Catholic values, to the society around us.

It is in the context of the royal office that a consideration of the role of the laity in the creation of a Christian politics properly belongs. Using their royal energies, the laity should seek to construct the foundations of a Christian civilization in this world, a civilization of which political ethics form a necessary part. Such a civilization will be at once for humanity and for God. As Jacques Maritain commented, speaking about the rise of that predominant civilization of the post-Renaissance West, whose weaknesses have produced such bitter fruits in the destructive ideologies of the modern period,

> Man, forgetting that in the order of being and of goodness it is God who has the first initiative and who gives life to our freedom, has sought to exalt his own proper movement as creature to the dignity of the first absolute movement, and to attribute to his own created freedom the first initiative towards goodness. Thus his movement of ascent has necessarily been separated from that of grace, and this is why the age in question has been an age of dualism, of division, of disintegration, an age of humanism apart from the Incarnation, where the effort of progress must needs follow an inevitable course and itself contribute to the destruction of what is human. In short, we may say that the radical fault of anthropocentric humanism has been its anthropocentric quality, not its humanism.[22]

The temporal task of the Christian in the world is to work for a realization in social and cultural terms of the truths of the gospel. Although the gospel is primarily concerned with the things of eternal life, and transcends all sociology as it does all philosophy, nevertheless it gives us sovereign rules of conduct for our lives, and traces a very clear chart of moral behavior, to which any Christian civilization, in so far as it is worthy of the name, should tend to conform, according to the diverse conditions of history.

This is not meant to downplay the search for personal perfection. The royal office is exercised first over ourselves, over our thoughts and our passions. Asceticism is the first duty of the royal office: for only those ignorant of the world of personality can mistake what is essentially the fruit of love and generosity for an egoistic enterprise forgetful of the collective neighbor. What is needed at the corporate level is a theocentric and integral humanism, integral because it is the humanism of the incarnation: the rehabilitation of humanity, not over against God or without God but in God.

The royal office, evidently, is concerned with preparing God's kingdom. But there is a vital distinction to be made here if the laity (and indeed the clergy) are not to become "worldly" in a pejorative, rather than exemplary, sense. The kingdom of God constitutes the ultimate

22. J. Maritain, *True Humanism* (London, 1938) 19.

end prepared for by the movement of all history and in which it concludes. Toward this there converge, first, the history of the Church, the world of the ecclesial mystery, and, second, the history of the secular world, including, most importantly, the political city. But there is a difference in the two paths: the Church is already the commencement of the kingdom of God, its beginning in time. It is the "crucified kingdom" (Charles Journet) that in the end shall be revealed in glory— whereas the history of the secular world will only come to its goal by means of a substantial mutation, described in the apocalyptic imagery of Scripture as its "conflagration," whereby in great travail it will be born again into the kingdom.[23]

In their *priestly* office, the faithful try to lead a holy life as the friends of God graciously redeemed in the blood of his Son. They practice Christian spirituality and share in the liturgy of the Church, which comes to its climax in the Eucharist, where we offer our souls and bodies to the Father, and, after the consecration of the holy gifts, co-offer the victim of Calvary glorified in the resurrection. Having received the power that Holy Communion gives, the laity are then called to go out and consecrate the world about them, baptizing its thought and culture in the life-giving waters of the gospel.

The baptism of culture is integral to the priestly office of the laity. What is culture? It consists of all those actions whereby people bring their gifts to perfection, whether as philosophers or scientists, artists or writers, social reformers or simply ordinary human beings concerned with the happy construction of human relations. The Christian must affirm the positive value of culture so defined, since it derives from God's command to "cultivate" the earth by sharing in his own creative action. Yet in a fallen world, culture is intrinsically ambiguous. In any case, the final transfiguration of the historical process—the gift of the kingdom—exceeds its capabilities. That this is so is only fully understood by Christian faith. Where the shadow of God's cross has fallen, and there alone, do people understand how deeply sin has engraved itself upon the created order. The flourishing of culture depends, therefore, on the Christian insistence that culture must fulfill its vocation eschatologically: by way of Christ's message of new life through death-to-self and by the descent of the Holy Spirit, the life-giver.

23. See C. Schönborn, "The Kingdom of God and the Heavenly-Earthly Church. The Church in Transition according to Lumen Gentium," in idem., *From Death to Life. The Christian Journey* (San Franciso, 1988) 65–98.

The mission of the laity is to use the charisms of the royal priest-hood, received in baptism and confirmation, in order to make of culture in its myriad manifestations a place of epiphany—a point from which God's glory shines out and converts the world in attracting it. Thus the cultural activities of the Christian laity are the expression of their universal priesthood. They are the efficacious calling-to-mind of the incarnation and atonement, whereby the divine Logos expressed itself in the world God so loved. They are also the efficacious calling-down of the Holy Spirit to transform the world of matter into an icon of the heavenly kingdom. Scientists, philosophers, social reformers, and artists must be able to rediscover the charisms of the royal priest-hood, and, each in their own field, as "priests" make their research a sacerdotal work, a "sacrament" transforming all forms of culture into acts of tacit worship, silently singing the name of God by means of science, thought, social action—the "sacrament of the brother"—or art. In its own way, culture joins with liturgy, echoes the cosmic liturgy, becomes doxology. In other words, to the *anamnēsis* and *epiclēsis* uttered by the ministerial priest during the Eucharistic Prayer there corresponds a whole variety of lay "consecrations" of culture (e.g., in an English context, the stone-carvings of Eric Gill, the homes and shops of Sue Ryder). It is only when the eye of faith has become blurred or lazy that such juxtapositions seem implausible. In reality, as Francis Thompson saw, Jacob's ladder can be raised at Charing Cross.

These notions offer a coherent and satisfying resolution of the unfinished debate lying behind *Gaudium et spes*, whose "optimism" was somewhat roughly handled by more "pessimistic" spirits at the extraordinary Roman synod of 1985. Is the watchword to be *incarnation* or *eschatology?* immersion in the world, or flight from it? This is a false dilemma.[24] Christians are meant to affirm the world precisely in order to open it to paradise and eternity. It is this eschatological dimension of incarnational humanism that gives the gospel its bite and verve. Our service of the *saeculum*, the "secular," will simply smooth a little the path of the world unless we carry it through with our feet firmly planted in eternity. In this way, we release in people that longing for the true home of undying light with which their own dignity is so intimately involved. The question of the kingdom—what is life finally for? what is its ultimate meaning?—is already found within culture. It will not be suppressed.

24. B. Besret, *Incarnation ou eschatologie? Contribution à l'histoire du vocabulaire religieux contemporain, 1935–1955* (Paris, 1974).

The multiplicity of the charisms and missions of the faithful displays the wonderful variety of vocation in the Church. Speaking of the Church as a visible society, Balthasar observes: "It is grace itself that assumes hierarchical and institutional forms in the Church in order the better to lay hold on man, who is of course a being bound by nature, structure and law." Yet he immediately goes on to add: "But it is also grace itself that takes shape in the most personal aspects of a believer's life through the charismatic mission of vocation in order to transform the unique talents and traits of the individual into what grace alone can envisage."[25]

Since the whole Church is a sacred order—a "hierarchy"—we must relate the place of the laity to that of priests and religious in an integrated view. The ministerial priest does not owe his specific place in the Church to the common prophetic and royal priesthood based on baptism, but to the sacrament of orders; he is configured to Christ as head of the Church, rather than representing the mystical body of the Church, the community. As the sacramental representative of Christ the head, the priest, in union with the bishops and the Pope, proclaims the Word with doctrinal authority; he leads the people of God in celebrating the sacraments of their salvation, playing the part of Christ in their worship; and he "pastors" them by seeing to it that the Church's canonical discipline—the expression of her own sense of identity—is realized in the community, and also that the community grows in the communion of charity which Church law is there to serve. The difference between the lay person and the ministerial priest lies in their different roles in the work of God the Son. The two priesthoods are distinguished in the apostolic foundation of the Church—and thus in the Lord himself. First, the Twelve as symbolizing the whole people of God possess as their foundation the common priesthood of all the faithful, which is united to Christ in his offering to the Father and so to his high priesthood. Second, the Twelve as the original apostolic ministers or envoys of the Lord share in Christ's mission as Lord of his Church, sitting at the Father's hand, ever interceding for us—and so are founders of the hierarchical or ministerial priesthood. Thus the Twelve are simultaneously, *in nuce,* the people of God and those sent into the world to form that people from the nations.

Religious do not owe their specific place in the Church to a sacramental difference from the laity, but to the vocation to respond by a

25. H. U. von Balthasar, *The Theology of Karl Barth* (San Francisco, 1992) 387.

special form of life to the Holy Spirit, as he brings to the Church some anticipation of the life of the kingdom of God. The life of religious is wholly centered on God, in communion with their brothers and sisters, without giving or being given in marriage (chastity), without self-definition by possessions (poverty), or by choosing one's own goals (obedience). It is a foretaste of the spiritual fruits of the age to come. The difference between the lay person and the religious lies in the different roles in the work of God the Holy Spirit.

These differences also make priest, religious, and lay person complementary. Christ as head (typified by the ministerial priest) and the Holy Spirit who rests on Christ (typified by the religious) need Christ's mystical body (typified by the lay person) for the will of the Father to be made effective in the world.

Over the integration of laity, priests, and religious there presides the bishop. He manifests his own place as chief ministerial priest of the local Church, bearing the fullness of the sacrament of orders, not least by unifying the work of the laity, priests, and religious, in relation to each other, as well as to what is happening in other local Churches within the communion of the single Catholic Church. The bishop carries out his ministry of unity first and foremost in personal ways (nothing can ever replace the personal touch), second by overseeing suitable organizational forms to serve unity. These should not replace spontaneous initiative (the "principle of subsidiarity") but help to render it coherent (the "principle of solidarity"). In practice this will mean informing, locating resources, putting people in contact with each other, discouraging needless reduplication of tasks, suggesting fresh initiatives to fit the needs of the Church's mission or apostolate and common life or ministry. It is vital to specifically ecclesial administration to avoid what has been termed "pathological synodalism": indefinite analysis and complexification, continual re-extending of time for discussion, excess of discourse over decisions, equivocations that enfeeble doctrine and spirituality, and the losing of time better given to evangelism.

But the bishop's position in serving the Church's horizontal or geographical communion is only one coordinate of his true situation. For there is also the matter of the apostolic succession which assures the vertical communion of the Church, guaranteeing her identity with the aboriginal Church of the apostles. The apostolic succession enables the bishop to carry out his task of uniting his Church here and now to the ensemble of the historic Catholic Church in all ages.

The analogue for communion with the apostles in the vertical dimension can only be, for the horizontal dimension, communion with the *centrum unitatis:* the Roman primate. It is to his special place in Catholicism that we must now turn. For the "Letter on Certain Aspects of the Church Understood As Communion" makes clear that while among the Eastern Orthodox communities, for instance, so many elements of the one Church exist that their own local Churches may be deemed true particular Churches, nonetheless their existence as such Churches is wounded because of their deprivation of that full communion with the universal Church which is represented and realized through the Petrine officeholder. As ministering to universal communion, the work of Peter's successor does not simply reach each particular Church from outside, but already belongs to its essence from within. Such a claim does not make sense geographically. It turns on the acceptance in faith of a fundamental mutual interiority, achieved mystically by God in Christ, between the universal Church and the Church particular. Defective understanding thereof accounts for the recrudescence of autocephalic and provincialist tendencies in some regions of the Catholic Church today.

The bishops always constitute the apostolic college *redivivus,* whether they are gathered together in one spot or spread out from Thailand to Tegucigalpa. But in their conciliar assembly—the ecumenical council—they are most visibly themselves, and, so gathered, constitute (along with the papal *ex cathedra* pronouncement of the Petrine ministry) an "extraordinary" or especially solemn form of the Church's teaching authority. The councils originated (beginning with the Montanist crisis of the third-century Church) in the need to come to a common decision about distortions of the gospel menacing the Church universal. Such a decision required the bishops, as the chief shepherds of the local Churches of the *oikoumenē,* to compare and unify the traditions which had reached them from the apostolic age, so as to confirm the Church in a common order and to assist each other in sound leadership. A council's function is to order and form the Church's faith and life in a given age. A council gives counsel *(concilium/consilium)* in the service of the communion of the whole ecclesial body. The content of what a council considers and promulgates is always, in one sense, the same: it is attestation of the Word of God, and on the basis of that Word, the right order of the Church. The ecumenical councils (and their regional and diocesan analogues) serve the purification and unity of the Church on the foundation of the Word.

Paradoxically, in Church history they have also been the occasion of numerous splits and schisms. That is because the "mystery of iniquity" of which the New Testament speaks is also at work in the Church, as the tares that break up the good wheat. Catholic fidelity to the teaching of the councils of the universal Church—on the principle that these inherit the words of Jesus to the apostles, "He who hears you, hears me"—continues the blood-flow of the Eucharistic heart of the Church toward the unity of human beings, in God, through Christ and his Spirit.

The relation between the conciliar institution and the Roman primacy (the two organs of the Church's unity in leadership) deserves clarification. Office in the Church, we may begin by noting, is of its nature collegial: it is not given individualistically but in such a way that it incorporates in a body. The Word of God is primarily, in the New Testament, a preached and heard Word, which takes the living form of witness. Though Tradition in its scriptural form is the measure of that witness for all subsequent ages, the written word cannot substitute for the living presence of Tradition in the person of the witness who takes responsibility for this word, and for its preservation. This is the task of the single bishop in the single Church: it carries with it no infallibility, but an onerous burden. It is when we move onto the level of the unitary proclamation of the Word by all the bishops in communion with the pope that the question of infallibility arises. In the normal life of the Church, when pope and bishops agree in teaching, the result of their concord is truth indefectible, the gospel articulated. But if the need is felt to bring forward some aspect of the doctrinal tradition in the special and express form of dogma, there are two means by which this can be done: the ecumenical council and the *ex cathedra* determination of the head of the college of bishops, the pope.

The First Vatican Council stigmatized as heretical a unilateral concentration on either the total episcopate or the papacy. On the one hand, it affirmed that the pope can of himself speak infallibly and does not stand under the censure of bishops gathered in council. There is no appeal from him to a council. On the other hand, it asserted that the bishops are not purely papally installed administrators: the episcopate is of divine right, which no pope can set aside, since it is the succession of the apostolic college and belongs therefore to the Christ-given formation of the Church. Council and pope cannot be set over against each other, but, in a relational unity, fill out and complement each other. On the one hand, only the defining judgment of the pope is juridically complete (that of the council without the pope is null). On the other hand, the word of the pope is not "judgment-ripe" (as the Germans say) unless it comes from the faith conviction of the whole Church, and thus of the many particular Churches with the bishops in their midst. There can be in the Church no dogma which is defined over against the conviction of the episcopate, or its greater part. The voice of the bishops without the pope is juridically incomplete, that of the pope without foundation in the preaching of the bishops is factually impossible.

A council is not a parliament. It does not represent the people of the Church but Christ from whom it receives its mission and consecration. Similarly, the pope is not simply an organ of the episcopate, but has a direct responsibility from the Lord to secure the unity of Christ's word and work among his people. And just as the papacy is not a monarchy in the worldly sense, for it is subordinated to Christ and necessarily referred to the episcopate, so the primacy and episcopate together are not an aristocracy (or oligarchy) in the worldly sense, since they belong within the living whole of the body of Christ. The Church is an order of ministries, among which the ministry of the Roman bishop in particular is key.

The governmental structure of the Catholic Church is unintelligible without an understanding of the place of the Roman bishop. A bishop is the chief ordained minister of a local Church. His task is to guard the faith and practice of that Church. "Faith" means doctrine, truths about Christianity. "Practice" means liturgy and ethical norms, the worship and moral standards that Christianity fosters. The Roman bishop differs from all other bishops by being guardian of the faith and practice not just of a local Church but of the universal Church. In this he does not displace the local bishops spread throughout the world but confirms, supplements, and sometimes corrects their efforts.

At the same time, the local bishops, whose particular Churches are themselves the Church in miniature, bring experience of those far-flung communities to the Petrine center, from where their concerns can be mediated to the rest of the Church universal. In fact, the particular Church and the universal Church interpenetrate in an unbreakable exchange, *perichōrēsis*, comparable to that of the Trinitarian persons in the life of God. In the Roman Rite, the Eucharist is celebrated "one with" *(una cum)* the pope as well as the local bishop, and this implies on the part of the local Church a real collaboration with the pope in the Church's daily life, and obedience to him both as guarantor of its unity and authoritative interpreter of that unity's demands. This *una cum* does not exhaust itself in bureaucratic and administrative structures, but also becomes, in the visit of the local bishop "to the threshold of the apostles" (*scilicet*, Peter and Paul, for each chief pastor must go to Rome at regular intervals) a personal encounter with the apostolic see's officeholder, the vicar of Peter, the one who continues the witness of Paul.

What then is the wider theological significance of the Petrine office for Catholics? In John 21, Christ tells Peter to "feed my lambs, shepherd, and feed my little sheep," the diminutive form *probatia* conveying a personal relation of affection. In return for his affirmation of love for Jesus, Peter receives from the master a personal bequest: a transfer of this loving relationship between the good shepherd and the members of the flock. Though the papacy is not a sacramental order it can be called a charismatic order: the charism of papal authority is conferred by a personal gift of grace through the direct action of the Holy Spirit which sets a seal of confirmation on the candidate for the papacy as a consequence of his election by procedures duly authorized by the Church. The papacy is not separate from the regular ministry which all bishops share, but it is unique in its mode of continuity and in the personal authority conferred by the charism of the papal office. The pope as spiritual father is, so to say, the "abbot" of the Catholic episcopate. The title of "the holy father," given to the pope by the Catholic faithful, is not, after all, a technical ecclesiastical term, but an expression of the experience of faith, putting into words the special relation between each member of the Church and the pope, the "universal pastor." What, then, of "bad popes," those who refuse cooperation with the grace of their ministry?

> The Petrine office is both central and "eccentric." Certainly, this office was placed in the "holy" centre of the Church (hence the demand for a declaration of love from the first pope). From this centre, however, it does not simply reach out to the sinners who are displaced from it and thus "eccentric"; it is not only *for* them but rather *with* them (it is Peter, who denied the Lord, who is given office), in such a way that the personal guilt of the office-holder does not vitally affect the indefectibility of the office. Peter is simultaneously though not in the same respect *justus et peccator, fallibilis et infallibilis*. . . . This is the central "scandal" of Catholicism: that a sinner should claim an element of infallibility.[26]

26. H. U. von Balthasar, *The Office of Peter and the Structure of the Church* (San Francisco, 1986) 181. Translation slightly modified.

Bad popes are, we trust, very much the exception, yet in all cases, Peter has to appear as an individual, and in this sense, over against (vis-à-vis) others, be they the people with whom he is in communion or the bishops with whom he forms a college. He does this not by domineering, however, but as a servant—not detaching himself from communion or college, but rather strengthening them, freeing them to be themselves in the true liberty of the fullness of the gospel.

The Four Notes

Both interiorly and exteriorly, then, the Church puts forth her four essential marks: she is one, holy, catholic, apostolic. These are the foundational properties, dimensions, or "notes" willed by the Redeemer for the life of the community he created. They are still recognizable in the *Catholica* today.

The ultimate source of the Church's *unity* is the Holy Trinity, whose interpersonal communion she reflects on earth. The mediate sources of that unity lie in the missions of Son and Spirit: the Church is one through the universally reconciling work of the incarnate Word, while the Spirit of the Son (himself from the Father) is her inner principle of unity. The means whereby her unity is guarded and fostered, though themselves divinely founded, are human. After naming charity as the first of these the *Catechism of the Catholic Church* lists those other "bonds of union" which theological tradition (not least at the Second Vatican Council, and in its canonical stepchild, the code of canons of the Latin Church) has identified: unity in a single faith; unity in worship, notably through sharing the same sacraments; and unity in the social life of the Church governed as that is by the successors of the apostles of Jesus Christ. It is because the continuing identity of the apostolic college cannot be located without reference to its primatial head, the successor of Peter, that communion with the Roman pope is essential to unity, that constitutive mark of the Church as Christ willed her to be.

That is not to say that the Church is meant to be a homogeneous monolith. Diversity, though not a theological mark of the Church, has certainly always been one of her features: the sheer profusion of the gifts of God in revelation and salvation, as well as the differences between human individuals and groups, guarantees that. Once those differences are baptized into the mystery of a Church possessed of the incalculable riches of the revealing and saving Word, the result is the precious pluralism of the various particular Churches. (How much poorer the Church would be deprived of either its Eastern or its Western "lung"!) This is not to say, however, that a light-hearted cry of "Vive la différence" solves all problems. As the *Catechism* points out, sin can turn the good of diversity into the evil of heresy, apostasy, and schism; legitimate pluralism can degenerate (as indeed the history of post-conciliar Catholicism demonstrates) into anarchy. In the past this phenomenon has bequeathed the historic schisms which have ruptured the unity of Christendom—to which "woundings of unity" the *Catechism* shows itself most sensitive. It echoes *Unitatis redintegratio* in finding outside the single Church's visible unity numerous elements of evangelical truth and apostolic order, such that the tragically separated Churches and ecclesial communities (the difference between the two turns on the presence or absence of a ministerial and thus sacramental life in the apostolic succession) can be instruments used by the Spirit of Christ for human salvation. At the same time, and once again in keeping with the conciliar decree, the *Catechism* does not treat these elements as autonomous and free-floating; rather, do they derive from the fullness of gracious truth Christ has given his holy Catholic Church, and coming from that source, carry a built-in gravitational pull back (or on!) toward the Church's unity.

Holiness is the second mark of the Church. Jesus Christ, whom the Gloria of the Western Mass salutes as "the only Holy One," has embraced her as his spouse, and the Church is necessarily affected by this unique contact with the infinite holiness of the divine Trinity, whose mediator Jesus is. Owing to her union with him, she is not only all-hallowed but all-hallowing, the agent of sanctification as well as its recipient. All her activities converge on human sanctification and the doxological praise of the God who has shared his holiness with humanity (as *Sacrosanctum Concilium* declares).

So far as her individual faithful are concerned, such is the war of sin with grace in our members that such holiness is far from complete in us as persons. Nonetheless each and every Christian is called to be perfect, and furnished, in the life of the Church, with all the necessary means for becoming so. The *Catechism* treats charity as the soul of holiness; as in Aquinas's theology of morals-under-grace, charity unifies the virtues in view of their common end, union through Christ with God in the Beatific Vision. Citing Thérèse of Lisieux's *Histoire d'une âme:* as the heart of the mystical body of Christ, charity is coextensive with the call of God to human destiny, despite the latter's innumerable concrete forms. And if, when contemplating the many counterforms that lovelessness can take, the faithful Christian is depressed at the thought of the tares that grow within Christ's field, the *Catechism* provides grounds for encouragement in rounding off its section on the Church's holiness with a mention of the canonized saints, and, at their center, the mother of God. Solemn canonization of those whose lives have shown forth heroic charity is a recognition by the Church of the power of the Spirit of holiness and a motive of hope for all believers. And in Mary, the Church's deepest nature is already radiantly apparent, for she is the *panaghia*, the all-holy Virgin.

This one, holy Church is also *catholic*. It is a theological commonplace that catholicity may be understood of the Church either qualitatively—as a statement about the integral nature of her faith and its capacity to meet human need—or quantitatively, as an expression of her worldwide mission. The *Catechism* places its emphasis firmly on the first. What is unusual is the decision to treat the holistic *(kath'holon)* quality of the Church's hold on divine revelation, and thus healing and sanctifying power for human life, in such determinedly Christocentric terms. The Church is qualitatively catholic only because in her Christ is present. If the Church is "his body, the fullness of him who fills all in all" (Eph 1:22-23), then she must have received fully, totally, and so in a catholic fashion all the means of salvation the Redeemer has to give. In this sense, the Church was already catholic in unsurpassable fashion while still gathered in the cenacle, at the first Pentecost. The second sense of catholicity, quantitative or geographical catholicity, is only applied to her, by contrast, when, impelled by the Spirit, her apostles tumble out of the upper room onto the streets of Jerusalem, and go forth through Judaea and Samaria into all the world (as the Acts of the Apostles suggests, cutting off its narrative on the outskirts of that Rome to which all roads led).

The last mark of the Church is *apostolicity*. The Church is founded on the witness of the apostles to the crucified and risen Lord; she preserves, assisted by the Spirit, the sound word of the apostolic preaching, and she continues to be taught, sanctified, and governed by the apostles in the persons of their successors, the college of bishops under its Petrine head. The *Catechism's* treatment of apostolicity is dynamic—as it must inevitably be, for the concept of apostleship is one of mandate for mission. The origin of all apostleship, all public representation, in the Church is the mission of the apostle par excellence, the God-man, from the Father: "As the Father has sent me, even so I send you" (John 20:21).

The perseverance of the Church in the apostolic tradition of faith and practice, as guarded by the succession of apostolic ministers, enables the revelation given definitively to the original apostles to be passed on by the whole Church, whether lay or ordained, in its integral purity and fullness. Apostolic faith and order serve, then, the wider apostolate of both clergy and laity: the diffusion of Christ's reign throughout the earth.

Of these four marks it is, we may say, the mark of holiness that signals most perspicuously the Church's rationale. For the unity which her catholic and apostolic being and mission would inaugurate is the unity of human beings with each other *in God*. Though the Church's holiness consists interiorly in her very nature as the bride of Christ, exteriorly—and so publicly and therefore most persuasively—it consists in the tangible holiness she shows in the lives of her saints. Denys the Carthusian, in his Commentary on the Song of Songs, had this to say on the text "Dark am I but beautiful, daughters of Zion":

> The Church calls herself dark because there are many imperfect, frail and sickly people, as well as sinners in her. . . . Still, she herself describes herself as beautiful, since there are always many virtuous and holy people who take their place in her, and all those truly incorporated in her are embellished with love and the infused virtues and the gifts of the Holy Spirit.[27]

Sinners are certainly in the Church, yet they do not embody the Church. Rather are they hospitalized there, with a view to being made well, and made saints.

27. Denys the Carthusian, *Enarration on Solomon's Song of Songs*, in D. Dionysii Cartusiani, *In Sacram Scripturam commentaria* 7 (Montreuil-sur-Mer, 1898) 302.

The Religious Life

Foundations

The religious life—also called, in its most ancient and pure form, the "monastic" life—is a special form of living highly prized within Catholicism. It is a life dedicated to God while renouncing even good things—property, family, personal independence—so as to cleave to him the more wholeheartedly and be free for his service. This basic impulse or project of the consecrated life is the same in all periods of Christian history. The various orders which, in canon law, are designated by terminology of a seemingly non-monastic kind (regular canons like the Premonstratensians, founded by Norbert in the eleventh century; friars like the Franciscans, founded by Francis of Assisi in the late twelfth century; clerics regular like the Jesuits founded by Ignatius Loyola in the sixteenth century) are *au fond* just so many different expressions or applications to special needs of the single monastic impulse in the Church. As Stephen of Muret, founder of the eremitical Order of Grandmont, put it:

> In my Father's house there are many mansions, and there are many ways which lead to it. These various ways have been commended in writing by diverse of the Fathers and they are called the Rules of St. Basil, St. Augustine and St. Benedict. These are not the sources of the religious life but only its offshoots. They are not the root but the leaves. The rule from which all others derive, like streams flowing from a single source, is the Holy Gospel.[1]

That statement would have been controverted by the Protestant Reformers. They maintained that there is no clear biblical justification

---

1. Stephen of Muret, *Book of Sentences*, prologue.

for Christian monasticism. But just as the overall logic of the New Testament writings points toward (for instance) the overt recognition that God is the Trinity, so too there are trajectories in that corpus that point toward Christian monasticism—even though the idea of a distinctive consecrated life within the Church may come later.

May come later . . . Yet we know that the idea of a life totally consecrated to God was no stranger to the world of the New Testament. There were Jewish "monks" in the time of Jesus. Historians have always known that there were Jewish ascetics who had hived off from the Temple worship because they disagreed with the priestly party of the Sadducees on theological grounds. Such ultra-pious Jews, practicing renunciation of worldly goods, celibacy, and life in community, were called "Essenes," and were in one sense a radicalized version of the Pharisees. In other words, they were the more radical spiritual descendants of the people who in the time of the Maccabees and afterwards, just before Jesus, had spoken out against the contamination of Old Testament revelation by new-fangled Greek ideas and pagan influence. Until 1947, not much, however, was known of how the Essene communities lived, but in the spring of that year an Arab shepherd boy in the Judaean desert found the cache of documents now known as the Dead Sea Scrolls. These texts, hidden away by the Essene monks of Qumran in some caves above the Dead Sea at the start of the Roman-Jewish War of A.D. 68–71, enable us to reconstruct a picture of Jewish monasticism in the time of Jesus.

The community rule portrays two groups, an inner and an outer, of which only the former were celibates and practiced common ownership of goods. The community was headed by two figures, who divided between them roles of teaching and pastoral care, on the one hand, and of presidency in worship, on the other. The "master" or "guardian" was responsible not only for admitting candidates and looking after their subsequent welfare, in the way of a father and shepherd, but also for teaching them the rule and providing ongoing spiritual instruction. Alongside this "lay (in fact, Levitical) abbot" was a priest, who took charge of the community's cultus. Each night, both the celibate and the married assembled for the studying of the Scriptures and prayer, though only the single could speak. Following the assembly, the priest led a common meal apparently restricted to the monastic household, in which the great communion supper of the messianic banquet was liturgically anticipated. The community's spirituality was focused in the idea that a life lived in concentration on

God and in sacrificial renunciation is redemptive and sanctifying. The notion that such qualities as poverty of spirit, humility, and purity of heart are so exalted in the sight of God as to form the true goal of the monastic life is just around the corner.

Are there indications within the New Testament, the sacred writings of the Church of Christ, of such a way of life, at once celibate, poor, communitarian, liturgical, engaged in study of the Word of God, and at the service of his will? The two crucial indications of the development of such an idea are the themes of consecrated virginity and of the common life as peculiarly apostolic life.

Jesus, in discussing with his disciples the topics of marriage and divorce, mentions in a laudatory way that some go to the length of making themselves "eunuchs" for the sake of *(dia)* the kingdom of heaven (Matt 19:12). Most probably, this is a praise of celibacy as more harmonious with the kingdom, since the generosity of the voluntary "eunuch" places him or her at the Lord's service in a thoroughgoing way. Again, in the call to the rich young man to sell all that he has in order to follow Jesus, the kingdom-bearer (Matt 19:16-22), Christ treats the life of the poor as chiming with the life of the kingdom. Although there is a place there for the rich, it needs all God's grace to propel them, weighted down with the goods of this world as they are, through the gate of the poor. Paul applauds the freedom of an undivided loyalty that is possible for the man or woman not committed to marriage (1 Cor 7). In the last times, the world is known to be transitory: in this context, celibate life becomes enacted prophecy. The Book of Revelation (14:4) describes the heavenly honor given to celibates because they were willing to follow the Lamb wherever he went. These sources evidently regarded celibacy as an especially blessed state, probably in the sense that its flowering in the Christian community is a sign of the presence of the messianic age, when God is to be all in all. To be able to live exclusively for God, offering one's sexual powers as a sacrifice to him, accepting joyfully the lack of ordinary human fulfillment because one wants no other partner than God himself, this is a characteristic grace and blessing of the last age of the world when God and human beings are entering on a new intimacy, a new closeness of covenant relationship.

By the beginning of the second century, the observance of virginity already constituted a sort of profession, a state, that members of the Christian community could take on *in facie Ecclesiae*. Linked with the apostolic nucleus of the Church through the daughters of Philip—

prophetically gifted women who, according to the early Church historian Eusebius, persevered in the single state until death—such virgins were greeted by Bishop Ignatius of Antioch on his way through Smyrna to martyrdom, and described by the apologist Athenagoras as the "many men and women who have grown old without marrying in the hope of being of service to God." In this perspective, it is not the men who went into the deserts of Egypt who originated monasticism, but the men and women who, soon after the resurrection, entered the desert of celibacy "in honor of the Lord." It was via such ascetics in the Churches of Syria, Cappadocia, Egypt, and Africa Proconsularis (present-day Tunisia) that monasticism evolved.

The second relevant New Testament motif (the common life) appears clearly in the early chapters of the Acts of the Apostles. The life of the apostolic community in Jerusalem is prophetic of later communitarian (cenobitic) monasticism. The Jerusalem Church had at its core a group of believers sharing a community life marked by fervent prayer and the celebration of the Eucharist. Acts 2:46 even suggests that the day was structured by the Temple liturgy, in which Jewish Christians at this time were still sharing. Right up to the close of the Middle Ages it was claimed that the religious life simply continues the apostolic life in the Church. This means primarily not a life of missionary activity (in later times, the more usual sense of *apostolic*) but a life in which Christians persevere in prayer, in community of goods, and in celebrating the Mass. We can safely regard this "apostolic" way of life as the continuance after the resurrection of the life Jesus' friends had shared with their Master during his ministry, with its atmosphere of prayer (summed up in the giving of the Our Father), its common purse (of which Judas was the bursar), and with Jesus himself—the Word incarnate, the Bread of Life—as its central focus.

So here we find our twofold trajectory: consecrated virginity and the apostolic life both point towards Christian monasticism, towards a baptizing of the kind of life the monks of Qumran lived in a surrender of self to the Old Testament revelation of God. There is even a case for saying that the monastic response, as a radical yes to the person and message of Christ, was the more natural evangelical response, in both its constitutive dimensions. Ascetics enter into the movement of Christ's death and resurrection. Insofar as they let the new life of the kingdom possess them, they become contemplatives, enjoying the intimate experience of the divine presence, and are drawn to a closer union with the rest of Christ's mystical body in the *koinōnia*, "community," of brothers or sisters who have entered likewise on this way. Whereas the laity have at once complicated and enriched their discipleship through such commitments as marriage, religious are content to be a basic expression of the Church.

Of course the Church of which religious are the basic expression is not the mediocre Church of sociology, the Church of statistically normative Catholics. It is holy Church, the Church "predestined to glory" of Ephesians, the Church of which that letter speaks as made holy and immaculate by Christ's blood, the bride of Christ of Revelation, the mystical body in Paul. The rationale par excellence of the religious life is the manifestation of the holiness of the Church. In both East and West, the rite for monastic profession is considered as a sacramental. Monasticism has a sacramental significance in that the public consecration of religious, as distinctive members of the body of Christ, reveals something about the nature and destiny of that body as a whole. As Karl Rahner put it, if the Church were present in history only through the preaching of the Word and the administration of the sacraments, she would be a sign, merely, of the grace that is *offered* by God. But the Church is not only that: she is also a sign of the actual acceptance and the final victory of God's grace. And that she is for Rahner in, principally, two ways: by the phenomenon of martyrdom and through the religious life. Each of these shows the Church forth as a community believing in the last things, aiming at a goal beyond this world, and held in the grip of God's victorious grace in the risen Lord Jesus Christ.

Early Monasticism

How did the two motifs of consecrated virginity and common life develop and interrelate in the monastic movement of the later Church? The answer to this question will also illuminate another: namely, how the monks and nuns of the first Christian centuries came to express the various dimensions of their calling (soteriological, Christological, ecclesiological).

Anthony of Egypt is called the father of monks, but we know that he was not the very first. Quite apart from the references to a "protomonasticism" already given, we find Jerome of Bethlehem speaking of a hermit, Paul of Thebes, in the Nile Valley prior to Anthony, while the *Life of Anthony,* by Athanasius, mentions both women ascetics into whose care the young Anthony placed his sister, and, near his village, an old man who had given himself to a life of asceticism from his boyhood. Anthony spent the first phase of his monastic life observing the practices of such believers, learning to imitate the special virtues of each so as to become a model ascetic in the eyes of God. If he stands therefore in continuity with certain predecessors, he also marks a difference from them in that in him the ascetic movement became aware of its own significance in the life of the Church, and found a leader who could attract many others to itself.

A well-to-do Coptic-speaking peasant, Anthony heard in the liturgy the evangelical counsel of perfection given to the rich young man, as well as Christ's appeal to trust in providence ("Be not solicitous for the morrow": Matt 6:34). In a radical step of *anachōrēsis,* "withdrawal," he made his abode in some deserted tombs (relics of the flawed pagan religion) where he fought off the "demons" of his disordered thoughts and passions. In the middle period of his monastic life, spent east of the Nile at the "outer mountain," he became in time the leader of an eremitical colony, as others came to join him. From these years we have his discourse on the monk's vocation. His themes were to remain major preoccupations of the Desert Fathers: first, self-knowledge (i.e., identifying the drives or demons that spoil our efforts at charity); second, how to discern whether particular bright ideas are more likely to be divine or diabolic; and third, how to grow in God, into absorption with his presence. Finally, Anthony's thirst for solitude drove him to the "inner mountain," flanking the Red Sea; even here monks came to him for sympathy and advice. Athanasius's *Life* stresses what a radiant and harmonious person Anthony was. In phrases chosen with an eye to the pagan reader, Athanasius suggests how others groped for comparisons in which to express his marked degree of human integration and fullness of spiritual presence. Indeed, what Anthony represents is celibate asceticism as the way to spiritual perfection. His psychological alertness is not naturalism, for it is lived in the spirit of Jesus' Beatitudes, of the Sermon on the Mount. But as yet the soteriological basis of such a way of life in the mystery of Christ and his sacraments is not clear. Neither is its ecclesiological significance. For that we must look elsewhere.

Anthony's influence in Egypt took different forms in different areas. Some twenty miles from Alexandria lay the partly cenobitic, partly eremitical settlement of Nitria. Founded in 330 by Amoun, a married man who lived in continence with his wife, Nitria resembled a village of scattered houses. On Saturdays and Sundays the monks assembled at the central structure—significantly called *ekklēsia,* and consisting of a church, *kyriakon,* with attendant conventual buildings—for their liturgy and common meals. The donations of guests and the making of rope and linen permitted a genuine monastic economy, supporting doctors, pastry cooks, and the sale and use of wine.

A lonelier settlement for those in this loose community seeking greater solitude was provided to the south and west. "The Cells" became a settlement of six hundred anchorites, whose houses were so scattered as to be out of earshot of each other, dependent on Nitria for basic foodstuffs, but with their own priest and church. Here the desert began. In marked contrast with traditions elsewhere—in upper Egypt with Pachomius and in Cappadocia with Basil—the Cells treated the cenobium not as a lifelong vocation but as a launching-pad for a strictly eremitical existence. The monks of the Cells considered themselves called to a life of perpetual solitude, broken only by the visits of those seeking their counsel or by exceptional calls on their charity. It is from them that the majority of wise sayings, or apophthegms, of the Desert Fathers have come down to us.

The collections of the lives and sayings of the Desert Fathers put into words their ascetic ideals and wisdom and allow us to glimpse the qualities that attracted others to them. Benedict recommends those who desire perfection to consult not only the "rule of our holy father Basil" (now thought to be connected with the monasticism of Syria) but also *Collectiones patrum et instituta et vita eorum* (the Egyptian sources). The desert tradition, as synthesized for the West by John Cassian on his monastic tours, gave later European monasticism its basic understanding of asceticism and penance. These activities are ordered to the acquiring of humility and purity of heart, the whole being held within the unity of an overarching quest for God. Monasticism can thus be understood as the supreme setting for what will soon be called the "practical" life—a life of development of the Christian virtues most relevant to salvation—and the "contemplative" life—a life where mind and heart are increasingly united with the Holy Trinity. The vocabulary of *practical* and *contemplative* comes from one of Cassian's theological mentors, Evagrius of Pontus.

By the time Cassian visited Egypt, the predominant tendency was the Nitrian one of gathering monks into loose communities. Source criticism of the sayings of the Fathers emanating from strictly eremitical milieux shows a trend there toward recognizing a common authoritative ascetic tradition and so a movement away from concentration on the individual monk alone with God. Cassian himself was in two minds whether to commend this development: the cenobium is a communion of charity, but it is also a concession to human weakness (the hermit life can prove just too demanding).

Cassian's attitude to the Liturgy of the Hours reflects the same ambivalence. His day, punctuated by five liturgical Offices, would have been impossible in the Cells or further still into the wilderness, the Marsh of Scetis, home of the most intrepid and "extreme" anchorites. But he adopts these Offices out of mixed motives. They are good in themselves—but it would be better still for monks to pray and make psalmody unceasingly. Still, feeble human beings need mutual support and the help that set times provide so as to be able to praise God. Benedict, influenced by the experience of the ascetics who gathered round the Roman basilicas, did not take from Cassian this rather low doctrine of the Divine Office. Neither did Augustinian monasticism, as found above all among the regular canons. That tradition was formulated in explicit association with the church and house of the bishop, the principal liturgist of the local Church.

However, the pure eremitism of the monks of the Cells did give to all later cenobitic monasticism one important idea, the "discipline of the cell." Keeping the cell in a spirit of alertness to God and his self-communication in salvation makes of the monk's dwelling a workshop of prayer. "The monk's cell is the Furnace of Babylon in which the three young men found the Son of God. It is the pillar of cloud from which God spoke to Moses."[2]

It is the focus of the Shekinah, the tabernacle of God's glory. And yet the sheer physical separation does not of itself make the hermit, any more than the cowl makes the monk. What is crucial is the eremitical attitude: standing before God, with all spirits to be saved in the heart. The true desert is of the heart but the hermit—whether the Church recognizes him or her canonically or simply informally—dramatizes this condition in a unique way. The hermit life, of all forms of the religious life, seems the least defensible to a socially conscious world. But the hermits themselves understood their vocation as a service to the wider Christendom. As Macarius of Alexandria put it, "I am guarding the walls." We begin to see a concern for the ecclesial significance of monasticism, here expressed as a ministry of holy warfare, or

2. *Sayings of the Fathers, Anonymous Collection*, no. 206. For the theology of the cell, see L. Gougaud, "Cellule," *Dictionnaire de spiritualité* 8 (Paris, 1938) cols. 396–400.

exorcism (negatively, against enemies without) and of intercession (positively, in favor of citizens within).

Far to the south, around Luxor and Thebes in upper Egypt, there grew up, *pari passu* with the movement in the north, a fully cenobitic monasticism centered on the figure of Pachomius. Pachomius was the first superior—administrator cum spiritual leader (one thinks of the guardian, both pastor and teacher, at Qumran)—of a strictly communitarian monasticism. Pachomian religious life took the form of alternative village societies with hundreds, possibly thousands, of peasant monks living in a context where mutual service was the dominant spiritual motif and the aural memorizing of Scripture (heart of the later *lectio divina* of the Bible) the chief spiritual exercise. Though both the Greek and Coptic lives of Pachomius were written by people who knew his successors rather than the man himself, it seems that he had lived a solitary life after Anthony's fashion until, around 320, he received (according to the Greek *Vita prima*) a vision that changed his way of seeking the monastic life. It was a sudden overwhelming recovery of his first conversion. "After this, when he was on an island with brethren cutting rushes for mats, and was himself keeping vigil alone in prayer to be taught the perfect will of God, an angel appeared to him from the Lord saying, 'The will of God is to minister to the race of men, to reconcile them to him.'"[3] Here we have the kernel of Pachomian monasticism: the creation of a reconciling community where men can be assisted by each other, and above all by the abbot, in the finding of God. Pachomius's disciples remembered him later as ceaselessly thanking God for three personal influences in his lifetime: "the bishop Athanasius, Christ's champion for the faith even unto death; the holy abba Anthony, perfect pattern of the anchoritic life; and this Community, which is the type of all who desire to gather souls according to God, to take care of them until they be made perfect."[4]

Distinctive of the Pachomian monasteries, and prophetic of the later Benedictine life in the West, were, first, their siting in rich agricultural land; second, their large, even enormous, numbers; third, the role of the abbot as Christ to his monks. Their rule anticipates both Augustine and Benedict in its provisions for weaker brethren, yet maintains a high ideal of observance, with the night Office lasting from midnight to dawn (in Egypt some four hours).

3. *First Greek Life of Pachomius,* 23.
4. Ibid., 136.

So far our sources have not been very explicit about the Christo-logical dimension of monasticism in the contemplation of the Savior, nor its ecclesiological foundation in the sacramental life of the Church. In these matters Syria is a better guide than Egypt. Some twenty years after the death of Pachomius, a Frankish lady, Egeria, went on pilgrimage to the Holy Land. Among other places, she called at Edessa, in Syria. She noted that there were monks actually living in the city: no self-respecting Egyptian monk would have stayed for more than an afternoon in Alexandria! A variety of Syrian sources report that religious were living cheek by jowl with the laity of towns and villages. The *ihidaye*, "solitaries" or "single ones," were central to the Syrian Church, which, at least at times, appears to have regarded a willingness to live in continence as a precondition for baptism. Though it did not repudiate married relations as wrong, the Church there saw monasticism as the sole form of radical discipleship fully compatible with the baptismal consecration. Everyone else should remain catechumens (hence, in the Church but not at its heart). Of particular interest is the vocabulary used. *Ihidaye* appears to translate not only *monachos* (one who lives the unmarried, ascetic life), but also *monogenēs* (the term used in the Gospels for Jesus' relation with the Father as the "only-begotten" or unique Son). At the baptism, the Father's voice declares, "This is my only Son in whom I am well-pleased," (Matt 3:17) and at the transfiguration, the voice from the cloud of glory says, "This is my Son, the Only One: listen to him" (Matt 17:5). Religious celibacy is, then, for the Syrians, a conformation to Jesus as the Single One: the Unique Son of the Father. The monk can have no other partner, since his entire life and being are invested in a relation with the Father. He is a son in the Son; and just as Jesus, absorbed in the Father's will and work, took no wife, neither will the ascetic. The solitary way thus entails singleness by leaving family and not marrying: single-mindedness, already emphasized by Paul; and a special relation with Christ as the only-begotten Son whom ascetics "put on" in a fuller fashion. Ephrem, reporting an "unwritten" saying of Jesus, "Where there is only a single disciple there I will be equally" comments that Christ said this "to remove from the solitaries all cause for sadness, for he is indeed our joy and he is with us."[5]

Here then the monastic life receives a clear Christological foundation. But what of its ecclesiological dimension? What was only implicit

---

5. Ephrem, *Commentary on the Diatessaron* 14.24.

in Egypt becomes explicit in Syria. The solitaries are *bnai qyama*, "sons and daughters of the Covenant," members of the Church par excellence. The root of the Syriac noun means "standing," and the implications are twofold. First, the monk as a "stander" stood up for Christ at his baptism, agreeing to fight the holy war with Christ, actively renouncing evil in all its forms. When the bishop summoned the catechumens to take ascetic vows, those who stood up became "standing ones," the exemplary or paradigmatic members of the Church. But second, there was also an angelogical aspect, which we could also think of as doxological, for the task of the angels is supremely the worship of God. The monk stands because the angel does so. As the fourth Eucharistic Prayer of the Roman Rite has it, "Countless hosts of angels stand before you to do your will." In both Jewish and Syrian-Christian tradition, the angels are heavenly "Watchers" who never sit or sleep since their life is ceaseless praise. In becoming a standing one, the monk shares in their assembly.

The experience underlying religious life, like all Catholic experience, is both one and differentiated. Continuity with Egypt is found among the Syrians in two respects. Living from the sacrament of baptism, the monk fights the holy warfare: as the Desert Fathers had already seen, this warfare consists first and foremost in the struggle with our demons, the destructive powers at work in our own hearts. Till we have identified our own demons we are unlikely to be of much use in dealing with anyone else's. Second, in living the angelic life the religious is called to continual prayer, what the *Liber graduum,* the earliest Syrian treatise on the Church, speaks of as a perpetual liturgy in the temple of the heart. The monk as a person in whom prayer bubbles up all the time to God: this is also the goal of the asceticism of Egypt.

In the practice of a largely interior monasticism, without external framework of life, the Syrian monks could go missionary, practicing homelessness in the service of the gospel in sharp contrast to the sedentary Egyptians or Benedict and his concern with stability of place. The insistence that a monk can remain a monk even on his travels, and may very especially serve the Lord there, prepares the way for the medieval friars, who, though they have a cloister, are also to be found outside of it, for God's sake and that of the Church. Syrian monasticism had a flexibility that enabled it to serve the wider Church, like the virgins of Revelation, following the Lamb wherever he goes. One reason for connecting the monasticism of Basil to the Syrians (quite apart from the geographic propinquity of Cappadocia to Syria) is that in him we see the monastic impulse being put at the Church's service, in a highly practical way. Though Basilian monasticism is primarily contemplative, it also gives itself to the needs of orphans, the sick, and the poor. While remaining urban, like the majority of the Syrian monks, it moves towards the idea that monks are normally better off spiritually when living with each other, since the hermit "has no one's feet to wash." What we do not find in Basil, however, is the notion that the cenobitic life is a re-creation of the *vita apostolica,* the ideal community of the Jerusalem Church. A clear perception of that awaits the Latin Catholicism of Augustine.

The interiority of the monastic life in, for instance, Ephrem also points toward the friars who emphasize likewise the experience of God in the heart—an openness to God touching us, giving us mystical touches of himself, "consolations." The desire for the sweetness of such mystical graces can be overdone, and lead one to forget the Crucified (as sometimes happens with the modern charismatic renewal) but it can also be underplayed and lead one to forget the risen One (as in some interpretations of the Carmelite mystics of the sixteenth century, which lead to a programmatic rejection of all experiences of spiritual delight).

If the "sons of the Covenant" in Syria frequently assisted the bishop by their teaching and philanthropic work (and not infrequently became bishops themselves), in Augustine we find a North African monasticism that is ordered from the start to the bishop's service. This is not, in the West, an isolated development. Both Cassian and Sulpicius Severus in his *Life* of the central Gaulish ascetic Martin of Tours suggest the development of ascetic anchoritism into a more structured movement capable of influencing the Church and (especially) the episcopate. Latin monasticism, like Egyptian, builds on the foundations laid by a proto-monastic asceticism (frequently found in the vicinity of famous sanctuaries of bishops). In Augustine's case, the preparation begins with what is virtually a pre-Christian asceticism of high-minded intellectual friends.

After his first, so-called moral, conversion, when he began to lead a chaste life, Augustine, along with a group of like-minded friends, adopted a common life based in a villa, with its surrounding estates. All were philosophically minded, being more than a little tinged with Neoplatonism. They were indeed typically Plotinian Catholics of the Milanese Church, except that a number, like Augustine himself, were simply catechumens, preparing for baptism. The basic feature of this pre-Christian model of celibate corporate life was the search for wisdom through study and discussion. Augustine would refer to it as *sacrum otium*, "holy idleness." It did involve a serious attempt to become better people: a moral and ascetic context. Still, it was basically a matter of Christian laymen working with a pagan picture of the monastic life.

Augustine's second model of the religious life—and one that transformed his theory and practice of it—was furnished by the *Life of Anthony*, and other reports of the goings-on in Egypt. Before his baptism, he met soldier-converts from the imperial city of Trier, where Athanasius had been exiled. In the *Confessions* he records the impact they made on him.

What most impressed Augustine about the New Testament in this connection was the account of the life of the Jerusalem Church in Acts 4: the community gathered around the apostles, listening to their teaching, celebrating the Eucharist together, having one mind and one soul and all things in common. At the same time, he was aware of the New Testament references to virginity as radical discipleship.

Augustine's theology of the religious life is of a piece with the rest of his teaching in that the leitmotif is unity: unity of Christians; unity of humankind; unity between the person and God. As a pastor, Augustine's main problem had been disunity: the chronic discord, tension, and conflict within African Catholicism which history knows as the Donatist schism. To his eyes, the fact that the three divine Persons share not only a common nature but a common life was highly instructive. Their mutual indwelling brings about an indescribable peace in the inner life of God.[6] This *pax unitatis* is realized above all in the person of the Holy Spirit, as the bond of unity and peace between the Father and the Son. Not surprisingly, then, he is also said to be *caritas*, charity itself.[7] The fire of this same Spirit—his self-communication to humankind—is to be found in the apostolic community, the Church. It is known to be present and active there precisely because the Church is a community, a being together in one: *anima una et cor unum in Deum*. Such unity of minds and hearts, so Augustine argues, is always the work of grace. It is, after all, not just any old unity, but that unity whereby people move harmoniously toward God. The mediator of this unity is the risen Christ who forms his disciples into a single

6. Augustine, *Letter* 238.
7. Augustine, *Tractates on John* 14.9.

"soul," modelling them so that they will form the *anima una Ecclesiae* and, finally, the single soul of the whole Christ, head and members— *anima unica Christi*. Christ sustains our unity in, above all, the Eucharist, which Augustine calls the "mystery of our peace and unity." At the Last Supper, Christ "consecrated the mystery of our peace and unity on his own table."[8] The monastic community represents all this to Augustine: it is an *ecclesiola*, a micro-Church or the Church in miniature. Because it is not of itself a ministerial expression of the Church, but an embodiment of her as a communion of life, its members may be either lay or ordained indifferently. Hitherto, monasticism had been very largely a lay phenomenon. But henceforth it can be thought of as supremely natural for priests or bishops to be monks also. Augustine's Rule is important evidence for the monasticizing of the Christian priesthood (presbyterate and episcopate) in the West. To read the Rule together with sermons 345 and 346 is to see how Augustine used the example of the Jerusalem Church to encourage the adoption of monasticism among the clergy of North Africa. In this he was not a total innovator. Ambrose had lived a common life with his clergy, as had another Italian bishop, Eusebius of Vercelli, just before him. But now with Augustine this becomes a whole program. In these sermons, Augustine gives an account of his clergy's way of life, and indicates that very few of them had been unwilling to give up all personal property: "You know . . . that we live in that house which is called the house of the bishop in such a way that we imitate as well as we can those saints of whom the Acts of the Apostles speak: 'none of them said that anything was his own, but all things were common to them.'"[9] And he finishes by roundly declaring that he will not tolerate in his Church any cleric who does not truly live the "social life," *vitam nostram socialem*. "May such a one appeal against me to a thousand councils, may he set sail against me wheresoever he wishes, may he in fact be wheresoever he can, the Lord will help me so that, where I am bishop, he cannot be cleric."[10] Only those who live the social life reflect the life of the city of God, and so Augustine will have no cleric, subdeacon, deacon, or priest who prefers the individualism (and by implication egoism) of the earthly city to the corporate (and by implication charitable) life of the city of God.

8. Augustine, *Sermon* 272.
9. Ibid. 345.2, with an internal citation of Acts 4:32.
10. Ibid. 346.4.

This did not mean, however, that Augustine eliminated the element of lay monasticism from his communities. All his clergy were monks but not all his monks were clerics. In *De opere monachorum* Augustine attacks monks who refuse to do manual labor, arguing that the distinctive marks of the monk are absorption in prayer and in the Word of God, together with the labor of one's hands. On the other hand, monks who are also clerics are entitled, as ministers of the Word of God, to live by the gospel. They may eat their bread gratuitously, receiving it from those to whom they preach "gratuitous grace." But it would be better still if they also did some manual work at certain times, and thus like Paul contributed to their upkeep. Augustine admits, though, that given pastoral demands, this may be impossible in practice.

Augustine's Rule falls into two parts. The first chapter states in a nutshell his basic vision of the monastic life: *unus in uno ad unum*—one together in the one Christ, in the way to the one Father (though that phrase actually comes from the *Enarration on Psalm 147*). For Augustine, the term *monachus*, so far from expressing a hostility to human ties, indicates the ideal of integration into a community. "They who live in unity in such a manner that they constitute one man are rightly called *monos*—that is, one alone. In them is verified what Scripture says, 'One soul and one heart': many bodies but not many souls, many bodies but not many hearts."[11] The rest of the Rule consists of concrete applications: Chapter 2 considers common prayer. Chapter 3 considers the common meal with an emphasis on the special needs of the weakly and sick. Chapter 4 deals with inner purity and the responsibility of each monk for all the rest. Chapter 5 describes the spirit of service in such things as clothes, illnesses, and the lending of books. Chapter 6 recommends the preservation of concord by avoiding what could be harmful. Chapter 7 investigates what counts as charity in relations involving authority. And in chapter 8 Augustine offers some concluding words of incentive to this common life.

In his treatise *On the Customs of the Catholic Church*, Augustine ascribes to the monastic life love, holiness, and freedom. Its holiness is composed of love (i.e., social life) and freedom (i.e., under grace). The Rule sees its subject not only from the angle of the common life of Acts. It also takes its color from the Letter to the Romans, where Christians are described as set free from sin to be made slaves of God, living by

---

11. Augustine, *Enarration on Psalm 132* 6.

his grace rather than law, and with their bodies placed at the service of righteousness, for their sanctification, which ends in eternal life. The unity which the Rule celebrates is not just group feeling. The perfect unity of the city of God is a future reality, which is why Christians must be not only *amatores unitatis* but *amatores aeternitatis*.

Is it possible to synthesize the material we have been looking at in order to produce an overall view of the monastic institution as it emerges from the New Testament through the later Church? We can say that, although the motifs of celibacy and the common life are originally distinct, they tend increasingly to converge inasmuch as people come to regard common life as a safeguard for celibates—providing them with a possibility of fraternal correction (as with Cassian), or a way of turning their energies to the service of the Church (as with Basil), or a necessary training ground (as with Benedict). By the same token, the common life is seen as a life essentially of celibates, and even, thanks to the influence of the notion of the discipline of the cell, of solitaries. A writer of the twelfth century will see the start of the monastic life in the "reclusion" of the disciples in the cenacle, after the ascension. It is a life simultaneously together and alone, alone by habitual prayer, together by common concord.

The concept of remaining unmarried for the honor of the Lord would lend itself not only to the fixed, geographically stable, existence of the hermit, but also to the more mobile, and even missionary, activities of the Syrian solitaries. Lacking *impedimenta*, they could travel light in the Church's service. However, the common life could also be devoted to that service: both as a manifestation of the Church's identity as a communion of charity (as in Cassian), or by enabling monks to take on institutionalized works of charity (as in Basil), or in constituting a resource for pastoral work and theologically informed preaching (as in the clerical monks of Augustine).

The foundations of monasticism in various relevant dimensions of Christian doctrine—particularly the doctrines of sanctification and salvation, of Christ and his sacraments, and of the Church—became gradually more apparent. In Anthony, the anchoritic life, where self-knowledge and knowledge of God advance in tandem, is a providentially created manner of laying hold on the sanctifying grace and (in hope) final salvation given by God. In Pachomius, monasticism is the instrument of the wider divine purpose to reconcile human beings with God and in this way stands at the center of the new covenant in Christ. In the Syrians, the monk is a son in the Son, and his life is plenary living out of the life in Christ given in baptism. In Augustine (antici-pated to some degree by Cassian and Basil) the monastic community is the expression of the archetypal Church: the Jerusalem Church of Acts, gathered by the teaching of the apostles, structured by "the Prayers," or Hours, and centered on the breaking of bread, the Eucharistic Lord.

The parallel development of these insights into the soteriological, Christological, and ecclesiological basis of the religious life brings in time a recognition that the monastic life is very much a liturgical life. It celebrates the mysteries of salvation in the liturgical cycle; it cele-brates Christ as the mediator of the liturgy, our great high priest; it celebrates the Church as his beloved partner, with the liturgy the voice of his bride. Thus the way is prepared for Benedict's declaration that to the *opus Dei* (the Mass and Office) nothing should be preferred. Among the canons regular and such mendicant orders as the Dominicans, this insistence is qualified by the need to make space for urgencies in the cure of souls or doctrinal preaching, yet in each case the clerical brothers are professed, significantly, "for the choir," while the nuns are indistinguishable in their liturgical life from those follow-ing the Rule of Benedict.

If the liturgy is, as the Second Vatican Council puts it, the source and summit of the Church's life; if it is the most inward form of our covenant response to God in Christ and the anticipation of the life of heaven, then both hermit and cenobite must find their deepest identity within it. The first testifies to its invisible reality (the presence of the heavenly Church to the earthly), the second witnesses to its visible re-ality (the solidarity of the earthly Church on its way to heaven). The monastic life is a full-time ritual-symbolic liturgical existence, memo-rializing through day and night that remembrance of God which the liturgy proper celebrates at set times and in limited places.

Development in West and East

The expansion of Latin monasticism passes crucially but not exclu-sively through Benedict of Nursia. The *Dialogues* of Gregory the Great show Benedict's predecessors and contemporaries living a life not un-like his. A comparison of his Rule with the "Rule of the Master," his main source, shows his work to be a codification—outstanding in sagacity—of what was widely held. Gregory's own monastery on the Coelian hill in Rome had a mixed rule, while Benedict dedicated Monte Cassino to Martin of Tours, whose influence, through his *Vita*, encouraged a monasticism in Gaul which normally included a semi-anchoritic life for mature monks. In Spain, the brothers Leander and Isidore of Seville represent a cultivated, humanist monasticism. Jerome's influence gave Western monks a taste for Scripture. Everywhere, in West as in East, cenobitic monasticism (and of an increasingly liturgical kind at that) gained ground.

The Celtic monks embodied the general trend in a remarkably short period of time. In the Patrician period, such monks and nuns as existed lived in modest groupings in connection with secular churches, rather than in monasteries proper, which seem to have emerged under Scottish and Welsh influence, though soon there followed the era of the great founders, Columba, Columbanus, and Ciaran. Celtic monasteries were gatherings of wooden or stone cells around an oratory and some conventual buildings. Their inhabitants practiced a rigorous asceticism: fasting, vigils, prostrations, standing with the arms spread out as a cross, immersions in streams. The ancient practice of manifesting thoughts to a spiritual father became with them private confession, sometimes daily. The Mass of devotion, celebrated by an individual priest-monk, was greatly valued. They developed a strong stress on literary culture from the sixth century onwards. Their interest in voluntary exile could be linked, but need not be, to evangelism. It seems that their basic orientation remained contemplative; the number actively engaged in mission was small proportionate to the whole. From the mid-seventh century onward exchanges increased between monasteries following the Celtic Rule of Columbanus. Sometimes the Rule of Benedict was taken as completing, and moderating, the Rule of Columbanus. This enabled it to spread in these milieus. From the eight century onwards we find the development of libraries and *scriptoria* in the continental Columbanian houses.

What of Benedict himself? Significantly, the vice to which Benedict was most opposed was subjectivism. Of such monks he says, "Their law is their good pleasure: whatever they think of or choose to do, that they call holy."[12] By contrast, the Rule stresses the need to accept a common discipline and the abbot's judgment, though this judgment must itself be informed by a realistic assessment of the needs of the community's members. Similarly, Benedict's objections to monastic wandering, at any rate when undertaken from caprice and fecklessness, leads him to stress the importance of stability in the sense of

12. Benedict, *The Rule* 1.

lasting attachment to one community and one abbot. Benedict himself had led the strict eremitical life for three years at Subiaco, but, as other monks gathered around him, a new idea hatched in his mind: a single monastic family living under an abbot with direct and intimate responsibility for each and all. Within the enclosure of his new monastery, Cassino (the word *enclosure* occurs here for the first time in monastic history), everything the monk needed could be found. In the life passed in God's presence to which the Rule directs Benedict's monks, there were three chief instruments: liturgical prayer, reading, and work. The Rule's horary allots some six hours daily to labor: Benedict was conscious that the ordinary man cannot spend a whole lifetime simply reading or praying vocally, it asks too much of human nature. Reading does, however, receive four hours per day. It is not intellectual study designed to help the monk enrich the mind of the Church at large (though this was already known in Benedict's day with Cassiodorus and in Spain), but a meditative poring over Bible and Fathers designed to be at once a spiritual education and a safeguard for faith and prayer. Normal persons need mental just as much as bodily activity. Such *lectio* for Benedict leads of itself to prayer: when a monk felt that reading had done its part he could simply enter the oratory and pray (as yet set hours of mental prayer are unknown). The monk's principal daily prayer was the liturgy, the offering of the whole person—voice, gesture, and all—and carried out in common, like every important action (seven times daily: cf. Ps 118:164).

What holds this way of life together is, outwardly, the spiritual relation of each monk to the abbot who stands in Christ's place. The monks are his that he may lead them to God who will hold him to answer for them at the judgment. He is to wait upon their different characters, knowing that sheep may be killed by over-driving, the vessel broken if scoured too fiercely. But the inner coherence of the Benedictine life comes from the promise of *conversio* or *conversatio morum*, "reformation of life." The phrase is close enough to Cassian's *conversatio actualis*: the monastic way of life as aimed at purity of heart. If Benedict does not follow Cassian in the latter's nostalgia for an age when hermits were the norm, and the Evagrian prayer of the pure contemplative the expected standard of the solitary, he is entirely at one with him in taking purity of heart to be the goal of all moral and ascetical endeavor, and the fount from which love of God flows.

Benedict's monk contemplates God primarily in others, in the abbot, the fellow monk, the guest, the poor. This makes the monastery a "school of the Lord's service." As to prayer, it should be short and sharp: more store should be set by compunction for our sins and by purity of heart than by length of praying. By distinguishing prayer so clearly from work (unlike the Egyptian attitude of pursuing meditation, including psalmody, while working with the hands), and by demarcating the Hours so sharply from other prayer (whereas in the desert tradition, as in Cassian, the Hours are there to stimulate unceasing prayer), Benedict prepares a path for two major developments of the Middle Ages and beyond: the rise of mental prayer, *oraison*, as a supplement to the vocal prayer of the liturgy, and a concept of the Office itself as not so much devotional and even charismatic (one thinks of the long silences, accompanied by prostrations, that punctuated it in Egypt) but rather as the formal, hieratic offering of the monastic Church to its divine sovereign. If the first tendency is especially typical of the early modern orders, the second is highly visible in later Benedictinism in the Middle Ages, and above all at Cluny.

The Western Middle Ages see other shifts also. In the Carolingian empire an attempt is made in the name of Church reform at strict classification and control. At the Aachen synods of 816 and 817, the emperor Louis the Pious imposed the Benedictine Rule on all "monks," restricting the title to those who accepted its authority. All other male religious were to take the Rule of Augustine and be termed "canons." Here the background was long prepared: monks living simply *iuxta canones*, rather than according to the Benedictine Rule and abbot, often merged with the clergy of the basilican monasteries to form an *ordo canonicus* from the sixth century onwards. Expected to live in one house, communities of such canons would be further reformed in the Middle Ages as "canons regular" (itself a tautology!). The Carolingian practice narrowed the future ambit of the term "monk" in the Latin Church. Benedict himself had recognized four types of monks: cenobites, hermits trained cenobitically, those who lived simply or in small groups, and wanderers. Though he is critical of the last, he never denies them the name "monk." With Louis' contemporary and collaborater Benedict of Aniane there originated the idea of customs, *consuetudines*, to complete a Rule, which had left too much to abbot and local custom. His *Concordia regularum* was written with the aim of creating a basic uniformity in the monastic life. This could not be achieved without a degree of centralization; the emperor gave him rights of supervision over monasteries in France and Germany. Here we have the "religious order" of later times *in nuce*. At the same time,

Benedict of Aniane's reform gave Benedictinism a more pronounced liturgical and contemplative character: missionary monasteries were no longer a critical need. Cluny took liturgical monasticism to its apogee. While the Benedictine Rule presupposes a comparatively short liturgy—it was influenced by the liturgy of the Roman basilicas, where the faithful still participated, and by Cassian, who was himself in reaction against the prolix Offices of the monks of Gaul and stressed rather the prayer of the heart—the Frankish implantation of the Rule brought it into a milieu used to more florid worship and, in certain pre-Benedictine circles, the *laus perennis,* "perpetual praise." Also at Cluny emerged the principle of exemption of a monastery, through papal patronage, from some at least of the juridical control of the local bishop.

Something more must be said about the canons before turning to the hermits and the White Monks, or Cistercians. The word *canonicus* denotes a cleric who lives according to a rule, *kanōn.* The appearance of the term *canon regular* precedes the creation of the orders of such canons in the eleventh century. Originally, it simply meant a presbyter, deacon or sub-deacon living in accordance with the rules characteristic of the eighth and ninth centuries (as distinct from others who lived more secularly). Canons living a common life were grouped in *chapters:* the term, which meant the same for the monks, came from the practice of reading a chapter of the Rule semi-liturgically after Prime in a room set apart for this purpose. Several (literary) Rules were used, not just Augustine's. The basic idea was simply that of living in conformity with the (juridical) rules or canons imposed by the Church, that is, the developing prescriptions of popes and councils, which began in the fourth century. From that time on, bishops tried to regulate clergy living in the *domus episcopalis,* the bishop's house, dissuading them from such secular activities as trading, hunting, and frequenting of shows, and getting them to wear the tonsure and a particular style of dress. The ecumenical Council of Chalcedon imposed stability within a diocese. Eusebius of Vercelli anticipated Augustine in establishing regular life for a cathedral clergy: his rule of life, known as the *Disciplina monasterii,* was not in fact intended to create an institution parallel to monasticism, but to order the lives of a *clerus* with its bishop, which should evidently be exemplary in its ecclesial authenticity. The name *canonici* emerged in the fifth to seventh centuries as bishops everywhere in the West took up this idea. Appealing to the example of the common life of the Jerusalem Church in Acts, it was not surprising that the reformed canonical life became known as the *vita apostolica*. The first person to give a precise rule to clerics living in community was Chrodegang of Metz, whose Rule would be imposed on canons by Louis the Pious's second Synod of Aachen in 817. Chrodegang's Rule prescribed the solemn celebration of the Divine Office (adapted from the rule of Benedict) as the *opus Dei*; it insisted on a common table and dormitory, silence, and some manual work and the wearing, as habit, of a tunic with cappa or cloak. Such regular canons differed from monks only by the lack of formal vows, and through their right to enjoy the usufruct of their own property (though not its bequeathing, which passed to their church of attachment). In the sixth century there is already some confusion between monks and canons. It is against this background that the Carolingian attempt to forge a distinction via the Rules of Benedict and Augustine must be seen. The Council of Tours (813) would distinguish between canons governed by a bishop (the later cathedral chapter) and those ruled by an abbot without being monks: the *abbas canonicus* (the later situation of the collegiate chapters). Frequently in this period monks gave way to canons, including Celtic monks unattracted by the Rule of Benedict.

The eleventh-century Gregorian reform definitely favored canons over against monks; the latter had proved more susceptible to decadence. From the end of the first millennium onward the new institutes of canons regular appeared: the canonical reformers both influenced by and influencing the monastic. A community of clerics of this kind could be referred to either as an *ecclesia* or a *monasterium*. The terminology for the superior varied: Augustine's *praepositus* became *prévôt* or *Probst* in the vernacular, but *abbas* could be borrowed from the monks though eremitical foundations usually rejected it; *decanus* was common in the chapters of cathedrals.

The liturgical horary of the canons was by now indistinguishable from that of the monks; but of course they also did pastoral work, preaching, visiting the sick, burying the dead, and baptizing the newly born. They had a pronounced intellectual life: each canonical church had a capitular school, frequently dependent on a famous master, such as Gerbert of Rheims, Anselm of Laon, Bernard Sylvestris at Tours, or Bernard of Chartres. Paris could boast two such schools: Notre Dame and La Montagne Sainte Geneviève. With the coming of the universities they took second place—and disappeared altogether with the founding of the seminaries.

So far we have hardly touched on the true orders of regular canons emanating from the Gregorian reform. The reform saw a renewal of the abbeys of canons inspired by the new white monasticism of the Olivetans, Camaldoli, Citeaux, and Chartreux. The institutes of canons regular stressed not only common life but also the renunciation of personal property and the need for a mortified life. In their desire for a perfect life the new canons were often more austere than the monks. The Congregation of St. Victor at Paris, for instance, was modelled on the *Carta caritatis* of the most ascetic of coenobites, the Cistercians. Some formed groups of hermits with a ministry to travellers and pilgrims, as in the hospice of the Great St. Bernard seated eight thousand feet high on a saddle of the Swiss Alps.

Hitherto Augustine had been considered simply one patron among many of the canonical order. Now he came to the fore. In 1126 Honorius II specified that the Premonstratensian canons are established "according to blessed Augustine's Rule." In 1135 Innocent II placed the canons of Grenoble cathedral under the same Rule, and did the same for all communities that sought his approval. It was in this pontificate that the canonical order became par excellence the Augustinian order, whose authoritative Rule, as the work of so eminent a Father was comparable only to that of the Rule of Benedict.

So defined, the canonical order prepared the way for the mendicant friars by popularizing the notion that the cult and common life could be combined with the *cura animarum*. With the friars there is a definite theory, prepared by the earlier debate between canons and monks, of the "mixed life," a life synthesizing contemplative and active elements. The earlier polemic had produced the idea of a religious life where the religious would not be confined to his cloister but would make periodic sorties to serve neighboring Christian communities. The first treatise on the mixed life was that of the regular canon Anselm of Havelberg, who argued that the supreme model of religious life, Christ, practiced contemplation and action equally.

When we turn to the hermits and the White Monks, we are dealing with religious who restrict their life to its contemplative dimension. What characterized the new orders of monks and hermits founded at the close of the eleventh century and the opening of the twelfth (Citeaux, Fontevrault, Tiron, Grandmont, Chartreux) was a greater sensitivity to the spiritual and social demands of evangelical poverty. According to William of St. Thierry, the distinctive ideal of Clairvaux was life *in paupertate spiritus*. Roger of Byland, one of the early English Cistercians, could write to a prospective postulant: "Poor we follow the poor Christ, so that we may learn to serve him with minds that are free. We work, we fast, we keep vigil, we pray; Christ does not ask for gold and silver from us—only that we love him with a pure heart and body."[13]

The first Cistercians embraced poverty (both physical and spiritual) not because of some abstract ascetical necessity, but, as with the Franciscans and the holy fools of the Christian East, because of their understanding of Christ's demands on his disciples and of his proclamation of good news to the poor. The original aim of the founders of the Cistercian order was to become really one of the *anawim*, one of the poor, voluntarily stripped of everything. As Dom Jean Leclercq has put it, the first Cistercians felt themselves called "not only to be poor, but to feel it, to experience it. Like the *saloi*, the "fools for Christ's sake," they felt they had to know the poverty and nakedness of Christ in their inmost being, in the depths of their hearts, and trust in God alone. Cistercian spirituality sees the monk's physical poverty as a sign of that total dispossession, that death of the acquisitive ego, which Jesus tells us is the only way to eternal life. It is a "letting go" of every security, including the security of the wisdom of this world. Bernard's denunciations of the humanism of later Cluny, the quest for the simplest decoration of churches and of liturgy, the undyed clothes, and the mystique of poverty all belong together. At the same time, there was a desire to return to primitive forms (somewhat idealized). The memory of fourth-century Egypt produced a tendency toward "collective eremitism": a life together *in eremo* unites the advantages of the common and the eremitical lives. It was not forgotten that Benedict had given as his own sources, apart from Basil, the sayings and lives of the Desert Fathers. Bernard goes behind Benedict to appeal to the Desert Fathers as the standard of a more integral and authentic monasticism; the same is true of William of St. Thierry, when speaking both of the early Cistercians and of the Carthusians. In the *Exordium Magnum Cisterciense*, Conrad of Eberback gives us the "desert myth" in its full form: starting with the "Do penance!" of Jesus and the Baptist, he traces this spirit through the Egyptian desert and via Benedict to the West, all in the service of a new fervor in asceticism and simplicity, stressing manual labor, poverty, and austerity. John Gualbert and Romuald also saw their hermit foundations in this light; the *Vita antiquior* of Bruno, founder of the Grande Chartreuse, agreed.

---

13. C. H. Talbot, "A Letter of Roger, Abbot of Byland," *Analecta Sacrae Ordinis Cisterciensis* 7 (1951) 218–31.

Since the founding of the Carthusian Order ("never reformed because never deformed"), the hermit life has been held in the highest regard in the Catholic Church. Aquinas declares its solitude to be a more powerful instrument of contemplative perfection than community life—on condition that the person entering it has already acquired a considerable degree of perfection, normally thanks to sharing in some kind of community or at least social life. In the hermit life, Aquinas continues, two of the essential means to perfection in the religious life (poverty and chastity) are carried to an extreme pitch, while the third (obedience) is radically altered. Actual obedience is no longer necessary: the solitary is led by the Holy Spirit. However, he or she has perfect obedience in a readiness of mind to obey God. The difference marking out the hermit life lies in this characteristic of liberty of spirit which alone is essential. To it the elements of solitude, simplicity of life, extreme asceticism, and humility must be judged secondary.

Such solitude can take many forms: the traditional "desert" of lonely places, whether on sand, or in woods or mountains; the anonymity of life in a great city; or some abandoned and despised state of life as with the beggar's existence of Benedict Joseph Labré. In Britain, hermit saints have hallowed all the terrains of our landscape. One thinks of Gwyddfarch on the summit of his solitary, steep-sided hill above the Vyrnwy Valley (near Welshpool); or the hidden valley near Bala preferred by the hermitess Mellangell, one of numerous Welsh women hermits who established cells in remote corners of the country in the mid-seventh century; or the marshy fens of East Anglia where in the eighth century Guthlac paddled his way to the "island" of Crowland, site of the later abbey of that name; and of course there were hermit-denizens of true islands, like Cadfan on Bardsey Island, off the Lleyn peninsula of North Wales, or the many hermit saints of Caldey Island, off Tenby, in South Wales: owing to the swift and dangerous currents that separated these islands from the mainland they could be true "deserts," unlike those other islands that, in an age of sea-borne communication, were crossroads and emporia of trade.

Pope John Paul II, writing to the minister-general of Chartreux for its ninth centenary in 1984, drew out the theme of the help given by hermits to the rest of the Church—and the world.

> Faced with the acceleration of the rhythm of life which marks our contemporaries, you must return without cease to the original spirit of your Order and remain unshakable in your holy calling. Our epoch indeed seems to need your example and service: minds are between different

opinions, very often they are perturbed and run great spiritual dangers under the pressure of the many writings which appear without discernment, and above all of the means of social communication, endowed as these are with a great power to influence hearts, while opposing themselves at times to Christian truth and morality. Men experience therefore a need to be in search of the Absolute and to see it in some sense guaranteed by a lived testimony. Your function is precisely to let them perceive it. For their part, the sons and daughters of the Church who are consecrated to apostolate in the world, at the mercy as they are of a perpetual mobility and evolution, need to rest on the stability of God and his love. This stability they contemplate manifestly in you who have shared it more specially than the rest here below.[14]

Indeed the Second Vatican Council spoke of solitaries as following more closely the Christ who contemplated on the mountain, and it saw their lifestyle as a secret source of fecundity for the Church.

With the Carmelites, however, we touch on yet a different synthesis: here eremitism and apostolate are combined. When the first Carmelites, who were solitaries living in a loosely connected group in caves and huts on the side of Mount Carmel, asked the patriarch of Jerusalem for a rule, they were given one that stressed solitude but also licensed a certain apostolate. In the words of the early Carmelite Nicholas the Frenchman:

> Conscious of their imperfection, the hermits of Carmel persevered for a long time in the solitude of the desert, but as they intended to be of service to their neighbor, in order not to be guilty of infidelity in their way, they went sometimes, but rarely, down from their hermitage. That which they had harvested with the sickle of contemplation, in solitude, they went to thresh on the threshing floor of preaching, and to show abroad on all sides.[15]

Hermits living on Carmel near the "springs of Elias," where the prophet had prayed alone and "sons of the prophets" had a "school," sought to express the prophetic spirit concretized in Elijah. A prophet is one who lives in direct submission to the Holy Spirit, so that by his life, actions, and words, he may at all times be a sign of God in the human world. The author of the fourteenth-century Carmelite

---

14. 1984 Letter of Pope John Paul II to the prior of the Grand Chartreuse.

15. *Ignea sagitta,* in François de Sainte-Marie, *Les plus vieux textes du Carmel* (Paris, 1944) 173.

Institution of the First Fathers describes the spirit of Carmelite contemplation by interpreting Elijah's hiding at the torrent of Carith as an embracing of the ascetic life, leading to the perfection of the love of God, and the drinking of that torrent as a reception of the light of contemplation from God, so as to be transformed inwardly by his wisdom:

> To taste, in a certain manner, in our heart, and to experience in our spirit, the power of the divine presence, and the sweetness of the glory from on high, not only after death but even in this mortal life. That is what is really meant by drinking from the torrent of the joy of God. . . . It is in order to accomplish this twofold end [asceticism and contemplation] that the monk must enter upon the eremitical way, according to the testimony of the prophet, "In a desert land where there is no way and no water, so in the sanctuary have I come before thee, to thy power and thy glory."[16]

The Carmelites, men and women, therefore see themselves in succession to the prophets as witnesses to the desert vocation of Israel. More specifically, by their witness and (in the case of men) preaching they aim to lead others in the ways of prayer, contemplation, and solitude. Carmel's is a contemplative apostolate to other potential contemplatives. As such its supreme model is not Elijah so much as Mary, "Our Lady of Mount Carmel," whose spiritual life—if it embodied her metaphor of handmaidship—was simple, unassuming, without drama and exaltation. Thus the mysticism of Teresa is rooted in an ordinary, commonsensical life, accepting all human life as it is; that of John of the Cross dispenses with everything that savors of display in favor of "dark faith"; the "little way" of Thérèse of Lisieux is a Marian way of humility, candor, and simplicity.

The spirit and practice of the desert tradition continued to exercise its influence—for instance in seventeenth-century France; among not only the solitaries of Port-Royal but also at La Trappe, the center of the strict observance reform of the Cistercians. The masterpieces of the desert life—notably Cassian's writings and the *Ladder of Divine Ascent* by John Climacus—revolutionized the tepid life of Armand Rancé, who when reading them still retained a number of (abusive) titular abbacies *in commendam*.[17] The chapels he had built, in honor of

---

16. Ibid., 114, with an internal citation of Ps 63:1-2.

17. "A commendatory abbot *(abbas in commendam)* is any person, ecclesiastic or layman, entitled to draw the revenues of a monastery without any responsibility whatsoever in regard to the discipline of the house" (A. J. Luddy, *The Order of Citeaux* [Dublin, 1932] 55–56).

Climacus and Mary of Egypt, suggest the Trappist aim of creating an ascetic context within which an intense mystical life, under the direct influence of the Holy Spirit, could grow and flourish.

The developed Byzantine monasticism of the Middle Ages, and its organic continuation in the Catholic and (to a more marked degree) Orthodox East today, show the stamp of the sources we have looked at. The two main strains, the eremitical or Antonian, and the cenobitic or Basilian, continued, and indeed complemented each other to some extent. The *coenobium* could serve as the training ground for those called to solitude, or it might send out colonies of experienced contemplatives to live in cells or lavras of their own (even Basil did this). The abbot of a monastery might retire into seclusion, delegating communal affairs to an elder. On the other hand, a great anchorite and hesychast like Athanasios of the Meteora could find himself the center of so large a group of disciples that he had to found a *coenobium* to cater for their needs.

The vigor of the eremitical tradition is shown in the development, beginning in the ninth century, of Mount Athos, that verdant protrusion into the Northern Aegean, and the fourteenth-century founding of the Meteora, monasteries of the air, perched on rocky outcrops of the Pindus mountains, as, with the waning Middle Ages, the ties linking the Byzantine Church to Rome grew ever weaker. But cenobitic communities were also clamoring for recognition in the hermit territories; and even the hermits themselves recognized the need for better organization, especially on Athos. In 1063 the Byzantine emperor Nicephorus Phocas founded the Athonite *coenobium* still called, misleadingly, the Great Lavra (for the lavras were definitely loose collections of hermits). The struggle for supremacy between eremites and cenobites was reenacted at Meteora in the fifteenth century, when the abbots of the Great Meteoron began to claim the functions of the *prōtos* of the anchorites.

The competing prestige of the cenobitic idea in the Byzantine Church and her daughters in the Slavonic world was due especially to the work of Theodore the Studite. The immaturity of many of the hermits of the late patristic period led that great Churchman to essay in an urban setting (not so unusual as might be thought, either in Constantinople or at Rome) a major cenobitic foundation of a strict kind and preach not only *apatheia* but also fraternal charity as the goal of the ascetic life. Taking further the programs of Pachomius and Basil for the common life, he regulated the devotions and daily lives of monks under his care to a hitherto unheard-of degree. The spirit of his *Hypotypōsis* or "testament," *Catechisms,* and the Studite *Constitutions* was at the opposite pole to the idiorhythmic temper of the hermits of the holy mountains of Byzantium.

What the Christian East, in the period of its full sacramental communion with Catholicism, and indeed much later, showed no sign of developing was the specialized apostolates which became so common in the Western Church with the reform of the sixteenth century: the communities, congregations, and orders devoted to such differentiated activities as nursing or teaching. Though some sisterhoods of this sort appear in the Orthodox world of the later nineteenth century, the concept of such functionally determined religious foundations (which has spread somewhat invasively to the Eastern Catholic churches in modern times) remains *au fond* a peculiarity of Western Catholicism. As this survey may have suggested, if it is to remain in touch with the historic sources of the religious life, it is important that such professionally "apostolic" religious retain a firm hold on the common basics of the monastic institution in the Church—however adapted to meet particular pastoral demands.[18]

A Theology of the Religious Life

The root of the religious life is the monastic movement, and the numerous religious orders, congregations, institutes, and communities of Catholicism represent the branching and leafing of the tree that grows from this root. Although modern religious take on many works in the service of the Church that would have surprised the monks and nuns of the patristic age, they are well advised to keep close in spirit to their ancient source.

As a sign of the holy Church, the Church that already lives with the life of the city of God in heaven, religious are called to witness to the unity of Christ's mystical body, because the salvation the Church is both offered and given is a sharing of the divine life in solidarity with each other. As Augustine sums up the goal of Christ's mediating work in his *De Trinitate:*

> It was God's will that we be justified by being made one in the one Just Man; that we would not lose hope of rising in the flesh itself when we

18. This plea is powerfully echoed by Archimandrite Boniface Luykx, Premonstratensian canon and historian of the Liturgy, in *Eastern Monasticism and the Future of the Church* (Stamford, Conn., 1993).

saw how the One Head had preceded us, his many members. By this
Mediator we are being cleansed by faith at the present time, but later on
we will be renewed by vision and reconciled to God. Then we shall adhere to the One, enjoy the One and remain one for ever.[19]

If the hermit testifies to the unity of the mystical body in its invisible
aspect, the cenobitic religious witnesses to the unity of that body in its
visible sacramental form on earth. Each religious community is a
micro-Church, the most intense or concentrated form of the Church as
communion that there is: more so than the diocese, more so than the
parish. Only the family as the "domestic Church" can rival it, but the
family church is essentially a cell of the parish. This means two things:
first, that the family is not called on in its own right to embody the total
mystery of the Church; and second, its task is in this world, it has what
the Second Vatican Council called an *indolis saecularis*, a "secular project," to transform little by little the environment around it. It is not intended, like the religious community, to point beyond this world to the
world to come.

The fact that the religious community is, in its own right, an embodiment of the mystery of the Church, and that it is so specifically as
an expression of the Church as the sacrament of the future, the glory
of the age to come, means that its life is centered on the sacred liturgy.
The liturgy is the source and summit of the Church's life, as the
Second Vatican Council expresses it; it is the most inward form of her
covenant response to God in Christ, and it is the anticipation of the life
of heaven. The rationale of such worship (apart from the glory of God)
is the upbuilding of the community in faith, hope, and charity, because
these are, as Aquinas says, the specifically theological virtues, the ones
that relate us to the God of glory himself.

It follows from what I have said that even a purely contemplative
community lives the apostolic life, understood as a replication of the
life of the Jerusalem Church in the Acts of the Apostles. A community
of "mixed" life reduplicates this by living out also the apostolic mission in some one or other of its modalities. Active religious, or indeed
contemplative religious when they accept active works in certain times
and places, have done historically a great variety of things. How can
we understand these theologically? To be authentic, the work of the
active Church, and so the religious as active, must be a legitimate

19. Augustine, *The Trinity* 4.7.

expression of the ministry or ongoing work of the Savior who, in his achieved work, salvation, is the center of the contemplative Church, the focus of the religious as contemplative. Christ was a healer, so there can be religious devoted to nursing; Christ was a teacher, so there can be religious engaged in education; Christ was, for the inspired theology of the New Testament writers, a priest and a king, so there can be religious who are ministerially ordained, and who are indeed actively involved in pastoral work, the shepherding or ruling office of Christ in his Church. But in each case, in order to correspond to the source of the religious life in a celibacy in honor of the Lord, pursued normatively with others in a communal liturgical setting, such active works must always return to rest in the contemplation that forms the primary basis of the monastic state.

Because the religious life is, in the ways I have been describing, an expression of the mystery of the Church, it follows that the hierarchical Church, the pope and bishops as the Church's supreme pastors (the pope for the universal Church, the bishop for his local Church), ordained as these are to oversee the welfare or proper functioning of the Church as a whole, have a right and proper interest in the *modus operandi* of the religious life. The hierarchical Church does not originate the religious life, which has always been understood as a free gift to the Church by the Holy Spirit. Yet the hierarchical Church has the duty to exercise its own charism of discernment, and once it has discerned the charism of a particular religious founder as authentic, to welcome it by what *Lumen gentium* calls a "willing response to the movements of the Holy Spirit." By the official sanction which it gives to a particular religious Rule or constitutions, to the authority of religious superiors, and to the personal commitment of individual religious, the hierarchical Church admits the embodiment of a particular charism as a legitimate institution within her corporate life. Although this institution is not merely a canonical one but has for those involved in it the meaning and value of a special consecration to God, and so is, for them, as *Perfectae caritatis* puts it, a never-failing source of grace, the hierarchical Church has a proper role in the regulation of its life and self-expression.

Because the monastic community is a consecrated expression of the mystery of the Church, by its life only or by its life and mission, it has a relation both to the universal Church, its overall context, and to the particular Church, the locality where it is. It must both be rooted in the diocese, the local Church, and yet represent to the diocese some aspect of the wider, universal Church. It must both be content to be within the bosom of the local Church, exhibiting to that Church's members, in depth, the basic Christian life which they already share, and also offer to them something different, a monastic tradition which draws on a wider Christian experience than that of one place or one time and so helps to draw the local Church out of a bad particularity, out of too narrowing a confinement within its temporal and spatial limits, its present culture, and into a wider catholicity. Needless to say, a monastic community can only succeed in these ecclesiological functions if it is a micro-Church, a communion in the profoundest Christ- and God-centered sense, if in other words its members are engaged as whole-heartedly as possible on growth in holiness through Jesus Christ and his Spirit, who is the Spirit of the Father.

This is true both of the purely contemplative religious life and of that religious life where contemplation has been placed at the service of action. For in each case the vows, or the substance of the vows, are the same. The vows are three expressions of the Church as a mystery of configuration to Jesus Christ (perhaps the more natural symbolism for the male religious) or of union with him (perhaps the more appropriate for the female). For the final salvation assured to the Church by the Son was achieved by him only in the poverty, chastity, and obedience—that is, the single-hearted service of the Father—of the man Jesus, while, correspondingly, the grace of God achieves the Church's definitive sharing in that final salvation only by arousing in her a bridal response—a desire to be similarly poor, chaste, and obedience, that is, single hearted—vis-à-vis the Son made man who is the human form of salvation, the Savior.

The religious life—monasticism—is a fact of comparative religion. The monastic systems of Buddhism resemble most closely those of Christianity, though one could add other examples both historic (e.g., pre-Christian Greece with its Cynic mendicant preachers; pre-Columbian America, with its "virgins of the Sun"; the Jewish Therapeutae of Egypt described by Philo) and contemporary (e.g., the Sufi Muslim communities which managed to eke out an existence in Communist Albania). The three elements of expropriation and common use of property, celibacy, and obedience to superiors are found as a fact of the *religiosum,* if not everywhere then in many places. The common element in their motivation is to foster a relationship with what is simply beyond the human being (variously thought of as the absolute, the transcendent, the ultimate reality, the world of spirits) or a personal God. Other subsidiary motives exist, but in Christian monasticism they are transformed, transposed, and reinterpreted in the light of the Judaeo-Christian tradition.

Though religious life has taken to itself motifs of non-Christian philosophy (and more recently, of political ethics, usually of a Socialist variety), and repristinated themes of the Hebrew Bible (e.g., the recovery of divine likeness, the restoration of the image of God, return to Eden, recreating the life-way of the ancient Israelite "schools of the prophets," preparing for final judgment, anticipating the life of the kingdom, living in fellowship with the angels), its predominant inspiration has always been evangelical.

People have wanted to "follow" Jesus as he invited them to: imitating him in his despoiling himself of earthly interests; his virginity and tender yet wholly exigent love of the Father; his submission to the Father's saving will. They have wanted to share in his mystery by uniting themselves especially to his cross, reproducing certain of his actions, such as his solitude in the desert, fasting, struggle against the evil powers, his lengthy praying and care for the sick, the poor, the stranger, as well as his urgent proclamation of his message—all of which constituted the concentrated preparation of his "hour." They have wanted to respond to his call for penitence, conversion, a change of life and outlook. They have wanted to embody more fully the commitment to him made at their baptism, to acquire his grace more abundantly and enter into that relationship of bride to bridegroom so frequently mentioned in the Gospels, the Pauline Letters, and the Revelation of John. And they have wanted to do all this so as to show they could serve, and suffer for, his Church as generously as did the earliest disciples.

In carrying out such inspirations the religious life stands as an incomparable icon of the mystery of the Church.

9

The Rites of the Church

If the Church is the mediation of the grace of Christ, we must look also at one of the main submediations of her mediation, namely, the sacraments. The actual grace that comes to us from the sacraments wells up within human nature, sanctified in the Church, from springs placed there by God (viz., the various sacramental characters and other sacramental titles to grace).

The Sacramental Principle

To appreciate the sacraments theologically—not just anthropologically, as rites of passage, or sociologically, as occasions for the building of community—we must backtrack and resume that constitutive principle of Catholicism, incarnational realism. The distinctive Catholic attitude to both Church and sacraments stems from the conviction that incarnation—the self-communication of God to humanity through embodiment in the human and visible—still remains, even after Christ's ascension, the principal form of God's covenant presence to us. Although Jesus Christ is no longer part of the public, observable space of this world, the incarnation continues, albeit under different modalities.

As we have seen, Christ is, for Catholic Christians, God's communication of his own inner life, the Word, and he is so both totally, absolutely, and yet in an incarnate, tangibly human fashion. For this reason Catholic theology often uses an expression not found in the New Testament by calling him the "sacrament of God," the primordial sacrament. In other words, he is the supreme instance of a sign that actually brings about what it symbolizes. Christ's human existence does not simply convey to us what God is like in the manner of an audiovisual aid. Then he would be no more than a teacher, albeit one who taught through his life, death, and resurrection. Rather, the sign which Jesus actually is brings to us the very presence of God. He is God's way to us, mediated by human embodiment, as he is our way back to God. He is God's sacrament. The continuing mediation of God through the human which follows on, with the ascension, from the work of Christ is nothing other than the Church and the sacraments. As the Letter to the Ephesians sees it, the Church, as the body of Christ, is the manifestation in history of the mystery of God's eternal purpose which was consummated in the glorified crucified Lord. The Church, then, is the visible sign, and mediation, of God's grace because she carries on the divine sacramentality. She is the sacrament of Christ who is the sacrament of God.

Catholic teaching about the seven sacraments follows from this principle of incarnational realism, since sacraments are focal moments, when the Church's life as the sacrament of Christ comes to fullest expression. As Pope Leo the Great puts it, "All that is visible in the life of Christ has passed over into his mysteries [the sacraments of the Church]."[1] Ambrose in his *Apology of the Prophet David* says, "You have shown yourself to me face to face, O Christ, I find you in your sacraments."[2] Not for nothing does Aquinas place his treatise on the sacraments immediately after his treatment of Christ's life and passion: they are the "sacraments of his humanity." Though it is the glorified Christ who principally ministers them to us, it is the humanity of Christ that became, through the passion, the glorified principle of grace. It is, then, the mysteries constitutive of the *Christus passus* (the dying and rising Christ) that actually sanctify souls in the sacraments. Christ's Passover enjoys a primacy here among the mysteries of his life because it is the divinely appointed fulfillment of his mission. Other mysteries of the *vita Domini* have saving efficacy only insofar as they are ordered to this principal mystery, being lived out by Christ as preparation for his death and exaltation. At the Lincolnshire church of Kirton-in-Lindsey a fourteenth-century wall painting, now lost, showed in its uppermost image the Crucified between Mary and John, while "from the wounds of the crucified body blood flows in seven trickling lines which create a semi-sphere radiating into scenes of the seven sacraments."[3]

1. Leo, *Sermons* 74.2.
2. Ambrose, *Apology of the Prophet David*, 12.
3. M. Rubin, *Corpus Christi: The Eucharist in Late Mediaeval Culture* (Cambridge, 1991) 102.

Similarly, on the octagonal "seven-sacrament fonts" of East Anglia, sadly defaced by Reformation-period iconoclasm, the passion of Christ and the risen Crucified One form the eighth image—challenged only by stone icons of the baptism of Christ (which, theologically, is a prefiguration of his death and resurrection).[4] In texts and images in other media as well, the Passover of Christ appears as the abiding source of sacramental life. The redemption becomes "re-actualized," not of course in its physical and historical detail but in the sense that the humanity of Christ and his saving acts are present actively and dynamically in the sacraments of the Church. In particular, then, as Aquinas points out, it is to the saving passion that any sign must be related if it is genuinely to count as a sacrament of Christ.

No sacrament could be such, moreover, unless Christ himself instituted it. No purely human symbolic creation could have this valency. Although the New Testament records "words of institution" only for baptism and Eucharist, the Catholic doctrine is that the other sacraments are not so much created by the Church as recognized by her. "In those pregnant engagements of her faith which we call the sacraments, the Church became increasingly aware that she was both doing and encountering Jesus' human will as the human expression of the *mystêrion* of God's eternal saving will, by analogy, then, with those engagements of her faith for which Jesus' command was explicitly given."[5] Each sacrament was instituted for the purpose of some chief effect, to be gathered from its signification, its symbolic texture. Because Christ is God, these sacramental signs, while they are humanly intelligible (were they not, they would be of no earthly use in our salvation) are ultimately signs in *God's* language. In them God speaks: he communicates by way of our languages, including our vocabulary of gesture. This renders the sacraments events in which the Church recognizes her own deepest identity as the sacrament of Christ, and events, moreover, by whose celebration she becomes more fully that sacrament.

Like all God's actions, the sacraments are never nugatory. They do not depend on our response for their constitution as acts of grace, though that response is needed for their fruitfulness. If they manifest the sacramentality of the Church, the continuing incarnation of Christ

---

4. A. E. Nichols, *Seeable Signs: The Iconography of the Seven Sacraments, 1350–1544* (Woodbridge, Suffolk, 1994)

5. C. Ernst, "Acts of Christ: Signs of Faith," in idem, *Multiple Echo: Explorations in Theology,* ed. F. Kerr and T. Radcliffe (London, 1979) 113.

as the sacrament of God, then they cannot be simply psychological stimuli to the exercise of faith and devotion. The world is never the same again after the celebration of a sacrament.

In their totality, the sacraments present a portrait of Christian existence under the regime of grace. They structure the organism of life in Christ. That life comes to birth in baptism. It finds its maturing, and acceptance of responsibility, in confirmation. It receives its nourishment in the Eucharist. When it falls morally sick it has the sacrament of penance, and in physical convalescence, or by way of immediate preparation for the kingdom in dying, the anointing of the sick. It acquires its pattern of common life through the sacrament of orders, and its realization in the family through the sacrament of marriage.

Above all, the self-communication of God for our salvation, through the Word of God which does not merely testify to a distant God but brings about his actual presence, has its sacramental climax in the Eucharist. In this sacrament, Christ himself in his Body and Blood—that is, in his personal presence—is the very medium in which we encounter him. In all the other sacraments, we are related in some way to Christ's redemptive *work*, through the instrumentality of creaturely realities like ourselves, be they animate or inanimate. In the Eucharist, however, we are related to his *personal presence* as our Redeemer, and that in no other medium than himself. That is the meaning of transubstantiation.

Even then, however, the ultimate goal of God's purpose is not that there should simply be such a sacrament for its own sake, just as it is not an end-in-itself that there should be the sacrament of Christ in the incarnation. The goal lies in our return through Christ, through the Church, through the sacraments, to unity in God, as his sons and daughters. Even in the Eucharistic presence, the ultimate reality involved is the mystical unity of the Church in charity—humanity sharing in the life of uncreated love which unites Father and Son in the Holy Spirit.

Communio Sanctorum

The Creed's commitment to a *communio sanctorum* is hard to interpret from an historical viewpoint. The ambiguity of the Latin—a communion "of holy persons" or "in holy things"?—allows for a reference here to the sacraments, and this is how much (but not all) of tradition has read it. A sermon on the Creed from the time of Charlemagne refers the clause to "that holy communion, through the invocation of the Father, the Son and the Holy Spirit, in which all the faithful ought to participate every Lord's day."[6] Medieval theologians who took this line sometimes integrated the two possible genders of *sanctorum* by saying that the clause's object is "the communion which the saints enjoyed," namely, the holy sacrament of the altar. In the eleventh century, Peter Abelard speaks of "that communion by which the saints are made saints, and are confirmed in their sanctity, by participation in the divine sacrament."[7] Aquinas, in his short commentary on the Creed, also tries to have the best of both worlds, remarking that "Because all the faithful form one body, the benefits belonging to one are communicated to the others. There is thus a sharing of benefits in the Church, and this is what we mean by *sanctorum communio*."[8] He explains that the "goods shared" comprise everything worthwhile done on earth by the saints, but particularly the seven sacraments, since they alone convey to us the *virtus* (the power, or in the archaic English sense, the "virtue," the peculiar property) of Christ's passion, the atoning act whereby Christ as head redeemed his body, the Church. The sacraments are, in other words, a uniquely privileged sphere of the action of the Holy Spirit transmitting to us the reality (insofar as we can share it here and now) of the Son's redeeming work, that highpoint of the Father's love and mercy to the world.

The conjunction of this reference to the sacraments in the pneumatological section of the Creed with Aquinas's Christological or Christ-centered theology of the sacraments as extensions, expressions, or manifestations of the victorious passion of the Son tells us something of prime importance. The sacraments involve the presence and action of both the Spirit and the Son, and as such they cannot really be described as "impersonal" realities (however useful that term may be in enabling us to distinguish between the two historical alternatives, based on grammatical gender, in the interpretation of this article). Just as a symbolic gesture like a birthday present or handshake is an embodiment of personal intention and activity, so too are the sacraments.

Although a purely symbolic understanding of the sacraments would already justify us in calling them holy things, the Church claims more for them than simply that they are a kind of vocabulary for ar-

6. "Symbolum Graeca lingua est" (anonymous sermon), cited in J. N. D. Kelly, *Early Christian Creeds*, 2d ed. (London, 1960) 393.

7. Abelard, *Expositio symboli quod dicitur apostolorum.*

8. Thomas Aquinas, *Expositio super symbolo apostolorum, scilicet Credo in Deum.*

ticulating the purposes of Son and Spirit. Or, better, because the Son and the Spirit whose purposes the sacraments articulate are the Son and the Spirit of the Father, the source of all creation, they cannot express those purposes without (to some extent at least) realizing them. We make this point by calling the sacraments "efficacious signs," symbols that actually tend to bring about what they symbolize. Indeed, when we reach the Eucharist we come to a sign that does not simply effect what it symbolizes—namely, our feeding upon Christ by induction into the movement of his sacrificial dying—but actually contains the giver of the sacrament, since the reality of the bread and wine are converted into the being of Christ, retaining only just so much of their own reality as will enable them to stay within the order of signs, important as that is to their functioning as sacraments. The sacraments are holy, then, not only because they are symbols for the work of Spirit and Son, but also because they draw on the creative power of the Father, being efficacious signs that bring about the active involvement of Spirit and Son they signify, and, in the case of the Eucharist, the personal actuality of the very being of the incarnate Son (on which there must also follow, thanks to the communion of life between the persons, the presence of the entire Trinity). We speak therefore of holy baptism, holy orders, holy matrimony, but we call the Eucharistic gifts the "most holy," *sanctissimum*, the "most holy sacrament of the altar."

Furthermore, the shared sacramental goods found in holy living in the Church have their center in the Eucharist. All the sacraments in their various ways find their meaning in relation to that center. Baptism and confirmation have to do with, respectively, entry into the Eucharistic community and taking on full responsibility as a member of Christ's priestly people. Penance and the anointing of the sick are about return to the Eucharistic table when one has been impeded from approaching it by sin or sickness, or, in the case of the last anointing (extreme unction), access to the eschatological fullness of the Eucharist, preparation for the banquet of heaven. Orders is about the provision of ministers to enable the continuance of the Church as a Eucharistic fellowship, and matrimony has as its goal the constitution of that community's most fundamental cell, the "domestic Church" of the family.

The Liturgical Principle

The sacraments are embedded in a wider structure of gesture and prayer: the liturgy. This too requires our attention, for in the ritual life of the Church—in Catholic symbolic activity at its most intense—the meaning of the whole Christian religion comes to expression. In the Catholic view, ritual is anthropologically necessary to religion. Without it, the attempt to express ultimate realities ruptures the life of the imagination. Ritual weaves speech, gesture, rhythm, and structured ceremonial into a form of worship expressive of the human person's being in the world. It unites our physical, mental, and emotional being in a single response to the unseen, all within the specific conditions of humanness.

Of course, there is more to liturgy than anthropology. Through the liturgy, as Catholicism understands it, Jesus Christ continues to exercise his priestly office. That office has two aspects or faces. With respect to the Father, Christ's priesthood consists of glorification; with respect to humankind, it consists in sanctification. Through his life and death, Christ glorified God and sanctified human beings; exalted at the resurrection, his priestly work goes on. In Jesus Christ, our humanity gives ceaseless adoration to the Father and through him the Spirit of the Father is poured out on to the world, to heal the wounds of human nature and raise up humankind to share the life of God. This priesthood of Christ the head is shared by his body the Church. The head does not separate himself from the body, so Christ's mediation between the Father and the world is participated in by the Church.

The proper approach to celebration of the liturgy may be exemplified from the biography of the priest-novelist R. H. Benson.

> At . . . the old Jacobean chest, with emblems of the Passion gilded on its panels, which served for altar, Hugh said his Mass, quickly and without mannerism, regarding it essentially as his priestly *business*, his *opus Dei*—sacrifice for God—and not edification for the populace, nor even an affair of personal devotion. He was fond of emphasizing the obliteration, by the conventional vestments, of the human outline; so, too, from tone and gesture must the merely personal be remorselessly eliminated. The idea of prayers elegantly "read to" an audience was repulsive to him; neither were pious sighs or inequalities of voice to be allowed as tribute to his own feelings. The whole action was hieratic.[9]

The liturgy is not subpersonal, however, but suprapersonal, for it expresses the communion of a multitude of persons—present visibly or invisibly—through the Church's great high priest, Jesus Christ, with the three-personed God.

9. C. C. Martindale, *The Life of Monsignor Robert Hugh Benson* (London, 1916) 2:142.

The value a Catholic places on the Eucharist in part comes from and is certainly sustained by an atmosphere of reverence. The Eucharist as rite, as drama, "works" in the same sort of way as does a play—hence the importance of care and objectivity in the manner of celebration of the Mass. If F. R. Leavis could say of tragic drama that in it we have "contemplated a painful action, involving death and the destruction of the good, admirable and sympathetic, and yet instead of being depressed we enjoy a sense of enhanced vitality," so too at the Mass we encounter the death of Christ and yet we come away with a "sense of renewed life and of hopeful joy," rather than one of "depression at the futility and pointlessness of human existence." In the impersonality of the liturgy, *mine* matters only "insofar as the individual sentience is the individual focus of experience." Significance is revealed, not because of conscious purpose or will on the worshippers' part, but simply because this rite is what it is, *ex opere operato*. In the liturgy we are concerned with *metanoia,* "repentance," "a transforming of perspectives and expectations, both in self-knowledge and in knowledge of reality, which *may* sometimes occur in observable moments of special insight or of emotion intensity, but is more commonly . . . a steady re-direction of the personality as a whole."[10]

The Ethos of the Liturgy

The ethos of the liturgy varies in the concrete from community to community—turning, above all, on whether a particular group of the faithful belongs to the Latin Church, or to one of the Catholic Eastern Churches. The language of their worship may be the vernacular, with its advantages of greater (at least surface) intelligibility and capacity for transfiguration of the profane world. Or it may be a specially preserved "sacred" language (Latin, patristic Greek, Syriac). The use of a sacred language underlines the truth which is the other side of the vernacular coin. It draws attention to the discontinuity between the public world of our everyday concerns and the space and time of the liturgical celebration in which, sacramentally and symbolically, the pilgrim Church steps into eternity. That salvation is both already given us and is still to come, the gift of the ineffably mysterious God, is well expressed in the coexistence, within the Church, of both vernacular and non-vernacular liturgical languages. Naturally, for this coexistence to

10. F. Kerr, "Liturgy and Impersonality," *New Blackfriars* 52 (1971) 436–47, citing F. R. Leavis, *The Common Pursuit* (London, 1952) 127.

flourish, the Latin liturgy must retain that degree of salience and mainstream use that makes it available as a shared inheritance. It appears that Jesus himself used Hebrew, in his day an archaic sacral language, rather than the vernacular Aramaic, at the Last Supper. Presumably he wished thereby to heighten the sacrality of the action and words, and to emphasize continuity with God's salvation celebrated in the Passover. An exclusively vernacular liturgy can tempt clergy and faithful to cast the Mass entirely into contemporary terms, and make it appear as something that we ourselves devise. But then we should not be doing what Jesus ordered us to hand on; the Mass would be deprived of strong roots in the past, and be less effectively something that forms us as we celebrate it.

Of course not everything in the ritual celebration of the Eucharistic drama, or the other rites of the Church, goes back to Jesus and the apostles, or even to the early post-apostolic community. Such things as vestments, incense, holy water, blessed ashes, and blessed candles appear in the Church's worship only with the "peace of the Church": her emergence to not only tolerated but also privileged status within the civil society of the Roman Empire. The domain of the sacramentals reflects in its own limited fashion the universality of salvation. The material elements are caught up into an incarnational scheme which can bestow good things upon human beings *ex opere operantis Ecclesiae* (that is, through the working of the prayer of the Church, not the direct action of God). We must stress that the objects themselves are but lightly touched: only a tenuous thread connects them with the grace of the all-hallowing Word. Though many of these "smells and bells" were anticipated in the Judaism of the Old Testament, some people regard their ecclesiastical re-emergence (or fresh creation) in and around the fourth century as distinctly suspect. Was this not a creeping paganization of the gospel? Just as the English historian Edmund Gibbon regarded the papacy as the ghost of the Roman Empire sitting crowned on the grave thereof, so the French political philosopher Charles Maurras saw Catholicism as Judaeo-Christianity tamed and civilized by the Greco-Roman ethos. Needless to say, this is not how the Church herself understands the development of her worship. For her, the evolution of these ritual appurtenances does not denature her primitive worship but helps her to bring out the meaning of the liturgical actions. Vestments interpret the standing of the deacon, priest, or bishop as recipients of the sacrament of orders; incense indicates the honor due the Eucharistic elements or the images of Christ, Mary, and the saints, and the people of God, *plebs sancta Dei;* holy water reminds the faithful of their own baptism and the need to continue in the graced life of baptismal existence; ashes invite them to remember the command of Christ that we should undertake penance; the candles carried by the congregation on Candlemas, the feast of the Presentation in the Temple, recall how Christ was there proclaimed a light to the nations, and indeed called himself the light of the world.

In such ways the ritual objects or actions created by the Church tease out the meaning of the liturgy; the sacramentals (as the chief ceremonial aids to our worship are called), subserve the deeper reality of the sacraments. Just because the Church's liturgy is the action of Christ the high priest, and because her sacraments are his continued activity as the risen Lord of the Church, her worship has a depth of significance which requires not only words but also gestures to unfold. Such words and gestures are not improvised but prescribed. For Catholics, canon law and rubrics are not, in principle at least, impertinent intrusions upon the expression of our faith. The sacraments are expressions of faith in which the Church realizes her being as the congregation of the faithful, prescribing ritual actions as bearers and witnesses of a faith continuous with her origins, acknowledging her Lord as the summary, concrete presence of God's eternal purpose of salvation and renewing on earth Christ's intercession with the Father.

The Liturgy of the Hours: The Sanctification of Time

In descending into hell, Christ entered both past and future time. With his resurrection, the total content of his saving work can be focused on different points in historical time. Not only are all ages open to God, but, with the atonement, all time is penetrated by the mystery of Christ. It is from this Christological background that the Church approaches the sanctification of that medium in which the narrative of human life unfolds.

Not only the year has to be sanctified, but also the week and the day. Sunday is the fulcrum of the liturgical week, for it is the weekly Easter: the commemoration of the Lord's resurrection and, as such, the fulfillment of the Sabbath, at any rate in time as we know it. Sunday is the "primary holy day of obligation" when all the faithful, of whatever ritual Church, must assist at the Liturgy of the Eucharist and "abstain from such work or business that would inhibit the worship to be given to God, the joy proper to the Lord's Day, or the due relaxation of mind and body."[11] With profound insight into the paschal mystery, the Irish-speaking Church called Christ *Rí an Domhnaigh* "King of the Sunday," and celebrated accordingly: "We bid you welcome, blessed Sunday, a fine lovely day after the week, a fine lovely day to speak to Christ. Stir your feet and make your way to Mass. Stir your heart and drive from it all spite. Stir your lips and speak words of blessing. Look up and see the Son of the blessed Nurse."[12]

Within the week, each day, including Sunday, must be hallowed within its own course, following the example of Israel. In the synagogue, prayer was said thrice daily, accompanied by readings from the Scriptures for purposes of instruction. As early as the *Didache* (and so in apostolic times), the Our Father, the dominical prayer par excellence, had supplanted the Shema, Israel's basic confession of monotheistic faith, at these three hours. Cyprian, Clement of Alexandria, Hippolytus, and Tertullian speak of liturgical assemblies for such non-Eucharistic worship. In the Liturgy of the Hours, the Church carries out the priestly office of her head by offering God a sacrifice of praise and by interceding through Christ for the salvation of the whole world. The special characteristic of the Hours in this regard is that they consecrate the flow of time, the course of day and night. The Hours extend the praise and petition of the Eucharist to the different hours of the diurnal round.

Each Hour is composed of four elements: a hymn, psalmody, the reading of the Scriptures, and prayer. Underlying this structure lies a deeper pattern: the dialogue between God and humanity. In each Hour we hear two voices, the word of God in the Bible, and the word of humanity in the other texts which are preparation for, commentary on, or application of the word of God. The *hymn* is meant to express the particular characteristic of each Hour or feast, so as to draw those present into the celebration, especially by its literary beauty. The *Psalter* constitutes the largest element in the Divine Office. It has a proven power to raise human hearts to God, to help them give thanks in happy times, to bring consolation in adversity. The psalms are always recited in the name of the Church; thus, even though the feelings expressed in them may not coincide with our own at a given moment, we can always find a reason for joy or sorrow in singing them. The antiphon helps bring

11. *Codex Iuris Canonici*, 1247.
12. Cited in P. O'Fiannachta and D. Forristal, *Saltair: Prayers from the Irish Tradition* (Dublin, 1988) 24–25.

out the character of the psalm, or color it to fit the tonality of some particular feast or occasion. Also psalm-like are the gospel canticles—the songs of Zechariah, Mary, and Simeon. These have a special dignity as acts of thanksgiving for human redemption and so are given the same solemnity as the liturgical proclamation of the gospel itself. The reading of the *Scriptures* forms the climax of the Office. Normally the reading is followed by a response or acclamation, aimed at letting the divine Word penetrate more deeply into mind and heart. In celebration of Lauds and Vespers with the people, a brief homily on the Scripture can be given. The last element is the *prayers*. The petitions, added in the liturgical reform of Paul VI, are always linked in some way to the praise of God and the recalling of the history of salvation. They include intercessions for the Church and world. At Vespers, the final petition is always for the departed. In accordance with tradition, the Lord's Prayer follows, and the entire Office is rounded off by a concluding prayer, either proper to the day or underlining the special character of the Hour.

The morning is, in its freshness and stillness, especially suited to the praise of God. Human beings and nature awake to their daily "resurrection." In the Office of *Lauds,* the Church rejoices at the renewed gift of life and light, acclaiming thereby the Creator. At the same time, the rising sun, referred to in the solemn canticle, the song of Zechariah (Luke 1:68-79), also symbolizes the resurrection of the Redeemer. Just as Zechariah, filled with the Holy Spirit, hailed the dawn of the day of salvation, with the birth of the forerunner, John, so the Church daily greets her risen Lord as "Oriens ex alto." Lauds highlights the praising psalms, often those with nature motifs. On Sundays and feast days the Benedicite (Dan 3:35-68) calls on all creation to join in this act of praise, acknowledging God's sovereignty, which means, in the New Testament context, the kingship of the risen Christ.

Vespers—a name originally used for the evening star, and the evening meal—was also called in early times *lucernarium:* the Office of lamp-lighting. Christians followed Jews in using blessing prayers for lighting lamps, and this preliminary rite lent its name to the prayer service that followed. Vespers is the Christian counterpart to the sacrifice of incense offered each evening in the Temple as mentioned in Psalm 140, a favorite Vesper psalm which prompted the use of incense, first during its own recitation but in later times during the singing of the Magnificat, the canticle of the Blessed Virgin Mary. The Church Fathers regarded incense as a symbol of Christ on Calvary. They read the psalm as a prayer of the crucified Lord who stretched out his arms on the cross and celebrated the first Vesper rite of the new covenant at the hour of the evening sacrifice. Although a Christianized evening prayer is already found in the third century, in Tertullian and the *Apostolic Tradition*, where it consists of *lucernarium*, psalmody, and an agape meal, the development of the classic Vespers services of East and West is the work of the fourth to the sixth centuries.

If the character of Vespers is essentially that of thanksgiving for the blessings, spiritual and temporal, of the day, *Prime* (now used only in the monastic Office) is basically a blessing for the day's work. The martyrology is read, the day's work distributed, and the superior's blessing closes the ceremony. The "little Hours" of Prime, Terce, Sext, and None were at first confined to monastic churches, but in the eighth century became obligatory for all clerics in the West. *Terce, Sext,* and *None* are the more venerable little Hours: they derive from the division of the day into three segments in the Roman Empire. Tertullian and Hippolytus commend private prayer at these times, citing the apostolic practice in Acts 2:15; 10:9; and 3:1-7. By the fifth century monks and devout people had turned these "apostolic prayers" into public rites in many places.

The same was true of *Compline:* John Cassian describes how Eastern monks would gather in huddles to recite some psalms before retiring, while in the Rule of Aurelian of Arles the apt choice of Psalm 90, later the classical Compline psalm, is enjoined. A preliminary rite, consisting of spiritual reading and a self-accusation of faults, was generally omitted in non-monastic settings, while the body of the service—a hymn, psalms, a lesson and responsory, the canticle of Simeon, a prayer, and a blessing—is faithful to the basic structure of the Liturgy of the Hours. Compline sees sleep as a daily rehearsal for death—both of which the Church faces with profound trust in the protecting presence of Christ.

Matins has the least traceable history of all the Offices. It may have started life as a night vigil (attested already in Tertullian and Cyprian), but it soon became a wandering Office which could be celebrated at various hours and notably, as its name indicates, in the later morning. When the Frankish pilgrim Egeria visited the holy places in the late fourth century she found the laity at Matins and Vespers, the ascetics at the other hours also. In the East, it has retained its nocturnal character as a vigil service, archetypally on Easter Eve, but this was extended early on to the festivals of the martyrs and to Sundays. The perseverance of monks in prayer after the corporate vigil of the local Church was an essential part of the monastic Office in the East after Basil, while Benedict gives it four chapters of his Rule before even considering the other Hours. In the period of Hilary and Ambrose (fourth century), homilies from the Fathers were added to biblical readings at the night Office, and this principle (widened to include post-patristic authors) survives in the modern Office of Readings in the Latin Church. In many monastic communities in the West, however, this is still celebrated as a lengthy Office at the end of the night (rather than, as originally, in the first half of the night).

The Divine Office is, evidently, the worshipping expression of the Church's identity. But it remains for all that a method of prayer as well. As such it is, first and foremost, a symbolic kind of praying, to be approached somewhat as one might a poem. Its meaning has to be grasped as a whole and from within, if the symbols of which it is to be composed (and much of it is, precisely, liturgical *poetry*) are to exercise their power and introduce us to the wider world whose key they hold. The Office is also a cosmic kind of praying, a prayer that embraces all humankind, disclosing the meaning of all history. Through it we enter the space of the kingdom of God, taking our places as members of a society that extends through time and space but finds its fulfillment in an order of being beyond them, in the new creation where God's incarnate Word has his human home. At the Office, we can apply to ourselves the words of the Letter to the Hebrews:

> You have come to Mount Zion and to the city of the living God, the heavenly Jerusalem, and to innumerable angels in festal gathering, and to the assembly of the first-born who are enrolled in heaven, and to a judge who is God of all, and to the spirits of just men made perfect, and to Jesus, the mediator of a new covenant, and to the sprinkled blood that speaks more graciously than the blood of Abel (Heb 12:22-24).

We have of course come there in signs and symbols, and so the Office is, finally, and in an extended sense, a "sacramental" way of praying. It is to the sacraments proper that we must now turn.

The Particular Sacraments

The Catholic Church holds that there are seven sacraments, all instituted by Jesus Christ. In these pregnant engagements of her faith, the Church became increasingly aware that she was both doing and encountering

Jesus' human will as the human expression of the mystery of God's eternal saving will.

1. Baptism

The Eucharist is the supreme sacrament, since it is the ever-renewed sacramental representation of the single sacrifice that has been constituted the source of all sacramental grace. However, it is baptism which is *the* sacrament of faith. Baptism is that fundamental sacrament which enables us to receive the Word of God not as foreign to our nature but as the renewal of our true nature, now assumed into the ambit of the life everlasting. It is the sacrament of that faith whereby, through the enlightening of the Holy Spirit, we respond to the gospel of Christ, adhering to him and entering into the new covenant he founded.

As a washing, baptism speaks of the cleansing away of sin (both original and personal), but in Catholic soteriology the forgiveness of sins is the same as the coming of grace. As water brings life in the desert, and flows at birth, so baptism is the means whereby God first plants his life in us. The water of baptism is therefore at least *bivalent*: as cleansing and life-giving. But more than that, it is *trivalent*, for water can also cause death—and death may be redemptive. Paul teaches that baptism is a dying with Christ: we are buried with him (something most clearly seen if baptism is by immersion [going under water] rather than simply aspersion [sprinkling]). We die to sin, which means leading a new and richer life. In baptism we start to share in Christ's resurrection.

> This is the meaning of the great sacrament of Baptism which is solemnized among us, that all who attain to this grace shall die to sin as (Christ) is said to have so died because he died in the flesh which is sin's likeness; and rising from the font regenerate, as he arose alive from the grave, should begin a new life in the Spirit, whatever may be the age of the body.[13]

We live out our baptism by continuing to put sin to death and let the new divine life shape our behavior. Not for nothing is the favored time for adult baptism the vigil of Easter. At the start of Lent, those preparing for baptism are enrolled—classically, they give their names to the deacon in the evening, and present themselves with their sponsor the next day to the bishop in his principal church. In the *Rite of*

---

13. Augustine, *Enchiridion* 42.

Christian Initiation of Adults (1972)—adults are theologically, though not statistically, the normative candidates for baptism—Lent serves as a retreat aimed at preparing for baptismal regeneration. At Jerusalem the candidates were told, "If your wedding-day were approaching, would you not leave everything else and devote yourself entirely to preparing for the feast?"[14] Penitence, prayers of exorcism, examination of purity of motive, catechesis: these preliminaries are still reflected in the Catholic liturgies of the sacrament and its preparation. In the Jerusalem Church, the bishop expounded the Scriptures first literally and then spiritually, prior to solemnly "handing over" the Creed on the Sunday before Easter. Theodore of Mopsuestia admonished the candidates: "By the recitation of the Creed you bind yourself to God by the mediation of the bishop and you make a pact to persevere in charity toward the divine nature."[15] During the Easter vigil, in the last preparatory rite, Satan is renounced—traditionally facing the West, the region of visible darkness, which Hilary takes as adhesion to Christ in his victory over the dark power. The contrast is underlined by the turning to the east, toward Christ as rising sun of the second creation. The leading to the baptismal font which follows signifies the candidate's entrance into the Church. Baptisteries were frequently octagonal, for eight is the number of the eschatological Sabbath and so of the life of the kingdom, to which this sacrament gives entrance. The removal of garments prior to the anointing with the oil of catechumens, with its agonistic symbolism (it recalls wrestlers in the arena) is a configuration to the naked Christ and a sign of the filial trust which replaces the shame proper to the sinner before God. On the oil Denys the Areopagite writes:

> The high priest [the bishop] begins by anointing the body of the postulant with holy oils, thus in symbol calling the initiate to the holy contests which he will now have to undertake under the direction of Christ, for it is he who, God as he is, orders the combat. He himself descended into the arena with the combatants, to defend their freedom and to assure their victory over the forces of death and damnation.[16]

This conformation to Christ who "in this Goodness was the first of athletes" was followed at Antioch by the consecration of the baptismal

---

14. Cyril of Jerusalem, *Procatechesis* 6.
15. Theodore of Mopsuestia, *Commentary on the Sacraments of Baptism and the Eucharist* 13.1.
16. Denys, *On the Ecclesiastical Hierarchy* 2.6.

water (still done today in the Roman Rite, unless the water was blessed on Easter Eve itself). The liturgies are rich in their deployment of illuminating types for this water: the Creation, the Flood, the crossing of the Red Sea, etc. Clement of Alexandria remarks that "the new birth of Baptism comes about by water and the Spirit, like the coming to be of the universe."[17] Justin Martyr holds that "Christ became the head of another race regenerated by him, by the water and wood which contained the mystery of the Cross, as Noah was saved by the wood of the ark when he was carried with his family on the waters."[18] Basil says that "the people came out of the sea whole and safe; we also come out of the water as living men from among the dead."[19]

Cyril of Jerusalem explains that the baptismal bath that follows is an antitype of the passion of Christ: both like and unlike it. It is unlike in that the historical fact of the passion is only imitated dramatically (in the "drowning" and "rising again"); it is like in that the grace-content is the same. By this rite, we have communion in the saving grace of the passion. What seemed to be a tomb is in fact a womb, a *maternal* womb as the Fathers love to point out. "You are blessed when you come out of the most holy bath of the new birth, and when you pray for the first time beside your Mother the Church and with your brothers."[20] And this statement leads to the perfectly rhetorical question: "Since the birth of the Christian is accomplished in Baptism, and since the baptismal birth only takes place in the one Bride of Christ who is able spiritually to bring to birth the sons of God, where could he be born who is *not* a son of the Church?"[21]

The newly baptized is now clothed in a white garment (the "christening robe" of baptized infants), which Theodore calls "the sign of that shining world, of that kind of life to which you already come by means of symbols."[22]

In the Roman liturgy, after the gift of a candle with flame lit from the paschal candle itself, there is a postbaptismal anointing which will be either the sacrament of confirmation (on which see below) or, if confirmation is not to be given directly (as with infants in the West) a seal-

---

17. Clement of Alexandria, *Prophetic Eclogues* 7.
18. Justin, *Dialogue* 138.2–3.
19. Basil, *On the Holy Spirit* 14.
20. Tertullian, *On Baptism* 20.
21. Cyprian, *Letter* 84.6.
22. Theodore of Mopsuestia, *Commentary on the Sacraments of Baptism and the Eucharist* 14.26.

ing with chrism—oil mixed with sweet-smelling balsam—which looks ahead to that second sacrament. In either case we are dealing with a sign of incorporation into the Christian community which is at the same time a pledge of salvation. Like the brand sported by soldiers or devotees of a god in the ancient world, this commits one to a public act of witnessing. The Fathers frequently stress what Cyril of Jerusalem calls the "holy and indelible" character of this seal: the ineffaceable nature of the baptismal character comes from the fact that it is founded on God's irrevocable promise. Sacramental initiation brings one into a new order: there is an objective holiness which is retained (sacramental character) even when the subjective holiness that should flow from the grace of the sacrament is imperilled or lost. Baptism (and confirmation) are never repeated.

Baptism is entrance into fellowship with the Holy Trinity. As the Trinitarian persons ceaselessly give themselves to each other in eternity, so in the love they communicate in time do they enfold the baptized Christian in their own communion. Since it thus grants access to the Father, the source of the triune life through the manifestation of that communion in the economies of Son and Spirit, baptism must necessarily be both Christological and pneumatological. As a celebration of the paschal mystery, whereby the barrier of sin is destroyed and humankind reconciled to the Father, baptism is a sharing in the mystery of Christ. Yet baptismal regeneration is the work of the Spirit, whose house is the Church. It incorporates into the community of the Church. The anointing with chrism which follows baptism shows that the neophytes now have for their vocation the offering of spiritual sacrifices, the sacrifices that belong to the spiritual house of which they are living stones (1 Pet 2:5). *The Shepherd of Hermas,* a text of the subapostolic age, records a vision:

> The tower which you see being built is myself, the Church. . . . I asked her, Why has the tower been built on the water, Lady? . . . Because your life was saved and shall be saved through water, and the tower has been founded by the utterance of the almighty and glorious Name and is maintained by the unseen power of the Master.[23]

The Church also recognizes that besides drawing adults to faith, God can plant in the minds and wills of children the new life, and this testifies peculiarly strongly to his initiative in grace.

23. *Shepherd of Hermas,* Visions 3.3, 5.

2. *Confirmation*

Confirmation, by its ceremonies—anointing, laying on of hands, the giving of the kiss of peace by the bishop—does not merely unfold the content of baptism. Distinguished from the gift of the Spirit in regeneration there is also a special outpouring of the Spirit for the promulgation of the gospel.

Since, moreover, the gospel can never be thought of save as the proclamation of the Church, confirmation also introduces the baptized into their full rights and duties as members of the *laos,* God's holy people as a royal and universal priesthood.

It is at once, then, the sacrament of mission and (therefore) of "ordination" to the laity, the entry on duties and rights befitting the general priesthood of the faithful. As in the life of Christ there were two stages to his paschal mystery—Easter and Pentecost—so, in the life of the Christian, which is typically modelled on Christ's, there are likewise two stages—baptism and confirmation to her initiation into that saving mystery in its evangelical and catholic form. Just as Pentecost strengthened the apostles with the power of the Spirit for their mission in the Church, so too this sacrament has been seen as an empowering: *robur ad pugnam,* "strength for the fight," something associated particularly, in the twentieth century, with Catholic Action, the social outreach of the faithful into a world increasingly unheeding of Christian truth and values. In all these respects, the Holy Spirit in confirmation completes or seals what is given in baptism: hence the common patristic name of this sacrament, the seal of the Spirit. Confirmation is the "Ite, missa est!" ("Go, you are sent forth!") of baptism. It publicly ratifies the baptism in water and the presbyteral anointing before the whole assembled Church, and links these to the Eucharist, where the Spirit is invited to descend in his fullness on the communicant. As reformed in 1971, the Latin Rite retains the laying on of hands but stresses the anointing as the main sign of conferring the Holy Spirit, virtually adopting the Byzantine formula. Where baptism is more Christic, confirmation is more pneumatic.

The new dignity of the confirmed person vis-à-vis the mission, worship, and social action of the Church would not be efficacious without a more ready disposition to be at God's service, and this is the primary sacramental grace of confirmation: a more abiding docility to the Holy Spirit, in his sevenfold gifts of wisdom, understanding, counsel, fortitude, knowledge, piety, and the fear of the Lord. Ambrose calls these gifts "the seven virtues that you receive when you are marked with the seal." Confirmation is thus a new outpouring of the Spirit having as object the perfecting of the spiritual energies given in baptism. This explains why in the Christian East, this sacrament is seen as the sacrament of spiritual progress. Cyril of Jerusalem in his *Mystagogical Catechesis* tells his neophytes:

> First you were anointed on the forehead, to be freed from the shame which the first man, after his sin, carried with him everywhere—to be freed so completely that you may be able to contemplate the glory of God with open face, as in a mirror; then on the ears, so that you may find again the ears with which to hear the divine mysteries; then the nostrils, so that, perceiving the divine perfume you may say, "We are the pleasant perfume of Christ." . . . Finally, you were anointed on the breast so that, putting on the breastplate of justice, you might stand up well against the attacks of the demons.[24]

In the Western Rite, by contrast, only one chrismation with oil takes place (on the forehead), while in all the Rites of Catholicism the laying on of hands is *de rigueur*—a gesture customarily amplified either by insufflation (a gentle blowing of breath, the principal symbol in Scripture of the Spirit) or by a striking (again, not *too* painful!) on the cheek, as a token of entry into holy warfare for the gospel. The bishop, who was in ancient times the only minister of both baptism and confirmation and retained a special link with the latter by retaining the sole right to consecrate its oil and, in the West, remaining the normal minister of the sacrament, then concludes the rite by giving the newly confirmed the kiss of peace, as a token of their deepened communion with the Church, and, through her, in the kingdom.

It is theologically normal for confirmation to precede the first Holy Communion of the newly baptized, but the Latin Church at large has, for pastoral reasons, frequently delayed confirmation: so as to form people in a more perfect obedience to Christ, that they may bear more effective witness to him. The universal *Catechism of the Catholic Church* comments presciently on the providential co-existence of the two forms of sacramental practice which results:

> That of the Eastern Church gives greater emphasis to the unity of Christian initiation. That of the Latin Church more clearly expresses the communion of the new Christian with the bishop as guarantor and servant of

---

24. Cyril of Jerusalem, *Mystagogical Catecheses* 3.4.

the unity, catholicity and apostolicity of his Church, and hence the connection with the apostolic origins of Christ's Church.[25]

Both baptism and confirmation (like, as we shall see, orders) confer as already mentioned a sacramental character, a permanent mark on the soul, for one is now a transformed man or woman. The grace the sacrament brings may be lost by infidelity, but not so this mark which endures as a standing reproach. As Matthias Joseph Scheeben explains, this sacramental character is a sort of "signature" which makes known that the members of the God-man belong to their head, configuring them to him and realizing their organic union with him. It extends to human beings the consecration of Christ's humanity achieved by the hypostatic union, as Christ takes possession of another human person through these sacraments. The sacramental character is then a holiness of consecration—which should be followed therefore by a holiness of grace. We should be in nature what we are in status. Such grace springs from the character because the character brings us into organic contact with Christ, the source of grace, and gives us a "right" actually to possess the grace in question. Human beings can set up impediments, alas, to the flow of this grace, but when they do so, Christ does not revoke his action in sealing us. Through the seal God's love binds itself so strongly to us that it remains ever ready to give grace back to us when we have trifled it away. Thus the mark is not in the moral or psychological order (though these are on the horizon), but rather establishes the one baptized and confirmed in the Spirit by God's self-gift, the process of initiation in which he has been active since the first conception of faith by the convert.

3. The Holy Eucharist

In his retreat notes for Corpus Christi, the Church's annual thanksgiving for the institution of this sacrament, the priest-poet Gerard Manley Hopkins wrote:

(1) Preciousness of our Lord's body, born of the
Blessed Virgin of David's line, crucified, raised
from the dead, seated in heaven; united to Christ's
soul; united to the Word. Appreciate. Feel your
unworthiness.
(2) Its mystery; it binds the Church into one, bodily
into one. It is the pledge and means of our

---

25. *Catechism of the Catholic Church*, 1244.

immortality. Revere this mystery.
(3) The good it has done, sanctifying Christians, in
Mass, Communion, as viaticum. Thanksgiving.
(4) It is put into my unworthy hands as a priest.[26]

A. SACRIFICE

In Catholicism, the Eucharist is first and foremost a sacrifice. It is the sacramental expression of the sacrifice of Christ. In itself, that sacrifice cannot be repeated. For one thing, the death of Jesus and his subsequent vindication are a unique historical event, and so by definition unrepeatable. For another thing, the significance and power of Christ's sacrifice are endless, making it, as the Letter to the Hebrews notes, something achieved once only, and for all time. But none of this excludes the possibility that in the Eucharist this once-for-all sacrifice might become present to believers in a sacramental fashion (i.e., through signs and symbols). Indeed, in the light of the sacrificial imagery used by the Lord at the Last Supper this would appear to be his plan. On the night before his death he instituted a meal filled with images of broken bodies and spilt blood, commanding that it be celebrated indefinitely by his disciples "in memory of me."

The ecumenical Council of Trent teaches that the Mass, the Eucharistic sacrifice, differs from that of Calvary solely in its mode, which is sacramental, located in the order of signs. The Eucharist can be thus identical with the sacrifice of the Cross because Jesus Christ's abiding state with the Father is one of accepted victimhood. His sacrifice was for the sake of our union with the Father; his reality as the accepted sacrificial victim remains forever the foundation of redeemed humanity's life of grace. A sacrifice is a sign expressing and, if possible, effecting humankind's deliberate, suppliant return to God. It is something seemingly negative, an immolation signifying our painful detachment from sinful or at any rate imperfect forms of attachment to ourselves and to other creatures. It is at the same time something entirely positive, an oblation signifying our movement toward, and meeting with, God himself. The sacrifice of Christ exemplified and fulfilled this pattern in a definitive way. As the poet, artist, and lay theologian David Jones put it:

> What was accomplished on the Tree of the Cross presupposes the sign world and looks back to foreshadowing rites and arts of mediation and conjugation stretching back for tens of thousands of years in actual

26. Devlin, *Hopkins,* 256.

pre-history. Or, to speak in theological terms, the Tree of the Cross pre-supposes the other Tree and stretches back to the "truly necessary sin of Adam" and the "happy fault" so that St. Thomas in the Good Friday hymn could write *Ars ut artem falleret* [that "the art (of man's deceiver) by (God's) art might be outweighed"].[27]

Christ realized in a visible way, in his own person, the entire meta-physic of man's return to God which humankind's ritual sacrifices out-lined in symbolic guise. The only Son made man, at once victim and high priest, whom all other sacrificial offerings and ministers fore-shadowed, lived out his sacrifice from Judas's kiss to the Father's Easter welcome. But that sacrifice was centered on the immolation of the Cross. There above all he carried through his disposition of ador-ing love in the hard conditions our sin imposed. There too the Father, in his answering love, accepted the homage of the incarnate Son on our behalf. Once the mystery of the atonement was thus achieved, in his-tory and beyond, the power and providence of God could furnish it with an effective rite owing all its value to that mystery but passing on to us its fruits.

Since sacrifice appears to have originated as a sacred banquet, where human beings recognized that their life comes from God and develops in tacit response to him, this Eucharistic sacrifice takes the form, by the Lord's own institution, of a communion meal. We associ-ate ourselves with Christ's sacrifice by means of the sacrificial sym-bolism of the offering involved in the communion meal; the offering only becomes identical with the sacrifice of Calvary when, in transub-stantiation, the bread and wine become what they represent: Jesus Christ himself.

Of course the Holy Eucharist does not look like a bloody sacrifice. The immolated God-man is the only common point between the sacra-mental sacrifice and the Lord's passion, death, and resurrection.

> We Catholics have that great freedom of mind through our faith in the reality of the Eucharistic sacrifice. We know that through this faith we move in a world which is entirely beyond human experience. We are true mystics, because we hold an infinite reality and yet hold it without any human factors. It is truly the *mysterium fidei*, the mystery of faith.[28]

27. H. Grisewood, ed., *Epoch and Artist: Selected Writings by David Jones* (London, 1959) 168.
28. A. Vonier, "A Key to the Doctrine of the Eucharist," in *Collected Works 2: The Church and the Sacraments* (London, 1952) 272.

Since Christ is alpha and omega, time's origin and its eschatological fulfillment, in him time can be united with eternity. The Lamb immolated in time under Pontius Pilate is identical with the Lamb glimpsed by the seer of Revelation, slain "before the foundation of the world." Hence the Spirit can effect, in the holy sacrifice of the altar, his sacramental parousia. As the Byzantine office for the preparation of the Eucharistic gifts recalls, this is the oblation God always intended for the world. The world's destiny is to become a messianic banquet, where God is wedded through the saving flesh of the Son to humankind.

B. REAL PRESENCE

The Eucharist is also our Lord's real presence. When Jesus calls the elements of the Supper his "body" and "blood," he identifies them with his life, personhood, existence. The saving sacrifice which summed up everything he was becomes accessible (present) through the symbolism of bread for eating, wine for drinking. Christ does not leave heaven; his transformed biology remains where it was. But the consecrated elements become the embodiment of his presence. There is a conversion of the medium in which our meeting with him is to take place. He himself becomes the medium in which we encounter him. This is what the Fathers of Trent, echoing those of the Fourth Lateran Council, called "that wonderful and unique conversion of the whole substance of the bread into the body [of the Lord], and of the whole substance of the wine into the blood, the appearances alone of bread and wine remaining."[29] The consecration destroys none of the natural qualities of bread and wine, but these no longer manifest its ultimate reality. Its true substance, what is supremely important about it, lies elsewhere. The Eucharistic sensibility of the English people of the Middle Ages was nourished on this doctrine. In the Sarum pontifical (although not the Roman) we find this dialogue between the consecrator bishops and the candidate for episcopal ordination:

> Dost thou believe that the bread which is laid on the Table of the Lord is only bread before the Consecration; but in the Consecration by the unspeakable power of the Godhead the nature and substance of the bread is changed into the nature and substance of the flesh of Christ—and the flesh of no other than him, who was conceived of the Holy Ghost and born of the Virgin Mary?
>
> (Bishop) I believe.

29. DH 1642.

> In like manner that wine which, mixed with water, is put into the chalice for satisfying, truly and essentially is converted into the Blood which by the soldier's spear flowed from the wound in Christ's side?
> (Bishop) I believe.

But what is the rationale of the real presence? Why, in all its glorious objectivity, is it there? So that we may be united with Christ and with each other in Christ. The Holy Eucharist is the source of both individual and corporate renewal as of the unity of the Church. That is well captured in the striking prayer *Salve salutaris hostia* regularly printed in primers for layfolk, for use before Communion, on the eve of the Reformation. In this prayer, the communicants greet Christ in the sacrament as the "saving victim" offered for them and for all humanity on the altar of the Cross. They pray that the blood flowing from the side of the crucified wash away their sins so that they may be made worthy to consume his precious Body. Pleading that Christ's suffering for humanity might be the means of mercy and protection the communicant asks for a renewal of heart and mind so that the old Adam may die and the new life begin.

> May I be worthy to be incorporated into your body, which is the Church. May I be one of your members, and may you be my Head, that I may remain in you and you in me, so that in the Resurrection my lowly body may be conformed to your glorious body according to the promises of the apostle, and so that I may rejoice in you and your glory eternally.[30]

The faithful are to approach communion "arrayed in God's livery, clothed in love and charity, not the fiend's livery, clothed in envy and deadly wrath."

The real presence is, then, to unite us both to God and to our neighbor. It has, therefore, both a Trinitarian and a humanitarian dimension. By means of it, the Church enters, through the Mass, into the life of the Trinity. Just as the Son is never found without the Father and the Holy Spirit, so the Mass is always offered, through the Son, to the Father in that same Spirit. In the Trinity icon of Andrei Rublev the Eucharist is displayed as a participation in the Trinitarian life. The fatherly angel on the left addresses the devoted, consenting filial angel on the right, while in the center the pneumatic angel consecrates the Eucharistic gifts, the symbol of Christ, on the altar. The Trinitarian God is not just

---

30. E. Hoskins, *Horae Beatae Virginis Mariae, or Sarum and York Primers with Kindred Books and Primers of the Reformed Roman Rite* (London, 1901) 127.

repose; he is also streaming life, abiding always in his self-moved movement, and drawing those redeemed by Christ's sacrifice, through the Eucharist, into the rhythmic pattern of his own communion of love. At the same time, the real presence, in uniting Christians to each other in Christ, sums up the humanitarian outreach of the Mass which is a petitionary prayer par excellence, embracing all sorts and conditions of persons in their differentiated unity. Here for instance is the intercession that joins the *epiclēsis* (the prayer for the descent of the Holy Spirit) to the *anamnēsis* (the solemn commemoration of the Lord's Passover) in the Chaldaeo-Malabar liturgy of India:

> Yes, Lord God Almighty, receive this offering for the supreme pontiff and the head and ruler of the universal Church, Mar N. Pope of Rome, and for our holy father Mar N. archbishop or bishop, now ruling our people, and for all the Holy Catholic Church, and for priests (kings and governors), the public authorities, and for the honour of all the prophets, apostles, martyrs and confessors, and for all the just and holy fathers who were pleasing in your presence, and for all those who mourn and are in distress, for the poor and the down-trodden, for the sick and the afflicted, and for all the departed who have died in your name, and for this people that looks forward to your mercy, and for my own unworthy self.

In receiving Christ in Holy Communion or in saluting him in the reserved elements, we come through him not only to the divine society of the Trinity but to the human society of all his brethren, all those for whom he died, whether or not they know it. The hermit Charles de Foucauld, kneeling in Saharan solitude before the consecrated Host, was not alone, but with a multitude of brothers and sisters whom he learned thereby to carry in his heart.

C. THE ORDER OF THE MASS

How then does the order of the Mass, its liturgical sequence, unfold? I concentrate here on the Roman Rite, since that forms the staple of worship of the great majority of Catholic Christians, but the basic program is reflected in the various Oriental liturgies too. In the main, I shall describe (in its fullest version) the reformed Roman Rite of Pope Paul VI, dating from the late 1960s, with explanatory reference to earlier Western and contemporary Eastern practice.

The Mass is a diptych: its doors swing apart to show us two distinct liturgical actions which are, however, integrated into one unitary rite. The Liturgy of the Word or of the Catechumens (those preparing for sacramental initiation) was sometimes even celebrated in a different place from the Liturgy of the Sacrifice. In the modern Roman Rite, the first is focused on the cathedral of the bishop, or the chair of the priest representing him, as these preside over the assembly in their role as apostolic ministers of the word of the gospel. The focus of the Eucharist proper, on the other hand, is the altar itself where they stand as icons of Christ the high priest.

The Mass begins with certain introductory rites: either a dialogue of bishop (or priest) and people (or server) or a polylogue, with a choir participating; by means of these we place ourselves in the right disposition for celebrating the liturgy. In the introit antiphon and psalm (often replaced by a vernacular hymn), we welcome Christ who is coming to preside among his people, as represented by the processional cross, the tapers, the book of the Gospels, and the sacred ministers. (A secondary motif is that of the Church herself, moving through Christ toward the kingdom of God.) When the procession reaches the altar, which is already dressed and honored with lights, the Gospel book is placed upon it, since it contains the word of Christ. Because the altar is the most important liturgical symbol in the church building, representing Christ as the "place" where sacrifice is continually offered by humanity to the Father, the rite cannot proceed without taking notice of this fact. The kissing of the altar salutes the holy place where the mystery will be celebrated. In pagan antiquity a kiss was offered to the threshold of a temple, to the images of the gods, and to the family table. In the liturgy the kiss of the altar is meant first of all for Christ—the cornerstone, the spiritual rock. An altar table should if possible contain some stone as well as wood, since it is both the place of a meal and the place of sacrifice (normally carried out on stone in natural religion). With the growth of the cult of the martyrs, the altar stone included from early times a little reliquary and the kiss would be planted at this point. The kissing of the altar is also a greeting to the whole Church triumphant which is to worship with us in the liturgy. Pope Innocent III, in his early thirteenth-century treatise *On the Mystery of the Altar* maintains that in the celebrant's kiss Christ greets his spouse, the spotless Church. In older forms of the Roman Rite the text accompanying the kissing of the altar prays that God might take away our sinfulness so that, at the prayers of the martyrs whose relics lie there, we may come with purified minds into the holy of holies: the Eucharistic presence and the heavenly banquet it prefigures. Altar and crucifix are incensed, as the prayer of the Church draws in the body with its senses at the opening of the act of worship.

In the Roman Rite as we have it today this is immediately followed by an invocation of the Holy Trinity, when all present sign themselves with the Cross: the sacred action is undertaken in the power of the triune God which flows from the Cross of Christ. Then the celebrant greets the congregation using a New Testament formula which asks that the congregation may be established by God in that awareness of what he had done for them which will enable them to share fruitfully in the Mass. They reply courteously (in the Latin paradigm), "And with your spirit," meaning, "and may this also be true of you in your special ministry, the gift of the Spirit whereby you are the Church's minister."

Next comes the penitential act which has as its theme sin, and the ensuing need for atonement and forgiveness. When first introduced, these prayers were virtually private prayers of preparation of the pope or bishop, and were said lying prostrate on the floor of the sanctuary, a gesture still used in the Roman liturgy on Good Friday. In the High Middle Ages this became a little drama in which several voices participated. In the Tridentine Rite, the priest bows, says the "I confess," turning to the servers when he comes to the words "and [I confess] to you, my brethren," and then receives the confession of the servers in similar fashion; finally, each "side" prays an absolution over the other. A profound bow during the *Confiteor* is theologically correct: the gesture of praying upright belongs to the Christian as forgiven, who is now found erect in the Father's presence. The gesture of beating one's breast here is copied from the Lucan parable of the Pharisee and the publican. The confession of sin is made not only to God but also to the Church, both the Church of the congregation and that of the saints. The reasons are, first, that all sin diminishes the life of charity that circulates between person and person, and second, that by Christ's command reconciliation with God normally takes the form of reconciliation with Christ's community.

The fact that the *Kyrie* (at least in its ordinary form) follows the priest's absolution should alert us to the fact that it is not simply a repetition of a statement of sorrow. As many of its plainsong and polyphonic settings demonstrate, it is, rather, a strong and confident act of praise of God as the merciful One. In a troped *Kyrie*, various acclamations bring out different aspects of this compassionate Lord. In the Byzantine liturgy, as at Jerusalem in the early centuries, the *Kyrie* is interspersed with petitions (in the Liturgy of St. John Chrysostom, petitions for the whole Church, the clergy, the people, the ruler, those on a journey, the sick, the benefactors of the Church, the poor, and others too, as well as for peace).

If in the *Kyrie* we acclaim Christ as the merciful Savior, in the *Gloria*, a venerable dogmatic hymn of thanksgiving, we remind ourselves that the true object of our religion is the Father with the Son in the Holy Spirit. Recited on Sundays (except in the penitential seasons) and feast days, it exemplifies the "spiritual canticles" in which Paul's churches abounded. The *Gloria* recalls the joy which broke on the world with the birth of Christ—the Lucan song of the angels on Nativity night. First praising the Father, it then invokes Christ's grace over all humankind, not forgetting at its close that this happens through the Holy Spirit.

The collect, or opening prayer, is the first point where the celebrant comes forward to address God in the presence of the assembly. The term *collect* refers to the prayer's functions, its gathering and summing up of the people's intentions. It is, however, not merely petitionary but always invites us to bless God in some way consonant with his character, as the *Kyrie* and *Gloria* have just declared it to be. The collects of the Roman Rite are distinguished by their economy, clarity, and majesty.

The readings with, at their climax, the proclamation of the gospel, the high point of the Liturgy of the Word, come next. Enormous variety has prevailed as to how many readings should precede the gospel, and on what principle they should be selected. The Syrian liturgy has five, the Chaldaean three (from the Law, the Prophets, and the apostolic letters). The most widespread practice in the early Church was two: an Old Testament reading chosen so as to point in some way to the New, and a lection from the epistle. This is the pattern observed in the Roman liturgy today on Sundays and the greater feasts. But on the vigils of certain solemnities, above all Easter, the number of readings may be extended to give the worshippers a vast panorama of their faith. The eight readings of the mother of all vigils, Easter night, begin with the world's creation and move on through the call of the patriarchs, the entry of the people into the Land and the teaching of the great prophets so as to throw light on the resurrection of Christ as a new genesis, a new exodus, a new return from exile.

In the selection of readings, two principles jostle. First, the people should hear as much of Scripture as is feasible. At its simplest, and if left to itself, this principle works itself out as *lectio continua*—the cover-to-cover reading of the Bible. That this was the case for certain books seems clear from the formula used by the deacon in announcing the gospel: *sequentia*, "the continuation" of the holy Gospel according to Matthew, Mark, Luke, or John. But second, and set over against the first, there is a need to select readings appropriate to liturgical time, to the celebration of various key events in the life of Christ and his Mother, as well as the anniversaries of the saints. In the ancient Church it was, for instance, the custom in places to read the Books of Job and Jonah during Holy Week, for they too were sufferers who had been vindicated. The juxtaposition of readings, especially from Old and New Testaments, can be striking. The compilers of the present Roman Lectionary show not only a scholar's grasp of how various texts were used in the ancient liturgy, combinations hallowed by long Christian usage, but also an impresario's flair for thinking up fresh couplings of their own (though this has its own drawback in dislocation of earlier readings cycles).

Liturgical reading should not be too prosaic: as a proclamation of the divine word a degree of stylization is appropriate, not through the injecting of the lector's own sentiments but through observing a certain objective solemnity. On the greatest feasts, the readings should be sung. Such cantillation can vary between the *tonus rectus,* where the only change of pitch is a slight modulation in questions, for the sake of intelligibility, to much richer, and more varied tones. In Augustine's North Africa the reading of the passion, for example, was already elaborate. In the Middle Ages a proper ranking in significance between texts (the gospel being higher than, say, the epistle) was audibly manifest in comparing methods of cantillation. Change of place was also important. Whereas the Old Testament lection and the epistle would be read from an ambo-stand, slightly elevated and sometimes adorned with mosaics and sculpture, a second ambo for the gospel stood higher still and possessed a fuller iconography, becoming in the pulpit a major locus of Gothic and later art.

Readings are followed by chant; the gospel is preceded by an alleluia. In the fourth-century *Apostolic Constitutions* the response of cantor and people to the lections comes from the hymns of David: the Psalms, chosen for their wonderful expression of so many pertinent attitudes and emotions, trust and confidence, contrition, need, praise. Elaborate melismas (lyrical expansion of the notes of a psalm verse) led in time in the West to the loss of the congregation's part; in the Byzantine East the psalm itself disappeared, displaced by postbiblical liturgical poetry, often of great beauty. The alleluia verse expresses the Church's joy at the gospel. In the Roman gradual the alleluia takes off in a *jubilus*—a stream of jubilant sound, regarded by many as the highest achievement of the chant.

There has never been any doubt as to which texts of Scripture hold highest place. The Gospels contain the good things, the fulfillment of all the past and the point from which all future ages radiate. How highly they were regarded can sometimes be seen in the sheer physicality of the gospel books. Written in the stately uncial hand, often in gold or silver script against a purple ground, sometimes decorated with miniatures, their binding, in the Dark Ages, would be covered with ivory or precious metal. A formal procession developed from the deacon's deportment in walking to the ambo. After seeking a blessing from the celebrant, he goes to the altar where the gospel book has lain since the entry. Reverently picking it up, he carries it, accompanied by torchbearers and thurifer, to the ambo to begin the reading. From ancient times people have heard the gospel standing, and turned to the East, symbol of the risen and victorious Christ, the unconquered sun. Men had to remove every head covering, even the royal crown of princes. Mention is made of setting aside one's outer mantle and sword, or, conversely, drawing the sword and holding it extended as a sign of willingness to fight for the gospel message. In earlier periods at Rome, the subdeacon took the book after its reading and brought it round to the attendant clergy, and perhaps the whole congregation, to be kissed before returning it to its casket in a place of safe-keeping. The Dominican use preserves the primitive custom of making a sign of the cross at the close of the gospel: this stands for a prayer that the seed of the word, now planted, will not be taken away from our hearts. In the Roman Rite, this signing, on forehead, mouth, and breast occurs only as the gospel is announced: we want to receive Christ's words with our minds, to give them assent intellectually; to be ready to confess and defend them, if need be, in conversation; to love them and to receive them (and him) in our hearts.

The liturgical sermon must arise from the gospel—either that of the day or the wider gospel message as rendered incarnate by the texts of a feast or commemoration. In the Coptic Rite the bishop when preaching is required to keep hold of the gospel book, to make this point. The homilies of the patristic Church are generally to be found as collections of conferences on the Gospels, like Augustine's marvelous *homilia super Joannem*. As an official act of one of her ministers, authorized for this purpose in her name, the Church expects a sermon to be an exposition of her common faith as manifested in Scripture.

The Liturgy of the Word closes on Sundays and feasts by saying or singing the Creed: the faith produced by the word just encountered in

Scripture. In the Greek liturgy the Creed comes later, as a foundation for the Liturgy of the Sacrifice, yet it still functions as a hinge between the two. The celebrant in the Byzantine Rite calls out to the people, to introduce it, "Let us love one another so that we may confess Father, Son and Holy Spirit, consubstantial Trinity, undivided Unity," thus bringing home the fact that the Creed is not just a bare recitation of facts about God but an act of loving homage made by a community conscious of itself as his household.

In the new Roman Rite the Creed is at once followed by the prayers of the faithful (what in Britain are called, following medieval English custom, the "bidding prayers"). They are the intimate household prayers of the Christian family, and, as prayer for each other, lead us into the Liturgy of the Sacrifice by fulfilling the command of Jesus about brotherly love as a precondition of authentic worship: "If you remember that your brother has anything against you go and make it up with him before you come to offer your gift on the altar" (Matt 5:24).

Now the gifts must be prepared, or, if already prepared, brought in to the sacred assembly. In the Byzantine Rite the bearing of the gifts from the place of preparation to the altar is a liturgical high point: people bow or even prostrate as the "Great Entrance" proceeds. For though the elements are not yet consecrated to be Christ's real presence they are already in a weaker sense consecrated inasmuch as they are set apart for the Holy Eucharist. The modern Roman Rite follows the medieval custom in France and England, where representatives of the faithful wended their way through the church, carrying bread, wine, and water to the sanctuary, where the celebrant and his assistants met them and took the elements on the final relay to the altar. In North Africa, at least, it was usual for the faithful to offer many other gifts at this point, most importantly alms for the poor and the upkeep of the Church's ministers (our collection-plate) but also gifts in kind. This continues in Masses for the canonization of saints when the pope is customarily handed two loaves, two barrels of wine and water, five candles and three cages containing doves or other birds, though nowadays gifts more redolent of the distinctive culture of the servant of God newly "raised to the altars" may replace these, at least in part.

The offertory prayers are intended to accompany the laying of the gifts on the altar. A natural tendency would amplify these texts so as to look forward to what will happen to the gifts at the consecration— but this should not entail duplicating the Eucharistic Prayer! In the Latin Church the bread used is unleavened, pointing back toward the

Last Supper itself. In the Oriental Churches leavened bread is the norm, which stresses the natural integrity of matter and the yeast of the resurrection. In both East and West the bread is to be as fine as possible; in a Ravenna mosaic it takes the form of a *corona,* a plaited crown. In some places its baking has itself been liturgical: among the Ethiopians each church has a little "Bethlehem" (house of bread) attached for the purpose; in some Western monasteries monks wore albs while milling flour for the altar. The wine presented is, by ancient custom, mingled with water—originally, no doubt, a practical measure to prevent dizziness. Cyprian was the first to interpret this symbolically: just as the wine receives the water into itself, so Christ has taken upon him ourselves and our sins. As the celebrant raises paten and chalice we should place in them, in imagination, our lives, work, sorrows, and joys, and all those to whom we are bound by love and responsibility.

The bread and wine, now presented on the altar and incensed, and the priest having prayed in simple and profound biblical language that we may be received by God as we come with broken hearts, and the people having joined their voices in the form of prayer for the celebration, the focus suddenly shifts. In the *oratio super oblata* the accent typically moves from the theme of the gifts as symbols of our interior surrender to the theme of the gift himself into whom our gifts will be transformed, Jesus Christ. For now we come to the heart of the Mass, often called, simply but impressively, "the Great Prayer."

Because what will follow is so hugely important the introduction is heightened: not just *"Oremus"* ("Let us pray"), said by the celebrant, but three invitations and responses in which the people present their assent. For Augustine the *"Sursum corda"* ("Lift up your hearts") affirms that in the risen Christ all humanity has its home with God, so that is where our hearts should be, *"Habemus ad Dominum"* ("We have raised them up to the Lord"). This enables the celebrant, Augustine continues, to pass on the last injunction, *"Gratias agamus Domino Deo nostro"* ("Let us give thanks to the Lord our God"); though we cannot, alas, always have hearts and minds fixed on God we should certainly give thanks at this moment above all, renewing our self-committal from our deepest personal center. The language appears to caricature the emperor cult: the Church too has a "Lord," but it is not Caesar. In this dialogue, she reminds herself of what she is to do, and gets into the right frame of mind for the Christian sacrifice.

The preface gives us the reasons why we should be celebrating the Eucharist. In a rapturous prose hymn the priest blesses God for all his wonderful works, especially in the world's redemption by the Son and inaugurated transfiguration through the Spirit. The Roman liturgy has vacillated wildly in the number of such prefaces it could countenance—from over two hundred and fifty in the Leonine Sacramentary to a mere fourteen in its Gregorian successor. The Missal of Pope Paul VI has just over eighty, many remarkably fine.

Every preface ends by bringing in the angelic hosts. Ronald Knox spoke here of

> the various ranks of Angels flashing past us like the names of suburban stations as we draw closer to the heart of a great capital. The holy Angels, I think, have a knack of drawing up one's mind to God by being at once so awe-inspiring and at the same time obviously inconclusive, the attitude of the Angel in the Apocalypse who will not let St. John worship him and bids him worship God instead, is permanently their attitude.[31]

The *Sanctus* follows as the people's punctuation of the praise of God the celebrant is offering and a reminder that the liturgy is a foretaste of the heavenly worship of the angels and saints. Its text is an outburst of praise, amplified by the ringing of a bell.

> All of God's benefits and the manifestations of his favour, for which in the Preface we are giving thanks are after all only revelations of his inmost being, his holiness, which is all light and brilliance, inviolable and without strain, before which creation can only bow in deepest reverence. . . . That the cry resounds three times must have but increased the joy the Christians had in this song, so even when a Trinitarian meaning was not expressly attached to the triple "holy" still there was inherent in it an echo of this most profound of all Christian mysteries.[32]

In France, during the dark ages, another motif was subjoined in the *Benedictus*. The glory of the Lord, filling heaven and earth, did not begin to shine in fullest splendor until the divine Son came to us in form of flesh. The liturgy took over the cry with which the crowds welcomed Christ into Jerusalem on Palm Sunday: blessed is he who is coming, as the Eucharistic action brings his presence, in the consecrated gifts, into the midst of his people.

The Canon or Eucharistic Prayer, the Anaphora or Offering, shows us, as it unfolds, six features. First, there is always an invocation

31. R. Knox, *The Mass in Slow Motion* (London, 1949) xv.

32. J. A. Jungmann, *The Mass of the Roman Rite: Its Origins and Development* (New York and London, 1959) 381.

(*epiclēsis*) whereby the Church begs God to effect the consecration by his power, asking that the communicants may be granted salvation by their sharing in the Eucharistic Lord. Second, we find an account of how Christ instituted the Eucharist, followed by the words of his command to renew it in his memory. Third, there is a prayer of recalling all that Christ did for our salvation, thus claiming the grace of the presence of the Son-made-man, offering himself in love. Fourth, the Church confesses how she is now joined with Christ in his sacrifice, taken up into it, and co-offering it with him. Fifth, there is alongside commemoration of the saints intercession for the living and the dead. Sixth, the Canon ends with an act of praise of God which the people seal by adding their "Amen." A clue to the meaning of the texts often lies in the gestures that accompany them. Thus, while the celebrant, in the Roman Canon, resumes, after the *Sanctus,* the basic *orante* posture—with arms outstretched—he has taken during the preface, at the "*Hanc igitur*" he holds out his hands palms downwards over the bread and wine in an epicletory gesture, one of imparting the Holy Spirit over the gifts as once that Spirit descended, in the Genesis poem, over the waters of creation, and in Luke's Gospel, on the womb of Mary. In reciting the institution narrative the celebrant places his hands on the altar-table, identifying it implicitly with the table of the Supper. When taking up the bread he follows the motions of Jesus, acting *in persona Christi,* playing the part of Christ. Bowing slightly over the gifts to express the holiness and solemnity of this moment, he raises them up for the people to acclaim and adore Christ before them, and genuflects in representative adoration. For the *anamnêsis,* in the Dominican use, he holds out his arms in the form of a cross to express the unity of the Church with the Christ who was sacrificed for us. Then, asking that God may make this sacrifice fruitful for those who will share its fruits in Holy Communion, he bows low with arms folded in a second epicletory gesture, asking that the reception of the gifts may be for the faithful a true encounter with Christ. After this the celebrant joins his hands to pray silently for a moment remembering by name the departed for whom he should pray, just as before the consecration he has done this for the living. Not dissembling either the unworthiness of the assembly or his own, he beats his breast in an ancient Jewish gesture of contrition. Finally, he takes up the gifts, now transformed into the living reality of the sacrificed God-man Jesus Christ, and proclaims that through, with, and in him the Father receives all glory possible from his Church gathered together into one by the Holy Spirit. As the priest lowers the gifts again the people call out their assent in the "Amen."

The rite of Communion follows. After the Lord's Prayer, the supreme Christian prayer and its coda, a prayer for peace, the celebrant breaks the sacred Host into pieces, placing one in the chalice as the Agnus Dei is sung. As the Liturgy of St. John Chrysostom has it, "The Lamb of God is broken and shared out, broken but not divided, ever eaten but never consumed, hallowing those who share it." In the Roman Rite, the fraction of the Host and the "reunion" of the Lord's Body and Blood as a particle is dropped into the cup signifies both the passion and the resurrection. It is from these that all grace comes. Showing the elements to the people, the celebrant invites them to prepare for Holy Communion. For this prayer and repentance are always required. We must prayerfully intend to receive Communion for some while beforehand; it is never to be taken on the spur of the moment. The Church suggests devotional texts to help the communicant make ready to receive the Guest. We must also come with a real desire to change our lives, not with resentments and unfinished moral business—which is why regular Communion implies regular confession. A canonical fast is also demanded, long from the Orientals, short from the Latins, though personal devotion may suggest more. In fasting, the people of God stand ready, awaiting the parousia of the Lord.

Communion is followed by the ablutions, the communion verse (or hymn) and a prayer of thanksgiving for the grace received, a petition that its fruits may endure, that the blessings of nature or supernature suggested by season or feast may be ours, as well as the unending joys of heaven prefigured in the reception of the Lord's person. The whole is terminated by the parting blessing of the priest—recalling in gesture the triumph of the Cross and in words the mystery of the Trinity in the glory of the Godhead—and the dismissal, *"Ite, missa est!"* ("Go, you are sent forth!"). This is not merely a formal dismissal: it is also an exhortation to bring the spirit of the Mass into daily living.

4. Penance

Jesus Christ as the God-man is the reconciler between God and human beings. He brings to their true home in God those who have wandered far away from him—and first of all by sin. One of the characteristic actions of Jesus in his public ministry was forgiving sins; this comes to its climax in his resurrection when he gives to the apostles the power to transmit the grace of God's forgiveness. This too has its sacrament.

Most popularly, it is called the sacrament of confession, for saying that one is sorry is the ordinary human action which in this sign is taken up and transformed by the Word of God. In contemporary Church documents it is called "the sacrament of reconciliation," because the forgiveness of sins is so central in Christ's reconciling work. Here it will be called by its medieval name, the sacrament of penance, which links it to the fundamental attitude of repentance, seen by Jesus as pivotal when he began his preaching: "Repent, and believe the Gospel" (Mk 1:15).

Prior to being a sacrament, we may say, penance is a permanent constituent dimension of the Christian life. It is a state of mind and heart (and even body) which, by turning into reality the death to sin promised in baptism, shares in the passion of Christ. Thanks to the detachment from sin that penance brings about, it progressively (though no doubt with many setbacks) assimilates Christians to Christ, conforms them to him.

As a Christian virtue, a permanent disposition to practice repentance of heart, penance is confirmed and brought to completion by a sacramental act: the sacrament of penance itself. Only in union with the Church, Christ's mystical body, can the sinner re-find peace and the Holy Spirit. Christian penance is only fully effective when united with the Church. For this reason, the Church does not simply require the faithful to frequent this sacrament in the case of very grave postbaptismal sin (classically summed up in the unholy trinity of murder, adultery, and apostasy). More than this, the regular submission of our actions, words, and even thoughts to sacramental penance is seen by her as a highly desirable moment in the practice of this crucial virtue. The sacrament of penance is a consecration, by an act of the Church, of our personal efforts at detachment from sin, our struggle with the evil within us.

As the patristic reception of biblical revelation took definite shape, this sacrament began to take on clear form—not, however, without attendant uncertainties. To the authors of fourth-century texts on this subject, such reconciliation with the Church is essentially an effective sign of peace with God, the Holy Spirit restoring to the penitent the graces given with baptismal regeneration. But soon a division appeared over just how rigorously rationed the celebration of such canonical penance should be. According to some, it was only to be permitted once, for fear of encouraging laxity. And even this one-off experience of "second Baptism" (as it was sometimes called) was placed beyond the reach of clerics who, it was thought, should be more exigent with themselves, and also of a married person in the event of the spouse withholding consent. Perhaps owing to the influence exerted by rigorists, resort to unofficial forms of penance became more common. Among such monastic founders as Pachomius, Basil, Cassian, and Benedict we find "private" confession highlighted as a means of spiritual direction and of growth in Christian perfection. The bringing together of the two—the canonical public penance and the alternative, more private kind—provided the sacrament of penance with its eventual, enduring form. From the seventh century on, the influence of the Irish Church was decisive. While for the Irish monastic teachers lesser faults of the baptized were to be pardoned by such means as prayer, lay confession, and other acts of humility, serious faults required the intervention of the power of the keys. Such recourse to apostolic authority of binding and loosing was made not to a bishop (as in the Continental canonical penance) but to a simple priest who, first, heard the penitent's confession; second, taking into account the penitent's dispositions, set a penitential action to be performed; and third, when such "sufficient expiation" or "satisfaction" was deemed complete, reconciled him or her by absolution. In the wider Latin Christendom of the early Middle Ages, confession increasingly came to be seen as an integral part of the expiation—not surprisingly, as the act of confession is hardly pleasant, involving as it does the baring of the less attractive features of one's soul to a fellow human being. In the tenth and eleventh centuries the liturgy of penance presupposed ever more clearly that reconciliation would take place at the time of the confession itself, usually by the imposition of the priest's hands. The priest prayed for the forgiveness of the sinner, gave him a "satisfaction," to remit the old canonical penance, and pronounced the words of absolution. By the twentieth century the penances people were invited to perform were usually token in nature, gestures that did not pretend to complete the healing suffering which penance entails. Postbaptismal sinners in the contemporary period require therefore a more conscious sense of sharing in Christ's liberating passion, expressed in works of self-denial and supererogation at other times.

In the eleventh century there was already some bemusement over general absolution as pronounced by pope or bishop over a multitude of people at the same time (without opportunity for the concrete confession of personal sins). Theologians of the period regarded this either as a prayer for absolution or as a remission of the satisfaction the penitent was otherwise obliged to make (notably through such major projects as pilgrimage to a distant shrine or participation in the Crusades). In the modern Roman rite of penance such absolution is foreseen for those who cannot make individual confession owing to their great numbers, and the relative paucity of confessors or time. But it is regarded as dependent for its sacramental actuality on the willingness to make a personal confession when circumstances at last permit.

How then may we sum up the significance of the sacrament of penance in Catholic eyes? The state of sin is one of separation from God through deprivation of grace and charity. It is comparable to a grave illness or a mortal wound: it cannot be, before death, definitive or total, but it can be serious and life-threatening. As an action incompatible with the *ordo amoris*, the "order of love," such mortal sin places its agent in an immediate condition of "aversion" from God. It may be contrasted with minor slackening in the momentum of the Christian life: venial sins, which leave intact the orientation towards God and the living out of his commandments while diminishing its effectiveness. Sin affects not only the individual in his or her relation to God but also the community, the Church. Mortal sin constitutes a spiritual rupture with the community of Christ, since the sinner in losing charity loses at the same time life-giving communion with others "in Christ." Venial sin is not so radical, yet it too enfeebles the flow of charity in the Church, lowering the tone of ecclesial existence. Now the redemption of sin is the proper work of God in Christ. The destruction of sin in each sinner demands a divine remedy: only God can wipe out the effects of disruption of the order of love. For fallen Christians, the remedy is this sacrament, adapted as it is to the human condition since in calling for persons' active collaboration it respects their freedom, the same freedom they abused in sinning and which now needs to be redeemed. This sacrament, however, can only be a redeeming action (and not just a piece of symbolism, more or less moving, but ultimately of only subjective significance) if it is founded on Christ's saving acts in the atonement, and if, furthermore, it expresses that mission and those powers which the Church receives from Christ so as to translate his redemptive achievement into reality for individual persons. The Council of Trent stressed that the locus of penance is truly a tribunal— a court that really acquits. Absolution is not some general declaration that God forgives sinners but the restoration of full friendship with God through spiritual communion in Christ by way of a judgment on the sin and repentance of this concrete person who has come here and now seeking reconciliation.

Neither shame nor pride is to inhibit the recital of one's sin, for, as in a Gaelic prayer from the Scottish islands, we are to condemn ourselves at the chair of confession lest we be condemned at the chair of judgment. In a good confession, such candor is married to asking forgiveness for the past and seeking strength for the future. The matter of the sacrament is the desire to say that one is sorry, the will to submit oneself to ecclesial penance. Its form is the priest's words which consecrate the penitent's manifestation of sorrow by the deed of God in Christ. Here the priest is to act not only as judge but also as spiritual physician. And while priests vary much in their ability to be helpful in the confessional, or to one penitent rather than another, they should at least convey the truth summed up by Francis de Sales when he called penance the "sacrament of reconciled friends."

The texts of the liturgy of penance bring out these themes. The Byzantine version is the richest, notably in its Slavonic form. It opens with a litany calling on Christ not only as Son of the living God and Good Shepherd but also as a Lamb, taking away the sins of the world, who forgave the two debtors their debt and the sinful woman her sins. Asking for the remission of sins and time for repentance of the "servant of God" who has approached the Church's tribunal, it also reminds the penitent of the sub-mediatorial role of the communion of saints in the work of our salvation when it prays, "Open to us the door of your loving-kindness, blessed Mother of God; in that we set our hope on you, may we not go astray, but be delivered by you from all adversities, for you are the salvation of all Christian people."

The penitent asks for divine pardon: "Father, Lord of heaven and earth, I confess to you all the hidden and open sins of my heart and mind, which I have committed until this day. Wherefore I beg of you, the merciful and righteous judge, forgiveness and grace to sin no more." Whereupon the priest comments, "Brother, inasmuch as you have come to me and to God, be not ashamed; for you are speaking not to me but to God, before whom you stand." In the Slavonic usage, the priest then brings the penitent before a desk positioned, commonly, before the "royal doors" of the iconostasis (the icon screen which is the dividing line between nave and sanctuary). On the desk has been placed the book of the Gospels and an icon of the crucified Savior. Standing at the side, he admonishes him:

> See, my child, Christ is standing here invisibly and receiving your confession; so do not be ashamed or afraid and conceal nothing from me. But tell me without hesitation all things you have done; and so you shall

have pardon from our Lord Jesus Christ. See, his holy image is before us; and I am only a witness, bearing testimony before him of all the things you have to say to me. But if you conceal anything from me, you will have the greater sin, so take heed lest having come to a physician you depart unhealed.

In the Greek practice, the priest questions the sinner about his sins; in the Slavonic, as in the Latin, the penitent takes the initiative in confessing as he or she desires. Absolution is given "deprecatively" (in a prayer form) in the Greek usage, both deprecatively and "declaratively" (in the form of an assertion) in the Slavonic. Thus the Greek celebrant prays:

> May God who pardoned David through Nathan the prophet when he confessed his sins, and Peter weeping bitterly for his denial and the sinful woman weeping at his feet and the publican and the prodigal son, may that same God forgive you all things, through me a sinner, both in this world and in the world to come, and set you uncondemned before his awesome judgement seat. Have no further care for the sins you have confessed; depart in peace.

And the Slavonic both prays and affirms:

> May our Lord and God Jesus Christ, through the grace and bounties of his love towards mankind, forgive you, my child, all your transgressions. And I an unworthy priest, through the power given me by him, forgive and absolve you from all your sins. In the Name of the Father and of the Son and of the Holy Spirit, Amen.

In each case the rite ends with reference to the communion of saints in which both priest and penitent are incorporated, thanks to the character of the philanthropic Lord of the Church. "May Christ our true God through the prayers of his most holy Mother and of all the saints, have mercy upon us and save us, for he is gracious and loves mankind."

From ancient times it was customary to ask for the prayers of confessors, just as the entire congregation would pray for the public penitents, offering them the *suffragium ecclesiae,* the Church's "suffrage" or "kind assistance." (The "confessors" here—the accent is placed on the second syllable—are those who have suffered for the faith. The principle of coinherence immanent in the communion of saints suggests that the closer members of the Church are to God, the deeper their charity, the more they can help their fellows.) The intervention of such holy confessors was taken, then, as justifying a diminution in the time of penance imposed by the Church in view of the sinner's reconciliation with her, and with God.

The first recognizably modern indulgences (i.e., those which correspond in evident form to the present practice of Catholicism) come from the south of France of the eleventh century. There, associated with almsgiving, or a pious visit to the sanctuary, we find the Church making an authoritative intervention, in the name of the communion of saints, in favor of her penitents. Such intercession is also found in the ante-Liturgy of the Eucharist, expressed in the old Latin prayers *Misereatur* and (significantly) *Indulgentiam*. The point of the intervention was to grant penitents a remission of the ecclesial penance due, signifying thereby the Church's role as corporate intercessor on their behalf before God. Such remissions derived from the commutation of a period of penance between confession and absolution, but as those two moments were increasingly united in a single rite, the remissions of penance were equally increasingly separated from the sacrament itself. This provided the sphere in which indulgences could operate. In 1215 the Fourth Lateran Council thought it proper to inveigh against "indiscreet and superfluous indulgences," and it was no doubt to avoid their trivialization that thirteenth-century sources insist explicitly that the recipient of an indulgence must be "rightly contrite and confessed." From the thirteenth century on, we find indulgences directed to the faithful departed, on the ground that even among them the power of the keys can operate, though only "deprecatively," *per modum suffragii*. The temporal penalty that both satisfaction and indulgence are said to remit is, then, both the penance imposed by the Church as discipline and the consequences of sin even after a sinner's conversion in depth. Indulgences exemplify how the Church's role towards sinners extends beyond the confessional: these acts of devotion or gestures of charity or exercises of penitence (all these descriptions can serve here) help relate to sacramental penance the daily penitence called for from the Christian. We should note that there is nothing magical about indulgences; the actualization of the remission which the Church accords depends on the degree of faith, the depth of devotion, and the fervor of charity which the recipient can muster: these are the basis for all union with Christ and his Church.

5. Anointing of the Sick

The reconciling work of Jesus Christ can also be regarded as a healing work. In both cases, the empirical facts—getting Pharisee and tax-collector to sit down together, curing Simon's mother-in-law—always have a parabolic significance. They are not done simply for their own sake, although for their own sake they were worth doing. In such reconciliations and healings in the gospel tradition there is a super-plus, since, as their handing on in the preaching and liturgy of the early Church demonstrates, they are meant to be pointers to a larger reconciliation and healing, that by which Jesus was affirmed as Savior of the whole human race. The evangelists, and notably John, are concerned to underscore this point vis-à-vis those who were satisfied with enjoying the material benefits of signs and wonders. The New Testament basis of the sacrament of the anointing of the sick lies in the Synoptic accounts of the Lord's commissioning of the Twelve for a work of healing, as that is further interpreted in the Letter of James (5:13-16), where the prayer of the Church and anointing with oil by presbyters (the delegated local form of the ministry) are said to "raise up" sick persons and "save" them. Here we have the sacramental instrument of apostolic healing. In the original Greek, both of these "doing-words" are ambivalent in meaning, hovering between physical healing and final salvation—the reconciliation of the whole person with himself, with others, and with God in a definitive fashion.

The shape of the sacrament is already clear. In the language of later analysis, the matter is anointing with (olive) oil, the form a prayer formula determined by the Church. Oil is a food marvelously suited to a ritual of healing, at once a soothing ointment and, in the Arabic proverb, the father of muscle. In Scripture oil connotes consolation, joy, peace, and gladness flowing from God's own abundance and toward human wholeness in him. Perfumed oil, in Jewish tradition, is not only this-worldly in its symbolic resonance, for it brings to mind the "oil of paradise," the restoring of life to the elect at the judgment. The form found in the present Latin Rite has the priest pray, "Through this holy anointing, may the Lord in his love and mercy help you with the grace of the Holy Spirit, Amen. May the Lord who frees you from sin save you and raise you up, Amen."

In the age of the Fathers, Christians saw anointing as, in Caesarius of Arles's phrase, *medicina Ecclesiae*, "the Church's physic." But soon the sense unfolded that this physical healing was ordered to, and therefore subordinate to, spiritual well-being. The shift of emphasis can be documented in the prayers of blessing the oil of the sick on Holy Thursday—between, for instance, the words *"ad refectionem corporis"* in the Gregorian Sacramentary and the more comprehensive *"ad refectionem* mentis *et corporis"* in its Gelasian counterpart. So a more holistic sense of what Christian healing might be gained ground, though never to the complete exclusion of the idea that actual physical recovery was a possible effect of this sacrament. The very primitive Sacramentary of Serapion, an Egyptian prayer book, has:

> We invoke you, who have all authority and power, Saviour of all men, Father of our Lord and Saviour Jesus Christ, and we pray that you may send forth the power of healing from heaven of your only begotten Son over this oil, so that to those, who are anointed by these your creatures . . . this oil may be used in riddance of any weakness and of any infirmity, in remedy against the Devil, in the expulsion of any unclean spirit, in the detachment of worthless preoccupation, in the cure of fever, of cold, and of physical weakness; let it be a channel of good grace and of remission of sins, a source of life and health, an instrument for the well-being and wholesomeness of the soul, body and spirit; thus perfect health may be restored.

Aquinas, in his commentary on the *Sentences* of Peter Lombard, considers that the sacrament was instituted to provide for spiritual enfeeblement, itself provoked by sin (both original and personal) and aggravated by the demoralizing effects of illness. Such enfeeblement would hinder a sick person from carrying out those acts of faith, hope, and charity that bring about in us the life of grace and glory. Subsequently, the Council of Trent produced on this subject one of its most balanced summings-up of the earlier tradition. The Fathers of Trent distinguished between the habitual and the merely occasional effects of anointing. The first consists in the grace of the Holy Spirit relieving and strengthening spiritually the sick person. In every case, Christ does this work in this sacrament (unless we, the receiving subjects, prevent him). The second category entails pardon and healing. These are not, however, different graces from the first, but the same grace insofar as in particular cases sacramental grace, in order to procure its proper (habitual) effect, must either purify the subject from his sins, or give him physical healing, or both. In other words, there may well be cases where a return to physical health is the fruit of this sacrament. It may be in God's will that a person comes to spiritual health by way of physical.

Anointing, then, maintains and strengthens communion with God and with others at times when that unity is compromised by the debilitating effects of sickness and old age. The tendency of the sick body to become an alien object to the mind is corrected by the grace of the Spirit of Christ. Similarly, the tendency of suffering to make me exclusively attentive to myself and to dislocate my relations with others is rectified by that Spirit, and the anguish of illness, prompted by the experience of finitude and mortality, is also healed as the sacrament enables me to accept the fact that I shall (eventually) die and to accept that fact in a manner both creative and sacrificial, which makes a death a way to God. In this regard, anointing welcomes the Christian into the mystery manifested in the Lord's person as priest and victim.

In the early modern period, and indeed until earlier this century, when grave illnesses were usually short and death-dealing, this sacrament was rarely conferred more than once, thus justifying the name "extreme unction" (the "last anointing"). However, the authors of the *Catechism of the Council of Trent* considered it gravely wrong to "defer holy unction until, all hope of recovery being lost, life begins to ebb and the sick person is fast verging into a state of insensibility."[33] Because of the progress of curative and preventive therapy and surgical technique, some illnesses can be prolonged or even permanent states, so that, paradoxically, the development of medicine has produced more sick people. In a period when many people, having been anointed, will live on and even recover, unction has generally ceased to be "extreme." Where it is not, then, *praeparatio ad gloriam,* part of the last rites, and in those cases where it does not entail cure, what it signifies is the task offered to the sick person under grace. That task is the preservation of a new sense of meaning which the crisis of sickness has created when believers affirm that only the life of the age to come will bring them the total fulfillment they desire. The sick are to pass, with Christ's help, from physical weakness to spiritual strength, from panic to tranquillity, from dereliction to a foretaste of immortality.

As Fr. Richard Conrad has insisted, although the sacrament of the sick does not always result in healing, this does not mean it does not always work. For all the sacraments are sacraments of hope: they point us forward to the kingdom, and enable us to lay hold of it.[34] Part of their action is deferred. In baptism we rise with Christ spiritually; we rise physically in the power of our baptism only at the end of time. (Even spiritually, we are not set free from the world, the flesh, and the devil straight away, but are enabled to withstand these so as to share Christ's victory over them more personally.) The Eucharist is in the

33. *Catechismus ex decreto Concilii Tridentini* 2.6, 9.
34. R. Conrad, *The Catholic Faith: A Dominican's Vision* (London, 1995) 182.

words of Ignatius of Antioch the "medicine of immortality," but we still have to die before we can fully enjoy the life it brings.

The sacrament of the sick brings healing, but only does so for certain when the body that was anointed rises to a life beyond sickness. Anointing is linked to the resurrection of the body, just as at Bethany the Lord's body was anointed for its destiny: to die and be buried so as to overcome death and rise in glory. Thus the holy anointing passes into the commendation of the dying, with its climax in the great *Profiscere* prayer of the Roman liturgy.

> Go, Christian soul! Depart from this world, in the name of God the almighty Father, who created you; in the name of Jesus Christ, Son of the living God, who suffered death for you; in the name of the Holy Spirit, who has been poured forth upon you; in the name of Mary, God's holy and glorious virgin-mother; in the name of her great consort, blessed Joseph; in the name of the Angels and Archangels, of Thrones and Dominations, of Principalities and Powers, of Virtues, Cherubim, and Seraphim; in the name of the Patriarchs and prophets, of the holy apostles and evangelists, of the holy martyrs, confessors, monks, and hermits, of the holy virgins, and of all the saints of God. In peace be your home this day and in holy Sion your abode: through the same Christ our Lord. Amen.

Fortified by the last Holy Communion—food for a journey, in Latin *viaticum*, in Greek *ephodion*—the faithful receive the Church's parting gift to the dying: a pledge of future glory that will give way before the eternal sacrament of the glorified humanity of Christ.

6. Orders

Orders is the sacrament whereby, through incorporation in the original ministry of the apostles, men come to share, not only in the royal and universal priesthood of all the baptized, entered by baptism and confirmation, but the ministerial or serving priesthood which aims to equip the members of the Church with the graces that flow from Christ as head upon his body, his people. Although those who share in orders are properly called bishops, presbyters, and deacons, the office of the first two groups (assisted by the third) is known not only as the "apostolic ministry" but also as "the *priesthood*."

For the Letter to the Hebrews, Christ is our great high priest whose work on the Cross has superseded the priesthood of Israel. By his sacrificial death Jesus is more truly and profoundly a priest than the priests of old. From the first moment of the incarnation to the ascension, and now for ever in heaven, he is the source of all priesthood. Moreover, this priesthood can be shared. If the Church is the "fullness of him who fills all in all," the body of Christ, then she must be included in his priesthood. And so the New Testament sees her: as "a royal priesthood" (1 Pet 2:9), "a kingdom and priests to God" (Rev 1:6). Catholicism finds here, as we have had occasion to note in the ecclesiological chapter of this book, two distinct ecclesial ways of sharing the priesthood of Christ. Interrelated and coordinated, they are nonetheless different in kind. The election of the Twelve and their consecration marks out the ministerial leadership of the Church as called to share in Christ's priesthood not simply through baptism—the foundation of membership of the Church—but in a sacrament specially devoted to the hierarchical structure of this people's Church: holy orders. The Twelve share Christ's priesthood because they share in his apostolate, his sending by the Father. They are chosen and consecrated for extending and continuing the mission of the Son in a public way. The Letter to the Hebrews calls Jesus "the apostle and high priest of our profession" (3:1), and the Gospel of John brings out the direct causal link between the sending of the Son and the Son's sending of the apostles: "As thou didst send me into the world, so I have sent them into the world" (17:18).

At the Last Supper, in commanding the Twelve to "do this" (a sacrificial term in itself in both pagan usage and the Septuagint) in remembrance of him (against its Jewish background, not human recollection but God's remembering, a divine *action*), Jesus bestows on the Twelve an active oblationary share in his priesthood. He empowers them to make present his sacrifice, efficacious for salvation, until he comes again. In the farewell discourse of the Fourth Gospel (the "high priestly prayer," which replaces, in John, the scene of the institution of the Eucharist in the Synoptics), the apostles are presented as sharing the dignity and destiny of the incarnate Son as priestly intercessor and consecrated apostle of the Father. "All mine are thine, and thine are mine, and I am glorified in them" (17:10).

Special *droits de cité* in the kingdom of Christ are, however, purely for the building up of that city and realm in its fullness. The Lord constituted his Church with a hierarchy within her so that the entire Church might become what she is called to be. The Council of Trent remarks of the Holy Eucharist that *the Church* celebrates by the hands of her priests: and here the Church can only be that great sacrament, the Lord's spouse, the totality of the people of God as a structured assembly.

If the New Testament then refuses the title *hiereus* to Christian ministers, this is not a denial of the priestly character of their ministry, but an attempt to avoid confusing it with that of the priests of the old covenant (and a fortiori, those of pagan religion). The Christian ministry is essentially apostolic: as such it can only be a "sacramentalization" of the one effective priest, Christ the Redeemer, whose death and resurrection the minister proclaims and actualizes in ritual. The apostolic college—and thus the sacrament of orders—is fundamental to the Catholic view of the Church. As Paul insists, in the Church as in the human body, the sign of organic life is organized structure, the diversification and coordination of parts. An undifferentiated Church could not be Christ's mystical *body*. Moreover, the place of the apostles in particular is, for the New Testament, indispensable: they are the foundation of the household of God (Eph 2:20) which is, therefore, not only a differentiated but a hierarchical assembly.

> The apostles are not "extras" in the drama of redemption, nor are they simply narrators; the institution of their college is itself part of the dramatic action, willed by God; their ministry is itself part of the economy of salvation. Jesus' appointment of the twelve, and their special consecration at Pentecost, are not functional devices, otherwise irrelevant to the preaching of the Kingdom and the redemptive work of Christ; no, it is precisely through these men, and through the Spirit who will indwell them and guide them, that the Lord's words and work will be communicated.[35]

A. THE OFFICE OF A BISHOP

The Second Vatican Council speaks of the bishop's sharing in the apostolic offices of teacher, priest, and shepherd as one of the great Pentecostal gifts of the risen Christ to his Church.

> For the discharging of such great duties the apostles were enriched by Christ by a special outpouring of the Holy Spirit who came upon them. . . . This spiritual gift they passed onto their helpers by the imposition of hands. . . . Christ whom the Father sanctified and sent into the world . . . has, through His Apostles, made their successors, the bishops, partakers of His consecration and His mission.[36]

Through what has been called "apostolic simultaneity," the sacrament of orders is a direct sharing in the mystery of Pentecost. Not secondhand

---

35. J. Saward, "Priesthood, Suffering and Sacrifice," *Christian* 4 (1977) 33.
36. *Lumen gentium*, 21, 28.

but directly do the bishops participate in that meta-event, thanks to the working of the one Spirit in the Church. "The extension of the apostolate and high priesthood to bishops is part of a God-created pattern, at the centre of which is the Paraclete. The fathers see a typological sequence in which the one Spirit descends upon Jesus at the Jordan, on the apostles at Pentecost, and on the bishop at his ordination."[37]

The content of the bishop's office is well summed up in its consecration prayers at the ordination Mass. Those of the Armenian Rite will serve as well as any to illustrate this. The chief consecrator begins by summoning forth the candidate and praying for him with the laying-on of hands (the ancient, apostolic ordination gesture):

> The divine and the heavenly grace that always provides for the ministry of the Apostolic church calls the priest . . . to the episcopate according to his own testimony and that of this people.
>
> I place my hands upon him and do you all pray that he may purely maintain the degree of the episcopate before the holy altar of the Lord.
>
> I thank you, the only-begotten Son of God, our Lord and Redeemer Jesus Christ, who have visited all mankind which is the work of your hands. You were sent into the world by God's will, to seek and save those who were lost. You humbled yourself to share our nature. You saved us from the condemnation due our sins by your Passion on the Cross. You subdue our enemy, and by renewing us from the ancient corruption, have shown us the new and holy way to eternal life, through your Resurrection. As you were sent by the Father, so you sent your Apostles. You gave them courage to preach to all peoples, inspiring them by your powerful Spirit with the promise to stay with them always till the end of the age. To them you never cease to raise up heirs and successors on the thrones of your holy Church, to shepherd and defend the rational flock which you purchased by your precious and life-giving blood. Accept, good Lord, the prayers of us your servants who are gathered here before you and implore your favour for this your servant whom you have chosen and called by grace to the office and dignity of the episcopate.

The rite asks more specifically for gifts equipping the bishop-elect to teach the faith, to convert the vicious and confirm the virtuous, to celebrate the sacraments worthily (especially the "wonderful mystery of the [Eucharistic] sacrifice"), and not to ordain deacons and presbyters hastily or inadvisedly. The bishop is to be a pattern of observance of the commandments and virtues of Scripture, and to pray and keep

37. Saward, "Priesthood," 34.

vigil for the salvation of the people entrusted to him. He will inherit the apostles' authority to absolve sins, "opening the door of heaven to those who come to you through him," to be a father to orphans, widows, and the poor.

The consecrator proceeds to anoint the head and hands of the candidate, asking that he may receive a share in the Pentecostal mystery: "Lord, may the unction poured out plentifully on the head of your elect run abundantly throughout his body. Through the strength of your Holy Spirit in him may it abound in his heart. May he keep himself always constant in the faith and in love of the truth." As he hands over the pastoral staff, he says, "Receive this crosier and staff of the dignity of pastor, with which you will judge the wicked with justice and severity, and pasture and feed at all times those obedient to the law and the commandments of God." Next, the ring is given: "Receive this ring as a sign of faithfulness and keep yourself prudent in your divine wedding with holy Church by right faith." Placing the pectoral cross around his neck, the main consecrator then hands over to the newly ordained the book of the Gospels, with the words, "Receive now the Gospel and go and preach to the people committed to you by God; may almighty God increase them by his grace, and reign over them to the ages of ages." The conferral of the mitre, the bishop's headdress, is accompanied by a prayer to the Father:

> Lord, we place on this bishop's head the helmet of strength and salvation, so that his face, adorned and formidable by the power of the New Testament, as of the Old, may appear terrible to the opponents of truth, and smite them vigorously with the grace you will grant him—as once you impressed on the countenance of Moses, resplendent from his converse with you, the radiant authority of your light and truth, and ordered the mitre to be set on the head of your high priest Aaron.

Lastly, the consecrating bishop puts on the breast of his new brother the *omophorion,* which corresponds to the *pallium* of the West, a sign of communion with the rest of the episcopate, and notably, for Catholics, with the pope: "For the glory and honour of almighty God, and of the most holy, ever-virgin Mary, and of the blessed saints Peter and Paul, and for our holy father pope . . . of the holy Roman church, and for the church of . . . we bestow upon you the *omophorion,* which signifies the plenitude of the priestly ministry." This rich symbolism, embodying high doctrine, is only comprehensible if, in the words of *Lumen gentium,* "By divine institution bishops have succeeded to the place of the apostles as shepherds of the Church, and . . . he who hears them hears Christ, while he who rejects them rejects Christ and him who sent Christ."[38] That statement is made of course not of an individual bishop as such, but only as such a one is conjoined in mind and heart with the whole episcopal college which has the Roman bishop, the universal primate, as its head.

B. THE OFFICE OF A PRESBYTER

Whereas the deacon is ordained as the bishop's servant, *in ministerio episcopi*, the presbyter shares his priesthood. Together—liturgically as a *corona*, "crown," surrounding him—the presbyters form with the bishop, the primary *sacerdos*, one priestly body, helping him in the governance of the Church. But while the ensuring of spiritual discipline and orthodoxy of faith (shepherding and teaching) must count high among a presbyter's duties, if indeed he shares, through and with the bishop, in the apostolic ministry, nonetheless the special priestly offering of the Eucharistic sacrifice takes pride of place. Indeed, for presbyters—commonly called, simply, "priests"—who are contemplative monks, it may be the *only* tangible expression of ministerial priesthood.

> It is not that the sacrifice is simply superior to the Word; it is rather that the sacrifice is itself the supreme preaching of the Gospel, not just in the sense that every Eucharist contains the liturgy of the Word, but because it is precisely the Christ really, substantially present in the Eucharist, offered and offering himself in the oblation, the Christ who pours himself out unceasingly in the Blessed Sacrament, whom we preach to the nations.[39]

It was the Donatist crisis that helped the western Church to formulate the doctrine of the *opus operatum*, the objective existence and influence of grace within a priest despite his unworthiness. Though the grace of orders does not require us to make a cult of failure (for God wants us to make good use of his gifts), it nonetheless challenges us to keep our eyes fixed on Christ crucified and to be configured to him.

> When a priest, groaning within himself at the thought of his unworthiness and the sublimity of his functions, has put his consecrated hands on our heads; when, humiliated to find himself the dispenser of the Blood

---

38. *Lumen gentium,* 20.
39. Saward, "Priesthood," 36.

of the Covenant, amazed on each occasion to utter the words which give life when, a sinner himself, he has absolved a sinner, we ourselves, rising from before his feet, realise that we have suffered no indignity. We have been at the feet of a man who represented Jesus Christ. . . . We have been there to gain the characteristics of free men and God's children.[40]

The grace of orders is nonetheless given for the cultivation of holiness. For that grace to show itself in its true glory, it must be accompanied by the cooperation of the priest's will, and that means his unrelenting pursuit of holiness of life through ascesis and spiritual combat, which in turn means unceasing prayer and thanksgiving, regular self-examination and confession, fasting, abstinence, and the conquest of personal sin. A priest's life and ministry can have no fruitfulness unless he acknowledges the priority of the glory of God in all he does and is.

The privileged contiguity of the priest to the sacrifice of Christ imposes on him the obligation to lead a sacrificial life. Paul defined the apostolate as the capacity to be wasted, poured out on behalf of the Church, seeing there its Christological configuration and thus its hidden fruitfulness. The poet Paul Claudel replied, in April 1945, to a young *curé de campagne* who had written to tell him of his sense of spiritual isolation. After mentioning his own experiences of isolation in a diplomat's life abroad, Claudel explained:

Thanks be to God: study and prayer enabled me to cross those desolate zones which lead to Horeb, the mount of God. However, it seems to me that, in your own part of the world, you have resources which I did not. The Mass which you say each morning pours out a torrent of inestimable, incommensurable blessing not only on your village but on all humanity. It empties Purgatory. And then each morning, as you awake, you can tell yourself that these men, women, children, have been specially entrusted to you by God himself. To others he gave cows or horses; to you these immortal souls. You are their Christ, able to give them life, fully invested with a power of vivification, illumination, resurrection. You immolate yourself for them each day on the altar. You have an inside knowledge of what is deepest in them—and of what is unknown to them—but what makes them who they are. You are the agent of their guardian angels. You stand in for them. In this sublime role, what do human *contretemps* and contradictions count? Were you promised a paper cross? Or a good honest heavy cross, which is just your size, precisely because it appears overwhelming? Besides the immense divine

---

40. A. Manzoni, "Osservazioni sulla morale cattolica," 18, in *Opere* (Milan, 1965) 1143–44.

joy reserved for you, and whose dispenser you are, how simply ridiculous these little pebbles in your shoes appear.

Believe me, the vocation of a priest, and I would add of a country priest (*our Lord* was a country priest) is the sublimest of all. That of writer pales in comparison. *Deus illuminatio mea, quem timebo?* ["God is my light, whom shall I fear?" (Psalm 27:1)].[41]

Like the bishop everywhere, the presbyter in the Latin Church is, with few exceptions, celibate. Sexuality is a divine blessing on, specifically, this life, whereas the priest's primary concern lies in preparing people for the age to come. In the Eastern Churches, where a married presbyterate coexists with a celibate or monastic one, this point is affirmed in the canonical requirement of abstinence from intercourse in the time before celebration of the (non-daily) Eucharist.

Minister of reconciliation and of the Eucharist, man of doctrine and prayer: the priesthood of the presbyter has an amazing concentration of representative significance, gathering up as it does so many of the roles of the whole Church. Its pattern includes most importantly the following elements

1. Evangelizing the unconverted
2. Teaching sound doctrine in faith and morals to the converted
3. Forming others to be apostolic
4. Celebrating the sacraments, and other rites of the Church
5. In particular, by the celebration of penance and the Eucharist, bringing the paschal mystery to bear on the lives of the faithful, who die to sin, and live with Christ to God
6. In the Mass, but also in the Divine Office, acting as intercessor for the Church, and for all creation
7. In union with the bishop, and, ultimately, with the pope, to build up, as pastor, the communion of the Church, gathering the faithful and opening them to the fullness of the Church's life
8. Visiting, and so counselling and encouraging, individual members of the Church community—especially the sick and the poor

41. Apart from the volumes of published correspondence, chiefly with literary figures, the Archives Paul Claudel contain many unedited items testifying to what Sr. Isabelle Bouchard had called his letter-writing "apostolate": *L'expérience apostolique de Paul Claudel, d'après sa correspondence* (Montreal, 1969).

9. Overseeing the community's wider attempt to meet the needs
of its members, and of the wider realm in which their lives
are set.[42]

In that last regard, the priest will naturally find himself in relation to
the deacon. But before moving on to look at the diaconate, some few
words must be added about the non-ordaining of women to the ministerial priesthood in the Catholic Church.

The two figures which *must* be displayed in any church building
where the Christian people gather to celebrate the mysteries are the
crucified Christ and the mother of God. The ministerial priest, iconic
in his male gender, stands for the one; the people, symbolized as
mother Church, find expression in the other. While Jesus Christ is the
Savior of all human beings, men and women, Mary is our mother, and
notably the mother of the members of Christ's Church-body. In the typological and iconic experience of worship, and of the Christian life,
the mother of God presents Christians before the Lord's throne; in the
one who gave human flesh to the Son of God they find a ready help
and intercessor. Mary represents the whole people of God in relation
to their Lord. The ministerial priest, by contrast, iconically presents to
this body of Christ her head and Lord, the high priest Jesus Christ.
This distinction belongs at the deepest level to the ethos and inner tradition of Church, such that all challenge to it disturbs the interrelation
of Christology on the one hand, and, on the other, Mariology, ecclesiology, and (ultimately) pneumatology. The choice, use, and combination of images made by Christ and the Spirit must be a supernatural
work, or else Christianity is an illusion. Among analogical forms in
Catholicism, none are more influential than those which make use of
the imagery of sexual differentiation, above all those which refer to
God as Father and Christ as bridegroom of the Church. The maleness
of the hierarchical priesthood is one vital way in which these great images are preserved in the Church. There is no question here of Jewish
male chauvinism in the Lord's non-selection of women for the
Twelve, much less any ascription of moral superiority to men. One
has only to think of the comparative performance, on Calvary, of the
Twelve and of the women disciples. What is at stake is, rather, a symbolic and ritual-dramatic significance in the polarization of man and
woman within the group of the Messiah's followers. The fruitful tension

42. I take this precis from A. Nichols, *Holy Order: The Apostolic Ministry from the New
Testament to the Second Vatican Council* (Dublin, 1990) 142–43.

of Christological and Marian principles must be structured in the life of the Church: it must, that is, find expression in a sacrament. The ministerial priesthood is the efficacious sign of the new Adam, with the bishop or priest at the altar imaging Christ the bridegroom. (It is also true that the very maleness of Christian priests guards a continuity between the two covenants, where the president at Passover was always male: a female Messiah could not have fulfilled the Exodus tradition.)

Woman becomes one with man not when she is and does all that man is and does, but when her womanliness and its distinctive charisms are acknowledged by man and integrated with his own. There are many tasks of a ministerial nature open to Catholic women along these lines: education, from elementary school to university; pastoral counselling; preparation for marriage, baptism, and confirmation; youth work, social service, especially with the sick and the deprived; iconographic and musical work. Some women may feel called to a full-time service of the Church in these ways not as vowed religious but in the form of specifically lay *diakonia;* the ancient order of deaconesses could well be revived in that context.

C. THE DEACON

The deacon is ordained above all for the assistance of the bishop. The Syrian *Didascalia Apostolorum* describes him as the bishop's mouth, ear, and heart. Deacons were, historically, approached on routine matters so that the bishop would not be continually interrupted. Owing to their position of confidence they sometimes—and especially at Rome—considered themselves superior to simple presbyters. But the normal rule is that the deacons are also at the service of presbyters whenever the bishop considers it desirable.

The deacons of the Church are ordained so as to represent Christ in the role of servant: serving the Father and serving human beings. Ignatius of Antioch calls them servants of the bishop as Christ is of the Father, and thus stewards of the *diakonia* of Jesus himself. They prepare the table of the Eucharistic feast in the liturgy, but they also act as go-betweens, joining the ministerial priest in the sanctuary to the common people of God in the nave, in the Byzantine Rite, and communicating, in the litanies for which that rite makes them responsible, the world's needs to the Church of saints and angels represented on the iconostasis. In the West, Prudentius calls them the "columns on which God's altar rests"; through them, the hierarchy of bishop and priest finds itself in closer contact with the world and the legitimate temporal concerns which are also germane to the making of the kingdom of God.

7. Marriage

In the Book of Genesis, marriage is presented as given in the very moment when God creates male and female in his own image and likeness. It images, then, something of God himself. As the revelation contained in Scripture unfolds, it transpires that this "something" is in fact the capacity for love in interpersonal relationship and its fruitfulness. However, marriage, like all human things, was soon distorted. With the Fall, that primordial going astray at the beginning of our race, marriage too fell; we see the emergence even within Israel, the chosen people, of such practices as polygamy and divorce. Yet, as the Old Testament presents it, marriage never lost the blessing of God. It remained a vehicle of relationship with him; even more, though a natural reality, it was spoken of by the prophets as a lived metaphor—the Bride, Israel, and her Bridegroom—for God's seeking out his people. In other words, it tended toward the sacramental order, the order of incarnational friendship with God, which Christians are privileged to share.

The Redeemer of marriage, as of all the other constitutive dimensions of human life, is Jesus Christ. With the incarnation, the union begins of "things in heaven and things on earth" (Col 1:20). The Gospels present Jesus as the bridegroom awaiting his bride—the human race provisionally embodied, as long as time lasts, in the Church. In word and deed, the bridegroom reveals what the Letter to the Ephesians describes as his "great mystery" (5:32). As *prophet* Jesus reveals the new kind of marriage to be practiced among his people, an indissoluble marriage based on the gracious origins of humankind, a restoring of the original creation. As *priest* (or rather, priest-and-victim, for the sacrifice which the God-man offers on Golgotha is himself), Jesus, goes up to Jerusalem, there to die for his spouse, offering his consent at the supper table and promising to take her to himself. From there his wedding procession leaves for the place of the actual celebration: Calvary. As in the medieval rood-screens, Mary, the mother of Jesus, and John, the beloved disciple—the two great personifications of the coming Church—act as the bridegroom's attendants, and the witnesses to the wedding. On the cross, the bridegroom dies for the Church his spouse, who is thus born from his pierced side, since human beings are reborn, accepted and cleansed, in that nuptial self-immolation of God's own Son, becoming one with him who loved us and gave himself for us. As *king*, Christ reveals in his resurrection that these nuptials of the Cross bring about a complete union between human beings and God for all eternity. By his royal power, as Lord of all, he draws those of the baptized who marry into the sphere of his own marriage covenant, enabling them to experience the nuptial meaning of their own bodies as sacraments of his sacrificial love for his bride, the Church. The baptized who marry as members of Christ's mystical body are thus consecrated by their act of mutual consent. They receive the Spirit of the Father and the Son who joins them together in the marriage bond. They are strengthened by a grace conditioned to their new state, helping them to make the love of Christ, crucified and risen, a present reality, sanctifying one another in the suffering and joy of daily life.

Without this high doctrinal background, it is impossible to understand the demands and specificities of the Catholic understanding of marriage and sexuality. That understanding cannot be set forth in simply pragmatic and empirical terms as though it were purely a matter of one particular presentation of the facts of human psychology. The reason why indissolubility is an integral aspect of the sacrament of marriage is, in the last analysis, that the union between God and humanity cannot be broken. Christ cannot separate from his Church. Divorce, in this context, is not so much a sin as a lie. Similarly, adultery is a falsification of the "one flesh" by (in the context) simulated self-giving. Again, the use of artificial rather than natural methods of birth control can be said to substitute technical control for the personal control which befits the eminently personal character of the marriage covenant.

Catholic married couples, and other married Christians who share this fundamental understanding, are not, therefore, the last bastions of a Victorian concept of sex and family. They are prophets, priests, and kings; the acting images of Christ the bridegroom and his bride; united to the power of his glorious Cross, journeying together towards the kingdom, the everlasting wedding banquet of the Lamb of God.

The conditions of a valid marriage are implied in the wedding rites of the Catholic Church. The couple are asked to undertake the fulfillment of three conditions. First, the marriage must be open to new life, that is, the couple must be willing to procreate and nurture children. (Couples where one partner or both are childless may still marry, but on the understanding that if ethically acceptable means of overcoming infertility are available, they will make use of them.) Second, a marriage must be permanent, abiding until the death of one partner or both. Third, the union must be "exclusive": this relationship is only possible if it has a unique recipient.

These specify, as it were, the minimum conditions of the marriage covenant which the sacramental order then elevates to be a medium of the grace of the incarnation. For in the first place, the basis of marriage lies in the created order—which is why the Catholic Church claims the right, as the accredited interpreter of that order, to counsel the state on the form of law conducive, in these matters, to the common good. The "Genetic" account of marriage shows Adam receiving Eve as his "helpmate": she brings him complementarity, draws him out of loneliness—and by mutual love each makes the other more himself or herself. Marriage is then for the sustaining of each partner. It is also for their task of co-creation, with God, of the new members of the human race. Companionate union is necessary for children to be born and brought up in a loving home; in these offspring, moreover, the couple re-discover themselves in a new way, as parents, the better to enhance their companionship. The Second Vatican Council's Pastoral Constitution on the Church in the Modern World calls children the ultimate crown of marriage, its most outstanding gift, and the greatest good bestowed on the parents. The spouses are to show forth the mystery of the fruitfulness as well as the unity that holds good between Christ and the Church.

Thanks to Christian initiation by baptism, a married couple share not only a natural, God-given covenant, but a sacrament of the Church. Incorporated in the redeeming work of Christ by baptismal regeneration, with its consequences (justification and sanctification), a man and a woman are now located within the new and everlasting "spousal" covenant of Christ and his Church. Marriage, with its call to self-giving love, acts as a sacrament of God's own love for humankind, as the prophet Hosea had already glimpsed in describing YHWH's union with Israel. More specifically, it is a sacrament of the love of God in Christ for the whole Church, as the Letter to the Ephesians so eloquently puts it (5:21-33). "Love one another as I have loved you" (Jn 13:34) is the new commandment of Christ on his way to Calvary. Marriage is a school of charity-love, entailing an overcoming of selfishness throughout one's life. Married love involves a deepening of both erotic love (the communion made possible by sexuality) and the love of friendship (made possible by shared interests and values). In the spirit of the marriage vows—"for better, or worse; for richer, or poorer"—the charity-love of marriage is a self-emptying, kenotic love, like that of Christ on the cross. It is, then, an unconditional commitment, which does not depend on one or the other remaining lovable, or even sane. One does not marry so as to reform, though love will of its nature reform and improve. Catholicism's opposition to divorce is not, then, a legalism, but an affirmation of the nature of true love. The other can only be truly loved by being continually forgiven until death do them part. (The Church recognizes judicial separation, "from bed and board," but not the concept of the irretrievable breakdown of marriage, and so of remarriage in the lifetime of a spouse. Given grace and providence, there is no total irretrievability.)

Like all sacraments, marriage is related not only to God's "crucial" work, the atonement, but also to what that work served: the mission of the Son now continued in his body, the Church. Marriage has a missionary task. This is directed first to the children. Father and mother are to minister Christ to the children in the whole of a life together. It must then extend beyond the children to a wider circle. The Christian family is a *foyer*, a radiating center of warmth and affection, into which the lonely, the troubled, the disadvantaged, and the poor should find an entry. The range of such hospitality is wide—befriending other families, welcoming newcomers, visiting the sick, helping single parents, etc., all come within its compass.

Like any sacrament, marriage has its ministers. On the overwhelmingly predominant Catholic view, these ministers are the couple themselves. The priest serves as a witness; if he cannot be located within a given period (as perhaps in Outer Mongolia, or the Antarctic), the couple may proceed to a fully sacramental union with lay witnesses instead.

Though the early liturgy of marriage is lost in the mists of scarcely documented time, in all probability it followed Jewish practice: betrothal leading to marriage, with the making of contract, all taking place by a domestic ritual, presumably with some version of the talmudic seven blessings, as appears to be the case in the third-century Syriac text the *Acts of Thomas*. In the medieval West, domestic rites (in the home or at the church gate) could both precede and follow the nuptial Mass. Commonly, there would be a domestic rite of consent, with the blessing of a ring (expressed in short pithy prayers, like those in the Anglo-Saxon pontifical of Egbert); a nuptial Mass, with a theologically fuller and indeed often florid prayer of nuptial blessing (one of the most ancient, that of the Gregorian Sacramentary, survives in the reformed Roman book of 1969); and then, at home again, the blessing of the bedchamber (and the couple). Although Scholastic theologians increasingly found the heart of marriage to lie in the exchange of vows, the act of consent (for *consensus facit nuptias*), the nuptial blessing constituted the liturgical high point, when the bridal pair were placed under a canopy (as in the Sarum Rite) or had a veil draped around their shoulders (as at Milan), both symbols of the Shekinah, or divine presence. In the Visigothic rites, they were bound by a special cord or golden chain. In the Eastern liturgies, the couple are crowned with wreaths of flowers or actual crowns of metal and stones. The East Syrian liturgy prays:

> O Christ, adorned Spouse, whose betrothal has
>   given us a type,
> complete the foundation and the building and
>   their [the couple's] laudable work;
> sanctify their marriage and their bed;
> and dismiss their sins and offences;
> and make them a temple for you and bestow on their
>   marriage chamber your light;
> and may their odour be as a roseshoot in paradise,
>   and as a garden full of scents,
>   and as a myrtle tree may be for your praise.
> May they be a bastion for our orthodox band and a
>   house of refuge.

The Eastern Churches retain often elaborate rites of betrothal, with anointing (Maronite), the blessing of robes and jewels (Armenian), and the drinking of a cup of water, ash, and wine, to symbolize dying to a former life and rising to a new (East Syrian). The *Order of Christian Marriage* for England and Wales (1995) restores a form of betrothal rite for those who wish it, with blessing of the couple and the engagement ring, as well as the lighting of candles to symbolize the convergence of two families. The provision of liturgically marked states of approach to marriage is seen not as archaeological revival but as good pastoral practice which will, through ritual acts, however simple, bond the couple more closely to the Church's understanding of what marriage involves.

The grace of marriage may be expected to be especially fruitful in crises. Love ceases to blossom; it wilts; but grace gives resurrection, a new start, and its effect is cumulative over time.

The Church Building

The building in which these rites take place is evidently a special space for Christians. As the place where the sacrifice of our redemption is celebrated and its fruits received in the seven sacraments, where the word of God is heard and the Christ present in the Eucharistic tabernacle adored, and where all manner of extraliturgical devotions, expressive of the faith of the Church, are carried on, it is a different kind of place. In a special way it is the dwelling of God among us (Rev 21:3), the place where God guarantees he may be found by the faithful. It is our Father's house, God's "royal palace" (the "basilica"); it is the place where the ecclesial body of Christ is molded and developed, and hence is a living symbol of his own blessed body; it is the place where God's ultimate union with his people by the Spirit is anticipated, and so is the new Jerusalem come down from heaven (Rev 21:2). It is a place of escape from what is merely peripheral, where we occupy ourselves with what is fundamentally important. Its architecture reflects human nature in the image of God: passionate for clarity, and enlightenment, as also for peace and quiet, warmth and shelter. In the world of late antiquity where the Catholic Church was born, churches were not, as one student has pointed out, "iconographical puzzles." Rather, they were

> *ho topos:* the "place," where it was possible to share for a moment in the eternal repose of the saints in paradise. Light seems trapped in the churches. The blaze of lamps and gold mosaic recapture the first moment of Creation: "Dark chaos is fled away." They are heavy with incense, which brought into this world a touch of paradise, conceived as a mountain covered with trees in full bloom. Their floors even attempt to catch the same sense of ease and release from care that forms such a poignant theme in the private mansions of the great from Hellenistic times up to the establishment of Islam and beyond: one church could even be described as a meadow blooming with flowers. In the northern Syrian church of Huarte, Adam sits with imperial serenity among the beasts in a paradise regained. Two churches, the one near the dangerous mountains of Isauria and the other set up by its bishop, "a man of subtle mind," in Apamea, a city with a tradition of philosophical leisure, have mosaics depicting the coming of the Kingdom of Peace among the wild animals scattered on the floor. Christians hoped to find in their shrines a "place of fulfilment and sweet perfume," the echo of a rest beyond the grave in what was still a very classical landscape—because it was a

human and a Mediterranean one, "in a grassy place by refreshing waters, whence pain and suffering and groaning have fled."[43]

As stylistic epochs give way to each other, Hellenistic and Byzantine, Romanesque, Gothic and Renaissance, Baroque and Romantic, we sense a connection between the Church's theology, her mission, and her feeling for the arts—more recently endangered, alas, by a functionalism which tends to the aniconic, without and within. Yet the *Rite of Dedication of Church and Altar* makes clear that the building is quintessentially an icon, achieved by way of a specifically architectural set of means (location, volume, massing, and working with the repertoire of earlier tradition in the new accents made available by materials and techniques of the present day).

The building of a church offers a wonderful opportunity to make, for the glory of God but also for the good of human beings, a thing of beauty in a world where there is so much ugliness, and to embody a symbol in a world where symbols are so largely forgotten. A house is but the night lodging of a pilgrim, whereas a church should be the reflection of eternal life and bliss.

A church is essentially a Mass-house, but owing to the organic character of the sacramental and ecclesial life, which flows from and surrounds the Holy Eucharist, a Catholic church contains more than simply the prerequisites of the Eucharistic celebration. The church tower (if it exists) may contain a bell or peal of bells, worked either by moving the bells, or moving the clappers (in which case the peal is known as a carillon). Alternatively a bell may be housed in a small building of its own, a campanile. Less essential today, in that we have clocks and watches, the sound of the bell expresses in its own medium the summons of grace, while smaller bells are used in the worship of the Eucharist to give added solemnity to the moment of the consecration (at Mass) or blessing with the Host (at Benediction). A second space that is sometimes separate from the main church is the baptistery, often round or octagonal, with the font surrounded by a railing. By the eighth century, in Western Europe at any rate, fonts were customarily resited just within the Church. By the thirteenth century the

43. P. Brown, "Art and Society in Late Antiquity," in *The Age of Spirituality: A Symposium,* ed. K. Weitzmann (New York, 1980) 25, with internal citations of an anonymous ancient Latin Christian inscription, the *Miracula sancti Demetrii,* and the Coptic Liturgy of St. Basil.

baptismal water was normally protected by a wooden lid. By the end of the Middle Ages the lid had been lovingly adorned with a spire, sometimes tall enough to reach the Church roof and worked by pulleys. Since the opening part of the baptismal liturgy takes place in the narthex or porch of a church it makes good sense to locate the font there, though nowadays, to permit congregational participation in some numbers at the climax of the rite of baptism, many fonts are relocated in the sanctuary. Since baptism is the "gate of the sacraments," this is not so congruent. If the font is not in the porch (or even if it is), a holy water stoup reminds the faithful entering the church of their own baptism: they take water, and make the sign of the Cross with it. By the nineteenth century, these stoups had become tiny niches in walls, surmounted by canopies. Earlier they could be much larger: the Renaissance Church favored vast shallow basins, frequently designed as shells.

The principal object to which the eye should be directed on entering the body of a church is the (high) altar. Early Christian altars were very small affairs, but gradually they underwent an expansion. Originally, nothing was placed on the "table of sacrifice" except the bread and wine, perhaps the book of the Gospels, and a small casket in which to place the consecrated elements for the communication of the sick. The expansion was due to a number of factors. First, when it became commonplace to "say" Mass rather than sing it, the epistle and gospel ceased to be chanted from ambos (the little pulpits in the early basilicas) and were read instead from two sides (ends) of the altar. Second, with the growth of popular devotion to the saints, reliquaries were placed behind, beneath, beside, and even upon the altars. In the Byzantine Rite, in which the altar is covered in silk or linen cloth embroidered with the instruments of the passion, the relic-bag *(antimension)* takes the place of the stone containers of the West. Sometimes an altar would have a retable, a decorated screen adorning a fixed platform behind the altar. From that there developed the higher reredos, sometimes a wonder work of statuary, which grew throughout the late medieval and early modern period until by the eighteenth century it filled the entire rear wall of the Church. Though the modern tendency is to reemphasize, by simplifying the surroundings, the starkness of the altar, it must still have a small cavity in which the relics of the saints are placed. It must also be related to an image of the crucified Savior; other images, of our Lady and the saints, are also appropriate in its near vicinity as a reminder of the entire worshipping Church made present in the liturgy.

Also highly prominent in a Catholic church is the tabernacle where the Blessed Sacrament is reserved. The earliest tabernacles appear to be in the form of a kind of small tower, on the gospel side of the sanctuary. Later there were metal doves suspended above the high altar, or a pyx (a kind of veiled chalice), or a small cupboard built into the lower part of the reredos. The modern tabernacle has evolved as a combination of the tower and the cupboard. It is covered in a veil, usually of silk, brocade, or damask, to signify the preciousness of its contents and the divine presence which is thus both concealed and revealed. The veil, in Latin *tabernaculum*, gives the sacrament house its name.

Candles were originally placed around the altar, having been carried there in procession. But by the twelfth century we find two candlesticks placed on the altar table itself for the whole of Mass. Later this was extended to six for high Mass (and seven when the pope was celebrating, or a bishop in his own diocese). The Dominican use retains the custom of lighting an extra candle during the Canon of the Mass.

The altar must be clothed: the antependium or frontal, hanging down at the front and the sides, is the most ancient furnishing for the altar. In the Byzantine Rite and other Eastern Churches it is close-fitting, of brocade or silk. Except in Rome, frontals in the West tended to disappear in the Renaissance, being replaced by carving or sculpture. In addition there are linen or hemp cloths of white: classically two to cover the altar table and a third, the topmost, to hang down on both ends.

An altar is also frequently dignified by a canopy, either free standing (a "civory") or suspended from roof or wall ("baldaquin"). The oldest known is at Ravenna, the best known is Bernini's 1633 baroque civory at St. Peter's, in Rome.

Required for the service of the altar are the sacred vessels and vestments. The chalice (for the wine) and paten (for the bread) are the most important of the former. In the Byzantine Rite the paten is surmounted by the *asterikos*, consisting of a crossed arch of two curved bands of precious metal, to prevent the veil touching the holy bread. A small spoon is used to give Communion while a metal knife (the lance) cuts the altar bread prepared as the liturgy opens. The ciborium, a sort of covered chalice, holds the consecrated bread in the tabernacle; when the sacrament is carried to the sick it is placed in a small round box, the pyx. If the carrying is by way of public worship and witness it is done in a monstrance, a kind of portable shrine; since the sixteenth century the usual tower type has been replaced by a sun shape, surrounded by rays.

Two kinds of vestments are used in the celebration of Mass. First, there are outer garments, made normally of silk: the chasuble, a tent-like garment (Latin *casula*, "little house") for the bishop or priest; the dalmatic, a robe with wide sleeves, originally made of Dalmatian wool, for the deacon; the tunicle, a simplified dalmatic, for the sub-deacon or, in the modern Roman liturgy, the cross-bearer; the stole, a scarf symbolizing the priestly office; and the maniple, a liturgical handkerchief, now confined to the older uses of the Roman Rite. Second, there are the linen garments worn underneath: the amice, a head-covering; the alb, a long white garment with close-fitting sleeves; and a girdle or cord. On special occasions, the sacred ministers (which in this case can include non-clerics, such as cantors) may use the cope—a semi-circular cloak called in Latin *pluviale* (literally, a rain-coat)—intended to give solemnity to festal occasions. A bishop wears a ceremonial hat called a mitre, originally a soft round cap, but now shield-shaped, and carries a crosier, a crook-shaped staff, as the emblem of his pastoral (shepherding) authority. The design of these garments and objects differs significantly in the Oriental Catholic liturgies, al-though occasionally there has been borrowing from the Latin Rite.

These special clothes and symbolic objects are not necessarily con-fined to a church building, for the procession—a characteristic feature of the public life of a Catholic culture—takes them out of doors. A Church "must be potentially and occasionally processional, must show itself for worship and jubilee in the open, must at times be pere-grinating and agoral, and wind, in rich pomps and gauds, through market-place, street and town. Pomps and gauds, chanting and sweet smells, ceremonious adoration and mystery—if these be not the fit cir-cumstance and habit of worship, the worshipping world has for many thousands of years erred."[44]

44. R. Macaulay, *Personal Pleasures* (London, 1935; 1968) 101.

10
Mary and the Saints

The Blessed Virgin Mary

Men are men, wrote G. K. Chesterton, but man is a woman. For Catholic Christians, Mary is the icon of how humanity should be before God, the paradigm of what it is to be a hearer of the word of God, a disciple. This she is by virtue of her special place in the interrelation between God in Christ, on the one hand, and the Church and ourselves, on the other. Mary is the mother of God: the *Theotokos,* the "God-bearer." The main significance of this divine motherhood is that it expresses a truth about Jesus Christ, and so is located within the whole scheme of the mystery of our salvation where he is fulcrum and center. Yet the divine motherhood cannot help but tell us something as well about Mary herself, as the daughter of God's predilection, a human being filled to overflowing with his redeeming grace, and so the preeminent witness to the transforming power of the gift of the Holy Spirit. Furthermore, Mary's motherhood has a value in connection with the life of grace in each of us: Mary is our exemplar because of the special link with her of each baptized person. She is the highest member of the mystical body of which all form part.

Clearly, the general picture which Marian doctrine gives us, as well as its specific details, has meaning in relation both to God and to ourselves. And this implies the special prerogative of Mary, what is called her "privileges." Those privileges in turn cannot be understood unless we bear in mind the double function she serves—towards God, towards us—because it is in that function that the degree and importance of her glory consist. Mary is totally relative to God. She is totally correlative to the Church. And she is these things in, through, and for her Son, Jesus Christ.

Mary is related to God by a total dependence which makes her unreservedly his. In being totally relative to God she must also be immediately relative to Christ, the way to the Father; she is indeed a sign pointing us to him (as in the Byzantine icons where, under the name *Hodegitria,* the "Way-pointer," she indicates her Son) by all she is and does. At the same time Mary is related to the Church. In two senses is she prior to the Church: chronologically, she preceded the Church born at Pentecost; ontologically, there is concentrated in her all that the grace of God brings about in the Church. The Church is precontained in Mary's spousal answer to the Father's messenger, her motherhood of the Word. Yet this does not prevent her from being a member of the Church also, and the highest member since her acting is consistently selfless in the Church's favor. Reciprocal dependence, mutual inclusion: these join Mary and the Church. Mary has priority as setting up Christ's relation with humanity, and so with the Church. Yet the ultimate finality is the Church where is made present the mystery of human salvation, the end for which the Son took flesh in the womb of his human mother.

The incarnation, so as not to overthrow human freedom, required the consent of the mother of Jesus to this unique mode of divine indwelling. At the Fall, humankind's original mother had received the promise that one of her descendants would triumph over the evil One (so the Hebrew and the Septuagint, the Syriac and the Old Latin Bible), and in that way the woman herself ("ipsa": Vulgate) would triumph through her seed. There would be a new Eve, a mother of all the spiritually living (Gen 3:15, 20). In the Hebrew of Isaiah, the woman is a maiden, "almah," an unmarried woman; and in the Septuagint, the authoritative Greek translation of the Hebrew Scriptures, this great woman who is to "conceive and bear a son whose name will be called *Emmanuel*" (Isa 7:14) is understood, unmistakably, as a virgin. (Those two concepts were in any case closer in traditional society than after the "sexual revolution" today.)

The teaching of the Catholic Church about Mary of Nazareth, the "Blessed Virgin," takes its rise from both the New Testament and the internal memory of the ancient community. Given the great prominence of the father in the birth narratives of the Bible, and his preeminence in social reality, there is no reason why Matthew and Luke should have wanted to sideline Joseph save under the pressure of reality. Luke, who stresses the parallels between the births of two prophetic children—John the Baptist and Jesus—leaves a gaping hole in the fabric of his literary construction, with the father singled out in one case, absent in the other. In the Creed, accordingly, the Catholic Church confesses the virginal conception of the Word made flesh: he was "born of the Virgin Mary." Sexual generation brings before us man as willing, achieving, creating, and so is unsuited to be the expression of the incarnation, which depends on the grace of God alone, while virginity, by contrast, sums up the helplessness of human beings in the face of God's sovereign grace: our human nature cannot, as such, contribute anything to the coming of the divine Word, now personally enfleshed, into the created world.

The Mysteries of Mary's Preparation

To be the mother of the Savior, Mary needed the special grace of God, indicated by the words of the angel at the annunciation, "Hail, full of grace!" (Luke 1:28), and described in Catholic doctrine as the *"immaculate conception,"* solemnized in the Liturgy on 8 December. Although this dogma was only promulgated in 1852, it is a product of the exploration of a memory, for, as we have seen, the development of doctrine is *anamnēsis*—a process of reactualizing an original awareness. She whom the Greek Fathers termed *Panaghia*, the "all-holy one," shared, from the first moment of her existence, in the saving and sanctifying grace of the only Son of God, he who, by the incarnation, would be her Son also. The Second Vatican Council speaks of the "unique resplendent holiness," coming to her from Christ, whereby she was "redeemed in a more exalted manner" than any other human creature.[1] The medieval Franciscan doctor Duns Scotus called this the *praeredemptio*—Mary's redemption by anticipation which made feasible the historical coming of humankind's Redeemer. The Roman liturgy audaciously applies to Mary a messianic prophecy from the book of Isaiah: Mary is the *radix sancta*, the "holy root" of salvation; through her the incarnation was possible. At the same time, Catholicism regards Mary's past as a clue to humanity's future: in the radically holy virgin is seen the destiny of the virgin mother Church, which is to be "without spot or wrinkle or any such thing . . . holy and immaculate" (Eph 5:27). Pope John Paul II summed up the tradition in his Marian encyclical, *Redemptoris mater:*

> From the first moment of her conception—which is to say of her existence—she belonged to Christ, sharing in salvific and sanctifying

1. *Lumen gentium,* 53, 56.

grace and in that love which has its beginning in the "Beloved," the Son of the eternal Father, who through the Incarnation became her own Son. Consequently, through the power of the Holy Spirit, in the order of grace, which is a participation in the divine nature, Mary receives life from him to whom she gave herself in the order of earthly generation— gave life as a mother. . . . And since Mary receives this "new life" with a fullness corresponding to the Son's love for the mother, and thus corresponding to the dignity of the divine motherhood, the angel at the Annunciation calls her full of grace.[2]

In Mary's immaculate conception, then, she becomes the image of holy Church. The Pope continues, saying that the liturgy salutes Mary of Nazareth as "the Church's own beginning, for in the event of the Immaculate Conception the Church sees projected and anticipated in her most noble member the saving grace of Easter."

In the Old Testament, the more charged with significance election was, the more interior it became. The grace of the elder covenant reached its acme of maximal penetration in Mary's conception by enabling the whole constitution of one Jewess to be transformed by God.

The bull promulgating the dogma of the "all-gracing" of Mary reads in the crucial passage of its doctrinal definition:

> By the authority of our Lord Jesus Christ, of the blessed apostles Peter and Paul, and our own, we declare, pronounce and define that the teaching, according to which, by a singular grace and privilege of almighty God and in view of the merits of Jesus Christ, Saviour of the human race, the most blessed Virgin Mary, from the first instant of her conception, was preserved from all stain of original sin, is a doctrine revealed by God and must consequently be firmly and constantly believed by all the faithful.[3]

As we saw in chapter 6, that "stain," or muddying of the waters of human living, means first and foremost the loss of divine friendship, and with that those gifts—both preternatural and supernatural— which God bestowed on human nature at its origin. But that very unbalancing of the human creature brings with it "concupiscence"—the phenomenon of misdirected desire, in the redeemed the raw material of our necessary spiritual warfare but otherwise the very badge of culpability. Mary, so *Ineffabilis Deus* explains, stands among the redeemed; yet she was redeemed "in a more sublime manner" than the rest of the

2. John Paul II, *Redemptoris mater*, 10.
3. DH 2803.

faithful. As with the other just people who lived before Christ—the saints of Israel and the "holy pagans" who crop up from time to time in the Old Testament's pages are the main examples used in Catholic theology—to her were applied by way of anticipation the merits of the Redeemer. The crucial difference is that the just men and women of ancient times had first contracted the hereditary fault of humanity and were subsequently delivered from it, whereas Mary was preserved from this sin in the first moment of her existence in her mother's womb. Her redemption was not so much deliverance as preservation.

Mary was always adorned, therefore, with sanctifying grace, as an adopted daughter of God, enriched with all the privileges of the state of first innocence—those gratuitous gifts which make up "original righteousness." If in point of fact she lacked some of those gifts (e.g., she certainly suffered, and her body was mortal), these negativities did not flow from original sin, in her case, but from her role as the new Eve, intimately associated with the new Adam. As with Jesus himself, passibility and mortality were not now sinful things. They were less deficiencies contracted than infirmities accepted in view of sin's reparation, humankind's salvation.

There are many ways in Tradition of expressing the immaculate conception. The Fathers and other writers may say that Mary has always been blessed, or enjoyed the grace of God, or that she was justified from the first moment of her conception. More tacitly the doctrine is expressed by saying that Mary is the holiest of all creatures, "more holy than the cherubim and seraphim," the *Panachrantos* or "spotless one," the virgin earth from which the new Adam was formed. Here speaks true radicalism, for the holiness given Mary by Christ reached right down to the roots of her being. From the very first moment of her coming to be, she belonged to him. "To be in the world and yet to be prevented from ever falling under the domination of the world is to be not less but more dependent on Christ our Redeemer."[4] Mary is more thoroughly redeemed than we are, and has the greater cause for gratitude to God in Christ.

In the symbolic thinking of the prophets about their people, "virgin Israel" has been set apart from the world, reserved for Israel's God alone. They called her "virgin" to symbolize her sacredness—her transcendence vis-à-vis all other nations of the earth. She has to do not just with the present age but with the world that is to come through the union of God and

4. H. McCabe, "The Immaculate Conception," in *God Matters* (London, 1987) 212.

humanity. In Mary this union of the Lord with the virgin Israel truly takes place, concentrating the holiness of the people of God in one unique person. The Holy Spirit did not come down out of the blue at the annunciation; he had already taken a radical hold on humankind as redeemed in Mary, just as he would on humankind as Redeemer in Jesus.

Mary's redemption is, then, presacramental—she has Christ in her existence in her very flesh. Accordingly, her redemption is a foretaste of the postsacramental life of the risen body, the world of the kingdom. She is, therefore, as immaculate, the image of our final condition, when there will no longer be any need for sorrow for sin, and we shall at last be fully free.

At the angel's greeting at the annunciation, Mary is declared to be all-enveloped by the divine favor: full of grace *already*, in the moment when the angel arrives, prior to the descent of the Holy Spirit. After Ephesus, and until the end of the Byzantine Middle Ages, the Greeks too (with few exceptions) held that Mary resembled Eve before her sin. Only in the sixteenth century did the idea gain ground that Mary was not "purified" until the incarnation itself. Catholicism holds, however, that she was redeemed in the very moment of incurring original sin. The immaculate conception is a demonstration of what the Greek Fathers so lovingly expounded: the cosmic power of Christ's redeeming death as that stretches both backwards and forwards in time.

Why was the doctrine defined? At a time when in Protestantism (not least in England) the doctrines both of baptismal regeneration and of original sin were under attack (and rejected completely in the increasingly secularized culture beyond the churches), it was a sign to a world full of self-sufficiency and pride. Bishop William Bernard Ullathorne defended the dogmatization of the doctrine in part as the ultimate in counter-culturality, a stumbling-block to give people pause in a society bent on perfection through human effort. In place of endless perfective amelioration through the industrial transformation of nature, exponential growth in commerce, new social arrangements based on ideology or force, rational enlightenment defined as the rejection of traditional wisdom, secular education, and mechanistic schemes of philanthropic improvement, the Church proposed in the foundational grace of Mary's life strength in weakness, stature in humility, glory in purity. She is the "one bright star which, in the universal night of human conceptions, makes the darkness still more visible."[5]

5. W. B. Ullathorne, *The Immaculate Conception of the Mother of God* (Westminster, Md., 1904) 207.

In art, the immaculate conception creates a problem: the iconographer is treating not of a narrative but of the visual representation of a concept. Not till the sixteenth and seventeenth centuries did the iconography of the *Immaculata* achieve a certain stability: the woman of Revelation, complete with crescent moon, solar rays, and a crown of stars; or the Virgin replete with all the symbols of her litanies, notably the *Lauretana*, the litany of Loreto. In Renaissance and medieval times, "immaculist" artists reframed existing Marian images—the tree of Jesse, the embrace of Joachim and Anna—to their new purpose, though often it is only the interrelation of image and text that brings this out. The Flemish manuscript known as the Rothschild Canticles is more transparent: its miniature of the Virgin alone in prayer, clad with the sun, standing upon the moon, gives overwhelming importance to a sun that nearly blots her out. Fulbert of Chartres had hailed the immaculate conception in the words "In gremio matris fulget sapientia Patris" ("From the mother's bosom the Father's Wisdom shines forth"); here the artist stresses how the Virgin had received her immaculate condition from Christ, the Sun of righteousness.

The Church's liturgy celebrates not only Mary's conception but also her *birth*. From the vantage point of the feast, two perspectives open up. First, the Church looks to the Old Testament, the story of mingled grace and shame which makes up the history of Mary's people, summed up in her "family tree," the genealogy, read at Mass on this day (8 September). Through Mary the Christ-child is rooted in this very human soil. Through her, the promises generated by Jewish history can point to him, and a knowledge of these promises is necessary for the understanding of his person and work. Mary links the old covenant to the new, introducing each into the other. But second, on this feast the Church also looks to the future destiny of Mary's child, acclaiming her as the "Gate through which the Light was poured" (as in the hymn *Ave maris stella*), the "exordium of our salvation," the place whence, humanly speaking, our salvation arose. Mary did not just lend her biological functions to God the Word. A mother does more than lend her body as a site for gestation. She builds up her child's life with her own flesh and blood, and forms their souls by her address and affection. Without a perfect mother, no perfect son can be imagined. Nor is calling Mary the matrix of human salvation simply a human *façon de parler*: the story of the immaculately conceived is from the outset a story of what was divinely given. As the mother of God, the Virgin united in her life the creation with its Creator, such that every creature can find in her person the gate of the true life, Jesus Christ.

On 21 November (possibly the dedication day of a Marian basilica in Jerusalem), the Church recalls the tradition, contained in the pseudonymous Jewish-Christian work known as the *Protevangelium of James*, that Mary's mother had promised, should she be fruitful, to dedicate a child to God, and that the infant Mary was indeed welcomed into the Temple of Zion by Zechariah, and dwelt in the sanctuary until she was twelve. Since Zechariah's wife was Mary's kinswoman it is possible that this Jewish priest played a part in her upbringing. But the legend of her living in the Temple's most holy place cannot be historical.

The Byzantine liturgy uses this commemoration to speak of Mary as the true temple: the dwelling place of God incarnate will be, not a shrine made by human hands, but the altar of Mary, the whole woman, body and soul. It likens Mary, on her entrance to the sanctuary, to a sacrificial offering dedicated to God. It takes the story of her *presentation* to represent the entire process of her predestination and preparation to be the mother of the Savior. As the "mother preordained before all ages," the entire history of the old covenant looks forward to her. The great Byzantine doctor Gregory Palamas sees Mary as prepared for her vocation by acquiring that inner depth which is conferred by silence. She is the supreme contemplative. The evangelists stress this, emphasizing her attitude of attentive listening, how she "kept" the sayings she heard (in Luke), and (in John) told those present at Cana to listen to her Son. She understood through stillness, acted out of it, conquered in it. "Her presence in the midst of Israel—a presence so discreet as to pass almost unnoticed by the eyes of her contemporaries—shone very clearly before the Eternal One, who had associated this hidden 'daughter of Zion' with the plan of salvation embracing the whole of humanity."[6] That connection becomes clear in the annunciation.

The Mysteries of Mary's Childbearing

Though the feast of the *annunciation* (25 March) is more centrally a feast of Christ than of Mary, its Marian component is, evidently, essential to it (and justifies the medieval English name, "Lady Day"). Unless Mary was prepared to turn her whole life upside down, by

6. John Paul II, *Redemptoris mater*, 3.

moving in faith toward whatever obscure future God was pressing upon her then the Word could not have become man. Her words to the angel, "Be it done to me according to thy word" (Luke 1:38), are the disclosure of her inner life, her basic attitude to God, and compose a model for how Christians themselves are to live. In Mary's receptive openness to God, we find the secret of living religiously. Here the human creature cooperates in humankind's redemption on the basis of prevenient grace, and to that extent constitutes the principle and type of the Church. This is how Catholic theology would understand the Irenaean doctrine (already encountered in chapter 4) that God made Mary "cause" of our salvation.[7] The Anglo-Welsh lay theologian David Jones draws attention in one of his haunting poetic sequences to the weightiness of that testimony to a high Mariology from a witness only one generation removed from the apostles: "This Irenaeus had known the holy man Polycarp who in turn had known Ieuan Cariadusaf [John the Beloved (Disciple)] to whom had been committed the care and safeguarding of Mair the Mother by the direct mandate of the Incarnate Logos, even when he was going from the terrible stauros [Cross], his only purple his golden bloodflow."[8]

Mary conceived Jesus, then, not only in her womb but also in her heart by faith. Her "fiat" ("let it be so") is discussed by the Fathers in the context of the typology of Eve and Mary. Just as the infidelity of Eve led to death and disaster so the fidelity of Mary led to salvation and life. Eve's disobedience is reversed by Mary's obedience. In the traditional iconography of paradise in the Eastern tradition, the mother of God is shown enthroned, with her Son on her knee, amid the trees and flowers of Eden, alongside Abraham, with Lazarus in his bosom, and the other patriarchs.

In the annunciation Mary stands as exemplar of obedient faith. In classical theology we do not speak of the "faith" of Christ, and the deepest reason for this is given by Cardinal Newman when he speaks of a "range of thought" where Mary, not her Son, is the proper center. Where common creatureliness is concerned, "If we placed our Lord in that centre, we would only be dragging him from his throne and making him an Arian kind of God: that is, no God at all."[9] Jesus remains the One who strides ahead of his disciples; the love and loyalty of their

7. See above, p. 117.
8. D. Jones, *The Sleeping Lord* (London, 1974).
9. J. H. Newman, *Certain Difficulties Felt by Anglicans in Catholic Teaching Considered* (London, 1907) 2:84–85.

heart's devotion can never lose the awe due to One who is different in kind as well as in degree.

"Rejoice," then, says Gabriel to Mary, "O lady full of grace!" (Lk 1:28a). The most memorable texts containing the verb "to rejoice" in the Old Testament signify the joy that comes to the whole people of God when God actively intervenes to deliver them from distress and bring them salvation. Here Mary embodies the corporate personality of Israel, and the language implies that the era of the fullness of grace is come (whereas, for instance, the language used of the parents of the Baptist marks them as saints of the old dispensation). "The Lord is with you" (Lk 1:28b): in the Old Testament these words are addressed to someone for whom God has great plans. Such is certainly the case here, for the Messiah will come to Israel only by coming to Mary. The creative power of God's Spirit will "overshadow" her, descend upon her, as the glory of the Lord had once descended on the tent of witness and filled it with a divine presence. Jesus enjoys divine sonship from the first moment of his conception (it will be manifested later, at the baptism and transfiguration).

In art, the annunciation is associated with two Old Testament figures: Moses and the burning bush, aflame but not consumed, as Mary's creaturehood was on fire with the divine presence; and Gideon, whose fleece received dew from heaven while the rest of the ground stayed dry, a type of Mary receiving the Spirit of God while the rest of the world remained parched by sin. Had Mary been an ordinary lass, the incarnation would still have been possible, but it would have been reduced to the level of a means or tool—a stage on the way to Calvary, with Mary just an instrument, to be cast aside once the need was passed. For the Logos to have an internal relation with his own embodiment in humanity, he had to have an internal relation with the humanity of his mother. And so at the annunciation, the Spirit came upon Mary just as in all eternity he had rested on the Son. As a result, the humanity of the Logos taken from Mary corresponded to, or was fit for, the being of the Logos himself. The annunciation is the Pentecost of the Virgin—but this would not have been possible had she not been uniquely open to the Holy Spirit before the moment of the annunciation itself.

At the *visitation* (2 July), Elizabeth bears witness to Mary, proclaiming that before her stands the mother of the Messiah. The babe in her womb shares this witness, leaping at the approach of Mary big with Jesus. Just so at the Jordan John the Baptist will point out Jesus as Messiah. Elizabeth exclaims in admiration at Mary's faith, "Blessed is she who believed that there would be a fulfillment of what was spoken to her from the Lord" (Luke 1:45). The obedience of faith is given to the self-revealing God: by it Mary entrusts her whole self to God. Mary becomes by the exemplary quality of her faith the mother of all believers in the New Testament, just as Abraham was their father in the Old.

Luke by his choice of language implicitly compares Mary's journey over the Judaean hills from Nazareth to Ain-Karem, the home of Elizabeth, to David's bringing of the ark of the covenant into the citadel of Zion from its resting place in the fields of Yearim. The same exultation and leaping for joy marks the arrival of the glory-seat of the Lord in each case. The Coptic liturgy is particularly rich in its vocabulary for Mary as bearing the glory.

> O blessed among women, you are rightly called the Second Tent, which is called the Holy of Holies, and within which are the Tables of the Covenant written by the finger of God. They signify for us in advance the Iota, the name of salvation, Jesus. He it is who received flesh in you without change and has become the Mediator of a New Covenant. Through the sprinkling of his holy Blood he has purified those who believe into a people that he justifies.
>
> The Ark which was covered with gold on every side was made of imperishable woods. It was made as a sign beforehand of God the Word, who became man without separation. He is one from two, perfect Godhead without corruption, consubstantial with the Father and consubstantial with us according to the economy, sacred humanity without confusion, which he took within you, O spotless one, and was united with it hypostatically.
>
> The Mercy-seat which rested upon the Cherubim forms an icon of God the Word who took flesh in you, O most pure, without change. He became a purification of sins and a pardoner of iniquities.

If Christ is the mercy-seat who rests upon the cherubim, then Mary is herself the cherubim throne, the *Merkavah*. The Syrian hymn-writers thus apply to Mary what the prophet Ezekiel has to say about that throne of Glory, central as it is to Jewish mysticism.

At the *nativity* (25 December), Mary's babe is declared by Luke to be a sign, because he is already preaching humility in his birth: he is already teaching the lesson of Calvary. For the New Testament, signs are not so much surprising events intended to stimulate confidence in a promise as they are things that can condense the gospel message, and so have power to pierce the heart. For the Fathers the manger is the mirror of the Cross.

To declare Mary to be mother of God is to proclaim the humility of God. The preexistent One humbled himself to be a little child. He emptied himself in the sense that he accepted the whole slow development of human life from conception to its last breath. "The Word was made flesh" means he became a woman's tiny baby. "The Word was made flesh, weak flesh, infant flesh, tender flesh, frail flesh, flesh incapable of work or labour."[10] In the words of John the Monk, taken up in the Byzantine liturgy:

> O marvel! God is come among men; he who cannot be contained is contained in a womb; the Timeless enters time; and, strange wonder, his conception is without seed, his emptying is past telling, so great is this mystery! For God empties himself, takes flesh, and is fashioned as a creature when the angel tells the pure Virgin of her conception: "Hail, thou who art full of grace; the Lord who has great mercy is with thee."

The doctrine of Mary's divine motherhood is the foundation of all other teachings of Catholicism about the Virgin. The Council of Ephesus proclaimed Mary *Theotokos*, the "God-bearer," the mother of God, in the course of its effort to preserve the Christian community's sense of the unity of Jesus Christ, at once human and divine. Jesus Christ is so thoroughly one in his Godhead and his manhood that this human mother really did carry in her womb the person of the eternal Word. She conceived one who was personally her own maker and Redeemer. As the Nun's prologue in Chaucer's *Canterbury Tales* puts it, "Thou Maid and Mother, Daughter of thy Son." She gave her own flesh in order that the Creator of all things might be born as a human creature and so know our human experience from inside. She carried, bore, nursed and educated One who in his own person is the almighty upholder of the universe and the all-holy foundation of morals. The medieval Irish poet Blathmac in his hymns to Mary never forgets the divinity of Mary's Son to whom all nature belongs: "Your Son of fair fame owns every bird that spreads wings; on wood, on land, on clear pool, it is he who gives them joy."[11] Nonetheless, she is simultaneously mother of a human child—as the iconography of Mary's breast-feeding, *Maria lactans*, underlines. He on whom all creation hangs hung from the breast of his human mother.

---

10. Bernard, *Sermons on the Nativity* 3.2.

11. J. Carney, ed., *The Poems of Blathmac son of Cu Brettan, together with the Irish Gospel of Thomas and a Poem on the Virgin Mary* (Dublin, 1964) stanza 195, cited in P. O'Dwyer, *Mary: A History of Devotion in Ireland* (Dublin, 1988) 53.

Tradition has much indeed to say in words and in images about the Madonna and Child. John Damascene regards the title *Theotokos* as a compendium of the entire dogma of the incarnation. "The name expresses the whole mystery of the Economy. If she who gave birth is the Mother of God, then he who was born of her is definitely God and also definitely man. This name signifies the one hypostasis and the two natures and the two births of our Lord Jesus Christ."[12] The reference to the two births alludes to the 649 Lateran Synod which had affirmed a birth incorporeal and eternal from the Father before all ages, and another, corporeal and in the last age, from holy Mary, ever-Virgin, the mother of God. The Gnostics had taught that the Word merely passed through Mary "like water in a channel," while for Irenaeus it is only because he receives real humanity from Mary that Christ can "recapitulate" us, sum us up, unite us under himself as head, join us with himself as the new man. We are related to Christ on his mother's side: we are his maternal relations.

The seventeenth-century French spiritual theologian François Bourgoing stresses how Jesus, in Mary's womb, is like every other child in dependence on his Mother for physical life: "Attached to her, like fruit to its tree, taking life from her and growing constantly in and through her."[13] But between any expectant mother and the child in the womb the physical co-presence is the foundation of an interior personal intimacy of knowledge and love. The depth psychologist C. G. Jung identified the qualities associated with the "mother archetype" as motherly solicitude and sympathy, wisdom and a spiritual exaltation that transcends reason, all that is benign, that cherishes and sustains and fosters growth. Though Jung warned against our offloading the whole of this archetype—that "enormous burden of meaning, responsibility, duty"—onto the shoulders of "one frail and fallible human being" who was the "accidental bearer of life for us," the election of Mary means that in her case, thanks to the light and power which was hers from the Holy Spirit, she could be all of this for her child. She mediated to him all the vitality of mother nature, he who was nature's own origin.

Recognition of the fact, and the appropriateness, of Mary's unique holiness came about in the Church before other Marian mysteries were explored. The Gospel of Luke notes her stalwart faith (1:45), profound humility (1:38-55), and prompt obedience (2:5, 22), and the singular

12. John Damascene, *On the Orthodox Faith* 3.12.

13. F. Bourgoing, *Méditations sur les divers états de Jésus-Christ notre Seigneur* (Paris, 1648) 42.

engracing to which these testify make Mary, for Catholicism, the model of both the active and the contemplative lives in the Church.

Yet Mary's holiness is for a wider purpose: it is inseparable from her office. At the annunciation, she represented all humanity, giving her consent to a spiritual marriage between the Son of God and human nature. For this she needed some knowledge of the divine status of her child. This came perhaps in an unarticulated way through a supernaturally illumined understanding of the texts of the Hebrew Bible, referring as these do both to a human mediator and a new presence of the God of salvation: the child that is Emmanuel. Mary's function within the mystical body of the Church was well expressed by the poet Gerard Manley Hopkins. As the bride of the Holy Spirit she brings forth Christ spiritually in human lives by her intercession:

> Merely a woman, yet
> Whose presence, power is
> Great as no goddess's
> was deeméd, dreamed.

Her role in the economy of grace adds the touch of feminine and maternal humanity to the work of her Son:

> Through her we may see him
> Made sweeter, not made dim,
> And her hand leaves his light
> Sifted to suit our sight.[14]

The Mysteries of Mary's Suffering

At the *presentation* of the Child Jesus in the Temple (2 February), the prophecy of Simeon reveals the conflictual or agonistic character of the coming of that kingdom of Christ which was promised at the annunciation. Simeon's words tell Mary of the actual historical situation in which the Son is to accomplish his mission, namely in misunderstanding and sorrow. It is as though a second annunciation by Simeon follows the first by Gabriel, the second revealing the modality in which the first will be achieved. The "sword" that shall pass through the soul of Mary/Israel is disclosed in Revelation as the sword of the word of revelation: coming from the Son of Man, it becomes, by reason of

---

14. G. M. Hopkins, "The Blessed Virgin Compared to the Air We Breathe," in *The Poems of Gerard Manley Hopkins,* ed. W. H. Gardner and N. H. Mackenzie, 4th ed. (Oxford, 1970) 93–97.

people's reactions to it, an instrument of God's judgment. Mary would watch the physical torments and hear the mockery directed at Jesus on Calvary. But in addition she had the sorrow of knowing that the appointed leaders of God's people had refused the message of salvation.

At *Nazareth* Mary was the first to whom the Father chose to reveal the Son. Yet not all was light: the tonality of the Gospels is chiaroscuro. Mary has to live through the night of faith in order to come to true contemplation of her Child. The infancy gospels show Mary as sometimes heavy of heart, baffled by the mystery of her Son's behavior, notably when she lost the twelve-year-old Jesus in Jerusalem. The child must be about the Father's business. Everything in Luke's Gospel leads up to Jerusalem, just as everything in Acts leads away from it. But the mystery of Jesus means a hard school for Mary: this is the first experience of the sword of Simeon. What form her suffering would take she could not know in advance, but the loss of the child Jesus in the Temple, and his uncomprehended avowal that there is where his place must be, provides a premonition of it that the public ministry will confirm.

In John's Gospel, the mother of Jesus is present at the first manifestation of his glory, at *Cana* of Galilee. By that glory, he testified to his "descent" from above and anticipated the hour of his "ascent" which, for John, is not only the ascension but also, and more fundamentally, the lifting up on the cross: the means of his return to the Father in glory. So even at Cana the intermingling of suffering and joy is found. Yet Cana does foreshadow the later spiritual motherhood of Mary, what *Redemptoris mater* terms Mary's "solicitude for human beings, her coming to them in the wide variety of their wants and needs."[15] More specifically, by her motherly solicitude, Mary's brings those needs within the radius of Christ's messianic mission and salvific power. In other words, she acts as a mediatrix, putting herself in the middle between her Son and humankind, not as an obstacle but as a facilitator.

In the Synoptics it is the darkness more than the light that Mary experiences during the *public ministry*. After the start of Jesus' public activity she evidently lived in close contact with relations who, as John reports, did not believe in him (7:3-5). In Mark, they fear indeed for his sanity (3:21). We need not suppose that Mary agreed with the opinion of the family council, but she evidently agreed with their purpose. When she comes with his brethren, he lets her wait outside the door

15. John Paul II, *Redemptoris mater,* 21.

and go home without achieving anything (Mark 3:31-35). In the Marian tradition of the Church, this is her training for the Cross.

The grief-stricken mother *at the cross* is celebrated with a feast of her own (14 September), but also in Lent and Passiontide. In the *Stabat mater,* the sequence of the Roman liturgy for the feast of the Virgin of sorrows, her pain on Calvary is presented as arousing and focusing sympathetic suffering in the heart of the onlooker.

> Come then Mother, the fount of love,
> make me feel the force of your grief,
> make me mourn with you.
> Make me weep lovingly with you,
> make me feel the pains of the Crucified
> as long as I shall live.
> I long to stand with you by the Cross,
> and to be your companion in your lamentation.
> Grant that I may carry within me the death of Christ,
> make me a partner in his passion,
> let me relive his wounds.
> Who is there would not weep,
> were he to see the Mother of Christ in so great anguish?

Here the Western liturgy appropriates the poems in which, in the Book of Lamentations, the weeping woman who is Jerusalem bewails her desolation. Woodcuts of our Lady of pity, in the later Middle Ages, were bordered by the emblems of the passion so that all Christians, in the words of the mystic Margery Kempe, should "think of the doleful death he died for us." François Poulenc's setting of the *Stabat mater* for orchestra and chorus (1950) retains a startling power to place the listener in touch with that event, ending with an alternation of passionate cries and the plea to be admitted, through Mary's intercession, into the glory of paradise. No wonder that Christians have sought to identify with the mother of sorrows. In the poetry of eighth-century Ireland, Blathmac describes himself as seeking out Mary's company so that he may keen with her, and so come to the quality of her response to the Word. "Had I, being rich and honoured, power over the people of the world as far as ever sea, they would come with you and me to keen your royal Son."[16]

In the Book of Revelation we read that "the woman . . . cried out in the pangs of birth" (12:2). Tradition sees this as a reference not to the lit-

---

16. Carney, *The Poems of Blathmac,* stanza 1, cited in O'Dwyer, *Mary,* 49.

eral birth of Jesus but to the interior torments which Mary experienced for his sake—from the annunciation to the resurrection and ascension. Jesus' "birth," therefore, represents his entire earthly life and encompasses, in the perspective of the seer of Revelation, the hidden life *and* the public life, the passion and death *and* the resurrection. The Virgin would not have fully brought forth the Savior unless he had become fully the Savior. According to the redeeming plan, he became so in completeness only with the passion, death, and resurrection. In saying yes to the incarnation of the Son, Mary says yes to his redemptive work, and repeats that yes throughout his life, supremely at the foot of the cross where she is God's privileged *collaboratrix* in the new covenant. Mary standing beside the Crucified is the prophetically envisaged daughter of Zion on the great and terrible Day of the Lord. As *Lumen gentium* puts it, Mary "associated herself with his [Christ's] sacrifice in her Mother's heart and lovingly consented to the immolation of this victim who was born of her." Nor is this a merely passive virtue. On the contrary: such unfailing readiness to surrender herself to the ever-greater demands of her Son's saving mission requires supremely active qualities—generous love, eager obedience. Mary's tears do not flow helplessly, simply in reaction to the tragic historical events in which she was involved. The tears of the *socia Redemptoris*, the "Redeemer's woman-companion," symbolize in a participatory way the purifying sacrifice of her Son, which washes sinners of all stain, and gives them new life.

The Mysteries of Mary's Glorification

Though the Gospels are silent on the matter, there is a tradition in the Church that the mother of Christ was not deprived of an encounter with the risen Christ. In the iconography of the Byzantine Rite, one of the Easter myrrh-bearers is always Mary: as the Easter liturgy has it, "You met the Virgin and granted life." Romanos the Hymnographer witnesses to the same conviction in his *Kontakion* for Good Friday where he has the dying Christ say to his Mother:

> Courage, Mother
> For you will be first to see me come from the tombs;
> I am coming to show you from what pains I have
> ransomed Adam,
> And how much I have sweated for his sake;
> I will reveal it to my friends, showing them the
> proofs in my hands;
> And then, Mother, you will see Eve

> Alive as before, and you will cry out in joy;
> "He has saved my forebears, My Son and my God!"

Because the cross drew forth from Mary an obedience of faith that took the form of a total darkness, a complete self-abandonment of mind and will to the God whose ways are inscrutable, we might expect that the effulgence of the risen Christ would include her first of all—albeit not as a public, legal witness—in its radiance. Such perfect union with Christ in his self-emptying brings in its train a unique insertion into his redemptive victory at its central point.

Made mother of the Church at the cross, when the community of the disciples is entrusted to her care in the person of John, Mary assists the infant Church with her prayers after the ascension (Acts 1:14). In the providence of God, she carries out the functions ascribed to her in the Old Slavonic "promises" of her shrine at Jasna Gora (Czestochowa, Poland): "I am standing by you, I am remembering, I am watching."

Mary was thus present at the beginning of the Church, the start of the Church's pilgrimage through the history of individuals and peoples. It is the conviction of Tradition that her presence was not limited to that, but belongs with the Christian community's whole journey through space and time, notably as that journey is found in the history of souls—the microcosmic inner personal journey which accompanies and helps to compose the macrocosmic public and corporate journey of the Church.

Mary exercises this motherhood most powerfully upon her own *assumption* (15 August) when, at the end of her earthly life, she is raised in her total integrity (body and soul) into glory. The "woman" of Revelation 12 is the mother at once of the almighty messianic child and of his brethren. Pursued by the "dragon," she is nonetheless safe and sound, for the worst that the enemy (sin and death, the "powers of hell") can do has failed to take her in thrall. Even so she remains one with those of her children who are still vulnerable to his attacks, in the warfare that continues on earth. Here we have *in nuce* the dogma of Mary's assumption as proclaimed by Pope Pius XII in 1950.

When the celebration of the assumption began to take shape, its main focus was Mary's falling asleep (*dormition*, from the Greek) in the Lord, her transit or passage to him on her "birthday," the day of her definitive entry into God's life. As soon as the Church emerges from her age of persecution, we find Fathers and other early Christian writers reluctant to ascribe the normal processes of death and corruption to Mary. If the earliest clear reference to her complete bodily redemption comes from Timothy of Jerusalem, writing around 400 (and other fifth-century Marian homilists in the Jerusalem Church show him not to be a sport), the great heresiologist Epiphanius of Salamis was writing even earlier in his *Contra haereses* that whether Mary actually died is unknown. He was aware of various hypotheses about the manner of Mary's "passage" to the Lord, and, committing himself to none of them, is thus an important testimony in the fourth-century Church to a positive tradition, claiming apostolic authenticity, on Mary's *transitus* from earth to heaven. (It is worth noting that all of these authors lived in Palestine, and were necessarily familiar with the tradition of the Jerusalem Church.)

Gradually the mind of the Church pondered these hypotheses and let through its sieve a secondary motif for the assumption celebration: the belief that Mary's body remained untouched by the decay of the tomb. Her flesh, which gave flesh to the Word incarnate, could surely never suffer physical corruption. As soon as Mary died or "fell asleep," she went straight to the Lord in her total personality. Mary, then, enjoys among human beings a unique privilege: not in that she has reached a goal which is not promised to others, but rather in the manner whereby God has brought her to that common goal. Our bodies will decay after death; the completion of our personal redemption is deferred because it is linked to the consummation of God's plan for the whole of his creation. But because of Mary's special place in God's redeeming plan, he brought her redemption to its completion straightaway. There was no sin to obstruct her union with him from the very start of her life. For her extraordinary task the mother of the Redeemer needed to be rescued from sin more than any of us, and so she was from the very outset. Similarly, at the end of her life there were to be no obstacles to prevent the perfect fulfillment of her redemption: not even the need of the material world for reordering, for harmonizing with the final end of humanity.

The assumption means a new intimacy of Mary with Jesus in the kingdom; on this is founded its salvational significance. The Byzantine liturgy sings: "Thy death, O pure Virgin, was a crossing into a better and eternal life. It translated thee, O Undefiled One, from this mortal life to that which knows no end and is indeed divine, and so thou dost look in joy upon thy Son and Lord." This latter note is picked up by the liturgies that employ as the Old Testament lection for the feast of the Assumption a passage from the Song of Songs (2:10-13):

My beloved speaks and says to me: "Arise my love, my fair one, and come away; for lo, the winter is past, the rain is over and gone. The flowers appear on the earth, the time of singing has come, and the voice of the turtledove is heard in our land. The fig tree puts forth its figs, and the vines are in blossom; they give forth fragrance. Arise, my love, my fair one, and come away."

For this "Summer Easter," the Roman Rite makes use of part of an ancient Israelite wedding song, "The queen stands at your right hand, arrayed in gold." Mary stands in glory at Christ's right hand, just as once she stood in humiliation by his cross. Since she remained close to her divine Son, she is taken into his destiny. The assumption draws the final implications from this closeness of Mary to Jesus, which is not a sentimental one but a real moral union working itself out at all levels and leading to a victory over the dehumanizing and disintegrating alien forces at work in the human world, namely, sin and death (as we know it). Mary suffered so intimately with her Son that she equally ultimately reigns with him: this is the logic of Christian salvation. Her standing by the crucified is the necessary and sufficient condition of her standing at the risen One's right hand.

Mary's assumption is not, however, a personal privilege irrespective of any wider function. In the work of salvation there are no privileges without responsibilities, no *noblesse* conferred that does not *oblige*, no sharing in the divine life that does not produce the most characteristic sign of that life: self-communication, self-bestowal. Mary's glorification is in one sense the end of her life, but in another sense its beginning. It is her entry upon her duties in the regime of transfiguration by which the world becomes the Church, sinful humanity the company of the redeemed, and the evil and mediocre are turned into saints. At the assumption, Mary initiates the activity prophesied by her dying Son when he gave her to the infant Church (represented in the last apostle) with the words, "This is your mother" (John 19:27). The assumption is a mystery of hope.

Because of the assumption, we can call on Mary as not only mother of God but also mother of the Church, and call for her to exercise her motherhood with efficacy in our regard, asking that, through her, we may glimpse and be drawn toward the glory in which she is bathed, the radiance of the uncreated love shining out in the face of the risen Son. Mary is called on, accordingly, as advocate, *auxiliatrix, adjutrix, mediatrix,* not to diminish the unique mediation of Christ but to show its power. For Christ's mediation flowers by stimulating participation in itself. The cultus of the Virgin is enormously varied in Catholicism. Its simplest form is a cry for assistance, as in the very early (possibly third-century) prayer *Sub tuum praesiduum:* "We seek refuge under the protection of your mercies, O mother of God; do not reject our supplication in need but save us from perdition, O you who alone are blessed." But it can also take complex forms, as in the Rosary, the "psalter of Mary," where prayers of acclamation and praise (the Our Father, the Hail Mary, the Glory Be) are fused with meditation on the principal events of the lives of Jesus and Mary, the whole being presented via the medieval symbol of the rose—a garland of devotion for the rose without thorn. Where mysticism is concerned, Mary's Rosary is the people's charter. It puts the gospel in a nutshell, and tells of how all can become contemplatives. The least sophisticated and most sophisticated can pray it in different ways, and by it all can become truly simple—looking to God with the prayer of simple regard, as Mary now sees him in her bliss.

Many natural symbols have been pressed into the service of Marian devotion: the moon, in its constancy and hegemony over tides, as in the Norman fisherfolk's prayer, "Veuillez toujours, belle lune"; or the morning star *(Phosphorus Hesperus)* in the *Ave maris stella*—"Bright virgin, steadfast in eternity, Star of this storm-tossed sea," prayed Petrarch. The blue of the sky is Mary's color, the color of light, space, eternity. The pine cone and pomegranate are more earthy symbols of her spiritual fertility and abundance of grace. In Giovanni Bellini's *Pietà,* the Virgin laments over the dead body of her Son, but the icon of sorrow holds the promise of resurrection. Behind her, the winter landscape blossoms with the first flowers of spring.

In heaven, Mary reveals the Church's most profound ambitions, both in the afterlife, when the bride hopes to be reunited, like the new Jerusalem, with Christ the bridegroom, and on earth, where as the messianic community she hopes to hold sway in plenitude of spiritual power. But this power is made perfect in weakness: as Bonaventure remarks of Francis's devotion to Mary (in this as in other respects the type of the Church): "He embraced the mother of the Lord Jesus with indescribable love because, as he said, it was she who made the Lord of majesty our brother, and through her we found mercy."[17]

The concern of the exalted Mary for the people of God is manifested in a number of visions and appearances vouchsafed in the

17. Bonaventure, *The Major Life of Saint Francis* 9.3.

course of Church history. The visions usually designate a new saint by a personal token of his or her communion with the "eschatological icon of the Church," while the appearances sanctify that portion of the earth where it took place with a lasting salvific effect—a kind of "geography of salvation," expressed in the many Marian shrines of Catholicism. These range from the well-known Lourdes, where the Virgin appeared by a cave in the Pyrenean mountains in 1858 to inaugurate a river of healings of the sick, who constitute Lourdes's central figures, to Guadalupe, where a Mexican peasant in 1531 saw the stones of the hillside and the desert cacti bathed in radiance, and heard music sweeter than birdsong as the Virgin approached him, star-crowned and wearing the sash of local women in pregnancy, and impressed her image on his cloak. This century other people and places have made their claim—Akita (Japan), Cua (Venezuela), Kibeho (Rwanda), Zeitoun (a suburb of Cairo), Damascus, and, perhaps best known, Medjugorje in Herzegovina.

Such visions and appearances, however their truth-claims be assessed, add nothing to Catholicism's doctrinal content and the faithful are entirely free in their regard. Indeed, they concern hope more than faith. Their fruit lies in the lives of those who return to prayer, charity, and the practice of community. In themselves they are doubly relative—relative to the capacity of the visionaries to receive them, and relative as well to their ability to express what they receive, for their words are not guaranteed as are those of Scripture. Still, as the leading Catholic student of these phenomena, René Laurentin, has pointed out, the cultivation of doubt per se is not a virtue, and especially when the human record offers its own verification according to the axiom laid down in the Fourth Gospel, "The man who does what is true comes to the light" (John 3:21).[18]

An Archetypal Litany

If humanity is an empty receptacle awaiting the presence of God, then the feminine element (the *anima*) concretely symbolized in woman is the heart of humankind, our most Godward side. Here, in woman, the vessel of humanity opens to receive life. Mary's role, and by inference that of all Christian women, is that of the "maternal feminine": the personification of love, the giver and protector of life, brooding over God's creation in the contemplative space of the heart, and bringing to

18. R. Laurentin, *The Apparitions of the Blessed Virgin Mary Today* (Dublin, 1990) 25.

birth in silence and patience. Just as Jesus' own archetypal significance is seen most clearly in the spiritual fatherhood exercised by the ministerial priest in the Church—a memorial and sacramental sign of Christ the high priest, communicating the mystery of the Son by the ministry of the word and sacraments—so Mary's archetypal significance is seen in the spiritual motherhood carried out by women in the Church, and notably by the women doctors like Catherine of Siena and Teresa of Avila. These are "charismatics," who communicate the mystery of the Holy Spirit as memorials of Mary and signs of the Church in her contemplatively fruitful heart. (In this sense, the nonordination of women to the priesthood is a way of expressing the indispensable and irreducible specificity of femininity.)

However, if Mary's archetypal significance begins in this "maternal feminine," it does not end there. For Mary is not only virgin and mother, she is also companion and *mediatrix*. The litany of Loreto—the most extended Marian prayer of the Latin Church—tries to do justice to each of these in a series of invocations. The first two are easy. The mother, warm, tender, caring, selflessly devoted, her whole being centered on the child is "Holy mother of God," "Mother of Christ," "Mother of divine grace," "Mother of the Creator," "Mother of the Savior," "Loveable mother," "Admirable mother," "Health of the sick," "Refuge of sinners," "Consoler of the afflicted." This mother is also a virgin: "Mother most pure," "Mother most chaste," "Inviolate mother," "Mother still virgin"; and her virginity, not only in its bridal readiness of self-giving but also in its strong independence, is both imaged in terms drawn from the Old Testament—"Tower of David," "Tower of ivory," "House of gold," "Ark of the covenant"—and invoked directly—"Virgin to be revered," "Virgin to be acclaimed," "Virgin most powerful," "Virgin most merciful," "Virgin most faithful."

Mary as companion, a reference to her companionate relation to both Jesus and the Church, is hinted at in "Mother of good counsel," "Virgin most prudent," and (clearly enough) "Help of Christians," as in the co-ruling imagery of "Queen of angels, patriarchs, prophets, apostles, martyrs, confessors, virgins, all saints." Mary's role as a mediator is suggested, finally, by the invocations which refer to her as a means of guidance or communication: "Mirror of justice," "Seat of wisdom," "Spiritual vessel," "Vessel of honor," "Vessel of outstanding devotion," "Gate of heaven." Thus in Mary the multiple forms of feminine consciousness and experience are summed up, and make her the "mystical Rose," a role model for all the daughters of Eve.

The Saints

Our Lady, however important for Catholic piety, is not to be separated from the throng of other saints which surrounds her. The final mystery of the Rosary is often presented as "the coronation of our Lady in heaven and the glory of all the saints." The fellowship of the saints, as persons redeemed, called, and hallowed by God, is indeed the comprehensive aim of the self-disclosure of the three-personed God, especially as the *communio sanctorum* finds its archetypal root in the *communio Trinitatis,* the Trinitarian source which posits its own creaturely image by creation, grace, and glorification.

Communio sanctorum: we have already seen, in dealing with the rites of the Church, how that phrase may have a neuter sense, and refer to the communion of holy gifts which is the sacramental life, with the Eucharist at its center. Now we must turn to its almost equally ancient personalist meaning. On that reading, this clause of the Creed will simply amplify the preceding article on the holy catholic Church. The visible Church of which those now alive on earth are members has further invisible dimensions comprising the holy dead of all ages, what Augustine called *ecclesia ab Abel,* "the Church since Abel [the first just human being]."

> What is the Church but the congregation of all saints? From the beginning of the world patriarchs, prophets, martyrs, and all other righteous men who have lived or are now alive, or shall live in time to come comprise the Church, since they have been sanctified by one faith and manner of life, and sealed by one Spirit, and so made one body, of which Christ is declared to be head, as the Scripture says. Moreover, the angels and the heavenly powers too are banded together in this Church. . . . So you believe that in this Church you will attain to the communion of saints.[19]

But if these words of a fifth-century Church Father living in what is now Romania are to be our cue, we must distinguish between devotion to the holy souls in purgatory (the suffering or sleeping Church: see above, chap. 6) and veneration of the saints strictly so called: the inhabitants of the Church triumphant, the glorified Church.

Veneration of the saints has been and remains one of the issues dividing the Catholic and Orthodox Churches from those of the

---

19. Nicetas of Remesiana, *Explanatio Symboli,* cited in C. P. Caspari, *Kirchenhistorischen Anecdota* (Christiania, 1883) 355–56.

Reformation. For the latter, such veneration is unacceptable, since it appears to detract from the honor due to Christ as the sole mediator between God and humanity. Reformed Christians may admire many saintly people of the past, yet they refuse to give them public cultus and, especially, to ask liturgically for their intercession. Were we to seek an idea which both sums up the Catholic view of the saints and also meets the Protestant objection, we could find it in the concept, already mentioned several times in these pages, of submediation. Christologically, we are familiar with the idea of mediation: God acts by the mediation of his Son, just as humanity responds to him by the mediation of Jesus Christ, thus enabling God's gift of salvation and humanity's reception of it to coincide perfectly, and therefore effectively. But the question then arises, can the mediatory work of the Son made man—a work which, as the Letter to the Hebrews reminds us, goes on throughout time and eternity—itself be mediated? Can God by grace enable other human beings to share in Christ's mediatorial activity so as to become its channels to others? The Catholic view is that such submediation is not only conceptually possible, it is also a familiar feature of Christian experience. Examples would be when people pray for each other "through Christ our Lord," that is, in the power of his high priestly prayer before the Father; or when they take the gospel to others, as agents or instruments of the Word of God, Jesus Christ. That Christ makes other human beings, the saints, into submediators of salvation is a more powerful testimony to what we can call his salvific creativity than would be his simply saving us without any further submediation of his atoning work. Few better ways to understand the cultus of the saints in Catholicism can be imagined than the graphic depiction of its rationale in the medieval Western rood screen. "The saints stood in the most literal sense under the Cross, and their presence on the screen spoke of their dependence on and mediation of the benefits of Christ's passion, and their role as intercessors for their clients not merely here and now but on the last day."[20]

Since Protestants do accept in practice the reality of such submediation by living Christians, and only deny it to the dead, they are saying in effect that the efficacy of Christ's generation of this submediatorial activity is extinguished by biological death. But this goes against the entire thrust of the New Testament's doctrine of the resurrection, which

20. E. Duffy, *The Stripping of the Altars: Traditional Religion in England, 1400–1580* (New Haven and London, 1992) 158.

holds that the continuum of life in Christ, established on the basis of the transfigured biology of Jesus' risen body, is now more fundamental to reality than is the biological continuum by which physical organisms come into being and pass away again, so forming the humus from which other organisms can grow.

Less controversial is the power of the saints to express something of the divine beauty, goodness, and truth. God's goodness is *diffusivum sui*: of its nature it tends to spread itself around. The light of the one Lord Jesus Christ streams out in the endless variety of the lives of the saints, drawing us to them. In each we see some facet of the God-man. But most notably, in the saving events chronicled in the New Testament, the Spirit of God, the giver of all holiness, has come to communicate himself in a new way in the midst of human life. Disciples of Jesus who have opened themselves without holding back to this communication of the Spirit of the Father in the Son are those we call the saints. In the preface of the feast of All Saints, the Church invokes Christ as "the only Holy One in so great an assembly of holy ones." This paradox indicates that the saints show us what pneumatic Christ-life is like.

The saints are not simply those canonized by the Church, persons placed on a list of servants of God whose lives were either the object of acclamation by the Christian people in some place, or (more recently) have met the test of a rigorous official examination (both in the local Church and at Rome, where investigation is made of the candidate's writings, reputation for holiness, and the evidence of miracles occurring in answer to his or her intercession). The Byzantine icon of the resurrection shows the victorious Christ raising up Adam and Eve as representatives of all humanity. "At the root of the Tree of Man, an urn/ With dust of apple-blossom./ . . . On the seventh step down/ The tall primal dust/ Turned with a cry from digging and delving./ Tomorrow the Son of Man will walk in a garden/ Through drifts of apple-blossom."[21] Those whom the Church recognizes canonically as saints are those in whom the Christian people have seen some outstanding manifestation of the single life in Christ which all are graced to share. It is because all are called to be saints that the Church is able to recognize in some an outstanding generosity of response to a universal vocation.

In the reciprocity of the uniqueness of the person and the singularity of his or her self-gift to the Church, the Christian rhythm of indivi-

---

21. G. Mackay Brown, "Good Friday and Easter."

dual and community becomes a real parable of the inner-divine Trinitarian life, but more specifically, the foundation of the theological personality and mission of the saints must lie in the mission of the Son as principal protagonist of the drama of salvation which the triune God is staging in the world. The center of the *vitae sanctorum* is always Jesus Christ in his universally representative mission, yet each life expresses adequacy of response to the personal and thus unique call to discipleship.

> The nature of Christian holiness appears from the life of Christ and of his saints; and what appears there cannot be translated into general theory. It has to be experienced in the encounter with the historical which takes place in the individual case. The history of Christian holiness (which is the business of every Christian since everyone is both sanctified and called to holiness) is in its totality a unique history, not the eternal recurrence of something always the same. Hence this history has its new, unique epochs.
>
> Hence too it must always be newly discovered (even though this takes place within the imitation of Christ who remains the inexhaustible model), and that by all Christians. Herein lies the special task which the canonised saints have to fulfil for the Church. They are the imitators and creative models of the holiness which happens to be right for, and is the task of, their own particular age. They create a new style. They prove that a certain form of life and activity is really a genuine possibility for people. They show experientially that one can be a Christian in the way they have been. They make their type of person credible as a Christian type. Their significance begins, therefore, not just with their deaths. Their death is rather the seal put on their task of being creative models, a task which they had in the Church during their lifetime, and their living-on means that the example they have given remains in the Church as a permanent form.[22]

The saints bring before the eye of the Catholic Christian, tacitly but no less potently for that, numerous wider aspects of the faith. These include the solidarity of living and dead Christians, the unity of the body of Christ over space and time, the presence of the Holy Spirit in the Church as the One in whom is wrought all communion and intercession, and the salvifically mediating power of the humanity of Christ. In the medieval Western text called the *Golden Legend*, a widely diffused work written on the eve of the Protestant Reformation, six rea-

22. K. Rahner, "The Church of the Saints," in *Theological Investigations* (London, 1987) 3:99–100.

sons are given in commendation of the cult of the saints. First, that veneration gives honor to God, since whoever honors the saints necessarily honors as well the One who has sanctified them. Second, we venerate them in order to provide "aid in our infirmity," so that we may deserve their assistance. Third, in celebrating their glory, our hope is augmented. As Augustine remarked of the martyrs: "They really loved this life, yet they weighed it up. They thought of how much they should love the things eternal if they were capable of such deep love for the things that pass away."[23] Fourth, we honor them so as to learn from their example. Fifth, just as the saints rejoice in heaven over our repentance, so it is right that we "make feast of them on earth." Sixth, in worshipping them with the worship of devotion, we honor the whole communion of the Church "for charity makes all to be common." All personal salvational situations before God are reciprocally co-determined, or as the French poet and social commentator Charles Péguy put it: "We must all be saved together! Reach God together! Appear before him together! We must return to our Father's house together. . . . What would he think of us if we arrived without the others, without the others returning too?"[24] The cult of the saints brings before us likewise the ecclesial dimension of eschatology, whether individual or general, as is well brought out in Bede's homily for All Saints Day.

> Brethren, today we are keeping as with one great cry of joy a feast in memory of all God's holy children, his children, whose presence makes earth glad; his children, whose prayers are a blessing to our earth; his chosen ones whose victories are the crown of holy Church; his chosen ones, whose witness is all the more glorious and honourable the more intense was the agony in which they gave it. So our mother, the Catholic Church, spread far and wide over the face of this planet, has learnt in Christ Jesus her Head not to fear shame, nor the Cross, nor death. Not by fighting but by enduring she has breathed into all the noble company of those who came to the starting-post for heaven the hope of conquest and glory which encouraged them manfully to start the race.
>
> Mother Church, how truly blessed you are! The full blaze of God's glory beats down upon you. You are adorned with the blood of victorious martyrs. You are clothed with the virgin whiteness of uncompromised orthodoxy in the faith. There is nothing that you lack. So you too brethren should each one strive to win the one crown or the other: the

23. Augustine, *Sermon* 344.4.
24. C. Péguy, *Le mystère de la charité de Jeanne d'Arc*, ed. A. Béguin (Paris, 1956) 44.

whiteness of purity of faith, or the red robe of suffering for Christ. For in heaven's army peace and war have each their own crown to place on the heads of Christ's true soldiers.

God is very good to us; we can find no words to express his love and care for his own. See how he does not make us wrestle and work for all eternity, nor even for a long time. Instead, he invites us to share in the Christian conflict for but a moment, for this short and fleeting lifetime that is ours. So the work is soon over, but the wages are paid for ever. And when the night of this world draws to its close, in the light of the rising Sun of Easter the saints see the brightness of the true light; and they receive a blessedness which far outweighs the pangs of any torments they could have suffered.[25]

The cult of relics in the Catholic Church is mainly but not exclusively concerned with the relics of the saints. (There are also Christological relics, mainly connected with the instruments of the passion. Supremely, these are staurological [from the Greek *stauros*, a "cross"], namely the fragments of the true cross traditionally held to have been discovered by the archaeological efforts of the empress Helena in 324.) A relic is defined as a sacred object which has been in real contact with Christ or the saints and so recalls their memory. It must possess an objective relation with the body of Jesus in his human life or a relationship of a more of less intimate kind with the saints and blesseds of the Church. The Church recognizes the duty to remove false relics from veneration, though in many cases historicity cannot be ascertained one way or the other—in which case a relic recognized as such by pious custom will generally receive the benefit of the doubt.

Relics are not necessarily vestiges of the bodily remains of a saint. They may also be examples of their clothing, of the objects they used in their daily life, or more biographically significant items like the instruments of their penance or of their martyrdoms. Lastly, there are the so-called representative relics: pious objects that have been placed in contact with their remains. Thus even a mediate relation with a saint or a *beatus* can make an object a relic.

The veneration of the relics of the saints is ultimately founded on two broad principles drawn from biblical revelation. First, the divine plan is to save us not atomistically (individually) but as persons in relation with others in Christ's mystical body, by incorporation into a redeemed community embracing this existence and the age to come into

---

25. Bede the Venerable, *Homily 70, for the Solemnity of All Saints* 1.

whose distinct temporality the saints have been drawn forward. The communion of the Trinitarian persons, Father, Son, and Spirit, which is the source of our creation and sanctification, can (we have seen) only find full reflection in a *communio sanctorum,* a communion of holy human beings. Second, our salvation, thus mediated through the solidarity of redeemed humanity in Christ, does not take place without reference to the body. For Scripture we are essentially embodied souls. The redemptive work of the Son necessarily entailed, therefore, the incarnation of the Logos, his embodiment within the bodily continuum of our interpersonal life, just as the final goal of his mission is the resurrection of the body to life everlasting.

These principles are more to the point than the allusions of the Bible which Catholics have regarded as pointing onwards to the specific practice of the cult of relics. Those would include, in the Old Testament, the ceremonial transfer of the body of the patriarch Jacob from Egypt to Hebron, where Abraham had established his family burial ground, and the belief of the editor of 2 Kings that a revivification took place of someone whose body was laid on the grave of the prophet Elisha. In the New Testament reference is customarily made to the incident of the woman with a hemorrhage in the Synoptic Gospels, for she was healed through touching the hem of Jesus' cloak. Then there is the claim of the author of Acts that God worked wondrous healings through "handkerchiefs and scarves" that had been in touch with Paul's skin. As Paul was still alive this is hardly an example of the relic cult *tout court,* yet it shows how objects that had touched Paul's person were honored and preserved by the faithful.

As so often, Thomas Aquinas best sums up the developed teaching of the Church.

> We are evidently bound to hold in veneration the saints of God as being members of Christ, sons and friends of God and our advocates. And therefore in memory of them we are bound to accord due honour to other relics, and this is primarily true of their bodies, which were the temples and instruments of the Holy Spirit dwelling and acting within them, and which are to be made like the body of Christ by glorious resurrection.[26]

So while we should hold dear every memorial of the saints as *aliquid ad sanctos pertinens,* "something belonging to them," we should regard

---

26. Thomas Aquinas, *Summa theologiae* 3.25.6.

as holy and holy-making the bodies of the saints, which are more than the former, being *aliquid sanctorum,* something of the saints themselves.

The communion of saints is rooted in the places where people have lived and seen the glory of God shining out in the common light of every day. There is a geography of the holy places, where the saints have dwelt: Avila and Athos, Iona and Assisi, Rome and Lisieux. Those who have been constantly with God become rather freer of time and space than others. Holy places remain full of a timeless presence, from which the rest of the Church benefits by pilgrimage and devotion.

This may be then a good point at which to mention the Catholic practice of making pilgrimages, not indeed only to the shrines of the saints, but also to those of our Lady, and—above all—the holy places of Palestine, sanctified by the Lord's own footsteps. Pilgrimage has a symbolic value: it is a lived metaphor of the whole of life as consecrated, a journey towards God's kingdom—as sources as diverse as *Piers Plowman* and the pilgrimage paintings of Hieronymus Bosch attest. It also has a practical religious value, providing a share in the graces of renunciation and discipline which those professional ascetics who are faithful to their calling typically receive. Finally, it provides an opportunity to review one's life, by way of a temporary release from ordinary norms and constrictions. The abandonment of known structures for a situation where such structures are absent, and the consequent release of spontaneous fellow feeling, are part of the enduring appeal of the experience of pilgrimage in settled societies.

11

The Cosmic Setting of Salvation

The setting of salvation is the realm of nature, the created world. For Catholic faith, this includes a dimension little thought of in ecology: the realm of the angels.

The Natural World

We are surrounded by an amazingly vast and delicately structured universe of which our more immediate environment, our "world," forms a part. The medieval English poet William Langland said, "Go to the giant Genesis and the engendering of all things." The Church Fathers, who anticipated this advice in their commentaries on the *Hexaemeron*, the biblical narrative of the creation, read Genesis with one eye on a mosaic of cosmologically relevant passages from both Testaments. These included not only the revelation of the divine name as "I am who am" (Exod 3:14)—the leitmotif of what has been termed the "metaphysics of Exodus" (3:14), making possible an account of finite being in its relation to him whose being is Being itself—but also the affirmation of the author of Wisdom that the Creator "has disposed all things in measure and number and weight" (11:21). For a Father like Augustine, measure, number, and weight (or order, *ordo*) are ontological principles interwoven into the very make-up of the cosmos, thanks to the nature of the creative act which leaves inscribed there a regularity, measurability, and interconnectedness that make the world a *vestigium Dei,* a trace or vestigial sign of the superintelligible Being of God himself.

This is remarkably relevant to modern natural science which, in probing the intricacies of physical reality, allows certain general patterns to emerge. The universe moves towards ever-greater complexity and diversification, with fresh entities—bearers of new properties and potential—emerging in interrelationships which both help to characterize those entities and also provide the environmental net in which further development can occur. Despite the staggering variety of the material world a unity pervades it because the same structures—atomic, molecular, genetic—enter into all entities and organisms. The panorama of the cosmos, where, within a quartet of fundamental forces—gravitation, electro-magnetism, and "weak" and "strong" nuclear reactions—billions of stars have sent out, in their death-throes, heavier elements as spores to seed new stars and planets, fills the mind (more fully than Kant could have known) with wonder and awe. As the mathematical physicist Roger Penrose has remarked, things at least seem to organize themselves somewhat better than they ought to, were one to consider only blind chance or a combination of evolution and natural selection.

Natural science also points negatively to the creative act thanks to its own inability to provide what the Jesuit astronomer William Stoerger has called "a theory of everything." Such hypotheses as unified field theory and the thesis of the initial boundary of the universe fail in their attempt at total explanation by having always to relate everything to something rather than nothing—to what already has a potentiality to begin the cosmic process and to account for that potentiality's actualization. The origin of the initial supreme symmetry of the cosmos, for instance, and the laws that govern its devolution into lower symmetries, always eludes the researcher. Thus, while the deliverances of natural science chime with, and even disclose, the basic theological idea of creation, the creation event itself is jealously hidden.

Not only is the Judaeo-Christian tradition indebted to modern natural science; it also helped to generate it. Contrasting that tradition with the predominant cosmological assumptions of antiquity, Peter Hodgson has written:

> Into this world of cyclic despair the Judaeo-Christian revelation of the one omnipotent God, creator of heaven and earth, came like a thunderbolt to shatter the dreary enslaving mechanisms of cosmic pessimism. The Incarnation of Christ was a unique event, decisively dividing the past from the future. Through belief in the only-begotten Son, there developed a vivid consciousness that the universe could not be a *begetting*, that is, an eternal and necessary emanation from the "divine" principle. Consequently, there emerged a broad cultural consciousness about a universe as a *created* entity with a clear beginning and a definite end, a

world of purpose, of freedom, of decision, of achievement. The world is rational because it was made by a rational God. It is contingent because it is the result of a free choice which the Creator made among an infinite number of possibilities.

Its workings are open to human minds because these are also the work of God, who told us to master it and use it in his service. Thus we can see that science was born in Christian Europe because the Christian revelation prepared the way by saturating the European mind with just those specific beliefs that are essential to the very existence and flourishing of science.[1]

We have spoken above of the way emerging physical structures provide the basis for the new property of livingness, and emerging biological structures likewise for the new property of intellectual livingness, the rational soul. To speak of "providing the basis" rather than "explaining" is only prudent. A particular difficulty attaches to explaining the evolution of the first replicating system equipped with stored information to control its own living processes. No one has yet encountered DNA (deoxyribonucleic acid) set up in its own shop outside an organism. The origin of life, the origin of sensation and consciousness, and the origin of human intellectual faculties beyond the ken of the rest of the animal species: these are the three points where there is need to posit an intelligent directing of the course of evolution. Newman commented: "Mr. Darwin's theory need not then be atheistical, be it true or not; it may simply be suggesting a larger idea of Divine Providence and Skill."[2] As it happens, those "three points" correspond to the presence within the world of inorganic ("inanimate") matter of three life principles, each higher than its predecessor. Aristotle had already identified them as vegetative soul, sensitive soul, and intellectual soul.

It is of course in respect to the last that the question of origin has maximum ethical and spiritual significance. For if it is by chance that intelligent beings have arisen (as the pure Darwinian form of evolutionism would maintain), then quite apart from any questions about how the powers of understanding, thinking, and self-reflection could have arisen from matter alone, this would or at least should fundamentally alter our view of human beings. If human beings are neither

1. P. Hodgson, "The Significance of the Work of Stanley L. Jaki," *Downside Review* 105 (1987) 263.
2. C. S. Dessain, et al., *The Letters and Diaries of John Henry Newman* (London, 1973) 24:77.

intended nor have an end, they should not look for either purpose or meaning in their lives. Thinking we are unintended must affect our view of the value and thus the dignity of any human being.

The existence of culture, reason, creativity, freedom, and religion marks off human life from animal, and gives us reason to expect a discontinuity not only of end but also of beginning. The radical distinction between the first humans and their hominid parents may be biologically unexpected, yet biologists have not regarded as impossible the notion that one couple could be the source of an entire population.

The prescientific character of the biblical form which encloses the revelation to Israel of God as, precisely, Creator ensured that the creation story's account of the cosmos was not separated from its account of the human world—the world as it appears to us. Save for such pure scientists as astrophysicists, such a cosmology of the environment remains of paramount interest for human beings, since it deals with the world as it can be experienced directly. It concerns, in other words, the meaning of both human beings and nature, and the relation which the one possesses to the other.

The doctrine of creation has it that the natural world originates in a sovereignly free act of an all-loving God. The doctrine of the incarnation goes on to maintain that this God became, in the person of his Word, his eternal self-expression, an integral part of his own creation— thus displaying not only matter's capacity for expressing God but also, and more profoundly (since this was an act, above all, of his own overflowing charity), the love with which he views the work of his hands. While the primary object of God's self-incarnation into the world of nature was human beings, and their redemption, such apostles and Fathers of the Church as Paul and Irenaeus did not hesitate to find a secondary objective for the redemptive incarnation in the transfiguration of the nonhuman world as well.

In the Genesis creation account, the Priestly source, before telling us that men and women are given dominion over all creatures, insists that they are themselves created in God's "image and likeness." The human rule over creatures is not to be autonomous, much less libertine; it is subject to God's dominion over all things. Similarly, in the Yahwist version, man's duty to till and keep the garden of the world, and to name all other living creatures, is related to the unique distinction whereby he alone of all creatures, endowed as he is with the power of decision, can dialogue responsibly with God. Thus the human being, set by God in the midst of creatures, and given possession of them, must deal responsibly with them, because through them he will enter into responsible relation with their, and his, Creator.

> The formative theological descriptions of the prelapsarian world strongly suggest that human beings are to be stewards rather than despoilers of nature. God puts Adam in a position of dominance, and he allows Adam to use nature for the fulfilment of his needs; but God intends Adam to learn moral lessons from the structure of nature and from the behaviour of animals.
>
> A careful reading of Basil and Ambrose, Augustine and Bede allows us to construct an ethic of cooperative partnership with nature. As Genesis makes plain, it is only with the corruption of the human will that the earth withdraws itself from the benign symbiosis that had characterised the prelapsarian world. Adam and his progeny must restore perfection both through the labour of the hands and through the reshaping of moral character.
>
> However, the restoration of perfection need not have as its means or goal the exploitation of nature. Even if it were unambiguously true that Genesis supported an ethic of human domination, it is by no means clear that this ethic need sanction a destructive attitude toward nature. The control of nature may be accomplished through the use of tools that extend human capabilities and put to efficient use the powers inherent in nature, rather than through machines that pit the inventive powers of man against nature. Indeed, ethnological studies of primate tool use suggest that *homo faber* might have been content to use nature's forces, including the body's own organic potential, in order to develop tools that enhance the ability of human beings to live within a particular ecology.[3]

For, while God is disclosed personally only through the human being, his "icon" in the temple of the world, his glory and power are also manifested in other creatures as well. For the Old Testament, God's Word is effectively active in all created reality; his life-giving Spirit moves over the face of the waters, renewing that earth which the glory of the thrice-holy Lord of Hosts (Isa 6:3) so abundantly fills. Nothing of creation, then, is to be sundered from the history of salvation which the Scriptures describe. "From the greatness and beauty of created things, there comes a corresponding perception of their Creator" (Wis 13:5). Just as Israel enjoys a ministerial role among the nations so, more widely, human beings act as priests of the world. In

---

3. S. Ovitt, Jr., *The Restoration of Perfection: Labor and Technology in Mediaeval Culture* (New Brunswick and London, 1987) 85–86.

them the Word of God is addressed to creatures, and in them too, through worship, the mute praise of their existence becomes vocal. The more human beings walk in the "paths of the Lord," in faithfulness to his covenant, the more they can sing with all creation, like the three young men in the fiery furnace of persecution, the praises of God (Dan 3:57-81).

Ancient Israel shared with neighboring cultures a belief in a divinely willed order which in a harmonious way links heaven with earth. Fr. Robert Murray has summed up the features of a widespread, if often subterranean, belief in this "cosmic covenant" in the Hebrew Bible under six headings: the binding of the cosmic elements by a covenantal oath, the breach of this covenant by rebellious spirits, its reestablishment by God in an "eternal covenant," the earthly effects of any breach of the cosmic covenant, the ritual preservation of cosmic and heavenly order, and an ideal picture of the cosmic harmony between humans and animals.[4] In Jeremiah, the Lord speaks of his "covenant of daytime and night, the statutes of heaven and earth" (33:25) as a paradigm for the covenant with the house of David, on whose basis the Messiah is to be born. The society over whose religion the kings of Judah ruled felt a need not merely to celebrate in word but to act out in symbolic ritual God's control of the world's terrifying cosmic forces. The covenant was disrupted by human beings, but also by higher beings with whom they were associated, and the consequences spread through both nature and society. But in the mystery of the Flood and its appeasement God restores the covenant of cosmic harmony in the promise made to Noah: "While all earth's days endure, seedtime and harvest, cold and heat, summer and winter, day and night shall never cease" (Gen 8:22).

For Murray, just as comparison proves that much of Israelite law coincides with Semitic common law, so biblical ideas of order and disorder, how they are caused and how repaired, show certain strands in Israelite ethics which agree with much ancient thinking on "natural law." The king had to maintain balance and harmony in society, just as God did in the cosmos, and an infringement of the one order might bring in its train the divine suspension of the other. Moral disorder is the inversion of those structures and relationships which keep society in harmony with the cosmic order. Moreover, the Jerusalem Temple

---

4. R. Murray, *The Cosmic Covenant: Biblical Themes of Justice, Peace, and the Integrity of Creation* (London, 1992).

bore a cosmic significance, befitting the place where God's justice ("rightness")—in all its senses of cosmic order, religion, justice, and peace—was praised.

The first chapter of Genesis, in portraying the divine Creator as a transcendent king whose viceroys are human beings made in his image and likeness, implies that the rule over other creatures conferred on the human being is in the pattern of such ideal kingship. The Wisdom of Solomon portrays its royal author as praying to the God "who by your wisdom formed man, to have dominion over the creatures you have made, and to rule the world in holiness and justice, and pronounce judgement in uprightness of soul—give me Wisdom, who sits by your throne" (9:2-4). When God warns Noah, the only human being who has not corrupted the divine image, to save not only his family but also representatives of all other land animals and birds, we see both God's and Noah's concern for the latter (though that theme is not greatly developed). Isaiah's poem on the paradise where the wolf is at home with the lamb (11:1-9) led Philo to imagine the wild animals returning to Adam, from whom they had been estranged, ready to recognize his sovereignty once again.

All of this has implications for the treatment of animals. Proverbs 12:10 states, "The righteous knows the soul of his cattle," that is, feels for the nature of his animals. The Torah's prohibition on killing the young of beasts on the day of their birth is probably to be ascribed to the "impiety" of giving needless suffering to their mother (whose milk, Philo remarks, will remain painfully within her rather than nurturing life, as was its purpose). Again, the ban on boiling a kid in its mother's milk forbade the pious Israelite from bringing death into shocking contact with the source of life, offending against due piety towards the Maker of beasts. Maternity in animals symbolizes divine care for life. The Law also requires certain forms of assistance to animals—partly as a question of property rights, but also by virtue of what the Talmud will term the duty of relieving the "suffering of living beings." The psalms praise God for his care of all creatures (especially 104; 145; 147), and see all creatures as themselves praising God by their sheer existence (148; 96; 98). At Nineveh, rebuking the angry Jonah, who has been deprived of the satisfaction of seeing his message of doom come true, the Lord invites him to attend, among other things, to all the animals in the city; these are the words on which the Book of Jonah ends. Even young fruit trees are the object of the Law's solicitude, ascribed by Philo to the Lawgiver's kindness and graciousness.

Nor is this perspective abandoned in the New Testament, where the fullness of God, dwelling in Christ, is said to be communicated to all creation through him and his body, the Church. As bearers of Christ's image, Christians, accordingly, are not to act toward creation in a way that betrays Christ's creative and sustaining lordship over all things.

Some exegetes have seen in Mark's testimony that in the wilderness temptations Jesus was "with the animals" a hint of the Messiah as center of a restored paradise, a new Adam (as Paul will explicitly call him). An early Syriac homily says, "He went about with the animals, which knelt and worshipped him; and the angels praised him on earth as in heaven."[5] Certainly in his preaching Jesus turned frequently to the animal and vegetable creation for his images, as well as reaffirming God's care for lilies and sparrows. Paul speaks of how the whole creation is groaning in travail until its final redemption (Rom 8:18-23): the thought appears to be that the divine healing will flow to all creation, repairing its unity and enabling its nonhuman members somehow to share in the blessings of the adopted sons of God. And in the history of sanctity in the Church, the Christian inheritance of the kingly function of Christ has entailed a call to share in the making of the new earth (as well as the new heaven).

> Again and again, from Syria and Egypt to Ireland and Northumbria, we find stories of ascetic saints being trustfully approached by wild animals or birds, and thereafter living in friendship with them; these stories are recounted not merely as wonders but with a sense that these saints showed the possibility of re-building a harmony that had been broken. Even in a world where hunting and killing wild animals was the normal state of affairs, the popularity of these stories shows a wistful admiration, even an implicit yearning, for the integrity of creation.[6]

As Helen Waddell, translator of such *legenda* as Pachomius and the crocodiles, Columba and the white horse, Cuthbert and the otters, Brendan and the sea monsters, says, these are stories of the "mutual charities" between saints and beasts.[7] The iconography of Christ as Orpheus, surrounded by animals and birds in a creation reharmonized by the "instrument" of the gospel, points in the same direction.

---

5. Pseudo-Ephrem, *Sermons for Holy Week* 1.95–96, cited in ibid., 7.
6. Murray, *Cosmic Covenant*, 146.
7. H. Waddell, *Beasts and Saints* (London, 1934).

In this respect, Catholic doctrine sees Christ as enjoying two roles: as the preexistent Christ, the Logos (protological) and as the Christ of the paschal mystery, the victor over sin and death (eschatological). As Paul's Letters to the Colossians and Ephesians make clear, in Christ all was created as in the supreme center of unity, harmony, and cohesion. He is the meeting point at which all the generating forces of the universe are coordinated in view of the end which only he can reveal. In the catacomb of Callixtus at Rome, artists learned this lesson well: on the ceiling of a cell Christ is depicted as the center of a cosmos symbolized by winds blowing in from every corner of space. But the Christ of the beginning is also the Christ of the end. Not only the Alpha, he is also the Omega, consummating the evolutionary movement of the universe in his own paschal triumph, which is the anticipation of the end of all things. Karl Rahner wrote, of the relation between the Easter Lord and the world of matter:

> Jesus himself said that he would descend into the heart of the world (Mt 12:40), into the heart of all earthly things where everything is linked together and is one, where death and futility hold sway in the midst of this consolidation. Down into death he has penetrated. He let himself be conquered by death—holy stratagem of eternal life—so that death would gulp him down into the innermost depths of the world. In this way, having descended to the very womb of the earth, to the radical unity of the world, he could give the earth his divine life forever.
>
> Because he died, he belongs all the more to the earth. For when the body of a man is embedded in its grave of earth, the man (his soul, we say), even though in God's immediate presence after death, enters all the more into definitive unity with that one mysterious basis in which all spatial and temporal things are linked together, and the soul lives on, as from its root. By this death the Lord has descended into this lowest depth. Now he is there; futility and death are there no longer. In death he has become the heart of this earthly world, the divine heart in the innermost heart of the world. And here the earth, "behind" her continual development in space and time, sinks her root into the power of the almighty God.
>
> Christ has risen from this one heart of all earthly things where realized unity and nothingness were no longer distinguishable. He has not risen for the purpose of departing once and for all from that heart of the world. He has not risen so that the travail of death which brings him forth anew might so bestow upon him God's life and light that he would leave behind him the dark womb of the earth, hopelessly barren. He has risen in his *body*. And this means that he has already begun to transform

the world into himself. He has forever taken the world to himself; he is born anew as a child of this earth. But it is now an earth that is transfigured, an earth that is set free, that is untwisted, an earth that is established forever in him and that is forever redeemed from death and from futility. He rose, not to show that he had forsaken the grave of the earth, but to prove that he has definitively transformed even this grave of death—body and earth—into the glorious, immeasurable dwelling of the living God and of the God-filled soul of the Son.[8]

In this daring speculation, Rahner could presuppose a highly positive account of creatures in the Catholic tradition. "The earth on which mankind lives in Jesus Christ" (wrote Cardinal de Bérulle) "is a new centre of the universe to which every spiritual and bodily creature tends."

The Fathers, thanks to their combined Platonist and biblical inheritance, see creatures as reflecting the eternal and unchanging exemplar by sharing in his goodness, beauty, and wisdom, albeit at a level which is only a distant echo of the infinite One. Origen of Alexandria writes that "Our mind cannot behold God as he is in himself, therefore, it forms its conception of the Creator of the universe from the beauty of his works and the loveliness of his creatures."[9] Consonant with both the biblical doctrine of the human being as made in the image of God and the Platonic idea of the human being as a microcosm of the greater world, Gregory Nazianzen can say of this unique creature:

> The Creator-Word . . . fashions man, taking a body from already existing matter, and placing in it a Breath taken from himself . . . as a sort of second world, great in littleness, he placed him on the earth, a new angel, a mingled worshipper, fully initiated into the visible creation, but only partially into the intellectual, king of all upon earth, but subject to the King above; earthly and heavenly, temporal and yet immortal, visible and yet intellectual; in one person combining spirit and flesh.[10]

For Basil the Great, our symbiosis with nature means that we have been welcomed into the embrace of all creatures and, through them, receive "visible memorials of (God's) wonders." It is *with* creatures, symbiotically, that we must manifest God's glory.

Not that the patristic view of nature always rhapsodized on so exalted a metaphysical plane. In *Adversus Marcionem* Tertullian does not

---

8. Rahner, *The Eternal Year,* 90–91.
9. Origen, *On First Principles* 1.1, 6.
10. Gregory Nazianzen, *Orations* 45.7.

neglect, in praise of the cosmic creation, "a single tiny flower from any hedgerow . . . a single shellfish from any sea . . . a single stray wing of a moorfowl."[11] Gregory of Nyssa notes in his *De virginitate* an ill-matched pair of horses pulling at the shafts unevenly, and the ripples on a pond's surface moving centrifugally when a stone disturbs it.[12]

Still, it is not primarily for exact observation that we turn to the Fathers. For the ninth-century Irish Platonist Eriugena, each thing is a symbol whereby God makes himself known to us, while in Alain of Lille's *De planctu naturae* (twelfth century), nature presents herself as the source of fecundity, order, and beauty—yet, referring to God, she is made to say: "His operation is single, mine is manifold; his work is self-sufficient, mine is self-undoing . . . he makes, and I am made; he is the workman whose work I am . . . he works with nothing, I beg for a matter with which to work; he works in his own name, I work in the name of God."[13] The Franciscan Scholastic Bonaventure drew the obvious conclusion: "Open your eyes . . . alert the ears of your spirit, unlock your lips, and apply your heart that you may see, hear, praise, love and adore, magnify and honour your God in every creature, lest perchance the entire universe rise against you."[14] And Bonaventure's outburst must be related to that of his "seraphic father," Francis.

The greatest Catholic statement of ecological cosmology is the "Canticle of Brother Sun" by Francis of Assisi. Firmly grounded in orthodox doctrine, it was written after a mystical experience in which Francis was promised that he would attain eternal life; its verses on forgiveness and suffering (23–26) were added in the context, some weeks later, of a feud within the community of Assisi, and the whole poem was first chanted at a meeting between the bishop and the *podestà* (temporal ruler). It contains, then, metaphysical, mystical, and ethical aspects fused into a unity of thought and sensibility. Verses 27–31 were written just before the saint's death in October 1226, thus producing the following text:

I   1   Most high, all-powerful, good Lord.
       2   Thine are the praise, the glory and the honour and every blessing.

---

11. Tertullian, *Against Marcion* 1.13.
12. For these and other references see D. S. Wallace-Hadrill, *The Greek Patristic View of Nature* (Manchester and New York, 1968).
13. Alain of Lille, *On the Lamentation of Nature,* "Natura Alano loquitur."
14. Bonaventure, *The Journey of the Mind to God* 1.15.

II	3	To thee alone, Most High, they are due,
	4	and no man is worthy to mention thee.
III	5	Be praised, my Lord, with all thy creatures,
	6	above all Sir Brother Sun,
	7	who is day and by him thou sheddest light upon us.
IV	8	And he is beautiful and radiant with great splendour,
	9	of thee, Most High, he bears the likeness.
V	10	Be praised, my Lord, through Sister Moon and the Stars,
	11	in the heavens thou has formed them, clear and precious and beautiful.
VI	12	Be praised, my Lord, through Brother Wind,
	13	and through Air and Cloud and fair and all Weather,
	14	by which thou givest nourishment to thy creatures.
VII	15	Be praised, my Lord, through Sister Water,
	16	who is very useful and humble and precious and pure.
VIII	17	Be praised, my Lord, through Brother Fire,
	18	by whom thou lightest up the night,
	19	and he is beautiful and merry and vigorous and strong.
IX	20	Be praised, my Lord, through our Sister Mother Earth,
	21	who sustains and directs us,
	22	and produces diverse fruits with coloured flowers and herbs.
X	23	Be praised, my Lord, by those who pardon for thy love,
	24	and endure sickness and trials.
XI	25	Blessed are they who shall endure them in peace,
	26	for by thee, Most High, they shall be crowned.
XII	27	Be praised, my Lord, through our Sister Bodily Death,
	28	from whom no man living can escape.
XIII	29	Woe to those who die in mortal sin.
	30	Blessed are those whom she will find in thy most holy will,
	31	for the second death will do them no harm.
XIV	32	Praise and bless my Lord,
	33	and give him thanks and serve him with great humility.[15]

As the early Franciscan source called *The Mirror of Perfection* explains, Francis was moved to write the canticle both by a sense of gratitude to God for creation and through sadness at the misuse of creatures "in whom the human race much offends their Creator."[16] While the

---

15. As translated by the late Eric Doyle, in his short study, "The Canticle of Brother Sun," *New Blackfriars* 55 (1974) 392–402. For its interpretation, see R. D. Sorrell, *St. Francis of Assisi and Nature: Tradition and Innovation in Western Christian Attitudes towards the Environment* (New York and Oxford, 1988).

16. *Mirror of Perfection* 100–101.

poem's main concern is to praise God as Creator, its chief originality lies in its presenting the world as a vast friary where each brother and sister holds a unique and indispensable place. From Brother Christ this cosmic friary extended via Francis's human brethren to brother wolf and to his sisters, the swallows and hooded larks. His love extended to embrace the strong brother fire, who lights up the night, and the humble, pure, and useful sister water, as well as sister moon and brother sun. Francis is linked here to his later disciple Duns Scotus because he affirms in this canticle the never-to-be-repeated identity of every creature in nature, the *haecceitas,* "thisness," of things, what Hopkins would call their "inscape." As Francis presents matters, while things are indeed useful, nature has a meaning and value of its own, as created by God. Brother fire is beautiful and merry, vigorous and strong, and not simply an aid to human beings.

A sense of wonder at the beauty, mystery, and fascinating intricacy of nature is part of the Catholic ethos: in the philosophy of Thomas, the science of Albert, the romance of Wolfram, the carving of, say, leaves of thorn and maple in a great mediaeval church like Southwell Minster. The scale of being is the splintered image of the fullness of being. But all is led back ultimately to the Lord of the cosmos who became one of his own creatures so as to transfigure all: the "Elder Brother and Firstborn of all creation, who came to cast fire on the earth and to give us waters that well up into springs of eternal life, the unconquered Sun of Justice and Only-Begotten of the one Father of heaven and earth." This raises the question of the sense in which, for Catholic doctrine, the universe is itself, like humanity, fallen and to be redeemed. Here *fallen* and *redeemable* can only be analogous terms. Yet we can say that a universe which has known, in human sin, an upsetting of its own internal order, is to some degree disintegrated. Material things' "obediential potency" to a human activity which should perfect them remains frustrated in a world where people are unable to control either themselves or their environment in a way that chimes with the will and way of the Creator.

It seems indeed that, as Margaret Atkins has written, the contemporary ecological movement needs a theistic (as in Judaeo-Christianity) not a pantheistic (as in, for instance, "new age" spirituality) basis.[17] In the first place, only belief in a Fall can ground a conviction that things could be—were meant to be—better. In the sec-

17. M. Atkins, "Flawed Beauty and Wise Use: Conservation and the Christian Tradition," *Studies in Christian Ethics* 71 (1994) 1–16.

ond place, judgment about the value of other creatures and about our failings in their regard has to be grounded in appeal to the higher order—of that which ought to be—as the apparently irresolvable differences between animal rights theorists and environmental ecologists (both working within a humanistic framework) show. The former exploit the idea of kinship with human beings, stressing evidence that points to a capacity for self-determination, or at least subjectivity, in certain animals, or (if they are utilitarians) the capacity for pleasure and suffering. But such commentators find it hard to "draw a line": for instance, why, on this view, should a plant matter? Ecologists, on the other hand, criticize the anthropocentric starting-point, which treats other creatures as incomplete humans. Surely other beings should be valued precisely in their distinctiveness, for they have their own existence and excellence. Thus conservationists tend to value highly non-anthropomorphized ecological systems for qualities such as integrity, stability, and variety. Both approaches raise the question of a ground of values, a ground that is nonsubjective and enables us to posit a good end or proper goal for this vast range of creatures, such that their flourishing is something we must respect for itself. For Catholic theology, it is because the wider world is a sketch of the ideas in the mind of God that we can see its point and at times disregard our own private interest in its favor. The fasts and feasts of the Church, if entered into in the right spirit, induce a proper sympathy for the cosmos. Eating is integrated with prayer, and by liturgical action—one thinks of the Byzantine Rite's blessing of water on the feast of the Theophany, or of grapes on the feast of the Transfiguration—we share with Christ in the gathering in and benediction of a scattered creation. The Word's entry into the world with the incarnation, and his provision in the resurrection of a new outflow of the Holy Spirit grants the material cosmos a new possibility of perfection and harmoniousness. The final gathering-together of the universe can only be in Christ, the perfect image of the Father who represents not only the Father himself but all creatures, flowing as they do from that same Word. Inevitably, then, the cosmos, beautiful with creation's radiance, yet groaning with the travail of salvation, forms the wider temple in which the Church's liturgy is celebrated—a point well made in the Saunders Lewis's poem *Ascension Day*.

> What's going on in the hills, this May morning?
> Look at it all, the gold of the broom and laburnum,

The shoulders of the thorntree bright with its surplice,
The ready emerald of grass, the quiet calves;
The chestnut-trees have their candlesticks alight,
Hedgerows are kneeling, the birch is still as a nun,
The cuckoo's two notes over the hush of bright streams
And a ghost mist bending away from the meads' censer.
Before the rabbits scatter, O man, come forth
From your council houses, come and with the weasel
See the earth lift up an immaculate wafer
And the Father kiss the Son in the white dew.[18]

The Angels

Scripture opens by referring to the creation of the angels: "In the beginning God created the heavens"—the world of the angels, or indeed
the angels themselves. That at least is how the Fathers of the Church
understood the word. Given the existence of God, who is infinite
Spirit, it seemed to them improbable that spiritual being should be represented in the world only in the minimal fashion that we find in ourselves. Old Testament people experienced the angels as filled to the
brim with divine activity, so much so that sometimes they had difficulty in distinguishing the angels from God himself (cf. Gen 16:7-13).
In the New Testament Jesus Christ overshadows the angels, because in
his person God and man are perfectly joined. Nevertheless, the members of the New Testament Churches occasionally venerated angels too
enthusiastically—earning a rebuke from Paul, and the warning voice
that corrected John in Revelation.

The "angelophanies" of Scripture fall into four main types: *historical*—when individual angels lend help to humanity, from the time of
the patriarchs, when Hagar is saved from the folly of her flight from
Sarah, to that of the apostles, when Peter is brought out of prison with
angelic assistance; *liturgical*—as in the allusions to the multitudinous
presence of angels in divine worship; *prophetic*—where angels are described as doing great things in the mysterious future; and what can
only be described as *ontological* references—mentions of the angelic
realm as a vital part of the supernatural world. The overall message is
that the angels are as wholly ready to do God's will as they are powerful to perform it; they are completely God's own, and at no time is
there any fear as to their future. In their world spiritual wealth is the
rule, and journey toward a moral or mental destitution unknown.

18. Welsh original in S. Lewis, *Byd a Betws* (Aberyswyth, 1941).

The angels stand in the burning light of God's countenance, yet the lowliest things of this earth are the objects of their attention—as when Raphael goes to the city of the Medes and finds Gaelus, giving him the note of hand and receiving from him all the money that was owed to Tobias. As Balthasar has written, the fact that they continually behold and adore God does not prevent them from existing in the mode of mission. From their home in heaven, their *mission* is to "provoke" and trigger history in the world.[19]

Until the ninth century, the only individual angel honored in the Church's liturgy was Michael. Michaeline devotion had spread rapidly from the fourth-century East to Italy and then to the rest of the West, leaving a trail of sanctuaries behind it, not least St. Michael's Mount, off the coast of Cornwall, and Skerrig Michael, on the west coast of Ireland. Among medieval theologians, Aquinas offered a rationale of the cult of the angels, which is based, he suggested, on two things: a recognition of their excellence as created beings, and a recognition of our dependence on them within the providence of God, who uses them to help us. As with the veneration of the saints, submediation (from God, through Christ) is no derogation from God's being God, but on the contrary a witness to his sovereign creativity and graciousness. By establishing the intermediaries through whom he accomplishes his will, God gives them the dignity of sharing in his causality, and by multiplying their number increases the sum total of those to whom gratitude is due.

In the later Middle Ages and the early modern period, Christians founded confraternities and other associations for the purpose of honoring the angels. This carried on until as late as 1950 when the society called the Philangeli, the "friends of the angels," was formed by an Englishwoman, Mary Angela Jeeves (its headquarters is now in the United States). In the Catholic Church, whole periodicals were dedicated to angelology, the study of the angels, and many paraliturgical prayers and other devotional aids were assembled. In the *Carmina gaedelica*, a collection of Celtic oral material made in the Catholic islands of the Hebrides and the adjacent Western Highlands by Alexander Carmichael (1832–1912), angels come and go as naturally as they ascended and descended upon the Son of Man (John 1:51). The shining presences, invisible except to the inner eye of love and self-giving,

19. H. U. von Balthasar, *Theo-Drama: Theological Dramatic Theory* (San Francisco, 1992) 3:491–92.

continued to play the role they had occupied for Jesus himself—for, despite his Godhead, it was by an angel that he was helped in the time of his deepest agony. He also spoke in his teaching of the angel guardians of children: for these "always see the face of God" (Matt 18:10). In the *Carmina,* hills, the sea and the heavenly presences are wonderfully blended.

> O Michael, victorious,
> Stand guard all around
> On your bright shining steed
> With your sword that tamed
> The dragon. Your name:
> Great Ranger of heaven,
> God's warrior man.
> Be thou at my back
> O Michael victorious;
> O light of my days,
> Thou shining and glorious
> Guard me always.
> My round I will make
> with my saint by my side
> On machair, on meadow-land,
> On the cold hills of heather;
> We'll travel together
> Round this hard globe of earth.
> No harm will come to me,
> For your shield is over me,
> O Michael victorious,
> Shepherd of God.[20]

Tradition maintains, indeed, that an openness to the angelic presences can transform our attitudes and activities toward wholeness, creativity, and a charity which is at once exacting and joyous.

Since human beings are spirit as well as flesh, they are naturally subject, in spirit, to the conditions of the spirit-world as they are, in body, subject to the conditions of the material world. In themselves, and in their bodies, part of the earth, they have a direct relationship with the celestial hierarchies with their cosmic scope and power. These latter are part of the mighty harmony of innumerable regions and orders of being, as we are.

---

20. Carmichael, *Carmina Gadelica,* 1:208–11.

It is an army at salute!
It is a people in the Dawn!
It is the ceaseless service done
by those who were, and are, the First
unto the Father, eternal rite!
In presence of the Unity
this is the Number which adores!
This is the soul attuned entire
and never parted from its source
in contemplation of the truth,
flawless and faithful children who
ever regard their Maker thus.
God the Father-God who knows
all his nestlings by their names—
has gathered in his mansion, sealed
with seven seals, these winged seeds
in all their myriad multitudes,
different each from each in kind,
being, from Angels to the Seraphim,
the types and prophecies of all
Creation and, within the Eternal
Zion, Preface to the Holy Mass.

No one who kneels, no one who prays,
no one who yields himself to God,
no one who weeps to see his life,
no one who with a grieving cry
opens himself to Mary's Son
but soon must feel his buried soul
gradually pervaded by
the adorable Angelic host:
O revelation of the Friend,
spiritual Brother and the Guide
chosen—assigned!—to grant us Heaven
and unite us in the hierarchy
of those concerning whom it is said
they give not nor are they given
in marriage of the flesh! For none
is welcome in the Father's Realm
who is not as his children are.[21]

---

21. P. Claudel, "Hymnes des saints anges," in *Oeuvre poétique* (Paris, 1967) 453–56.

The ending of this segment of Claudel's poem, by raising the question of the dialectic of the spiritual and the fleshly, reminds us that the Logos became man at two levels: that of spirit, and that of body. He who asked a woman for water when he was thirsty could also be helped throughout his life by the good spirits, and challenged by the evil ones. Though the Gospels were written from the stand-point of the historical and visible realm, they are not enclosed by its limitations. Openings into the invisible recur throughout their course, from the annunciation to the ascension when the Lord passed from one to the other.

The light of the Word—in itself altogether sufficient for the world's redemption—must be appropriated, and it is in our spiritual relations with the angels as well as in our physical relations with matter in its organization and extension in the empirical realm and our practical ac-tivities there that we must do so. When the Son addressed the Father he did so in intimacy, certainly, but not in isolation: the Father is the Lord of Spirits, the "I Am" whose angels stayed the hand of Abraham, and appeared in the burning bush (Acts 7:30), the Lord who rides above the cherubim, the Lord of hosts. All this is expressed in the opening invocation of the Lord's Prayer: "Our Father, who are *in the heavens.*" At the passion Jesus remarks that if he asked the Father, he would send his angels to save him. All prayer is an asking of the Father, yet the angels are our helpers in presenting our asking and ado-ration. To discover this for themselves, Christians must give the angels an active place in their own lives of prayer and meditation, where the mind reaches to its source. What the angels can do most naturally is to clarify the human spirit, to open human minds to the light of God which shines around them. The glory of the Godhead has so much in excess of what we can take in and is so different from our own sinful being that were the parousia to take place immediately, few could look upon the face of Christ and find in it love, not judgment. But—and this is true likewise of that analogue of the parousia which is our indivi-dual dying, instead he sends his angels before his face to prepare the way for his coming. The return of Christ will be the definitive opening of heaven into earth, the irreversible throwing open of the threshold. Co-involved with the Father and the Son in all "sending" (and the angels are certainly God's messengers, as the etymology of their name implies) is the breath of God, the Holy Spirit, in whom the parousia, as also the incarnation, of the Son is achieved, and whose personal econ-omy Christ's second coming will reveal. The angels are breathings of this Spirit: the relation of the doctrine of the Spirit to that of the angels is, as the Irish Carmelite theologian Noel Dermot O'Donoghue has pointed out, an area as yet undeveloped in the story of Catholic theology.[22]

The belief of the Church about *guardian* angels is expressed only in the liturgy. It is not dogma, but it is doctrine in the sense that *lex orandi* equals *lex credendi*: what is laid down when we pray is a norm for our faith. Though it may seem excessively pious, ecclesiastical, and specialized, in the hands of the traditional theologians who have written about it angelic guardianship is presented as something absolutely natural. It has no special relationship to the Christian economy, or to the mystery of the Church. One's guardian angel is acquired at birth, not baptism. This guardianship is a general dispensation of providence to keep the human race, and human individuals, in perfection of nature. For Thomas Aquinas, its most direct and constant effect is the illumination of the human mind. Humanity is kept in approximate mental equilibrium through the unceasing watchfulness of these spirits. It is a remarkable thing that, despite the many fatuous or aberrant things that individuals or even entire cultures can come to believe about why or how we are here, the human race can be expected to respond to a call back to some fundamental truths about beliefs and behavior. Because of the angel guardians, for instance, a papal encyclical on morals can be addressed to all human beings with some hope of a hearing.

Yet the guardian angels are not concerned with world-historical forces as such, but with each person. Aquinas points out that the secrets of grace are God's personal providence—the dealings of the Trinity with ourselves not *en masse* but as individual rational creatures. It is not astonishing that individual angels are chosen to watch over individual human souls treated with some preference by God himself. This is how the divines of the English Catholic revival saw them. In Newman's *Dream of Gerontius,* the angel guardian greets Gerontius, "My friend and brother, hail!" and in F. W. Faber's hymn *Angels of Jesus* they wait, ready to greet the pilgrim whose *Doppelgänger* they have been: "Angels of Jesus, angels of light, / singing to welcome the pilgrims of the night."

22. A rich angelology can be constructed from O'Donoghue's writing in *Heaven in Ordinarie* (Edinburgh, 1980); *The Holy Mountain* (Collegeville, Minn., 1983); *The Mountain behind the Mountain: Aspects of the Celtic Tradition* (Edinburgh, 1993).

But there is the negative side: the doctrine of the *fallen* angels. To the extent that God, the infinite Spirit, is thought of as thoroughly distinct from the world, it becomes possible to conceive of a disharmony between him and some finite spirit. Thus the notion of spiritual evil becomes intelligible—and for the New Testament not merely a possibility, but a reality. The devil and his angels are also realities, in Catholic teaching. These realities are not to be encountered by human beings chiefly in the spectacular form of satanic possession, which happens only under the most extraordinary (and rare) circumstances. The reality of angelic evil is to be sought rather in the ordinary realm, in the alienation from the divine image of the individual person as also in the demonic character of pathologically deformed institutions. Evil lives in the human heart, and that heart's refraction in the pattern of human coexistence; yet it cannot be completely demythologized as a simply human reality. Although we are the subject of evil, we are not altogether its initiator, and the sin in us can be experienced as the work of a stranger; furthermore, morally criminal activity (Hitler, Stalin) can take on more-than-human proportions. The struggle between good and evil has a cosmic dimension. The article of the Creed that deals with the descent of the Word incarnate into hell affirms among other things that the victorious Christ confronts Satan in a world utterly beyond the everyday, and that as a result of that conflictual meeting evil is now, in principle, directly subjected to the victory of God's goodness in Jesus Christ.

Aquinas's account of angelic sin is subtle. An angel's nature is so perfect that there is nothing he can wish for or to which he can aspire. How then is angelic sin possible? Only if the spirit be taken out of his natural order and placed in another, higher, supernatural one where the possibility arises that he may resist this relocation, and rebel against God. The share given him in the supernatural order is not only elevation, for it means also community with all others so favored, including the human race. A spirit may choose to enter into community with the supernatural or to remain entirely within his own sphere, preferring his own natural excellence to the communion of the universal family of God. The *malitia angelica* consists in wanting to possess the resemblance with God that comes from grace not through the divine help, according to God's order, but through the power of his own nature alone. All other perversities ascribed to the evil angels follow from this: for what they have freely chosen is not a passive state of personal excellence but an active opposition to a higher order. With every means in their stupendous power, then, they fight against the super-natural ordering of the world—which means above all the world drama's center in the Cross and resurrection of Christ.[23] That is why the Revelation of John the Divine concentrates the activity of the "dragon" in the time from incarnation to parousia, and why too the human embodiment of angelic evil can only be the "Anti-Christ": one who is systematically opposed to Christ, and to that extent para-sitic upon him—even, as in Luca Signorelli's fresco at Orvieto, his dreadful parody.

The Gospels, or at any rate the Synoptics, are barely conceivable without the presence of the fallen angels. One of the strongest impressions Jesus made was as someone who healed by exorcism. Nowadays, we may tend to understand the demons in psychopathological terms, as a disease of the mind, or a disease of the body induced by the mind. But we do not need to regard such a subjective view of the demonic spirits as an alternative to an objective account of them, of the kind that the doctrinal tradition furnishes. The devil and his angels are present wherever there is disintegration of God's creative work, wherever what should be orderly, harmonious, a unity, begins to fall into chaos and anarchy. These spirits are personal beings but they are not persons: they lack the unity that goes with being a person. Their thoroughgoing, clear-sighted commitment to evil makes them not only the disintegration of others but, more profoundly, disintegrated beings themselves. Small wonder, then, that we encounter them only as a pattern of symptoms, a disorder in the body or the mind. Whereas the angels who said yes to God are self-consistent spiritual realities who share actively in the construction of his kingdom, the satanic angels do not hold together: their act of saying no disintegrates themselves not least of all.

The Church's Christological faith proclaims Christ to be Lord of these fallen principalities and powers by right of his victorious Cross, and the supereminently personal reality (at once divine person and human personality, inseparably united) whose omnipotence, working patiently through created forms, can nullify and reverse the processes of disorder in the universe. The cosmos is, then, not only the setting of salvation; it is also, in and through humanity, salvation's wider objective.

---

23. K. Foster, "Satan," in Thomas Aquinas, *Summa theologiae*, vol. 9: *Angels*, ed. K. Foster (London, 1968) 306–21.

The bliss of the redeemed will be to possess all truth, to be in contact with all reality, to see all beauty. In this the enjoyment of the company of the angels will play its part.

> We must always keep alive within us that essentially Catholic principle of life, that the possession of the supreme Goodness, God himself, never destroys the appetite for created goodness, but, on the contrary, enhances it; to see God face to face produces in the minds of the elect a new capacity to see him in his creatures, and where is he seen to greater advantage than in the world of angels, which mirrors back, with an almost infinite power of radiation, the glory of the invisible God?[24]

Whereas the modern Italian philosopher-aesthetician Benedetto Croce thought Dante was wrong to fill his vision of ultimate reality with highly selved beings, for that medieval predecessor of his it was vital that in the light of God the angels and saints are yet more distinctly themselves.

> And all around that Centre, wings outstretched
> I saw more than a thousand festive angels,
> each one distinct in brilliance and in art.[25]

In the eschatology of the Church, by contrast with Hegelianism, opposites do not combine and disappear in higher syntheses. Rather is there stronger identity and sharper distinctiveness even or especially within final harmony, indissoluble unity. As one Dantist has put it:

> All this is no doubt a medieval embarrassment, even to the postmodern Christian who is usually convinced both that the spiritual needs to become virtually indistinguishable from everydayness and that paradise, if it exists, will simply be unlike anything we know. Some future intellectual antiquarian will have to explain why the twentieth century tried to make God a subdivision of this world, and push the transcendence of the next world beyond all human relation. That investigator will no doubt still be reading Dante, who thought, with all Christendom before us, that unexpected beings sometimes visit our world and that the next world will be like this one, only more so than most of us can imagine.[26]

24. A. Vonier, *The Angels* (London, 1928) 84–85.

25. Dante, *Paradiso,* canto 31, lines 130–32.

26. R. Royal, "The Good, the Bad and the Ugly: Dante's 'Birds of God,'" *Crisis* 13.2 (1995) 29.

12
The Good Life

For the Catholic Church, morality has high doctrinal significance. There are two reasons for this. First, Christian morality sets forth vital aspects of our vocation as sons and daughters of God. Second, for those who do not have the good fortune to possess revealed truth, living an upright life may be a highway on which, unknowingly, they can walk towards the God of all salvation. The moral teaching of Catholicism is that dimension of its wisdom which states and explores the principles that should govern human behavior vis-à-vis the final destiny of humankind: the vision of God. Though chiefly based on divine revelation, the theological expression of Catholic morality also incorporates much rational ethics. When looking at the nature of salvation we saw how our human substance is neither destroyed nor displaced by its supernatural elevation in grace to glory, but is, rather, ennobled and perfected. Here and now humankind's ultimate goal, the enjoyment of almighty God, can be anticipated in his conscious and willing service. And this is not only an obligation laid upon us. It is also the proper finishing of our nature, an exercise of our faculties that gives them final satisfaction. If God is the Creator of human beings who wills salvation for them and gives them a revelation for this purpose, they have, evidently, a duty to attend to that revelation and adapt themselves to what it commands. But if it were possible to isolate the commands from the revelation, they would still be recognizable as the way to our full flourishing. Happiness lies in so ordering the goods of this world that by way of them we can efficaciously elect the infinite good. For no finite good is so necessary, sufficient, and irreversible that it can constitute the final resting-place of the heart in its open-ended "eros" (both negatively, its power of desiring, and positively, its capacity for living).

The Church's Concern with Morals

The ethics of Jesus, though bulking large, belong within his teaching on salvation. The behavior of the disciples in the present age is to reflect as much as possible of the love and unity which typifies the life of the kingdom in the age that is coming. As prophet of the good life, Jesus is an ethical maximalist. The good one must do to gain eternal life is a striving after nothing less than perfection. But everything turns on how such "perfection" should be understood. Jesus reaffirms the validity of the Ten Words, the foundational pillars of the moral life registered in inspired fashion by Moses on Sinai, but arising more primordially still from the created pattern inscribed in the being of the human animal by its maker. In the Sermon on the Mount, however, Jesus transforms the ethos of the Law, the spirit in which these commands are to be received. The Beatitudes, in privileging such dispositions as humility, penitence, mercy, peacefulness, purity of heart, and vulnerability for righteousness's sake, propose a new manner in which to obey the commandments, and so define ethical holiness in a novel, distinctively evangelical, way. For these qualities express, in a form appropriate to fallen creatures, their own archetypes in the attributes ascribed to God—his patient mercy, flaming justice—by the gospel itself. Of these, Jesus gave ostensive definition in his own deportment: he did divine things humanly. The *imitatio Patris* for which he called—"Be perfect, as your heavenly Father is perfect" (Matt 5:48)—takes the concrete form of the *imitatio Christi*, for Jesus is the incarnate visibility of the Father. Finally, the setting of Jesus' ethical teaching within a message of salvation implies the provision of fresh resources of grace for keeping the commandments—summed up in the two imperatives of loving God and loving neighbor—in this perfect spirit. Through the grace of God we can keep the commandments: this is one important way in which the God of grace enables us to claim his own promise of life everlasting.

After our Lord left the public space of this world, we find the apostles treating the moral life as vital to the new "way" which was Christianity. They were as vigilant over the conduct of Christians as they were over their beliefs. There has been a development in the ethical understanding of the Church since apostolic times, but, as with all development of doctrine, this has happened homogeneously (consistently) and not heterogeneously (by sudden unrelated new starts). The later teaching of the Church in moral matters underscores the permanent validity of the words of Jesus himself.

Faithful to her master, the Church's ethical concern was clear from the outset. The apostolic letters betray a regular pattern. First, converts to the faith are enjoined to abandon various vices (recognised as such elsewhere in the ancient world, an important link to the Fathers' notion of a law of nature or rational ethics presupposed by the teaching of the gospel, and first appearing with Justin Martyr). Next they are invited to develop some typical virtues of the Christian life: gentleness, humility, generosity, purity, the readiness to forgive, and so forth. Characteristically, neophytes are then advised of the need to deal uprightly with their pagan neighbors, to obey the lawfully constituted state authority (though without prejudice to the integrity of the faith), and are reminded of the specially onerous time in which we now live: the "last age" with its attendant responsibilities.

The gospel changes the context of ethics. In the first place, the world looks smaller, God greater. The conviction that this world-order is definitively surpassed in the new order of the resurrection makes what would survive the passing of the old heavens and earth alone seem finally worthy of attention. And yet the same eschatological consideration makes more urgent the need to use one's gifts ethically while time lasts. Moreover, the justice of God, and his mercy, looms larger in human affairs than ever before in history—for the death and resurrection of the divine Son are their supreme manifestation. In the second place, the moral life is now to be lived within a new society—the body of Christ, the Church—a community at once deeper and, in principle, wider than any community heretofore existing. *Deeper* because as wholly subordinate to the divine glory in Christ, this one society alone can make total demands on its members without totalitarianism. *Wider* because the Church is the nucleus of a new humanity, formed from the riven side of Christ who died and rose again as representative of all humankind. The ethos of this new society is fashioned by the *imitation of Christ*. Insofar as God in Christ can be a model for creatures he is so in such virtues as forbearance, gentleness, self-giving, charity—the last of which is not simply one virtue among many but that all-embracing attitude brought about by exposure to the love of God expressed in Christ's sacrifice, and manifesting itself in unselfishness, kindness, compassion, courtesy.

In the Church Fathers, the aspect of natural ethics—the good life as a life in harmony with the creation—came more to the fore. The Fathers quite consciously adopted the wisdom of the philosophers of the ancient world so as to understand better the progress of human beings toward God. Under Stoic influence, they spoke of the "mind-possessing soul": and it is this human capacity to grasp the meaning of existence which founds the role of rationality in ethics. For patristic thought, humanity is at once solidary with God (since the human mind is a tiny reflection of the divine mind) and with the universe, which, in the words of Jacques-Bénigne Bossuet, man "gathers up in himself." If Justin was the first Father to use the term *natural law,* Irenaeus could say that the Lord in his incarnation willed to perfect the *naturalia legis,*[1] while for Tertullian the law as revealed by God renders more precise the wisdom of nature. Clement of Alexandria declares that "from God is the law of nature and the law of revelation, which together makes but one."[2]

We are dealing here with not only the integration of ancient ethics but also their transcending by the demands of the gospel. The Fathers, like the great Scholastics after them, did not know the much later separation of morals from spirituality, or of morals from dogmatics, or even (to some extent at least) of theology from philosophy. All these subject matters, or distinctive approaches, formed part of a continuous wisdom. The Fathers' moral theology is found in their Scripture commentaries and homilies, as well as in their general writings: it is not confined to *opuscula* devoted to particular moral problems. The Fathers took the Bible as the main source of their moral theology—not surprising when one considers that they viewed the main question in morals as beatitude (final happiness) and the ways in which one might attain it. Their exegesis expresses an understanding that has penetrated into the heart of the mysteries of which Scripture speaks and whereof it is a sign.

Little by little there emerges a picture of the moral life as ordered love, a discipline of loves great and small. For Augustine, supremely, love calls for order and a rectitude which gives it beauty and makes it true. Here a philosophical ethics and a theology of grace can greet each other and embrace.

In the medieval period, and notably with the reception of Aristotle's psychology in the West, a greater effort is made to integrate the orders of nature (creation) and grace (redemption and transfiguration), so as to show how, in the Christian life as a concrete whole, the human being enters on the moral good. In particular, a Christian

---

1. Irenaeus, *Against the Heresies* 4.24.1–3.
2. Clement of Alexandria, *Miscellanies* 3.73.3.

Scholastic like Aquinas usefully supplies a lacuna in his account of the structure of the human act. In his theology, the reciprocal influence of knowing and loving is expressed in terms of causality. Mind affecting will resembles a formal cause, which gives shape and meaning to some action, while will affecting mind is closer to an efficient cause, setting up a movement in accord with the dialectic of love for which motion goes from soul to thing, not from thing to soul. (These are not, we should note, full causes, for mind and will are only aspects, albeit dynamic ones, of human persons.) The role of perception, wish, judgment, intention, deliberation, consent, decision, choice, command, application, performance, and completion, explored by Aristotle above all, is explained within a Christian anthropology by Thomas in the West as by Maximus the Confessor (seventh century) in the Byzantine East. The last of these terms—"completion," *fruitio*—in Aquinas's use is more indebted to Augustine as well as to Scripture with its imagery of the Sabbath rest: *quies*, with its joy (*gaudium*) and delight (*delectatio*).

The humane holism of Aquinas's account is remarkable. For him, the moral good is an inner modulation of the common end sought by all love; the activity of virtue belongs to the metaphysical dialectic of love, and "right" wells up from the very nature of things. Moreover, since Aquinas conceives the good as, above all, *actuality,* the proper response to it is *appetite,* including even the unconscious drives of "natural appetite," given with our nature as such. Yet the proper good for human beings, rational animals, is answered by their proper appetite, the rational appetite—the *will*—which indeed works on and through a kind of blind instinct for wholeness (*consistentia naturalis*), yet seeks what is appreciated as good by the mind. The good is, in other words, for the classical Latin theology of the thirteenth century, not only a term to reach and rest in, but an objective to grasp and hold. The will has a capacity for the all-good which, were it present (as in the Beatific Vision), would transport it into unpremeditated rapture; in this life, however, God appears to us only as the greatest of particular goods, though we can correct that misperception mentally by denying limit to God's goodness (the *via negationis*) and affirming its supreme transcendence (the *via eminentiae*). Our sharing in God's beatitude turns on our adjusting ourselves to an environment composed of many other, and conflicting, goods, and on our picking our way to him, aided by the judgment—both an influence from reason and an assurance from revelation—that any goods distracting us from God will in the end profit us nothing.

> The unity of the *Summa theologiae* is not merely logical and intellectual. It can also be called ontological and dynamic, since it tries to reproduce the very movement of the divine Wisdom and action in their work of creation, terminating as this does in man as the image of God, and in the work of governance, which leads back to God, as ultimate end and beatitude, all creatures, and especially the human being—thanks to the free will which makes him master of his acts and capable of enjoying God. This work at once divine and human cannot come to completion, however, without Christ who in his humanity has become for us the way to the Father.[3]

Here moral theology has its own final outcome in the loving vision of God: it is truly a wisdom both natural and Christian. Aquinas is concerned both to do justice to the internal demands of the natural world order (a metaphysical quest) and to ensure that these demands are truly "finalized," that is, receive their own ultimate meaning and fulfillment, by an account of the human being's supernatural destiny in Christ (a theological vision). Thus Thomas's discussion of the virtues—the concrete forms of moral goodness—is, in effect, an account of the relation between the natural law, seen as a law of moral progress for the human being as spiritual creature, and the law of Christ, regarded as a law of moral progress for men and women as sons and daughters of God.

The disintegration of Aquinas's beautiful synthesis had a deleterious effect on the moral theology of Catholicism. Morals and mysticism moved further apart, though the new emphasis on obligation did bring out the holiness of the moral law, the seriousness of the moral life. Beginning in the late fifteenth century, handbooks for confessors provided help for people placed in difficult situations of moral choice *(casus conscientiae)*, while the sheer range of ethically relevant subject matter in human life was displayed in manuals of "special morals," frequently divided into the areas of living typified by each of the Ten Commandments. Justice became more and more important with the new problems of political ethics raised for Catholic Christendom by the discovery (and ultimately conquest) of the New World.

The early modern period, and notably the seventeenth century, was the age par excellence of casuistry. By discussing moral cases and taking them as patterns theologians could throw light on the true mean-

---

3. S. Pinckaers, *Les sources de la morale chrétienne: Sa méthode, son contenu, son histoire* (Fribourg, 1985) 226.

ing of the basic principles involved and disengage the values present in complex data. Good casuists avoid futile questions or an excessive concern with calculating the minimum needed to fulfill the whole duty of a Christian. For the earlier tradition, our best hope in quandaries lies in practical reason, fortified by prudence, and assisted by discretion or discernment (in the monastic tradition especially), faith, and the gift of counsel. But in the seventeenth and eighteenth centuries the Church tried to take stock more systematically of her resources for arguing in such hard cases: the criteria of judgment for uncertain cases were themselves argued over, until in 1831 the papacy declared for the view of the Neapolitan lawyer and mystic Alphonsus Liguori: for there to be true doubt, the arguments in favor of liberty (including "external" ones from Church authority) must be at any rate equal to those favoring the law. Such a view was declared to be something that confessors may follow safely (itself, then, a prudential judgment by the Holy See!) and in 1871, significantly, Liguori was declared a doctor of the Church.

Alphonsus's view reflects Paul's teaching in the Letters to the Corinthians that it is not conscience that is supreme but Christ the Lord. The Second Vatican Council says the same in affirming the Lordship of Christ over conscience, and the consequent obligation to form conscience by the teaching Christ gives through the Church. As Christians, we have already exercised our conscience—our moral judgment—on the fundamental question of whether we accept Christ and his Church as holding authority from God to teach. Once we have made this act of acceptance, we are obliged by our conscience to follow the authoritative guidance that comes from these sources, though of course they may offer such guidance with more or less binding degrees of authoritative utterance, and in ways that are more or less clearly pertinent to our situation. Nor is this alien to conscience for, as Newman stressed in his 1830 university sermon on "The Influence of Natural and Revealed Religions Respectively," conscience "implies a relation between the soul and a something exterior, and that, moreover, superior to itself,"[4] a tribunal, judge, or lawgiver to whom, it realizes, obedience is owed.

In the centuries between Liguori and Vatican II, the biblical, patristic, and Thomist revivals in Catholicism restored morals to its place

---

4. J. H. Newman, *University Sermons: Fifteen Sermons Preached before the University of Oxford, 1828–1843* (London, 1970) 18.

within Christian spirituality as a whole: the moral life is centered on God's kingdom; it is the life of a child of God within Christ's mystical body; the theological virtues and the beatitude they set before us belong intimately to its texture.

On the other hand, Catholic ethics remain distinguished from general Protestant ethics by their insistence that, within the law of Christ, the practice of which proceeds from the Holy Spirit by charity, the *natural* human virtues are assumed and assimilated. Faith transcends them, yet it requires incarnation in them. The wisdom of God can purify reason and the heart, assuming human wisdom and knowledge in a living conjunction of faith and reason. Nevertheless, the pride of place in moral theology belongs to the act of faith, which submits and opens our intelligence to the Word of God—the external Word in Scripture, read in the Church; the internal Word in the action of the Holy Spirit.

The Church's doctrinal authority, her mandate to teach, covers not only faith but also morals. The Catholic tradition accepts that the principal revealed moral truths are open to our natural reason. As Paul remarks, Gentiles who lack the Mosaic Torah nonetheless have what the Law requires written on their hearts (Rom 2:12-16). Following Irenaeus and Aquinas, the Louvain theologian John Driedo could write in the throes of the Reformation crisis:

> The teachings of natural and moral philosophy have nothing to do with faith, just insofar as they are entertained by philosophers or by peoples. But many of those teachings are *de necessitate fidei,* insofar as they could be demonstrated from Sacred Scripture, either expressly or by silent implication. . . . Thus, for example, it is heresy to persist in asserting that adultery, or theft, or false testimony are not wrongful.[5]

God's revelation, whose authentic transmission is entrusted to the Church, enables certain truths *per se* accessible to reason to be known by everyone, even in the present condition of humankind, with ease, with certitude, and without admixture of error, as the two Vatican councils (1869–70; 1962–65), would later insist. At the Council of Trent, the fathers were anxious to distance the Church from the potentially subversive implications, for Christian morality, of the Reformers' *sola fide.* They maintained, accordingly, that the last stage of that conversion which disposes one for the forgiveness of sins, and sanctification,

---

5. J. Driedo, *De ecclesiasticis Scripturis et dogmatibus* (Louvain, 1533).

is a determination to keep the divine commands which Christ charged his apostles with teaching. Keeping these commands is vital if faith is not to be dead and fruitless for us. Trent affirms, in a passage taken up by the Second Vatican Council,[6] that the gospel, whose purity is to be preserved in the Church by the elimination of errors, Christ first promulgated by his own mouth, and then ordered to be preached by the apostles to every creature, as the source not only of all saving truth but also of moral discipline. On such matters as polygamy and divorce, controverted by the Reformers, Trent insisted upon moral norms as intrinsic to revealed and salvific truth. The phrase *fides et mores* was already classic in the twelfth century, and has roots in Leo and Augustine.

Some such precepts derive from the natural law. We should note that not only is revelation's help morally necessary for us to know the natural law: since the whole human being is embraced by the order of salvation, the Church quite properly claims the right to speak authoritatively in questions of the natural law—not merely as pastoral directives but as doctrinal assertions. In part, the order of nature can be regarded as the order of God's creation. In this sense, we are asked to recognize our place within this order, to appropriate it in freedom, and to realize those goals of nature which the rest of creation aims at instinctively. In part, too, however, we are charged with shaping the world of nature we have inherited. We must not simply accept passively the goals of creation but exercise a reasonable dominion over nature, giving her new goals and meanings—however, such humanization, or personalization, of the world can never take the form of a flight from nature or a disregard of the preestablished meanings already embedded in the structures of the world. It falls to the magisterium to formulate norms for Catholic believers, in the light of the gospel and with the collaboration of the laity (with their Christian experience). Christian moral teaching on the new issues of the day is to flow from revealed faith without contradicting human reason but without being limited to human reasons. The faithful owe the bishops in communion with the pope a *religiosum animi obsequium* when the latter teach doctrine about (faith and) morals in the name of Christ (not, of course, when they simply propound a personal opinion). This religious assent is not, it should be said, an absolute assent, but it is still "religious," that is, supernaturally motivated.

6. *Dei Verbum* 7; see DH 1501.

Some further nuances must be added. The obligation of submission to the bishop or the pope in their exercise of teaching authority is measured according to the quality of that exercise. Between the careful attention which is appropriate to some merely prudential judgment of the Petrine officeholder and the glad inhesitancy which should greet his definitive interpretation *in persona Petri* of the Gospels a great gulf is fixed. As for the bishops, what is said of the pope applies also to them when considered as a body, a college. Though bishops individually, or in groups, can err, the *charisma veritatis* can enfold them even before they pack their bags for Nicaea or Constance. The Second Vatican Council speaks of their collegial infallibility on three conditions: that they remain in hierarchical communion with the pope; that their common teaching is on matters of faith and morals; and that they show an official and manifest consensus not just on the proposition concerned but also on its absolute and obligatory character. Naturally, the infallible character of such ordinary magisterial teaching is most easily perceived in the context of an ecumenical council. A zeal for giving clear and firm moral guidance may be tempted to treat all moral norms of the magisterium as of equal weight: but this backfires in the long run, by lessening the magisterium's own credibility. Yet it is an even more serious mistake to suppose that, because some concrete norms lack perfect certitude, they may be ignored or minimized. It is typical of a legalistic mentality to think of moral norms as obligatory only when they are certainly binding, rather than to be grateful for whatever guidance they can give, even if this is only probably correct.

Some have questioned whether the Church can teach specific moral norms, rather than the most universal ethical principles—either on the grounds that, since faith and love determine salvation, specific moral practices are only secondary, or by appeals to the constantly changing concrete nature of humanity. But if the magisterium is to apply concretely the faith that works through charity, it has to teach specific norms. If it cannot be specific then it cannot teach Christian morality in any challenging fashion. As to the historicity of morals: while the magisterium must teach with morally binding efficacy for the formation of conscience and the conduct of life, the quality of its teaching may be differentiated. On the one hand, it can teach some norm—arrived at by interpreting the law of the gospel, or the natural law—as an absolute norm for all times and places; on the other, it can present some norm as the historical application of an indeterminate and dynamic gospel principle. In his commentary on Aristotle's

Politics, Aquinas points out that as a society progresses it may become more perfect through enrichment with new dispositions: for instance, a greater awareness of the need of general education. There may not be progress in moral behavior, but there can be a fuller explicit awareness of particular precepts of the natural law. Recognizing this should not, however, lead us to the conclusion that the magisterium's moral norms are in every case historically conditioned in value, and hence changeable as cultures change. The religious import of this lies in the fact that even universal moral laws serve an interpersonal responsive morality: they are the abstract expression of God's call to us.

Yet the "words" they speak are altogether concrete. John Saward remarks, tellingly:

> As the Fathers of Orthodoxy taught against the abstract Christology of the Iconoclasts, the divine Word assumed into the unity of the divine person a complete *and concrete* human nature, not a mere "general idea" of humanness, and he merited our salvation by specific historical human acts. In becoming man, he entered into human relationships both universal (he united himself, somehow, as Head, with every man) and particular (he became the Child of the Virgin Mary of Nazareth). Now that he is in glory at the right hand of the Father, his human words and actions on earth live on, in the Sacraments and teaching of the Church, with a sanctifying and normative force that is inseparably universal and concrete, applicable to all men at all times and in all places, and to all their specific acts. St. Gregory Nazianzen says of the incarnate Word that "he bears me wholly within himself, with my weaknesses, in order to consume in himself what is evil." How could that be true if he did not, through his Church, give me not only grace to heal the weakness of my will, but also certain knowledge, with respect to specific actions, of what is good and what is evil?[7]

We hear much nowadays about the respect due to liberty of conscience; yet that theme can be expounded in ways that falsify the truth about the human being as a creature of God, a being, that is, with a God-given nature and called to a God-provided fulfillment. In *Veritatis splendor,* the most comprehensive document of modern Catholicism on "fundamental morals," Pope John Paul II pointed out that, for the gospel, we are neither autonomous (a law unto ourselves), nor heteronomous (puppets whose strings are pulled by a being quite other

---

7. J. Saward, *Christ Is the Answer: The Christ-centred Teaching of Pope John Paul II* (Edinburgh, 1995) 97, with an internal citation of Gregory Nazianzen's thirtieth *Oration.*

than ourselves), but "theonomous": we find our inner law in God, who is not another being set beside us, because, as our Creator and Redeemer, he is most intimately identified with us and is in fact the only cause and source of our ultimate happiness.[8] God has not just made us beings who can set up moral laws for ourselves. He has given us in our moral reason a participation in his own eternal Wisdom, so that we can discover, in a human way, his divine will for us. The capacity to identify the natural moral law—in effect, a form of access to the divine counsels—is a far higher dignity than would be the mere ability to set out our own rules for living.

Frequently, philosophical mistakes underlie bad ethics. The trouble usually starts with a wrong understanding of how nature and freedom are related. Some people reduce freedom to nature: the way "most people do things" determines how we should act. Others regard freedom as possible only when one denies nature, which is just a brute "given," without intrinsic meaning. Our natural life (the body, and, through the body, the emotions of the psyche) are seen as just so much raw material from which, by freedom, we construct or invent our humanity.

The norms of the natural law, already implicit in the forms of our bodily and psychic life though given only through our practical reason (assisted if need be by faith in revelation), are growth-lines along which our nature can develop in freedom. As such they are the same for all men and women of all ages. They unite in the same common good all human beings in every period of history, and as they do so they express the same divine calling and destiny we all share. Since we are a single human family it is only right that one ethical truth should bind us together.

The call to respond to the moral law is not in any case a call to legalistic obedience: it is an invitation to live out those actions and intentions which enable us to share eternal happiness. The teaching authority of the Church should not be regarded as an imposition, an exercise in legal power. Only if the Church can exercise her sacred obligation to penetrate and proclaim the truth about God's plan for our salvation can she set us free to discover and enjoy that which, in the end, will make us most happy. For no action of mine, however conscientious, based on error about the moral good can have the value of a moral act founded on a correct conscience.

No doubt in some sense every act we perform is unique. It is also true however, that every act has common features with other acts. In

---

8. John Paul II, *Veritatis splendor*, 41.

every area of human life there is need for generalization. Life is too short for innumerable agonizing appraisals made from scratch. Rules, customs, habits, and the like capitalize on human experience, sustaining human existence as they do so. The opposing position—radical situationism—subverts the very idea of a moral community. It assumes an extraordinary degree of moral sensitivity in those expected to read the demands of a situation. It barely recognizes how distorted our consciences can be: prohibition can be protective, saving us from our worst selves.

The Holy Spirit is the inner law who enables us to imitate and embody the love of Christ, but the formulation of moral norms helps us to translate the Spirit's bidding through the ages. Some kinds of human acts, indeed, are so intrinsically evil that no intention, circumstances, or consequences could ever purify them.

For the Christian, morality is religious: it is the confession of God (we live to the "praise of his glory" as Ephesians puts it), and witness before human beings ("See how these Christians love each other"). Such has been the total respect for the Commandments in salvation history, that, beginning with the holy woman Susanna in the Old Testament, the martyrs have gone to their deaths rather than commit, even under duress, one mortal sin (of idolatry, say, or fornication). These martyrs are hailed, nonetheless, as champions of life. Since the Commandments always envisage the supreme human good, their martyrdom was not a denial of the value of human living but its consummate celebration.

The Moral Vision of Catholicism

Just as, however, Catholicism's faith-vision of the world in relation to God is not simply a collection of the Church's defined doctrines, but entails a more holistic penetration of the contents of Scripture and Tradition, the sources of divine revelation, so in morals too Catholicism has a vision which is wider than its norms. The Church's moralists are concerned not simply with the articulation of moral rules. They study human acts so as to order them to the loving vision of God as humanity's true, plenary beatitude or happiness, its ultimate end. By their free choices, human beings integrate themselves around, and in a sense synthesize themselves with, the ends and means they adopt. Those who intend to destroy, damage, or impede a human good incorporate into their will, their own subjectivity, the evil which, on choosing it and making it their own, they treat as if it were a good.

While the divine goodness is both the self-sufficiently adequate object of human love and the cause of all other goods, the loving vision of God takes place in a redeemed city: God has freely created a universe of goods distinct from himself. The "society of friends," as Aquinas puts it, is necessary to the "well being" of perfect beatitude. The vision of God in heaven unifies the goods found in the moral life, the goods that make our nature flourish "blessedly." Such integral human fulfillment is not available in this life, but what is now only an ideal regulator of action is, for faith in divine revelation, an attainable reality for the future, through the power of the gracious God. To see God in his essence will be to see the triune Lord personally causing all the goods—including the finite, created persons—of the universe. To see God will be really to understand, for the first time, the point of all created goods, including created persons and the love of friendship between them. To love oneself and others like one in fullest measure would be more possible and appropriate then than now. The full understanding of the goods we know in this life—such as friendship, practical reasonableness (virtue), and human life itself—and the realization of them in sufficient degree to satisfy our nature, is possible only through a sharing in God's creative understanding and personal existence beyond anything we can (even under grace) appreciate now. The reward so insistently proposed by Scripture is intrinsically connected to the rightful pursuit of the good fruits of our nature and choices: in similes suggested by Professor John Finnis, it is not like the prospect of a beach holiday rewarding long hours of hard work, but more like an orchestra's prospect of performing, really satisfactorily, a symphony after hours of self-discipline, work, and study. Thus the Christian life is not so much a flight from the world as a flight ahead with the world.

The roles of revelation and grace are, evidently, essential to the constituting of this "vision." Catholic moralists understand human actions as rightly ordered not least by the means of grace, the virtues and the gifts of the Holy Spirit, and (as we have seen) they exercise this understanding in the twin light of revelation and of reason. The aim of the Church's moral doctrine is the formation of Christian personalities, seen at one and the same time as ethical personalities where the flux of subjectivity and the passions has been temperately mastered, and also as centers of spiritual spontaneity and creativity. But this is not a technique: the spinal column of the question of happiness is formed by the question of meaning—which is why moral doctrine, in formulating its answers to the problems of human living, conjoins rational reflection with the revealed word of God. The resources with which it works are not only the natural resources of the human affections, the will, and the intellect, but also the secret spring of the Holy Spirit, poured into our hearts by the sacramental economy of the Church. Though concerned with what needy human nature demands, the Church's ethic goes beyond a naturalistic eudaimonism: human beings are capable of a true love for God for God's own sake, and for their neighbors for their neighbors' sake, and, this being so, the desire for happiness, for the fulfillment of their capacities, can open them to God and to others. A desire for happiness that is *amical,* open and generous, is itself set to work, in the Catholic understanding, for the construction of the moral life.

Let us look now at some of the underlying principles in the Catholic appreciation of ethics—notably at (1) the existence of a specifically Christian morality; (2) the recognition of nature as an ethical norm; and (3) the virtues, and the development of the ethical personality. After such a *tour d' horizon,* we should be well-placed to consider how the Catholic Church treats substantively of the main questions of ethics typically controverted by secular society today—especially of social and familial morality.

Christian Morality

For Catholicism, morality is the movement of rational creatures towards God. Every action is good insofar as it has that perfection of being which it ought to possess, and whose presence (or absence) is determined by the object, the circumstances, and the intention involved. As already indicated, the moral life is essentially connected with the spiritual, because for successful practice the moral life requires some grasp of *scientia cordis,* the "science of the heart." After all, most of morality is a matter of harnessing, and transfiguring, our emotions. In moral action, God in his Law provides the external principles—the norm, the contents, and the sanctions of moral action—but the internal principle of habit, both natural and supernatural, is also unavailable to us unless in his grace he moves, supports, and raises us, implanting supernatural energies in our acting. Such sanctifying grace is a communion in the *agapē* which is God's own being. It generates in the soul a new reality: charity-love in its "primal act," its primordial reality within us. Through the Word incarnate and his Church, the divine *agapē* creates in me a kind of echo of itself, a created gift enabling me to respond to it, an infused virtue whereby I can produce acts of divine worth. In charity what we do—loving God as his children and each other in him and for his sake—is raised above itself by God's action.

Christian action consists in translating this *modus vivendi* into a way of acting, a *modus agendi*, or "second act." Though each distinct virtue retains its proper character, virtue is, in the Christian economy, and in the words of Augustine, "the ordering of love." The basic movement of love for God—our insertion into the dynamic interrelations of the Holy Trinity—must express itself in us by an outreach toward all those who are related to God as well. The primacy of God's love means that his charity now indwells, and acts through, ourselves with a view to bringing all rational creatures into his presence.

That reaching, with the neighbor, into God's infinity, is summed up in the Sermon on the Mount, which Augustine regards as our chief mirror of perfection.[9] It is the transmission of our Lord's teaching on the specifically Christian virtues which lead to perfection: poverty of spirit, humility, docility before the Word of God, penitence, hunger and thirst for justice, mercy, purity of heart. These Beatitudes can be seen as so many degrees or stages which lead the Christian from humility and poverty of spirit up to the heights of wisdom and the vision of God. That is where we locate our perfection: in the loving vision of God which will perfect all our powers.

The specificity of Christian morality is above all then a Christological specificity. The incarnate Word, taking on our entire condition (except sin, from which he frees us through his cross and resurrection), has simultaneously restored it, not least in its ethical dimension. He did not come to abolish or replace human ethics. Instead, that "perfecting" of the Law which the Sermon on the Mount announces radicalizes its demands. From out of the gift of a new heart in justification morality can deploy new energies; the resultant actions stem from a human freedom regenerated by the Passover of the Lord. In the Christian regime of life, human morality is reconstituted as the consequence and fulfillment—albeit still within our sin-pocked condition—of the love-gift of God. That is why Christian morality is paschal longing. The commandments remain its rudimentary requirements, the agapeistic minimum, but the *agapē*-life is not content with them, and rises (super) naturally to the self-giving spirit of the evangelical counsels.

9. Augustine, *Commentary on the Sermon on the Mount* 1.1.

Nature

Nature herself is nonetheless an ethical norm in Catholic morality. This does not mean that the cosmic process, with its vast evils of waste and suffering, is itself an exemplar for human conduct. That the moral life is a life "in accordance with nature" is a proposition which, in the first place, draws our attention to the objectivity of the good. We cannot be content with a purely psychological theory of value. We cannot help asking, Why do we desire something? Why do we take an interest in it? Why do we approve of it?, which means, What is it that makes this or that an object of desire, interest, or approval? No one could be content, then, with a purely psychological, subjective theory of value unless he or she had despaired already of finding an objective one. The Cambridge philosopher G. E. Moore's view that the good is a simple unanalyzable quality (like, for example, yellow) which we directly recognize as belonging to certain situations and states of mind is, again, a theory of value which no one would be likely to hold unless he or she had first tried to analyze the notion, and failed abysmally. Nor can Catholic ethicists be content with the suggestion that the good is the pleasant, even though one of their masters, Aristotle, taught that pleasure is a normal consequence and accompaniment of the attainment of good—however twisted some people's pleasures may be, the pleasure always results from some element of positive attainment and not precisely from the twist, the evil in the activity. More fundamentally, however, the good of anything appears as the actualization and fulfillment of its potential nature. Its complete good will involve the completest possible actualization of its nature as a whole, sponsoring a harmony and due order for its different powers. Human good ought therefore to be investigated, in the first place, by examining the functions of human nature, for that good must include their harmonious fulfillment.

Examples of such "appropriate operations" for human nature, both suggested and stirred by our deepest inclinations, would come from: the human being's social character (hence the precept against injuring others in society); the due hierarchy of his or her being (hence precepts concerning the use of "lower things" like food and drink); the human soul-body relationship (thus moral precepts inhibiting actions that disturb the body sufficiently to hinder the work of human reason); and human nature as that of a worshipping being, on which Aquinas comments:

> Since the good, taken universally, is God himself, and since . . . all human beings . . . exist as contained within that good—because every

creature, precisely in respect of what it is by nature, belongs to God—it follows that the instinctive love of each . . . human being is for God first of all and for God more than for self. Otherwise, if this were not true, if creatures by nature loved themselves more than God, then natural loving would be perverse; and would not be perfected, but destroyed, by charity.[10]

Insofar as human nature is constant, it makes permanent demands which form a basic human morality. Catholicism is opposed to ethical relativism. It sees the gospel as a transcultural, transhistorical universal standard, which both confirms and surpasses the order of creation.

Confirms *and surpasses*—for right action is directed not simply towards the good of the agent but towards the good of all affected by the action. Morality frequently calls for self-sacrifice: that is, the surrender of one's own good for the sake of the good of another. Complete rightness does not belong to the kind of action in which the claims of self and of others are anxiously weighed, for it belongs to the activity of love, which is in one sense an enlargement of the self but in another transcendence of the self. An action done through love is necessarily both completely unselfish and yet completely satisfactory to the agent. Morality itself is fulfilled when it becomes true love of God and of human beings. So while the concept of nature provides the ethical norm, nature is not the culmination of ethical life and activity. Morality is not complete until the contrast of self and other ceases to be relevant, and that belongs to the sphere of *agapē*—that charity in which alone duty and happiness are fully one—as we have seen already above.

Virtue

In Catholicism, the theory and practice of the good life is bound up with the virtues. Not only does right action express itself theoretically in the formulation of moral norms, the truths of practical reason. It also expresses itself by way of concrete living, in the form of the virtues, which may be called "life-enhancing habits." Right from the time of Homer, the virtues have been recognized as those qualities which sustain free persons in their roles, and manifest themselves in the actions their roles require. In epic, heroic, and tragic writers, a view of the virtues is at the same time an attitude to human life in its story-like or narrative structure.

10. Thomas Aquinas, *Summa theologiae* 1.60.5.

> If a human life is understood as a progress through harms and dangers, moral and physical, which someone may encounter and overcome in better and worse ways and with a greater or lesser measure of success, the virtues will find their place as those qualities the possession and exercise of which generally tend to success in this enterprise and the vices likewise as qualities which tend to failure. Each human life will then embody a story whose shape and form will depend upon what is counted as a harm and danger and upon how success and failure, progress and opposition, are understood and evaluated.[11]

Or, in Aquinas's perspective: that a thing should reach its proper perfection is both God's will for it and its own way of reaching God. But the instinct for God which carries a human being, via a certain self-transcendence, towards the supreme good (the "natural desire for God") is not by itself enough to teach persons what their end is, much less to lead them to pursue it. Our responsibility lies in acting so as to attain the end once it is seen. While some dispositions may be innate (for some people are better endowed temperamentally in this or that respect than others) most dispositions are, by contrast, the result of the agent's own activity. When we reflect, our reasoning affects the faculty of desire, generating dispositions in the will and the sensory appetite. In this sense, virtue is a benison upon morally disciplined attention. Virtuous habits can never be compulsive or impulse-ridden tendencies; they are, rather, the tendency to perform right acts where moral reason would call for them. Thanks to the virtues, we can have such things as virtuous passions. Even at the level of physiological engagement, we—that is, our bodies—can be the subject of virtues.

The virtues that the Catholic moral tradition regards as cardinal ("hinge-like") in importance are justice, prudence, temperance, and fortitude. They come from the ancient pagan world, but are now to be supernaturalized: that is lived in the new, divinely given, evangelical spirit. Prudence is the virtue that disposes us to discern the golden mean of all the moral virtues, and inclines us in the choice of right means of action. Without prudence, no other moral virtue could truly be exercised: for example, the virtue of mercy bids us help the needy, but only prudence tells us how and when so to do. Justice is the moral virtue that moves us to give others their due. Fortitude is the virtue that urges us to action where we would otherwise and unreasonably be apt to shrink back because of difficulties foreseen. Temperance is

---

11. A. MacIntyre, *After Virtue: A Study in Moral Theory* (Notre Dame, Ind., 1981) 135.

the virtue that holds us back from pursuit of pleasure where appetite would urge us unreasonably to go forward.

In the ancient world, before the gospel, it was realized that these virtues—and others—must be interrelated.

> Because of the different types of achievement in different types of situation; because of the different character of the goods which are at stake in different types of situations, it will be impossible to judge justly, and consequently, impossible to act justly, unless one can also judge correctly in respect of the whole range of the virtues. . . . But since on Aristotle's view it is impossible generally to judge consistently aright concerning a particular virtue without possessing the virtue, it seems to follow that someone who makes just judgements must not only be just but also temperate, courageous, generous and the like. . . . [Moreover] since practical reasoning, as Aristotle understands it, involves the capacity to bring the relevant premises concerning goods and virtues to bear on particular situations, and since this capacity is inseparable from, is indeed a part of, the virtues, including justice, it is also the case that one cannot be practically rational without being just.[12]

But we can go further. Once the gospel enters the picture, not only does prudence unite the virtues at the natural level, but charity enters to unify them more deeply still at the level of God's grace. Here is the result, according to Augustine:

> If virtue leads us to the happy life, I dare to affirm that virtue is nothing else than the sovereign love of God. For in saying that virtue is fourfold, one is speaking . . . of the diverse movements of love itself. And so I would not hesitate to define these famous four virtues (if only their force lay in all spirits as their name is on all lips!) in the following way: temperance is love giving itself integrally to what it loves; courage is love bearing everything with ease for what it loves; justice is love serving exclusively what it loves and for that reason governing with rectitude; prudence is love separating wisely what is useful and what is harmful to it. But this love is not just any love, as we have said, but the love of God, that is, of the sovereign Good, Wisdom and Harmony.[13]

Thomas will go on to speak of charity as the form of the virtues. For him, it is the highest of the three "theological" or God-conjoining virtues, of which the other two are faith and hope. We must say something about each of them. Faith is the virtue that enables us, in recog-

12. A. MacIntyre, *Whose Justice? Which Rationality?* (London, 1988) 106, 123.
13. Augustine, *On the Customs of the Catholic Church* 15.

nizing God's revelation for what it is, actively to believe his promise. As a gift of God, it unites our minds with the God whom we believe on, making us rely on his truthfulness. In so doing, it prepares our intelligence for the final union of heaven. Hope gives us the strength to continue to strive for the eternal life which is the goal God holds out to us. Impossible through our own efforts, it is possible by God's help.

> The essential and chief good that we ought to hope for from God is an unlimited good, one matching the power of the God who helps us. For it belongs to unlimited power to lead to the unlimited good. Now this good is eternal life, which consists in the enjoyment of God himself. For nothing less is to be hoped for from him than what he is. . . . No one can rely too much on God's help. . . . Hope does not chiefly rely on grace already received, but on God's omnipotence and mercy, through which even one who does not have grace can receive it and so come to eternal life. And whoever has grace is certain about God's omnipotence and his mercy.[14]

By charity, God enables us to love him more than all else, so that our lives are shaped by the love of God—our decisions so taken that they imply we prefer nothing else to him, and our actions such that they show we love him and will to share his love for others. In charity, we love God not simply as our maker but more characteristically as our freedom, who wishes to share with us his life and happiness. Of its nature charity flows into love for those whom God loves. But the union of love for God and love for the neighbor is not only in their source; it is also in their goal. "You do not love your neighbor as yourself unless you try to draw him to the good towards which you tend yourself."[15] Charity, then, orientates the other virtues toward their last end: it is, in the language of the Scholastics, both their "efficient" and their "final" cause. The human virtues find their value reaffirmed, not denied, by their integration in the order of grace. Yet the theological virtues remain outstanding, for unlike the moral virtues they have no "mean"; we can never love God inordinately, nor believe in him excessively, nor hope in him too much.

The ugly reverse of virtue is of course vice. The ascetic tradition of the Church normally numbers seven "capital" vices: pride, covetousness, lust, anger, gluttony, envy, sloth. They are at their worst in "mortal" sin, the sin that destroys charity (i.e., friendship with God), robbing

---

14. Thomas Aquinas, *Summa theologiae* 2–2.17.2.
15. Augustine, *On the Customs of the Catholic Church* 26.

us of sanctifying grace and the right to eternal happiness and so killing off the spiritual life of the soul. Such sin involves an awareness that one is turning from the supreme good, not only to find satisfaction in some created finite good, but to do so to the exclusion of God. Though there may be no act of direct hatred of God, one knows that what one is doing is seriously evil: this constitutes the fact of one's "aversion" from God. Such a sin must involve some intrinsically grave moral matter, thorough advertence to that gravity, and full consent in the act of sinning. It is a major decision in favor of wrong priorities. The greatest good is to be the friend of God, and if I break off that friendship, only God can reach out to draw me back to himself. He must re-invent charity in me, re-orientate me so that I once more live for and in him. Because we often repent of mortal sins, it seems natural to do so. But this is because God is so gentle in his rich manifestation of mercy.

Venial sin is called sin only by analogy with mortal sin. It is really a slackening in the momentum of the life of grace. Though it is not rebellion against God it nonetheless slows down our pursuit of him and makes it easier to commit truly grave sins. It calls not so much for repentance as for a reinvigoration of our Christian effort.

There has been much talk above of effort. But in fact the good life in Catholicism is meant eventually to be easy, we might even dare to say facile. The strain we experience in trying to live well is not an inherent part of Christian ethics. On the contrary, the glorious freedom of the sons of God promised us under grace involves learning how to do the good in a spontaneous fashion, as though it were second nature. Aquinas speaks of the God of grace as rendering the acquired moral virtues easier for us by his bestowing of infused moral virtues, whose whole point is to give us greater facility in the exercise of the basic decencies. Analogously, the theological virtues become easier for us to practice when the Holy Spirit gives us himself in the full form of the seven gifts bestowed in embryo at confirmation. In the saints, those gifts are seen in their full flower, and they make the saints docile— readily responsive—to the mind and will of God, to his truth and goodness. The good life becomes a song for them, rather than a slog.

Controverted Areas

The Church's ethical vision and teaching enable her to lay down ground rules in a variety of controverted areas of ethical debate, ranging from bioethics (the ethical investigation of human interventions vis-à-vis the beginning of life and its ending), to matters of social politics. The love she owes human beings moves her to help them to recognize their rights and duties. As she contemplates the mystery of the incarnate Word, she comes to understand as well the human mystery, and by proclaiming her gospel of salvation discloses to human beings their dignity, inviting them to discover more fully the truth of their being.

Social Ethics

For some thinkers such as Hobbes, society, as distinct from brute animal-type relationships of domination and submission, is constituted by the state. More moderately for Hegel, society only enjoys a fully rational and thus proper moral existence via the state. On the opposite end of the spectrum, anarchism holds that the state is a parasitic by-product of society which should be dismantled as soon as possible. Less radically, for Marxism the state is a necessary by-product of society, in all phases of social development save the last, socialist, one where it will wither away. Between these two poles (thus briefly sketched) there stands the Church. For her tradition, the authority that underlies the state is divine authority, though it can be and often is grossly abused by those responsible for carrying out the state's functions. Those functions are intended both to serve and to enhance the common good of society. Society can attain via the state a level of value and virtue which, in some respects, it could not achieve without the state. Yet society exists in its own right prior to the state and has values and institutions (such as the family) that the state must respect, not revise. This distinctness yet interrelatedness of society and the state is one major reason why Catholic social doctrine cannot ally itself with many currents in either left-wing or right-wing theory.

In the eyes of the Church, then, the state is a good: social life is not possible without the recognition of authority as nurse of a common good. Moreover, as Aquinas remarks, those who excel in knowledge and justice do so uselessly unless they can dedicate their gifts by some instrument for the benefit of others. But since morality is ultimately the movement of rational creatures towards God, civic society must conform to the human being's final end—the possession of God. "No man belongs wholly to the State, to the political community. Man belongs wholly only to God, to whom he is wholly oriented, with all that he is, can do, and has."[16] Not that this licenses the Church in taking over

---

16. Thomas Aquinas, *Summa theologiae* 1–2.21.4.ad 3.

temporal power: for Thomas, the Church has a role in *temporalia* only insofar as they are related to *spiritualia,* the natural to the supernatural. Still, the Church sees herself as called to play a vital part in the life of the *polis,* and that in two respects. First, the Church's divinely authorized access to the truth about the human being enables her to speak with authority about the principles that underlie moral coexistence in the human city. Catholicism is sometimes attacked for its concern with authority; yet such concern is evangelical. Christianity's basic postulate is the kingdom of God, and a kingdom implies authority. It was controversy about authority that brought Jesus to his death. Second, the Church also regards herself as an animator of culture, the many-sided human exchange that sustains—or subverts—the life of the *polis* and its common good. The most truly common features of a community should be its religious feasts and civic celebrations, its moral, intellectual, and artistic culture. All of these are highly pertinent to the fullness of social peace found by way of more mundane matters, such as the achievements of a system of justice, of public health, communication, transport. Even these earthly empirical issues are not alien to penetration by moral thinking, because in moral thinking we are not trying to show people how to achieve the vision of God but why a certain pattern of living is a necessary (but not sufficient) condition for that vision.

In such matters, the Church's authority underpins the natural, yet divinely ordained, authority of the civil order. Such natural authority is a good in itself, because it unifies the creative but non-self-regulating functional differentiations found among agents engaged in common action. It is wrong to think, as individualists do, that the restraint that comes from authority is wholly alien to the good of individual persons: the common good is meant to be fruitful in the life of each person in the community, for their perfecting. Because of the social nature of human beings, every person should find an inclination in themselves to the love of what benefits all. When authority is appropriately wielded, it frees people for a more concentrated pursuit of those matters that most interest them. It is communal prudence. In the absence of total unanimity (hardly to be expected) there can be no common action without it.

The Catholic Church accepts a variety of ways of arranging the apparatus of the state. So long as state authority truly aims at the common good, objectively conceived, and retains the consent of the population for its exercise, it may be monarchic, oligarchic, or democratic in form (or some combination thereof). But Catholicism's insistence on the reality of civil society "prior" (i.e., logically, not necessarily chronologically) to the state means that it does not envisage state authority as confronting naked individuals, but presupposes that other levels of corporate entity (such as, in different historic periods or geographical regions, fraternities, trade guilds, village assemblies, municipal communes, trade unions) will provide an intermediate space for responsible action. At the same time, the mutual interdependence of all human beings (the principle of solidarity) encourages us to look beyond our more immediate sphere of responsibility (the principle of subsidiarity) in the prosecution of the common good. It is not the function of a country's government to create a completely integrated system, including economic machinery, for the people to accept and to which they must conform. The task of government is, rather, actively to create and sustain the conditions which will provide an opportunity, a lead, and an encouragement for the civil society in question itself to develop that organizational pattern which accords with its ideals and tradition, and can secure the welfare of its members. In the Thomistically influenced social thought of the Welsh Catholic convert Saunders Lewis: "A nation's civilisation is rich and complex simply because it is a community of communities, and for that reason also the freedom of the individual is a feasible proposition. . . . His liberty depends on his being a member not of one association but of many."[17]

The removal of an obstinately entrenched governing power opposed to the common good is a difficult matter which in recent decades especially has led moralists to apply to civil revolution the principles of just war theory, building thereby on the earlier discussion of the possibility, in extreme circumstances, of regicide. In traditional Christendom, many societies recognized in the pope a useful instrument for confirming or deposing rulers, on the basis of their faithfulness or unfaithfulness to the general principles of an ethical politics. The moral force of such a pontifical intervention could hold out the possibility, at least, of a more irenic transition. This was an extra-evangelical prerogative which the Petrine office had acquired in the course of (as Catholic Christians saw it) a providentially guided Church history. Even today, this role survives in the form of the pope's moral interventions either to state general principles of social morality or (speaking, evidently, with less authority) to interpret the "signs of the times" in secular history, or comment on particular historical

---

17. A. R. Jones and G. Thomas, *Presenting Saunders Lewis* (Cardiff, 1973) 34.

developments. By virtue of the universal kingship of Christ, the Church has an indirect authority over the entire temporal domain.

The object of freedom is truth and goodness. So the state cannot be indifferent to the dissemination of falsehood in religious and moral matters. This conviction separates the Catholic view of civil authority from that of modern liberalism. Though there may be no coercion of conscience (i.e., no one may be pressured into accepting the gospel), religious liberty is not unlimited. It does not extend, for example, to the dissemination of gross error directly productive of moral evil. Natural law provides the general principle of a limited religious liberty for all persons, but God himself has left to the changeable discretion of his Church, under her power of binding and loosing, the judgment of what those limits should be in different times and circumstances. The *Catechism of the Catholic Church* affirms (art. 2105) that she will strive to "penetrate the mentality, customs, laws and structures of society with a Christian spirit," thus "manifesting the kingship of Christ over all creation and in particular over human societies." The redemption of social life cannot be undertaken independently of the inner spiritual renewal of society's members.

At the same time, however, it would be a mistake to conceive of redemption individualistically as a purely inner spiritual transformation with no tangible societal manifestation. The virtue of justice contradicts such a thought. Justice in its most general sense—whatever is required by the common good of a community—is sometimes called "social justice," precisely because it is the justice of society as a whole (and not simply, therefore, its political and economic aspects). A society deemed just will be so at all levels—in the life of the family, the locality, the city, the nation, and its participation in the international order as well.

Subordinate to this, yet vital, are distributive and commutative justice. Distributive justice is both public and personal. Government must see to it that the cost of public provision is equitably borne and that all have equal access to those services provided at public expense. At the same time, the principle of subsidiarity—which is also a principle of justice!—forbids government from taxing people to provide services they could perfectly well furnish for themselves. At the interpersonal level, distributive justice allows people to make reasonable provision for the enjoyment of their own property, since they are by rights the first beneficiaries of what is theirs; it also insists that they should treat the rest of their property as held in trusteeship for the benefit of the wider community.

Commutative justice concerns exchange (e.g., between buyer and seller, debtor and indebted). Price justice requires that neither buyer nor seller dominate the other, and that there be some parity in the value of a commodity or a service and the price paid. Wage justice is more complex, for it adds a consideration of social justice, namely, a sufficiency of payment to support workers and their dependents, while also sustaining the viability of business. It is now widely recognized that where families need help part of this burden should be born by the community at large.

A just society is one where all acknowledge their duties to others; for its full expression, and for any real chance of its success, it requires charity. Only so can it provide a reflection, however distant, of that transfiguration of Old Testament "righteousness" by New Testament *agapē* which is the hallmark of the kingdom.

Justice also applies in the international order: in matters of rich and poor nations, it concerns the equity of international trading relations. Here, justice demands that countries that produce consumer goods, especially farm products, in excess of their needs should help other countries where people are suffering from hunger. Because it is, moreover, integral to the moral nature of civilization that it honors the unity of the human race, it is inappropriate for developed nations to use such aid to gain political control over others.

Not surprisingly, the Catholic social ethos leads to special concern for the poor, for the poor have always had a special place in the heart of the Church.

> This wonderful City, whose foundations God himself has laid, has its laws and its security officers, by whom it is governed. But, since Jesus Christ, its Founder, came into the world to invert the order which pride established, its policy is directly opposite to that of this world—something I note particularly in three points. First, in the world the rich have all the advantages and hold the first rank, whereas in the kingdom of Jesus Christ, pre-eminence belongs to the poor, who are the first-born of the Church and its true children. Secondly, in the world the poor are subject to the rich, and appear to be born only to serve them: on the contrary, in holy Church, the rich are only admitted on the condition that they serve the poor. Thirdly, in the world, favours and privileges are for the powerful and rich, the poor sharing in them only by their support: in the Church of Jesus Christ, by contrast, favours and blessings are for the poor, and the rich have no privileges except through their mediation.[18]

18. J.-B. Bossuet, "De l'éminente dignité des pauvres dans l'Eglise," in *Oeuvres choisies* (Versailles, 1822) 6:15–16.

For Aquinas (and his viewpoint is reflected in the contemporary social teaching of the Church), on the one hand the appropriation of property should be individual because this is dictated by the needs of the human personality, who works on and elaborates matter, subjecting it to the forms of reason. On the other hand, the primordial destination of material goods is the benefit of the human species, and the need that all human beings have for such goods as a means to direct themselves toward their final end. Thus the use of the goods that are individually possessed should serve the common good of all. The problem is thus not how to suppress private interest but how to purify and ennoble it; to hold it in a social structure directed to the common good, and also (and this is the capital point) to transform it inwardly by a sense of communion and fraternal amity.

Modern papal statements have characteristically shifted, however, from basing rights statements directly on the law of God to founding them indirectly on that law—passing by way of the idea of the dignity and task of the human person. Human beings are the proper ends of social institutions. Society exists to serve the interest of its members and to create the conditions in which they can live and develop as God intends. Catholic Christians are not social humanists: they believe that we have here no lasting city, but seek one that is to come, being kept safe for us as it is in the heavens (that is, in the crucified and glorified humanity of the Son of God). Their concern for society is a concern for the world which God loved so much that he both forgave it and ordained for it a new condition, wholly supernatural and divine: his kingdom, in which human life is not only repaired but raised up to enjoy the friendship of the Trinity, the social God, in ways that surpass its own potentialities. This is why the Church rejects both doom and despair about society and a millenarian utopianism. As Leszek Kolakowski has remarked, the Church holds that "the philosopher's stone, the elixir of immortality, these are superstitions of alchemists, nor is there a recipe for a society without evil, without sin or conflict: such ideals are the aberrations of a mind convinced of its own omnipotence, they are the fruits of pride."[19]

Criminality, both of the person and of the state, to which this citation draws our attention, takes its clearest form in murderousness. The Church does not deny that the state may at times legitimately declare a criminal's life forfeit. The point here is that penalty must bear a rela-

19. L. Kolakowski, *Modernity on Endless Trial* (Chicago and London, 1990) 30–31.

tion to truth. The outcome of a person's actions must reflect the nature of those actions. By the decision to commit murder, a murderer loses the kind of claim to inviolability of life made by or for an innocent. Yet many prudential motives would stay the executioner's hand, and a Christian state may well commute such sentences by way of prolongation of the divine mercy. But of course the state itself may also behave murderously—by internal tyranny or, externally, through its attitude to war and peace. No state may go to war against another unless, first, some injustice is clearly established and proved to be very grave; second, every other means has failed; and third, the destructive consequences of armed conflict will be less than those of the injustice that occasioned it.

This macro-social level is not, however, the only one on which the social good can be found. At the micro-social level (and there are others in between—local community; workplace; cultural and philanthropic societies; the family) we have the smallest social group possible: the circle (and, at the smallest, the duo) of friends. "All men are to be loved equally, but since you cannot do good for all, you are to pay special regard to those who, by the accidents of time, or place, or circumstance, are brought into closer connection with you . . . as by a sort of lottery."[20] Within this providential "lottery," our friends and family hold a special place.

The good life cannot be evoked for the Church without reference to the idea of friendship, which is both a constitutive part of the moral vision of her greatest theologians, and lived out in her exemplary ethical heroes, the saints. Its spirit is well expressed in Hrabanus Maurus poem to the "very sweet brother and most reverend abbot Grimold" (abbot of St. Gall, in Switzerland):

> Then, live, my strength, anchor of weary ships,
> Safe shore and land at last, thou, for my wreck,
> My honour, thou, and my abiding rest,
> My city safe for a bewildered heart.
> What though the plains and mountains and the sea
> Between us are, that which no earth can hold
> Still follows thee, and love's own singing follows,
> Longing that all things may be well with thee
> Christ who first gave thee for a friend to me,
> Christ keep thee well, where'er thou art, for me.

20. Augustine, *On Christian Teaching* 1.28.

Earth's self shall go and the swift wheel of heaven
Perish and pass, before our love shall cease.
Do but remember me, as I do thee,
And God, who brought us on this earth together,
Bring us together to his house of heaven.[21]

Christianity learned from the ancient writers—notably Plato, Aristotle, and Cicero—a high regard for friendship. This was in any case immortalized in her own Scriptures, in, for example, the friendship of David with Jonathan, or that of the Savior himself with Lazarus or the "beloved disciple." Friendship is extolled by many of the Fathers and medieval authors, including Aquinas and the English Cistercian abbot Aelred. Friendship can flourish between members of the same or of opposite sexes. In a society where the language of love has been corrupted it will often be misunderstood. It requires self-control and sacrifice. Christian tradition shows that the road to happiness for some lies through friendship without marriage, and that such people, whether publicly consecrated to celibacy or not, have an honored place in the Church.

According to Aelred, God has willed to create human beings in the image of his own triune happiness: they promote their own happiness by doing good to one another. In his *De amicitia,* Aelred teaches that God willed that friendship should exist between his creatures, so that they might be true images of himself. Love is friendship's principle, but friendship is love's perfection, since love tends to union and unity. Spiritual friendship is not for that reason easy: it is demanding, for it requires the formation of a "single will." It provides a medium for the activity of Christ who remedies the disharmonies of human wills with each other in the good and in God; it constitutes therefore an element in sanctification. If the friendship between two Christian friends is true, then Christ himself becomes more and more their common center of attraction and union. In the *osculum spiritua,* the "spiritual kiss," Christ breathes the sacred affection of Father and Son into such friends. Yet the coiling-back of the soul on itself, gradually untied by Christ, is not fully undone till the life of heaven, when charity will become all-embracing friendship.

If friendship saves us from placing ourselves at the center of things, and thus helps us to want the good, the highest good, for ourselves and our friends, it does not restrict our love; while we can only be

---

21. Hrabanus Maurus, *Dulcissimo fratri et reverendissimo abbati Grimoldo.*

friends with a few, we can do good to many. The most basic unity of that "many" in Catholic ethics is the family. The Holy See's *Charter of Family Rights* (1983) spells out the ethos of the family in twelve articles on

> the right to free choice to marry or to remain single; to free and full consent to marriage; to found a family and to decide on the spacing of births; to the protection of life from the moment of conception; to the original primary and inalienable right of parents to educate their children in conformity with their religious and moral convictions; the right of families to exist and progress as a family unit; to profess publicly and to propagate their religious faith; to form associations to protect and foster family rights; to be able to rely on public policy without discrimination; to a social and economic order which permits the family to remain together; to decent housing; and for migrant families to have the right to the same protection as other families.[22]

The family is the hearth in which the most basic values of human and Christian living are focused, and from which they must radiate. Husband and wife are called to share their common love in a fruitful giving of self which has its first, but not its only object, in children. Their mutual support should sustain them in a call to shape a cell of civilized living—"civilized" not in its modern sense, which has connotations of fashion and snobbism, but in the sense of all that which, through culture and grace, makes a person most human. The lifelong dedication of spouses to each other, and the sturdy acceptance of responsibility for how their children grow up, is the foundation on which all else can be built, creating the confidence which is a necessary condition for the successful transmission of values.

Familial Ethics

The basis of Catholic sexual ethics lies in the affirmation that certain values are part and parcel of human nature and should, accordingly, be fostered and developed. "Values" tell us what is more important than what, what takes precedence over what, and therefore, inevitably, what is to be sacrificed for the sake of what. All of this is to be found by exploring human nature—what it is to be human. In accord with our nature, we have certain basic deep desires. We may hide them from ourselves, but if they are frustrated or contradicted, we will inevitably live in self-contradiction and be unhappy. Many things that

---

22. Cf. *Catechism of the Catholic Church,* § 2211.

look as if they will make us happy in the long run will not do so because they involve the frustration of deep natural desires. Our deepest sexual desires are only fulfilled in marriage, or as the Roman *Declaration on Sexual Ethics* of 1975 put it, "sexuality meets the demands of its own finality in marriage." Sexual activity is only humanly natural when it involves mutual self-giving, procreation, and the proper context of true love—a socially directed compact of life-long reciprocal commitment by two people. Sexuality is not a merely animal function, and the sexual act is not a kind of compulsive discharge of no intrinsic moral significance. Sexual desire is a longing to be united with another person and tenderness (and so mutual consent) is the essence of its bond. Modesty and shame are essential to it, and the attempt to abolish its mystery by replacing these ideas with sexual hygiene also abolishes true desire. Moreover, human life is so great a good that the sexual act, which results in the coming to be of life, can never be treated cavalierly.

It is because homosexual activity lacks the full complementarity of the man-woman relationship, and also procreative openness to new life, that the Catholic Church cannot recognize it as a legitimate expression of the human sexual inclination. As the 1988 letter to the bishops of the Catholic Church by the Roman Congregation for the Doctrine of the Faith observes, while the Church must be open to enlightenment from the human sciences, she must also remain confident that her own more "global vision," transcending that of the particular sciences, "does greater justice to the rich reality of the human person."

Empirical investigation of the causes of the homosexual condition has produced no generally accepted results. This is not surprising since, in fallen humanity, human sexual instinct is highly pliable; early erotic feeling is diffused and therefore potentially polymorphous. The idea of exclusive homosexuality is a modern one. In the ancient, medieval, or even early modern periods, same-sex liaisons were not thought of as something engaged in by a sexually distinct class of persons. Exclusive homosexuality, it would seem, was a social creation ("construct") of modern times. For ancient Israel—by contrast with surrounding cultures—all genital activity between persons of the same sex was considered a moral offense. As revealed by God to Israel, humankind's sexual nature is meant to have physical expression only within certain definite limits. This has to do with, first, the spousal or nuptial significance of the human body and, second, the complementarity of the unitive and procreative dimensions of sexuality in the divine plan. And, as Paul points out in the Letter to the Romans, when by idolatry human beings put the creation in place of the Creator it can be expected that they will also pervert the created order itself. Homosexual practices constitute in the "household code" laid down by the Apostle in First Corinthians one of the things that Christians are not to do, on pain of exclusion from the coming kingdom of God (1 Cor 6:9–10). Paul maintains that the union of body and spirit is such that in intercourse the whole personality is committed, and the "one flesh" which two personalities thus become can only be that man/woman relation of the original creation of humankind where the two—Adam and Eve—became one flesh, one reality. "To choose someone of the same sex for one's sexual activity is to annul the rich symbolism and meaning, not to mention the goal, of the Creator's sexual design."[23] Such an option is neither complementary nor life giving. While it recognizes that the abandonment of habitual homosexual activity may require a demanding collaboration of the person with God's liberating grace, the congregation also insists that to regard homosexual behavior as compulsive is unfounded and demeaning. Theologically, the ultimate origin of this condition is the Fall, which produced an inner dislocation among our human powers so that these different faculties tend to their proper objects only in an uncertain, unstable way. The capacity for companionable love, the love of friendship, which should be aimed indifferently at those of one's own and the opposite sex, can become mixed up with the desire for erotic love, whose rationale is the complementarity of male and female.

Contraceptive activity can also be seen in its true light as intrinsically unfitting to the human being, for the Creator so arranged the sexual act that it is simultaneously per se generative and per se expressive of intimate oblative love. He has so ordered things that procreation would take place from an act intimately expressive of conjugal love, and this act of conjugal love tend towards procreation. Unfortunately, a perverse and dehumanizing ideology of irresponsible sexual pleasure stands in the way of the reception of this ethics in Western or Western-influenced cultures today. The mastery of sensibility in the moment of adolescence, a mastery whose goal is a true love, alone gives young persons the chance within marriage to be able to regulate their fecundity and space the births of their children as they wish without falling

---

23. *Letter to the Bishops of the Catholic Church on the Pastoral Care of Homosexual Persons*, 7.

victim to a contraceptive practice that substitutes technical control for the self-control which alone befits the virtue of parental responsibility.

The heart of the Church's objection to artificial contraception lies, then, in her insistence that the unitive (relational) and procreative aspects of marital intercourse should not be sundered. Contraceptive intercourse does not express an act of total self-giving, for it withholds from one's spouse one's fertility, with all that that entails. The yielding of this point in matters of family planning turns out to unravel the entire logic of the Christian sexual ethic. If sexual intercourse can be turned into something other than the reproductive *type* of act (for clearly, not every act of intercourse is reproductive, any more than every acorn becomes an oak), if sexual union can be deliberately and totally separated from fertility, then it becomes quite unclear why sexual union must be married union at all. The Church inherited from the Old Testament people of God a fundamental objection to what Augustine called "base ways of copulating for the avoidance of conception"—for contraception excludes God from an arena designed by him as the special locus of his creative action. The earliest situation in which she explicitly reaffirmed the moral ethos of Israel appears to have been third-century Rome, where free-born Christian women, who had married slaves so as to have Christian husbands, used contraceptive methods so as to avoid bearing children who, in Roman law, would themselves be slaves. When, in the early twentieth century, Western society became increasingly contraceptive, but also gained a much fuller physiological understanding than the ancient or medieval worlds had enjoyed, Catholic married people came under great pressure "rationally to limit" their families. At first only cautiously, but later with more confidence, Catholic authorities recommended the identification and use of the "safe period"—where no question arises of a moral intention to prevent the coming to be of a new human life. Couples need not desire children in every act of intercourse, yet that does not license their abrogation of the natural ordination of the marriage act. This remains the basis of the "natural family planning" advocated in Catholicism and it is in process of rediscovery, from differing perspectives, by ecologism and "moderate" feminism alike.

Pre-marital intercourse is not necessarily a caricature of the procreative dimension of sexuality (as is homosexual intercourse) or its denial (as with contraception), for it may of course lead to parenthood. Instead, it gravely damages the oblative dimension. Though such intercourse may express a love the partners sincerely feel for each other at that particular time, they do not as yet share a community of life, to be sustained by the subordination of their individual desires. Hence the sexual exchange tends to become a mutual receiving and giving of pleasure, separated from the sacrificial context necessary to give authenticity to sexual love. Pre-marital intercourse in a subtle way generates selfishness, and so destabilizes in advance the marital union. Moreover, the couple loses the opportunity of *limerence:* the cementing of their union by the marriage-act at a moment when it has most power to facilitate their mutual adjustment in married life.

Similarly, auto-eroticism reinforces an attitude of seeking immediate satisfaction rather than of self-giving. The practice of abstention, not from an irrational fear (of medical or psychological consequences that are no doubt largely non-existent) but as a freely willed preparation for marriage or for permanent celibacy, should promote a greater capacity for love. Characteristically accompanied by fantasy, sometimes of a bizarre kind, its origins are several (desire for sexual release, or boredom, but also, and worthy of greater concern, loneliness and self-hatred). It must be treated with compassion. Yet Christ was very clear in his condemnation of lustful desire—which this certainly is.

Such practices belong with a culture where sex has been severed from spirituality and even from humanity. Pornography authorizes lust by freeing it from moral scruple. It delivers excitement from the obstructions of tenderness and enables interest in another body to be pursued without deflection by awareness of another soul. It is the perfect preparation for a sexual ambition which aims to disconnect soul and body, possessing the second without paying the price exacted by the first.

The feminist myth that the institution of the family, the division of sexual roles, and the ideals of modesty and chastity are all male inventions, designed to confine and thwart women, exacerbates this situation. These "confines" are in fact the bonds from which men have always sought to free themselves. Feminist ideology, as Professor Roger Scruton has pointed out, enables men's relations with women to be regulated by the laws of supply and demand, so that claims of power can replace those of allegiance.

Bioethics

The Church holds that every person has the potential for a knowledge of God so complete as to involve sharing the divine nature. Because of this, every life must be treated as precious. A given life may have little chance to obtain the things the world cares about, but it always has this far more profound potential. The conviction that governs the Church's ethical teaching in this area was well expressed in Pope John Paul II's encyclical *Evangelium vitae* ("On the Value and Inviolability of Human Life").

> Even in the midst of difficulties and uncertainties, every person sincerely open to truth and goodness can, by the light of reason and the hidden action of grace, come to recognise in the natural law written in the heart the sacred value of human life from its very beginning until its end, and can affirm that right of every human being to have this primary good respected to the highest degree. Upon the recognition of this right, every human community and the political community itself are founded.[24]

Catholicism's teaching on a range of questions raised by this topic is conveniently summarized in *Donum vitae*, a document promulgated on the Pope's behalf by the Congregation for the Doctrine of the Faith in 1987, and confirmed in *Evangelium vitae*.

What respect is due to the embryo, given its nature and identity? *Donum vitae* took its cue here from *Gaudium et spes*, where the fathers of the Second Vatican Council used the strongest language on this subject: "All offenses against life itself, such as murder, genocide, abortion, euthanasia, and wilful suicide . . . are criminal. They poison civilisation, and they debase the perpetrators even more than the victims. . . . Life must be protected with the utmost care from the moment of conception: abortion and infanticide are abominable crimes."[25] The life sciences can support the notion that in the zygote the biological identity of a new human individual is already constituted, but leaving that aside, it is at the very least a counsel of prudence to hold that the adventure of human life begins from fertilization. Since the embryo must be treated as a person (indeed, for divine revelation there was once a Redeemer in the womb), it must also be defended and cared for to the extent possible, in the same way as any other human being, so far as medical assistance is concerned. No objective, however noble, such as a foreseeable advantage for science or society, can ever justify experimentation on living human embryos, whether viable or not, inside or outside the mother's body. For the Catholic Church such practices of advanced medical technology form part of a "culture of death," where

24. John Paul II, *Evangelium vitae*, 2.
25. *Gaudium et spes*, 27.

researchers choose arbitrarily whom they will permit to live, transgressing the foundational moral axiom according to which no human being may be reduced to the status of a mere instrument for the benefit of others.

Another concern is those techniques—artificial procreation and fertilization—aimed at obtaining a human conception in some other way than by the sexual union of man and woman. Though every human being is always to be accepted as a gift from God, the tradition of the Church and a sound anthropology alike find in stable marital union the only setting worthy of procreation. Every child has the right to be conceived, carried in the womb, and brought up, within marriage. Through a recognized relation with its own parents it discovers its proper identity, while for their part the parents find in their child the completion of their reciprocal self-giving. The deepest reason for this is that the procreation of a new person, whereby man and woman collaborate with God's creativity, must be the fruit and sign of their mutual love. As *Donum vitae* puts it, the child is the "living image of their love, the permanent sign of their conjugal union, the living and indissoluble concrete expression of their fatherhood and motherhood."

In the light of these principles not only heterologous artificial procreation and surrogate motherhood (in both of which third parties are involved) but also homologous artificial fertilization appear as evidently misplaced. Though the desire to have a child of one's own and to obviate a sterility which cannot be overcome in any other way are in themselves thoroughly understandable and even praiseworthy aspirations, to introduce a rupture between genetic parenthood, gestational parenthood, and responsibility for upbringing can only threaten the unity and stability of family life at large.

Homologous artificial fertilization, since it involves no third party (save by way of medical help) is a distinct category. Yet it too brings the procreation of a child outside the act whereby the marriage covenant of its parents is renewed. As the means of seeking an offspring which is not the fruit of a specific act of conjugal union, it brings about a separation between the meanings of marriage analogous to that wrought by artificial contraception. Procreation is deprived, ethically, of its proper perfection when it is not desired as the result of that act, sexual intercourse, which is specific to the union of the spouses. A fertilization achieved outside that meeting in the flesh which is simultaneously the meeting of two souls is bereft of the meanings and values that the nuptial language of the body articulates. Such fertilization entrusts the life and identity of the embryo to the power of doctors and biologists, and, once again, establishes the dominion of technology over the origin and destiny of human beings.

The intrinsic evil of the abortion of the unborn is manifest from this discussion of the context of conception. It is for Catholicism a mystery of iniquity that

> choices once unanimously considered criminal and rejected by the common moral sense are gradually becoming socially acceptable. . . . Broad sectors of public opinion justify certain crimes against life in the name of the rights of individual freedom, and on this basis they claim not only exemption from punishment but even authorisation by the State, so that these things can be done with total freedom and indeed with the free assistance of health-care systems. . . . In this way the very nature of the medical profession is distorted and contradicted, and the dignity of those who practise it is degraded.[26]

No pope could speak otherwise than in these accents were he really to act in the name of the Savior who himself at the annunciation took flesh as a human embryo in the womb of Mary and, at the visitation, was heralded while still an embryo by his fetal cousin. His birth was attended by a slaughter of the innocents; there are now millions of such little ones to whom life has been denied because others felt threatened on their throne of self-love, as Herod did on his throne in Judaea.

Although few countries have introduced legislation permitting the deliberate termination of inconvenient life at its other end, in old age and advanced chronic sickness, the mind-set analyzed by the Pope leads ineluctably in this direction also.

Euthanasia is the alleviation of suffering through the purposeful destruction of the life of the sufferer. Reflection on the nature of the human person generates the axiom that no one has the right to make another person's death the goal of his or her action; therefore, the institution of therapies designed to promote death earlier than would be otherwise expected cannot be countenanced. Like suicide (and "assisted suicide" is its most frequent form), it "represents a rejection of God's absolute sovereignty over life and death, as proclaimed in the prayer of the ancient sage of Israel, 'You have power over life and death; you lead men down to the gates of Hades and back again' (Wisdom 16, 13)."[27] To be carefully distinguished from such so-called

26. John Paul II, *Evangelium vitae*, 4.
27. Ibid., 66.

positive euthanasia there is also, however, what has been termed nega-tive euthanasia: the shortening of a fatal disease through the planned withdrawal of life-prolonging treatment. This, for the Church, is not morally objectionable so long as it is simply a response to a new situ-ation caused by the unusual progress of medicine. There is no obliga-tion to keep a person alive indefinitely by means which the "reasonable man" would regard as more than ordinary, more than expected. But this does not extend to such absolutely minimum treatment as basic hydration, nutrition, and ventilation (except for the person actually dying where, commonly, keeping the mouth moist is the sole tradi-tional nursing care deemed appropriate). *Jura et bona,* a 1980 declara-tion of the Congregation for the Doctrine of the Faith on these issues, reiterates the point that persons in a "vegetative" state cannot be dead: their brain-stem is functioning. If the supplying of nutrition, hydra-tion, and ventilation to such patients benefits them and causes neither undue burden of pain or suffering, nor an "excessive" expenditure of resources, then it is a duty.

Bioethics are not the whole of Catholic medical ethics. The two most important principles governing Catholic medical ethics at large are the principle of totality and the principle of integrity. A whole per-son is a multi-dimensional person and each dimension must be re-spected simultaneously. As a result there is both an imperative to improve the integrated workings of a system where one part may be deficient or another part hypertrophied, and a recognition that the parts of an organism exist in, by, and for the existence of the whole and are therefore properly expendable for the good of that whole.

Relevant to the questions raised by medical practice vis-à-vis the use of drugs, surgery, sterilization, organ transplantation and sex-change, psychiatry, and medical experimentation, these principles re-flect both the real existence of unities and *differentia* in a creation-based account of the cosmos, and the incarnational personalism of the gospel. However much it seeks a hearing—and so common ground—in the public, philosophical realm, Catholic ethics never loses touch with the wider revelatory (and so theological) vision that issues from Scripture and Tradition.

The Ethics of Labor

All the human activities which Catholic ethics evaluates require labor, whether intellectual or manual. The Genesis author who portrays God as a worker in his creative labor evidently intended to signal work's dignity and the possibility of treating working as an imitation of the Creator. The Church's Tradition treats humankind as called to sub-creation, continuing God's creative work. Though human art is the fabrication of formless material into formed, whereas divine art creates the material from which all objects and the acts which beget them take their origin, nonetheless divine artisanship can be the paradigm of human because it is concerned with the infusion of meaning into matter. For Basil, in the fourth century, the mark of the Creator can be discerned in the durability of the creative arts—architecture and wood-working, metal-work and weaving—whereas the products of the practical and theoretical arts pass away more quickly. The world as a whole is a work of art through which the wisdom and power of the crafting Creator may be contemplated.

Insofar as everything that human beings do can have skill applied to it, all human action can be called in a wider sense "art." In a maxim beloved of Eric Gill, every man is a special kind of artist. Our work flows from God's, and this dependency shows the limits of our dominion and the desirability of conforming that realm to the "laws of creation," work's ecological aspect. Our inheritance is not, however, directly from God alone; we also have a patrimony from the accumulated work of other people.

The second Adam, Jesus Christ, worked, and made reference to workers of many different kinds in his parables. His hidden life, on which I made some comment in chapter 4, speaks eloquently of the dignity of work, especially the manual work despised by classical culture.

It would be, however, unrealistic to deny a negative, destructive side to work. Work is toil, it can seem to destroy rather than recreate us, something well evoked in the language of Adam's "curse" after the Fall. There is a hard, mortificatory—though possibly redemptive—aspect to work.

We have a duty to work, but only those who need to do so in order to support themselves have a right to employment. Though involuntary unemployment is always bad, we cannot expect the state to guarantee employment in every case without simultaneously granting it the right to direct labor where it thinks fit, irrespective of talents or wishes—something manifestly counter to social justice in its widest acceptation.

There is no normatively "correct" level of human technology or, indeed, science. Each culture can to a degree create for itself the view of the natural world it considers most suited to its needs. A society might, for instance, prefer a more custodial (rather than exploitative) attitude towards nature, and some science other than physics or biology as its preferred paradigm.

In Catholicism, the approach to technology will normally be human-, person-, or worker-centered. Emphasis will lie on the human purposes fulfilled or thwarted by particular technologies and their effects in human lives. Material life should sustain spiritual value: this is the message of the personalistic understanding of work at the heart of Pope John Paul II's encyclical on this subject, *Laborem exercens*. The subjective aspect of work, whereby we grow more fully into the image of God, is more fundamental than the objective, the economic gain to be enjoyed—though the honesty, utility, and even beauty of good work well done has, irrespective of market valuation, a kind of objectivity that enriches subjects, both individually and socially.

Conclusion

In many contemporary societies, the Church has difficulty not only in commending her metaphysics and account of history (thanks to the secularization of pure reason) but also in encouraging the pursuit of the moral life in her terms (thanks to the secularization of practical reason). Once the notion of essential human purposes or functions disappears from morality, there seems to be no reason to treat moral judgments as factual statements; gradually, then, ethical argument becomes interminable because it is indeterminable. At the same time, the notion of moral judgments as reports on divine law also founders. And since mere imperatives—as distinct from reports of what the law requires or commands—cannot be judged true or false, the question of what it is in virtue of which a particular moral judgment is true or false has come to lack a clear answer. Furthermore, where virtues are seen as dependent for their justification on a proper authentication of certain rules and principles, when the latter are called into question so too are the former. It is the function of the canonized saints in Catholicism to draw our attention in the first place to the (as it were) canonical virtues, from which vantage point we can proceed to develop our understanding of the function and authority of rules. And there is, one supposes, normally no way to possess the virtues *efficaciously* except as part of a tradition in which we inherit both them and our understanding of them. The virtues belong to a city, a *polis,* and the virtues ordered by charity belong to the city of God. In the Church's tradition, the grasp of virtues found in the pagan city (the heroic literature of Greece, Plato, Aristotle) is married to the sensibility of Scripture (chiefly narrative in form) in order to create an understanding of the virtues as permitting us to live in, and respond to, history—to live human life as a quest or a journey. Encouragement of the virtues does not of course exclude the identification of absolute norms of action. There are whole kinds of action that a virtuous person would do or refrain from doing. Finally, in the Christian perspective there is no evil that can exclude, ultimately, from the human good those who practice the virtues—as defined by charity—unless they willingly become evil's accomplice. The good entertained in biblical (and so ecclesial) eschatology shows us the virtues' final point.

13
Ways to Holiness

The Doctrinal Foundations of Spirituality

The Catholic Church knows various spiritualities, but we must begin by outlining what they have in common. According to Catholicism, the heart of spirituality, prayer, is determined by the structure of the Christian faith itself, where the truth of both God and creature shines out.

Distinctively Christian prayer takes its ethos from the historic revelation. In the Old Testament, the prayer of Israel (most notably in the Psalms, but also in canticles and odes scattered throughout the historical, prophetic, and wisdom books), tells in the first place of God's works on behalf of the chosen people. Not only in creation but also, and especially, in redemption Israel meditates and contemplates these *mirabilia Dei,* reappropriating them for herself. In the New Testament, the self-revelation of the Father in the Son by the Holy Spirit enormously enriches the content of biblical prayer and changes its axis. For Paul, the mystery of God par excellence is Jesus Christ "in whom are hid all the treasures of wisdom and knowledge" (Col 2:3). As the Second Vatican Council puts it, by means of his revelation the invisible God "from the fullness of his love, addresses men as his friends, in order to invite and receive them into his own company."[1] Hence the role in spirituality of the prayerful reading of Scripture *(lectio).* To meditate is, in the first place, to rehearse the biblical text, constantly repeating, murmuring, its words. The medievals called this *ruminare*—as a cow chews the cud, so a Christian digests the word of God, tranquilly, engrossed. If the biblical word is to be a seed of life germinating within us, we must let it sink down and enter the heart. Such *meditatio* turns naturally into prayer, a response of self-surrender to God in Christ via this text; on the classical medieval scheme, this is called

---

1. *Dei Verbum,* 2.

oratio. Finally, such prayer tends to become silent adoration of God's presence, *contemplatio*. The movement is not of course inevitable, yet it is self-correcting. When distractions take over, one has a remedy: returning to the text, one lets the language pour over oneself again until the prayerful and contemplative spiral resumes.

This is not simply the result of the individual's effort. The missions of the Son and the Spirit enable human beings to welcome and contemplate the words and works of God in the "new and everlasting covenant," and thank and adore him in the liturgical assembly and the "cell" of the heart. Because Christian prayer is always a participation in the prayer of Christ and the "groaning" of the Spirit, it bears a necessary relation to the Scriptures, where these realities are disclosed, and also to the communion of the Church, where they are sacramentally present. Even when a Christian prays alone, his or her prayer remains within the framework of the communion of saints.

Among those "saints" the masters and mistresses of prayer have always constituted an important group. Since the time of the Desert Fathers, teachers warned of spiritual dangers such as the false "gnosis" which hates matter and treats supernatural grace as an attribute of the soul, rather than the free gift of God; or "Messalianism" which deifies spiritual experience, and regards its deprivation, or transmutation into the experience of affliction and desolation, as signs that the Holy Spirit has abandoned the soul; or again that Neoplatonism (in the pejorative sense of that in some ways admirable movement of philosophical thought) which regards prayer as the attempt to ascend to, or immerse oneself in, the sphere of the divine, understood as a realm beyond both sense perceptions and intelligible concepts. Over against these temptations, teachers of the art of prayer in a Christian context also stressed, more positively, the human and earthly mediation of a divine and unearthly reality, whose center is the life, death, and resurrection of Jesus Christ and the Pentecostal communication of his (characteristic) Spirit. Referring to that model of all praying, the 1989 Letter of the Congregation of the Doctrine of the Faith *On Some Aspects of Christian Meditation* drew the attention of its readers to the practical test of the authenticity of prayer: from the desert and the mountain, Jesus passed to his saving work in the human city. "Contemplative Christian prayer always leads to love of neighbor, to action, and to the acceptance of trials and precisely because of this it draws one more closely to God."[2]

2. *On Some Aspects of Christian Meditation,* 13.

Purgation, Illumination, Union

On the basis of a commonplace of late antiquity, various schools of prayer and individual writers on prayer have expounded their sense of the dynamic development of a Christian life in terms of three phases: purgative, illuminative, and unitive. Though such categories can be abused by failure to fill them with a distinctively evangelical and ecclesial content, they are in themselves a helpful way in which to structure an account of this dynamism. First, seeking God through prayer has to be at once prepared for and accompanied by a serious effort to uproot the tares of sin and error: *purgation*. By (negatively) self-denial, or "mortification," and (positively) exposing oneself to the message of the gospel in an integral and wholehearted way, evil thoughts and passions are to be rooted out: the lack of truth and love, the endemic selfishness that follows from the Fall are to go. In disencumbering the self of sensuous representations and of concepts, an emptiness is created which can then be filled by the richness of God. This emptiness is, however, not a rejection of the creaturely, nor is it simply an entry into the depths of the self: rather is it a re-evaluation of the world in the light of God, who wills to draw us totally into his triune life, his eternal love. Consequently, in orthodox mysticism the human figure of Jesus is not, in this context, something to be left to one side. On the contrary, it is through the manifestation of Jesus, as a figure perceivable by the senses and still so perceivable through the spiritual eye of faith, that the praying person knows the Father.

"After" purification (the stages are to some extent not so much chronological as [theo-]logical) comes *illumination*. Church tradition links this inextricably to the grace or "unction" bestowed on believers by the Holy Spirit in baptism. On the basis of the grace of baptism, the faithful are called to make progress in understanding of, and witness to, the mysteries of faith, helped by the interior penetration of those realities provided by the Spirit of Christian initiation. "Any subsequent graces of illumination which God may grant help to clarify the depth of the mysteries confessed and celebrated by the Church, as we wait for the day when the Christian can contemplate God as he is in glory."[3] Through the sanctifying grace of baptism, the theological virtues of faith, hope, and charity are infused within us, to act as the foundation of our disposition towards God. They are, as the last chapter showed, the operative principles of the supernatural life: the rest is icing on the

3. Ibid., 21.

cake. However, given that these gifts are received into our normal human faculties they are to some extent subordinate to rational knowledge and functioning. The "gifts" of the Holy Spirit—wisdom, understanding, counsel, fortitude, knowledge, the fear of the Lord (Isa 11:2)—are given so as to render our faculties more receptive to the movement of the Holy Spirit. They are bestowed *in nuce* in that "seal" of baptism which is confirmation. As with all the gifts of grace that make for holiness, however, the sacramental manifestation will often await a more "charismatic" manifestation; it unfolds in our lives when factors, both exterior and interior, are favorable.

Baptism, together with (above all) the Holy Eucharist, forms likewise the sacramental foundation to the state of *union.* That state must be distinguished from any particular experience of union. All are called to the profoundest union with God by charity, but not all are necessarily called to mystical union: a specific type of union, based on a special grace of the Spirit. Every Christian can quicken the normal gifts of the Holy Spirit through zeal for the life of faith, hope, and charity, and these gifts provide, for any baptized person, a certain experience of God and the other realities of faith. Other charisms are bestowed on persons specifically that they may bear fruit in the life of the Church; every Christian has a specific task (and in this sense a charism) for the edification of the Lord's house. In addition to these, those endowed with mystical gifts experience certain momentary foretastes of the age to come; when their experience is intense, habitual, they lead the person (not without suffering) into that deep union often called—in the imagery of the Song of Songs—the "mystical marriage." The medieval English Cistercian Aelred of Rievaulx would appeal rather to the imagery of the Sabbath:

> We are drawn into his glorious light and are lost in his unbelievable joy. Everything that belongs to our human nature, everything that is fleshly and perceptible and transitory is stilled. All we can do is to gaze on the One who is forever changeless, and as we gaze on him we are perfectly at rest. So great is the delight we find in his embrace that this is indeed the Sabbath of Sabbaths. . . . In each Sabbath we find rest and peace and joy for the spirit, but the first Sabbath belongs to a man's own quiet conscience, the second to the community of men living happily together, and the third consists in the contemplation of God.[4]

---

4. Aelred, *Mirror of Charity* 6.

An ecstatic understanding of transcendent verities may be purely natural (as perhaps in the ancient philosopher Plotinus) or enjoy the assistance of the Spirit, but it is not strictly mystical contemplation, which is always based on love of its own object. Indeed, according to Augustine in his *Confessions* (7.10; see also 9.10, the famous vision at Ostia shared by Augustine and his mother, Monica) such "intellectual ecstasy" discloses to the soul its weakness and distance from God. Union—a habitual and steady harmony between God and the soul—can only be the fruit of a long and costly process, the appropriation of the Lord's death and resurrection. In describing the state of union, John of the Cross tried to express a level of contact deeper and more comprehensive than that available through any of our faculties—something other than ordinary subject-object perception. The "substantial touch" (as he terms it) reflects the soul's protracted reaction to what it is coming to know ever more certainly: it is held in God's love and is being united with his will and work in the very ground of its motivation. This may occasion joy, tears, ardent love, and praise, but what is constitutive of mystical union is not these sensations but the fact of divine action in the heart of the self, so stripped of self-seeking that it erects no barriers to God's loving will.

Christian mystics habitually speak of this condition in terms of what at first sight appears to be quite conflicting imagery: a suffusion of light, or an entering into darkness. The disorientation caused by God's profound activity in the soul (in the case of the mature contemplative), when grasped by the recipient in its thorough pervasiveness, can be called either darkness or light, void or plenitude, depending on traditions of religious rhetoric, exegetical interest, and even temperament.

Through the active and passive purification of its knowledge, the adherence of the believing intellect to God's revelation comes to depend less on its natural operation as a mind and more on the infused light it owes to its engraced sharing in God's own knowledge. However, because the mind's infused understanding comes from the light of faith, its object can be nothing other than the revealed truth to which the assent of faith is given. Therefore, even in the mystical encounter with God of a mind purged thereby of concepts, the adherence of the intellect must still be given to the "substance" of the truths it has already learned through historical revelation. The charity operative in living faith gives the soul the strength it needs to adhere firmly to that gospel "substance" in its interior life of prayer.

It follows that growth in faith can never be equated with increasing clarity in the mind's conceptual knowledge of God. On the contrary, the growing firmness with which faith, vivified by charity, adheres to God must be attributed to the increasing ability of the mind to dispense with a conceptual knowledge of God in its ascent through the stages of active and passive purification. That is why the mind, in journeying from the world to God, must rise above the conceptual science of theology—in mystical prayer, a Gregory the Theologian, a Thomas, is not simply thinking about God—in order to adhere more firmly to the "substance" of revelation in the non-conceptual wisdom of prayerful contemplation. Yet at the same time, contemplative wisdom retains its source in faith. No knowledge of God's own inner being available to the human mind can be more direct or immediate than the knowledge given by God himself in revelation and humanly accepted through faith. Mystical knowledge can never rise above the historic revelation. The Catholic mystic remains firmly solidary with his "even-Christians," the community of the Church.

The position adopted here belongs to the mainstream of the Catholic theology of mysticism: all may aspire to "acquired" contemplation, the non-discursive "prayer of simple regard" or "prayer of loving attention." But contemplation in the fullest sense—infused contemplation—is entirely God's gift in such a way that it can never be expected as something quite predictable. Although some may doubt whether the Christian contemplative tradition forms a coherent enough whole for any theological generalizations to be legitimate, that tradition does (consonant with sound doctrine!) expect and encourage all baptized believers to enter into transforming union with God. It does not, however, predict or require that all will become reflectively aware of this condition. All Christians receive a general and (in the language of the Neoscholastic divines) "remote" call to contemplation, but not all have a proximate and immediate call. Given certain conditions and circumstances it may well be impossible even for a saint to reach the higher degrees of contemplative prayer—as Gregory the Great recognized in his pastoral rule. For the Dominican school, there can be a genuinely mystical life, with the gifts of the Holy Spirit in play, when the gift of wisdom exists in a Christian in practical, rather than contemplative, form. Thus the gift of wisdom enabled that eminently practical Church reformer Vincent de Paul to see the suffering members of Christ in the unfortunate; it did not give him contemplative glimpses of that final Sabbath which is the goal of the whole Church in the kingdom.

The norm for most devout Christians is nonetheless for periods of conscious loving attention to become longer and steadier, according to the helpfulness of circumstances. (This, in the Sanjuanist scheme, is the threshold of "infused contemplation," the night of sense.) It was the great contribution to Catholic spirituality of Francis de Sales to insist that such a "devout life" is in principle open to all, whatever their station or situation. As Abbot Cuthbert Butler put it, "A contemplative life does not lie in the absence of activity but in the presence of contemplation." Any devout layperson can live a genuinely "contemplative" life, though without the dramatic commitment (and the helpful concomitants) of the full monastic life, lived at the heart of the Church as a celebration of, and witness to, just such contemplation.

Various attempts have been made in the history of spiritual theology to "grade" the Christian ascent up the ladder of spiritual perfection. It is characteristic of the Carmelite school (and especially Teresa of Avila) and those influenced by the great Carmelite mystics of the sixteenth century to distinguish states of soul by the criterion of psychological accessibility. This has its place, but it is not the whole story. A typical medieval text such as *De septem gradibus contemplationis,* with its steps of fire, unction, ecstasy, speculation (contemplation), taste, quiet, and glory, is more concerned with the objectivity of the Spirit's gifts (seven being the number of his fullness), and less with our capacity consciously to experience them.

The Diversity of Spiritualities

How, then, do spiritualities differ? Not only in the sense that there is in the Church a variety of spiritual schools; there are also different states of life. The individual Christian life, founded in every case on the evangelical charity revealed by Christ, is nevertheless lived out in differing mediations of his work of recapitulation—which nothing escapes save the sin he came to destroy. The indispensable subjective condition without which an objective mediation of Christ's recapitulating work would remain sterile for spiritual progress must always be charity. But charity means not only attention to the concrete needs of our neighbor in the most elementary, pragmatic sense of the word "need." Those who work to bring to the world more intellectual light or greater aesthetic beauty can also be moved by charity, as can those who consecrate their lives to prayer as a service to humanity. The chief loci at which the Lord's transfiguring presence makes itself available for contemplative appropriation may be said to be, first, oneself; second, one's neighbor; and third, the world at large in which one's life is set, and all these modes of his epiphany are operative in the classical spiritualities of the Church. Reaching the God who is actively present in the embodied soul, seeing God in the neighbor, and finding God in nature and all things: these three are found time and again in the history of Christian spirituality. Let us look at each more closely.

Hunger for God—a deep desire of the soul to seek the Lord whom she wishes to possess fully—is a dominant theme of all spirituality, appearing most clearly in the Carmelite school. It has its roots in Paul's desire "to go away and to be with Christ" (Phil 1:23). This desire for the life everlasting can be, if God wills, directly illuminated by him, nourished with the very life of grace the Spirit gives at baptism. Though God cannot be possessed except beyond death, as the "reward" of a life of loving obedience, the soul can seek him (above all) within. Since "the love of God has been spread abroad in our hearts by the Holy Spirit who has been given us" (Rom 5:5), the active presence of the Spirit of Father and Son in the human soul is a privileged mediation of the divine being itself. The interior life, founded on the theological virtues of faith, hope, and charity, testifies to the real inauguration here and now of the life eternal. As Paul puts it in his Second Letter to the Corinthians: "Though our outer nature is wasting away, our inner nature is being renewed every day" (4:16). While the body, like the soul, is preparing for the resurrection, life in the body, during the present age, carries with it a consciousness of exile from the life of the age to come (cf. 2 Cor 5:6-8).

The fourteenth-century English hermit Richard Rolle wrote:

> O honeyed flame, sweeter than all sweet, delightful beyond all creation! My God, my Love, surge over me, pierce me by your love, wound me with your beauty. Surge over me, I say, who am longing for your comfort. Reveal your healing medicine to your poor lover. See, my one desire is for you; it is you my heart is seeking. My soul pants for you; my whole being is athirst for you. Yet you will not show yourself to me; you look away; you bar the door, shun me, pass me over; you even laugh at my innocent sufferings. And yet you snatch your lovers away from all earthly things. You lift them above every desire for worldly matters. You make them capable of loving you—and love you they do indeed. So they offer you their praise in spiritual song which bursts out from that inner fire; they know in truth the sweetness of the dart of love. Ah, eternal and most loveable of all joys, you raise us from the very depths, and entrance

us with the sight of divine majesty so often! Come into me, Beloved! All ever I had I have given up for you; I have spurned all that was to be mine, that you might make your home in my heart. Do not forsake me now, smitten with such great longing, whose consuming desire is to be amongst those who love you. Grant me to love you, to rest in you, that in your kingdom I may be worthy to appear before you world without end.[5]

Of all mediations, the interior life is the one where the transforming action of grace is at its most immediate. Despite its risks of delusion, error, false mysticism, and self-absorption, the Church's tradition prizes it as the best way to union with God in his own action, in the manifestation of his presence. Starting from this luminous truth, it becomes possible moreover to look at all things in a transfigured way, after the fashion of the seraphic father, Francis.

If the intimacy of the divine indwelling is the most immediate way to serve and find God, the approach to God through our neighbor is the most accessible. This "neighbor" may be a friend, a spouse, the poor, the sick. Neighbors, though mediations, are not means: precisely as persons, they are ends. One does not use neighbors: one serves them, and in serving them one is united to Christ the Savior. Realities always exercise their mediating function according to their own structure, and with their own inalienable value. Persons, therefore, do not merely offer occasions for doing good; rather, as made to the divine image, God is present in them as in his icons, though some be engrimed. To see our neighbors as mediations of the Lord presupposes that we have already grasped the spiritual significance of fraternal relations with others.

That great contemplative, John the Divine, asks rhetorically: "If any one has the world's goods and sees his brother in need, yet closes his heart against him, how does God's love abide in him? Little children, let us not love in word or speech but in deed and in truth" (1 John 3:17-18). As the parable of the Good Samaritan makes clear, my "neighbor" is anyone I pass on the highway or, more precisely, the needy towards whom I go. The love of others for the sake of the Father is a share in the love of the Son for human beings; it is to open oneself in the Spirit to the benevolent influx of the charity of Christ. In the consequent "wasting" of energies on the poor, sick, and old is seen the supernatural

---

5. Richard Rolle, *The Flame of Love* 2.

reality of the Church as "holy mother Church": and every Christian should take after this mother.

Epiphanies in spiritual experience are not restricted to the flaring of the "spark of the soul" or glimpses of treasure in the earthen vessels that are our neighbors. The wider world, too, both as nature and as creatively affected by human beings, addresses itself to the contemplative awareness of human beings, while also inviting them to contribute to its own movement by their actions. Since the same Logos is disclosed in both Scripture and nature, both must be spiritually "read," deciphered. The medieval Doctors frequently speak of the "twofold book." Scripture, as a new world of meaning, is given to sinful humankind by the divine mercy, to help it rediscover the sense of the primal world. Though the heavens proclaim God's glory, carnal ears cannot hear their music until the book of the re-creation, Scripture, received by faith, restores to us an understanding of the primordial creation. Only so are both the pagan deification of nature, and its naturalistic reduction, equally avoided. In the same perspective, the world of art also rediscovers its just meaning. If human beings, in their aesthetic self-expression, perceive themselves as without relation to the God who alone maintains their dignity, they will naturally reproduce in art their own distorted image. Again, their marked tendency to assert their own autonomy engenders, when unchecked, a narcissistic attitude to the rest of creation, and so a disfigured portrait of the world in art. To find its mediating function, art demands considerable ascetic and spiritual effort as the Byzantine tradition is especially aware.

So much for contemplative activity via the world (though art is at once contemplation and productive action). But what of practical activity? In all the variety of their daily occupations, Christians try to live the will of God. But more than this: they attempt to revalorize the world spiritually by consecration. Every Christian, as one sharing in Christ's priesthood, can be the locus of the offering of the world to God. This can take receptive form, as in Teilhard de Chardin's *Mass of the Universe*—a becoming thankfully conscious of creation as participation, with the gift of being at its beginning and the prospect of being's fulfillment at its end. Or it can take transformative form— infusing gospel values into the human milieu, making the human environment, accordingly, a sign of the world's relation to God. Spirituality practiced as consecration of the world made possible the ramifying sacramental sense of the Middle Ages, and, in modern idiom, the work of such very different poetic thinkers as Paul Claudel and David Jones. Such world-consecrating *poiēsis* (from which our word *poetry* arises) is not itself salvation, but it is a condition of salvation in a world of signs. The stuff of the world is only rightly called "profane" if we abstract from its origin and its goal, for it is within the wider, if diffuse, sacramentality ascribed by human agency to the world as a whole that the Savior steps forth as salvation's sign. Since God himself is continually at work in creating and re-creating his own world, it should be possible for us to rediscover him there. We can associate ourselves therefore with that divine action which leads the world by countless tracks and paths from wasteland to paradise.

This principle underlies the spirituality of the "sacrament of the present moment," beautifully brought out by the seventeenth-century French Jesuit Jean-Pierre de Caussade in his *Abandonment to Divine Providence:*

> The designs of God are the fulfilment of all our moments. They manifest themselves in a thousand different ways which thus become our successive duties, and form, increase and perfect the "new man" in us until we attain the full stature destined for us by divine wisdom. This mysterious growth to maturity of Jesus Christ in our hearts is the end and fulfilment produced by the designs of God; it is the fruit of his grace and his divine goodness. This fruit . . . is produced, fed and increased by the duties which are successively presented to us and are filled with the will of God.[6]

Or as the Second Vatican Council puts it in its Dogmatic Constitution on the Church:

> All of Christ's faithful . . . whatever be the conditions, duties and circumstances of their lives, will grow in holiness day by day through these very situations, if they accept all of them with faith from the hand of their heavenly Father, and if they co-operate with the divine will by showing every man through their earthly activities the love with which God had loved the world.[7]

Though in many areas of human engagement the concrete will of God cannot be determined in an absolute way, it is all the more necessary to seek it wholeheartedly in the outworking of a history where the good wheat and the tares still grow together.

6. J.-P. de Caussade, *Self-Abandonment to Divine Providence* (London, 1959) 10.
7. *Lumen gentium*, 41.

Ways of Prayer

The Prayer of the Heart

The simplest understanding of prayer known to Catholic Christendom is that characteristic of the Desert Fathers of the early centuries. It is the attitude of one who stands before God "with his mind in his heart": a resting in the presence of God in pure faith. At the same time (and this distinguishes it from the heretical quietism of later centuries in the West), there is no attempt to annihilate the will, but an active love for the Savior and an ardent longing to share more fully his divine life. Though the intelligence cannot be forced to cease its restlessness ("distractions"), its activity may be simplified and unified by the continual repeating of a short ("ejaculatory") formula of prayer. Generally, this takes the form of some kind of invocation of the name of Jesus. "When we have blocked all the outlets of the mind by means of the remembrance of God, then it will require of us at all costs some task which will satisfy its need for activity. Let us give it, then, as its sole activity the Lord Jesus."[8] In the Byzantine tradition, the "Jesus prayer," so understood, helps to focus the dis-integrated personality of the fallen person upon a single point, assisted by the use of a prayer-rope (in Greek, *komboschoinion,* or in Slavonic, *tchotki*). Such an approach to prayer—where it is accepted that the flow of images and thoughts will persist but the persons praying are gradually enabled to detach themselves from that flow—is also found in the monastic West of the Middle Ages. In his treatise on the anchoritic life, Aelred advises his sister: "She must apply herself very frequently to prayer, throw herself repeatedly at Jesus' feet, and by repeating his sweet name very often draw forth tears of compunction and banish all distraction from her heart."[9] Among the English Cistercians, Aelred prefers the prayer formula *O dulcis Domine;* Gilbert of Hoyland, *O bono Jesu;* John of Ford, *Domine Jesu.* Dominic's prayer was very much a prayer of "immediate acts," marked by hundreds of prostrations. As Augustine had written in his *On the Care for the Dead:*

> I do not know how it is, but though such bodily actions can only be due to mental acts that precede them, it is a fact nonetheless that by the repetition of such visible external actions the interior invisible movement that produced them is thereby increased, and those affections which had

8. Diadochus of Photike, *On Perfection* 59.
9. Aelred, *On the Life of Recluses* 11.

to precede if those actions were to be performed grow by the very fact that were so performed.[10]

The Prayer of the Memory

The most common account of prayer in the medieval monastic sources, however, follows the quadripartite division of labor—*lectio, meditatio, oratio, contemplatio*—mentioned at the outset of this chapter. However, these categories shade imperceptibly into one another. The heart of the monastic ideal was continual prayer, or the habitual thought of God, termed most commonly the "memory of God," *memoria Dei*, in Latin, and in Greek, *mnēmē tou Theou*. The powers of the soul have fallen away from God, and the way back is founded on meditation on the Scriptures. It is a re-actualization of the mysteries of salvation and a sacramentalizing of the action and events of Scripture (and above all the Gospels) so that they may become really present for us, *hodie*, "today," that clarion call of realized saving time in both Bible and liturgy. "The bride finds Christ through her desire for him; she holds him by retaining him in her memory; she will not let him go because she gazes on him with continual contemplation."[11] So *lectio* and *meditatio* provide the atmosphere or setting for *oratio*, whose aim is ultimately *contemplatio:* God himself contemplated in the vision of his glory.

The Prayer of the Imagination

Such prayer of the memory lent itself, especially with the advent of the more psychologically aware sense of subjectivity in the Renaissance, to a further development. This we can call the prayer of the imagination. Its clearest expression is perhaps the *Spiritual Exercises* of Ignatius Loyola. The aim of the *Spiritual Exercises* is to convert the soul by therapy from worldliness and selfishness to a state of unhesitating obedience to God's will and the cause of Christ. They propose to harness together all the natural faculties of a person to that end. Intellectual considerations about God and Christ, on the one hand, about the soul and its condition, on the other, are put forward; affective attitudes follow, on the one hand wonder and thanksgiving, on the other, confusion and contrition; then, by the mediating role of the imagination which pictures God speaking to the soul via a biblical scene or a moral

10. Augustine, *On Care for the Dead* 5.
11. Gilbert of Hoyland, *Homilies on the Song of Songs* 9.2.

allegory, the will translates these affections into resolutions about what one must do in one's life. The meditation habit which the success of the *Exercises* engendered in Counter-Reformation Europe was perhaps predictable in an age passionate about method (as the French historian of spirituality Henri Bremond pointed out). The purpose was, in Ronald Knox's words, to "make the thoughtless, whose attention was all directed to outward things, turn back upon themselves and see their own souls in the light of eternity; he [Ignatius] would turn extroverts into introverts."[12]

The Prayer of the Will

But perhaps because the succeeding age was itself so given to introversion, thanks to the "anthropocentric turn" and the morally analytic interest in distinctively human awareness, there was a danger that the mind could not make its affectionate acts of the will happily while watching to see whether it was making them successfully. Hence the reaction against formal meditation which took the spiritual teachers of the seventeenth century back to the medieval Western tradition, and also to the Carmelites Teresa of Avila and John of the Cross, for whom prayer was essentially a loving attention to God as present to the soul. The new teachers recommended the "prayer of simple regard," a sort of natural counterpart to the prayer of quiet of which those mystical saints conscious of a bonding to God not of their making had made so much: a François de Sales, a Jeanne de Chantal. In this prayer of simple regard there was an elemental "heaving up of soul" to God, as the *Cloud of Unknowing* had put it. Recommended in many "short methods" of interior prayer its success was startling; mysticism was widely diffused indeed in the seventeenth-century Church.

The orthodox mystic has a sense of being carried away by a power greater than one's heart, by infused charity, yet one is not just passive, automated. In Knox's words, the recipient of mystical grace "remains in an attitude of bewildered sacrifice." The apprehension of God becomes at once more direct and less distinct. In trying to love God more, the soul makes less apparent use of its affections, for more of its activity goes on in the apex, center, or foundation of the soul, where it springs from the divine creative act. The will, increasingly, is the center of prayer, yet its acts become decreasingly perceptible. What re-

---

12. R. A. Knox, *Enthusiasm: A Chapter in the History of Religion with Special Reference to the Seventeenth and Eighteenth Centuries* (Oxford, 1950) 246.

mains is a sense of dependence overflowing into daily occupations—as described so graphically by Br. Lawrence of the Resurrection in his "practice of the presence of God." Some contemplative saints have found that the more they pray, the less they ask for—even spiritual concerns are left to God by an exercise of holy in-difference (this produced the controversy over "disinterested" love, whose chief protagonists were Bossuet and Fénélon). The more the soul enters into itself the less it is self-conscious: the Salesian school was particularly hostile to *repli sur soi,* which François de Sales himself compared to the bride looking at her wedding-ring instead of the groom who gave it. The soul, moreover, as it advances in contemplation becomes less not more conscious of living virtuously; François de Sales, again, counsels against supposing we can rest content with wanting the virtues so that they may be *ours.*

The danger that a mysticism of the soul alone with God would bypass the humanity of Christ was a real one in such austere theocentrism. In reaction, the French Oratory and the "French School" which it inspired devised a scheme of praying which Knox regarded as a compromise between meditation and the prayer of simple regard. Its aim was that the Christian could so identify in intention with the states of Christ's life that he or she would enter the presence of God by contemplative prayer but "with the mantle of the incarnate Christ thrown about us."

The Prayer of Devotion

The ordinary Catholic will, however, understand prayer much more straightforwardly, as the saying of certain devotions. The day of the good Catholic takes on a certain rhythm from moments where set prayers are said or at any rate a brief set period is left for praying. Morning prayers and night prayers—a quarter of an hour given to God at the start and close of the day—form the basic skeletal structure of such devotional praying. The "morning offering" of the day in union with the Sacred Heart; acts of faith, hope, love; the Our Father, Hail Mary, and Glory to the Father; such Marian prayers as the Rosary, the *Angelus,* the *Salve Regina,* the *Memorare;* the kind of commonplace formal prayers found in Catholic prayer books for the multitude; a simple examination of conscience; intercessions for one's loved ones: all of this can release a genuinely contemplative life, for after all, as Thomas Merton remarked, the important thing is not to live for contemplation but to live for God. One can turn to God with devotion at many suitable times: We should pray when we are about to do something, or when we have just finished something. . . . We should pray while we are reading and studying, or when we see something going wrong. . . . We should especially pray when we have just received any grace or blessing from God, because that is a time of great risk. We should pray in accordance with what is actually going on in our lives. If we cannot pray without ceasing in any literal sense, at least we can make sure that every thing that we do is permeated by prayer.[13]

It is not a matter of trying to bring about ideal conditions of prayer, but of "breaking through" whatever conditions actually obtain, and finding God there. "There is a proper time for everything except prayer; as for prayer, its proper time is always."[14] This is well illustrated in one of the Gaelic prayers collected in the Hebrides by the late Victorian Celticist Alexander Carmichael:

> Jesus! Only-begotten Son and Lamb of God the Father
> Thou didst give the wine-blood of thy Body to buy me from the grave.
> My Christ! My Christ! My shield, my encircler.
> Each day, each night, each light, each dark,
> Be near me, uphold me, my treasure, my triumph.
> In my lying, in my standing, in my walking, in my sleeping.
> Jesu, Son of Mary! my helper, my encircler
> Jesus, Son of David! my strength everlasting.[15]

In such daily praying, the Catholic makes prudent use of helpful external aids to devotion. In the Catholic home, the crucifix, the image of the mother of God, and other holy pictures (icons) should be prominently displayed. In the Byzantine tradition, it is a recognized practice to venerate the icons in the host's home on arriving for a visit. The family, after all, is a "little church" of its own. Images of patron saints are especially meaningful to children. It is good to have a light burning before the holy images, at least at special times such as meals. It may be an oil lamp, or a votive candle. Holy water is also a sacramental of the devotional life of Catholics. It is sprinkled when a house is first blessed by a priest, but this "aspersion" can be renewed by the lay members of the Church wherever they feel the need to invoke God's protection of the home, his care for the sick, and even for animals. Among Byzantine

13. W. Peraldus, "De justitia" 7.6, in *Summa virtutum ac vitiorum* (Antwerp, 1588) 1:162–63.

14. Antiochus of St. Saba, *Pandect of Sacred Scripture*, 91.

15. Carmichael, *Carmina Gadelica*, 3:76–77.

Catholics it is customary to offer incense with a small hand censer—traditionally on the eves of major feasts and name days. A Catholic home will also have a Church calendar, and a missal and lectionary for keeping up with the Eucharistic worship of the Church, as well as an Office book or other prayer book containing some of her chief canticles and prayers, whether for the sanctification of time, for preparation for and thanksgiving after Holy Communion, or for other occasions. A memorial book or list of those for whom the family or individual wishes to pray frequently is also useful.

Grace at meals unites the family in the presence of the Creator, and reminds us that every meal is an echo of the Eucharistic feast. Numerous graces in fact link the ordinary meal, via the Holy Eucharist, to the banquet of the Messiah at the end of time. A traditional Gaelic grace asks, "May the blessing of the loaves and fishes which our Lord shared among the multitude, and Grain from the King who made the sharing, be upon us and on our partaking," while a Latin table-prayer petitions "the King of Glory to bring us to his heavenly Table."

The making of the sign of the Cross at the day's opening and close, at grace, when setting out on journeys, and at other significant times, roots family and individual in the mystery of the Trinity revealed on the redeeming tree. As the Anglo-Saxon poem *The Dream of the Rood* puts it,

> Lo! the Prince of glory, the Lord of heaven, honoured me
> beyond the trees of the forest
> even as almighty God
> honoured his mother Mary
> above all the race of women. . . .
> none there need fear
> who bears in his heart
> that best of signs,
> the Rood;
> for by that Rood
> shall all who seek the kingdom
> come from earthly life to dwell
> for ever with the Lord of the Rood.

The Prayer of Petition

It is the teaching of Christ that we should ask God for the things we need, that he delights to give us what is in his will for us by way of response to such petitioning. This does not, however, excuse us from the attempt to discern what we should be praying for. Good petitionary praying does not stem from wanting one's own way no matter what, but rather flows from a waiting on God, where we are able to look at matters as objectively as possible, only wanting his will to be done. Next we ask ourselves to which side of this matter we seem drawn; we then go forward believing that the whole matter is now in the hands of One who can make it all come right—in his own time.

Thomas Aquinas gives petitionary prayer a central place in his spiritual doctrine because it is a particularly pure expression of dependence on the Creator. "Man pays God reverence by praying, in as much as he subjects himself to God and confesses, by praying, that he is in need of God as the source of all his good."[16] Aquinas also points out that "We do not pray with a view to changing God's purposes, but to win from God in prayer those things which God purposes to bring about through prayer."[17] Petitionary prayer can make a difference—not in the sense of doing something to God, but "by being part of creation as willed by him, and an essential part at that."[18] Of course it is common experience for such prayers to go apparently unheard. The inability to ascribe a ground for this in many cases is not theologically troubling. The goodness of God means that he (unlike us) never wills evil directly and for its own sake. It does not enable us to determine what positively he will do. But petitionary prayer lost in the divine silence is never futile. Often enough it is an act of charity and has its own beauty; always it bears intrinsic value as an acknowledgment of the creation relationship, the bond between creature and Creator.

Extraordinary Visitations

If we take the theologically realist view that in spirituality and prayer we are caught up into and enfolded by the divine persons themselves, so that in us through grace God himself communes with God, we shall not be surprised to find that there are from time to time some dramatic consequences of praying.

Mystical visions are those whose content concerns the personal religious life and perfection of the visionary. By contrast, prophetic visions lead, or even commission, the visionary to address those around him or her—and ultimately the Church at large—with a message that

16. Thomas Aquinas, *Summa theologiae* 2–2.83.3.
17. Ibid. 2–2.83.2 and ad 2.
18. B. Davies, *Thinking about God* (London, 1985) 319.

instructs, warns, demands, or foretells. What they have in common is the presupposition that God, since he is free and personal, can make himself perceptible to the created spirit, not only through his works, but also his word—free and personal like himself. He can do so, in the words of Karl Rahner,

> in such a manner that this communication of God is not simply himself in the direct vision of the Godhead, or in the dimension of a blessed intellect emptied of all that is finite, but also—and for a Christian who believes in God's incarnation this is essential—in such a way that this communion is bound up with a particular place and time, with a concrete word or command, with an "apparition" of an object presented to the internal or external senses, which object represents and manifests God, his will, or the like.[19]

Rahner emphasizes that this adherence to God in a sign is more appropriate to the economy of the redemptive incarnation than would be a mystical union devoid of images.

The Catholic Church, however, does not regard revelations given to her members in the postapostolic period as in any way constitutive of her faith. After Christ, no further revelation which would essentially change the conditions of salvation is thinkable for Catholicism. "Private" revelations (the word must be used carefully, for what is at stake is the prophetic element in the *corporate* Church), are imperatives showing how the Christian people should act in some concrete historical situation. They are essentially new commands, not fresh assertions.

Such imaginative visions must largely conform to the given structures of our spiritual faculties of understanding and willing. Yet if they are to be deemed authentic, they must be God-given, in a supernatural fashion which goes beyond the laws of our physiology and psychology. Even then it is not as a rule the vision as such that is primarily and directly effected by God; the vision is an overflow and echo of a more intimate process. For John of the Cross, the "forms, images, and figures" are husks; the kernel is the "spiritual communications." And since in the nature of the case such communication is a two-way process, there is a difficulty in disentangling the divine from the human component. In Rahner's terms, the "graphic content" of a vision is a "picture" of not only the divine contact but the person who receives it as well. Since that contact cannot impinge on the recipient's

---

19. K. Rahner, "Visions and Prophecies," in *Studies in Modern Theology* (Freiburg and London, 1965) 95–96.

consciousness until it is already a synthesis of the divine influence and the seer's subjective limitations, proof that the imaginative content is really intended by God could only be offered through examining external criteria. (In the history of visions in the Church, even saints and *beati* report what, to the Church's informed judgment, are distortions—historical, theological, aesthetic.) As one professional explorer of such apparitions, John Cornwell, has written of their Marian genre: "To the extent that apparitions symbolise Mary's promised availability, they offer the promise of her living participation in the narrative of the children who see and address her. Such apparitions could be said to be the language, the theatre, the liturgy of folk mysticism, the authentic imaginative perceptions of people steeped in traditions of local spirituality."[20]

Certain extraordinary gifts of the Holy Spirit—such as prophecy, healing, and speaking in tongues—have been associated with the church of Corinth in the Pauline Letters, with a number of the lives of the saints, and with a deliberate movement of revival (the "charismatic renewal") started in the Catholic Church in 1967. The Church officially recognizes the importance of such gifts, bidding us receive them "with thanksgiving and consolation," but she also warns against seeking them with a wrong attitude, and against presumptuously exaggerating the fruits to be hoped for. In Catholicism, the reception of the Holy Spirit belongs with the common initiation of Christians—which is why in the early Church baptisteries were decorated with paradisal imagery, for the baptized are enfranchised in heaven (Phil 3:20). But without, then, falling prey to the (heretical) Pentecostalist notion that there is a "baptism in the Holy Spirit" (by laying on of hands, and manifested in tongues) distinct from the sacrament of the Church, we can say that in the baptismal life, God seeks to create in his disciples an ever-greater capacity to receive the fullness of Christ.

What is the significance, then, of an extraordinary gift such as the gift of tongues? A tradition in the early Church (especially in the Syriac *Odes of Solomon*) saw salvation as including the opening of human mouths by the Holy Spirit, himself released into the world thanks to the incarnation and atoning work of the Son, so that we may utter God's Word with Christ, in praise of him and proclamation of his triumph, and in that way escape the baleful silence of death and damnation. The Anglo-Saxon poets called the human being "the bearer of

---

20. J. Cornwell, *Powers of Darkness, Powers of Light: Travels in Search of the Miraculous and the Demonic* (London, 1992) 386.

speech." Pentecost is the definitive reversal of Babel for it allows human beings to share once again in the holy speech to which, in the beginning, man was privy when he named the animals—a continuation of the creative act. The gift of speaking in tongues, in this perspective, is a celebration of our salvation from dumbness by the Word of God, who allows us to express our identity in him through the worship of faith.

The tradition is well aware indeed that there can be a very distinct experience in the Holy Spirit, a "manifestation of baptism," whether in tears or in shouts of joy, an experience of spiritual purification or exultation lacking at sacramental baptism because of the candidate's own lack of faith or carelessness about the commandments, his or her deliberate sin, heresy, or psychological bondage. But unlike Pentecostalism, Catholicism locates such a "baptism of the Spirit" in the initial total gift of grace in baptism of water. It seeks, moreover, to keep us always open to further gifts of the Holy Spirit, and to preserve us within the Church's unity, in the fellowship of those who have received the same baptismal grace, even if not all have experienced that grace in the same way. To claim some definitive "fullness" is always mistaken. As Bernard remarks in his second homily for the feast of Andrew the only sure sign of the Spirit's presence is our desire for yet more.

It is natural that people who are seriously embarked on the spiritual life—and especially those who have received (or *think* they have received) such extraordinary visitations—will look for assistance and counsel from time to time. They will find this in various ways: in providential events or encounters, in books, in priests or laypersons who are gifted in the advising of others on the way of holiness. So far as the latter are concerned, the Church expects certain qualifications of them. First and foremost, they must have a good grasp of the dogmatic essentials of Catholic Christianity, for spirituality is but dogma lived and prayed. They must be deeply soaked in the Scriptures as the word of God, and in the spirit of the liturgy as the living response of God's bride, the Church. They must have a reasonable acquaintance with the classical literature of Catholic spirituality, to be able to advise on reading, in accordance with need and ability, and to inform their own response and give it depth. At the same time, the spiritual director should have some understanding of human psychology—not necessarily of a bookish kind, for many of the great spiritual teachers of the Church showed a remarkable grasp in practice of the unconscious motivations of conduct. Above all, the spiritual counsellor needs personal humility, freedom from self-seeking, possessiveness, and authoritarianism, as well as the capacity to make genuine contact with others.

Such things as levitation, the stigmata, and the incorruption of the body after death appear very often in the lives of the saints, and have sometimes been regarded as a normal condition of pronouncing someone a genuinely God-possessed person. Some of the greatest of the saints have protested against this belief, but none has disputed that such phenomena occur. Catholic writers usually hold them to be strictly supernatural and even miraculous in origin—signs and wonders worked by God to attest his invisible working in the souls of the saints. For these commentators, to question this assumption smacks of rationalism: a refusal in principle to accept the possibility of miracles. A second school of thought is more cautious. Because the relationship between soul and body, or mind and brain, is so intimate, if God *were* working on the soul of a mystic then strange things might happen to the person's body even though God may not have willed this directly. On such a view, these phenomena are side-effects of grace, the body reacting in abnormal ways under the stress of divine action in the soul.

The construction one puts on these phenomena will depend partly, perhaps crucially, on one's basic picture of reality. If one believes that this world is set within a wider order of reality, one may allow that surprising things might sometimes happen. If the ultimate agent in history is a God who has created the human person, body and soul, and wills the transfiguration, body and soul, of that same being, then these phenomena do not look so bizarre. They can be considered as hints, clues, pointers; consolations; anticipations of the final destiny of the person in the total self-surrender of the soul to the loving purposes of an infinite God and the raising up of the body, which in baptism was sacramentally conformed to the crucified Christ, to share the soul's glory.

Spiritual life is life anchored in God, where all we do comes from the center; it is a life soaked through with God's reality and claim and given over to the movement of his will. This is why prayer is vital to it, since the heart of prayer is throwing ourselves away in self-oblation. Its "waste" of time enables us to share in the absolute "waste of time" which is the interior life of the Holy Trinity. Such prayer molds the human being into the Trinitarian pattern, relating him or her by adoration and surrender to the Father; by communion, and closeness, in a prayer of wanting to be with him to the Son; and by co-operation in the purposes of God to the Holy Spirit. In this way, the spiritual experience of the Church reintroduces the believer into that union with God which was Adam's before the Fall, and more than that—as heaven is more than paradise—into a participation in the sense of God's nearness enjoyed by the blessed. To say that every member of the Church is called to spiritual perfection is simply to say that every Christian is called to share in the redemptive work of Christ as he restores the lost grace of Eden and promotes humankind to the vision of God. The soul's transfiguration is also its fullest personalization.

> The mystery which [Ezekiel] saw was that of the human soul as she is hereafter to receive the Lord and become herself the very throne of his glory. For the soul that is thought worthy to partake of the Spirit of his light and is irradiated by the beauty of his ineffable glory (he having, by that Spirit, prepared her for his own seat and habitation) becomes all light, all face and all eye. . . . She . . . appears to be altogether face, by reason of the inexpressible beauty of the glory of the light of Christ that rides and sits upon her.[21]

---

21. Pseudo-Macarius, *Macarian Homilies* 1.2.

14

Catholicism and Other Religions

The guiding text of Catholic reflection on the topic of other religions must now be *Nostra aetate,* the declaration on this subject by the Second Vatican Council. For while statements of this relationship are to be found scattered among individual Church Fathers and theologians, it has not previously come to expression at a theological "place" so important as an ecumenical council. The text in question limits itself, rightly, to pointing out *features* of the complex and mysterious relation between the Church and other religious traditions. While faith in Jesus Christ involves belief that he is the pre-existent Logos and the ultimate Lord of history, it does not entail the claim to know the consequences for every aspect of created reality of this immanent presence and lordship. That would be to anticipate illicitly God's own discriminating judgment, which is either salvation or condemnation for creatures.

In the opening chapter of the document, the council Fathers teach that all people have a single origin and one ultimate end, namely, God himself. His "providence," the "witness of his goodness," and "counsels of his salvation" extend to all human beings. His salvific will is universal (the document refers to a chain of scriptural texts), but this means that he owes it to himself to offer all human beings whatever means are necessary and sufficient to attain salvation.

Does this mean that other world religions should be thought of as such "means of salvation"? The text does not say so. Scripture speaks of the Noachic covenant, made with all the peoples of the earth. But this is little more than a promise of God's fidelity to his own created work. It has no obvious bearing on the providential character of the particular religious traditions with which the Christian missionary or theologian must deal. These religions are historical creations with debts to a conditioning society and culture. The Noachic covenant may be illuminating for Jean Daniélou's "holy pagans" of the Old Testament, but it cannot be taken to legitimize, without more ado, all existing world religions. Yet it may be *relevant* to them.

On the one hand, Scripture has it that it is God's will that "all should be saved, and be led to recognize the truth" (1 Tim 2:3), while, on the other hand, the same biblical revelation insists that "Nobody reaches God's presence until he has learned to believe that God exists and that he rewards those who try to find him" (Heb 11:6). Yet the latter conditions are realized, it would seem, among a rather sizeable human constituency. Not only such heterodox Christian communities as Unitarians but Judaism and Islam too propose this minimum material object of faith to their adherents. The same may hold for segments of those religions which can claim no connection with the main stem of historic revelation, and can boast only some distant echo of "primitive" revelation. Paul's address to the Athenians assembled on the Areopagus in the Acts of the Apostles, with its citation from the pagan Greek poet Aratos, refers to the Creator Lord of the biblical tradition: "In him we live and move and have our being, for we are his off-spring" (Acts 17:28), a text written in praise of Zeus, father of gods and humans. The Pauline critique of human religions in the Letter to the Romans presupposes, as did the Hellenistic-Jewish author of the Book of Wisdom, that the *goyim* grasped well enough the one divine Creator (Rom 1:20); the reproach that they mistook the creature for the Creator in abusive worship of the former would be meaningless otherwise.

If the same mystery is approached less by way of the material object of faith, and more by way of its subjective condition, a still more generous conclusion is possible. The "intention of faith," in Catholic theology, consists in the good disposition of the person to his or her last (supernatural) end, and, consequently, to the necessary means for attaining that end. Those necessary means are of course the regime of grace, while the subjective disposition required is faith. In the normal scheme of things, it is through the apostolic preaching that this intention of faith encounters the object adequate to it, namely God's redemptive and reconciling work in Jesus Christ and his Spirit. Failing that, at least it finds the "minimum material object," as it were the minimal sacrament of salvation.

A question is raised by Catholic writers in the modern period, conscious, inevitably, of the massive cultural facts of paganism and atheism of which the Fathers and medievals were either unaware or which they happily escaped: If the intention of faith does not encounter even this minimum object, and the person remains invincibly ignorant of God—for many doubt or ignore the existence of a personal absolute—may it not be said to find an outlet in adhering to some substitute for God, like devotion to a great cause (e.g., justice, truth, brotherhood, peace; one might add, in the postmodernist context, reverencing the "other"), treated as though that mighty preoccupation were an absolute? Objectively, these values could be considered the idols—the alternatives to God—of the contemporary world. But on the subjective level, may they not function instead as so many "species" (really, appropriating instruments) whereby, tacitly and unconsciously, the human conscience seeks and honors the true God? Some Catholic theologians would answer, mindful of the Hebrews text already quoted, no: there must always be explicit knowledge of the object of salvific faith, albeit granted "by God himself or through an angel," as Augustine puts it, in the moment of death. The *pars gravior* of Scripture favors this view. In the Bible, whenever the field of salvation is extended beyond the limits of the people of God (with, say, the Ninevites in the Book of Jonah, or the "queen of the South" in our Lord's reference in Matthew 12), it presupposes not only explicit faith in the existence of God but also some reference to the positive economy of the Judaeo-Christian revelation. Yet there is a second strain as well in Scripture: that *catena* of texts which opens up wide possibilities of, at any rate, non-damnation (for some commentators would speak of those who cannot reach theistic assent as moral infants, destined for "limbo"), on the principle that God will render to each according to his or her work. For Paul, persons who, lacking the law of Moses, have for law their own conscience will be assessed on that basis before the judgment seat of God. Although performing good works for fallen humanity is impossible without the help of grace and entering into the orbit of the sovereign plan of Christ (cf. Eph 1:19-23; Col 1:15; 2:9), Paul nonetheless envisages a reward at the end of time to which no other name than "salvation" seems appropriate for those who, on the basis of conscience, carry out such deeds. By extension, presumably, for followers of various religions (or anti-religions), bound to travesties of God, the *unum necessarium* would be to maintain such an attitude in their works—humility of heart and openness to the promptings of the light—as would not deprive God's ultimate plan of efficacy. In such persons of good will, the intention of faith would be present, though it would only reach its proper term eschatologically.

None of this affects the basic grounding of Catholic missionary activity. The latter is dogmatically based in two claims: first, that grace cannot take its birth except through our mother the Church, the second Eve and spouse of Jesus Christ; second, that God has commissioned the Catholic Church, and her alone, to be the institution that provides salvation for all human beings in Christ. Whatever grace is found in other religions, then, has its source in the incarnation of the Word in Mary's womb, and the atoning work of the Logos enfleshed through the paschal mystery. The yearning of the Church for the entry into her of nations whose cultures flow from other religions is founded, therefore, on the desire to recuperate aspects of her own being: for her own corporate consciousness—the *sensus Ecclesiae*—will have an increase of light as revelation becomes more luminous to us through its expression by way of all the nations of the earth. As Abbé Jules Monchanin put it, referring to the example of India:

> What Justin and Clement said of Greece may equally well be said of India. The Logos was mysteriously preparing the way for his coming and the Holy Spirit stimulated spiritually the gropings of the purest minds among the Greeks. The Logos and the Holy Spirit are again at work and in a similar manner in the depths of the Indian soul. Unfortunately, Indian philosophy is spotted with error and does not appear to have found its proper equilibrium. And neither did the Greek until the message of the risen Christ had been humbly received by Greece. Outside the unique revelation and the one Church, man everywhere and always is incapable of filtering the good through the evil, truth through error. But once christianized, Greece rejected the errors of her ancestors—especially their too cosmic perspective and their forgetfulness of the transcendental aspect of the Absolute—and having been baptized in the blood of her martyrs, she became mistress of the world in philosophy, theology, and mysticism. So, in the same manner, with confidence in the unwavering direction of the Gospel, it is our hope that India, once baptized in the depth of her "quest for Brahman" which has endured for centuries, will reject her pantheistic tendencies; and, discovering in the Holy Spirit the true mysticism, will engender, for the good of humanity and the Church, and for the glory of God, dazzling galaxies of saints and doctors.[1]

How, then, does the Catholic Church see other religions? We must begin with *Judaism*, the Church's own root and mother. Not only does

---

1. J. Monchanin, *Ermites du Saccidananda* (Tournai and Paris, 1956), cited in H. de Lubac, *The Church: Paradox and Mystery* (Shannon, 1969) 80–81.

our New Testament still contain a letter to the Hebrews—Hebrew Christians, Jewish Christians—but its whole canon bears witness to the pangs of birth as the Church emerges from Judaism. We may be tempted to think of this as the butterfly emerging from the chrysalis, but this would be to ignore the tragic sense of loss, breathed by so many pages of the New Testament, at Israel's failure to recognize the Christ. There is nothing tragic about the metamorphosis of a caterpillar.

It is true that many Christians understand the Old Testament better than some Jews. It is also true that the Church's own understanding, as the englobing subject of revealed faith, surpasses in range what Judaism can say of its own Scriptures. Nevertheless, it seems obvious that there must be a special inwardness or intimacy in the way that Jews live with the Hebrew Bible and the other literature that made, or reflects, the world of the Gospels. No Gentile can, for instance, feel the devotion to the Torah that a Jew feels. No Gentile Christian can grasp the implications of Jesus' identification of himself as the Torah in person in the way that a Jew might. In this perspective it is extremely unfortunate that the church of the Hebrew Christian failed to survive within the *Catholica*. Had it done so, the universal Church would have included within the unity of the same faith, sacraments, and governance communities especially devoted to the memory and observances of the Jewish ancestors of the Christian way—a living witness not only to non-Christian Jews but to Gentile Catholicism also.

The principal Jewish objection to the Church where doctrine is concerned is her affirmation of the divinity of Christ. However, it can be noted that in the first centuries of the Christian era, the same theological principle guided a process of internal clarification among both Jews and Christians: the infinite qualitative distinction between the uncreated and the created, ruling out as this does any suggestion of intermediate beings or conditions. Just as Judaism pruned away its more extravagant apocalyptic imagery, and a tendency to angelolatry, so the Church shunned the *homoiousion* ("like in being [to the Father]") of the semi-Arians and clove to the view that either Christ is consubstantial with God or he is of no transcendent significance whatever. It is possible that it was an initial encounter with an implicitly heretical Christianity rather than direct confrontation with the orthodox tradition of the Nicene faith that accounts for the vehemence of rabbinic Judaism's rejection of patristic Christianity.

The main Jewish objection to Catholicism in the realm of practice must be the Church's mixed record of treatment of the Jews in her midst. There were indeed numerous verbal and physical attacks on Jews carried out more or less under Christian auspices. Yet on the whole, and this is not so often adverted to, higher ecclesiastical authority tended to moderate negative action towards the Jews either by the populace or by secular princes. It can be suggested that hatred for Jews on the part of European Christians was fundamentally a reaction of the residual pagan—the "old Adam"—against the originators of "bondage" to pure worship and high ethical norms. In this sense, violence against Jews was a rebellion against Christianity itself, under the figure of a less powerful proxy. By the time of the Holocaust in Nazi Germany, we are dealing not so much with a Christian civilization but with a European civilization which a century-and-a-half previously had embarked on a rapid process of de-Christianization.

Judaism's distinctive continuing light can add to the Church an orthopractic concern with the *mitzvoth*, the divine precepts, whose actualization is a sign that makes present the Creator's reign and a celebration of a total liturgy, referring the creation to the Creator and so consecrating it to God through human agency.

Since Judaism is not in the fullest sense a different religion from Christianity, there can be and are such a thing as "Hebrew Catholics," Jews who have entered the Church but with every intention of maintaining their Jewish heritage intact. They insist with Paul that "God has not rejected his people whom he foreknew," for "the gifts and the call of God are irrevocable" (Rom 11:29). A Catholic Christian, contemplating the mystery of Israel, can be, accordingly, only a qualified supersessionist. Inasmuch as Israel's Messiah has come, and fashioned his new community, the call of Israel is indeed superseded. Yet the vocation of Israel, to witness that the One who has come is truly her long-expected Savior and that the salvation he wrought is the genuine fulfillment of the promises of the Hebrew Bible, remains intact. For the Paul of Romans, the prospect of this perduring election of Israel reaching full term is a cause of eschatological joy: "If their trespass means riches for the world, and if their failure means riches for the Gentiles, how much more will their full inclusion mean!" (11:12). Hebrew Catholics, meanwhile, have a special place within the Church; their association enables them to experience a common identity as the prototype of the Israel of the end, and not merely a random collection of assimilated Jews.

We can now turn to the case of *Islam*. The genius of Mohammed was to provide a rationale for the Arabs in their self-involvement in

Jewish messianism. Proclaiming the descent of the Arabs from Ishmael, brother of the patriarch Jacob (Israel), Mohammed gave his people both a claim to the inheritance of the Holy Land (Palestine), and, more importantly, a monotheistic genealogy. The Second Vatican Council declared of Muslims:

> They adore one God, living and enduring, merciful and all-powerful, Maker of heaven and earth and Speaker to men. They strive to submit whole-heartedly even to his inscrutable decrees, just as did Abraham, with whom the Islamic faith is pleased to associate itself. Though they do not acknowledge Jesus as God, they revere him as a prophet. They also honour Mary, his virgin mother; at times they call on her too, with devotion. In addition they await the day of judgement when God will give each man his due after raising him up. Consequently, they prize the moral life, and give worship to God especially through prayer, almsgiving, and fasting.[2]

But the declaration also refers to the "many quarrels and hostilities" between Christians and Muslims in the course of the centuries. It is natural that there would be some hostility toward a distinct religion originating from the Abrahamic root at a time when salvation through faith in Christ had already been available to humankind for six hundred years—a cult, moreover, that proceeded, largely by force of arms, to displace Christianity as the dominant religion throughout the Near East and much of the Mediterranean world, including the Holy Land itself. In the last century or so, Catholic scholars have made a great effort of sympathetic understanding in the study of Islam, but there have been few signs of reciprocation by Muslim scholars. The 1985 invitation from the king of Morocco, who claims descent from Mohammed and the title "Commander of the Faithful," to Pope John Paul II to address an audience of young Muslims from a number of countries was a rare (and eagerly accepted) opportunity for dialogue. Muslims know Jesus only via polemics, of which, among more gracious materials, the Koran provides the earliest example: the idea that Jesus is the Son of God appears there as absurd and indeed blasphemous.

Catholicism, however, welcomes Islam's grasp of the divine aseity— the terrible distinctness of God from the world—not least in a post-Christian epoch in the West where to a vague "new age" religious sensibility the distinction between what is divine and what is not divine is altogether elided. The God of Islam is indeed adorable, but not

2. *Nostra aetate,* 3.

lovable. To introduce an account of the God-world relation able to sustain a mysticism of love between God and humanity, the Sufis found themselves rejecting the doctrine of creation and adopting in its place a Neoplatonic monism adapted to the Muslim emphasis on God's word or command. Here the human spirit is treated as a direct emanation of that divine command, and loving devotion to God is misinterpreted as an anticipation of some final obliteration of the finite self and its absorption into eternal reality. The wonderful Sufi literature in praise of God's love and beauty, and its magnetic effect, is thus flawed by the wrong aim of a vanishing away in God—a state of bliss shared in now by either sober abstraction or spiritual intoxication.

Nostra aetate speaks of the way *Hindus* "contemplate the divine mystery and express it through an inexhaustible abundance of myths and through searching philosophical enquiry," while also "seeking freedom from the anguish of our human condition either through ascetical practices or [through] profound meditation or a flight to God with love and trust."[3] This is, evidently, an attempt to seize what is essential in Hinduism's bewildering variety of forms, while at the same time judging their truth and goodness within a Catholic Christian perspective. The conciliar statement is notable for its restraint, for some Catholic authors have seen in certain features of Hinduism a prefiguration of the Christian revelation. The Hindu worship of a supreme deity, whose nature is described as "being, knowledge, and bliss" (the absolute of the Vedanta), but who is also conceived as having a personal form (manifested as Shiva or Vishnu, Rama or Krishna), can lead to an emphasis on the love of the deity, shown to his worshippers by the bestowal of grace. Further, the notion of the *avatara* bears a resemblance to that of incarnation, while the final human bliss is sometimes presented as union with God in a total surrender to his goodness. Such intimations are from the Church's standpoint engraced intuitions of true eschatology. Unfortunately, this is by no means the only strand in Hinduism. The mythological world, pullulating with gods, symbols of a divine multiplicity, stands over against the critique of both myth and pantheon by the prophetic spirit of Israel. The non-dualist *(advaita)* monism of the medieval metaphysicians of India, firmly grounded as it is on a majority of the Upanishadic scriptures of Hinduism, is incompatible with the Creator/creation divide which lies at the root of the attitude of adoration in Judaeo-Christianity. In both of these ways,

3. Ibid., 2.

the experience of the divine presence—at the core of both the cosmos and the human heart—has been, to a Catholic Christian sensibility, misinterpreted by Hindus. Yet there remains, hidden within Hindu asceticism, something that Catholic theology can recognize as an impulse of the Holy Spirit. Long before the Word incarnate appeared on earth, before, indeed, the prophets uttered the word spoken to Israel, many in India had already heard from the Holy Spirit speaking within them the call of a life of complete renunciation of worldly things. The *sannyasi*, living hermit-like in the forests of India, or wandering from place to place with no fixed abode, can also represent the Spirit's call to the Church to deepen the interior life of Christians, to give contemplation primacy in the Church's common life, to re-examine the mystery of God's presence in the depths of the heart, to become as aware of the cosmos as a manifestation of the glory of God as of history as manifestation of his providence.

If it is encouraging to a Christian observer to see how, in the development of Indian religion, a tendency arises to displace impersonal categories in favor of personal, a similar trend can also be noted in *Buddhism*.

In the same pre-Christian period to which the personalist elements in the Vedanta belong, we find the beginnings of devotion in the austere religion of Buddhism. The cultus of the Bodhisattva, the enlightened one, who in love and compassion for the world refuses to enter Nirvana till all living things have been delivered, is a kind of premonition of the Savior (to be further ratified in the "Amida Buddhism" of Japan). Without any direct influence from Christianity (though some Hindu scholars have speculated about possible Nestorian influence on the rise of devotion to Krishna, frequently portrayed as a babe in his mother's arms), both Hinduism and Buddhism took a personalist turn on the eve of the incarnation. But the task of Christianity in India today is to show how Christ, in the fullness of his divine and human natures, comes to answer the problem posed by the Vedanta itself.

Buddhism is now almost unknown in its Indian birthplace. At its beginning, it appears to have taken the form of an atheism. One might perhaps interpret the state of Nirvana, into which Gautama, the Buddhist founder, is held to have passed by the cessation of all finite cravings, as a negative expression for the life of the Godhead (comparable to the "cloud of unknowing" of Christian mysticism); apart from this possibility, Buddhism knows no God. On his death, the Buddha became inaccessible: he was not prayed to, but his images were, rather, icons of calmness, wisdom, and enlightenment. In Nirvana, all desires are extinguished, and there is no becoming of any kind. "Conservative" Theravada Buddhism looks on the craving for continued individual existence and personal relationships, and a bond with a more knowable absolute, as thoroughly misplaced. The doctrine of "no-self" entails that there is in the human being, finally, no person who could relate to a God, nor in any case is it possible to think any thought or speak any word about an ultimate reality beyond all conception. The Mahayana tradition, in a spirit of innovation, would come to wax lyrical over the delights of heaven. Unfortunately the fuller doctrines about the absolute gradually developed by more philosophical Buddhists of this persuasion show markedly monistic or theopanist tendencies. Where a God-concept has developed, it is generally some impersonal, omnipresent Buddha-nature. The refusal of the Buddha to answer questions about God or the destiny of the soul (maybe because the Brahmins of his day, like the Athenians of Paul's, exploited argument on these subjects to avoid the demands of repentance) created an epistemological void.

Zen's deliberate inarticulateness points in this direction with peculiar force. The moment of enlightenment, *satori*, is an experience of total oneness with what is other. Zen tries to grasp existence, deprived of essence: to seize being in act, abstracting from its content or meaning.

Both Buddhism and Hinduism, therefore, struggling with the mystical problem of how the utterly transcendent can be experienced as immanent, are forced to conclude that the human being must be overwhelmed by, and absorbed into, the absolute, and that this in turn requires the elimination of the ego, either by affirming its oneness with the absolute (Brahman) or by allowing it to pass into the extinction of Nirvana.

Lastly, we must not forget the so-called *traditional* (*olim:* "primitive") *religions,* so persistent in, for example, sub-Saharan Africa. The myths, rituals, and proverbs of tribal society frequently carry an echo of a "high God," a supreme deity, yet his presence is tenuous, distant. Here the Fall is not so much perceived as humans being driven from paradise but rather as God disappearing from the world. In his place, the religious sense operates centrally with the concept of the human organism—tribe, clan, family—seen as lasting beyond death, and engaged in a complex intercourse with nature. Such African religiosity knows well what it is to be "in" the first ancestor ("in Adam," as Paul expressed it), to live with his destiny and disposition working themselves out in time. Fundamental to that destiny and disposition is the inability to find the face of God, a terror that compels the raising of a hierarchy of intermediaries, and the inhabiting of a microcosm that makes the family unit all in all.

To redeem the world, however, as this study has testified, the All-present himself passed into the closed circle of the human family. Stage by stage he was initiated into it: by birth, by circumcision, by presentation with sacrifice, by instruction, by attendance at the feasts. In the baptism of repentance, he immersed himself in the spiritual reality of our sin and its effects in estrangement from himself. In all this he acted as the new head of the human family. Willingly incorporated into the old Adam for our sake, by the perfection of his obedience he won back all things to what we were meant to be. He reconstituted the whole organism upon himself as the Second Adam—as Irenaeus showed in his great theology of recapitulation. He then offered us a sharing in this humanity, that we might become a new tree from a new stem.

What, in conclusion, is the practical attitude of Catholicism today to other faiths? It was well expressed at the Assisi "world day of prayer for peace" hosted by Pope John Paul II at the shrine of the peace-lover Francis on 27 October 1986. There, in welcoming "representatives of the Christian Churches and Ecclesial Communities and World Religions," the Pope drew attention to the fact that "the form and content of our prayers are very different . . . and there can be no question of reducing them to a kind of common denominator," while also insisting that a "common ground" could be found in the "dimension of prayer, which in the very real diversity of religions tries to express communication with a Power above all human forces." The structure of this occasion, at which the Pope presided, gave body to this nuanced position. This took the form of (1) separate prayer, in distinct locations for each religion, (2) common silent meditation on what had been prayed, and (3) a symbolic corporate self-commitment (to peace). At the same time, in his sermon the Pope witnessed to the faith of the Church that Jesus Christ is the universal Savior, the sole divine-human mediator.

Indeed, only Christ, as the Word of God made human, can offer a reasonable explanation as to how a transcendent God, totally Other, can also be experienced from within this world: consciously by mystics, unconsciously by graced individuals, without persons losing their identity and becoming subsumed into God. The principle and instrument of all grace is the hypostatic union, the archetype of a new form of relationship between God and the human being and the foundation for the unsurpassable covenant between them made in Christ's atoning work. Here lies the scandal of particularity: while the mystical practices of the other world religions are designed to facilitate the laying aside of material impedimenta so as to let being be reabsorbed into the world's origin, Christianity alone dares to contradict this program by its assertion of a God who entered into and became a part of history, making his own body, on the cross, the unique bridge between the finite and the infinite realms. *Avatar,* even when historicity is claimed (as sometimes for Krishna) is not incarnation in this sense. The figure of Krishna is a symbolic expression of that which cannot be directly expressed: the unique reality of our divine self of which the I, the Thou, and the world itself are only transitory mirrors.

Only in Christ, in whom all apparent opposites are unified without mingling, can the partial insights of the various world religions reach a satisfactory account of the God-world relation, within a narrative that situates their own story of sin and grace between the beginning— the pre-existent Logos—and the end—his glorious parousia as the Word incarnate. This is the context in which the Second Vatican Council proposed to the Catholic Church a dialogue, in the contemporary period, with the other world-religions:

> For all peoples comprise a single community, and have a single origin, since God made the whole race of men dwell over the entire face of the earth. One also is their final goal: God, his providence, his manifestations of goodness, and his saving designs extend to all men against the day when the elect will be united in that Holy City ablaze with the splendour of God, where the nations will walk in his light.[4]

It is precisely according to her own revelation that the Church is able to find nuggets of gold in these other religions. "The Catholic Church rejects nothing which is true and holy in these religions. She looks with sincere respect upon those ways of conduct and of life, those rules and teachings which, though differing in many respects from what she holds and sets forth, nevertheless often reflect a ray of that truth which enlightens all men."[5] Jesus Christ is *totus Dei,* "wholly God," but he is not *totum Dei,* "the whole of God." Without the Son we cannot speak

4. Ibid., 1.
5. Ibid., 2.

of the Father, yet that speaking is never completely exhausted in history, for the Spirit constantly calls us into a deeper understanding of God in Christ, not least through the challenges of the other religions. Catholicism itself condemned the (Jansenist) position that "outside the Church no grace is granted."

The riches of the mystery of the Father are disclosed by the Holy Spirit, and both measured and discerned by conformity to, and illumination from, Christ, the Son. The basis for a theological understanding of the religions lies in the universality of God's presence and action in the world. These religions are human responses to God's all-encompassing presence and activity, where God works, as in all forms of created being, as the ground of being and meaning, and the source and end of being's fulfillment. However, this universal claim is based on the particularity of the incarnation and atonement in Jesus Christ: it is in the particularity of his unique epiphany that Father, Son, and Spirit are disclosed as interacting with the world as the single source of creation, of reconciliation for an alienated world, and so for the fulfillment of creation itself.

All religions and ideologies have within them spiritualities which are not of God, described in Scripture as forms of darkness or idolatry, or as anti-Christ. The discernment of spirits will sometimes exclude, at other times include, and at still other times accept a degree of pluralism. The Church, so Newman wrote:

> began in Chaldea, and then sojourned among the Canaanites, and went down into Egypt, and thence passed into Arabia, till she rested in her own land. Next she encountered the merchants of Tyre, and the wisdom of the East country, and the luxury of Sheba. Then she was carried away to Babylon, and wandered to the schools of Greece. And wherever she was sent, in trouble or triumph, she was still a living spirit, the mind and voice of the Most High.[6]

Newman was thinking of the Church as pre-existent in that community of faith whose father is Abraham. She had garnered the good wheat of truth from fields set in the wilderness of pagan culture, for the better understanding of her own Christ-centered mission, when once it came. "We are not distressed to be told that the doctrine of the angelic host came from Babylon, while we know that they did sing at

---

6. J. H. Newman, "Milman's View of Christianity," in *Essays Critical and Historical* (London, 1890) 2:232.

the Nativity; nor that the vision of a mediator is in Philo, for in very deed He died for us on Calvary."[7]

In the radiance of the Epiphany—light to enlighten the Gentiles and the glory of God's people, Israel—the Church can see more, not less, even though the historic revelation is completed and we can expect no fresh truths but only the unveiling of truth's own face in the age to come. The Church, en route between Pentecost and the parousia, can continue to find analogues of her own truth in the cultures of the unbaptized; not merely, indeed, echoes of the truth she knows consciously, but instruments for the fuller appropriation of its inexhaustible richness.

7. Ibid., 2:233.

15

Coda

God so loved
A small ball, spun
On its own axis round a lesser sun;
And on the ball that lemur creature, man,
Standing upon the ground as one who can
Perceive and know and name the beasts and birds
With whistles and with clicks, his early words.

God the Word made
Flesh in a daughter of Eve
At prayer by the well
Of a Syrian village, born
In the chill of a cold stable,
Done to death on a hard tree,
Be merciful to all, have mercy on me.

"Sequence," by George Every

Suggestions for Further Reading

General Sources

The Catechism of the Catholic Church. London, 1994.

Neuner, J., and J. Dupuis. *The Christian Faith in the Doctrinal Documents of the Catholic Church.* London, 1983.

Reference

Attwater, D. *The Catholic Encyclopaedic Dictionary.* 2d ed. London, 1951.

The Catholic Encyclopedia. 15 vols. London, 1907.

Hellwig, M. (ed.). *The Modern Catholic Encyclopedia.* Collegeville, Minn., 1994.

Komonchak, J. A., M. Collins, and D. A. Lane, eds. *The New Dictionary of Theology.* Dublin, 1987.

The New Catholic Encyclopedia. 17 vols. Washington, D.C., 1967–78.

Rahner, K., et al. (eds.). *Sacramentum Mundi. An Encyclopaedia of Theology.* 6 vols. New York and London, 1968–1970.

Introductory Studies of Catholicism and/or Catholic Theology

Burghardt, W. J., and W. F. Lynch, eds. *The Idea of Catholicism: An Introduction to the Thought and Worship of the Church.* London, 1960.

Butler, B. C. *An Approach to Christianity.* London, 1981.

Conrad, R. *The Catholic Faith: A Dominican's Vision.* London, 1994.

Knox, R. A. *The Belief of Catholics.* 2d ed. London, 1957.

Lubac, H. de. *Catholicism: A Study of Dogma in Relation to the Corporate Destiny of Mankind.* New York and London, 1950.

_____. *The Structure of the Apostles' Creed.* London, 1970.

McBrien, R. *Catholicism.* 2 vols. Minneapolis and London, 1980–81.

Nichols, A. *The Shape of Catholic Theology: An Introduction to Its Sources, Principles and History.* Collegeville, Minn., and Edinburgh, 1991.

Ratzinger, J. *Introduction to Christianity.* London, 1969.

Scheeben, M. J. *The Mysteries of Christianity.* St. Louis, 1946.

Sheed, F. J. *Theology and Sanity.* London, 1947.

_____. *Theology for Beginners.* London, 1953.

Smith, G. D., ed. *The Teaching of the Catholic Church.* 2d ed. London, 1952.

Chapter 1: A Christian Philosophy

Blondel, M. *Letter on Apologetics and History and Dogma.* London, 1964.

D'Arcy, M. C. *The Nature of Belief.* Dublin, 1958.

Davies, B. *An Introduction to the Philosophy of Religion.* Oxford, 1993.

_____. *Thinking about God.* London, 1985.

Duméry, H. *Faith and Reflection.* New York, 1968.

Geach, P. T. *God and the Soul.* London, 1969.

Gilson, E. *Elements of Christian Philosophy.* New York, 1960.

Kolakowski, L. *Religion.* London, 1982.

Latourelle, R. *Man and His Problems in the Light of Christ.* New York, 1983.

Lattey, C., ed. *God.* London, 1931.

Lubac, H. de. *The Discovery of God.* London, 1960.

MacGillivray, G. J., ed. *Man.* London, 1932.

Maloney, G. A. *Man the Divine Icon: The Patristic Doctrine of Man Made According to the Image of God.* Pecos, N.M., 1973.

Maritain, J. *The Degrees of Knowledge.* London, 1959.

_____. *A Preface to Metaphysics.* London, 1939.

McInerny, R. *The Logic of Analogy: An Interpretation of St. Thomas.* The Hague, 1971.

Mouroux, J. *The Christian Experience.* London, 1955.

_____. *The Meaning of Man.* London, 1948.

_____. *The Mystery of Time.* New York, 1958.

Nichols, A. *A Grammar of Consent: The Existence of God in Christian Tradition.* Notre Dame, Ind., and Edinburgh, 1991.

Owens, J. *An Elementary Christian Metaphysics.* Toronto, 1985.

Chapter 2: Revelation and Its Sources

Butler, B. C. *Why Christ?* London, 1968.

Charlier, C. *The Christian Approach to the Bible.* Dublin, 1958.

Congar, Y. M. J. *Tradition and Traditions.* London, 1966.

Daniélou, J. *Christ and Us.* London, 1961.

_____. *From Shadows to Reality: Studies in the Biblical Typology of the Fathers.* London, 1960.

Dulles, A. *Models of Revelation.* Dublin, 1983.

Dvornik, F. *The General Councils of the Church.* London, 1961.

Holmes, J. D., and R. Murray, eds. *John Henry Newman: On the Inspiration of Scripture.* London, 1967.

Jones, A. *God's Living Word*. London, 1961.

Latourelle, R. *Theology of Revelation*. New York, 1966.

Levie, J. *The Bible: Word of God in Words of Men*. London, 1961.

Mackey, J. P. *The Modern Theology of Tradition*. London, 1962.

Orchard, B., ed. *A Catholic Commentary on Holy Scripture*. London, 1953.

Rahner, K., and J. Ratzinger. *Revelation and Tradition*. New York, 1960.

Shorter, A. *Revelation and Its Interpretation*. London, 1933.

Sullivan, F. A. *Magisterium: Teaching Authority in the Catholic Church*. New York and Dublin, 1985.

Synave, P., and P. Benoit. *Prophecy and Inspiration*. London, 1961.

Tanner, N., ed. *Decrees of the Ecumenical Councils*. 2 vols. London, 1991.

Tavard, G. *Holy Writ or Holy Church*. London, 1959.

Vorgrimler, H., ed. *Commentary on the Documents of Vatican II*. 5 vols. New York and London, 1969.

Chapter 3: The Historian's Jesus

Brown, R. E. *The Virginal Conception and Bodily Resurrection of Jesus*. London and Dublin, 1975.

Kopp, C. *The Holy Places of the Gospels*. St. Louis, 1963.

Lagrange, M.-J. *The Gospel of Jesus Christ*. 2 vols. London, 1947.

Laurentin, R. *The Truth of Christmas beyond the Myths: The Gospels of the Infancy of Christ*. Petersham, Mass., 1988.

Meyer, B. F. *The Aims of Jesus*. London, 1979.

_____. *Christus Faber. The Master Builder and the House of God.* Allison Park, Pa., 1992.

Pixner, B. *With Jesus through Galilee According to the Fifth Gospel*. Rosh Pina, 1992.

Studies by Non-Catholics:

Bockmuehl, M. *This Jesus: Martyr, Lord, Messiah*. Edinburgh, 1994.

Hengel, M. *The Cross of the Son of God*. London, 1988.

Wright, N. T. *Who Was Jesus?* London, 1992.

Chapter 4: The Church's Jesus

Adam, K. *Christ Our Brother*. London, 1931.

_____. *The Son of God*. London, 1934.

Balthasar, H. U. von. *Mysterium Paschale: The Mystery of Easter*. Edinburgh, 1990.

Bouyer, L. *The Paschal Mystery: Meditations on the Last Three Days of Holy Week*. London, 1951.

Fitzmyer, J. *A Christological Catechism: New Testament Answers*. New York, 1982.

_____, ed. *Scripture and Theology: A Statement of the Biblical Commission with a Commentary*. London, 1988.

Galot, J. *Who Is Christ? A Theology of the Incarnation*. Rome, 1980.

Grillmeier, A. *Christ in Christian Tradition*. 3 vols. London, 1965, 1987, 1995.

Kasper, W. *Jesus the Christ*. London, 1976.
Kereszty, R. A. *Jesus Christ: Fundamentals of Christology*. Staten Island, N.Y., 1991.
O'Collins, G. *Interpreting Jesus*. London, 1983.
_____. *Jesus Risen*. London, 1987.
Saward, J. *Redeemer in the Womb: Jesus Living in Mary*. San Francisco, 1993.
Schlitzer, A. *Redemptive Incarnation: Sources and Their Theological Development in the Study of Christ*. Notre Dame, Ind., 1956.

Chapter 5: The Trinity

Congar, Y. *I Believe in the Holy Spirit*. 3 vols. London, 1983.
Durrwell, F. X. *Holy Spirit of God: An Essay in Biblical Theology*. London, 1986.
Hill, W. J. *The Three-Personed God: The Trinity as a Mystery of Salvation*. Washington, D.C. 1982.
Kasper, W. *The God of Jesus Christ*. London, 1984.
LaCugna, C. M. *God for Us: The Trinity and the Christian Life*. San Francisco, 1991.
Margerie, B. de. *The Christian Trinity in History*. Still River, Mass., 1982.
O'Carroll, M. *Trinitas: A Theological Encyclopedia of the Holy Trinity*. Wilmington, Del., 1987.
O'Donnell, J. J. *The Mystery of the Triune God*. London, 1988.
Tavard, G. H. *The Vision of the Trinity*. Washington, D.C. 1981.

Chapter 6: The Nature of Salvation

Durrwell, F. X. *In the Redeeming Christ*. New York, 1963.
Fransen, P. *Divine Grace and Man*. New York, 1965.
Guardini, R. *Freedom, Grace and Destiny*. London, 1961.
Journet, C. *The Meaning of Grace*. St. Louis and London, 1960.
Lattey, C., ed. *The Atonement*. Cambridge, 1928.
Lubac, H. de. *A Brief Catechism on Nature and Grace*. San Francisco, 1984.
Ombres, R. *The Theology of Purgatory*. Dublin, 1978.
Ratzinger, J. *Eschatology: Death and Eternal Life*. Washington, D.C., 1988.
Rondet, H. *Original Sin: The Patristic and Theological Background*. Shannon, 1972.
_____. *The Theology of Sin*. London, 1960.
Scheffczyk, L. *Creation and Providence*. London, 1970.
Schönborn, C. *From Death to Life: The Christian Journey*. San Francisco, 1995.
Sullivan, F. A. *Salvation outside the Church? Tracing the History of the Catholic Response*. London, 1992.
Yarnold, E. *The Second Gift: A Study of Grace*. Slough, 1974.

Chapter 7: The Church

Adam, K. *The Spirit of Catholicism*. 2d ed. London, 1959.
Auer, J. *The Church: The Universal Sacrament of Salvation*. Washington, D.C., 1993.

Balthasar, H. U. von. *The Office of Peter and the Structure of the Church*. San Francisco, 1986.

Bouyer, L. *The Church of God: The Body of Christ and Temple of the Holy Spirit*. Chicago, 1982.

Butler, B. C. *The Church and Infallibility*. London, 1954.

_____. *The Idea of the Church*. London, 1962.

Congar, Y. *Lay People in the Church*. London and Westminster, Md., 1965.

_____. *The Mystery of the Church*. London, 1960.

Dulles, A. *Church Membership as a Catholic and Ecumenical Problem*. Milwaukee, 1974.

Hamer, J. *The Church Is a Communion*. London, 1964.

Journet, C. *The Church of the Word Incarnate*. 2 vols. London, 1955.

Latourelle, R. *Christ and the Church: Signs of Salvation*. New York, 1973.

Lubac, H. de. *The Church: Paradox and Mystery*. Shannon, 1969.

_____. *The Motherhood of the Church*. San Francisco, 1982.

_____. *The Splendour of the Church*. London, 1956.

McNamara, K. *Vatican II: The Constitution on the Church. A Theological and Pastoral Commentary*. London, 1968.

Mersch, E. *The Theology of the Mystical Body*. St. Louis, Mo., 1958.

Osborne, K. B. *Lay Ministry in the Roman Catholic Church: Its History and Theology*. New York, 1991.

Rahner, K., and J. Ratzinger. *The Episcopate and the Primacy*. London, 1962.

Sullivan, F. A. *The Church We Believe in*. Dublin, 1986.

Catholic Ecumenism:

Congar, Y. *Divided Christendom*. London, 1959.

Leeming, B. *The Churches and the Church*. London, 1960.

Meyer, H., and L. Fischer, eds. *Growth in Agreement*. New York, 1984.

Storman, J., ed. *Towards the Healing of Schism*. New York, 1987.

Stransky, T. F., and J. B. Sheerin, eds. *Doing the Truth in Charity*. New York, 1982.

Chapter 8: The Religious Life

Chitty, D. J. *The Desert a City: An Introduction to the Study of Egyptian and Palestinian Monasticism Under the Christian Empire*. Oxford, 1966; non-Catholic.

Knowles, D. *From Pachomius to Ignatius: A Study in the Constitutional History of the Religious Orders*. Oxford, 1966.

_____. *Christian Monasticism*. London, 1969.

Ladner, G. B. *The Idea of Reform. Its Impact on Christian Thought and Action in the Age of the Fathers*. Cambridge, Mass., 1959.

Leclerq, J. *The Love of Learning and the Desire for God: A Study of Monastic Culture*. New York, 1961.

Luykx, B. *Eastern Monasticism and the Future of the Church*. Stamford, Conn., 1993.

Vandenbroucke, F. *Why Monks?* Washington, D.C., 1972.

Chapter 9: The Rites of the Church

Adam, A. *The Liturgical Year: Its History and Its Meaning after the Reform of the Liturgy.* New York, 1981.

Casel, O. *The Mystery of Christian Worship, and Other Writings.* Westminster, Md., and London, 1962.

Conlay, I., and P. F. Anson. *The Art of the Church.* New York, 1964.

Crichton, J. D. *Understanding the Prayer of the Church.* London, 1993.

_____. *The Dedication of a Church: A Commentary.* Dublin, 1980.

Dalmais, I.-H. *The Eastern Liturgies.* London, 1960.

Daniélou, J. *The Bible and the Liturgy.* Ann Arbor, Mich., 1979.

Kellner, K. A. H. *Heortology: A History of the Christian Festivals from Their Origin to the Present Day.* London, 1908.

Martimort, A. G., ed. *The Church at Prayer: Introduction to the Liturgy,* vol. 1: *Principles of the Liturgy.* London, 1987. Vol. 4: *The Liturgy and Time.* London, 1986.

Mazza, E. *Mystagogy: A Theology of Liturgy in the Patristic Age.* New York, 1989.

O'Neill, C. *Meeting Christ in the Sacraments.* Staten Island, N.Y., 1963.

Schillebeeckx, E. *Christ the Sacrament of the Encounter with God.* London and New York, 1963.

Taft, R. *Liturgy of the Hours in East and West: The Origin of the Divine Office and Its Meaning for Today.* Collegeville, Minn., 1980.

Vagaggini, C. *Theological Dimensions of the Liturgy: A General Treatise on the Theology of the Liturgy.* Collegeville, Minn., 1976.

Wegman, H. *Christian Worship in East and West: A Study Guide to Liturgical History.* New York, 1985.

The Mass and Other Sacraments:

Anciaux, P. *The Sacrament of Penance.* New York, 1962.

Austin, G. *Anointing with the Spirit: The Rite of Confirmation.* New York, 1985.

Bohen, M. *The Mystery of Confession: A Theology of the Sacrament.* New York, 1963.

Crichton, J. D. *Understanding the Sacraments.* London, 1993.

_____. *Understanding the Mass.* London, 1995.

Cuschieri, A. *Anointing of the Sick: A Theological and Canonical Study.* Lanham, Md., 1995.

Dujarier, M. *A History of the Catechumenate: The First Six Centuries.* New York, 1978.

_____. *The Rites of Christian Initiation: Historical and Pastoral Reflections.* New York, 1979.

Elliottt, P. *What God Has Joined. The Sacramentality of Marriage.* New York, 1993.

Hellwig, M. *Sign of Reconciliation and Conversion: The Sacrament of Penance for Our Times.* Wilmington, Del., 1982.

Jungmann, J. A. *The Mass of the Roman Rite: Its Origin and Development.* London, 1959.

Kavanagh, A. *The Shape of Baptism: The Rite of Christian Initiation.* New York, 1978.

Martimort, A. G., ed. *The Church at Prayer: Introduction to the Liturgy,* vol. 2: *The Eucharist.* London, 1986. Vol. 3: *The Sacraments.* London, 1987.

Masure, E. *The Christian Sacrifice.* London, 1944.

_____. *The Sacrifice of the Mystical Body.* London, 1954.

Neunheuser, B. *Baptism and Confirmation.* New York, 1964.

Nichols, A. *The Holy Eucharist: From the New Testament to Pope John Paul II.* Dublin, 1991.

_____. *Holy Order: Apostolic Ministry from the New Testament to the Second Vatican Council.* Dublin, 1990.

O'Connell, M., ed. *Temple of the Holy Spirit: Sickness and Death of the Christian in the Liturgy.* New York, 1983.

Poschmann, B. *Penance and the Anointing of the Sick.* New York, 1964.

Schleck, C. A. *The Sacrament of Matrimony: A Dogmatic Study.* Bruce, Milwaukee, 1963.

Stevenson, K. W. *Nuptial Blessing: A Study of Christian Marriage Rites.* London, 1982, non-Catholic.

Vonier, A. *A Key to the Doctrine of the Holy Eucharist.* London, 1931.

The Ministry of Women:

Bouyer, L. *Woman in the Church.* San Francisco, 1979.

Hauke, M. *Women in the Priesthood? A Systematic Analysis in the Light of the Order of Creation and Redemption.* San Francisco, 1988.

Chapter 10: Mary and the Saints

The Book of Saints: A Dictionary of Servants of God Canonized by the Catholic Church. Compiled by the Benedictine Monks of St. Augustine's Abbey, Ramsgate. 6th ed. London, 1989.

Brown, P. *The Cult of the Saints: Its Rise and Function in Latin Christianity.* Chicago, 1981, non-Catholic.

De la Potterie, I. *Mary in the Mystery of the Covenant.* Staten Island, N.Y., 1992.

Douillet, J. *What Is a Saint?* London, 1958.

Graef, H. *Mary: A History of Doctrine and Devotion.* 2 vols. London and New York, 1963.

Laurentin, R. *The Apparitions of the Blessed Virgin Mary Today.* London, 1965.

_____. *Mary's Place in the Church.* London, 1965.

McHugh, J. *The Mother of Jesus in the New Testament.* London, 1975.

O'Carroll, M. *Theotokos: A Theological Encyclopedia of the Blessed Virgin Mary.* Collegeville, Minn., 1982.

Polan, S. M., M. C. McCarthy, and E. R. Labande, "Pilgrimages," *New Catholic Encyclopedia* 11:362–72.

Rahner, H. *Our Lady and the Church.* London, 1961.

Rahner, K. "The Church of the Saints." *Theological Investigations,* 3:91-106. New York and London, 1974.

Ratzinger, J. *Daughter Zion: Meditations on the Church's Marian Belief.* San Francisco, 1983.

Chapter 11: The Cosmic Setting of Salvation

Bouyer, L. *Cosmos: The World and the Glory.* Petersham, Mass., 1988.

Daniélou, J. *The Angels and Their Mission.* Westminster, Md., 1976.

Guidici, M. P. *The Angels: Spiritual and Exegetical Notes.* New York, 1993.

Hart, R. van der. *Theology of Angels and Devils.* Cork, 1973.

Jaki, S. L. *The Relevance of Physics.* Chicago, 1966.

_____. *Science and Creation: From Eternal Cycles to an Oscillating Universe.* Edinburgh, 1974.

_____. *Cosmos and Creator.* Edinburgh, 1979.

_____. *The Road of Science and the Ways to God.* Chicago and Edinburgh, 1978.

_____. *The Saviour of Science.* Edinburgh, 1990.

Jones, D. *Can Catholics Believe in Evolution?* London, 1991.

Messenger, E. C., ed. *Theology and Evolution.* London, 1950.

Midgley, M. *Evolution as a Religion.* London, 1985, non-Catholic.

Murray, R. *The Cosmic Covenant: Biblical Themes of Justice, Peace and the Integrity of Creation.* London, 1992.

Pearce, E. H. V. *Who Was Adam?* Exeter, 1976, non-Catholic.

Peterson, E. *The Angels and the Liturgy.* New York, 1964.

Schlier, H. *Principalities and Powers in the New Testament.* New York, 1961.

Chapter 12: The Good Life

Basterra, B. J. E. *Bioethics.* Slough, 1994.

Caffara, C. *Living in Christ: Fundamental Principles of Catholic Morality.* San Francisco, 1987.

Cataldo, P. J., ed. *The Dynamic Character of Christian Culture: Essays on Dawsonian Themes.* Lanham, Md., 1984.

Charles, R., and MacLaren, D. *The Social Teaching of Vatican II. Its Origin and Development.* Oxford and San Francisco, 1982.

Dawson, C. *The Historic Reality of Christian Culture.* New York, 1960.

Fairlie, H. *The Seven Deadly Sins Today.* Notre Dame, Ind., 1979.

Gilleman, G. *The Primacy of Charity in Moral Theology.* London, 1959.

Grisez, G., and R. Shaw. *Fulfilment in Christ: A Summary of Christian Moral Principles.* Notre Dame, Ind., and London, 1991.

Grisez, G., et al. *The Way of the Lord Jesus,* vol. 1, *Christian Moral Principles.* Chicago, 1983. Vol. 2, *Living a Christian Life.* Quincy, Ill., 1992.

Geach, P. T. *The Virtues.* Cambridge, 1977.

Häring, B. *Medical Ethics.* Slough, 1972.

Lebreton, J. *The Spiritual Teaching of the New Testament.* London, 1960.

MacIntyre, A. *After Virtue: A Study in Moral Theory*. Notre Dame, Ind., 1981.

Malone, R., and J. R. Connery, eds. *Contemporary Perspectives on Christian Marriage*. Chicago, 1984.

Maritain, J. *The Person and the Common Good*. London, 1948.

_____. *True Humanism*. London, 1964.

Musto, R. G. *The Catholic Peace Tradition*. Maryknoll, N.Y., 1986.

Pieper, J. *The Four Cardinal Virtues*. London, 1965.

Reidy, M. *Freedom to Be Friends: Morals and Sexual Affection*. London, 1990.

Rommen, H. A. *The State in Catholic Thought*. St. Louis and London, 1975.

Schnackenburg, R. *The Moral Teaching of the New Testament*. London, 1975.

Schuck, M. J. *That They Be One: The Social Teaching of the Papal Encyclicals*. Washington, D.C., 1991.

Smith, J. B. *"Humanae Vitae" a Generation Later*. Washington, D.C., 1991.

Todd, J. M., ed. *The Springs of Morality: A Catholic Symposium*. London and New York, 1956.

Vann, G. *Morals Makyth Man*. London, 1938.

Chapter 13: Ways to Holiness

Aumann, J. *Christian Spirituality in the Catholic Tradition*. San Francisco and London, 1985.

Bouyer, L. *The Spirituality of the New Testament and the Fathers*. New York and London, 1963.

Butler, C. *Western Mysticism*. London, 1951.

Cayre, F. *The First Spiritual Writers*. London, 1959.

Cognet, L. *Post-Reformation Spirituality*. London, 1959.

Graef, H. *The Light and the Rainbow: A Study in Christian Spirituality from Its Roots in the Old Testament and Its Development through the New Testament and the Fathers to Recent Times*. London and Westminster, Md., 1959.

Gutierrez, G. *We Drink from Our Own Wells. The Spiritual Journey of a People*. Maryknoll and London, 1984.

Knowles, D. *The English Mystical Tradition*. London, 1961.

_____. *What Is Mysticism?* London, 1967.

Leclerq, J., F. Vandenbroucke, and L. Bouyer. *The Spirituality of the Middle Ages*. New York and London, 1968.

Lubac, H. *The Religion of Teilhard de Chardin*. London, 1967.

Murray, P. *The Mysticism Debate*. Chicago, 1977.

Sitwell, G. *Mediaeval Spiritual Writers*. London, 1959.

Squire, A. *Asking the Fathers*. London, 1973.

Thurston, H. *The Physical Phenomena of Mysticism*. London, 1951.

Vann, G. *The Divine Pity. A Study in the Social Implications of the Beatitudes*. London, 1945.

Walsh, M. *A Dictionary of Devotions*. London, 1993.

Chapter 14: Catholicism and Other Religions

Anderson, G. H., and T. F. Stransky, eds. *Christ's Lordship and Religious Pluralism.* Maryknoll, N.Y., 1981.

Balthasar, H. U. von. "Catholicism and the Religions," *Communio* 5 (1978).

Cornille, C., and V. Neckebrouck. *A Universal Faith? Peoples, Cultures, Religions and the Christ.* Leuven, 1992.

D'Costa, G. *Theology and Religious Pluralism.* Oxford, 1988.

_____, ed. *Christian Uniqueness Reconsidered.* New York, 1994.

Daniélou, J. *The Salvation of the Nations.* Notre Dame, Ind., 1962.

Fisher, E. J., et al., eds. *Thirty Years of Jewish-Catholic Relations.* New York, 1986.

Straten, H. van. *The Catholic Encounter with World Religions.* London, 1966.

Index of Names

Abel, 130, 360

Abelard, *see* Peter Abelard

Abraham, 15, 47, 123, 172, 196, 345, 347, 366

Adam, 28, 47, 110, 113, 120, 125, 127, 132, 141, 159, 174, 175, 177, 178, 179, 184, 186, 329, 372, 374, 423, 430, 455, 465

Adam, K., 104

Aelred, 27, 121, 420, 436, 444

Ahab, 82

Alain of Lille, 378

Albert, 380

Alphonsus Liguori, 397

Ambrose, 147, 197, 251, 273, 285, 290, 372

Amos, 33

Amoun, 243

Amphilochius, 143

Anaxagoras, 8

Anaximander, 7

Anaximenes, 7

Andrew, 82, 84, 452

Andrew of Crete, 183

Angela of Foligno, 12

Angelus Silesius, 63

Anna, 343

Anna, prophetess, 124

Anselm of Canterbury, 134, 136

Anselm of Havelberg, 260

Anselm of Laon, 259

Anthony of Egypt, 242, 243, 246, 253

Antiochus of Saba, 448

Aquinas, *see* Thomas Aquinas

Aratos, 457

Aristotle, 8, 9, 394, 395, 410, 420, 431

Arius, 108, 155

Arnold of Bouneval, 117

Athanasius of Alexandria, 53, 111, 155, 156, 160, 167, 197, 242, 243, 246

Athanasius of the Meteora, 265

Athenagoras, 241

Atkins, M., 380

Augustine, 11, 23, 24, 53, 69, 126, 138, 139, 160, 161, 163, 168, 185, 187, 192, 203, 204, 212, 222, 238, 246, 249, 250, 251, 252, 253, 254, 257, 258, 259, 260, 266, 267, 286, 301, 302, 304, 360, 368, 372, 394, 395, 396, 398, 399, 406, 411, 419, 424, 437, 444, 445, 468

Augustus, 80

Aurelian of Arles, 284

Balthasar, H. U. von, 127, 137, 180, 190, 191, 199, 228, 233

Bañez, D., 188

Barth, K., 18, 228

Bartimaeus, 78, 96

Basil, 53, 120, 162, 238, 244, 248, 253, 254, 261, 265, 285, 288, 309, 333, 372, 377
Bede, 123, 364, 372
Bellarmine, K., 188, 195, 216
Benedict of Nursia, 238, 244, 248, 253, 254, 255, 256, 257, 259, 260, 261, 285, 309
Benedict of Aniane, 257, 258
Benson, R. H., 58, 212, 278
Bernanos, G., 173
Bernard of Chartres, 259
Bernard of Clairvaux, 24, 27, 109, 110, 116, 118, 261, 348, 452
Bernard Sylvestris, 259
Bérulle, P. de, 377
Besret, B., 227
Blathmac, 348, 352
Blondel, M., 10, 11, 52
Bockmuehl, M., 76
Boismard, M.-E., 70
Bonaventure, 202, 357, 378
Boso, 136
Bossuet, J. B., 189, 190, 394, 417, 444
Bouchard, I., 324
Bourgoing, F., 349
Bremond, H., 446
Brown, P., 333
Brown, R., 99
Bruno, 261
Buddha, *see* Gautama
Burridge, R. A., 99
Butler, B. C., 154
Butler, C., 439

Cadfan, 262
Caesarius of Arles, 314
Callixtus, 376
Camus, A., 27
Carmichael, A., 197, 383, 384, 448
Carney, J., 348, 352
Caspari, C. P., 360
Cassian, *see* John Cassian

Cassiodorus, 255
Catherine of Siena, 359
Cesarini, G., 29
Challenor, R., 217
Charlemagne, 275
Chaucer, G., 348
Chesterton, G. K., 17, 201, 224, 337
Chrodegang of Metz, 259
Chromatius of Aquileia, 143
Ciaran, 255
Cicero, 420
Claudel, P., 323, 385, 386, 442
Clement of Alexandria, 282, 288, 394, 459
Climacus, *see* John Climacus
Clough, A. C., 176
Collingwood, R. G., 13
Columba, 255, 375
Columbanus, 255
Conrad of Eberback, 261
Conrad, R., 316
Constantine, 100, 218
Cornwell, J., 452
Croce, B., 390
Cu Brettan, 348
Cuthbert, 375
Cyprian, 215, 216, 282, 284, 288, 304
Cyril of Alexandria, 108, 159
Cyril of Jerusalem, 287, 288, 289, 291

Daly, C. B., 60
Daniélou, J., 457
Dante, 8, 24, 203, 390
Darwin, C., 113, 370
David, 46, 77, 109, 130, 172, 184, 273, 301, 323, 420, 448
Davies, B., 450
De Caussade, J. P., 443
De Lubac, H., 57, 168, 207, 218, 459
Demetrios, 333

Denys the Areopagite, 287
Denys the Carthusian, 237
Denzinger, H., 16
Dessain, C. S., 379
Devlin, C., 165, 293
Du Perron, J.-D., 168
Diadochus, 444
Dickens, C., 17
Dilworth, T., 23
Dominic, 444
Domitian, 81
Dostoevsky, F., 170
Doyle, E., 379
Driedo, J., 398
Duffy, E., 217, 361
Duns Scotus, 339, 380
Durrwell, F. X., 145

Egbert, 330
Egeria, 247, 284
Elgar, E., 195
Eliot, G., 48
Elisabeth, 346
Elisabeth of the Trinity, 166
Elijah, 48, 81, 82, 85, 94, 128, 263, 264
Elisha, 81, 366
Empedocles, 7
Ephrem, 113, 120, 121, 247, 249
Epiphanius, 355
Eriugena, 378
Ernst, C., 274
Eusebius of Caesarea, 86, 241
Eusebius of Vercelli, 251, 258
Evagrius, 244
Eve, 141, 175, 214, 328, 345, 353, 359, 423, 470
Every, G., 470
Ezekiel, 347, 455

Faber, F. W., 387
Farrer, A., 70
Fénélon, F. de la Mothe, 447

Finnis, J., 404
Flavius Josephus, 65
Forristal, D., 282
Foster, K., 214, 389
Foucauld, C. de, 297
Francis of Assisi, 238, 357, 378, 379, 380, 441
Francis de Sales, 311, 439, 446
François de Sainte-Marie, 263

Gabriel, 346
Gardner, W. H., 194, 350
Garrigou-Lagrange, R., 190
Gautama, 464, 465
Geiselmann, J., 51, 52
Gerbert, 259
Gibbon, E., 280
Gilbert of Hoyland, 444, 445
Gill, E., 227, 430
Gilson, E., 10
Goethe, 103
Gougaud, L., 245
Gray, J., 126
Gréa, A., 216
Gregory the Great, 254, 438
Gregory Nazianzen, 162, 177, 377, 401, 438
Gregory of Nyssa, 162, 378
Gregory Palamas, 344
Grelot, P., 45
Grimold, 419, 420
Grisewood, H., 294
Grosseteste, R., 5
Guardini, R., 170, 183, 210, 211
Guerric of Igny, 109, 110
Guthlac, 262
Gwyddfarch, 262

Hagar, 382
Handel, G. F., 48
Hardy, T., 48
Hegel, G. F. W., 21, 22, 413
Helena, 365

Heraclitus, 7
Herder, J. G., 72
Herod the Great, 80, 81, 428
Herod Antipas, 84, 90, 99
Hesiod, 8
Hilary, 47, 111, 285, 287
Hill, E., 164
Hill, W. J., 152
Hippolytus, 145, 282, 284
Hitler, A., 388
Hobbes, T., 413
Hodgson, P., 369, 370
Holmes, J. D., 49
Homer, 8
Hopkins, G. M., 42, 65, 193, 194, 292, 293, 350
Hosea, 33, 215, 329
Hoskins, E., 296
Hrabanus Maurus, 419, 420
Hume, D., 13, 61
Hünermann, P., 16

Ignatius of Antioch, 241, 317, 326
Ignatius Loyola, 42, 238, 445, 446
Innocent II, 260
Innocent III, 298
Irenaeus, 21, 59, 118, 127, 158, 222, 345, 349, 371, 394, 398
Isaac, 15, 130, 196
Isaiah, 374
Ishmael, 462
Isidore, 255
Israel, *see* Jacob

Jacob, 15, 130, 196, 227, 366
Jaki, S. L., 370
James, cousin of the Lord, 80, 88, 314
James bar Zebedee, 84
James VI and I, 168
Jeanne de Chantal, 446
Jeeves, M. A., 383
Jehuda, 92

Jeremiah, 373
Jerome, 242
Jesse, 77, 343
Jezebel, 128
Joachim, 343
Johanan ben Zechariah, *see* John the Baptist
John, apostle, 52, 62, 65, 70, 74, 79, 80, 82, 83, 84, 87, 88, 99, 100, 152, 153, 154, 158, 166, 168, 186, 199, 221, 222, 270, 273, 300, 305, 314, 318, 327, 345, 351, 354, 382, 389, 420, 441
John the Baptist, 66, 81, 82, 83, 85, 89, 90, 96, 99, 126, 261, 283, 338, 346, 428
John Cassian, 244, 245, 249, 253, 254, 256, 257, 258, 264, 284, 309
John Chrysostom, 132, 299, 307
John Climacus, 195, 264, 265
John of the Cross, 32, 264, 446, 452
John of Damascus, 26, 349
John Eudes, 117
John of Ford, 444
John Gualbert, 261
John the Monk, 348
John Paul II, 131, 182, 207, 262, 263, 339, 340, 344, 351, 401, 402, 426, 428, 431, 467 (*See also* Wojtyla, K.)
Jonah, 35, 91, 374, 458
Jonathan, 420
Jones, A. R., 415
Jones, D., 23, 293, 294, 345, 442
Journet, C., 214, 226
Joseph, 80, 87, 125, 126
Joseph, patriarch, 30
Joseph of Arimathea, 100, 101
Judas, 294
Julius Africanus, 77
Jung, C. G., 349
Jungmann, J. A., 305
Justin Martyr, 288, 393, 394, 459

Kant, I., 13, 14, 369
Kelly, J. N. D., 276
Kempe, M., 352
Kereszty, R., 105
Kerr, F., 274, 279
Knox, R., 307, 446, 447
Kolakowski, L., 418
Krishna, 463, 464, 467

Labré, B. J., 262
Lagrange, M.-J., 102
Langland, W., 368
Latourelle, R., 35, 37
Laurentin, R., 358
Lawrence of the Resurrection, 447
Lazarus, 95, 96, 345, 420
Leander, 255
Leavis, F. R., 279
Leclerq, J., 260
Leo the Great, 42, 123, 219, 273, 399
Leo X, 192
Leo XIII, 49, 217
Lewis, S., 381, 382, 415
Ligier, L., 179
Locke, J., 61
Lonergan, B., 185
Louis the Pious, 257, 259
Luddy, A. J., 264
Luke, 48, 53, 69, 70, 71, 74, 78, 79,
    80, 81, 82, 95, 99, 153, 300, 306,
    338, 344, 347, 349, 351
Luther, M., 199
Luykx, B., 266

Macarius of Alexandria, 245
Macaulay, R., 336
MacIntyre, A., 409, 410
Mackay Brown, G., 362
Mackenzie, N. H., 194, 350
McCabe, H., 341
Manzoni, A., 213, 323
Marcion, 53
Maritain, J., 19, 224

Mark, 69, 70, 71, 72, 74, 78, 79, 86,
    91, 92, 95, 96, 99, 300, 351, 375
Marrou, H.-I., 72
Marsilio Ficino, 192
Martin of Tours, 249, 254
Martindale, C. C., 278
Marx, K., 21, 22
Mary, 33, 79, 80, 88, 97, 111, 112,
    118, 122, 125, 126, 130, 156, 187,
    202, 215, 236, 264, 273, 280, 283,
    295, 297, 301, 306, 311, 312, 321,
    325, 327, 335, 337-359, 360, 367,
    385, 401, 428, 448, 450, 459
Mary of Egypt, 265
Mary Magdalene, 97, 101, 143
Matthew, 48, 69, 70, 71, 74, 78, 79,
    80, 85, 86, 96, 97, 99, 153, 300,
    338
Maurras, C., 280
Maximus the Confessor, 395
Meier, J. P., 73, 105
Melangell, 262
Melchizedek, 47
Melissus, 7
Melito, 127, 130, 137
Mersch, E., 186
Merton, T., 447
Michael, 383
Milman, J., 468
Milton, J., 175
Mohammed, 461, 462
Möhler, J. A., 51
Molina, L. de, 188
Monica, 437
Monchanin, J., 459
Moore, G. E., 407
Moses, 15, 33, 48, 94, 128, 130,
    392, 458
Mourroux, J., 61
Muncey, R. W., 215
Murray, R., 49, 373, 375

Nathanael, 83

Nestorius, 108
Newman, J. H., 16, 17, 49, 52, 56, 57, 119, 120, 178, 182, 195, 196, 199, 345, 370, 387, 397, 468
Nicephorus Phocas, 265
Nicetas of Remesiana, 360
Nicholas of Cusa, 28, 29, 191
Nicholas the Frenchman, 263
Nichols, A. E., 274
Nicodemus, 94, 100
Noah, 47, 288, 374
Norbert, 238

Oakes, E. T., 180
O'Donoghue, N. D., 387
O'Dwyer, P., 348, 352
O'Fiannachta, P., 282
Origen, 45, 211, 377
Orpheus, 375
Ovitt, S., 372

Pachomius, 194, 195, 244, 246, 247, 253, 265, 309, 375
Parmenides, 7
Pascal, B., 17, 176
Paul, 16, 19, 30, 55, 63, 88, 91, 107, 109, 110, 134, 148, 153, 158, 166, 176, 177, 186, 198, 210, 224, 233, 240, 242, 247, 252, 319, 321, 340, 366, 371, 375, 376, 382, 397, 423, 440, 457, 458, 461, 465
Paul VI, 61, 214, 283, 297, 305
Paul of Samosata, 108
Paul of Thebes, 242
Paulinus, 134
Péguy, C., 364
Penrose, R., 369
Peraldus, W., 448
Peter, 69, 82, 84, 88, 92, 94, 103, 107, 200, 221, 222, 230, 233, 234, 321, 340, 382, 400
Peter Abelard, 137, 276
Peter Lombard, 315

Petrarch, 357
Philip, apostle, 82
Philip, one of the Seven, 240
Philip the Tetrarch, 90, 95
Philipon, M.-M., 165
Philo, 151, 269, 374, 469
Pico della Mirandola, G., 192
Pinckaers, S., 396
Pindar, 8
Pius X, 49
Pius XII, 135, 208, 354
Pixner, B., 76, 86
Plato, 8, 9, 420, 431
Pliny the Younger, 65
Plotinus, 437
Polycarp, 345
Pontius Pilate, 65, 99, 295
Pope, H., 79
Poulenc, F., 352
Prudentius, 326
Pseudo-Chrysostom, 121
Pseudo-Ephrem, 375
Pseudo-Macarius, 455

Quirinius, 80

Radcliffe, T., 274
Rahner, K., 139, 140, 198, 242, 363, 376, 377, 451
Rama, 463
Rancé, A. de, 264
Raphael, 383
Read, P. P., 103
Richard of St. Victor, 161
Riesenfeld, H., 70
Roger of Byland, 260
Rolle, R., 440, 441
Romanos the Hymnographer, 353
Romuald, 261
Royal, R., 390
Rubin, N., 273
Rublev, A., 296
Ruskin, J., 5

Ruysbroeck, J. van, 129
Ryder, S., 227

Sanders, E. P., 76
Sarah, 382
Sartre, J. P., 34
Saward, J., 202, 319, 320, 322, 401
Scheeben, M. J., 292
Schelling, F. W. J., 14
Schönborn, C., 226
Scruton, R., 425
Second Isaiah, 215
Sedulius Scottus, 145
Serapion, 315
Shakespeare, W., 163
Shaw, G. B., 181
Shiva, 463
Signorelli, L., 389
Simon the Pharisee, 94
Simeon, 124, 283, 350
Socrates, 8
Solomon, 35, 86
Sophronius, 124
Sorrell, R. D., 379
Stalin, J., 388
Stein, G., 46
Stephen of Muret, 238
Stoerger, W., 369
Storey, G., 42
Sulpicius Severus, 249

Tacitus, 65
Talbot, C. H., 261
Tavard, G. H., 155
Teilhard de Chardin, P., 12, 27, 113, 442
Teresa of Avila, 264, 359, 439, 446
Tertullian, 282, 284, 288, 377, 378, 394
Thales, 7
Theodore of Mopsuestia, 287, 288
Theodore the Studite, 265
Theodotus of Ancyra, 119

Thérèse of Lisieux, 75, 235, 264
Thomas, apostle, 336, 348
Thomas Aquinas, 9, 18, 38, 46, 54, 110, 113, 118, 133, 138, 146, 163, 164, 167, 174, 185, 193, 200, 219, 235, 262, 273, 274, 276, 294, 366, 380, 383, 387, 389, 401, 404, 407, 408, 409, 410, 411, 412, 413, 414, 418, 420, 438, 450
Thomas More, 192, 197
Thomas, D., 176
Thomas, G., 145
Thompson, F., 227
Timothy of Jerusalem, 355
Torrance, T. F., 135, 147
Trajan, 65
Turner, H.E.W., 34
Turner, J.M.W., 5

Ullathorne, W. B., 342

Vincent de Paul, 438
Vishnu, 463
Vonier, A., 294, 390

Waddell, H., 375
Wallace, A. R., 113
Ward, W., 17
Weitzmann, K., 333
Wilde, O., 115
William of St-Thierry, 24, 25, 27, 260, 261
Wojtyla, K., 26 (*See also* John Paul II.)
Wolfram, 380

Xenophanes, 7

Yarnold, E., 181

Zacchaeus, 96
Zechariah, 283, 344
Zeus, 457

Index of Main Subjects Treated

Act of faith, 37–43
Analogy, 15
Angels, 382–390
    devotion to, 383–385
    fallen, 388–389
    guardian, 387
    role in human salvation, 385–387
Animals, 373–375
Anointing of sick, 313–317
Apologetics, 33–37

Baptism, 286–289
Bible: see Scripture
Bioethics, 425–429
Bishop, office of, 319–322
Blessed Virgin Mary, 337–359
    annunciation to, 344–346
    appearances of, 357–358
    assumption of, 354–357
    birth of, 343–344
    doctrine of, 337–339
    holiness of, 349–350
    immaculate conception of, 339–343
    litany of, 338–339
    motherhood of, 347–349
    mysteries of her child-bearing, 344–350
    mysteries of her glorification, 353–358

mysteries of her preparation, 339–344
mysteries of her suffering, 350–353
presentation of, 344
virginity of, 338–339
visitation of, 346–347
Buddhism, in Catholic perspective, 464–465

Canon law, 217–219
Canonical order, 258–260
Carmelite tradition, 263–264
Christ: see Jesus Christ
Church, 206–237
    apologetic value of, 36–37
    authority of in morals, 398–401
    as bearer of Kingdom, 214
    as born of Spirit, 212–214
    Catholic definition of, 207–209
    infallibility of, 54–59
    as mediating salvation, 206–207
    as mother, 215–216
    notes of, 234–237
    as one and many, 219–221
    role in interpreting Scripture, 45–46
    as sacrament of Christ, 211–212
    as social institution, 216–217
    as Trinitarian communion, 210
Church building, 332–336

Common life, in New Testament, 241
Confirmation, 290–292
Consecrated virginity, in New Testament, 240–241
Contemplation, call to, 439
Cosmos, as Christ-centered, 370–377
    as convivium of man with animals, 371–373, 373–375, 377–380
    in natural science, 368–371
Covenant, 97–98
Creation, 11–13, 169–170
Crucifix, 140
Crucifixion, 100

Deacon, office of, 326–327
Death, 194–196
Death penalty, 418–419
Direction, spiritual, 454
Doctrinal development, 56–57
Dogma, nature of, 55–56

Ecology, 380–382
Episcopate, in relation to primacy, 230–233
Eschatology, 191–205
Eucharist, 292–307
    as real presence, 295–297
    as sacrifice, 293–295
Experience, role of in revelation, 61–64

Fathers, role in Tradition, 53–54
Friendship, 419–421

Gifts, charismatic, 452–453
    of Holy Spirit, 412
God, existence of, 15–18
    imaginative sense of, 13–15
    in history, 32
    philosophical concept of, 11–13

rational notion of, 18–20
    as Trinity, 151–168
Grace, actual and habitual, 185–186
    created and uncreated, 186
    in history, 32
    justifying, 18,
    predestining, 188–190
    sanctifying, 185–186
    as transformative of history, 190–191

Heaven, 199–201
Hell, 198–199
Hermits, 262–263
Hinduism, in Catholic perspective, 463–464
History, as open to God, 23–24
Holiness, ways to, 433–455
Human being, complex nature of, 24–25
    destiny of, 27–28
    as metaphysical animal, 20–23
    as person, 25–26
    as theomorphic, 28

Illumination, in spiritual growth, 461–462
Imagination, in awareness of God, 13–14
Immortality, of soul, 192–193
Incarnation of Word, 107–117
    anthropological significance of, 21
    purpose of, 112–113
Indulgences, 312–313
Infancy narratives, 78–79
Islam, in Catholic perspective, 461–462

Jesus Christ, in apologetics, 33–36
    ascension of, 146–148
    atoning efficacy of death of, 129–139

baptism of, 126–127
birth of, 79–80, 119–122
burial of, 140–141
as center of faith, 41–43
childhood of, 80–81, 122–126
Church's perspective on, 106–107
circumcision of, 122
descent into Hell, 141–142
epiphany of, 122–123
finding in Temple of, 126
hidden life of, 125–126
historian's sources for, 65–67
historical method in studying, 67–76
as key to man and God, 28–29
life of, in historian's perspective, 76–105
life-setting for, 76–78
moral teaching of, 392
mysteries of life of, 117–148
parousia of, 149–150
passion of, 97–101
presentation of, 124–125
public ministry of, 81–97
resurrection of, 101–103, 142–146
as sending Spirit, 148–149
temptations of, 127–128
transfiguration of, 94, 128–129
virginal conception of, 117–118
Judaism, in Catholic perspective, 459–461
Justification, 182–183

Labor, ethics of, 429–431
Laity, as prophetic and royal priesthood, 221–228
in relation to priests, religious and bishop, 228–230
Liturgical principle, 277–279
Liturgy, ethos of, 279–281
Hours of, 281–285

Magisterium, and theologians, 59–61
and moral doctrine, 399–401
Marriage, 327–332
Mary: *see* Blessed Virgin Mary
Mass, order of, 297–307
Messiahship, 92–94
Mission, dogmatic foundation of, 459
Monotheism, trinitarian, 167–168
Monasticism, Antonian, 242–243
Augustinian, 249–253
Benedictine, 255–258
Byzantine, 265–266
Celtic, 255
Carthusian, 261–262
Cistercian, 260–261
desert, 243–246
Pachomian, 246
at Qumran, 239–240
Syrian, 247–249
Trappist, 265
Morals, Catholic vision of, 404–405
Church's concern with, 392–432
as confluence of revelation and reason, 404–405
distinctively Christian, 405–406
doctrinal significance of, 391
in Fathers of Church, 393–394
in mediaevals, 394–396
in modern period, 396–398
role of nature in, 407–408
role of virtues in, 408–412
in teaching of Jesus, 392
Mysticism, in act of faith, 40–42
in Christian holiness, 437–439

Old Testament, Catholic use of, 46–49
Orders, holy, 317–327

Parousia, 149–150, 201
Penance, 307–313

Perfections, divine, 19
Person, human, 24, 25–26
    Trinitarian, 162–164
Petrine office, 233–234
Phenomena, extraordinary mystical, 454
Philosophy, ancient as preparation for Gospel, 7–9
    in relation to theology, 9–10
Pilgrimage, 367
Pope: *see* Petrine office
Prayer, of devotion, 447–449
    of the heart, 444–445
    of the imagination, 445–446
    of the memory, 445
    of petition, 449–450
    of the will, 446–447
Presbyter, office of, 322–326
Providence, 170–172
Purgation, in growth in holiness, 435
Purgatory, 196–198

Redemption, need for, 172–174
    in Christ, 176–179
Reign of God, in teaching of Jesus, 89
Relics, 365–367
Religious, in relation to laity, priests, bishop, 228–230
Religious life, 238–271
    development in East and West, 254–266
    early monastic form of, 242–254
    foundations of, 238–242
    theology of, 266–270
Repentance, 183–185
Resurrection of body, 192–193, 201–205
Revelation, 30–33
    private, 451

Sacramental principle, 272–273

Sacraments, in general, 273–277
    in particular, 285–331
Sacred Heart, 139–140
Sacred Wounds, 140
Saints, 360–365
Salvation, nature of, 238–271
    possibility of outside Church, 456–458
    in teaching of Jesus, 88–89
Scripture, Christocentric character of, 44
    inerrancy of, 49
    inspiration of, 44–49
    interpretation of, 43–44
    and Tradition, 51–53
Sexuality, ethics of, 422–425
Sin, personal, 310–312
    original, 174–176
Social ethics, 413–419
Son, divinity of, 154–157
Spirit,
    descent at Pentecost, 148–149
    divinity of, 157–162
Spirituality, doctrinal foundations of, 433–434
    legitimate diversity of, 439–443
State, significance of, 413–416
Supernatural, 180–182

Tradition, 50–54
    as Christ-centered, 50
    in relation to magisterium, 54–59
    in relation to Scripture, 51–54
Traditional religions, in Catholic perspective, 465–466
Trinity, 151–168
    inhabitation of, 165–167
    in life of Jesus, 152–153
    in Old Testament 151–152
    as one being in three persons, 162–164
    in Paschal mystery, 153–154, 165
    as "social program," 165

Union with God, 436–437

Visions, 450–452

World religions, other, 456–459, 466–469